Larry McMurtry

ALSO BY TRACY DAUGHERTY

Hiding Man: A Biography of Donald Barthelme

Just One Catch: A Biography of Joseph Heller

The Last Love Song: A Biography of Joan Didion

Leaving the Gay Place: Billy Lee Brammer and the Great Society

Larry McMurtry

A Life

TRACY DAUGHERTY

St. Martin's Press

New York

First published in the United States by St. Martin's Press, an imprint of St. Martin's Publishing Group

www.stmartins.com

Library of Congress Cataloging-in-Publication Data is available upon request.

ISBN 9781250282330 (hardcover)
ISBN 9781250282347 (ebook)

Our books may be purchased in bulk for promotional, educational, or business use. Please contact your local bookseller or the Macmillan Corporate and Premium Sales Department at 1-800-221-7945, extension 5442, or by email at MacmillanSpecialMarkets@macmillan.com.

First Edition: 2023

10 9 8 7 6 5 4 3 2 1

For Padgett Powell, Glenn Blake, and Thomas Cobb,
in memory of books and a place called Houston

CONTENTS

The gold song, the gold stars,
The world so golden then . . .
He died a hard death long ago
Before the Road came in.

—Willa Cather

PART ONE

Heart's Country

1

On the day Larry McMurtry died, the River Oaks Theater on West Gray Street in Houston closed its doors for the last time. When the theater first opened in 1939, three years after McMurtry was born, it featured the film *Bachelor Mother,* starring Ginger Rogers and David Niven, a better-than-average confection offering the typical Hollywood fare of mistaken identities and romantic misunderstandings. *Bachelor Mother* was the kind of light comedy promising a serious social message (in this case, "Don't abandon your children"), drawing tens of thousands of citizens to palatial movie houses in America's cities prior to the Great Depression. The movies also played to popular acclaim in homelier small-town venues.

After the market crash of 1929, movie attendance dropped nationwide. In the years following World War II, motion picture palaces were prohibitively expensive to build because they required the fresh technology needed to screen the "talkies." Houston's River Oaks was an art deco extravaganza nestled among curling oak trees. It was two stories tall and featured abstract undersea designs carved into its stone walls along with bas-relief goddesses on either side of its screen. Its construction was made possible by the neighborhood planning restricting this part of Houston, west of downtown, to wealthy white families, excluding Jews and African Americans.

Bachelor Mother was a delightful, somewhat titillating distraction presenting a gentler America than existed in the places it played. Such movies continued to serve this ameliorative function for decades to come, even in the nation's small towns. In 1966, Larry McMurtry would publish a novel, *The Last Picture Show,* "lovingly dedicated to my hometown," he wrote: Archer City, Texas (375 miles northwest of Houston). The novel was set in the 1950s. Early in the story, a teenage boy smooches with his girlfriend in the dark at the town's lone movie house, but his interest in the girl is "muted": "He wanted to keep at least one eye on the screen, so if Ginger Rogers decided to take her clothes off he wouldn't miss it."

The River Oaks managed to survive for eighty-three years, in a city noto-riously indifferent to its history, by reinventing itself, weathering Hollywood's CinemaScope, VistaVision, and Techniscope years, outlasting the threats of television, videocassettes, and DVDs. In the 1970s (once the neighborhood was no longer restricted), the theater became a repertory house, running classic, alternative, foreign, and independent films along with new releases. In 1987, its owners, the Landmark Theatres chain, tore out its balcony and added a second screen to pack more people in. But by 2020, skyrocketing rent and the coronavirus pandemic had doomed the place. Nationally, box office revenue had decreased by 76 percent.

On March 25, 2021, at roughly the time McMurtry died of congestive heart failure in Tucson at the age of eighty-four, the River Oaks screened its final feature, *Nomadland,* a somber look at America's elderly indigent working poor. The movie starred Frances McDormand as a victim of the industries such as copper mining that collapsed and never recovered in the financial crash of 2008. Along with thousands of others who'd lost their life savings, she was forced to live on the road, traveling and sleeping in a van, seeking temporary jobs, throwing herself on the mercy of Ama-zon, Walmart, and other corporate lions (like the theater owners and the managers of the shopping center in which the River Oaks could no longer afford to operate). As a backdrop to this peripatetic existence, *Nomadland* offered austere big-sky emptiness, reinforcing the characters' alienation. Certainly, no one in the Houston audience that night could miss the fact that they were watching a latter-day Western—Frances McDormand as a good ol' gal spurring her van up the trail to the next violent encounter, even if *this* film's violence was mostly psychic and emotional.

Nor would Houston film buffs be unaware that *Nomadland*'s unusual pedigree, still rare in the film business—a female-centered Western directed by a Chinese woman, Chloé Zhao—might not have been possible at all without the example of the boundary-shattering American movies of the 1960s and 1970s. Among those movies was Peter Bogdanovich's version of *The Last Picture Show,* coauthored by McMurtry. McMurtry was one of the many American artists moving, mid-century, from the rural hinterlands to the cultural ferment of the cities. This movement transformed every region of the country; it especially altered places like Texas, just then *discovering* its own rich culture and figuring out how to nurture it.

"Houston was my first city, my Alexandria, my Paris, my Oxford," Mc-Murtry once wrote. "At last I was in a place where I could begin to read, and I did." For him, migration from Archer City was not just a practical decision or a forced march. It was a stirring in the blood. "The tradition I was born into"—as the son of a Great Plains cattleman—"was essentially nomadic, a herdsman tradition, following animals across the earth," he said. He confessed he was incurious about the animals; from his earliest youth, he was after different game. In Houston, he immersed himself in a world of books and movies—more accurately, in book*shops* and movie *theaters,* repositories of culture. "The bookshops are a form of ranching," he said. "Instead of herding cattle, [booksellers] herd books. Writing is a form of herding, too; I herd words into little paragraphlike clusters." As a young man in his teens and early twenties, he began to learn the rhythms of narrative in his local five-and-dime, in the secondhand shops, in the Fondren Library at Rice Institute, and at the River Oaks.

In the decades ahead, hundreds of budding artists would follow his trail, enriching culture in a region largely hostile to its production. Mc-Murtry became one of the seminal figures alerting the next generation of artists to the existence of Texas culture. For instance, *The Last Picture Show,* a River Oaks favorite, had a profound effect on at least one Houston-born filmmaker, Richard Linklater, director of *Slacker, Dazed and Confused,* and *Boyhood.* Like McMurtry, he completed a substantial part of his education in the theater. "I would sit really near the screen . . . in the middle, a few rows from the front," he said. The seventies movies he watched there would eventually lead him to develop the spare, naturalistic look of his films, translating that style to Texas, as Bogdanovich and McMurtry had done with *their* early influences (Orson Welles, Howard Hawks, Cervantes). "I remember . . . leaving the theater in a daze and missing the next screening," Linklater said. "I finally figured out the schedule—just never leave."

At around ten P.M. on March 25, 2021, the theater locked its doors. A small crowd milled beneath the marquee's yellow bulbs, not wanting to scatter, staring up at the neon letters spelling out River Oaks—some of the shapes blazed yellow, others green, replacement lights being hard to find these days. A mild breeze stirred loose sweater sleeves (nothing else moved; oaks no longer swayed next to the building). As word began to filter out on smartphones that Larry McMurtry, Texas's most famous novelist, was terminally ill, an overwhelming sense of loss—loss of stories, of ways of knowing, ways of understanding an entire American era—passed among the moviegoers.

"I'm drawn to stories of vanishing crafts . . . or trades," McMurtry once said. "I've seen cowboying die, and also bookselling, to a large degree. And both those things sadden me." Now, the movie houses.

From the first, in McMurtry's apprentice stories and poems, loss was the major theme of his writing. He began with elegy and ended there: the land that whelped him was the essence of "American bleakness . . . empty socially, intellectually, culturally," he said. It was a "place of unpeopled horizons."

"One of the things I have been doing, in [my] novels, is filling that same emptiness, peopling it, trying to imagine what the word 'frontier' meant to my grandparents . . . building their first cabin and begetting yet more McMurtry quail on [a] hill in Archer County."

This aching need to fill the hollowness of his raising drove him to Houston and eventually to other cities, whose losses he also noted—but "I can't escape [that original emptiness] in my fiction," he admitted. "I can work away from it, but I always start here. And whatever place I'm writing about, I'm still describing this same hill [in West Texas]."

In more than forty books, in a career spanning over sixty years, he staked his claim as a superior chronicler of the American West and as the Great Plains' keenest witness since Willa Cather and Wallace Stegner. He brought as much depth to his enterprise as William Faulkner brought to the South.

As a young writer starting out, he once wore a T-shirt, given to him by a friend, proclaiming himself a Minor Regional Novelist—a sly swipe at the provincialism of New York publishers, many of whom seem to believe that literacy stops on the west bank of the Mississippi River. "Being a writer and a Texan is an amusing fate," McMurtry wryly observed. A bestselling author, public intellectual, Pulitzer Prize winner, Academy Award winner, and National Humanities Medal recipient, he felt eastern critics never gave him his due. His late-life writing partner, Diana Ossana, said, "Larry straddles literary and popular fiction—how many contemporary writers do that? You could say Dickens—but no one now. That's what's so unusual about him . . . I think the literati in New York don't quite know what to do with him."

Perhaps deliberately, McMurtry left the T-shirt in a laundromat one day. It always irritated him that in the popular imagination (fed by New

York and Los Angeles marketing firms), he was considered a mere purveyor of cowboy myths.

His story was far grander than that. Writing in *The American Scholar* in 2010, William Zinsser lamented the fact that "men and women of letters were [once] the workhorses of the literary enterprise; they saw that the caravan kept moving . . . their universe was held together by a specific object (the book), sold in a specific place (the bookstore)." But now, he said, "The republic of letters has largely sputtered out. Little bookstores where writers once dropped in to chat were put out of business by big bookstores where the general populace dropped in to drink coffee: the republic of *latte*."

He was hard-pressed to find *any* men and women of letters now, he wrote. "Down in Archer City, Texas, I see Larry McMurtry, author of novels, articles, essays, book reviews, and screenplays, but also proprietor of Booked Up, one of America's largest used-book stores, with more than 400,000 titles. In 2004, hurt by competition from on-line bookselling, McMurtry wanted to close the store, but he changed his mind after an outpouring of public support. That's a man of letters."

America—especially in recent years—has produced few such engaged, enduring figures.

All his life, the bleakness of Archer County drove McMurtry's nomadism. "When I was a boy," he said, "one of the first questions I asked my parents and grandparents was, where does the road go to? I meant [Highway] 281"—the rare paved path bypassing the McMurtry ranch where his family remained stuck in mounting debt. As an adult, McMurtry loved driving America's highways coast to coast, crisscrossing the plains. (When I mentioned to McMurtry's friend, the esteemed art critic Dave Hickey, that I was writing McMurtry's story, he said, "Knowing Larry, it's going to be a real episodic book.")

McMurtry had an early, powerful memory of sitting in his father's car at the age of six, on a "long, long stretch of route 66." The plains were so level, the horizon so vast, "I thought my father was driving us into the sky," he said. The image always haunted him: a vision of escaping emptiness by heading into an even greater blank, as clean as a piece of paper.

In keeping with tales of vanishment, McMurtry spent a number of years before he died feeling "more and more like a ghost, or a shadow," following quadruple bypass surgery in 1991. "What I more and more felt . . . was that while my body survived, the self that I had once been had lost its life." Maintaining the strict work ethic he learned from his father, he nevertheless continued to write at a prodigious rate, the books, on the whole, getting sparer and sparer. "Prose must accord with the land," he said, suggesting that as the emptiness of death closed in on him from one direction, the vast stretches of his beginnings still yawned behind him.

Every summer, classes of aspiring writers from the University of North Texas's journalism program made a short pilgrimage to Archer City, to McMurtry's multi-building bookstore there. They came at his invitation. Starting in the late 1980s, he had begun filling his old hometown, once a bookless place, with more books than people. In the summers he would leave the stores open late at night so the students could browse—the best education they could have. One of his old Hermes 3000 typewriters, on which he had written many of his novels, sat in the open in one of the buildings on a cluttered desktop. No one was likely to steal it (or even to know what it was): it was outmoded technology.

The man himself—always dressing the same, in jeans and a Dr Pepper polo shirt, and exuding an air of quiet humility—rarely appeared. "Larry was an elusive idea," said one student. "It's like he was a ghost or something because he wasn't there. Everybody was talking about him and everybody has stories about him—nobody's meeting or seeing him."

He had vanished behind a wall of books.

Though he knew that "as soon as something's ended, people will flock to get at least a glimpse of what it was like . . . it's human nature," he did not want to be bothered by people wishing to honor him as a major author or as a distinguished public figure. He discouraged one would-be biographer, saying, "My women friends will never talk to you."

By the 1990s, the University of North Texas wasn't the nation's only academic institution paying him heed, though as a popular writer of plainly written texts, he was not a favorite of theory-laden professors. Still, a fair number of young teachers seeking tenure and historians writing revisionist appraisals of the West analyzed his books in monographs, articles, and dissertations. Many of them (for instance, D. L. Birchfield, writing on "Texas-American Myth" or Alexander Lalrinzama examining McMurtry's modes of representation) chastised McMurtry for citing so frequently the emptiness of West Texas or of the Great Plains stretching north of the Red River. They charged him with offering a narrow, privileged view. The plains were never empty, they argued—Indigenous peoples populated the deserts and the grasslands long before white settlers arrived to stake their claims. McMurtry never disputed this point. He agreed with revisionists recasting western expansion as "an irresponsible white man's adventure, hugely destructive of the land itself, of the native people, and even of the white male's own women and children," but the revisionists' problem, he thought, was their uninformed arrogance: they believed they were the first to notice "how violent, how terrible, how hard" western life really was: "My boyhood among the old-timers leads me to exactly the opposite conclusion: everyone noticed how hard it was."

Readers had reasons to challenge McMurtry's depictions of various peoples in his novels, but the notion that the plains weren't really as lonely as he made them out to be, that he was somehow blind to the presence of the original settlers, missed the point badly. The people who held these convictions read McMurtry metaphorically and politically—any way but how the books instructed readers to approach. They weren't familiar with the realities of his landscape, his starting point; they had not seen that wind-scoured vastness, that sky, that uninterrupted horizon. Nary a soul for miles. They interpreted McMurtry ideologically, through the myopia of professional specialties and agendas. They did not grasp the need for escape (and the failure to do so), the self-exile, the nomadism, producing one of the unique bodies of work in contemporary American literature. And they would be among the first to die if left alone in McMurtry country.

The place was damned *empty*.

2

————

arry Jeff McMurtry was born on June 3, 1936, into a dying way of life. "I knew as I was growing up something was wrong," he said. "I didn't know what. My father couldn't . . . have articulated it. But I could tell something was over and it [was] not going to come back. And I knew my father knew that."

A few months after the heaviest dust storms of the Great Depression razored the plains, McMurtry's mother, Hazel Ruth, brought her boy into the world in the Wichita Falls General Hospital. The hospital had been established in 1915, five years after scores of veterinary surgeons settled in town, the region's priorities being clear. As late as the 1980s, a triple-A travel guide, offering visitors places to see in Wichita Falls, listed nothing.

Hazel brought her infant back to the McMurtry ranch, located about forty miles southwest of Wichita Falls, eighteen miles from Archer City, on a grassy humpback in otherwise flat land known locally as Idiot Ridge. *Who* gave the place its designation is difficult to trace, but it's not hard to guess the reason *why*: the dirt was parched in every direction, if *direction* meant anything in the barren sameness one saw, turning in a circle. The ranch sat near several hundred acres once owned by Mark Twain. Twain never set foot in Texas, but he purchased the property following the Civil War to help one of his wife's cousins get started in the world. The land was eventually sold to a rancher named Sanford Wilson, the McMurtrys' neighbor, though neighbors had to travel sometimes hours to visit: back then, only some five people lived in any square mile in Archer County.

Hazel and McMurtry's father, William Jefferson Jr.—known to family and friends as Jeff Mac—lived with Jeff Mac's parents, Louisa Francis and William, in a shotgun house built by the men from a design obtained through the Montgomery Ward department store and mail-order chain. The family referred to the place as the Monkey Ward house on Idiot Ridge. It overlooked a small spring and a defunct old military road turned cattle trail. One of the last massacres on the southern plains, the Warren Wagon Train raid, occurred just a dozen miles from the ridge a few years before the McMurtrys settled in the area in 1889. A band of Kiowa under war leaders Satanta and Satank (whose son had been murdered by settlers) attacked a convoy of wagons hauling goods from one outpost to another, slaughtering and burning seven men.

The McMurtrys, nomads from the start, were of Scotch-Irish descent. The name can be traced back to the Scottish islands of Arran and Bute; restless wanderers brought it to Ulster. In ancient Gaelic, the name's origin, Mac Muircheartaigh, translates as "sea navigator." Once the Mc-Murtrys crossed the ocean, early in the eighteenth century, they settled in what would become Kentucky and Missouri. In the aftermath of the final battle of the American Revolution, on August 19, 1782, Captain John McMurtry was captured by unidentified Natives. Reportedly, he was about to be burned at the stake when a violent thunderstorm doused the flames. "The Indians, believing the Great Spirit had taken their prisoner under his protection, spared his life . . . [whereupon] an Indian and his squaw adopted him and he was saved from persecution," wrote an early family historian, establishing tale-telling as a McMurtry trait long before the family produced a famous novelist.

McMurtry's grandparents married in Benton County, Missouri, just after the Civil War ended. Later, they never spoke of the South, as if the past were too horrible to contemplate. In search of a sustainable life, they crossed the Missouri River, a "huge deformity of waters," the "River of Sticks," according to the American painter George Catlin, the Missouri being well-known among boatmen for snagging vessels with underwater branches and stumps. In 1877, the McMurtrys arrived at a place barely more endurable, near the present town of Denton, Texas, where William broke horses for a living. The great conflicts over land between white settlers and the Comanche and the Kiowa were only just finished—and maybe *weren't*, entirely. Satank and Satanta had been arrested and sent to Fort Richardson in the Texas Panhandle to become the first Natives tried in U.S. civil courts. On the way to the fort, Satank, singing a "death song," tore the fetters from his wrists and leapt from his horse onto a startled guard's back, inviting the other soldiers to shoot him. At his trial, Satanta warned the jurors, "If you kill me it will be like a bolt of lightning making a spark in dry prairie hay." Before he could be hanged, he committed suicide in prison. The chiefs' deaths left a leadership vacuum among their people. Still, an unhappy party would occasionally slip out of its cramped reservation in the Indian Territory, cross the Red River, and crouch among scrubby salt cedars waiting to attack, reminding settlers that the current accommodations were not to their liking. In addition to dreading her husband's consumption of home-brewed whiskey, Louisa—who claimed to have a little Sioux blood in her—feared sudden raids every day.

"My grandparents were among the very first white settlers in [West Texas]," McMurtry wrote. "In settling the land, [they] acted upon and developed a set of values, a set of beliefs, a set of traditions and customs that really went with the frontier way of life and that were designed to insure certain things, namely survival . . . not only survival of the individual but, hopefully, survival of the group."

For three dollars an acre, the McMurtrys bought a half section of bluestem prairie in Archer County, by the road running from Buffalo Springs to the old Fort Belknap. There, among twisted mesquite scraps (grown from hard seeds deposited in the soil in the waste of imported Mexican cattle), they raised twelve children: nine boys, three girls. McMurtry's oldest sister, Sue, recalled hearing family stories as a child—how her grandmother always refused to attend rodeos because "she'd had one at her back door for fifty years." While William tended cattle and guzzled whiskey, Louisa cut the wood to shove into her cast-iron cookstove and made sure her children got fed, year-round; the kids particularly liked her wild plum preserves, stocked with plum kernels wrapped in candied skins.

The girls took to sewing. The boys all wanted to be cowpokes. From atop the fence rails around the ranch they'd stare into the empty sky above the Indian Territory to the north and watch the last of the great American cattle drives heading out to the Chicago and Dodge City rail yards. They imagined the adventures awaiting them on the trail. "Cowboys are romantics, extreme romantics, and ninety-nine out of a hundred of them are sentimental to the core," McMurtry learned in early childhood, listening to his uncles' stories—often secondhand yarns tricked up with fabricated drama. "[Cowboys] are oriented toward the past and face the present only under duress, and then with extreme reluctance." In the 1980s, McMurtry wrote his friend the novelist Max Crawford that with the exception of E. C. "Teddy Blue" Abbott's *We Pointed Them North* and J. Evetts Haley's biography of Charles Goodnight, he found books on cattle herding pallid, probably because "my 9 cowboy uncles could tell trail drive stories so well that the written words [*sic*] has rarely competed."

The realities of cowboying were the precise opposite of romantic. When McMurtry's Uncle Jim, the second eldest of the boys, was fifteen, his father, convinced of his son's riding prowess, put him on a wild bronc. Jim remained in the saddle, finally exhausting the animal, but at the cost of a broken neck. William pulled him off the horse, placed his hands on either side of his son's head and attempted to snap his neck back into place. Jim lived with a severely pinched nerve ever after and spent forty years in a wheelchair (which did not prevent him from becoming a successful rancher and banker).

For a short spell just after World War I, the family moved to a plot of land near the town of Clarendon in the Texas Panhandle. The town's founder, a Methodist minister, had envisioned the community as a "sobriety settlement"—trail herders referred to it derisively as "Saint's Roost"—which suggests that perhaps Louisa was trying to tame her rowdy husband.

Right before the move, Jeff Mac enlisted in the U.S. Army, but the war ended before he could be trained. He was becoming a rather sophisticated young man. Growing up, he had attended school only about three months a year, when no cattle needed tending, but now he was driving with his friends into Wichita Falls on the weekends to see the moving pictures. At a pie-throwing farce one night he couldn't stop laughing and had to be dragged out of the theater by his brothers.

He even took classes at the small college in Clarendon, graduating with a general science degree in 1921. But soon after that, the old folks grew tired of the High Plains winds (against which "people lean west and trees lean east," an old saying went). William, now sporting a great gray mustache, had had enough of his boringly sober neighbors. He moved with Louisa back to Idiot Ridge. Jeff Mac went with them, hitching his fate to the ranching life.

At that time, Archer County, named after a former secretary of war for the Republic of Texas, had been an officially organized community for just over two decades. The first white child was born in the county in 1879, a year after Satanta's suicide. The 1890 census listed sixteen "Negro" residents, almost all of them chuck-wagon cooks on the open range. Single men predominated, itinerants more attached to horses and cattle than families.

The county had a police force now—largely replacing the Texas Rangers, who had once patrolled the area looking for Comanche and Kiowa—and a brand-new sandstone jailhouse complete with a gallows. The first prisoner was a horse thief. Mostly, the jail hosted cowboys who'd come to "paint the town red"—firing their pistols into the night to celebrate the end of a trail drive. The county had a dirt-floor schoolhouse, built inside the shell of a former saloon. And it laid claim to being the source of one of the earliest cowboy ballads, "The Dying Cowboy," written by a singer who'd come across a small grave marker on the banks of the south fork of the Little Wichita River. Carved into the sandy stone, barely legible, were crude letters spelling "cow boy" and "last words."

In 1916, the Panther Oil Company of Wichita Falls began drilling in and around Archer County, pocking the open range and—from the point of view of men like William and Jeff Mac—desecrating it. Oil—which was ugly and smelly, requiring the use of ponderous stationary equipment—had no heroic potential as far as the cattlemen were concerned.

A full seven years before Larry McMurtry entered this conflicted scene in the Wichita Falls General Hospital, the *Archer County News* announced the area's death throes: "People had more religion, more freedom, more Americanism apparently than they have today," an editor wrote. "We had more respect for womanhood, more respect for mankind in those good old days, when modesty, virtue, and true Christianity were looked upon as the true attributes of a lady or gentleman."

Jeff Mac's mother would have agreed wholeheartedly—she couldn't believe her boy had married a woman who'd been married before. One tenet of the cowboy ethos said that a dusty, unkempt trail rider could never be worthy of a good woman. Jeff Mac had reversed the situation, as far as Louisa could see.

Hazel Ruth McIver was the daughter of a Methodist minister in Haskell, Texas, eighty miles west of Archer City. The fact that Hazel's father was a man of the cloth didn't console Louisa. A roving preacher roistering about the oil-soaked Permian Basin boomtowns of Snyder, Haskell, Colorado City, and Big Spring couldn't possibly provide a child with a stable upbringing. Sure enough, before marrying Jeff Mac at the age of twenty-five (Louisa's boy was thirty-four when they wed), Hazel had been hitched to a philandering man of whom she never spoke afterward. The experience had humbled her, heightened her fretful nature, left her always expecting the worst, but Louisa could still sense the free-spirited girl Hazel could be, dancing, flirting, and playing basketball in the wastes of West Texas. Hazel had swiftly divorced her first husband—Jeff Mac had embraced a "soiled dove" and Louisa never let him forget it.

He defended his wife to his mother, but he also absorbed his mother's point of view. As a boy, he had watched Louisa haul water from the spring to the McMurtry cabin every morning, and he never forgot how hard she had worked. "To the end of his days, my father found it difficult to forgive women the ease of modern arrangements—something as simple as tap water," McMurtry wrote. "The old woman, Louisa Francis, recognized my father's unease and used it, becoming a gifted martyr and exploiting his sense of guilt." Whenever Hazel wanted to take a short trip to go shopping or to plan a picnic, Jeff Mac believed she was shirking her duties at the ranch. Whenever Hazel tried to help Louisa with the chores, Louisa let her know she did nothing right. She was only in the way. One day, as the women argued over who would fix Jeff Mac's breakfast, Louisa slapped Hazel. "My parents, like the Tolstoys, were thus sadly undone at the very outset of a long marriage," McMurtry said. He believed that slap reverberated throughout forty years of his parents' life together. In an attempt to ease the tensions, Jeff Mac borrowed $150 for lumber, built a tiny three-room cabin fifty yards south of his parents' house on Idiot Ridge, and moved into it with his pregnant wife.

Larry McMurtry spent the first six years of his life in that claustrophobic cabin.

His earliest memory, at the age of three, was of his parents screaming at each other in a hot, stifling room. He would grow up easily irritated at domestic disorder, quick to quibble with partners and friends over minor matters of day-to-day existence, enthralled by drama but fearful of major conflicts in his relationships with women. He worked strenuously to avoid such trouble.

His memories of his grandparents were hazy. His grandfather died when he was four. Before that, McMurtry, perched behind the saddle on his grandfather's big horse, would ride with William into Windthorst, a nearby town, to pick up the mail at the general store, or he'd sit with his grandpa on the roof of the scorpion-plagued storm cellar, listening to stories of the county's settlement, or he'd ask the old man where the road went—Highway 281, a bright river of lights at night. William grunted. "Oklahoma," he'd say, in a tone of voice suggesting no one need ever go there.

McMurtry got the impression early that western depredations, while strengthening women, had also silenced them. His mother was a fine storyteller—tales brimming with laughter, glimpses of dances and child-hood friendships—but she picked her moments and knew when to keep her stories to herself, which was most of the time. And occasionally her tales revealed a rock-bottom uneasiness with life, particularly as it was lived in the West: "At some point in her childhood two mules ran away with a wagon she was in; though not injured physically . . . from that moment on she was frightened, not just of mules but of everything . . . In her mind's eye, swimming led inevitably to drowning, flying to falling, driving to car wrecks, walking to snakebite, the highways to murder and rape," Mc-Murtry said.

As for Louisa, he couldn't remember her ever saying a thing to him. It was as if the wind had stolen her words. In fact, she was worn out. It was no longer worth it, to her, to try to reason or argue with the world. Prior to her tiff with Hazel, the last time anyone in the family remembered her raising her voice was sometime in the early 1920s, when she issued Wil-liam an ultimatum: stop drinking or I'll leave you. For nineteen years, his half-full jug of whiskey hung on a wall in the barn's saddle room until the nail rusted and the jug fell to the dirt.

Looking out across waving oat grass at dusk, in the direction of the red diesel truck lights swimming along 281 or of the low whistle of the brand-new *Zephyr* bound for Denver or of the winking blue and yellow glare of Wichita Falls on the northeast horizon, McMurtry felt loneliness blow through him; he felt isolated, imagining the vast, empty prairies to the north, the semideserts to the west; he felt lonely for the mother he could never know, listening to her stories and not recognizing, beneath her sternness, the carefree girl she had started out to be; he felt the romance and wistfulness of his uncles' trail-driving tales. They talked often of the Great Drift—when, in the years 1886 and 1887, before even *they* were cowboys, the cowboy life took a hit as Archer County's springs dried up and folks shriveled in oppressive heat. Maddened and thirsty, cattle drifted down dry streambeds searching fruitlessly for water. Ranchers, already parceling out the open range with the relatively new invention of barbed wire, built even more tight fences to keep wandering cows away from their dwindling water supplies. It was one of McMurtry's earliest, deepest lessons: the scariest word in the language was *drought.*

Aridity, he would learn, had determined every inch of his country, every pattern of thought behind the culture shaping him. In this land of rocks and clay and roots and wings, it was no accident that the brittle native plants assumed twisted shapes, writhing and fighting in the soil for the slightest traces of moisture; no accident that animals here developed a capacity to resist thirst for long periods and grew short, high-crowned teeth in order to eat the harsh grasses yellowing in the heat; no accident that prehistoric peoples here achieved sophisticated cultural practices unsurpassed by any other Indigenous groups on the continent—if they hadn't, they wouldn't have survived—and no surprise that the region's scarce resources prevented nearby settlements such as Santa Fe, which predated Boston and New York, from keeping pace with the rest of the country's growing urban centers.

The plains on which McMurtry dreamed as a boy were formed when the vast mid-continental sea erupted with lava, creating the Rocky Mountains. The mountain chain upended the rugged ground running east of its peaks, tilting the land, a dramatic slope slanting all the way to the mighty Mississippi, draining the old seabed. The Rockies cast a long rain shadow, blocking huge pockets of moisture from accumulating eastward, killing the trees, making way for the grass. The mariner winds swooping in from the Pacific Ocean mixed with the warm, salty air flowing up from the Gulf of Mexico, establishing in the atmosphere above present-day California, Arizona, New Mexico, and Texas a moving sheet of water a foot thick, 350 miles long, and 340 miles wide—but because of the Rockies' presence, the water fell sparsely and erratically over the plains, leading to frequent droughts. The McMurtry family's trail-riding life was doomed before it even began.

The plains Natives' buffalo culture evolved before Spanish horses arrived in the New World. (Horses had been here before, but had fallen extinct after scores of them migrated across the Bering Land Bridge to Asia and Europe.) The Natives based their economy on tracking herds of bison—a compact species especially suited to short grass—and killing only as many as they could butcher and consume at a time. It was a largely predictable, satisfying way of life. When Hernán Cortés arrived from Spain in 1519, he brought six hundred men and sixteen horses. Two hundred and fifty years later, the horse population had grown enormously, altering the Natives' practices, giving their nomadic rituals greater scope, enabling them to better guide and trap herds, and increasing their efficiency. Their customs remained sustainable: free-ranging fit the land, allowing over-grazed patches of ground plenty of time to regrow.

By 1870, two million bison had vanished from the region, after the U.S. Army's deliberate campaigns to thin their herds in order to cripple Native cultures and after the arrival of the railroads, enabling cattlemen to ship animals to distant markets, east and west. The plains were effectively cleared for white men to free-range their cattle, based on rituals developed by the Spanish-speaking vaqueros in northern Mexico. Immediately, these green new cowboys commodified the land: "Grass is worthless until a cow sticks its nose into it," they'd say.

The long-horned, long-legged Spanish cattle adapted easily to the grass-lands, standing tall enough to clear brambles and thorny brush. But for economic reasons, the cowboys began importing smaller, less robust Mexican cattle and cows from England, animals less suited to the environment, the *wrong animals*—further damaging any long-term future in which the McMurtrys might have partaken.

"The American West as we know it today came about in response to European—particularly Spanish—disappointment," McMurtry wrote. North America's treasures could not match the Aztec or Inca vaults, so old-world monarchs lessened their investment in the region, leaving set-tlers to their own, frequently misguided ways.

As McMurtry well knew, the great American cattle drives—foundation of so many cowboy myths in newspapers, dime novels, pulp fiction, and movies, ranging from the mid-nineteenth century to the present—lasted only about twenty years, reaching a peak in the 1870s.

The earliest drives out of Texas, lasting six months or so, headed west to California after the discovery of gold in the 1850s. Cattle worth five to ten dollars a head in Texas brought twenty times that much in San Francisco. Seven years later, the California market was glutted, so ranchers contracted to supply beef to army forts and Indian reservations in West Texas, the Indian Territory, and in what became New Mexico. In 1866, as railroad-loading facilities spread, over 260,000 head of cattle crossed the Red River, bound for northern, eastern, and western markets.

McMurtry's uncles taught him the deep lore. A drive usually began in the spring after a roundup when grass was plentiful and the northers hadn't commenced. A twelve-man crew, paid about thirty dollars a month, could handle a herd of two to three thousand head. An uninterrupted drive could make about ten to fifteen miles a day. Usually, lightning caused a stampede. Drovers would get in front of the cattle and turn the leaders to the right, forcing them to run in a circle. Slowly the cowboys would bring the rest of the herd into the circle, riding around it, making it smaller and smaller until the cows, barely able to move, settled.

By 1880, major droughts, refrigeration, the zigzagging of low-hanging telegraph wires across steep prairie gullies, and the branching out of the railroads diminished the efficacy of long drives. Cattle were bred not to roam but to graze in smaller spaces, growing ever fatter to suit market demand. In 1874, the appearance of barbed wire spelled the end of the open range, of unrestricted motion. "I believe the grassland was where we destroyed democracy because of our inability to accept and understand freedom," said the historian Richard Manning.

And though McMurtry's uncles had not experienced the heyday of cowboying, the majesty of vast herds of animals on the move would always bring them to tears.

McMurtry participated in his first cattle drive at the tender age of four: a matter of moving lazy cows fifteen miles from the McMurtrys' 150,000-acre ranch to a place called Anarene, once a town but now just a series of corrals about to collapse near a railroad yard, where the cows were shipped. McMurtry trailed the herd at a slow pace, watched by an old cowboy named Jesse Brewer, charged by Jeff Mac with looking after the boy and keeping him out of trouble. Brewer was not cut out for this much responsibility—age and trail injuries had left him barely able to control his own horse, a feisty bay gelding. Rather than *prevent* trouble, he expected and even courted it, sunk in self-pity over what he felt was his wasted life. If McMurtry waded through a puddle, Brewer yelled that he was probably going to be attacked by water moccasins. If the boy got his horse up to a galloping trot, Brewer warned him he was going to break his horse's leg in a prairie dog hole. Still, McMurtry considered Brewer his first childhood friend. He loved riding beside the old fellow, listening to sorrowful stories of the past.

On that first cattle drive, the only trouble was Brewer's gelding. Whenever the horse got away from him, hauling Brewer off in a swell of dust over the western horizon, McMurtry's horse, sensing opportunity, turned and tried to bite the boy, or he'd brush the boy against a tree, or he'd deliberately fall and try to roll the fidgety rider off his back. Horses would never be dear to Larry McMurtry.

His father gave him his first pony at three, which he promptly rode into a swarm of yellow jackets in a mesquite thicket, getting stung twelve times. Before his grandfather died, McMurtry's most intimate acquaintance with a horse was with his grandpa's old nag, "so big and slow that I could have danced a jig on his rump," he said. Once, on a trip to Windthorst to pick up the mail, William and his grandson plodded straight into a hailstorm—another fine example of the messes a horse could get you into, McMurtry thought. Man and boy rode out the storm under an oak tree as balls of ice crackled like shattering glass on the rocks.

Back at the ranch, McMurtry discovered that dismounting was no guarantee of safety. Immediately, on the ground, he'd be surrounded by pecking hens, guineas, roosters, peacocks, and turkeys, many of them taller than he was and apparently afflicted with some unquenchable anger at the world. Or you could fall into a pigpen and nearly be trampled to death as an object of the pigs' curiosity. Or you could be slapped in the face by a flurry of wings when a white snowy owl emerged unexpectedly from the outhouse just as you rushed toward it urgently in need of discharging your business.

When he was six, McMurtry's favorite old dog, Scraps, died of a rattlesnake bite. Sometime later, the boy watched his father battle a ten-foot rattler with a shovel. The rattler had struck at Jeff Mac's boot and barely missed. Jeff Mac bludgeoned the powerful thing as its tail buzzed, but he had to sit a long spell afterward to collect himself. A neighbor thought he might be having a heart attack. Eventually, Jeff Mac got over his shakiness, but McMurtry never did. From earliest childhood, he developed a decided antipathy, if not an outright dislike, for animals in general, with the exception of domestic cats and dogs. It was clear to Jeff Mac and all McMurtry's uncles that the boy was not going to be a cowpoke. He was too myopic to see cattle at a distance, on the horizon. And he "wasn't particularly mean," his uncles said: a major liability on the plains.

The unspoken corollary to this observation was that there was no future in cowboying, anyway. "To me [that life] was hollow and I think it was hollow for my father," McMurtry said. "He totally loved cowboys . . . but he knew perfectly well that it wouldn't last another generation." Every year on his birthday, McMurtry's mother would stand him up on an overturned galvanized washtub and take his picture to celebrate the occasion. The overheated tin scorched his bare feet. The grimace on his face revealed how ill at ease he was in this world despite his love for his family. "I [now] regard ranching as a form of slavery," he'd proclaim many years later.

If he was insufficiently mean, he did *not* lack courage or curiosity. He wanted to see *everything,* and from the first he demonstrated amazing recall. At sunset, he'd sit on a fence rail, mulling over the day's events in his mind, the prairie's openness offering his imagination free rein. It was almost as if an ancestral memory kicked in. "Lacking a tail and the agility necessary for treetop life, humans were disadvantaged in the forests, but with the ability to stand erect and see over the grass, humans fit [the place] . . . This is where our deepest knowledge and love lie," Richard Manning wrote in a book called *Grassland,* always a great favorite of McMurtry's.

"[I was] . . . conscious of looking north and not south," he said. "I don't like the trees"—or even *imagining* the timbers of Southeast Texas. "I like looking straight up to the guts of the Great Plains."

In West Texas—the *malpais,* the "bad country," to the Spanish—colors are vivid, the only contrasts being stark light and shade, the air, devoid of particles and water vapor, assuming an excessively crisp quality, especially in summer when the sun climbs to an almost vertical position above the land and the hard ground reflects the light back into the sky with an intense focus. Red clay, yellow stones, the gray-green of the creosote, smelling like fire smoke after a brief, hot rain. "A huge sky . . . I simply took [it] for granted, when I was growing up," McMurtry said. Anywhere else, for the rest of his life, he'd feel "sky deprivation . . . gloomy without knowing why" until he realized he was suffering "sky longing." Beneath the sky—

his *father's* sky—he mostly contemplated his father and his father's way of life. Several years later, after countless travels far from the ranch, he would reflect: "I have looked at many places quickly—my father looked at one place deeply . . . [For him,] land, grass, and sky composed a great, ever varying text whose interest he could never exhaust. What Proust [became] to me, the grasslands were to my father, a great subtle text which would repay endless study."

Just as he felt the loneliness of sitting, exposed, beneath a wide, purple dusk, he felt the sadness hollowing out his father, leaving him blank behind the ribs, grieving, in advance, everything he had ever known.

And why was it worth mourning? Any of it? McMurtry ached to know because the question so clearly pained his father. From the boy's perch on the fence, little here seemed worth preserving. The past may have been glorious, as his uncles insisted, and the nature and intensity of the work may have made sense once, but they no longer did. His father was perennially in debt. Going forward, wouldn't it be best to shuck it all? Not the camaraderie, not the fun of learning to shoot a .22, of hunting antelope, birds, and deer, which McMurtry would learn to enjoy with his father and his uncles. No, not the family's daily rituals—but the harsh legacy of what Jeff Mac, Uncle Johnny, Uncle Jim, and the rest referred to as the Old West. As a boy, McMurtry experienced enough traces of the Old West, lingering in the present, to be fascinated and frightened by the essence of the past.

Once, when he was very little, his father took him on a cattle-buying trip to South Texas near a border town called Alice. Jeff Mac told McMurtry to wait in the car while he rode off on horseback with the ranch owner to inspect the cows. As soon as the men left, four dusty and possibly drunk vaqueros appeared at the car windows. They'd ridden up on horses. They laughed, tapped the glass, and grinned with dirty teeth, trying to coax him out of the car using spurs, rope, and mountain oysters—calves' testicles—to snack on. He imagined being abducted into the brush and never seen again. "No sabe," he said over and over, the only Spanish phrase he knew. Far from being romantic figures, these vaqueros—the only cowboys McMurtry had ever seen aside from his uncles and his father's men—were reckless and appalling.

On another cattle-buying jaunt to South Texas, this time at Laredo, McMurtry again watched his father disappear on horseback into thick mesquite, leaving him to "fret in the car." That night, in a cow camp on the Texas-Mexico border, a vaquero rode into the light of the fire, carrying a dead javelina slung across the back of his horse. After a supper of wild pig and frijoles, shared with the most desperately hungry men McMurtry had ever seen, Jeff Mac and his son got eaten alive by bedbugs in a Laredo motel. By now, cowboying had completely lost whatever luster it might have had for the boy.

Closer to home, in the small community of Windthorst, a settlement of German immigrants where McMurtry and his grandpa used to grab the mail, a rancher walked into his barn one morning, milked his cows, then picked up a shotgun and took off the top of his head. For young McMurtry, greater than the shock of learning that people could kill themselves was the fact that the man had completed his morning chores before doing himself in: it seemed to say something profound—charming, tragic—about cowboy life.

Locals called the German families "Dutchmen"—Europe being, to them, an unimportant, blurry rock halfway across the globe. The McMurtrys had little to do with the Germans. Even as relative newcomers they seemed marked by the Old West's melancholy scars. One day when McMurtry was ten, he was riding with his father in the car, checking the state of their pastures, when they spotted a tiny barefooted boy running screaming along a parched dirt road. The boy said his little brother had drowned in a horse trough over by Windthorst. Jeff Mac turned the car in the direction of the boy's pointing finger, found the ranch, snatched the limp wet child from his mother's arms (the woman spoke no English), and managed to revive him, pumping his chest on the wooden porch. For many years afterward, the McMurtrys were the recipients of the grateful woman's sauerkraut, delivered regularly, year-round, in large glass jars.

For McMurtry, the woman's passivity that day suggested the fatalistic outlook imposed on individuals by the cowboy way of life: the acceptance of catastrophe as a natural condition of the land.

He would frequently see another silent, broken woman on his way into Archer City on the school bus. Bent, she would stand by the side of the road near the west fork of the Trinity River until a driver (often Jeff Mac) gave her a lift into town. The story went that many years earlier a skunk trapper had taken a fancy to the woman in a cow camp and offered a winter's catch of skunk hides for her. Ever since, she'd lived near the river, in a shack hidden among post oak scrub.

As McMurtry sat on his father's fence at dusk, watching scissortails chase crows across the sky, gazing out at the yellow shine of the grass or at the ball lightning rolling across the prairie, he'd wonder why the old ways were worth a second thought. Mentally, he'd link his own harsh experiences to his uncles' stories and the Roy Rogers or Gene Autry Westerns his mother took him to see at the Archer City picture show: a complex approach to comprehending "legacy." It had something to do with what his father called "character," a topic of concern every time Jeff Mac tried to beat back another invasive growth of mesquite—a struggle against impossible odds.

The point wasn't whether the Old West as an ideal was worth holding on to; the point was proving that you *could* hold on, under *any* circumstances. Self-denial was at the root of western character, a commitment to stoicism and duty so fierce, it fixed your soul as hard as your jaw. McMurtry saw this grim tenacity in his father and in his father's brothers, and he felt it growing in him. Instinctively, he'd come to believe that whenever his father was away on business, it was up to *him* to keep the world together. In the 1960s, in a letter to Ken Kesey, he would write: "My father could no more be optimistic than he could fly—pessimism was bred into him, as it was bred into most people of his place and era. A lot of it got bred into me."

After a while—it didn't take long, at the ranch—McMurtry began to connect self-denial with self-extinction.

Change came to Archer County the year McMurtry turned three. A young United States senator named Lyndon Baines Johnson—elected suspiciously, it was said, when somehow a bunch of dead people in South Texas managed to vote—wore down President Franklin Delano Roosevelt. "Now, Lyndon, now what in the hell do you want?" FDR would yell. Johnson managed to finagle money from the feds and funneled resources to a contractor buddy of his to bring electricity to rural Texas. Now a bright bulb hung in the outhouse, attracting mosquitoes and gnats but at least scaring away the owls. Women on ranches and farms could now "set aside their corrugated washboards and let their red hot cook stoves cool off while they iron on a hot August afternoon," Johnson announced. This raised Louisa's hackles: the coming of the wires meant that young women in general, and Hazel in particular, had caught a break *she'd* never got.

Hazel drew Louisa's wrath again three years later, when, in 1942, she said she wanted to move into Archer City. Louisa figured this flibberti-gibbet just wanted to play bridge with the stuck-up oil-field folks in town rather than stay home and make soap for her child's bathing or butcher pork for the family's supper. In fact, Hazel didn't want her boy riding the school bus anymore. (Sitting on the bus "in the company of older farm children whose behavior verged on the brutish, was too much for me," McMurtry said.) Reluctantly, Jeff Mac bought a small wooden box of a house in town, painted dull white. It resembled most of the other houses, with the exception of the Slack family's shingled two-story prairie cottage—McMurtry would spend much time there in the years ahead—and Old Man Taylor's spread (a mansion by Archer City standards).

Will Taylor had earned most of his money in petroleum, but happiness had eluded him. His boy had died in an oil-field accident and the old man had withdrawn into his house, just beyond the McMurtrys' hayfield on the south side of town. From his small bedroom window McMurtry could see a light burning all night on Taylor's second floor. When he asked his father what the old man was doing, Jeff Mac said he was probably sitting up, reading—an intriguing idea, as Hazel had ordered a subscription to *Reader's Digest* and bought a cheap set of encyclopedias as soon as the family moved from the ranch: the first books to assume a place, like furniture, in the McMurtry household. Hazel seemed keenly aware of the need to expand her boy's world; that same year, the year of the move, the family took a whirlwind automobile trip through Arizona's Petrified Forest to the Grand Canyon. McMurtry didn't take in much of the scenery. He caught a fever and spent most of the trip vaguely hallucinating in the back seat.

The radio, boosted by the miracle of electricity, was another world-expander. In between comic episodes of *Fibber McGee and Molly,* and concerts by Pappy O'Daniel and the Light Crust Doughboys, McMurtry sat riveted in the evenings by the voice of Franklin Roosevelt, whom his father had voted for, saddling up and riding to the one-room schoolhouse McMurtry attended to slip a piece of paper into a ballot box. Galvanized by Roosevelt's pleas with U.S. citizens to support the war effort any way they could, McMurtry, returning on weekends for visits to his grandparents' ranch, climbed the windmill to serve as a junior plane spotter, scanning the sky for German bombers over listless, graying sorghum fields. The only planes he ever saw were Piper Cubs belonging to local oil companies, checking their pipes. He didn't understand the war, but he liked what he heard about the power of hand grenades. If he could get his paws on a few of those, he thought, he'd blow the nasty pigs out of their wallows.

Jeff Mac sat no stiller in town than he did on the ranch. He was always driving out to Idiot Ridge to look after cows. His only quiet times were at the breakfast table, when he'd sit and drink coffee and read the comics in the paper, particularly enjoying J. R. Williams's *Out Our Way*. McMurtry (whenever he got up that early) liked these peaceful moments; Jeff Mac's reverie with the funny pages brought out a side of him—mirthful, calm, the opposite of self-denying—the boy rarely saw and grew to cherish.

The act of reading brought McMurtry another early pleasure: in addition to the *Reader's Digest* and *Field & Stream,* his father left copies of *The Cattleman Magazine,* a trade journal, lying around the house. One day Jeff Mac showed his son an article the writers had done on the family, with the title "McMurtry Means Beef." It thrilled him to see his name in print. The spiked and curly letters possessed a kind of permanence that nothing else in his world could match.

Two events coincided when McMurtry was six to strongly shape his sensibility. The first was the move to town. Archer City was hardly urban, but living there after growing up surrounded only by family on Idiot Ridge gave McMurtry his first experience of a movement that would define his life—and of a broader American movement. "[I] formed my consciousness in the period when (a very fortunate period for the development of any novelist, I have to think) one set of values and traditions was being strongly challenged by another set of values and traditions," he said. "That is, I grew up just at the same time when rural and soil traditions . . . were really, for the first time, being seriously challenged by urban traditions." The lure of what he called the urban—the appearance of books, the presence of a local movie house, the warmth of cafés serving as community centers where whatever passed for culture could spread—led McMurtry into a generational clash with his father and his uncles (aided by his natural tendencies). "When the conflict of the generations . . . can be joined with such a structural and stylistic difference as exists . . . between the country life and the city life as it developed in the '40s and '50s, then you have something very rich, something that is very often painful to the people that are making the transition from one way of life to the other, nonetheless something very rich," McMurtry said.

The second important event in his development was the appearance of his cousin Robert Hilburn at the house's front door. McMurtry was sick in bed at the time—or malingering, listening to the radio, trying to avoid school. Hilburn was on his way to enlist to fight in the war in Europe. McMurtry didn't know him well—they were far apart in age—but Hilburn was shedding possessions and he thought the boy might like his old adventure books. He handed McMurtry a box filled with nineteen Grosset & Dunlap editions of popular children's books, among them *Jerry Todd in the Whispering Cave, Poppy Ott and the Stuttering Parrot,* and *Sergeant Silk, the Prairie Scout,* the story of a Canadian Mountie. McMurtry had his own private library now. It was dusty. The pages smelled a little like tree bark and the sweat of sticky palms. He was thrilled to discover that people were allowed to *make up* stories (not like the pieces in the newspaper); comforted to experience the solidity of print, a "stability I could always depend on," he remembered feeling. He imagined the stories he'd heard all his life from his uncles transformed into solid blocks of prose on a page, and a new understanding of "legacy" grew in him, still unarticulated—how a feeling for life, for the past, could be formed into a package that finally made some sort of sense. And it *lasted,* unlike words on the wind, unlike the subjects of the stories being spun.

"What I don't remember is how I learned to read," he said. "I had only briefly been to school, and no one, that I can recall, bothered about teaching me my ABC's. Yet I *could* read, and reading very quickly came to seem what I was meant to do."

Bill Broyles, who would study literature and writing with McMurtry in the 1960s, said, "It was like he was starved, and once he tasted it, he embraced it."

Hazel felt her boy's need for privacy and concentration. To his delight, she moved him and his box of books into a small garage apartment behind the house. Briefly, the family cook had stayed there (another move-to-town experiment), but they couldn't afford to keep her, so she'd traveled on. The place was sometimes freezing, but McMurtry didn't mind. He'd sit up late reading about exciting lives on the road. He'd glance out his window at the burning light in Old Man Taylor's house and imagine the curious fellow lying in bed cradling a book in his lap. They were the only two people awake in the whole town.

_R_eflecting on what made him unique in the world of American letters, McMurtry once wrote, "I am one of the few American writers who can still claim to have had prolonged and intimate contact with first-generation pioneers." The trek from oral to written storytelling, from country to city, from natural to artificial light, from simple to more sophisticated technology; the arc in American literature from the late nineteenth century to the early twentieth, tracing the European domestication of the continent in such novels as Willa Cather's _O Pioneers!,_ the harshness of rural family life in Laura Ingalls Wilder's _Little House on the Prairie,_ the ruin of the land and the land's economy in John Steinbeck's _The Grapes of Wrath,_ and the migration of the innocent from isolation to the complexities of city life as conveyed in Theodore Dreiser's _Sister Carrie:_ McMurtry had lived it all before he graduated high school.

The Archer City public school, a three-story redbrick hulk housing grades one through twelve (replacing the old one-room school) was, according to McMurtry's classmate and friend Ceil Slack, "one long snore. The teachers went over and over the same material every day, like maybe they were trying to memorize it themselves." McMurtry skipped as much of the first and second grades as he could, feigning illness so he could stay in his garage bedroom rereading the books his cousin had brought him. Additionally, "[Larry and I] had the same early mentor: my mother"—Margaret Ellen—"a talented, inventive woman of great depth and curiosity," Slack said. "Far ahead of her time, she questioned conventional wisdom. She was a reader and a writer, and a nurturer of both . . . a kind of a misfit in this place . . . She provided the only intellectual backboard for the brilliant son of her closest friends, [the McMurtrys]."

Like Hazel, Margaret Ellen was a fine front-porch storyteller. She wrote poetry and painted. She read the plays of Arthur Miller and subscribed to _Life_ magazine. Her husband was a teacher in the Wichita Falls public school system. The Slacks were a bookish family, congenial to McMurtry, and he spent much of his free time at their house. (Ceil would grow up to become an editor, a journalist, and a university professor.) McMurtry lived just two blocks away. He'd play with Ceil's brothers, sneaking around Old Man Taylor's tall brick house at night, trying to glimpse the man's shadow against his lamp-lit curtains on the second floor, making up stories about him, peering into his basement windows, seeing there a ghostly, cobwebbed Cadillac (the boys *swore* it was there!). Most intriguing to McMurtry were the book catalogues discarded in Taylor's trash cans: pamphlets from book-sellers across the country, offering strange and exotic titles for sale. So it was possible to buy from libraries, to build and expand your *own* library, as McMurtry dreamed of doing with his cousin's gift.

In the summers he spent most of his time at the ranch, digging post holes, erecting fences, daubing cattle wounds with screwworm dope. He was skinny and tall with thick black hair, strong without being particu-larly muscular. He saw himself as a whippet. Despite his early mishaps with animals and his general dislike of the work, he was good with horses, confident in the saddle, never a shirker of duty.

In the fall he'd return to school, among the same eighteen kids he'd march in line with year after year. As someone who hadn't been raised in town, he maintained an outsider stance, often standing aside to listen to his classmates or to watch their boisterous behavior. Not that he lacked so-cial confidence—he learned quickly that the way to become popular with other boys was to talk dirty, which simply meant using standard barnyard terminology no one thought twice about in the country. Words like *shit, piss,* and *goddamn* (necessities in his uncles' conversations about cattle) seemed to cause a stir in town, particularly among his classmates' parents. His classmates loved it. And the big one—*fucking*—really made a hit: using the word allowed him to sound more knowledgeable than he was.

He didn't walk around cursing. He used language carefully, in love with the sounds of the words as much as their layers of meaning.

The shift from summers at the ranch to the Archer City town square, an increasingly disorienting split, made the Westerns he watched at the Royal Theater—*Fort Apache, Red River, The Kid from Texas*—more curious than ever. The films had always been sources of ridicule to his uncles. "The movies could never get it right," they'd say: the way cowboys dressed, the way they sat in their saddles, the way they talked. Especially off the mark was the phenomenon of trotting cattle. Cows were "driven across the screen at a pace so rapid that even the wiriest Longhorn could not have sustained it the length of Hollywood Boulevard without collapsing," McMurtry said. Yet he noticed that even as his uncles dismissed the details, they "believed the main message [of the movies], which was that the cowboy was an extraordinary man with an extraordinary code, a true symbol of virility and character." Though he didn't grasp the reasons, McMurtry saw that "the *selling* of the West preceded the *settling* of it," and he began to ponder how myths and legends were made. Narratives had an enormous capacity for establishing and holding their spells.

The radio was another case in point. Its "heroes and heroines soon came to obsess me," McMurtry said. "I remember sitting sadly in the living room of our ranch house, with my parents and my grandmother, as the radio informed us that President Roosevelt was dead. The crackly reports continued for a long time—the president's body, it seemed, was being brought to Washington by special train . . . Thousands of Americans were lined up beside the railroad tracks, weeping as they waited for the president's body to pass. The image of those thousands of weeping people . . . remained in my mind for many years." He didn't doubt that Roosevelt had been a great man, but recalling the Westerns—the gap between message and details—he wondered what the narrative was getting wrong. What was it hiding?

He could ask the same question of Archer City. Every day, folks emerged from the front doors of their houses, went respectably about their business, and returned in the evenings to disappear again behind their drab walls. *Respectability* was the public narrative—and yet, what homelier realities were those locked doors concealing?

The McMurtrys, no less than anyone else, made a social show of respectability, but their little house on Ash Street was a good deal more chaotic than one might wager from the outside. Jeff Mac and Hazel bickered all the time, often over some new household appliance Hazel wanted to buy for convenience's sake—a freezer or a pressure cooker—while Jeff Mac argued that a little hard work never hurt anybody. Just look at his mother.

The house grew even more hectic with the arrival of McMurtry's sister, Sue, in 1942 and his second sister, Judy, five years later. A fourth child, Charlie, was born in 1951.

Talk about *shit* and *piss*! A passerby glancing at the backyard clothesline might hazard a guess as to the mess in the house, seeing the heavy cloth diapers flapping in the breeze. In the summer the diapers would grow too hot in the searing sun. Hazel would unpin them, letting them drop straight into the basket on the ground. Then she'd stick them in the icebox for half an hour before wrapping them around her baby's waist. In winter, the diapers froze on the line as hard as linoleum tiles. Hazel thawed them out in front of a fire.

The town-and-country split in the family, running like a fault line through McMurtry's character, showed up early among the siblings. Sue put it this way: "Two of us liked horses and two of us didn't. [Larry] and my sister didn't." Sue grew up loving the ranch, riding as often as she could—in time, she'd become the county's Rodeo Queen. Judy was studious, like her older brother. Good with numbers, she'd eventually open a real estate title company. Charlie would drift for a number of years, seemingly caught in the rural-urban limbo, working on the ranch, becoming a welder, going off to college, teaching, welding again, moving back to Idiot Ridge . . .

What would the town-square gossips say about the McMurtrys? As early as fifth or sixth grade, walking to school, McMurtry learned where to go to hear the details lurking beneath Archer City's narratives: the Walsh brothers' Mobil filling station at the crossroads of Highways 25 and 79. It was just around the corner from the Royal Theater, sitting in the shadow of an old water tower. Most folks, eager for the latest news, gathered at the First Baptist Church on Sundays to catch up with their neighbors. McMurtry didn't especially trust this form of community. It was part of the respectability charade. (Two years after graduating from high school, he would write, in a statement for college, "I am agnostic . . . I take a great deal of pleasure from spoofing religious people about some of the more obvious absurdities of their particular dogma. This is a raging controversy in my hometown." Early on, he was an independent thinker: in the fourth grade, he had written a Methodist pastor, informing him that he wouldn't be returning to the fold. For the rest of his life, he kept his word.)

Far more reliable than the First Baptist Church as a barometer of the town's atmosphere were the Walsh brothers, Frank, Fred, Jay, and Tom. They'd stand in front of their open garage bays, watching the butane trucks roll down the streets, and discuss the local kids' latest devilment—pelting the sheriff's car with tomatoes, running a pair of girl's panties up the schoolhouse flagpole—or the Klan's rumored activities, or who was sleeping with whom (*sleeping*, in this context, meaning something quite mysterious, McMurtry surmised). The gab sessions got to be so popular among the locals, with old men especially, the Walsh brothers referred to them as meetings of "The Spit and Whittle Club." Years later, a former regular of the sessions would claim that McMurtry's novel, *The Last Picture Show*, was "stimulated by knowing a hell of a lot of gossip." Fred Walsh, he said, was the "source of rumors and information in this town like nobody in this world. If you want to know what's going on, you ask Fred and Tom, and *they* know. Lots of times it ain't rumors, it's the truth." McMurtry tucked it all away, even the stories he was too young to understand.

Around the corner, at Mr. Wilson's five-and-dime, near the barbershop (which proudly displayed a poster entitled *Custer's Last Fight*, a lurid painting of the massacre at Little Big Horn published by the Anheuser-Busch Company), McMurtry encountered still more enticing mysteries. He'd stare at the comic book covers—not Batman or Superman, which held no interest for him, but the racy, sadistic pictures adorning *Sheena, Queen of the Jungle, Wings Comics, Rangers*, or the scenes of torture on the covers of the 35-cent men's magazines, designed to appeal to war vets: *Rage, Man's Exploits*, and *Escape to Adventure*. Mr. Wilson was known to kids in town as Mr. Tee-Hee-Hee because of the way he would giggle as he walked from the back of his store to greet customers, turning on overhead lights by pulling long strings. When he'd see that McMurtry was only browsing, he'd turn and head for the back again, tugging at the ceiling as he went.

Comic books, men's magazines, and the popular fiction of the day, soon to be readily available in paperback format, overlapped in McMurtry's mind. The silly, formulaic narratives of the funnies and the movies shared certain qualities—suspense, momentum, a central problem to be solved—with the supposedly more serious narratives of full-length novels. But McMurtry was also interested in the business of *selling* narratives. In whatever form, they were packaged alike, with titillating covers, often involving women being brutalized by Nazis. In time, McMurtry would see some of the same writers' names—Mario Puzo, Mickey Spillane—moving seamlessly back and forth between writing for the comics, the men's rags, and the paperback market. The writers tended to work for the same companies: Fiction House, the publisher of *Sheena*, Funnies, Inc., and Magazine Management Co., purveyor of what the trade called "armpit" publications, postwar pulps balancing advice to veterans with lurid drawings of female flesh and adventure stories featuring the word *nympho* at every opportunity.

McMurtry's cousin Robert Hilburn had returned from the war bringing the boy another present, a Japanese rifle which he liked but didn't cherish as much as the original gift of the books. McMurtry noticed that his cousin's reading tastes had evolved from accounts of Canadian Mounties to the "girl pinching" or "animal nibbler" stories of the men's magazines (in the tales of rampaging beasts, "even the rhinos were nymphos," according to one of the writers).

Standing quietly at the five-and-dime's magazine rack, McMurtry studied the editorial pages and the publications' mastheads as keenly as he did the exciting pictures. His knowledge of the business of narrative expanded, combined with an acquisitiveness bred in him by the plains, the daily witnessing of how easily everything blew away. He developed a need to organize and keep, to hold close what would otherwise be lost, beginning with *all* Fiction House titles, an entire set of Dell's hard-boiled detective novels . . .

This impulse would grow in intensity throughout his life until he wanted to possess not just titles and books, but the *stores* where books were sold, libraries, all the houses he'd ever known, his hometown, right down to Old Man Taylor's cobwebby Cadillac.

But for now, as a preadolescent dawdling in the dime store, listening to Mr. Wilson tug at his lights, he collected knowledge, nurturing a sense of himself as someone who might be able to add to the world's stock of narratives.

After all, the magazines' evidence was inescapable: the superhero tales, the war adventures, the animal encounters, and the rescues of damsels in distress (exactly as in the Republic Pictures serials he saw every weekend at the Royal)—they all came from the westerns. From his uncles' stories. The GI was the new gunslinger. The enemy Indian had become an Arab, a Nazi, a Japanese fighter pilot, any evil person of color threatening a white woman. Furthermore, the pure western remained as alluring to readers as ever, judging by such stories as "Redman's Trail of Death" in *Fury* magazine, "The Scalping of Isaac Greer" in *Escape to Adventure*—"My God, My Guts are Coming Out!"—along with "'Joy Girl' Prisoners of the Apaches," in an issue featuring a "serious" article on Henry Miller's *Tropic of Cancer* (the "all-time sex novel").

In the context of war news and postwar analyses on the radio, the pulps answered a pressing question for McMurtry: now he knew that the selling of the West preceded its settling because a heroic narrative was necessary to excuse the aggression of greedy land grabs. It assuaged the inevitable guilt over what was happening to usurped Native populations. The story continued now against Asians, Germans . . . whatever actions may or may not have been justified in war, the simple narrative of Heroes versus Villains sanctioned the official *desire* to act.

And desire was clearly the point. The frank material raised further questions in the boy as he stood on the brink of adolescence in the dime store. Why could he not take his eyes off the cover of Mickey Spillane's *I, the Jury*, featuring a disrobing blonde, or *One Lonely Night*, depicting Mike Hammer's lovely secretary, Velda, dangling from a rope and being tortured by Nazis?

The sexy covers remained on his mind as he left the store, as he wandered past the Mobil station, the movie house, the sandstone courthouse. Women were disrobing—right now—behind the houses' closed doors! Did they look like Mickey Spillane's slender blondes?

One day after school, full of excess energy, he clambered up a street sign downtown. In an essay entitled "Eros in Archer County," published in 1968, he wrote: "I had no purpose in mind but casual exercise, but about the time I got to the top, the flexing activity . . . produced what I learned years later was an orgasm. I had not been expecting anything so delightful to happen at the top of that pole, and I hung for a moment in amazement before sliding down." He was so excited by this new experience that he hurried to report it to a woman his family knew. She happened to be shopping, standing nearby. "Ssh," the woman told him, glancing nervously up the street. "Just don't tell anybody."

The graphic language of the barnyard may have ruffled the town's cloak of respectability, but it certainly made clear what was happening in the barn. The reproductive lives of the animals, their natural paths from birth to death, were rendered unsentimentally, without any judgment or fuss. The same could not be said for the sex lives of people. For the most part, silence greeted curious adolescents, leaving them to wonder how their grandparents and parents felt about their bodies, what they *did* with them, what *anyone* should do or want to do. Archer City remained buried in nineteenth-century attitudes about sex, at least as old as the Civil War.

If lack of language was the first sexual problem for McMurtry—an inability to discuss or analyze the matter rationally—lack of variety was the second. The difficult puzzles of controlling sexual urges, judging attractiveness (one's own and others'), calculating appropriateness, and testing behavior had to be negotiated among the same eighteen kids he'd go to school with for nearly two decades. The restricted circumstances induced erotic claustrophobia. The town felt more than a little incestuous.

Year after year, he'd look at the girls in his class—Lenn (whom other boys claimed was "frigid"), Jeter (a "pretty shell," he thought), Anne, Tissa, and Douglas—and consider his options, running through the pros and cons of their appearances and demeanors, which did and did not change as they grew older.

McMurtry was a personable young man, but he had reason to act smug in school. He'd read a great deal more—and he read more often—than his classmates. To be a superior student, all he had to do was show up and stay awake. In his college statement, he wrote: "In . . . school I did a number of things mediocrely . . . Unfortunately, the area I lived in was so devoid of talented competition that . . . I was convinced I could look down my nose at Aristotle." This was a lonely condition, he discovered, adding an extra dimension to his sexual longings: he ached for someone who could stimulate him intellectually, who'd match, if not share, his interests and tastes. Girls who lacked these qualities (Lenn, Jeter, Anne . . .) were not as attractive to him as they might have been otherwise. As powerful as it was, a physical urge, swiftly if temporarily satisfied, was not as important as friendship.

Ceil Slack was the only person who regularly earned grades as good as his and collected honors in school. She was "constant and will never change," McMurtry told a friend. Auburn-haired and pale, she was certainly physically attractive, and under her mother's tutelage, she read almost as much as McMurtry, even if most of her reading involved fashion magazines—after all, how else was a girl to learn how to become a woman? For girls *and* boys, adolescent urgings were all the more maddening for being strange echoes of childhood games played with the same people over and over. Slack remembered climbing trees as a youngster with Bobby Stubbs and other neighborhood boys, laughing when her father warned her not to climb so high the boys could see up her dress. After puberty, she became well aware of the boys' attempts to peer up her skirts or to slip a hand inside them, and their good-natured laughter did not hide the fact that *these* games were far more serious than scaling trees.

The school, the kids' parents, and the town worked hard to socialize girls and boys into channeling their energy appropriately. While the boys sat in assembly listening to a presentation on the character-shaping values of competitive sports, the girls sat in an auditorium watching a film reel about their bodies' imminent changes. The jerky images unspooled against a white sheet stretched across a map rack: Tinker Bell touching a little girl with her wand and the girl shooting up in size. A voice intoned, "Be prepared! Buy Kotex *before* you need it!"

At the Walsh brothers' filling station after school each day, McMurtry listened to stories of *failed* socialization—whispered talk about the school's band director, run out of Archer City for "stepping just a little too high," or the "limp-wristed" kids in town, the "sissies" and "pantywaists" who didn't play sports. (They were like McMurtry's young cousin from Childress, he thought—the one the family rarely mentioned, yet "we had no reason not to be nice to him. He was a perfectly nice man.")

Then there was the preacher's son—always duck-footing around, starry-eyed, *something wrong with that boy*. Such talk found its way to school from time to time. One day, a group of bullies caught the preacher's son in the gym, held him to the lacquered floor and painted his toenails red, just because he was different.

Still, against heavy odds, the mighty civilizing efforts continued. Each day, articles in the *Archer County News* outlined the approved activities for girls, to wit: "Last Saturday morning, on May 17, Miss Bethalice Berry was given a 'brunch' kitchen shower in the home of Mrs. W. J. McMurtry . . . Hostess was Sue McMurtry . . . The calendar of events began with brunch. This consisted of dainty cookies, strawberries, juice and hot chocolate, which was served on pink and brown covered tables, centered with roses. Following were games concerning home life. The first game tested the girls' ability to determine spices by smell . . . Next on the agenda was the presentation of aprons worn by the hostesses, who are majorettes in the Wildcat [High

School] Band." Offered as proof that the town's daughters were safe and learning proper home-care etiquette, these notices appeared alongside such reports as "Charlie Spraggins and Ray Riner [set pipe] at 3,718 ft. [the other day] . . . a sure-enough shot in the arm" to the local economy. Altogether, the paper's news strengthened the local narrative of respectability.

The truth was trickier: however finely honed the girls' spice-sniffing may have become, by the time they got to tenth grade, they had also picked up the barnyard terms floating around school and managed to use them expertly. Sue McMurtry wore her apron sparingly; in later years, she was more likely to parade around in T-shirts proclaiming something like "You Can't Be First, But You Can Be Next."

Little by little, McMurtry began to glean society's *actual* purpose: mollifying people with uplifting narratives so they'd work all their lives without complaint and settle into a quiet and irrelevant old age. This truth presented itself to him at the regular sad cowboy reunions at the Clarendon Country Club, where the heavy uncles would arrive, many of them half-crippled by a lifetime of horse- or cow-related injuries, or speaking through buzz-boxes in their throats after cancer operations brought on by smoking. Their doughy wives helped them painfully to their chairs. They'd sit beneath a windmill, feasting on barbecued chicken and Dr Peppers, extolling the glories of trail-riding, hay mowing, or cotton picking, recalling their run-ins with Geronimo or Quanah Parker, capping their careers (as the narrative meant them to do) with tales to entice the next generation. All the while, the women flitted behind the rickety folding chairs, fulfilling *their* roles, pampering the men, keeping them stunned with mounds of potato salad.

McMurtry knew there was little to entice the next generation—his father was so deeply in debt he had to haul lumber for county construction projects just to pay the bills—but the narrative persisted with intoxicating power.

Years after graduating from high school, McMurtry, in his twenties, dropped by a senior citizens' home in Electra, Texas, near Wichita Falls, to say hi to his childhood buddy Jesse Brewer. Brewer was in his nineties then. Still chewing tobacco. "How you doin', Larry?" he said. "Where you livin' now?" McMurtry told him he was living in Houston. "Hard to breathe down there, ain't it?" Brewer said. Then a nurse wheeled him into the television room.

The cowboy narrative would never sanction such a pathetic ending, yet here was the truth.

McMurtry wondered: Is this where he and Ceil Slack would end up if they obediently followed the path laid out for them?

I had a nice, manageable boyfriend . . . in high school. He was tall and intelligent and sweet and was going to make something of himself in later life. I thought a good boyfriend was one who was not boring and who wanted to leave [Archer City] as much as I did," Slack wrote of McMurtry. "The things I loved most to do—like read, write, and sit around listening to porch stories—were not what normal [Archer City] school kids did, which led to some of them thinking I was stuck up. But I wasn't . . . I [just] thought that, by and large, people in books had better ideas to think about, and mostly I preferred them to live people."

McMurtry agreed. He and Slack were friends, really, more than girlfriend-boyfriend, an important distinction to them both: they managed to separate sex from friendship, but they also believed, based on their experiences together, that the best male-female bonds always contained an erotic component, acted upon or not, giving them the energy they required for staying power.

McMurtry's regard for Slack as a friend, his sexual attraction to her, and his recognition that these were distinct yet related feelings gave him an insight he expressed years later in a letter to Ken Kesey: "While I have talked a good deal about myself to all my friends, male or female, I have generally drawn a more consistent response from the females. So that I have a long string of female confidants, stretching back to high-school, in each of whom I have invested a good deal emotionally, and from each of whom I have taken some self-discovery."

Self-discovery was necessary because there were damn few models of successful male-female behavior in Archer City. Kids went to the Royal now not to see the Westerns but to watch Lauren Bacall pucker her lips and teach Bogie how to whistle. Women kissed back on the screen. They appeared to enjoy intimacy as much as men did: a revelation. "We probably derived a more realistic view of women from the movies than we got from our home-life," McMurtry said. In neither sphere was male-female friendship exhibited. The husbands and wives in town did not seem to be buddies. Most of them appeared to lead separate lives, enjoying vastly different activities, satisfying their desires through consumerism (those who could afford to buy things), ignoring each other in order to survive their marriages. "Most West Texas husbands of [my father's] generation were notably insensitive to their wives, and I find it difficult to believe that very many of them even wanted to understand their wives' sexual [needs]," McMurtry said. "Understanding would have increased responsibility and most of them seemed to feel themselves heavily enough burdened with female demands as it was." His own mother and father, always sniping at each other, were "roughly as neurotic as Kafka, Rilke, and Proust put together," he said.

Ceil Slack had as much trouble as he did trying to fathom what it meant to be a romantic partner. Since—with rare exceptions, like McMurtry—teenage boys did not communicate clearly (or at all) with girls, she understood vaguely that "men see women not as we are, but as they think we are, or maybe want us to be," based on the movies or their home lives or their fantasies. Right away, she learned that she had no desire to conform to most of the boys' fantasies about her, but she could use their imaginings—the promise of availability without ever delivering—to get what she wanted from them. "Boys [to me] were . . . secondary creatures, necessary when there was a dance or a picture show in Wichita Falls, to which [my father] would not let [me] go without an escort," she said. Boys "seemed so dumb they didn't even know that I was making them do and say this and that sometimes."

At home, she practiced with her makeup at the "kidney shaped dressing table I just had to have after seeing one in a picture show." She dreamed that Arthur Miller would swoop into her room one night to take her away. The boys in town thought of her as untouchable and bragged to their buddies that *they'd* be the one to break the taboo.

Bragging was an important part of sexual initiation for the boys—maybe, for most of them, the *crucial* part, since their first experiences rarely lived up to their expectations. "Most of the boys in my hometown had accomplished [losing their virginity] by the age of fourteen, 99% of them with the same accommodating girl," McMurtry wrote in "Eros in Archer County." He was no exception, though his initiation occurred "through a fluke," he said—a dare, an unexpected opportunity with a girl he didn't know particularly well. Convinced he'd probably contracted syphilis, he "went home determined to rot quietly away." After a few days, relieved that he hadn't died, he was grateful to spend time at his friend Ceil's house with Ceil and her mother.

Besides his obsession with girls, McMurtry had a growing passion for book collecting. He snatched up and studied the book catalogues he found in Will Taylor's trash cans—evidence of an alien world, vastly different from his bookless environs. Whenever his father had to go to Fort Worth on a cattle-buying jaunt, McMurtry accompanied him to browse newsstands and bookstores. Once when he was fourteen, he found an abandoned book in the parking lot of a livestock auction in Wichita Falls. The book was called *The Road to Disappearance,* and its dust jacket said it had been written by an Oklahoma historian named Angie Debo. The volume had been flattened a few times by pickups, smeared with tread marks, but McMurtry grabbed it out of the dirt. His father wouldn't let him take it home straightaway. Put it in the lost and found, he said, and if it's still around after two weeks, it's yours. The book sat on a shelf among chewed-on pencil stubs and a plug of tobacco. No one touched it. McMurtry brought it home and tried to read it—it was the story of the Creek Indians—but it sailed over his head, minutely analyzing the arcane language of U.S. government treaties. Still, after "reading a few of Angie Debo's sinewy sentences, [I] gradually arrived at a great notion, which was that it might be possible to organize one's life around literature . . . just read it and, in some ways, live with it," McMurtry said. "I could look off the porch of our ranch house, straight up the length of the Great Plains, all the way into Canada, but the only evidence I had that there were such things as writers in all that stretch of land was this book I had found in a parking lot, by a woman from Oklahoma. I didn't know about Willa Cather . . . And yet, a woman from Oklahoma had somehow ordered her life around books and study. Having that fact to contemplate was . . . an inestimable gift."

Shortly after this, at a bookshop called Lovelace's in Wichita Falls, he bought his first book, a faux-leather copy of *Madame Bovary.* It was remarkable, he thought, how closely the narrative followed certain stories in the pulps, gossipy yarns blowing the lid off seemingly placid communities, revealing the seamy doings of people who were not so respectable after all. Studying Flaubert, McMurtry saw how such narratives could fill the gap between the raw rumors at the Walshes' Mobil station and the cheerful brunch notices in the newspaper. Clearly, manners (including delicate language) had been invented as a cover for peoples' barnyard behavior; a well-structured story could examine and explore the consequences of social manners, their reach, and the many ways in which they were breached.

Archer City was *crying out* for such treatment—especially after a well-publicized local trial swirling around a case of infidelity. Everyone knew the participants: B. L. Pink had come home one day from the Fat Stock Show in Fort Worth and caught Floyd Pratt with his wife Bonnie Lou "in my own damn bed!" This was Archer City to a tee (*c'est moi!*). McMurtry knew the town's dark quirks. He just didn't know how to stitch them together.

His parents didn't know what to make of his reading, but they didn't seem to mind it. They left him alone in his garage. ("Larry can read a whole book before I can read the title," Jeff Mac muttered.) Even more than *Madame Bovary, Don Quixote* seized his attention—initially because it was about men traveling on horseback across a desolate plain. But then he became intrigued by the men's dynamic, their friendship based on opposition (a little like men and women): the visionary and the pragmatist. "I [long] pondered the grave differences (comically cast) between Sancho and the Don. Between the two is where fiction, as I've mostly read and written it, lives," he later wrote.

At first McMurtry embraced Sancho, regarding himself as a highly practical boy. But then he'd catch himself dreaming on the ranch's fence or imagining building a library as big as a barn, and he'd admit he had more than a little Quixote in his soul. A good narrative let you enter the minds of both types of men and see yourself in them.

All his life, he would never break the spell of the great Spanish epic.

The 1954 *Wildcat* yearbook from the Archer City schools shows Larry McMurtry and Ceil Slack, both members of the school's Who's Who, competing for top honors and vying to be named Town's Most Active Teen. By his senior year, McMurtry was "as popular as you can be in Archer City without playing football," said Ceil's sister, Mary. Ceil and McMurtry appear on several pages together, as writers and editors of *The Cat's Claw,* the school newspaper, and debate team colleagues, McMurtry particularly excelling at extemporaneous speaking, a fact that would surprise later audiences in lecture halls who often heard him drone in a monotone.

In pictures, Slack always struck a demure pose, Audrey Hepburn–like, her long neck highlighted by the bateau neckline of her black dress. McMurtry, wearing a light-colored suit and tie and a pair of wire-rimmed glasses, assumed an extremely serious expression but could not hide the twist in his lips suggesting emerging laughter. Beneath their photographs, the list of their respective accomplishments indicated they had each channeled their energies in appropriate directions. "I was already several Miss Somethings by the time I finished high school, but every once in a while the thought crossed my mind that standing up and being looked at was not the way a writer, artist and world traveler ought to be spending her time," Slack said. McMurtry was a track runner and a basketball player ("third tallest member of the team"—a team that once lost a game to Crowell High School 106–4), a clarinet and trombone player in the band, a member of the Hobby Club, and a 4-H club officer.

He was hardly a serious athlete, though he displayed fine coordination and a competitive spirit. Once, at a track meet in Fort Worth, he skipped several events, took a city bus downtown, and spent hours browsing through Barber's Bookstore, especially fascinated by skimming the Bhagavad Gita. That day, he bought a copy of Hugh Walpole's *Rogue Herries*. Decades later, when Barber's was going out of business, the acquisitive McMurtry would purchase the store's entire inventory.

As a 4-H member he excelled, despite stories he later related about his youthful ineptitude at cowboying. His parents had to prod him, but once he started working with animals, he paid attention to details and always got the job done. "The 4-H boys from Archer County did not get grand championship at the Wichita Falls Calf Show but . . . Larry McMurtry 'placed' a calf," the *Archer County News* reported on March 3, 1949. In 1953, in the West Texas Judging Contest, he scored eighth in individual rankings among three hundred and fifty-four boys.

His efforts earned him an all-expenses-paid trip to the 1953 4-H Club Congress in Chicago, a gathering of local 4-H club members from around the country—his first visit to a major city. He had never traveled on an airplane or a train, never ridden an elevator, such as the one in the Conrad Hilton. He had never been seated at a long banquet table in an elegant hotel ballroom, served by a host of waiters wearing cloth gloves and pressed white coats. He had never heard a symphony orchestra (Arthur Fiedler's first Pops concert at Orchestra Hall) or visited an art museum—or seen a movie on a giant screen (dwarfing the Royal's facilities) using the brand-new wide-screen process of Cinerama, in which three 35-millimeter projectors simultaneously cast an image on a large curved surface. He met representatives from the U.S. Department of Agriculture, International Harvester, the Ford Motor Company, U.S. Rubber, and Sears, Roebuck. He returned to Archer City in such an exhausted daze, he was hardly able to remember, much less describe, what he had seen in such a blur. But his world had just expanded, stirring his acquisitive juices. Highway 281, curling away from the ranch, had once seemed to him a mysterious gateway to worlds unknown, but now he saw it was just a tiny path in a complex maze of trails crossing the planet.

Driving those trails *away* from Archer City . . . that was a must, he thought, though it would seem to his father and the rest of his family a betrayal. Jeff Mac wanted him to go to vet school at Texas A&M. The thought depressed McMurtry, though in the statement he later wrote for North Texas State College, he conceded that "horses, dangerous devil-may-care stampedes, and the general stimulating variety of . . . out-door enterprise strikes a very elemental chord in my nature, and it is a chord that could very well draw me [back home] from more civilized sophistries."

In the meantime, as he waited to graduate from Archer City High, the only driving he did was with his buddies—the Slack brothers, Bobby Stubbs, occasionally Mike Kunkel, a friend from the town of Bowie nearby (and a fellow reader). They'd go round and round the town square at night, stopping in at the picture show or the pool hall. They knew that pickups and cars were the keys to their sexual freedom, tools for escaping their parents and going away somewhere private with a girl. The trouble was, most of the boys had no idea how to talk a girl into going away with them. Some of the rougher guys in town bragged about satisfying their desires using heifers in the field. Years later, when McMurtry wrote about the practice of adolescent bestiality, he was accused, he said, of "hyperbole," of making "unkind cuts against my hometown. It was, however, sober realism. Masturbation excluded, bestiality was the commonest and by far the safest method of obtaining sexual release available to adolescent boys in those days. Indeed, if adults were tolerant of anything sexual, they were tolerant of bestiality—or at least passive toward it." McMurtry and his friends, circling the town square in one of their father's flatbeds, never engaged in the practice.

Bobby Stubbs was essentially orphaned, his family having fractured. He lived with various friends in town and worked late at night for the pool hall owner and a local oil outfit. He recalled that McMurtry, always at ease around the opposite sex, used to urge him to talk to girls. "He would just say, 'Why don't you go with Ceilie? Why don't you try to get a date with her?' and that sort of thing."

Bobby "was a mischief-maker and a fun, good-humored guy," Slack said. She went out with him a few times. One day, another fellow she was dating showed up at his house "and invited me down the street to talk with him," Stubbs said. "I went down and got hurt pretty bad. Hit me in the eye and pretty well put me out." Twelve years later, this incident would reemerge as a central scene in *The Last Picture Show.* Already, Slack and Stubbs were seeding the creation of fictional characters.

It was long past time to get out of town. McMurtry spent his last year in high school stealing books from the school's meager library to add to his collection. (The teachers observed him but didn't try to stop him. "I was a kind of special case," he said. Eventually he gave the books back.)

While Ceil Slack applied to North Texas State College in Denton, close by, McMurtry set his sights on the Rice Institute in Houston, a tuition-free (whites only) institution of higher education promising students an in-depth, well-rounded knowledge of the world. As far as McMurtry was concerned, its qualifications were that it was free, it was in a big city, and it was hundreds of miles from his hometown. Initially, the school rejected McMurtry (his grades were good, but the Archer City High School math curriculum stopped at Algebra II, a liability). Placed on a waiting list, McMurtry got into Rice at the last moment.

After a campus visit there with his parents early in the summer of 1954, the McMurtrys drove to Galveston and saw the ocean for the first time, the Gulf of Mexico, "gray as dishwater," the beach "littered with dead jellyfish, horrifying my mother," McMurtry said. After a hot, sticky swim, the family hopped in the car and hightailed it back to the plains. That August, before he set out for school, McMurtry was riding horse-back in a mesquite-filled pasture alongside his father, inspecting cattle for screwworms, when his father dismounted and said he had something to say to his son. Patiently, in a quiet voice, he explained the mechanics of sexual intercourse, warning that pregnancy, and very often disease, followed the brief pleasure. McMurtry nodded solemnly, revealing nothing about his sexual experience. The lecture over (all of five minutes), father and son mounted their horses again and began looking for wormy cows.

A few days later, McMurtry was off to Houston—his Paris.

4

McMurtry's first sojourn in Houston would be short-lived—right away he fell in love with the city, but three and a half years would pass before he could embrace it. The Rice Admissions Office had calculated correctly: mathematics would be his undoing.

He arrived on campus in the late summer of 1954. Rice—officially, the William M. Rice Institute for the Advancement of Literature, Science, and Art—was located on nearly three hundred wooded acres, formerly farmland, on either side of Houston's Main Street. Established in 1912, initially designed by a Boston architectural firm, Rice was a tree-lined oasis of Mediterranean Revival–style buildings, adorned by cloisters, arched windows, and spires looking vaguely Moorish. The buildings' pink-and-sand-colored facades faced a series of grassy quadrangles and side paths shaded by cypress, oaks, hickories, and maples. A combination of scents—scarlet flax, bluebonnets, red salvia—swirled among whiffs of tree bark and brick, thickening the air with a woody, nutmeg smell.

It was a long way from the modest ranch on the plains.

Within a week, McMurtry had discovered his home away from home, the relatively new (1949) Fondren Library, funded by money from Humble Oil & Refining. It was Rice's first air-conditioned building—reason enough to hunker there, in Houston's killing humidity—and its floors were slick and silent, courtesy of the Mexican maintenance staff running giant waxers up and down the halls at night, past thin leather couches where McMurtry often dozed after spending hours reading books he'd pulled from the shelves: Chaucer, Henry James, C. S. Lewis, Northrop Frye.

He was particularly intrigued by a volume called *The Romantic Agony* by Mario Praz, which mentioned, among other European writers, the Marquis de Sade and Charles Robert Maturin, author of a novel called *Melmoth the Wanderer*. Praz became McMurtry's initial guide to European literature, leading him from one book to another. He found a copy of *Melmoth the Wanderer* in the library's rare-book room, a dark, chilly space.

The book was bound in boards. "I had never read, or even touched, a book that old . . . I was so impressed I could barely breathe," he said.

As much as he would like to have lived in the library, his actual dwelling was a garage apartment on North Boulevard, shared with three roommates, all of whom were studying to be engineers, and all of whom reeked of science labs and beer each night. Houston smelled much different once you got away from Rice's quads. It was fishy and sumpy and dank.

The city was founded on a scam. McMurtry relished its history. Its roguish legacy gave the place its spirit, along with its generally slovenly demeanor (Houston had no zoning laws, so an icehouse could operate next to a church next to a residence next to an auto-wrecking yard next to an industrial dump). It all started in 1836, when two entrepreneurial brothers from New York, John Kirby and Augustus Chapman Allen, moved to Texas to barter for land, issuing loans through real estate speculation to support the revolution and establish the Republic of Texas. (They were a Quixote and Sancho pair, with mighty appeal for McMurtry—both pragmatic and heedlessly visionary.) They paid $5,000 for a plot of mush at the confluence of Buffalo and White Oak Bayous and convinced investors that "when the rich lands of this country shall be settled, a trade will flow to it, making it, beyond all doubt, [a] great interior commercial emporium." Visitors called the new town, named after General Sam Houston, "one of the muddiest and most disagreeable places on earth," scattered about with "a few linen tents which were used for groceries [and liquor] together with . . . shanties made of poles set in the ground." Residents raised fattened pigs, setting them free at night to clean the streets.

In the next three decades, ten yellow fever epidemics would wipe out a substantial portion of the families who'd been suckered into settling in the Bayou City. John Allen died of a "bilious fever" at the age of twenty-eight and Augustus escaped legal trouble, fleeing to Mexico. By then, Houston had indeed become a "great interior commercial emporium" just because its founders said it would. (When Augustus skipped out, he deeded everything he owned in Texas to his wife, Charlotte, who stayed in Houston, invested in cattle, and helped develop what became the Rice Hotel.) Houston had functioned with the same reckless, brash confidence ever since, and McMurtry cherished the continuing energy of its "fuck you, I'll do whatever I want" persona.

Like the boy from Archer City, Houston in 1954 was poised to discover and nurture its deep talents, but it hadn't yet hit its stride.

McMurtry was lonesome. He played tennis and Ping-Pong to burn off excess energy. He had no car, so he quickly learned the city's public transportation system. "I was often the only white person on the bus," he said: another novel experience for him. As a central port for shipping oil and cotton (and as a beneficiary of Lyndon Johnson's DC deals), Houston had emerged from the Great Depression in better shape than most American cities. Its jobs boom drew a diversified population; relations among the races remained fairly calm (if systemically unequal) since, relatively speaking, there was money to go around. At the time, "all three of Houston's main secondhand bookstores were downtown, reachable without even changing buses," McMurtry said. Surprisingly, for a place focused so intently on business and land speculation, Houston developed a literary bent early in its history, largely through the efforts of Edward Hopkins Cushing, a Dartmouth graduate who served as editor of the *Houston Telegraph*. Like the Allen brothers, he hummed with boosterish energy. He had the foresight to recognize that a major center of commerce needed its own voices, powerful spokespeople, so in 1866 he opened a bookstore in Houston to promote local writers—Mollie Evelyn Moore Davis, Maude Jeannie Young, and John Sayles, among the first Texas authors. They had all been forgotten by the time McMurtry took the bus to Cushing's successors: Fletcher's Book Store on the corner of San Jacinto and Rusk, the Brown Book Shop on Studemont Street in the Heights, specializing in technical books for workers at the petrochemical companies lining Houston's Ship Channel, and the Book Mart, owned by J. W. Petty Jr., a generally disheveled man who made McMurtry feel right at home. ("One reason I'm comfortable in dusty bookshops is that I have no sartorial interests," McMurtry said.)

Through his limited exposure to serious reading in his classes at Rice, he had become interested in the notion of tradition, in the conditions *necessary* to create a culture supportive of an extended literary life. A lengthy history was one required element—something Texas sorely lacked. (Even if he *had* known about Mollie Evelyn Moore Davis and her compatriots, their meager output would not have comprised a tradition.) Europe was the model, he thought: he had to get his hands on every book ever published in the old Western world.

In one of his early forays into Ted Brown's shop, he found a copy of Robert Burton's *Anatomy of Melancholy* tucked among the technical books. He bought it for $7.50. From Petty's store he purchased a few volumes of Romain Rolland's ten-novel cycle *Jean-Christophe,* about a German musical genius. McMurtry didn't find the books particularly compelling, but he knew that Rolland (just as forgotten, these days, as Texas's early writers) had won the Nobel Prize for Literature and was a pal of Sigmund Freud's.

Meanwhile, McMurtry had spent enough time, now, in the Fondren Library to know how many volumes it contained—roughly 600,000 (a number his collection would nearly match by the end of his bookselling days)—and to know, by sight, where every conceivable subject would be shelved among the stacks. He was devouring, as much as he could, Shakespeare, Joyce, Swift, and Proust (who made him "schizophrenic," he claimed). "I read omnivorously, with more of the enthusiasm of a curious neophyte than that of a savant," he said. He taught himself the history of bookmaking. The subject interested him as much as books themselves. For one of his English classes, he wrote a paper on William Morris and the Kelmscott Press, known for publishing a highly ornamented edition of Chaucer's work.

One evening, the famous evolutionary biologist Julian Huxley arrived to deliver a lecture at Rice. Huxley was a self-declared atheist and a proponent of natural selection as the driver of evolution. McMurtry cited a meeting with him as deepening his agnosticism.

As much as he was lapping up new experiences, new books, and appreciating Houston's energy, he was surprised to find himself "dreadfully homesick." It was hard to disentangle this feeling from a "small inferiority complex" that "finally got the best of me," he said—his fellow students, many from wealthy urban families, were better prepared for the rituals of higher education than he was. He relished learning about "The Love Song of J. Alfred Prufrock" in Professor Will Dowden's English class, but each new discovery reminded him of the inadequacy of his high school education. His self-doubt erupted most forcefully in his Calculus, Trigonometry, and Analytics class. He got a 2 on the first test (out of 100), and never scored higher than a 4 throughout the first term.

In letters to his friend Mike Kunkel ("Kunk"), he masked his doubts in dour, defensive terms, writing off Rice as a "vastly overrated aggregation of uppermiddle class snobs and first rate psychopaths." "I hope I get famous, so I can denounce this hole from the pages of every learned magazine in America."

But he was panicked. He began to consider transferring closer to home—under those hot, open skies he missed so much. He thought about North Texas State, where his friend Ceil Slack had gone to school. But then, "I couldn't stand the thought of losing even a *teeny tiny* bit of *some people's* respect," he wrote Kunk. "I suppose I'd have lost some self respect."

The agony continued until the end of the school year and well into his return to Archer City for the summer. He didn't want to go back to Rice in the fall, but he did, convinced by "well-meaning friends." He got a new apartment by himself on Bissonnet Street, by the art museum. "Damn it, I knew better—all summer I knew better—then all the chiding took effect," he told Kunk. "Well, I'm paying out the ass for it now, I kid you not."

In what would become a pattern in his life, he said he had fallen in love with two different girls, Tissa and Douglas, before leaving home again in the fall. For years, they had been his classmates in Archer City; he had "been just friends" with them "till late in the summer" when he knew he was departing: a way of avoiding commitments, perhaps, but also a way of securing his ties to Archer City even as he continued to doubt it was still his place.

In any case, *longing*—emotional *and* geographic—requiring long letters as part of the courtship process would be central to McMurtry's conception of sexual romance. "I['d] be on top of the world no matter which [girl] I end[ed] up with, so long as it's one of them," McMurtry wrote Kunk. In fact, neither infatuation would survive his semester at Rice. Already, Tissa was "no longer the fun loving jolly gal everybody loved"; he wished he "had platonism back" with her.

To distract himself, he played more tennis and Ping-Pong. He went to the symphony. He got a job shelving books in the Houston Public Library. "I feel silly, but I feel the urge to write a novel," he wrote Kunk. "I don't know what about, or anything . . ."

Finally, he cast aside his self-respect and chose to drop out after the fall semester. The decision made, his remaining days in school settled into an almost pleasant routine.

Meanwhile, the city—more than his classes—presented him with thoughtful paradoxes in the matter of literary tradition. This was becoming his obsession. If a writer from Texas was to approach the subjects of history, the loss of the past, social manners, the bedrock of culture as a European would, where would he begin? Before even *contemplating* tradition and its evolution, one had to ask: what the hell was *Texas*?

To judge from the massive weeded lots in the center of Houston, abandonment was a core element of Texas's identity. Benjamin Moser, a Houston writer, once pointed out that the French didn't really want to deal with Texas when it got tacked on to their conquest of the Louisiana Territory. The Spanish didn't seem to like it much, and the Mexicans, uninterested, rented it out to gullible American settlers. The Republic never grew beyond a few unconnected towns, and the Confederacy had little to do with it. The brash boosterism characterizing Houston (mostly based on falsehoods) was about all the place had going for it. Could a literary tradition be built on that?

McMurtry pondered the question as he walked the vacant lots west of the old Montrose neighborhood, past the few remaining shotgun houses of Freedmen's Town, where the first freed slaves after the Civil War—following Juneteenth 1865—made their family homes. In place of history texts, Houston had tax codes encouraging the erasure of history (tearing down, rather than preserving, old houses gave an owner a greater return on investment). The city's humid air was hostile to paper and ink, dampening and weakening them, leaving history no home.

And yet Houston, forward-looking, was funding libraries and museums as if it *did* have something to preserve, some rich tradition to document and expand, a contribution to make to Western culture. In 1941, a pair of New York philanthropists, Mr. and Mrs. Percy S. Straus, whose son lived in Houston, had donated their extensive collection of paintings from around the world to Houston's Museum of Fine Arts, making it instantly competitive as a national arts center. Margo Jones had founded the Community Players, staging, in a sanitized incinerator converted into theater space, plays such as Oscar Wilde's *The Importance of Being Earnest*. Dominique and Jean de Menil had arrived in Houston in the late 1940s (Jean having survived several perilous missions with the French Resistance). Dominique said they'd fallen in love with "[all] things . . . *Texan!*" In the years ahead, with her family's oil money, the de Menils would shape Houston's arts and architectural scene, drawing to the city such talents as Philip Johnson and Mark Rothko. McMurtry could feel the vibrancy of these currents, even as he prepared to slip away from them and slink back home.

The homesickness he had felt for Archer City wasn't assuaged by his return this time, which meant it was something more complicated than homesickness. A deep ambivalence, at the very least. He wrote Kunk: "Archer City is rather a mess. If I didn't love the place I'd hate it violently. A bunch of almost inextricably mixxed up kids [*sic*]."

L arry] soon joined me at North Texas [State College], just as I was about to drop out and—what else?—get married. That's what girls did in those days," said Ceil Slack.

McMurtry was disappointed in her: it seemed that even the best of Archer City could not escape the worn paths meant for them. He was also upset with himself. Immediately, he regretted his decision to leave Rice. In retrospect, as he admitted in his statement for North Texas State, abandoning Houston because he'd felt intimidated and lonely was "a very foolish thing to do. Rice is . . . undoubtedly the best school in the Southwest, and hasn't more than a half-dozen peers in America. But, c'est la vie."

In the winter of 1955, traveling through a ferocious ice storm that left a two-inch hole in the windshield of the falling-apart Ford he'd purchased to slide around in, he arrived at a "kind of gulag operation in the boondocks, a mélange of ugly buildings surrounded by greasy eating joints," said Grover Lewis. Lewis would soon become McMurtry's closest friend on campus. The school, already feeling the dampening effects of McCarthyism, was "freighted toward business and education degrees," Lewis said. "You could be judged violently nonconformist just by liking jazz." Generally, intellectual freedom was not rewarded. In fact—as Lewis and McMurtry would discover—it was often severely punished.

If nothing else, McMurtry's year and a half in Houston had solidified his sense of himself. Clear-eyed (and brimming with the self-importance of youth), he summed himself up in his college statement: "I am a pure Caucasian Democrat . . . so far as I have been able to discern, no earthquakes, comets, or other singular cosmological phenomena (not a single wiseman) heralded my birth . . . My more remote ancestry is dubious. Snobbish aunts on my maternal side claim Scottish lairds among their progenitors, while my paternal grandmother spoke familiarly of Sitting Bull . . . [I have] a Renaissance outlook on life that has since proved perhaps more beneficial than specialization and mastery of any one of them would have been . . . For a while, I collected books, and I have a library of about 600 volumes . . . I have a great many friends. I have a bad habit of forming friendly alliances that are too deep to last. My friends and I are, consequently, occasionally prone to be disillusioned about one another.

"What is more," he added, "I love to write. I cherish fond hopes of being a writer. I shall almost certainly make some weird combination of writer-rancher-professor out of myself."

Armed with such cogent self-knowledge, he faced the problem of what to do with himself in the repressive atmosphere he'd landed in.

He was fortunate to find a pair of teachers—"better men than the institution they served," Lewis said—who could challenge and advise him. The first was Dr. Martin Shockley ("the first man I ever knew who actually twirled his mustache," Lewis recalled). He was a generalist who quoted long passages of *The Adventures of Huckleberry Finn* from memory, who railed against "picayune and stew-pid" people (like McCarthyites), and who defined literature as that "which distill[ed] truth from the bulk of human error." McMurtry's second mentor was Dr. James Brown, a creative writing instructor. He suggested that McMurtry write of his "world." "So, so will I," McMurtry informed Kunk. "I don't think (or expect) it'll sell though." Already, he felt his world was dated. Technically, Brown's one useful piece of advice was to correct a sentence in a story McMurtry had written—"the soft white hands of a dentist." Brown insisted that McMurtry had violated verisimilitude here: most dentists' hands were rough, he said, from all that damned yanking. He steered McMurtry to submit work to the school's literary magazine, *Avesta*.

In classes with these men, McMurtry met the only other boy on campus with a genuine aptitude for serious reading and writing: Grover Lewis, legally blind, a hard-luck kid scarred, literally and figuratively, from his raising in Dallas's rough-and-tumble "other side of the river," Oak Cliff. He'd gotten into the college on a generous scholarship. Dave Hickey, who would befriend McMurtry and Lewis in the 1960s, said Lewis had a tendency, out of the blue, to pass "some outrageous, absolute judgment on your life and work, while appealing to your sympathy by bumping into a chair. Which is pretty much my definition of 'exasperating'—that uncanny ability to break your heart while making you smile."

As for "Larry—he was a very *good* person," Hickey told me. "He was always right about a great many things."

Grover Lewis's essential biography had been written early, and his version of it, while not entirely matching the facts, was the first thing Mc-Murtry knew about him. Lewis would repeat the story often and eventually he'd write it down in unforgettable prose: "In 1943, my parents—Grover Lewis and Opal Bailey Lewis—shot each other to death with a pawnshop pistol. Big Grover had stalked us for a year, fighting divorce tooth and nail, and when he finally cornered Opal alone and pulled the trigger, she seized the gun and killed him, too." (Police evidence suggested that an old man scrubbing the bathrooms at the boardinghouse where the murders occurred may actually have grabbed the gun and shot Big Grover after he'd pumped five bullets into Opal. Apparently the cops, believing the old man had been justified, let him go.)

On many late nights, McMurtry sat up with Lewis while Lewis drank, telling the story, and McMurtry let him go on.

Encouraged by James Brown, the boys soon found themselves running *Avesta* and engaging in a friendly competition to win the campus literary prizes. "We [did it] three or four times running, splitting the prize money between us," Lewis said. In photographs in *The Campus Chat,* the college newspaper, commemorating their achievements, McMurtry stood a head taller than Lewis, grinning confidently (skinny as ever) while Lewis looked bemused, on the verge of vomiting. They both wore thick black glasses.

McMurtry wrote poetry and short stories—attempts to describe the Great Plains, baby steps toward his first novel. His dialogues carried on for pages, his situations were contrived, and his setting descriptions awkward ("The grass on the low hills being made beautiful by oblique rays of sunlight"). "Don't be too critical, 'cause I'm learning," he pleaded with Kunk in a note attached to the draft of a story. He did best when he started with characterization. "You clearly have the ability to do creative writing of the highest quality," Brown told him after McMurtry had produced several pieces (145 pages of prose in his first semester). "Included are a sensitivity to beauty, [and] an appreciation of the more indefinable but nonetheless powerful emotions."

Grover Lewis wrote poetry, fiction, and nonfiction. "Grover was regarded as the guy with the brilliant future in writing, not McMurtry," said Don Graham, who later took a class from Lewis (Graham would eventually become a preeminent Texas literary critic). McMurtry agreed that "Grover's stories and poems were a lot better than my stories and poems." Additionally, Lewis founded a student-faculty society for the "study of cinematic arts" and frequented local jazz clubs (McMurtry didn't have much of an ear for contemporary music, of any sort). He acted in campus theater productions. Soon Lewis developed "a very loyal following," McMurtry recalled. Some of his fellow students began "follow[ing] him almost like disciples . . . I was never a disciple, which is fine. He didn't want me as a disciple . . . But that was the difference between me and some other people in his life."

With McMurtry he could *really* talk books. "McMurtry and I were both 'country' measured by frat-rat standards—but far too sophisticated from our reading to be considered hayseed," Lewis said. "Between us, we had devoured hundreds, perhaps thousands, of books . . . and we were perpetually on the lookout for more."

With Jeff Mac's grudging financial help (he was still perpetually debt-ridden), McMurtry rented a small apartment on West Congress Street in Denton, near a noisy middle school, and he still drove the old Ford. He'd park beneath Lewis's apartment window and honk the horn.

"Got your toothbrush?" McMurtry would yell up at the window from behind the steering wheel.

"Sure."

"Any money?"

"Not much."

"Let's go to Juárez."

"Anywhere would do," Lewis recalled. "We would drive a hundred miles for a milkshake." All the while, talking books. "Dallas and Fort Worth were nearby, and gas cost only twenty cents a gallon."

One night, they heard T. S. Eliot read poetry at an SMU sports arena. (After the reading, a Dallas official made Eliot an honorary deputy sheriff of Dallas County.) On another evening, Lewis said, they witnessed a roughneck, an irate country music fan, whale "the living tar" out of a

relatively unknown Elvis Presley "in the parking lot of a rural dance hall."
(McMurtry later disputed Lewis's memory of this incident.)

"Larry knew a trick that would have outshone Dean Moriarty in Kerouac's *On the Road*," Lewis noted. "He could drive and read at the same
time on the barren stretches of highway out in the middle of nowhere."

Jeff Mac "took a rather dim view of his oldest son's education," Lewis
recalled. "Frequently [he] summoned him home for a weekend of forced-
march cowboying. Once in a while, I tagged along to help with the
chores—always . . . intimidated by the stern old man."

Their fellow literature students were intrigued and a little dazzled by
these "young turks." They'd remark that the boys were very different yet
somehow "just alike." The macho "frat-rats" couldn't stand them.

One day, Dr. Shockley, wearing his usual tweed coat and matching
billed cap, called to the pair from his office doorway, drawling in his deep
Virginia accent, "Mistah LOO-WIS! Mistah MUG-MURTRY! Step over
here closah, if you please, gentlemen."

"I hope he doesn't have a magic bulldog or anything," McMurtry whispered to his friend.

Shockley twirled his mustache. Slowly, painfully, he looked his students
up and down. "I've seen you two boys togethah . . ." He paused and shook
his head. "And I still can't make up my mind which one of you is in low
company."

Dave Hickey loved imagining "Grover and his old running-mate
Larry . . . at North Texas State in the 50s: as campus pariahs, as
these two skinny, four-eyed geeks in goofy '40s shirts, scuttling along the
sidewalk head to head, toting copies of *The Evergreen Review* and plotting
their mutual apotheosis—in the aftermath of which they would both be
famous authors, claiming any female who fell within their view."

"By the time I met them in the early '60s, they were no longer geeks,"
he said. "They were 'promising Texas writers' . . . [who'd] actually *achieved*
their apotheosis (and its consequent surfeit of feminine companionship)."

The papers McMurtry wrote in his undergraduate literature classes reveal a young sensibility stretching itself while simultaneously settling
into its groove. It was clear that he read as an aspiring novelist rather than

as a critic, though his critical abilities were sharp and his hunger to understand literary tradition, especially as it had developed in Europe, was keen.
Always, in reading fiction, his concerns were for authentic characterization
and a prose style matching its subject. In an analysis of *The Adventures of
Huckleberry Finn,* he chastised Mark Twain for giving Huck "Boy Scout
virtues," but he praised the book's prose for being "as completely free of af-
fectation as Huck himself, a prose of remarkable fluidity and naturalness."

His teachers, appreciative of his intelligence and creativity, gave him
leeway to experiment. In a meditation on "Steinbeck, Okies, and Hu-
manism," he imagined a Platonic dialogue between Huckleberry Finn and
Henry Adams concerning *The Grapes of Wrath.* Adams lights into Huck
for his shallow reading habits. It is easy to imagine McMurtry as Henry
Adams admonishing his fellow students, though in fact both characters
speak for McMurtry, Adams railing against Steinbeck's "diluted . . . journalism" and Huck arguing that "anybody that's been around at all could
follow the story." Steinbeck's crowning achievement, McMurtry wrote,
was his "sincerity," a difficult quality for any writer to convey (McMurtry
greatly appreciated another Steinbeck novel, *The Red Pony,* for its natural
style and its heartfelt lament for the West). Still, *The Grapes of Wrath* fell
short for him, presenting most of its characters as examples of social types.
In a statement predicting the literary controversies McMurtry would create as a mature writer, he wrote, "[Steinbeck] won a Pulitzer Prize for that
book . . . That's not saying much for the Pulitzer people . . . American letters has sunk so low that any ambitious journalist with a typewriter and a
handbook of aberrations can become a literary lion these days."

He admired James Joyce, though Joyce's modernism would not mark
his path. Joyce's early short-story collection, *Dubliners,* impressed him
more than the radical formal experiments of *Ulysses* and *Finnegans Wake.*
"The portraits [in *Dubliners*] are sharp, realistic (the first Irish realism), and
exactly as complete as the author chooses them to be," McMurtry wrote.
"The last story, 'The Dead,' is both a virtuoso performance and a preview
of things to come." (McMurtry always closely studied the way authors
consciously developed their bodies of work.) Most telling in his consideration of Joyce was his rapturous response to the end of *Ulysses*: "Molly's
soliquoy [*sic*] is the one part I can 'dig' completely." As in life, McMurtry
was most drawn to the characters of women; as he prepared to write his

first novel he was wrestling with the problem of a male artist conveying a female sensibility with nuance and accuracy. "I can scarcely think of a harder literary task than the one Joyce accomplished [here]," he wrote. "To take the mind of a woman and project it to the reader so convincingly that he loses all trace of the artist is hard. Joyce did this."

In a letter to Ken Kesey years later, referring to Joyce and his fiction experiments, McMurtry would further explain why Joyce had not emerged as a model for him: "I . . . don't think one has to worry about giving the world a product it's never bought before, or about surprising the reader . . . Innovations in form is . . . not anything I worry about because I don't think any one author can make major innovations [Kesey disagreed]. A major innovation is a new form and seems to result from the needs and habits of the audience or the people as much [as] anything. Epic, greek tragedy, elizabethan tragedy, the novel seems to me major kinds of things and no one writer formed them. That the novel evolved over a period of a hundred, two hundred years and became the various form[s] it is seems to me more important than the individual techniques brought to it by Sterne or Flaubert or Joyce."

No, the "obscurantist school" was not for him, he announced to his friend Kunk. "[Joyce] forfeited a great deal of art to vocabulary, and Eliot a great deal of music to erudition." McMurtry was, and would remain, a strict realist.

In late 1957 or early 1958, during his senior year, at an undergraduate party—and probably through Grover Lewis—McMurtry met Jo Ballard Scott from Florence, South Carolina, a junior at Texas Woman's College in Denton, across town from North Texas State. She was tall and classically beautiful, with thick blond hair, wisps of which jittered like compass needles across her forehead, indicating the several directions she appeared to consider at once. She often closed her eyes just a little when she smiled, so intense was her happiness.

Denton, full of returning Korean War vets in the mood to party, was in the process of becoming "a very pleasant little town," she told me. "The courthouse square was the place to go. There was a movie house that showed foreign films; we could feel very sophisticated. There was a department store that sold the latest fashions, the sack dress (what! no waist line!), and a coffee house, very dark interior, with folk singers and guitars. The sixties had begun, or maybe the pre-sixties. Everybody was reading Ginsberg and Kerouac."

She relished the loosening atmosphere, her freedom from the "sand" of South Carolina which her father often said he didn't want to be buried in. He was a public health official, a man who'd spent World War II eradicating mosquitoes and rats on U.S. air bases, and he'd had difficulty shielding his family from the harsh responses his decisions could prompt. James, the son Jo and McMurtry would produce, remembered his mother telling him that his grandfather "in the postwar summers . . . had to take the extremely unpopular action of closing the public swimming pools in attempts to stop the spread of polio . . . Public pools generally had baby sections which weren't really sealed off from the rest of the pool . . . It had to be done, the pools had to be shut down or a bunch of kids would end up paralyzed. But people complained . . . They just knew it couldn't happen to their kids." Jo had not escaped the shaming and the fear caused by her father's job, and she grew up determined to earn community acceptance. A picture in the April 23, 1954, *Florence Morning News* showed her standing proudly in a nearly ankle-length floral print dress, clutching a small white handbag, her hair darker than it would later be, and immaculately coiffed, above a caption lauding her for giving a "preview of one of the dresses to be modeled" at a fashion show and tea sponsored by the Twentieth Century Literary Club.

Three years later, far from the clutching "sand" of her home state, she had become the "Queen of Bohemia" in Denton, Texas, according to Greg Curtis, who would later befriend McMurtry. "I don't know if Grover ever went out with Jo," Curtis said. But they were close. "That Larry won her was really something."

Her first impression of McMurtry was that he "seemed rather quiet . . . in comparison to the rest of us. He . . . was said to be writing a novel. He was unusual in being interested in books as such, knowing about different editions, going to secondhand bookshops in Dallas and Fort Worth. When the rest of us bought books, they were usually Modern Library editions or maybe Grove Press paperbacks."

Her descriptions of him suggest that today he might be diagnosed as being "on the spectrum," single-mindedly focused and precocious in an uncanny way. As for her, she met his need to be with a woman who was stimulating both intellectually and physically.

He still spent a hellacious amount of time with Grover Lewis on the road. (Lewis seems to have replaced Mike Kunkel in McMurtry's world as an intimate, book-loving friend. At this point, Kunk vanishes from McMurtry's narrative, to assume a shadowy afterlife as a correspondent in a literary archive.)

"McMurtry and I justified our excursions as 'bookscouting,' but we were nosing around, really, poking into obscure nooks and crannies," Lewis said. "We checked out distant truck stops, county fairs, and junk auctions, the fading towns bypassed by the new interstates. We went to old fiddlers' contests, rodeo dances, favorite shoot-'em-up movies playing half the state away. We nursed beers in the strident honky-tonks on the infamous Jacksboro highway outside Fort Worth, trying experimental conversations with the B-girls and earnestly hoping not to get caught in the Wild West gunfire that periodically erupted there." (McMurtry insisted that Lewis embellished many of these recollections.)

Together, they found an old copy of *The Dial* in Lloyd Harper's used bookstore in the Deep Ellum section of Dallas, a Black neighborhood. A portion of Eliot's *The Waste Land* had first appeared in the issue. They bought it for a quarter. Harper got used to the frequent appearance of these "college gentlemen" among his book stacks. "You blame boys float through here just like ghosts, carry away all my best stuff," he groused affectionately.

But their road trips were wistfully colored now, not just because their time together as college buddies was approaching an end, but also because the "Southwest was literally perishing in front of our eyes, its old landmarks and heroes being nudged aside by tract homes and SAC bases—and the likes of Elvis Presley," Lewis said. "McMurtry had already pegged the theme of changing values in the region as his own literary territory."

They were both increasingly upset that the college administration was trying to "shape" their writing by complaining about some of the material appearing in *Avesta*. McMurtry had published in the magazine an essay about the cornetist Bix Beiderbecke (less interested in the music than in the "novel folk-literature, rich in romance and fabliaux" surrounding jazz). He'd written a mostly laudatory piece about Kerouac's *On the Road.* He would later claim Kerouac as a "historical," rather than as a literary, influence (his heart remained with the nineteenth-century Europeans). "At the time *On the Road* was published, American writing had been stodgy for quite a while," he said. "The English departments had been dominated by the New Critics for twenty years, and everything was very symbolical and academic and heavily written. Kerouac came along and opened it up. A lot of writers of my generation were stimulated by Kerouac . . . He was very important at the time we were developing."

Over supper one night, McMurtry and Lewis decided to flaunt the Beat sensibility in a literary journal of their own (the publication of which, they hoped, would also be an homage to Drs. Shockley and Brown). They recruited a friend, John Lewis (no relation to Grover), because as a pre-seminarian, he had a key to the mailroom of the Episcopal Student Center. There, the three young men typed cardboard plates, cranked the duplicating machine, collated, bound, and stapled the pages of the first issue of what they called *The Coexistence Review.* "The title . . . signified to us that we were all embarked on separate paths but getting along amiably just the same," Lewis said. At this point, McMurtry claimed to have written sixty-three short stories at North Texas State, all of which he'd destroyed in shame— though his shame was frequently balanced by a soaring confidence. While he was struggling with stories he hoped to stitch into a novel, Lewis was gaining recognition from magazines such as *The Carolina Quarterly* and *The Nation.* He won the Samuel French Playwriting Award. He was on his way to what would be a brilliant but woefully short career writing long-form magazine journalism, most notably for *Rolling Stone,* covering the burgeoning cultural revolution of the 1960s. If his addictions to meth and alcohol hadn't crippled him, he might well be spoken of today as one of the leading lights of that period's New Journalism, along with Tom Wolfe, Hunter S. Thompson, and Joan Didion.

McMurtry opened the first issue of *The Coexistence Review* with a Beat-infused credo:

BOO! You sanforized people.
You with TIME on your hands and LIFE on your ipana consciences.
You who hate NEGROES JEWS CATHOLICS NEIGHBORS

VIRGINS POETRY TAXES
& ANYTHING ELSE THAT LACKS UTILITY.
You who hid JESUS with other old easter eggs and beat your kids . . .
Run on to your sleazy heaven and check the trade in on haloes for me.
In case I can't find a flannel suit to match my SOUL.

(His other contributions to the magazine—a poem beginning, "beauty,
bear my wounded aprils ever- / green to your long day's fair"—as well as
early excerpts of a ranch novel he was already calling *Horseman, Pass By,*
indicate that his literary identity had yet to coalesce.)

Grover Lewis's credo, printed directly below McMurtry's, consisted of
the phrase "Let me alone" repeated twenty-seven times, the words and letters running closer and closer together on the page, culminating in a rant
against "stinking skincrawling fat-hog cannibal sonsofultimatebitches."

But it was John Lewis's contribution that got the trio in the biggest
trouble with the college administration. It was the clearest rejection of campus conformity: "I would rather be a Communist than a Southerner . . .
I would rather be anything than a Southerner. You have no culture; you
have but one tradition . . . and that is a *lack* of tradition . . . You are afraid
of Moloch, and your guts stink because of it."

The word *Communist* along with a large red star on the cover (a grotesque parody of the Texas Lone Star, though it struck the higher-ups as a
Soviet symbol) prompted official talk of forcing students to take a loyalty
oath to the United States of America. Meanwhile, at fifty cents a copy, the
two hundred issues of *The Coexistence Review* sold out on campus.

"On impulse, McMurtry dropped by the office [of the college vice
president] to offer a cowboy handshake and a copy of the magazine with
the compliments of the editors," Lewis said. The vice president said "he
didn't care to read such trash. He said we were nobodies who would never
be genuine writers."

McMurtry and Lewis were barred from publishing again in *Avesta,*
though, once more, they had just won that semester's literary awards. The
magazine ceased publication altogether for the next five years.

Under the threat of not being allowed to graduate, the boys hastily
released the review's second and last issue, blank on the cover except for

a standard loyalty oath ("I swear or affirm that I believe in and approve the constitution of the United States . . . and will not aid or assist in any efforts or movement to subvert or destroy the government of the United States . . ."). It was signed by the editors. If bitter cynicism had a hue, it would have been the color of the ink.

In the journal's brief run, McMurtry published two poems by Jo Scott. She was absolutely his peer.

L arry and I started dating seriously the following year, when I was a senior," Jo said. "Larry had finished his BA and was in his first year of graduate school at Rice. He came to Denton often as he still had friends there, and it was on his way if he were going home to Archer City."

In fact, before starting Rice again in the fall, he spent the summer of 1958 on the ranch, mending fences and moving cattle to Anarene, riding alongside his father. Jeff Mac would shake his son's foot in the mornings to wake him up, just as he had done when McMurtry was a boy.

McMurtry also wrote poetry that summer, and nearly finished a first draft of *Horseman, Pass By.* The novel's story line was evolving: the death of the old cattleman remained central in draft after draft, but the manner of his passing changed from a "kind thing," a mercy killing to end his suffering, to a more ambiguous act of aggression toward everything he stood for.

McMurtry's poetry that summer was heavily elegiac (he seemed to know that his second crack at Rice signaled a firmer, more permanent, break from life with his family). In a Fort Worth museum, he had seen Erwin Smith's photographs of horses, cowboys, and cattle. He had learned that Smith, raised in Bonham, Texas, was only four years old when the 1890 U.S. census declared the closing of the American frontier. In response to this news, Frederick Jackson Turner had written: "Now, four centuries from the discovery of America, at the end of a hundred years of life under the Constitution, the frontier has gone, and with its going has closed the first period of American history." Turner's sentiment would guide Smith's artistic career: like McMurtry, he noted the rise of the cowboy legend just as the actual life was disappearing. He would become the preeminent photographer of the final demise of the open range.

In the evenings, in Archer City, after a day spent working beside his father in the fields, McMurtry wrote a poem addressed to Smith ("Lead me along the hills, / where naked young mesquites / Shiver in the twelve-day wind / by stumps of burned ancestors"). He was in a particularly somber mood, seeing how much his father had aged in the unforgiving sunlight since he'd last been home. His poem whispered the same valedictions as Yeats's "Under Ben Bulben," from which McMurtry had taken the title of his novel ("Cast a cold eye / On life, on death. / Horseman, pass by!"):

And here, the last cracked bones
of my grandfather's horse [McMurtry wrote],

The gray one who stood in grave
infirmity under

Horsepasture elms through
my boyhood.

An old horse, youth
and the cantering after cattle

Lost, and lost calves,
and myself, lost

To the white bones and the hills—

He sent the poem to the *Southwest Review,* a journal still produced on the campus of Southern Methodist University, the third-oldest literary review published in the United States. McMurtry admired its history. It had distinguished itself with its first Dallas issue (after starting its run in Austin) with a one-act play denouncing the Ku Klux Klan. This was a time, 1924, when the Dallas chapter of the Klan was the largest in the country, claiming among its members the mayor, the county sheriff, the police commissioner, the police chief, and the district attorney. In subsequent years, the *Review* had published all the men deemed by regional critics to be the fathers of Texas literature: J. Frank Dobie, Walter Prescott Webb, and Roy Bedichek. No wonder, then, that McMurtry, finding a note one day in the mailbox accepting his poem, was, he said, "so thrilled that I went out into the burning streets of Archer City—115 degrees that day—and took a long, triumphant walk." It was his first publication in a nationally recognized journal. "For the very first time I began to feel that I might be a writer."

The burning streets of Archer City were preparing for the opening day parade of its annual summer rodeo in which his sister Sue would be featured. (Two years later, riding a pony called Scallywag, she would be asked to present the colors throughout the three-day event and be crowned Archer County Rodeo Queen.) McMurtry himself had ridden in the rodeo parade when he was nine years old. As long as he could remember, the county had held amateur calf-roping and bull-riding contests, originally sponsored by a man named "Goat" Mayo who wanted his events to be wholesome family affairs, finished by ten P.M. each night. To ensure that no one got hurt, he shaved the bulls' horns. In the mid-1940s, the Archer City Livestock Association slicked up the rodeo, professionalizing it, expanding the number of contests to include such things as bareback bronc riding and girls' breakaway roping. The association awarded saddles to the winners. Archer County hosted one of the most popular rodeos in the state, along with Fort Worth and Pecos, reportedly the site of Texas's first rodeo in 1883. The rodeo craze—and its link to patriotic events—had begun just a year before that with Buffalo Bill Cody's choreographed staging of what he had witnessed on struggling Nebraska ranches, the spontaneous competitions among cattlemen using their downtime to perfect the techniques of their labor.

In that sweltering summer of 1958, on the burning streets and in the cramped, dusty arenas smelling of animal sweat, McMurtry could not shake his elegiac mood. The rodeo simply seemed to him a sad, cynical, and sanitized parody of the cowboy life (despite its brutal risks), a show put on for ticket sales rather than a calling embodying a set of principles. It didn't matter that the *Southwest Review* had validated *his* calling. It didn't matter that he genuinely admired the competitors' skills. It didn't matter that the broncs came with adorably cute names—Double Diamond, Brown Jug, Crawfish, Strawberry Roam. It didn't matter that his sister loved the pageantry and the fireworks and the colors, her way of showing how much she worshiped her daddy and his chosen life in a way McMurtry wished *he* could do but couldn't.

In his growing literary mindedness, it all had the feel of Paradise Lost:

the clowns who weren't really funny, the crowds laughing at the torturing of the animals.

He walked the burning streets, amid the cow-dung reek, watching the rodeo circuit's repeat winners drive into town in big white Lincolns, honking their horns at the girls, at the café waitresses leaning out of fly-buzzed open doors, while the rest of the lonesome boys, carrying saddles, arriving on foot to scrabble for whatever they could win in whatever competitions they could talk their way into, looked for shady spots to toss their bedrolls. The old-timers emerged from their paint-peeling houses, hunched over, chawing about the good ol' days. Children tore off their clothes and blurred their chubby faces with red and blue Sno-Cone slush. It would soon become apparent which of them had no homes to go to—or none to speak of: they'd still be filthy by the end of the week.

By sundown that first day, beer-soaked bull riders would snuggle in flatbeds or the busted seats of cars with partners looking like every girl McMurtry had dreamed of in high school. Only the slow appearance of the stars above the grandstands, as the sky darkened and the sun's last glare lingered in the west, gave him any peace, honest reminders of the distances and the isolation against which rodeo sports had been created as distractions in the first place.

He'd go home to his father's kitchen table and stare at the pages of his novel. He'd scratch out a sentence. Add another. "Things used to be better around here," he wrote. "I feel like I want something back." "Granddad made something good," he typed. "It didn't stay made." And: "All of them wanted more and seemed to end up with less; they wanted excitement and ended up stomped by a bull or smashed against a highway; or they wanted a girl to court; and anyway, whatever it was they wanted, that was what they ended up doing without."

The Bayou City welcomed him back in the form of a fifteen-dollar-a-month basement apartment (basements being one of the worst ideas a builder could have in swampy Houston). It was filled with perpetually damp matting in lieu of carpets. It was a five-minute walk from campus. The whole place shook whenever the owner of the house sitting above the apartment pulled his Chrysler into his garage.

McMurtry had applied to several graduate schools as he was finishing his BA, but had received only two offers, from the University of Illinois, Urbana, and from Rice. Mathematics would not be a requirement at the graduate level. Rice extended him a "minute" but livable stipend.

"My time in Houston had not been long enough," he explained. "I was eager to go back." He had "missed [the city] as much as I've missed certain women," he wrote later. "And there are women I have missed so much that I've become afraid to see them again: it becomes too big a risk, because if you miss them that much and then see them and they turn out not to like you anymore—or, worse, you turn out not to like *them* anymore—then something important to you is forever lost."

But Houston enveloped him with its "old fishy smell . . . moist and warm, a smell composed of many textures," and he eased back in. Driving the Gulf Freeway in the late afternoon, under watery, boiling clouds sucking his car straight off the pavement (at least that's how it seemed), he felt like he had never left.

Among his new graduate companions, the main concern was finding good bars you wouldn't get killed in. Houston's story was told in its bars (and a few of the Mexican food and Cajun dives): the upper-class bars floated in the air atop steel-and-glass high-rises far removed from the filthy parking lots (the "city [was] only forty-one feet above sea level; [such bars] put their members well above the masses who cannot afford [the] relief of heights," McMurtry said); the middle-class pubs hunkered closer to the ground, usually in "generally squat one-story affairs, converted restaurants with imitation-Las Vegas furniture and deafening acoustics"; while working-class patrons and students slithered into dwellings hardly distinguishable from the elements of the earth except for their pulsing jukeboxes, the jars full of pigs' feet, and the red-haired waitresses tipsy on Thunderbird wine. On Telegraph Road, on Griggs, on Elysian and Almeda, a student could drink cheaply if he stayed quiet and huddled, glancing at no one, in a corner by the bathrooms in the back. Almeda was along a major ambulance route, so late-night conversations were limited.

There was the Angel Bar, serving tattooed pachucos. There was the Gulf-Air, a café-bar catering to Cajun cowboys, long-haul truckers, and pool-playing roustabouts. There was the Last Concert Café in the Warehouse District, north of downtown on the banks of Buffalo Bayou, where

"Mama" Elena Lopez, the owner, opened her arms and her patio picnic tables to a motley assortment of vagrants and students, along with large, extended Mexican families.

These loose-limbed establishments, relaxed and edgy all at once, made the pretentious, candlelit jazz clubs of Denton, where his old compatriots liked to congregate, seem blander than ever, whenever McMurtry returned on the weekends to visit Jo and other friends.

"The people in Larry's life were of tremendous importance to him," Jo said. As much as he relished living in Houston again, he felt the pain of transition, of leaving old pals behind, watching them scatter, developing and pursuing different interests. Raised as he was in the midst of a major cultural transformation, he would always be wary of change, ready to retreat into comforting old habits. It was already becoming clear, so soon after graduation, that many of his friendships in Denton had little left to them but fading habit. Things had even turned tense with Grover. "The first inkling I had that he had somewhat complex feelings about me . . . came at a party in 1959, when I was in Denton, visiting," McMurtry said. During his time at North Texas State, McMurtry had kept a running list of books he wanted to read as soon as possible, foremost among them James Agee's *Let Us Now Praise Famous Men*. The North Texas State library had a copy of the book, but it was always checked out, exasperating McMurtry. At the party, Lewis, drunk, admitted sheepishly that *he* was the one who'd sat on the book for over a year, just so McMurtry couldn't get his hands on it. He seemed to think he was being funny. "It was at that point that I stopped thinking of him simply as a friend, though we continued to see one another for most of the sixties," McMurtry said.

He didn't want what had happened with Grover to happen with Jo. The couple knew that his departure for Rice had brought them to a decision point. Long-distance dating was too difficult to maintain. Jo had embraced change when she'd first left South Carolina and experienced the independence of college life, but she had not completely abandoned her upbringing—the need for community acceptance. She felt the same urgency that Ceil Slack had responded to: a girl went to college to get married, no matter what other ambitions she may have pursued. Now, faced with uncertain prospects after earning her degree and involved in a relationship whose logistics worked against her, she became exceedingly nervous, hesitant, shy

around friends, even withdrawn. McMurtry, too, responded to the prompt-
ings of traditional values even as he chafed against them. Moreover, he had
established an easygoing *habit* with Jo, who shared his passion for reading.
It was pleasant. They discussed marriage.

Tooling down the highway between Denton and Houston, past waffle
houses, truck stops, and petroleum tanks, he considered the prospect of
life in a basement apartment smelling of damp rubber mats and dirty
laundry, sharing books with a wife.

He'd pull into Houston on Sunday evening and go immediately to the
air-conditioned hallways of Fondren Library, to nod off over heavy volumes while the waxers groaned, circling the green leather couches.

The next day, he'd walk to his seminars and classes, past the Mexican
gardeners wearing straw hats and khakis, clipping sweet-smelling bougain-
villea. He'd watch shadowy cloudscapes roll across the quad lawns. His
favorite teachers were the old-fashioned scholars—Alan McKillop, Will
Dowden. They adhered to the close reading of the New Critics (focusing
on the text, rather than regarding literature through a particular ideolog-
ical or biographical lens). They were opposed to the more theoretical approaches to reading—drawing upon linguistics, psychology, and European
philosophy. These were disseminated by their colleague Jack Cope, who
intimidated McMurtry by strolling across campus with an immaculately
groomed collie and bragging about working out in a gym where Sonny
Liston trained.

McMurtry avoided theory, gravitating toward literary history (F. R.
Leavis's *The Great Tradition*) and texts on writing craft (E. M. Forster's
Aspects of the Novel and Percy Lubbock's *The Craft of Fiction*). He had men-
tors, but his intellectual development had always been self-directed. He
concentrated on his personal obsession: the problems of realism in fiction.

For an advanced seminar he wrote a twenty-six-page paper on "Elizabethan Realism: Realistic Prose in England from 1525 to 1610." He maintained that "realistic fiction" was "concerned primarily with the activities
of humble people," and that formally, it consisted of "jeremiads, fanciful
journalism, and a variety of anecdotal material . . . Some of it purports to
be solemn fact, and some of it can accurately be called gossip. Even so, the
gossip is uncommonly good and the fact imaginatively handled. I . . . call
[this] fiction."

In the main, he dismissed Elizabethan realism as "lurid and aphrodisiac," pandering to the tastes of a lowbrow audience, "confused about what good fiction ought to do" (which was to create its *own* audience). He commended Elizabethan authors for being well-read and aware of international trends (something he would later condemn Texas writers for *not* doing), "but this wide reading did nothing for them as realists . . . As fiction all [of Elizabethan writing] is defective." A reader could pore over multiple volumes, he said, "without getting the slightest idea of how an Elizabethan tavern looked, or how an Elizabethan street looked, or even, for that matter, how the garden variety Elizabethan looked." From the first, McMurtry never met a literary tradition he liked—or, more accurately, one that could meet his high standards.

He was so hard on the poor dead scriveners, the paper became a slog; at one point, aware of this, McMurtry addressed his teacher: "A fuller discussion [of this topic] might be interesting, but very likely it would only double the length of this paper and leave you more sullen than you already are, a risk hardly worth taking." McMurtry's flagging interest in the subject spiked again only at the end, when he decided to "say a word about the bibliography," listing the various editions of the major works and their respective qualities. (In one case, he said, "The print . . . is really the worst I ever encountered, and seems literally to fade off the page after a chapter or two.") The nascent book dealer in him was stirring.

In the middle of the paper, and largely incidental to his discussion of Elizabethan realism, McMurtry revealed *his* aspiration as a writer of fiction—to become "one of those haunting young-old men who give literature so much of its poignancy, those who gasp and fumble . . . for a more complete speech than they ever attain, and who manage in their quick shatter to leave us writing that remains somehow profoundly warm."

B y October 1958, McMurtry had completed drafts of two full novels, *Horseman, Pass By* and a manuscript he called *Memories of the Old Tribe,* later to be revised and titled *Leaving Cheyenne.* Both novels were elegies for the cattleman's lost way of life, *Horseman* culminating in the death of an old cowboy after his cows are slaughtered following an outbreak of hoof-and-mouth disease, and *Leaving Cheyenne* tracing the lifelong friendship of a Quixote-Sancho pair, both in love with the same woman, both struggling to find their place in a changing world. It was while finishing the draft of *Horseman, Pass By* that he'd begun sketching the new story, and then he just kept writing each day, five pages every morning, a habit he would continue for most of the rest of his life (on the ranch he'd gotten used to rising early). The fresh pages accumulated to seed his second novel.

Writing was the one thing in his life he was not ambivalent about. At a certain point, in his mid-thirties, that would change, but for now, he was twenty-two, he had kicked out two novels—a process over which he maintained complete control, one of its chief pleasures—and he was living the highly specialized life of a graduate student, spending his days and nights in libraries and bookstores, his mind often in another century. In spite of his love of learning, he knew he was not a scholar—his reading proclivities were too eclectic to be channeled into a narrow academic discipline, and most often now his studies served as craft lessons for his own scribbles. His lack of a scholarly pedigree made him ambivalent about grad school; it was a splendid way to stall for time before entering a professional track, but what was he preparing for? Teaching? Already he suspected he was not cut out for that. If every student was as needy as he was, the responsibilities would be too great to bear. His doubts led to ambivalent friendships—his companions were serious academics or, as in the case of a fierce, fiery fellow from Louisiana named Bill Corrington, a self-professed poet and novelist, they felt a need to compete with him for literary fame. For a while, McMurtry's closest friends in Houston were a couple named Ray and Linda Waddington. They lived in a trailer home camp on South

Main near Rice. Ray had earned his BA at Stanford and was now working on a graduate degree, specializing in the aesthetics of seventeenth-century Platonic poets. McMurtry invited the couple to his parents' ranch, where Hazel introduced Ray to pecan pie. "She was very friendly, but we didn't see much of Larry's father. I got the impression that the younger brother, Charlie, was anxious to get Larry out of the way because he wanted to inherit the ranch someday," Ray said.

McMurtry studied Ray closely, to observe the scholarly demeanor, to see how it fit (or didn't) in the world, to extrapolate from his friend's plans and dreams what it might be like to follow an academic path. (Ray Waddington would eventually wind up teaching Renaissance literature at the University of Wisconsin and then at UC Davis.) McMurtry watched Linda because he found her very attractive, both physically and temperamentally. (Linda's wits were as quick as Jo's, but she was far more relaxed.) She was the *roundest* person he had ever known—round shoulders, round face, round hips. She was beautiful even when pregnant—she gave birth to two boys in rather quick succession.

McMurtry had noticed how the older academic wives at Rice exhibited remarkable patience and calm. These seemed to be emotional requirements of the role, in what was a rather sedate and decorative life. He was curious to see how, or even if, the necessary qualities would develop in a young woman as vibrant as Linda, who was not without patience, but who also enjoyed a good bit of fun. He watched her, thinking of Jo, with whom he was still discussing marriage. Could Jo settle into academic domesticity? (Of course Jo herself was talking about becoming an academic.)

Ray and Linda told McMurtry about the bohemian lives of the students they'd known in California, on the street where they lived, Perry Lane. Some of their friends practiced what they called open relationships, scoffing at the notion of traditional marriage, with its exclusivity and possessiveness. A far cry from Eros as it was pursued, or purported to be, in Archer County, much less on Idiot Ridge.

An Oregon boy named Ken Kesey had just moved into the house the Waddingtons had vacated on Perry Lane when they came to Houston. They'd heard he was a crazy man. He claimed he would be America's next great novelist.

McMurtry went often with friends to the River Oaks Theater.

Watching movies with pals like the Waddingtons was like reading books with a crowd—he didn't go just to be entertained, but to analyze the films' narrative structures, to try to understand what formal decisions, made by the director and the editors, gave the story lines the power they had. The River Oaks became another library.

McMurtry saw *South Pacific* and took wry delight in singing for his friends a song from its soundtrack, "Some Enchanted Evening," on Houston's broiling nights. He saw Richard Brooks's adaptation of Tennessee Williams's *Cat on a Hot Tin Roof.* The film starred Paul Newman and Elizabeth Taylor. The story, involving a close male friendship (minus the homosexual overtones, in Brooks's watered-down version) made turbulent by a volatile woman, bore similarities to McMurtry's evolving *Memories of the Old Tribe.* It impressed him that Newman was almost as eye-catching as his costar, though McMurtry thought Elizabeth Taylor "as beautiful as any woman on the planet." Even more intriguing to him were the stories he had read about her. She had saved Montgomery Clift's life one night following a terrible car accident by running into the road and pulling broken teeth out of his throat so he wouldn't choke. Clearly, the woman had a great capacity for friendship; this humanized her, brought her down off the imposing screen. Like millions of other moviegoers, McMurtry fantasized about getting to know her. Unlike millions of others, he *would* eventually meet her—and he'd spend time with Paul Newman even sooner than that.

On the weekends he drove to Denton to visit Jo. Back in Houston, during the week, he attended classes and frequented bookstores, as well as the Goodwill shop on Washington Avenue and a place called Trash and Treasure on Westheimer, which sometimes tucked quality books among its ripped and yellowed paperbacks.

He immersed himself in the novel, from Samuel Richardson to Anthony Powell. He bought books to improve his education as well as to satisfy his growing collector's urge. He rekindled his interest in the pulps, recalling the sexy paperback covers in Mr. Wilson's five-and-dime. He recognized that the covers "were the advance guard of the rapid breakdown of sexual restraint among the middle classes almost everywhere." As such, they were historical documents. Cultural markers. (The *Lady Chatterley's Lover* obscenity trial in Britain, in which Lawrence's novel was found not to be pornographic, was only two years away.) Too, the pulps were valuable for being descendants of the nineteenth-century dime novels, so essential to selling the romance of the Old West.

He also knew the value of erotica. Beyond whatever prurient pleasure he may have taken from nude photographs, he'd learned that wealthy collectors were willing to pay huge sums of money for them. Like dime novels, pulps, comic books, and bandes dessinées (*The Adventures of Tintin—Le Temple du Soleil!*), certain erotic series were likely to increase in price in years to come. He was an early collector of the Betty Page bondage photographs taken by Irving and Paula Klaw, a Brooklyn brother-and-sister team largely responsible for introducing S and M into the American mainstream when their bookstore began to fail and they turned to other opportunities. For a while, they sold pinup photographs of movie stars and bathing beauties—the pictures moved much better than rare books and first editions. Then, Paula said, customer demand "brought us that particular interest—bondage, girlie stuff, garter belts and high heels. They were mostly wealthy lawyers and doctors. A couple of them offered to put up the money for the project—models, photography and all, providing we kept their names anonymous . . . and that's why and how we did it . . . We hired the models and the studios and these guys showed us exactly what they wanted done. They taught us."

McMurtry also collected the fetishistic illustrations and strip cartoons of Eric Stanton, intricate offshoots of the Mickey Spillane covers featuring dominant women and subservient men. For Irving Klaw, Stanton developed the comic series *Battling Women* and *Fighting Femmes*. Like the Spillane books and the Betty Page pictures, Stanton's drawings helped lift kink out of the shadows. Eventually, Betty Page would pose for *Playboy* (itself an avenue for casual sex into the mainstream) and Stanton would wind up working with Steve Ditko, later a Marvel Comics artist and co-creator of *Spider-Man*. High and low aesthetics were beginning to blur—a hallmark of what some culture critics would soon be calling postmodernism. Though these same critics would never consider McMurtry anything other than a strict traditionalist, his interest in literary genres and esoteric items made him aware of trends—and of culture's porousness—far earlier than most observers of the time. He grasped the long ties between soft-core smut sold in small-town dime stores, nineteenth-century erotic doggerel from England, and Pietro Aretino's *Sonetti lussuriosi*, a book published in Venice in 1527 featuring sixteen woodcuts by the artist Giulio Romano, illustrating unusual sexual positions.

The time may have come to part or marry, but, for myself, I put no trust in either alternative. Parting would not leave me free, nor marriage make me happy." McMurtry wrote these words in 1968, regarding his relationship to the state of Texas, but they could well have expressed his ambivalence about Jo in the fall of 1958. She was finding long-distance dating increasingly unsatisfactory. For him, it was not so bad (and it established a lifelong pattern), putting some distance between him and the object of his affections, necessitating bittersweet longing, letters, and phone calls. To some extent, it *was* the distance and the longing he loved; they were what he'd grown up with, streaking the Great Plains sky; they supplied the romance behind what was lost before you even had it. He seemed most at home in transit, between commitment and escape, neither denying nor embracing, loving and wanting to be left alone, ticking off another day's set of miles.

He explored his contradictions in the characters Johnny and Gid at the heart of *Leaving Cheyenne*: Gid the pragmatic rancher loyal to the land in spite of the hardships it brings him, Johnny the restless cowboy, carefree (or trying hard to be), convinced that richer pastures lie just down the road. For decades, they love and sleep with their friend Molly, though neither settles down with her—she is as restless as Johnny and just as bound as Gid to her lonely oversight of the land. Johnny can romp with Molly and leave in the morning without a second thought, lighthearted and brimming with enjoyment of life; Gid can never spend time in Molly's bed without a guilty conscience, worrying that sex outside of marriage is wrong, or fearing that his intimacies with Molly amount to a betrayal of Johnny or others or of his duties to the ranch.

In the early 1960s, Ken Kesey read *Leaving Cheyenne* and suggested to McMurtry that Johnny and Gid represented opposing sides of him. McMurtry replied: "No, I am not quite Johnny and Gid. They lived a dialogue that interested and absorbed me, but I am not really that two-sided . . . I am at least nine/tenths Gid, and have practically no capacity for taking life easy. Though I enjoy my enjoys very intensely."

In the novel, Molly says of Gid, "He just couldn't believe sex was right. I don't guess he left my bedroom five times in his life that he wasn't ashamed of himself . . . I had to be careful where I touched him or he would jump like he was electrocuted. But he was the thoughtfulest man I knew, and took the most interest in me. He just wasn't able to understand that I . . . wanted him to enjoy himself—he got it in his head, but he never got it in his bones." And "If I made him sit around and talk when he didn't want to talk, he would just get self-conscious, and get ashamed of himself, and that would spoil things for him before he ever touched me. The only way . . . was to keep him from having to face what was on his mind until he was already in the bed. When I could manage that, he loved it . . . but it was just very seldom that he could let himself go."

To Kesey, McMurtry wrote: "[I] am not, alas, very seducible. Love lighthearted sex but never begin with it. That is, my body follows my emotions, and seldom precedes them." In another letter to Kesey written in the mid-1960s, he said: "It may just be that sexual relationships are basically destructive, though I suppose if that were true the world wouldn't be overpopulated. I agree [that] convention . . . is inescapable—to escape it you have to set up a counter-convention that traps you and conditions you just as surely as the one you try to escape."

These melancholy reflections did not encourage a positive approach to marriage. In spite of McMurtry's protests to Kesey, *Leaving Cheyenne* did constitute a self-debate. Gid's father tells him: "If you stay loose from [Molly], she'll make you the best kind of friend you can have. If you . . . marry her, you'll have ninety-nine kinds of misery." And Molly concludes: "I never had been able to talk [him] out of his conscience"—his inability to "let go"—"or love him out of it, either . . . [We] were in a situation where neither one of us could completely win."

Perhaps to test the terms of the debate, McMurtry considered initiating an affair with Linda Waddington. What would a romance feel like in the serious confines of academia, in the context of academic ambition (Linda serving here as a substitute for Jo)? Could he ever learn to temper/change/live with his conscience? Could the notion of an open relationship, which had clearly intrigued Linda since her Perry Lane days, really be viable? Presumably, McMurtry did not feel the answers would be clear enough in the end, or worth the trouble they'd require. His affair with Linda Waddington remained merely speculative—for now.

I n the fall of 1958, the students of Rice Institute produced the first issue of a literary magazine called *The Rice Mill*. McMurtry published two brief sections of *Horseman, Pass By* in it—the editor's note said "the following are two excerpts from a recently completed novel which Mr. McMurtry is now in the process of revising." He did not receive first billing on the cover. He was named third, after the titles of a scholarly article on Malraux and Nietzsche and a rather pretentious poem, "The Anatomy of Love," by William Corrington.

If Corrington considered himself the top literary canine on campus, the way Grover Lewis had at North Texas State, McMurtry nevertheless doggedly pressed his case. Earlier, he had sent a slice of *Horseman, Pass By* to Margaret Hartley, editor of the *Southwest Review*—it was the scene of the old cattleman's funeral, which McMurtry intended to be the novel's first chapter following the advice of his old teacher Martin Shockley. Hartley had responded favorably but just sat on the story, neither publishing it nor accepting McMurtry's ideas for revisions. Eventually, he wrote to her, asking that *Southwest Review* relinquish its rights to the story so he could send it to *Esquire*. Hartley responded curtly, agreeing to release the piece but chastising McMurtry for his poor literary etiquette. *Esquire* passed.

He then tried a different tack with the *Texas Quarterly*, a journal under the aegis of the fledgling University of Texas Press. The state of Texas letters, such as it was in 1958, depended almost solely on three men in Austin: J. Frank Dobie, Roy Bedichek, and Walter Prescott Webb, the first Lone Star literary giants, two of whom would soon take notice of McMurtry, and all three of whom McMurtry, in his young-upstart phase (lacking literary etiquette), would take the piss out of in print.

Bedichek had come out of Falls County, Texas, to work as an itinerant reporter and teacher before settling in Austin to head the University Interscholastic League. His lifelong love of camping led him to write a book called *Adventures with a Texas Naturalist* (1947), establishing him as the state's foremost essayist. Webb, a farm boy from Panola County, turned his childhood love of stories about the Texas Rangers into a successful career as a historian. In a book called *The Great Plains* (1931), he speculated that the ninety-eighth meridian, a fault line separating the North American continent's eastern woodlands from the aridity of the West, stalled westward expansion; not until the technologies of six-shooters, windmills, and barbed wire appeared did America come into its own. Dobie was born in South Texas in 1888, in a part of the state, he said, where "Mexicans were, and still are, more numerous than people of English-speaking ancestry." The stories he heard as a boy from vaqueros and curanderos set him on a path to become Texas's preeminent folklorist, collecting transcribed oral tales in numerous books. The men became fast friends. Dobie and Webb wound up teaching at the University of Texas. In the 1950s, "the university cherished a thin tradition of open-mindedness and a heavy strain of suspicion about thought in general," according to the historian Frank Vandiver. "Dobie and Webb and Roy Bedichek pretty well represented the campus thinking men, with a few stray scientists and others on the flanks. And they were under fire from dubious regents, legislators, even a tough cadre of alumni iron-heads." In fact, Dobie was eventually dismissed by the Board of Regents, who, he claimed, "tried to build a Maginot line around the institution to keep ideas out." Vigorously, he'd defended academic freedom when the board tried to purge "radical" professors.

In the meantime, the university's "thinking men" had proposed forming a university press, to document and promote the region's history and literature. In 1951, Webb interviewed a young man from South Carolina named Frank Wardlaw, "a big, shambling, deep-voiced man" given to "Biblical phrasing," Frank Vandiver remembered—a man, in the words of another acquaintance, "bred to mint and bourbon." He had worked for years as a journalist and had developed keen editing skills. Webb thought he was just the fellow to head the press. Wardlaw admitted to him that he had been forced to drop out of school when his father died. He didn't have an advanced degree, surely a liability in seeking an academic post? "Forget it," Webb said. "[A BA] is largely meaningless, the master's is very little better, and the Ph.D. has begun to shrink in value." On such wisdom, Texas letters took another leap forward.

As part of the press's mandate, *Texas Quarterly* was established as an intellectual journal, occasionally excerpting books in progress and printing book supplements. McMurtry tried Wardlaw with the full manuscripts of *Horseman, Pass By* and *Memories of the Old Tribe*. He did so at a crucial time, when the University of Texas Press was starting to set the terms of mature literary/historical debate in Texas.

A young Mexican American scholar named Américo Paredes had submitted a book to the press entitled *With His Pistol in His Hand.* The book examined the long tradition of corridos, or border ballads. Along the way, Paredes leveled severe criticisms at Dobie and Webb. Dobie ("that great Texas liberal," he sneered) had never claimed that Texas culture began with the arrival of white settlers; to his credit, he had acknowledged the rich storytelling traditions of indigenous peoples and Mexicans. But his limited knowledge of their cultures mired him in stereotypes and simplifications. In his role as folklorist, he had exploited rather than properly celebrated the traditions he had helped preserve. Paredes was even harder on Webb, accusing him bluntly of racism in romanticizing the murdering Texas Rangers, and for writing: "There is a cruel streak in the Mexican nature, or so the history of Texas would lead one to believe."

Wardlaw wanted to publish Paredes, but he feared offending Dobie and Webb. He asked Paredes if he would excise his critiques of the men. The author refused, explaining that if he did, "there would be nothing left but a pretty story." Finally, it was Dobie and Webb who smoothed the way for publication; in the spirit of intellectual debate, they did not object to Paredes's charges. Webb was on the press's board and fully supported publication, admitting his own shortcomings. Dobie underlined two sentences in his copy of the book—"One notes that the white Southerner took his slave women as concubines and then created the image of the male Negro as a sex fiend. In the same way he appears to have taken the Mexican's property and then made him out a thief." Next to these lines, Dobie wrote, "Just about the truth." In later years, he and Paredes became friends.

Wardlaw took a bold step in publishing the book, but the press timidly refused to promote it. Nevertheless, a former Texas Ranger got wind of it. He objected to the portrayal of Rangers as cold-blooded killers. One day he showed up at the press offices swearing he was going to "shoot the sonofabitch who wrote that book."

In the wake of this excitement, Wardlaw received the manuscripts of *Horseman, Pass By* and *Memories of the Old Tribe.* Though McMurtry would later dismiss his first two novels as hopelessly sentimental, Wardlaw was impressed with what seemed to him their blunt portrayal of the harshness of the plains, of the sadness of the cowboy's disappearing way of life. Like Paredes, McMurtry had pulled no punches. His characters were not the mythologized giants of Webb's Texas Rangers, nor were they the quaint figures from Dobie's folktales. Here was something new in Texas writing.

Unfortunately, at the time, the University of Texas Press did not publish fiction and Wardlaw could not see an excerpt of either novel fitting comfortably into the *Texas Quarterly.* He set the manuscripts on his desk, next to a copy of *With His Pistol in His Hand,* wondering what to do with them.

Oddly, Jell-O salad came to mind whenever McMurtry considered his options with Jo. Jell-O salad was the most exotic dish he could recall his mother making for the family when he was a child. Usually, the meal consisted of chicken or beef and one or two vegetables. It was served as the workday ended—on the ranch, this meant four-thirty or five in the afternoon, on a day that began with sunrise. The men would work from "can to can't" (that is, as long as daylight allowed them to see), and the women would always have supper ready. The elders were served first—they got the best portions. Children had to remain patient and be content with whatever was left on the platters. It was like that old Little Jimmy Dickens tune, "Take an Old Cold Tater (and Wait)."

Among the objections McMurtry's mother had to Jo was the fact that she nurtured ambitions beyond just staying home fixing food for her husband. Did she even know *how* to cook? McMurtry got tired of sighing, "*Momma . . .*" whenever he went home to Archer City and listened to her talk about the girl he was dating. His father was just as bad. In Jeff Mac's view, Hazel had developed lazy habits, lulled in the kitchen by various electrical appliances, but now this *new* generation of young women, God help them, surrounded by fancy sewing machines and coffee percolators and this damned noisy contraption known as television . . . the country was going to end badly.

And of course, McMurtry figured, deep down they probably know we're having sex, though they'd never admit *that* disturbing image to their conscious minds.

He was glad Jo was not as conventional as his mother. He didn't *want* her to serve him Jell-O salad, though he wouldn't mind being waited on from time to time. But it was easier to know what Jo *didn't* want than to puzzle through what she was asking for. He had begun to suspect a tremor of instability in her emotional makeup, tied almost certainly to her need for acceptance. This was bred into her by her father's tenuous relationship to his community whenever he needed to make an unpopular public health decision. When it came to love, Jo had an almost overwhelming need for round-the-clock reassurance. McMurtry was beginning to observe this now as their long-distance love affair heightened her fear that their bond was starting to loosen.

For his part, he was thinking it meant more to him to be able to move than to settle somewhere. His ranch-fed stoicism was probably not the best complement for Jo's particular requirements. But he *did* care for her, and he worried about what she would do if she saw herself as someone no one could love—a distinct possibility, he thought, if he left her. She was like a girl plucking petals off a flower: *He loves me not. He loves me not. He loves me not . . .*

These were his somber preoccupations as he drove the four hours between Houston and Denton on I-45, past garlic and wild onion fields searing the air, the *chrrr* of the silver automated sprinklers in the ditches, a muddy rain smell rolling in on thunderheads from the east. He'd lower the windows of his Ford—he hated the noise of air conditioners in cars. He'd reach for the melted Hershey bar on his dash. He liked the candy best when it was nothing but goo and you had to lick it off the wrappers.

Like lumbering animals just coming awake, semis shimmied by him on the sweltering asphalt.

He'd pick up Jo, and they'd head in the direction of Oklahoma on FM 156 until they got to Ponder, Texas, a town no bigger than a gnat but a place where you could get the best twenty-four-ounce Porterhouse or chicken-fried steak, with mashed potatoes, green beans, and grilled onions. Not a Jell-O salad in sight. Just a pretty girl sitting across the table from you, telling you how much she'd missed you.

"Larry and I were married on July 15, 1959, by a justice of the peace in Missouri City, Texas, not far from Houston," Jo said. The fact that they did not hold a large family affair and that they said their vows in the vicinity of the big city rather than on the open plains indicates just how unresolved Hazel and Jeff Mac's feelings about Jo were. She simply didn't *behave* like a wife. She intended to "[spend] our marriage reading Proust and Gibbon,"

McMurtry said. "That was fine with me. I was happy to have a wife who read Proust and Gibbon, rather than, say, *Ladies' Home Journal.*"

As far as Jo's parents were concerned, McMurtry was no prize, either. A *cowboy?* A teacher? Well, maybe that would be okay . . .

Houston was growing—I suppose it always is," Jo said. "The freeway system was getting started. The art museum, not far from where we lived, had just finished an extension, all sheets of glass, and I remember a wonderful exhibit of Giacometti sculpture. Larry knew all the bookstores and booksellers and scouted for early editions."

To help pay his tuition at Rice, he also taught night classes at the University of Houston, a "bright shy white new university on the Gulf Coast [surrounded by] gulls and oleanders and quick howling hurricanes. The teachers [were] brown burly men with power boats and beer cans," in the words of Donald Barthelme. At the moment McMurtry was making his opening remarks in class, Barthelme was working nearby on campus, making long-distance phone calls (unbeknownst to the university's administration), hoping to convince Jean-Paul Sartre, Leslie Fiedler, William Carlos Williams, Walter Kaufmann, Walker Percy, and Norman Mailer to contribute work to an unknown journal, *Forum,* with no budget, published in, of all places, yes, believe it or not, the University of Houston down in Texas . . .

McMurtry and Barthelme would not meet for a number of years, but on those autumn nights in 1959, they worked in close proximity to each other—McMurtry, who would one day become one of the nation's most celebrated writers of realism, and Barthelme, one of the country's most admired postmodernists, both enormously influential, two extraordinary talents.

McMurtry's night-school classes consisted largely of "cops who failed to see the virtues of *Beowulf* or Dylan Thomas," he said. "I was widely disliked because—idealist that I was—I expected the students to read their assignments. Since few did, I sometimes resorted to reading the assigned text aloud . . . Generally about half my class fell dead asleep."

Along with a new puppy, Putnam, he and Jo moved into a garage apartment on South Boulevard, across the street from the Edgar Allan Poe Elementary School. (Twenty-five years later, Barthelme would live in that same block, when he returned to Houston after years in New York, to help spearhead the University of Houston's—by then—nationally acclaimed creative writing program.)

McMurtry had joked with Jo that, because of its boomtown mentality and Wild West character, Houston was the easiest city in the country to get killed in. His jests assumed a grim reality for her on September 15, 1959, when a mentally disturbed parent of one of the students detonated a bomb across the street from their apartment on the campus of the Poe school. Three children and three adults died. Nineteen people were injured, some critically. Jo heard the blast from her living room and felt the apartment shake.

She was more nervous than ever after that, not fearing for her life, exactly, just—*perpetually* in need of knowing that everything would be fine, that she was loved and protected. McMurtry felt inadequate, trying to give her such assurance. He felt frightened, too.

Jo's insecurities were not helped by the fact that she had no set daily routine. McMurtry's routine was extremely rigorous. He'd get up early to write, both on his novels (tinkering while waiting to hear from Frank Wardlaw) and on his master's thesis, a consideration of Ben Jonson and the London theater scene in 1600. At night, he'd drive to the University of Houston to teach.

He was even busier by the end of the year, taking on book reviewing for the *Houston Post*. (He would become a distinguished voice in the paper. In 1963, he was one of the few reviewers in the nation who refused to snicker at the theme of homosexuality in John Rechy's groundbreaking novel *City of Night*. While other critics made poor jokes or disparaging moral judgments about Rechy, McMurtry declared the book was not about sex, but was, rather, a brilliant portrait of human loneliness.)

On December 29, 1959, he reviewed *The Henry Miller Reader*. J. Frank Dobie noticed the review and sent a clipping of it to Frank Vandiver, along with a note: "Frank. This newspaper critic can think; he can write; he knows. Who is he?"

At the time, Vandiver was serving as the president of the Texas Institute of Letters, a loose affiliation of Lone Star literati, founded the year McMurtry was born. They met once a year in old hotels to drink and eat and argue about what the hell Texas literature even was. In 1939, the organization had awarded its first literary prize to Dobie for *Apache Gold & Yaqui Silver* despite almost unanimous agreement that Katherine Anne Porter's

Pale Horse, Pale Rider was the better book. But Porter had had the temerity to leave Texas for New York, so that was that.

Dobie urged Vandiver to consider this young unknown, McMurtry, for the Texas Institute of Letters; in time, McMurtry *would* become a member, if not a very active one. As with everything else in his life, he felt conflicted about it. He wasn't sure he wanted to join an exclusive, self-congratulatory club. But the Texas Institute of Letters was also a healthy gesture in the direction of recognizing and promoting Texas culture. Culture didn't just happen. It required critical mass, an awareness of the past, active campaigns to preserve what was good about the past, a set of rituals designed to establish traditions, schools to teach them, and an adventurous spirit of extending traditions in new forms. Europe had worked hard to nurture culture for thousands of years. Texas had only had two decades to get the hang of it. It was a matter of engagement and citizenship.

Frank Wardlaw understood literary citizenship. Neither the University of Texas Press nor *Texas Quarterly* had a place for McMurtry's work, but its quality demanded attention. Rather than return it to the author with regrets, by far the easiest course of action, he forwarded it to John Leggett, an editor he knew who was just beginning to work at Harper & Brothers in New York.

Leggett, known to his friends as Jack, had been raised and educated in the East, earning a drama degree at Yale. After a stint with the Navy Reserve during World War II, he got a job as a publicist at Houghton Mifflin before moving to Harper & Brothers as an editor (all the while, writing his own novels). McMurtry would become one of his first authors.

Leggett was remarkably handsome, but "he always had an instinct for the underdog . . . identif[ying] with people who had not had proper chances [in life]," said Allan Gurganus. Gurganus would become Leggett's student many years later, when Leggett directed the venerable Writers' Workshop at the University of Iowa (from 1970 to 1987). "He once told me that what he looked for [in literary work] was a sign that someone was just extraordinary at doing one thing," said the writer Lan Samantha Chang. "Then that one thing would become their signature or part of their voice. He was extremely good at locating people's strengths . . . and cultivating them."

When he glanced at *Horseman, Pass By*, he saw right away that the author was up to his elbows in authentic material—as McMurtry put it, "I had a bedrock of observation accumulated throughout my childhood and adolescence about life in West Texas." For the time being, Leggett set the second manuscript aside and concentrated on the first one.

"Hooray!" Jo crowed when, in the early spring of 1960, McMurtry told her Leggett had offered him a $250 option against a possible advance, if he was willing to make extensive revisions on *Horseman, Pass By*. "I was really fortunate," McMurtry recalled later. "In those days, there was still a considerable interest in publishing fiction and in developing fiction writers among American trade publishers . . . I was learning the complicated business of writing a novel. I was making a lot of mistakes, most of them so obvious that even *I* could recognize them as mistakes. I was exploring this fascinating genre . . . What I had going for me [was] a receptivity in the publishing industry to developing talent."

Though he was stubbornly confident in his vision—even in the face of his mistakes—he was willing to listen to Leggett's suggestions, if for no other reason than his determination not to blow a publishing opportunity. "I would have published it in gibberish," he said.

On April 7, 1960, Leggett sent McMurtry a three-page letter listing several cuts to streamline the novel, most of which McMurtry accepted. He lost a cyclone and an extended scene in a dreary storm cellar. In what would prove to be prescient insight, Leggett wrote: "[T]here's much evidence that you are going to write some fine novels about the panhandle and its people. If there is a weakness . . . (and in your modesty you seem willing to go along with that idea) it's in story . . . people talk and reflect but without direction."

A few weeks later, Leggett urged McMurtry to make Lonnie, the youngest character in the book, the focal point: "There's something awfully appealing about an adolescent for a viewpoint character." (*The Catcher in the Rye* had been the most-talked-about novel of the decade.) At this stage, McMurtry was toying with third-person point of view; Leggett thought that wise: "[It] allows maximum freedom and yet permits as much subjectiveness as you want to give it." Ultimately, McMurtry rejected this advice, and switched the novel to first person, through Lonnie's eyes. That way, his own remembered experiences could become his character's stories.

Leggett felt that Lonnie revealed too many "genital turns of mind." "Sex and Lonnie. Easy, boy," he said. "Just a hint will do the trick. The reader's imagination will do the rest." He pleaded with McMurtry to preserve the boy's essential innocence.

Thus began months of back-and-forth between the two men concerning changes to the novel. Initially, Leggett expressed his pleasure in "work[ing] with an author who is so responsive and productive," but within a few months, tensions erupted. "Now what disturbs me is you dismiss [my advice] as though . . . the reader's train of logical curiosity . . . didn't matter," Leggett wrote after a particularly strong pushback from McMurtry. Despite his desire to please, McMurtry had become irritated by Leggett's lecturing tone. "[T]his is where you and I get into trouble," Leggett said. "It's my belief that in a good novel every detail is nailed down tight. That a motivation which might be one thing or another is not a motivation. That people who act off the top of their heads have no place in a good novel. That a character who is moved to an important course of action by 'half-hoping . . .' is half-destroyed by the halfness." Harper's publicity department had complained about McMurtry's title—too arch, the publicists said. In a snit with his author, Leggett quipped, "How . . . would [you] feel about the title THE BUM STEERS?"

Meanwhile, McMurtry was trying to finish his master's thesis and plan the immediate future. On Ray Waddington's advice, he decided to apply for a Stegner Fellowship at Stanford University, the finest postgraduate writing position in the country, established by the novelist and historian Wallace Stegner. "Minds grow by contact with other minds . . . as clouds grow toward thunder by rubbing together," Stegner believed. He had "arrived at Stanford just as the GI students were flooding back [from World War II]," he said. "Many of them were gifted writers. They had so much to say and they had been bottled up for two or three or four years. They were clearly going to have to be handled somewhat differently from the ordinary eighteen-year-old undergraduate." (In 1946, when Stegner secured funding to support a handful of writers on an annual basis, the Iowa Writers' Workshop was the only creative writing degree-granting institution in the country.)

Ray Waddington had studied with Stegner, briefly—"pure luck," he said. "When I applied to get into his seminar, my writing sample got lost, so he never read it. He felt badly about the mix-up and said the only fair thing to do was let me into the class. There was one fellow in the seminar who had already published two novels, and another with a novel in production. That ended any idea I had about becoming a competitive writer, but I knew Larry would do well there."

The program's prestige, and the Waddingtons' rapturous descriptions of California, appealed to Jo as well as McMurtry. With drafts of two novels and a book option under his belt, McMurtry thought he had a shot.

His finished thesis, "Ben Jonson's Feud with the Poetasters, 1599–1601," was as dry as his novel was fertile—even to him. But he *had* managed to focus his scholarship on what was essentially literary gossip, a quarrel among Elizabethan playwrights: a satisfying subject for the mind of a curious novelist. At the center of his study was Ben Jonson: "He had the most earnest interest in and devotion to literature, and was for the most part a very acute appraiser of the writing produced in his time; here his honesty made him enemies. He was always perhaps too well aware that his own work was far superior to much of what was being produced around him . . . When he saw poor work he seldom tried to conceal his scorn." It was no surprise that McMurtry felt an affinity with him.

The study's broader topic was the "satiric spirit at work in the times"—again, a subject of vital interest to McMurtry. In just a few years, he would say of his third book, *The Last Picture Show,* "[I was] not in a sentimental mood [when I wrote it]." He had passed out of a "sentimental phase into what bordered on a satiric phase," he said, discussing himself as though his emotions were distinct, traceable literary periods in a long developmental arc.

In any case, his scholarship phase was over—at least formally. His master's degree meant he could teach in most colleges, should he need to. The prospect did not excite him, especially when he received word from Stanford that he had been awarded a Stegner Fellowship. Perhaps a path different from the purely academic lay ahead of him.

The Waddingtons expressed their envy. They longed to return to California, away from Houston's paralyzing heat. This was no place to raise a family. Jo bid a happy goodbye to the shadowy Poe school. McMurtry tossed books and clothes into the car, a stale, shambolic pile. Putnam settled into the back seat. Like Steinbeck's dusty Okies, they headed west toward the Pastures of Plenty.

I n the late fifties and early sixties, [Perry Lane] was the only liberated
ground in the Mid-peninsula," insisted Vic Lovell, one of the lane's residents. "There aren't many crackpots at Stanford, but they all live on
Perry Lane," said Hughes Rudd, another local. By the time McMurtry and
Jo arrived to see the place, it was ruled by a jester-king named Ken Kesey,
at first glance a loud, hulking rube just off a dairy farm in Oregon, but on
further reflection, a man of many talents and depths. Like Grover Lewis, he
came to life when surrounded by an admiring coterie. He thrived on the energy of disciples, as the center of friendly competitions—pickup basketball,
croquet—or as the organizer of elaborate charade sessions or costume parties
(where he'd transform himself into a motorcycle-riding Brando, complete
with leather boots and jacket) or as a jam-session singer, pounding out Okie
tunes on an old guitar, or as a master chef, roasting a pig on a spit, or most
especially, as the leader of late-night, alcohol-and-pot-infused poetry readings.

McMurtry called him "the last wagon-master."

Perry Lane was located in an unincorporated section of Menlo Park,
two miles from Palo Alto, on former Stanford farmland now owned by the
university. In the First World War, the area had served as a military training camp. The army built small wooden cabins to house soldiers. After the
war, the university began renting the cabins to students, altering some of
them, modestly, into single-story cottages with little brick chimneys, and
adding a courtyard at one end of the lane. Artists and writers were drawn
to the low rents, and soon Perry Lane became Stanford's Left Bank. It was
dominated by a huge, forked oak tree, hundreds of years old, under which,
according to one press account playing up the neighborhood's bohemian
atmosphere, residents could "contemplate the heavens or escape from their
wives."

Kesey and his wife, Faye, had arrived in Palo Alto in 1958, shortly after
Kesey graduated from the University of Oregon. While in school there,
he had met William Faulkner when Faulkner came to give a reading on
campus. The meeting galvanized Kesey—he had never been much of a

reader, and though he wrote well, it was not something he particularly liked doing. But the grandeur surrounding the stately Faulkner—the mantle of the Great Man of Letters—appealed to the competitor in him. Being a writer was a way of gaining attention, one he might be able to pull off, he thought. His other ambition—to become an Olympic wrestler—was thwarted when he suffered a severe shoulder separation. Faye considered the injury a blessing. She had not much relished the thought of following Kesey to sports venues around the world. She had grown up with him and been his high school sweetheart—many times already, she had seen how quickly his dreams materialized, then vanished.

Faye Haxby, quiet and always a bit physically frail, despite her steady fortitude, came from a poor family in Springfield, Oregon. Throughout high school and college, she tolerated Kesey's "sport" with other girls because she knew she encouraged his best instincts, he was devoted to her, long term—and because he was so much *fun*. She majored in dietetics at Oregon State College and at the University of Oregon. But her main focus was keeping Kesey from derailing as he veered from one wild adventure to the next. He later called her "a deep keel in the raving waves, a polestar in the dark, a shipmate."

They were married in the spring of 1956. Events prior to the wedding captured the opposing sides of Ken Kesey, which Faye would learn to balance throughout her life with him—the great charmer who surprised her with an engagement ring tucked inside a giant Christmas package, and the reckless fuckup who planned a wedding ceremony on the day the Lane County Courthouse was closed for an election. The couple went ahead with an invalid marriage license, forcing them to recite their vows again later, following an incident in which Kesey, ingesting rum, gin, beer, and bourbon, pissed all over a University of Oregon fraternity house before passing out on a couch. The next morning, for the second wedding, Faye slipped into a long white gown she'd made herself, and entered a life she'd make and remake for decades to come.

In 1958, when Kesey received a scholarship to attend Wallace Stegner's creative writing seminar, Faye traveled to California to find them a place to live. She discovered a small garage apartment in Palo Alto, above a gravel driveway fouled with mounds of dog shit. It was the neighborhood pets' favorite gathering spot. At the time, Palo Alto, a former summer vacation retreat for rich San Franciscans, consisted of little more than a mediocre restaurant and a J. C. Penney's. Kesey spent most of his time at Kepler's Books & Magazines, in Menlo Park.

In accounts of Kesey's life, much has been made of his clash with Wallace Stegner—the Counterculture Clown versus the Staid Old Master. The story makes a neat parable about the generational divide of the 1960s, but it has been overstated. "I was never sympathetic to any of his ideas because I thought many of his ideas were half-baked," Stegner said. "[But] we got along in the class perfectly well. I liked his writing most of the time." The trouble occurred a few years after Kesey left Stanford. Very publicly, he accused Stegner of no longer "writing to people," but "to a classroom and his colleagues." Understandably, the teacher was hurt.

That first year in the writing seminars, Kesey quietly ignored Stegner's advice about developing discipline and avoiding self-indulgence. He worked on a Beat novel called *Zoo,* "full of the worst and best writing of anyone in the class," according to Stegner's colleague, Richard Scowcroft.

At midyear, the Keseys moved into cottage number 9 on Perry Lane when they heard that the Waddingtons were moving to Houston. Ray and Linda left the place a mess, according to Kesey—trash scattered everywhere, no electricity, a sickly pale blue paint on the walls. But by then the Keseys had met most of the residents and liked the atmosphere. Kesey had found a battalion who'd follow his commands.

The McMurtrys arrived in California in September 1960. They'd soon be frequent visitors to Perry Lane, but they lived in San Francisco. "It was an easy commute to Palo Alto," Jo told me. "Nothing like today's traffic. I found San Francisco enchanting—all hilly and misty, vertical houses close together, a city to walk in [unlike car-crazy Houston]. This was before the more colorful era of the mid-sixties, Peter Max designs, Haight-Ashbury. In those earlier days people wore lots of black and the place to go was North Beach. And it was definitely before the houses turned into gorgeous Painted Ladies. In the early sixties the buildings were somber, mostly gray. Local lore talked about surplus paint intended for battleships, left over from World War II. Larry and I had an apartment on Clay Street, across from a park that went up in terraces, sort of Babylonian. Alta Plaza Park. There was a grove of pines on top, and an amazing view."

Wallace Stegner went on leave at the beginning of autumn, but McMurtry met him briefly. Unlike Kesey, he would always have a cordial relationship with the man. With good reason, Stegner had always felt snubbed by the New York publishing world, which was generally dismissive of the West. Yet Stegner had persisted. His novels, histories, and meditations on pioneers and visionaries and the forging of new civilizations influenced readers to take the West seriously as subject matter. He opened up fresh literary territory for his students. The problem was, Stegner's West, predominantly white, Eurocentric—fashioned roughhewn from heroic feats of labor, education, and technology—was not the terrain sixties youth had come to know. *Their* West had been fenced by the rich; it had been urbanized and poisoned by nuclear tests. It had become a far more diverse and cynical place than Stegner could acknowledge. He was most at home with the students of the 1940s and '50s, especially the GIs returning from war, discussing, in their written stories, themes of sacrifice and duty. By the time men like Ken Kesey and Edward Abbey showed up in his classes, Stegner no longer recognized his fellow citizens. Abbey shared Stegner's passion for conservation, but showed little of Stegner's optimism, writing, at one point: "If the world of men is truly as ugly, cruel, trivial, unjust and stinking with fraud as it usually appears, and if it is really impossible to make it pleasant and decent, then there remains only one alternative for the honest man: stay home, cultivate your own garden, look to the mountains." For Stegner, such an approach—"[telling] the world to kiss your behind"—amounted to "social irresponsibility." As for Kesey's drug-fueled pranksterism—forget it.

McMurtry's elegiac stance didn't accord with Stegner, either, but the older man recognized the youngster's talent. In any event, he would not be McMurtry's teacher. The writing classes would be led that year by Malcolm Cowley, a poet, a critic, and an editor, a member of the Lost Generation in Paris in the 1920s (his introduction to *The Portable Hemingway* was, in large part, responsible for establishing Hemingway as a critical favorite), and by the Irishman Frank O'Connor, a man McMurtry described as a "beautiful short story writer." "He didn't really like to be a teacher, and he rebelled in various ways," McMurtry recalled. "Malcolm Cowley didn't like to be a teacher either, and so he rebelled by turning his hearing aid off as soon as he got to class every day, letting us fight it out, which [was] okay."

McMurtry remembered vividly the instant Kesey walked into the class that fall. "He made it plain that he meant to be the stud-duck . . . There were about a dozen of us assembled when Ken made his entrance, and he was hardly the only competitive person in the room. Like stoats in a henhouse, we were poised to rend and tear. Except for the lovely Joanna Ostrow, protected by her elegant Afghan . . . we were all young males. Ken plopped himself down at the right hand of Mr. Cowley and got set to read what turned out to be the first chapters of *One Flew Over the Cuckoo's Nest.* This was stud-duckery indeed."

McMurtry wondered "who *was* this lumberjack, a figure so Paul Bunyanesque that I would not have been surprised to see Babe, the Blue Ox, plod in behind him? . . . Ken cleared his throat, we bristled, and then relaxed and decided to be bemused, rather than annoyed. Why? Because Ken Kesey was a very winning man, and he won us . . . [He was] determin[ed] to be the center of attention: he wanted it so badly; so we let him get away with it, and . . . he kept getting away with a good deal of it for the next forty-one years."

Cowley may not have enjoyed teaching, but he liked his students and got to know them fairly well. "It was a pretty brilliant class that year, including as it did some professional writers already launched on their careers," he recalled (among them Peter Beagle, James Baker Hall, Gurney Norman, and Christopher Koch). "Larry McMurtry . . . was working on what I think was his second novel, *Leaving Cheyenne.* He was a light, sallow, bespectacled cowboy who wore Texas boots and spoke in a pinched variety of the West Texas drawl. Gradually I learned that he had read almost everything in English literature, besides a great deal of French . . . Larry supplemented his Stanford fellowship by finding rare books on the ten-cent tables of Salvation Army outlets and reselling them to dealers; *Book Prices Current* was his bible."

Writing in support of McMurtry's failed application to the Rockefeller Foundation for funding, Cowley praised this "extraordinary character: Texas drawl, cowboy mannerisms, combined with an unusual knowledge of contemporary and seventeenth-century literature . . . [H]e is a gifted and serious writer who is likely to contribute some new qualities to American fiction."

In a private letter to C. P. Snow, Cowley described McMurtry as a "wild young man from Texas, expert in pornography."

Kesey later claimed Cowley taught him the most valuable lesson he ever learned about writing etiquette: "Be gentle with one another's efforts. Be kind and considerate with your criticism. Always remember that it's just as hard to write a bad book as it is to write a good book." McMurtry appreciated hearing Cowley's stories about Hemingway and Faulkner, about championing the publication of *On the Road.* "Gossip about the great does as much as anything else to pull young writers deeper into the great stream of literary endeavor," he said. "[I]t gives them something to hold in their imaginations as they live in those grubby garage apartments, scratching out their first poems or fictions."

In the spring, when O'Connor assumed control of the class, it was like the sheriff had come to town. *This is not a short story!* he would shout of anything placed before him. "With his grand white hair and roguish good looks, Mr. O'Connor kept himself at a patrician distance from the big table at the head there," said James Baker Hall. "[He] turned away, not exactly listening over his rumpled shoulder, but with suspicion . . . staring off into the knowing distance, a pipe sticking up out of the handkerchief pocket of his seersucker jacket."

McMurtry was not much interested in writing short fiction, though he made some efforts (a section of *Leaving Cheyenne* would appear as a stand-alone piece in *Stanford Short Stories*). O'Connor "brought some of the passions of the Irish Rebellion into our modest classroom," he recalled. "Occasionally he would be brought to tears by the folly of our sentiments or the ineptness of our stories . . . His firm belief was that if the essence of a short story couldn't be conveyed in three sentences, then it was no story at all." The man couldn't believe McMurtry had read, much less appreciated, Smollett. "'Jesus, Larry—Smollett!' he said often, to my bewilderment," McMurtry said. "Smollett he found unnecessary, if not actively pernicious. He was an extremely good critic of the nineteenth-century novel, but showed little interest in the novels of the eighteenth century. His problem with Smollett may simply have been that he didn't think Scots should write books."

In class, Kesey fiercely challenged him, asking *why* something was not a story. "It doesn't bend the barrrr!" O'Connor would growl. Kesey quit the workshop.

Though McMurtry's affinity was for the novel, not the story, he learned a good deal from O'Connor; the men shared a sensibility. O'Connor's famous study of the short story, a book called *The Lonely Voice,* asserted that the "short story remains by its very nature remote from community—romantic, individualistic, and intransigent" (like the cowboy myth), "[conveying] an intense awareness of human loneliness." O'Connor's crowning achievement in this regard was "Guests of the Nation," one of the finest stories ever written in English. It concerns two British men executed by Irish nationalists during the independence struggle; it explores the alienating effect the moral quandary of killing has on one of the lonely executioners. It was a frontier story, familiar to McMurtry, masterful in its modulation of humor and sentiment.

The year at Stanford "was very special for Larry, I think," Jo said. "He had always known he was a novelist. Now he could feel confident that other people knew it, too. And being with his fellow workshoppers who not only wanted to become better creative writers but were doing something about it, very energetically . . . charged up the atmosphere and made him feel less alone and more part of a bigger world."

That bigger world included the Bay Area bookstores. Palo Alto offered slim pickings: Bell's College Bookshop, whose crotchety owner, Herbert Bell, showed little patience with college students—they were not, in his view, serious connoisseurs of his stock: ancient medical treatises, seventeenth-century herbals, and botanical woodcuts. He tried one day to order McMurtry away from the rare books on his second floor, underneath the low-hanging tin-plated ceiling, even though McMurtry had found there, and eventually purchased, a copy of *Annals of English Literature.* There was also, in Palo Alto, a bookseller operating out of his house, a gentle man named William Wreden, to whom McMurtry sold "a pile of local fine printing acquired at a library sale," to supplement his student income.

The real book treasures awaited him in San Francisco. While Jo went to work each day for Crown Zellerbach, a paper and pulp company also specializing in timber and plastics (it produced the slick-coated paper for *Time* and *Life* magazines), McMurtry rented a three-dollar-a-day hotel room on Geary Street to which he lugged his typewriter and worked on revising both *Horseman, Pass By* and *Leaving Cheyenne.* Magazines were piled haphazardly on squat tables in the hotel lobby, and molted black birds squawked from a birdcage near the door. Around the corner from the hotel were two bookshops, Dunlop's and McDonald's. McMurtry was still searching for a good copy of *Let Us Now Praise Famous Men* (a seller offered him, instead, Agee's first book, *Permit Me Voyage*, a particular volume once owned by the poet Weldon Kees, but at $35.00, it was beyond his means). One day in McDonald's he met a man named I. R. (Ike) Brussel, a self-styled book scout. McMurtry had not heard of book scouting—not as a professional activity, anyway—but he learned that Brussel, born in Minsk, Russia, had taught himself to be a specialist in various editions of nineteenth-century British and American literature. He traveled around the world personally scouting books for discriminating collectors in the United States and abroad. He made most of his money finding books for public, school, and research libraries.

Brussel carried a business card proclaiming him to be the Last of the Great Scouts, but in fact he was among the first to do what he did with such persistence and imagination. McMurtry was intrigued by the vision of such a life—on the move, among books. Soon he met Brussel's son-in-law, a carpenter and book scout named Miles Caprilow. From these early days in San Francisco, McMurtry dated his true beginnings as a book scout and dealer. "I went around with Miles . . . learning the rudiments of scouting, at a time when there were workingmen's bookshops in Oakland and along Market Street where all the books were a dime," he said.

In North Beach, McMurtry met the Beat poet, jazzman, and cabalist David Meltzer, who'd left Brooklyn for California when he was twenty, got a job in a Bay Area book warehouse where he mostly sat around smoking dope, and then began managing the Discovery Bookstore at night, right next to City Lights Books. Both stores stayed open past midnight, and McMurtry often hung with Meltzer until closing. "One day he . . . asked me to go scouting with him in the East Bay. I [still] knew little of book scouting but I did have one asset David lacked: a car. Soon we were off," McMurtry said. "The dominant East Bay bookshop in those years was the Holmes Book Company in Oakland, a wonderful large bookshop with a big wraparound balcony devoted to fiction. That balcony, not to mention the Holmes Book Company in general, could always reward as much time as I could give it." He bought there a copy of Lady Anne Blunt's travel account of the Nejd; one day he would own over two thousand volumes of women's travel narratives.

He avidly sought Gershon Legman's 1949 attack on sexual censorship, *Love & Death.* Legman was a culture critic specializing in the history of sexuality and erotic folklore. For a while he worked as a bibliographic researcher for the Kinsey Institute. *Love & Death* was a quirky, self-published polemic against censorship that nevertheless derided American comic books for their glorification of violence. Copies of Legman's book had been seized by U.S. Post Office authorities, who had declared its contents "indecent, vulgar, and obscene." No serious collector of high-end pornography should be without it, McMurtry thought—especially given the obscenity battles he could see brewing in the American legal system that would soon change the face of publishing.

On Thursday nights, usually in Kesey's cottage on Perry Lane, the Stanford writers and their friends, some of whom were also working on novels or poems, gathered for reading sessions, an extension of the workshop geared toward sharing rather than critiquing. "We were all learning how to smoke dope, and we would read our work to each other," said Ed McClanahan, who'd first attended Stanford in the late fifties. He'd made his way back, growing long hair and a bushy mustache, after a brief teaching stint at Oregon State College. There he'd taken over Bernard Malamud's writing classes once Malamud resigned (Malamud had written a scathing novel about the college and figured it was time to get out of town). "What was really nice" about convening on Perry Lane "was that it was an opportunity to try stuff out on an audience before you went into the more formal atmosphere of the seminar," McClanahan said.

"These parties were full of life and laughter," Gurney Norman recalled. "It is hard to see anything in the least bit decadent about them. They were very sweet and dear and above all, extremely literary . . . I'm in no way envious of Paris in the twenties because we had Palo Alto in the sixties."

McMurtry would drive in from San Francisco, bringing Chris Koch with him (Koch would write the novel *The Year of Living Dangerously*). Sometimes Jo came along. Someone would pass around a bottle of cheap Chianti or a jug of moonshine that Kesey had gotten from his Arkansas grandma. Faye would cook up a pot of rice and beans or pineapple chili, and Kesey would fire up a joint. He'd read from *Cuckoo's Nest*. McMurtry brought pages from *Leaving Cheyenne*—"those mesmerizing dialogues between Gid and Johnny, both in love with Molly: that would have been my nominee for the keeper among us," said James Baker Hall.

In addition to Hall, McClanahan, and Norman, the gatherings usually included Kesey's pal, Ken Babbs; his neighbor Chloe Scott, a striking redheaded dancer; Vic Lovell and Jim Wolpman, longtime Perry Lane residents who appreciated the neighborhood's contrast to the "oppressive air" of the campus; Lovell's roommate Dirk Van Nouhuys; Wendell Berry; and on occasion, a friend of McClanahan's, a quiet young man named Robert Stone, then working fitfully on what would become his first novel, *Hall of Mirrors*. He had been in the Navy, had traveled the world, and had a far more sophisticated sense of global politics than his peers. He was already suspicious of the U.S.'s early, still largely unheralded activities in Southeast Asia (at least, most of these activities remained hidden from the American public). Because of his time at sea, Stone had no idea how to talk to people. His mumbled comments on military movements convinced Kesey, still an Oregon country boy, that he was a Communist. Kesey told McClanahan he didn't trust Stone. He didn't want him coming to the reading sessions. McClanahan persuaded Kesey otherwise, and Stone's recitations on Thursday nights riveted everyone.

Van Nouhuys immediately found McMurtry "empathetic, interested in other people." Most folks caught Van Nouhuys's eye because of their behavior; McMurtry engaged him merely with his presence—a calm, accepting, if penetrating demeanor. He felt no need to show off. At first blush, "he seemed as country and as shy and as intimidated by the great world as I felt then," McClanahan recalled. In spite of the sessions' indulgent practices, "to my knowledge, Larry never dropped acid or even smoked a joint," McClanahan said. "I think he was probably judgmental [of us all], probably drawing conclusions."

McMurtry didn't hesitate to argue with Kesey about writing and its relationship to the larger culture, but he rarely did so in front of others. He had no desire to perform for the crowd, as Kesey did. "To enjoy the strength of Ken's friendship it was necessary to separate him, for a time, from the court, because if the court was sitting around he would play to it, meddle with it, charm it, vex it," McMurtry said.

("I wasn't the only one who found Ken's life more compelling than his work," James Baker Hall remarked.)

McMurtry shared Kesey's enthusiasm for the example of Jack Kerouac—the way *On the Road* had shaken the primness of American prose—but finally he could not abide what he saw as a nihilistic strain in Beat writing, whereas Kesey tumbled completely for the romance of sex and death on the edge. "[We] disagreed about most of the important issues of the day—beatniks, politics, ethics, and, especially psychedelics—in fact, about everything except for [our] mutual fondness and respect for writing and each other," Kesey recalled. "Larry defend[ed] the traditional and [I] champion[ed] the radical . . . [he was always] claiming conservative advances, listing the victories of the righteous right, and pointing out the retreats and mistakes made by certain left-wing luminaries." (McMurtry was not as thoroughly conservative as Kesey made him out to be, nor was Kesey the fully enlightened progressive he claimed, as his initial response to Bob Stone's views on Vietnam indicated.) McMurtry liked to tease Kesey, "So. What has the Good Old Revolution been doing lately?" but he quickly learned to defuse serious fights with the "wild boy from the hills." "There was a lot of the frontiersman in him, an unwillingness to accept conventional answers to a lot of profound questions," McMurtry said. "We argued and debated a lot of things. But I never would not listen to him, even if I thought some of what he said was gobbledygook, because there would always be the perception of genius if you waited him out."

The times they were a'changin.' The "Cold War was in the not-too-distant background. Elvis was in the air. Ike [had been] campaigning for Nixon," James Baker Hall said.

"We all came from conservative backgrounds—Kentucky, Texas, Oregon—but everybody was tired of being bored, it being the Eisenhower era," McClanahan added.

Yet Dirk Van Nouhuys cautioned, "As to the politics, I wouldn't stress its importance too much. [We] were not much interested in being active. Kesey wanted to change the world, but into his own image of how people should live, which didn't have much to do with electoral politics or government policy."

Overall, McMurtry was not terribly impressed with the stud-duck's bohemian pond: "To me Perry Lane looked not unlike cheap graduate housing anywhere; similar hotbeds of low-rent revolt could have been found in Iowa City, Ann Arbor, or New Haven." The examples he knew of the neighborhood's radicalism—say, the night the residents blew up a fifty-gallon oil drum with firecrackers, summoning a mostly amused squad of Menlo

Park cops—struck him as third-rate party pranks. McClanahan and others, under Kesey's spell, believed they were all living a grandiose vision, an extension of the Beat ethos. "One night we decided to have the gathering at my house on Alpine Road, within easy walking distance of Perry Lane," McClanahan said. "A half dozen of us were there—Kesey, Larry, Bob Stone, Vic Lovell—all sitting on the floor in this graduate student cottage. Larry read a piece of *Leaving Cheyenne,* and in the middle of our evening, the door burst open and in came Neal Cassady. It was an astonishing moment. Here were all these would-be novelists and in strode a character [from Kerouac's *On the Road*]. It was like some kind of cosmic convergence!"

McMurtry was not so blown away. "[I] found little about [Cassady] to like," he said. "[He] had no achievement to put beside the novels of Kerouac or the poetry of Allen Ginsberg; all he had was his vitality. He reminded me of certain cowboys I've known, men with a scrap or two of education who happen to be very capable in physical ways—they can ride any horse, fix any machine—but few of them ever bring their mental equipment up to the level of their physical abilities. So it was with Cassady."

Ultimately, what made Kesey's court different, and important, was the introduction of an unexpected chemical element into the mix and the hullabaloo surrounding it later in the press and in books such as Tom Wolfe's *The Electric Kool-Aid Acid Test.*

In early 1960, right before the McMurtrys arrived in San Francisco, Vic Lovell introduced Kesey to Dr. Leo Hollister at the VA hospital in Menlo Park. Lovell was an intern at the hospital. He had become a test subject in Hollister's experiments designed to analyze the physiological impacts of psychotropic drugs on reasonably well-adjusted individuals. Hollister's funding came largely from the National Institute of Mental Health and the National Institutes of Health, both of which funneled money from the CIA directed toward research on the uses of LSD-25 as a mind-control drug. After a few sessions ingesting hallucinogens, Lovell quit. "I was all turned on with no place to go," feeling anxious and scattered, he said. He suggested Kesey take his place in the trials. After that, every Tuesday morning Kesey arrived at the hospital and was taken to a "ward. All the other people in it were nuts. I went out and looked through the window, a little, tiny window, and the door there with a heavy, heavy screen between two panes of glass. There was no way to break out." (*One Flew Over the*

Cuckoo's Nest was gestating.) "I'd look out there and see these people moving around, and I could understand them a whole lot better than I could understand the doctors and the nurses, or the interns—and they knew this."

Week after week, for hours at a time, Hollister gave Kesey LSD, mescaline, psilocybin, MP-14, and IT-290. The first time he was dosed, Kesey noticed a squirrel playing with an acorn outside the window of the little room in which he sat. The squirrel dropped the acorn and thunder exploded in Kesey's ears, accompanied by a shimmering blue aura bouncing off the walls. Six hours later in the doctor's office, he was handed a check for twenty dollars for his participation in the test. He asked what was in that little blue pill he'd taken. "It's called lysergic acid diethylamide twenty-five," Hollister told him.

"I knew [then] that LSD couldn't be stopped," Kesey said.

In a study called *It's All a Kind of Magic,* historian Rick Dodgson reports that tape recordings still exist of Kesey speaking during early trials while under the influence of acid. "It's quarter to one and I'm high out of my mind," Kesey slurs on one reel. "Wild color images. There's this great colored frog of a man outside standing at the door . . . I am suddenly filled with this great loving and understanding of people . . . [LSD] seems to give you more observation and more insight, and it makes you question things you ordinarily don't question."

When Kesey began "sneak[ing] nameless pills out of the hospital in the cuffs of his jeans," brought them back to Perry Lane and, according to James Baker Hall, "passed them around, if he liked you and thought you needed goosing," the 1960s took a giant leap out of the boring Eisenhower era: "[I]n my staid opinion," McMurtry said, "a thoroughly bad idea."

On certain evenings, when the pills were plentiful and the reading sessions completely unraveled, McMurtry sat silently in a corner, watching. McClanahan assumed he was intimidated and frightened by what he was witnessing. In retrospect, "I think I was deceived by Larry's apparent shyness," he said. "I think Larry was a lot more sophisticated than I knew. He was skeptical of everything around him—and justifiably so."

Throughout the early fall at Stanford, McMurtry's correspondence continued with Jack Leggett at Harper & Brothers. Leggett was pleased, even astonished, by McMurtry's productivity and his willingness to revise

Horseman, Pass By. He sent McMurtry a contract: Harper offered an advance of $1,000 payable on delivery, with a royalty scale of 10 percent to five thousand copies. Publication was scheduled for May 24, 1961.

The men still bristled at each other, but they had developed a favorable working rhythm. "That's what I like about you—hard-headed, mule-hoofed but with the forgiving heart of a whale," Leggett wrote McMurtry.

His objections to certain of his young author's writing habits predicted the complaints critics would make against McMurtry throughout his career: his "carelessness" as a result of his prolific swiftness—"You ought to read over what you have written," Leggett advised him; his reluctance to explain his characters' motivations ("[Hud is] such a prick from the start," Leggett groused); and his unique sense of verisimilitude—he insisted that, to be true to life, a novel should not be tightly plotted. It had to make room for happenstance and unprepared-for events. "By god, that's a novel *I* don't want to read," Leggett assured him. "Larry, listen to me. This is your uncle talking . . . [You can't] shrug [things] off as the kind of pointless thing that so frequently happens. Carried an inch further, you'd have us believe that in a novel, you can present characters that are 'pretty uninteresting types' behaving arbitrarily." (During the period of American literary minimalism, in the 1980s, influenced by such writers as Raymond Carver, Mary Robison, and Ann Beattie, the student stories Leggett encountered at the Iowa Writers' Workshop would perfectly match this description.)

In letters to Bill Corrington, his old classmate at Rice, McMurtry examined his relationship to Leggett, and his general attitude toward editors. Corrington had drafted a novel about the post–Civil War South, inspired by his reading of Hodding Carter's history of Reconstruction, *The Angry Star.* (Within a few years, McMurtry would cross paths, significantly, with the Carter family.) Without reading the manuscript, just as a favor to his friend, McMurtry recommended it to Leggett, who liked the material well enough to discuss potential revisions with Corrington. Almost immediately, the men clashed. In a series of missives advising Corrington how to handle the editor, McMurtry revealed his own feelings about the man who had shepherded *Horseman, Pass By* to publication. "Leggett is a good honest guy with a heart of granite," he said. "He and I like each other a lot, but don't trust each other one bit." "Jack has his limitations, clearly. But one thing he's seldom guilty of is beating around the bush . . . and as he says, he's only right half the time or less." "He may ask for [revisions] that you are not enthusiastic about . . . But it can be done, without making the book any less good as literature, and Jack does not want it to become less good as literature . . . You should just distinguish between his desires and his demands. His desires you can ignore or think about as you choose." Finally, McMurtry warned Corrington (whose novel, *And Wait for the Night,* would be published—not by Leggett—in 1964), "Keep in mind that the world of publishing is cold and nobody alive or recently dead, not even Mr. Faulkner, gets through it without some frostbite or amputation. The hardy only lose toes and fingers."

Never again, after working so closely with an editor on his first novel, was McMurtry so amenable to changing what he had written—even after advising Corrington to listen to Leggett. He later regretted acceding to Leggett's vision of the novel's structure, believing it ruined the entire book. From the beginning, he had intended to open the story with the funeral of Homer Bannon, the old cattleman, and spend the rest of the novel exploring the suppressed family tensions released by the loss of its patriarch. Such an arc made sense to him. Instead, Leggett insisted the narrative needed stronger elements of suspense. Were the old man's cattle *really* riddled with disease? Would they need to be exterminated? Could the old man survive such a loss? McMurtry complained that he wasn't writing a suspense novel. Cows turned up sick all the time. A veteran cattleman, like Homer Bannon, outlived so many hardships in life; one more incident, such as a herd's eradication, wouldn't be enough to do him in. Yet McMurtry sensed Leggett wouldn't budge on the suspense argument, and he wanted badly to be published. He agreed to end the book with Homer Bannon losing his bearings and his will to live following the slaughter of his cows. The old man's death—clearly symbolic of a way of life's passing—gave the novel's finale mythic resonance, precisely what McMurtry had hoped to avoid by writing so brutally of the North Texas plains. His attempts and his failures to puncture western myths would characterize the rest of his literary career, particularly in the case of his best-known novel, *Lonesome Dove.* McMurtry was adamant: mythic trappings rendered what he had to say about the world unbelievable.

On September 25, 1960, while McMurtry was still revising *Horseman, Pass By*, Dorothea Oppenheimer, an independent literary agent operating out of her small apartment on Vallejo Street in San Francisco, wrote him, inquiring if he had an agent and if he had completed any new work. She was forty-two years old, a German immigrant, born in Berlin, from a wealthy family that fled the rise of Nazism in Germany in the 1940s, after the Nazis had pilfered the family's money. She'd gone to school with Philip Mountbatten, the future Duke of Edinburgh. An avid lifelong reader, with astute editing skills, she'd worked briefly for *The New Yorker* upon her arrival in America. She began her agency in 1956 after seeing a short story by Ernest Gaines in a small San Francisco magazine called *Transfer*. She contacted Gaines, asking if he had any other work, and from that moment on, she became his patron, his benefactor, his editor, and his friend. Not only did she help shape his fiction and handle his literary business, but she gave him a cultural education, taking him to art galleries, symphony halls, and the cinema. She taught him the value of understatement and repeated motifs in fiction. She encouraged patience and dedication, warning him not to rush his work, to hone it until it was ready for the "big city." "She was there when no one else was," Gaines said later. "There'll never be another person like that in my life."

She made a point of perusing the West Coast literary quarterlies and of keeping an eye on the Stanford writing program, where Gaines had studied. She knew Stegner and had a friend at the university who alerted her to promising writing samples among the fellowship applicants. In time, her other clients would include Frank Chin, whose 1971 play, *The Chickencoop Chinaman*, would become the first Asian American drama to be performed in a major New York venue, and Thomas Sanchez, author of *Rabbit Boss*, a multigenerational California epic concerning Native American communities. On each writer Oppenheimer lavished copious personal attention and indefatigable professional dedication.

McMurtry answered her query politely, informing her that Harper & Brothers held the contract to his first novel and that he had "nothing publishable loose right now." He told her he was working on a second novel, with a third book already in mind, and wondered if she handled short stories. He offered to meet with her at a mutually convenient time.

Over the next few weeks, McMurtry corresponded with Oppenheimer and spoke to her on the phone, warming to the idea of securing an agent, unsure about settling in for the long haul with Leggett as his editor (assuming Leggett wished to keep *him*). McMurtry became comfortable enough with Oppenheimer on the telephone to tell her how restless Jo was in her job; Oppenheimer offered helpful tips on what else Jo might try.

Finally, in late October, McMurtry dropped by Oppenheimer's place to discuss the possibility of doing business with her. She was striking, tall, dark-haired with an angular face, somewhat formal in manner but with an overall loose-limbed ease that immediately relaxed him. She charmed him with stories of her skiing trips to Europe and her annual vacations to Lake Tahoe. He was impressed with her professional demeanor and the breadth of her literary knowledge—they shared a passion for the Europeans. He also believed she was the most gorgeous, sophisticated woman he had ever met. He left Vallejo Street as her newest author.

Though the scene at Perry Lane had underwhelmed McMurtry, Linda Waddington had not exaggerated its tolerance for erotic horseplay. The antics were heightened by the effect of Kesey's little blue pills. "We'd recently been initiated into a *new* head space when we smoked pot for the first time," said Jane Burton, an undergraduate philosophy major (a native Texan) and a resident of the lane. But then LSD blew people wide open.

"We all hallucinated the same thing! It was grand!" Ed McClanahan said. "The commonplace would become marvelous; you could take the pulse of a rock, listen to the heartbeat of a tree, feel the hot breath of a butterfly against your cheek."

"I don't remember anyone having a bad trip," Burton said. And the shared mind expansion only enhanced the sexual freedom already buzzing in the small community (aggressively encouraged by Kesey, more often than not). "Everybody was sleeping with everybody," Chloe Scott claimed.

It was "an incredibly supportive group love affair," Burton said.

McMurtry was not tempted by the psychedelics or the grass. But the unspoken sexual offerings implicit in nearly every Perry Lane gathering were hard to ignore. At one point, in a letter to Kesey after the fact, he confessed he had developed "a lot of feeling" for Jane Burton, "but the one time we were together under possible circumstances [for a tryst] was such a down night for both of us that no moves seemed worth the effort." On another occasion, quite a bit later, he was drawn to Helen "Gus" Guthrie, a lively young woman who entered Palo Alto's orbit. She was the daughter of A. B. Guthrie, the Pulitzer Prize–winning novelist and historian who also wrote the screenplay for *Shane*. She had worked for the Viking Press in New York and was a superb editor of fiction. "Did I tell you of the night when Gus and I decided that it was time we worked out a moral system for ourselves, so as not to fuck-up . . . the future[?]," McMurtry wrote Kesey. "We started with categories: family, friends, sex, marriage, kicks, etc., and made a pretty good beginning." As with Burton, he passed up the chance for a quick affair with Guthrie for a deeper emotional connection, and he maintained his strong friendships with both women.

"[Without] a context for emotion, [sex] is more often, for me, like gambling for troublesome amounts of money: exhilarating to win, depressing to lose," he told Kesey.

The temptations to step outside his marriage were made more urgent by the fact that he and Jo had hit a rough patch. A combination of youthful naiveté about the state of connubial bliss and the confusion of *too many* options unsettled them both—not to mention the disorientation of living in new surroundings, however beautiful, and adjusting to fresh habits. Jo was dissatisfied with her job, no longer with leisure time to read, and McMurtry was away every day, in his room on Geary Street, writing to fulfill a contract, an unfamiliar pressure on his work routine. At night he'd often go book scouting with David Meltzer.

In an early draft of his second novel, he had written that marriage should automatically provoke delight in a husband and wife; it should be a natural condition, requiring little effort; later, in a letter to Kesey, he mentioned much the same thing. A couple should "delight . . . in one another, in order to counterbalance the inevitable frictions and make it worthwhile over a lifetime pull," he said. "Jo has a fine capacity for delight; much greater than mine, I'll admit, but few things in marriage have delighted her."

While at Stanford, between revisions of *Horseman, Pass By* and *Leaving*

Cheyenne, he kicked out a few rough pages of what would eventually become, after many changes, his fourth novel, *Moving On*—pages centered on a young married couple, very like him and Jo. Jack Leggett, knowing from McMurtry about the "marital crisis," read the pages sometime later and suggested that McMurtry was too close to the material to write about it objectively or effectively: the couple's problem is "never defined," he said. "They emerge as two whining, self-pitying, self-indulgent figures. Miserable with one another sexually, spiritually and intellectually and with neither the wit nor the guts to find a solution. The effect on the reader is numbing . . . Jesus, Larry."

Habitually, the couple in the story becomes mutually irritated when making love (or failing to), both partners upset that the other is unable to intuit moods or body signals. They utterly fail to communicate. The man can't tell when the woman wants him to back off or to press his amorousness, the woman isn't sure whether pleasing him when she doesn't feel like it is generous or degrading. No moment seems natural—even a pleasant shoulder rub is freighted with awkwardness: can it simply be enjoyed for what it is or must it inevitably lead to something more? The couple plays at open-mindedness and bohemianism, but each suspects the other of prudery.

(At a Perry Lane party one night, Jo told Kesey, "Larry's hung up and can't see it.")

In the novel, social situations are invitations to terror: the woman wants her friends, and even strangers, to admire her beauty—she feels she's earned such regard—but the boundaries are hard to keep clear. Her insecurities, her need for constant reassurance that she's loved, are deepened by the "uncivilized or ambiguous admiration" of men appraising her sexually. The "disadvantage" of such attention, flattering as it might be, is that she begins to feel like "easy prey." She lies awake at night, panicked by the thought of total freedom: "[H]ow terrible and complicated life would be if she didn't belong to [her husband]—if that simple truth weren't true, or weren't all-covering. What if [he] didn't absolutely and automatically belong to her?"

The woman tells a friend of hers, "Why people sleep with the people they seem to sleep with is beyond me. Why anyone sleeps with anyone is sort of a puzzle, actually."

In fact, Jo—whose blond beauty struck Jim Wolpman as "ethereal"—crept around most Perry Lane parties as if she were being stalked. She didn't trust the outrageous flirting; she didn't trust Kesey. Like McMurtry, she failed to participate in the acid-stoked tree climbing or the impromptu dramas involving Shakespearean soliloquies and catsup-soaked axes or the attempts to create the World's Largest Cat's Cradle using a fifty-foot clothesline. She felt so at sea at some of these gatherings, she'd sit demurely, almost paralyzed. Dirk Van Nouhuys, who thought her "smart, pretty, open, kind of zany," recalled her at a party one evening "sitting on the floor with her knees up and her arms around them." Her dog, Putnam, in a horny mood that night, "came up and began humping her legs, thrusting his penis between her calves. She just let it happen."

Ed McClanahan found her "passing strange. She seemed peculiar to me," he said. "She got so unsettled at parties that she carried a vessel to vomit into. She was shy. Bunches of people upset her."

Kesey spread a story about her. He said he'd come to the McMurtrys' apartment one day and Jo had answered the door, casually nude, explaining that she suffered from stress, and a therapist had told her to walk around naked to relax. It was helping, she claimed, though as she paced the apartment, Kesey said, she carried a bowl into which she might puke at any moment.

It was disingenuous of Kesey to talk about Jo this way—nudism was a fairly common and unremarked-upon practice in and around Perry Lane. The truth was, Jo was suffering from a problem with her pyloric valve, the smooth ring of muscle connecting the stomach to the digestive system. She experienced severe abdominal pain. "She threw up a lot and tended to not eat and to lose weight," Van Nouhuys recalled. Sometimes the condition was exacerbated by stress, and doctors suggested relaxation techniques, including breathing and diaphragm exercises. It's likely that Kesey had caught her at her exercises one day.

In any case, her physical discomfort increased her general unhappiness, especially in the extreme social chaos of Perry Lane. McMurtry knew it wasn't fair of him, yet he couldn't help but compare her sullenness to Faye Kesey's sunny smile, always at the ready, it seemed, despite the trials her husband put her through. He began to see Faye as "the unwobbling pivot and the unmeltable glue that kept a very complex domestic situation from spinning into fragments." He didn't get a chance to know her well, complaining that Kesey wouldn't let him speak to her. But he felt comfortable with Faye. And friends remarked that she'd get a wistful look in her eye whenever McMurtry's name was mentioned. She'd talk admiringly of his discipline as a writer.

Her husband's growing legend, even in these early stages before the appearance of *Cuckoo's Nest,* fascinated McMurtry more than his actual behavior, which was boorish. It was like witnessing the transformation of the callow ne'er-do-well, William Bonney, a violent failure at everything he tried, into the colorful, charismatic figure of Billy the Kid ("How could [Bonney] have produced a legend, and a bibliography with thousands of items in it?" McMurtry always wondered. "There's an element of sheer publicity in it."). Already, Kesey was on his way to becoming "a very famous man in an Age of Groupies," and "Faye's forbearance was great," McMurtry observed. "I don't know a wife I respect more."

I n 1963, after Kesey confessed to McMurtry that he'd just commenced an affair with a married woman and was suffering hell as a result, McMurtry wrote him, employing an uncharacteristically macho tone matching Kesey's swagger (a dare to which McMurtry usually refused to respond): "If you're lucky or unlucky enough to be in love . . . with a woman another man loves you may fuck her or not fuck her as your conscience and hers dictates—I was in love that way once and did fuck her and don't pretend to regret it—but by no known laws of human nature (as valid on perry lane as anywhere else) can you expect the other man to continue buddybuddy with you. And you can't change human nature, for which I thank all the gods there never have been."

McMurtry was referring to an incident that occurred over Christmas break 1960, when he and Jo traveled briefly from San Francisco to see their families and old friends. Hazel and Jeff Mac were no more disposed to welcome Jo freely into their house than they'd ever been, and McMurtry was no more comfortable with Jo's folks. He despaired of his family's fierce holiday rituals. He was dispatched to Wichita Falls to pick up his mother's mother from an assisted living facility and bring her to Archer City so there could be loud and pointless family arguments over food baked and boiled to within an inch of inedibility. "I dislike Xmas so much I contrive to have car trouble if I can and spen[d] it alone usually in the vicinity of El Paso, where I know no one," he'd write Susan Sontag years later. "[Xmas is] the one day of the year when the bleakness of the Permian Basin fits my mood."

On this particular holiday, he and Jo returned to Houston as well. He spent much of his time there trying to avoid Ray Waddington. In a letter to Dorothea Oppenheimer (with whom he had become extremely close—she was very attentive to him), he said Ray "may create some mild bad scene (he has a genius for that kind of bad scene) because he suspects I intrigued with his wife at Xmas, and if he doesn't, Jo, who knows I intrigued with his wife at Xmas, may."

He had finally acted upon his attraction to Linda Waddington—less out of passion than a need for mutual comfort. He and Jo were miserable, and Linda felt all but abandoned by a husband preoccupied with his graduate classes and preliminary exams. He seemed to be having an affair with the Fondren Library, leaving her exhausted amid the squalor of domesticity, feeling unattractive and unwanted. McMurtry saw her as abidingly grounded and normal, sensible and calm—like Faye Kesey. He sought her nurturing qualities. She sought reassurance from him that she was still a desirable woman. "I don't love Linda [the way] I love . . . Jo . . . I just have a comfortable warm sexthing with her," he told Oppenheimer. He and Linda spent most of their time together just holding each other in a house full of dirty dishes and soiled clothes. Afterward, they felt plenty guilty. In January, he returned to California resolved to repair his marriage. "I can't kid myself that [Jo's] parents . . . screwed her up . . . Certainly they screwed her up— but [not] I fear so much as I have. Because she cares for me more than she does or has for . . . them, and I'm the one who continues to destroy her confidence in herself; in her own adequacy," he wrote Oppenheimer. "Well, I will be more careful from now on and can perhaps correct the damage done there. She feels she has failed repeatedly to establish a place—anywhere. She hasn't [failed], because she's established a place in me which is her own and which no one threatens."

Almost immediately, dreariness descended upon them once more in San Francisco—McMurtry working on his fiction every day; Jo slogging through her job, not eating, losing weight; and Perry Lane cranking up each week like a frenzied carnival. McMurtry's attention began to wander again from his marriage, and so did Jo's. He told Oppenheimer: "[By now] you have become one of the strange and compelling horde . . . of people who stand at the center of my world." Months later, like a lovesick boy, he wrote her from Texas: "Miss and want you a lot." He confessed to his agent he was beginning to see life as a gargantuan melodrama. "I'm thinking immoral thoughts about you right now."

McMurtry spent the spring of 1961, his last months at Stanford, listening to Frank O'Connor complain about the anemic state of the American short story, collecting rare books, steering carefully around Jo, and anticipating the publication of his first novel. It should have been a joyous time, but he felt suspended; trepidation about the future had become a palpable force, giving him migraines.

He didn't frequent Perry Lane as often as he used to. He had little tolerance remaining for what would evolve into Kesey's full-blown pranksterism, but he did enjoy meeting a handsome new couple, Laurence and Geraldine McGilvery. Dirk Van Nouhuys brought them around. They owned a bookshop in La Jolla. A year after McMurtry met them, the McGilverys were arrested for "selling obscene matter"—Henry Miller's *Tropic of Cancer.* The police chief, a zealot who'd previously warned Elvis Presley he'd be tossed in jail if he came to California and gave a "pelvis-grinding" concert, locked Geraldine away among shoplifters, drunks, and prostitutes even though she was nursing a brand-new baby girl. She remained bitter, the rest of her life, "about the inquisition-like treatment she received," McGilvery said. He spent time in a cell, too. At the couple's trial, the judge insisted the entire novel be read aloud to the jury—nine hours of "dirty" prose, performed dramatically by a local writer. To reduce the salacious edge, he referred to the main characters as "Mama Bear" and "Papa Bear," eliciting relieved laughter from the jurors.

After fifteen days, the McGilverys were acquitted of morals charges. In 1964, the Supreme Court ruled that *Tropic of Cancer* was not obscene, establishing free speech in literature and making possible the publication of—among others—a pair of novels McMurtry would produce in the early 1970s.

These novels, *Moving On* and *All My Friends Are Going to Be Strangers,* revolved around frank tales of adultery and sexual encounters among graduate students, rendered unsentimentally. The material, sad, dispiritingly aware of human failure, came to him naturally. He reported to Kesey that Jo had slept with a mutual friend of theirs, a man Kesey had angered by sleeping with *his* wife. McMurtry knew he had no moral high ground to seize against Jo. He wasn't angry as much as confused about how and why their bodies and minds had fallen so badly out of sync. The possibilities for delight were fading fast.

He believed Jo's indiscretions were "so obviously not a thing connected with [him]," but rather with her need to understand her own ambivalence toward sex. "I assure you I am unoffendable," McMurtry told Kesey. "As I keep insisting (to everybody) and as nobody believes, I am a pretty simple organism." He carried no animosity toward the other man. "I truly think jealousy is an emotion I have never known, except as a writer, when it is more accurately envy . . . That may make me a narcissist, I'm not sure."

Soon McMurtry's peers in and around the writing program, including Jo's lover, would envy him—*and* Kesey—as the publication dates approached for *Horseman, Pass By* and *One Flew Over the Cuckoo's Nest.* A couple of older writers whom Jack Leggett had approached for blurbs expressed astonishment at McMurtry. "Just between you and me, I think it's pretty damned disgusting for a 24-year-old man to write so well, to retain such freshness in his disciplines, such a sure touch. He ought at least to have to struggle a few more years before coming anywhere near this," John Howard Griffin, author of *Black Like Me,* wrote Leggett. "I spent a good deal of time in the ranching country he describes, and this is probably the starkest, most truthful, most terrible and yet beautiful treatment of it I've seen. It will offend many, who prefer the glamor treatment—but it is a true portrait . . . Technically, McMurtry has brought his poetic insights, which are first class, under the controls of a style that springs directly from the language rhythms and concepts of his subject—a most difficult and selfless thing."

A. B. Guthrie wrote, "Reluctant as I am to admit that a twenty-four-year-old can write a book like HORSEMAN, PASS BY, I must admit the fact that here is a young man who somehow knows so much about the language of fiction that I cannot understand . . . This boy is good."

By contrast, J. Frank Dobie groused dismissively, "The beatnikers ought to buy it"—perhaps a darker form of envy, a recognition that Texas writing was about to take a generational leap.

Back in Archer City, once the Stanford year was done, McMurtry spent the summer cowboying for his father while he and Jo contemplated their future. From Jack Leggett he learned that 2,720 copies of *Horseman, Pass By* had been shipped to stores on publication day. "[If] we get up close to 4000, we've made it. If there are few or no re-orders, we'll get back a lot of those 2720 and we'll not have made it," Leggett reported bluntly. In the next few weeks, sales slowed to a trickle, and though Leggett said the book had a "pulse," "she breathes," it was clear that the novel would not become a commercial success. McMurtry already felt the book was a literary failure because of the structural compromise he had made, though he admitted proudly to Oppenheimer that "the reviews are extraordinarily good." Once he had finished the actual writing, the project seemed to have nothing to do with him, and he was grateful for the purely physical challenges of rounding up cows and digging post holes, keeping Leggett's "irritating" news at bay. For once, his ambivalence about Archer City was overshadowed by other concerns, and the blood-orange sunsets and the heat and the open plains soothed him with their rugged familiarity. "I feel I've truly come home, and I'm sort of settling back into Texas and finding it satisfying," he wrote Oppenheimer. "I like it here right down to my marrow."

If only daily life with his family was as fulfilling. "Jo's stomach [has] temporarily buckled under the strain of coping with" the relatives, he said; their beloved dog, Putnam, "unleashed, and unused" to the place "panicked, ran off, and got run over and killed." McMurtry's younger brother, Charlie, eager for attention he felt he wasn't getting with the arrival of newcomers, somehow set three old cushions on fire in the garage, prompting local volunteer firemen, happy to have an "excuse to go play with hoses," to come rushing in swirls of dust amid "great sounds of bells and ambulances." The tension in the house became so pitched, McMurtry promised Jo, who was more and more gloomy, he'd find them a separate domicile, necessitating visits to "various vacant and rotting houses." Still, Jo sulked and got sick in the mornings. For a while, she thought she was pregnant, a possibility to which McMurtry was "not resigned." He was so exasperated with the domestic doings, so wistful in his longings for Oppenheimer and even Linda Waddington, he blurted in a letter to his agent that "marriage for my generation is an absurdity."

Years later, writing to Susan Sontag, he'd push this observation further: "When I look at families, any families, I see too much pain," he said. "I've always too great a tendency to see what's missing, not what's there."

Other than professional critics, perhaps, few readers of *Horseman, Pass By* in 1961 would have guessed that its author was widely read in eighteenth- and nineteenth-century English literature, that he was anything other than a modestly educated West Texan writing his own coming-of-age story using the natural dialect of his region. Mc-Murtry's skillful use of dialect belied the effort required to render regional speech in a manner both readable and seemingly authentic. Like Mark Twain in *The Adventures of Huckleberry Finn* and Ernest Hemingway honing his sentences to an elemental spareness in his short stories, McMurtry had created the illusion of offhandedness and ease on the page, hiding the fact of *literary production*.

And though the novel "follows a conventional structure," in the words of Mark Busby, one of McMurtry's most astute early critics, "exposition (Lonnie's prologue), rising action/complication (discovery of [Homer Bannon's] dead heifer), climax (slaughter of the herd/the death of Homer), falling action (Homer's funeral/Lonnie's response), and denouement (Lonnie's leaving)," the story is uniquely complicated by ambitions exceeding its streamlined structure. The conventional order owes more to Jack Leggett's insistence on narrative suspense than on McMurtry's vision of what he was up to.

Already, before adding his voice to the great ongoing conversation of Western literature, McMurtry had wrestled mightily with the form he had chosen—the novel—and with the contexts, both broad and specific, guiding the novel's contributions to national and regional cultures. On one level, then, *Horseman, Pass By* was the young McMurtry's distilled encyclopedia of his understanding of the uses and aesthetics of literature, and his place in it.

To begin with, he had faced down Texas. He asked himself the question posed so elegantly by critic Paul Christensen, who wondered "why [Texas literature] did not mature faster or produce more interesting results in the century or more of its evolution. Texas was at the heart of American history during that time, and its character was of interest to the rest of the nation. But all through the charged decades of the nineteenth century, Texas writers ignored developments in the arts of the north and midwest and clung tenaciously to traditional modes of story and poem, and to a stale romantic style."

McMurtry had learned that the earliest examples of Texas literature were the oral tales and pictographs of Native cultures, many of which were ignored, lost, or destroyed with the coming of the Europeans, replaced by travelogues, the notebooks and journals of explorers. These forms of writing privileged Anglo supremacy, the Europeans' right to claim the land and impose upon it racial and religious absolutes that remained unexamined for decades.

Texas took a long time to solidify as a *place,* as something to be considered in literature. Mexico did not recognize it until 1850; Native resistance to the European presence was not quelled until 1875; Texas then became a republic, then a state, then a secessionist member of the Confederacy, then a state again; all the while, the disorderliness of pioneer movements and uprooted settlers prevented easy establishment of principles that might have defined a society. "Texas isn't as religious as it thinks it is," McMurtry declared, acknowledging the region's shaky foundations. "Underneath there is a strong current of heresy and paganism."

Moreover, historian Louis Cowan said, "Texans from the beginning were confronted with a dual consciousness: were they transplanted Americans or a new breed? Should they look to the aristocratic landed gentry for their ideals or to Rousseau's noble savage? Should their allegiance be with the Anglo-Saxon or the Spanish culture? Should they be cultivated or primitive? . . . Was the new territory they settled garden or desert? Caucasian, Christian, Yankee, Southerner, Westerner—Texans found themselves to be all of these."

When Texas first appeared as a subject in a novel, it was observed from afar, by an anonymous French writer celebrating "free thought," using Texas as an exotic example. *L'Héroïne du Texas* (1819) followed the adventures of a young Protestant who marries a Spanish Catholic, and is forced to escape ecclesiastical condemnation; thus, the free, rugged individual was firmly established as *the* Texas trope. It was repeatedly reinforced in the dime westerns published by the New York firm of Beadle & Co., beginning in 1859—a series of cheap novels lauding the pioneer settlers' civilizing of wilderness by beating back dark savages.

McMurtry stored this knowledge away before writing his first novel. He also recognized that it was the development of modernism in Europe, following World War I, and its importation into the United States (through Mexico) that began to loosen the bedrock of white supremacism in Texas stories, making possible a more complex literature.

The devastation of the global war challenged Europe's formerly fixed assumptions about civilization, progress, and moral righteousness. It profoundly upended artistic production. At the time, historian and poet Herbert Read wrote:

> There have been revolutions in the history of the arts before today. There is a revolution with every new generation. . . . But I do think we can already discern a difference in [this moment]: it is not so much a revolution, implying a turning over, even a turning back, but rather a break-up, a devolution, some would say a dissolution. Its character is catastrophic.

Modernism was the expression of trauma. One of its hallmarks was a fervent embrace of "primitivism," "purer" stories and images from cultures older, steadier (or imagined to be) than the now-frayed European experiment unleashing horrifying destruction on the world. Picasso's 1907 painting *Les Demoiselles d'Avignon*, superimposing bold African masks on the faces of fallen French women, was a harbinger.

By 1920, Mexico City rivaled Paris as a center of modernist activity, with the concentration there of politically engaged muralists such as Diego Rivera, José Clemente Orozco, and Rufino Tamayo glorifying the peasantry over landowners. Their compatriot, the poet Octavio Paz, declared, "I began to feel that poetry and revolution, as the surrealists [say], are equivalents."

This turbulence in the arts, brewing on Texas's southern border, spilled over just as the original *Texas Quarterly,* the state's first serious literary journal, moved from Austin to Dallas to become the *Southwest Review* (McMurtry's first major literary home). This shift recentered the region's imagination from the South to the Southwest, expanding its boundaries even as the old sureties of Anglo identity started to wobble.

Having thoroughly explored the development of the novel in Texas, Mc-Murtry took one more step before tossing his little pebble—his plains story—into the long-flowing stream. What *kind* of novel, of the many possibilities offered by writers over the course of four centuries, best suited the Texas *he* knew? As it turned out, the question was an easy one, he thought: the contemporary Texas novel was Victorian in temperament—not just because Eliot, Hardy, Trollope, Thackeray, and Dickens were among his favorite writers, but because the Texas of his moment shared with Victorian England certain social ruptures: a movement from regional roots to foreign territories (rural to urban); a loosening of preindustrial values in a time of rapid technological development; a questioning of authorities in all fields of thought and endeavor; an unrealistic pressure on social manners, on family bonds, on all intimate ties, to compensate for every one of these agonizing uncertainties.

Horseman, Pass By would not be a historical novel or a revolutionary tract or an example of modernism or a nineteenth-century knock-off, but McMurtry's extensive familiarity with each of these ingredients powerfully shaped his story of the old cattleman broken by the death of his cows.

Homer Bannon is the last of a breed. A guardian of the cowboy's frontier order, he believes "nature [will] always work her own cures, if people would be patient enough, and give her time." The High Plains of West Texas are his cathedral, reserved for the running of cattle, and *only* for the running of cattle. He denies the encroachment of modern life, the new technology, the new money of oil, intent on destroying the land: "What good's oil to me, what can I do with it? With a bunch of fuckin' oil wells? . . . I can't breed 'em or tend 'em or rope 'em or chase 'em or nothin'. I can't feel a smidgen a pride in 'em, cause they ain't none a my doin'. Money, yes. Piss on that kinda money."

Admirable—to a point—in his tenacity and steadfastness, he is finally pitiable in his inflexibility, his refusal to acknowledge the tragic consequences of clinging to a passing way of life.

Ironically, his stoicism is largely responsible for forming his stepson's rotten character. Hud—scoundrel, drunk, crook, rapist, and by the end of the book, possibly a cold-blooded murderer—had wanted to go to college, but Homer saw no need for it. It didn't fit the old ways. "You thought I should drive that goddamn feed wagon for you . . . Yeah. You held on

tight," Hud spits at him. Once Homer's cows turn up sick, and the local
vet declares they must be slaughtered to prevent the spread of disease to
other herds, Hud understands that Homer and everything he ever valued
is done for. "Why, I used to think you was a regular god," he tells the faltering old man. "I don't no more."

If steadfastness and tenacity are the shining qualities of cowboys, Hud
embodies the cowpoke's vileness, especially when changing times have rendered such an existence untenable, leaving a man like Hud with nothing
to hope for. His mistreatment of women and people of color are embedded in the cowboy's selfish, superior self-image—along with a glorification
of violence—but in Hud they have hardened into chilly contempt. In a
shifting world, old certainties, old behaviors, having lost their center, can
only corrode, and Hud's corruption becomes complete when he rapes the
family's Black cook, Halmea.

In an essay later published in *In a Narrow Grave,* McMurtry addressed his intentions with Hud: "Hud, a twentieth-century Westerner,
is a gunfighter who lacks both guns and opponents. The land itself is the
same—just as powerful and just as imprisoning—but the social context
has changed so radically that Hud's impulse to violence is turned inward,
on himself and his family."

Like Hud, Jesse, a cowhand on Homer's ranch, is increasingly adrift as
his reason for being dries up. He channels his cowboying skills into unsat-
isfying rodeo events, in impersonal arenas proclaiming the "steady shrinkage" of his world. "I went all over this cow country, looking for the exact
right place an' the exact right people, so once I got stopped I wouldn't have
to be movin' again, like my old man always done," he says. But now there
is no longer any "right place" for him to find.

Just as Homer had thwarted Hud's character, he has caused his own
downfall by buying diseased Mexican cattle, infecting the rest of *his* herd.
He is forced to kill his longhorn steers—"I been keeping 'em to remind
me how times was"—and to allow the vet and his men to destroy the rest
of his cattle. After the slaughter, disoriented and distraught, he stumbles
toward death—the only territory still opening its vistas to him. But his
dying is protracted and painful; Hud shoots him, either an act of mercy or
a cold seizing of what's left of the old man's world: his property, on which,

it is clear, Hud will not hesitate to drill for oil. Hud's ambiguous killing of the old man encapsulates the novel's ambivalence toward its subject: the Texas of McMurtry's childhood.

"That life died, and I am lucky to have found so satisfying a replacement as [literature] offered," McMurtry wrote. "And yet, that first life has not quite died in me—not quite. I missed it only by the width of a generation and, as I was growing up, heard the whistle of its departure. Not long after I entered the pastures of the empty page I realized that the place where all my stories start is the heart faced suddenly with the loss of its country, its customary and legendary range."

In *Horseman, Pass By*, only Lonnie, Homer's teenage grandson, has any possibility of escaping the death rattle he's heard all his life. He is not really suited to the ranch. He rides a horse named Stranger; one day, startled by a fence, Stranger halts abruptly, throwing Lonnie violently to the ground. Lonnie would rather cling to books—*From Here to Eternity*—than to shiny saddle horns. At night, he lies awake listening to the swish of cars on the highway heading north to Amarillo or the whistle of the *Zephyr* across the dark prairie, imagining the "airplane beacons flashing from the airport in Wichita Falls," like the green signal at the end of the dock in *The Great Gatsby*, glowing with American promise. These sirens of travel, visual and auditory, may portend a better world or a false Eden overgrown with the taint of corruption, but either way, it is clear that Lonnie will follow them once Homer is gone. As he leaves, he will hear "the music of departure," as McMurtry wrote elsewhere, discussing his own farewell to early youth, the sound of a "god almost out of hearing." The reference was to a poem he'd read by Cavafy noting a Shakespearean scene—the god Hercules's abandonment of Mark Antony. As the god vanished, Antony's guards heard an odd music. McMurtry said, "Sometimes I see [the departing god] as Old Man Goodnight, or as Teddy Blue, or as my Uncle Johnny . . . but the one thing that is sure is that he was a horseman, and a god of the country."

Typical of the generous reviews McMurtry's first novel received was the notice in *Kirkus*: "The isolation and the homely, tangible beauty of small ranch life remove the taint of melodrama from this tale. The people . . . the country, the cattle are real."

Writing in *The New York Times*, Charles Poore said: "McMurtry is already well up among the most promising first novelists who have appeared this year. What's more, his promise is the kind that lasts . . . There is a gnarled pastoral side to Texas life that has not yet been shown fully to the world. It lies in Mr. McMurtry's province. He should not pass it by— remembering that the best of our southwestern writers is still Willa Cather, who showed the value of great underemphasis in lands that somehow stir most authors to prose shouts."

The book was barely in the stores when McMurtry pressed Leggett to offer him a contract on his second novel. He sent a new draft to the editor. He had decided to call it *Our Revels Now Are Ended*. Leggett responded, "On the positive side, it's a smoothly flowing job. You're a master of dialogue and the speech cadences cast a spell over the reader all by themselves. Your characterizations—particularly of Gid . . . are excellent and the more admirable because you do it all in dialogue without recourse to visual images or exposition of any kind, and on the whole this is a better written, a far less careless, book than HORSEMAN. BUT it has one huge flaw. It's static. It is boring. It is boring in spite of the good characters and the good writing because you don't tell the story of these people . . . [Y]ou have no structure, simply a string of arbitrary scenes which don't build any intensity. I remember trying to persuade you in the midst of HORSEMAN that any line or word which wasn't working for you to further story, to build suspense or reveal some <u>new</u> element of character ought to go."

McMurtry wasn't going to compromise a second time on the suspense issue. Leggett insisted: "You don't have to deliver every bit of information about Johnny, Molly, and Gid—but you have to deliver the <u>essential</u> information and the essential is why they married who they did and what effect this had upon them. If you can do this from the summit of their old age, you'll have a hell of a novel." McMurtry offered several ways around the need for exposition, including tucking footnotes into the text, to supply the information Leggett demanded. ("I'm skeptical" of the footnote approach, Leggett replied.)

McMurtry complained to Dorothea Oppenheimer, "I grow more and more annoyed with Leggett's way of working, so don't be surprised if . . . you have to find me another editor . . . I intend to be extremely obdurate about what stays in and what goes [from the new novel]."

Meanwhile, he was fiddling with still another idea for a novel—this one about a musician's son—but the story of Johnny, Molly, and Gid kept tugging at him: "[D]amn it I like it. It's a good bit better than Horseman technically; its [*sic*] pretty funny and pretty poignant." Once again, Leggett wouldn't budge on the structure.

"I do feel . . . that the time will come when Leggett will provoke me to some sort of nasty rejoinder," McMurtry told his agent. "I really feel that he would have been sort of tickled to see Horseman get slammed a few times, in hopes that I would pay more attention to him on the next book. Which hope would have shown a basic misunderstanding of my character."

Oppenheimer flew to New York to advocate on McMurtry's behalf. Perhaps at his insistence, she had come to see Leggett as a poor editor, full of "unsound notions." Leggett reported to McMurtry that he and Dorothea liked each other but couldn't avoid a shouting match in a restaurant. Finally, on his own, McMurtry worked out a structure for the novel that satisfied all parties: he divided the book into three sections, narrated by Gid, Molly, and Johnny, respectively, each telling the story of their lifelong friendships and the men's love for Molly, from the perspective of youth (Gid's section), middle age (Molly—in an echo of the final soliloquy in James Joyce's *Ulysses*), and twilight (Johnny). It wasn't suspenseful, but it was, in McMurtry's view, rich with the texture of life. As McMurtry said in an interview published in *Collage,* "I . . . am most interested in situations in which a person loves or is loved by more than one person. One man loves two women, one woman loves two men, etc.," he said. "Such situations seem to me extremely rich for the novelist, rich in textural possibilities. I'm a great deal more sensitive to texture than I am to structure. I think, humanly, it's a very interesting question, how many people one can love."

Wryly, perhaps wearily, Leggett wrote him. "I've gone over the manuscript again and see you've let me win here and there—but not enough to get a Max Perkins complex or a swelled head or anything like that." He sent a contract for the book to Oppenheimer and scheduled publication for September 25, 1963. McMurtry was now calling the book *Leaving Cheyenne,* explaining in a note at the beginning of the novel, "The Cheyenne of this book is that part of the cowboy's day's circle which is earliest and best: his blood's country and his heart's pastureland."

Despite his initial struggles with his editor, he conveyed to Ken Kesey that, at last, "*Leaving Cheyenne* met with an unexpectedly smooth reception [from Leggett] . . . No revisions beyond the level of good proofreading were asked for, and none volunteered. I figure this may be a unique experience for me, and am savoring it." From here on out, he said, he would not listen to editors. He knew what was best for his writing.

Like *Horseman, Pass By, Leaving Cheyenne* chronicles the end of the Old West. Gid, an aspiring High Plains rancher, dutiful, pragmatic, stoic, befriends a freewheeling, restless cowboy named Johnny when they are still just boys, and they both fall in love with a girl named Molly. Molly's father, an irresponsible rancher, is abusive toward her; he dies, leaving her with few prospects in life. Though she genuinely loves Johnny and Gid, remains intimate with them all her life, and even bears them sons, she marries a crude and feckless oilman named Eddie—he can give her the financial stability her devoted lovers, out of step with the modern world, cannot deliver.

It is Texas, post–World War II. As Dave Hickey points out, "Texas emerged from that war with a host of honored dead, a host of men with dead professions (ex-soldiers, ex-ranchers, ex-farmers, ex-oilmen, ex-railroadmen), and a host of men whose professions had gone sour." Gid and Johnny exemplify possible responses to this threadbare spiritual landscape: pursuing a life of duty and moral honor (Gid marries a girl he doesn't love just because she's needy and poor) or escape (Johnny is always riding off to what he perceives to be greener pastures). We first meet Gid when he arrives at a voting station during a local election on the day he turns twenty-one. Though he is there to keep Molly company, the scene establishes his fundamental character: he is a responsible citizen—so much so that, throughout his life, he never overcomes the guilt he feels each time he makes love to Molly, though she is a loving and willing partner, the mother of his son. By contrast, our last glimpses of Johnny, in his old age, show him wrestling futilely with modern machinery—irresponsibly, he has refused to learn how to negotiate the implements of a changing world. His sex with Molly is uninhibited, lighthearted, carefree, though he, too, has a child with her. The men's contrasts, one silent and tight, the other open, easy, sensual, anticipate McMurtry's most beloved characters, Call and Gus, in *Lonesome Dove*.

Molly bears the burden of most of her frontier foremothers—that of holding her social world together, what little of it there is, and of keeping her men whole under difficult and dangerous conditions. Her section of the novel is entitled, after a line from Shakespeare's Sonnet 64, "Ruin Hath Taught Me."

As in *Horseman, Pass By*—and as would be the case in *Lonesome Dove*—*Leaving Cheyenne* offers a portrait of a father who refuses to recognize his son or his son's true character. Gid's sexual guilt keeps him stiffly distant from his boy Jimmy. Like Hud, Jimmy grows up psychologically stunted from the absence of a loving patriarch.

And as with Homer Bannon, Gid's inflexibility dooms him. Stubbornly, he insists on climbing a windmill on his ranch to repair a busted sucker rod, though he is too old and frail to attempt such a feat. He falls and dies from his injuries.

The novel ends starkly, unsentimentally with "THREE GRAVE-STONES." The names Gideon Fry, Molly Taylor White, and Johnny McCloud appear along with their birth and death dates—a footnote to the story, placing the story in perspective in the thick of life's long, muddy texture: all is passing, and will pass. Nothing suspenseful about it; all we have is the richness of specificity as our short lives unfold.

Because *Horseman, Pass By* and *Leaving Cheyenne* shared similar themes, characters, and settings, many critics and reviewers assumed McMurtry was writing purely autobiographically. He conceded he drew from his life, but he pushed back hard on the notion that he was just a vessel for witnessing and reporting. He said, "The job of the writer is to make up shit."

Reviewing *Leaving Cheyenne* in *The Dallas Morning News*, Lon Tinkle complained that McMurtry "created effects but not people": the "nobly but harshly upright" father, the "all-purpose woman." But Marshall Sprague, writing in *The New York Times Book Review*, said, "Larry McMurtry's narrative moves at an easy lope and it occurred to me that if Chaucer were a Texan writing today, and only twenty-seven years old, this is how he would have written and this is how he would have felt."

8

Fort Worth had a chip on its shoulder—the size of the city of Dallas. McMurtry never much cared for Dallas. It was an uptight banking center, as far as he was concerned, producing little on its own, swimming in money generated elsewhere by people who couldn't afford to live there. He believed its municipal leadership was hysterically conservative, mean-spirited in its greediness, jingoistically patriotic as a means of excusing its greed (*hey—it's the American way!*). Since all it did was fatten itself on accumulated wealth, it developed an inferiority complex, a brash defensiveness aimed at promoting itself at the expense of the rest of the world. "Dallasans . . . are tentative, not quite sure who they are supposed to be, not really confident that who they are supposed to be is worth being. It is, consequently, the city of the instant put-down, and the higher one goes in the Dallas establishment the more true this is likely to be. Nowhere else in [Texas] does one find so many bitter, defensive, basically insecure people in positions of power," McMurtry observed (and he was referring to Dallas *before* the Kennedy assassination). Among the major targets of Dallas putdowns was its bustling brother to the west, the thriving railroad hub of Fort Worth.

Novelist Jim Thompson, who spent much of his youth in Fort Worth, once wrote: "Neighboring Dallas started an evil rumor about its rival. Fort Worth was so rustic, the libel ran, that panthers prowled the streets at high noon. Fort Worth promptly dubbed itself the Panther City, and declared the lie was gospel truth. Certainly, there were panthers in the streets [city boosters said] . . . Every morning they were herded down to the east-flowing Trinity River, there to drain their bladders into the stream which provided Dallas' water supply."

In the late summer of 1961, McMurtry loped along the streets of Fort Worth (encountering no big cats), looking for places to live. He and Jo, struggling with their marriage—living together, then separating for short periods—hoped that a steady income could stabilize their domestic situation (since book money could obviously not be counted on). Reluctantly,

McMurtry had accepted a position teaching five classes a semester in the English department at Texas Christian University.

He was fond of the Fort Worth Stockyards, which had given the city its other nickname, Cowtown. Between 1866 and 1890, drovers had run over four million head of cattle through Fort Worth, a last stop before crossing the Red River and wading into the dangers of the Indian Territory. The railroads arrived in 1876, making Fort Worth a major artery in the nation's food chain, and eventually attracting Armour & Company, Swift and Company, and other meat-packing outfits. The pens, barns, and the Livestock Exchange Building, an adobe structure with stately arches and an octagonal cupola, housing telegraph offices, railroad headquarters, and livestock commission companies, were soon surrounded by saloons, gambling halls, and brothels catering to cowboys. The brothels included the notorious Two Minnies, where customers in the bar downstairs could glance up through a glass ceiling and glimpse naked prostitutes cavorting in their rooms. The downtown area around the Stockyards was known as Hell's Half Acre; it remained untamed as late as the 1960s, and it gave Fort Worth a loose, rough-and-tumble quality (unlike ramrod Dallas) exciting to McMurtry. It reminded him of Houston's wildness.

As a boy, he had visited the Stockyards with his father when Jeff Mac had business there. He described the place in *Leaving Cheyenne*: "[T]hings looked . . . cheerful; the sun was up and the cattle were bawling and people were charging around everywhere. They had big wide planks nailed on top of the fences, so you could just walk around above the pens and see the cattle without having to get down in the cowshit." He'd sit at the lunch counter in one corner of the Exchange Building's rotunda, "feeling good," watching his father commune with other cattlemen, believing he "could handle anything." He'd watch men in rolled-up shirt sleeves scrawl the latest cattle prices reported from Chicago, Kansas City, and Omaha on a big chalkboard along one large wall in the open space, then swiftly erase the figures as new information rolled in.

(In 2015, McMurtry would get a star on the Texas Trail of Fame inside the Stockyards, a walkway established in 1997 to honor men and women who'd made a significant contribution to the "Western way of life.")

The TCU campus, nestled among dark oaks, and consisting of a series of Beaux Arts buildings made of pale golden brick under red-tiled roofs, was beautiful but awfully sedate compared with the Stockyards—except on the weekends, when the TCU Fighting Horned Frogs took the football field to pursue what appeared to be the university's main business, big-time sports. Its Christian mission had long been muted; it had affiliated itself with the Disciples of Christ in the late nineteenth century mostly as a means of securing finances.

McMurtry knew that he didn't want to teach. Already, he believed he was of "the generation of American writers that stayed in school a little too long," reading and talking about life rather than living it. Teaching classes was merely an extension of taking them, but it required much more work. Shortly after school began in the fall, he was complaining to Ken Kesey in long letters that he'd seen all he ever wanted to see of the inside of a classroom. The trouble was, he *did* get attached to individual students. Some of them were so eager to learn he couldn't help but try boosting them, giving them loads of extra time outside of class. "I got to teach the jocks," he said. Most of them didn't care for literature, so he challenged them to Ping-Pong games. "If I won, they'd get an F. If they won, they got an A." He was exaggerating—but not by much. "None of them got an A."

The lasting value of his year at TCU was the friendships he formed with John Graves and Dave Hickey. Graves was teaching at the school; a veteran of World War II, an experienced traveler—he had lived in France, Mexico, and Spain—he had returned to Texas when he learned that a beloved stretch of the Brazos River that he canoed many times was slated to be dammed. Out of this sense of loss, he wrote his masterpiece, *Goodbye to a River,* an elegy to Texas's rural past. He was a generally solitary fellow, and McMurtry had little time between his five classes, so the men didn't get to know each other well, but they developed a mutual respect. Published within two years of each other, *Goodbye to a River* and *Horseman, Pass By* signaled a literary turning point: a recognition that pastoral Texas was no more.

Dave Hickey was Graves's student, a precocious young man who'd started college at fifteen. He got the urge to write from Graves's passion for literature. "I didn't take Larry's classes, but I was hanging out with the writers he hung out with," Hickey told me. "I remember, at the time, some lady on the TCU English faculty was trying to get *Horseman, Pass By* banned from the university library because of its filthy language. Larry didn't take it too seriously."

In a halting, peripatetic career, Hickey would open art galleries and write country and western songs, travel with rock bands, edit magazines, teach, take crate loads of drugs; eventually, he'd develop into one of the nation's most brilliant and eccentric art critics. McMurtry credited him with writing one of the finest sentences ever scribbled by a Texan, a warning about the challenge of surviving in the Lone Star State: "Even if one succeeds in making a silk purse out of a sow's ear, there remains the problem of what to do with a one-eared sow."

Before leaving Archer City in the summer to move to Fort Worth, McMurtry wrote Dorothea Oppenheimer: "Jo has found a small, stray, starving black and white cat which she figures is a reincarnation of Putnam, so we have two cats now. She has also—a surprise move—dyed her hair a chocolate brown, and her hands the same color (though I believe the latter were done accidentally). Possibly this presages some transformation in personality; right now it's too early to tell."

At another point, he wrote Kesey: "We both know [Jo] is two people, if not more: some of her selves, surely, incline toward wife-and-motherhood, but probably the majority of them don't, at least not right now."

He was keenly aware of "all the pain" he'd caused Jo, pursuing the affair with Linda Waddington. Ray Waddington heard a rumor that Jo had been cutting herself. On July 14, 1961, while McMurtry and Jo were temporarily separated, McMurtry confessed to Oppenheimer, "I feel that I've established a life-time relationship with Jo . . . but I do not know that Jo and I will ever live together again as husband and wife . . . I hurt her terribly but she's recovered; one curious thing about her is the speed with which she recovers. She made a small suicide attempt nowhere near successful, and I am not worried now that she will ever make a real one; she screamed and shrieked and cried all one afternoon and when she got through it was all out of her system and she was okay. I'll probably go see her this weekend— it's our—ha—anniversary. But she agrees with me that marriage as we've known it is an absurdity."

That mid-July, Jo was reacting not just to Linda Waddington but also to Dorothea Oppenheimer. McMurtry's agent, to whom he was now writing openly flirtatious letters, had flown into Dallas and come to Archer City to see this exotic place for herself, to ride horses and watch a rodeo. She met and charmed McMurtry's parents—they were used to Germans, having known the Windthorst families. She and McMurtry talked business—Leggett had held out "a straw in the wind" to McMurtry: there might be some movie interest in *Horseman, Pass By*—but Jo could see their ease together, and she felt deliberately excluded from their conversations. Oppenheimer was cooler and more sophisticated than any woman who'd ever set foot in South Carolina, much less Archer City, Texas.

Before Oppenheimer's return to San Francisco, she and McMurtry drove to Lubbock to see Grover Lewis, possibly with the intention of seeing if she might represent him (though the trip was mainly an excuse to be alone). Lewis had earned a National Defense Act fellowship and moved to Lubbock to pursue a Ph.D. at Texas Technical College there. He edited the school newspaper and literary magazine and worked as a teaching assistant. (Eventually, his graduate career would crash when he penned a scathing piece in the school paper about the popular radio evangelist Billy James Hargis—his professors abandoned him as a heathen, and he received multiple death threats and was hastily driven out of West Texas.)

Lubbock was a cattle town, smaller and more godforsaken than Fort Worth, ringed by pump jacks, overrun with tumbleweeds, and redolent of fresh cow manure. Dark thunderheads massed in the sky each evening, teasing rain that never came (oh, but that distant, moist smell, almost like a rose blooming, and the slight cooling edge . . .). Oppenheimer was getting the true Texas tour.

She and McMurtry took a room with separate beds at the Sands Motel on Avenue Q near campus. It advertised "56 deluxe units with free TV and a 24-hour switchboard," but it resembled a low wall of bricks stacked in a vast parking lot. Semis groaned up the road past its triangular neon sign; washed-out mercury vapor lamps lit the pale bricks just enough to shade their rough, shallow pores.

Grover Lewis was missing in action. Oppenheimer never met him.

One night she took a walk with McMurtry by a tiny artificial lake, lightly touching hands, and he got the sense that she wanted him to kiss her. Later, back at the motel, as moths batted the dusty windows like bird shot, McMurtry and Oppenheimer explored sexual intimacy to the brink, without ever quite crossing the line.

As a souvenir of her rendezvous in Texas, she stuffed her purse with black Sands Motel matchbooks. A week or so later, after she'd returned to California, McMurtry wrote her: "You'll never know how close I came to not leaving you in Lubbock; leaving hurt me as bad as I've ever been hurt . . . [but it] had to be done; you had to go [to San Francisco], I had to come back [to Archer City], we couldn't have got around that, tearing as it was." He drove to Archer City with Lewis, who'd finally turned up: "[W]e had a crazy drunken time that I've barely recovered from now." He arrived to a "blow-up" with Jo, a tense visit from the Waddingtons and their rambunctious boys (adding to Jo's misery), and the need to firm up plans for finding a place to live in Fort Worth.

He apologized to Oppenheimer for being "pretty cold the last morning" in Lubbock, "but if I hadn't watched close you might not be in S. F. by now, or else I not here. One of my current projects is to slightly uncomplicate myself."

Then he launched into "second guess[ing] both of us." "I don't know how it would have been physically, that's always problematical, but I think emotionally, psychically and otherwise it was wrong of us to hold back," he said. He had done so because he thought she was "completely inaccessible." "[Y]ou seemed quite above me, mysterious . . . I have seen touch at the wrong time destroy a thing or two, and I was determined not to risk spoiling your friendship until I was sure you wanted me to. Obviously it takes a good deal to make me sure . . . and I kept faltering . . . primarily because I felt you were fighting it and feeling that [there] would be something wrong in our having sex."

"I do love you Dorothea—whatever I manage or fail to do about it—and I think you love me . . . those facts in my book give us the right to know one another as deeply as possible[;] if making love is a way [we] are free to use it." He had regrets, but they weren't "terrible": "I think I did find you in Lubbock to a depth that night, after all, [that would] only have been obscured by sex. There's so much about love I don't know—we might not find each other that deep without sex. Who can say . . . I do want you a great deal, and will go on wanting you, so that [if] you come this fall I will undoubtedly try to make love to you."

He ended: "All I can offer, as you so well know, is some of me, but it will always please me much for you to take that." He said he would install a second phone in his house, so he could speak to her privately.

Soon after this letter in mid-July, he reached a crisis point concerning any future he could imagine in Archer City: "[L]ast night . . . I glanced over my shoulder and saw into the abyss," he confided to his agent. "I think for the first time ever"—not true—"I've really had to doubt my ability to live in Archer City . . . too many of the people I love and want to be with the most cannot live here—and my beliefs and way of life have just become too different from those of my parents—so that if I stay here I fear doing the folks harm. Maybe I'm being melodramatic again, but I fear not. I very much do not want to go into exile, but even less, I think, do I want to relinquish the things I'd have to relinquish to live in peace in Archer City. These are sad reflections."

As a result of such concerns—the long distance between them, the tension in his marriage, the upcoming move to Fort Worth, and the possibility of a movie springing from his book—the romance with Oppenheimer lost a bit of its edge. ("I'm frequently in a frenzy for you but frenzy by it's [*sic*] nature is a very temporal state & I'm confident I can survive.") He said he was often depressed about matters as they stood ("I'm gloop," is how he put it). He told Oppenheimer: "I've caused you a lot of misery and will probably cause you a lot more . . . you've offered me a lot more than I have offered you."

He and Jo celebrated a melancholy anniversary together, commiserating about how much they missed Putnam, investing their emotions in a safe secondary source of pain rather than fully confronting their problems. More and more, McMurtry believed their trouble was sexual incompatibility—or perhaps a design flaw in human beings, concerning the sexual act. He kept wanting a *breakthrough* in his intimacies with Jo, a revelation enabled by skin tickling skin, leading him to the essence of this woman, a soaring expectation placing enormous burdens on the slightest touch. Jo felt he blamed her for inadequacy; she felt unloved. The irritations of daily life—faucet leaks, bills to be paid—drove them both crazy.

Readers and critics would honor McMurtry, throughout his career, for being unusually insightful about women and sympathetic to them in his writing, but here in his mid-twenties, in the early years of his first marriage, confused, restless, he kept "thinking that if I really examine how I've behaved and felt . . . I'll know what to do with myself, or at least what kind of self I have to do with." But then he thought: "Probably not."

To Ken Kesey, he wrote: "I think a writer's needs are unusual where women are concerned; personally, I would like to have on hand at all times a wife, a mother, a mistress, a whore, and two or three good girlfriends, but if that kind of variety isn't available, and it seldom is, practically any one of them will do."

On July 14, in a letter to Oppenheimer, he noted the passing not just of a literary giant but of an era in American literature: effectively, the end of the pre–World War II generation of writers. Ernest Hemingway had died. The sixties circus was about to hit town, horns ablare, heralded by the publications of *One Flew Over the Cuckoo's Nest, Horseman, Pass By,* Philip Roth's *Goodbye, Columbus,* Walker Percy's *The Moviegoer,* and Joseph Heller's *Catch-22.* (The fine new work produced by women—Grace Paley, Margaret Atwood, Ursula K. Le Guin—did not yet cause much of a stir in male-dominated critical/publishing circles.)

Of Hemingway, McMurtry wrote: "I'm glad he pulled the trigger—it was a very moral thing to do [under the circumstances]—but I'm sad that he's gone; and all out of proportion to my love of his work; I guess along with my father and my uncles he represents an attitude, tradition, or way of life that I hate to see vanishing; it so surely is. The American decline has touched the cowboy too. I had hoped he was safe."

One day in early August, Jo—whom McMurtry now referred to as his "sometime wife & sometime mistress"—announced she was pregnant. "One grows numb in some areas," he reported to his agent.

In the weeks ahead, he wrote: "I'm afraid this pregnancy may not work out too well. But then perhaps it will," and, "Getting [Jo] pregnant . . . was perhaps foolish, I don't know . . . I remember . . . being in a terribly reckless mood . . . I can really be extremely reckless when I become fatalistic."

Jo experienced debilitating morning sickness but generally seemed pleased about having a baby, despite the uncertainties she felt about her marriage. Meanwhile, McMurtry heard from Linda Waddington that she was about to separate from *her* husband. McMurtry believed Ray didn't appreciate "what a jewel she [was]"; he offered to give her and her two little boys a place to stay, even though he could barely stand the kids. They were the noisiest children he had ever encountered, always bickering. In the event, Linda did not accept his offer, but he continued to feel partly responsible for the Waddingtons' "storm." He believed he was "on the permanent shitlist of everybody who knows us." He began to welcome the idea of moving to Fort Worth. It would be a blessing to his parents: "I'll probably be more help [to them] just staying far enough away that they won't witness the frequently sordid truth about my way of life," he wrote Oppenheimer, before trying hard to convince her to come see him.

He figured bookselling would supplement his teaching income—they'd need as much money as they could get once the child arrived. Bookselling might also deliver him, someday, from academia. Right before the move to Cowtown, he befriended a man named Bill Gilliland who ran McMurray's Book Store in Dallas. Gilliland paid him ninety cents an hour to sort through books and clean out his warehouse on Industrial Avenue. McMurtry was tempted to steal from the warehouse a copy of Edward Dahlberg's novel *Bottom Dogs* with an introduction by D. H. Lawrence, but resisted the impulse. With the books he purchased from Gilliland then resold to other stores, he earned enough to consider going into business for himself (Dust Bowl Books, he'd call it), but for now the operation would have to be part time; he was due to begin at TCU.

In late August he sold 656 books in one marathon evening and "was up till dawn . . . listening to immoral proposals," he told Oppenheimer. Along its seamy underbelly, "Dallas [was] a pretty wild town." More people than he would've supposed wanted the kind of kinky material that tempted Irving Klaw into the S and M business. "What I need most is—of course—pornography, about $10,000 worth of it," McMurtry said. "Met a rich boy the other day who buys about $40,000 worth a year—he has decided to establish a library for sex research. Some customer."

McMurtry settled into a tiny apartment on Lubbock Street in Fort Worth (which TCU later demolished to build a parking lot). Sometimes Jo stayed with him; at other times she lived separately in a place he'd found for her, with "an incredible yard." One week he'd report to Oppenheimer that Jo was doing just fine on her own; the next week he'd say, in passing, that Jo was getting so big he could barely get past her in the bed.

The one consistent refrain in his letters was that TCU was a dreary, mediocre school and he'd made a mistake accepting the teaching post. His department head had an office full of Edna Ferber books—certainly not an indicator of revved-up intellect, he thought. He went home with a migraine after his first day.

He suffered from insomnia. Oppenheimer suggested he ask Jo to show him some yoga poses, for relaxation.

He backed away from his earlier invitation to his agent. He regretted she was wrestling with her conscience concerning him; he had no regrets at all, he said. He loved her and that was that . . . *but,* given his heavy academic schedule, a visit was not a good idea. He'd have no time for her.

Nor was he feeling very companionable. Harper & Brothers had arranged a few autograph parties in bookstores in Dallas and Fort Worth. Nothing made him feel worse about himself than these depressing episodes—a smattering of people, none of whom really cared to read his book but insisted on asking him how *they* could be published. He was supposed to sit there being proud of a book he was not actually fond of. (One old lady kept calling his novel *The Four Horsemen of the Alamo.*)

The strict teaching load disrupted his writing. He thought about fiction more than he wrote it, and his brooding led him back to his obsession about the ending of *Horseman, Pass By.* To Oppenheimer, he railed against Leggett for talking him into changing the novel's structure: "[I've] decided that in the future, excepting very minor emendations, I won't accept or even consider any more editing . . . If they won't take them the way I write them, then from now on they won't get published." Shortly after declaring his literary defiance, he raised the stakes. He told Oppenheimer: "I come closer than anybody to knowing what's best for me. There are exceptions (very rare), but as a rule I only screw up when [I] am temporarily lulled into believing that someone else knows as much about what is best for me as I do. I don't believe anybody does."

Oppenheimer read this as a warning to her not to push him. Their romance was cooling. She wrote: "Larry, I feel I've lost touch with you almost entirely." She said wistfully that she'd used the last match from her Sands Motel matchbooks. Then, in a "stern letter," which "wash[ed] off me like water off a duck's back," McMurtry informed her, she accused him (as Jo had) of being repressed. Rather defensively, McMurtry replied: "Coming as you do from a more worldly, or at least an older and more educated background, I doubt you fully realize how much there is in 19th century American low protestant background to be pushed against; I know there are some good things about it but I think there are some bad things too, and the latter easily get embedded in one very deeply. [In] Fact I doubt they can be eradicated; but one can fight to minimize them. I'm existential enough to believe one creates oneself—quel struggle. The alternative is letting someone else create you."

Then he softened his tone. By way of apology for his emotional withdrawal, he said: "I seem to have been in constant motion all summer . . . I'll probably be permanently rushed from now on forever, I'd better just learn to think while in motion."

Oppenheimer remained concerned about him: "Dear, poor Larry . . . Please take better care of yourself . . . I'm sure you're eating inadequately. Also you seem somehow against yourself." She never confused her professional obligations with her personal entanglement, and she worked hard to promote him. He had managed to complete a pair of short stories (revising drafts of pieces composed a couple of years earlier). Dutifully, Oppenheimer sent them to magazine editors. The prologue to *Horseman, Pass By* appeared as a stand-alone story in *Southwest Review,* but the other pieces fared less well. "I'm afraid this is much too dirty for us. I don't think you should be reading such things," Rust Hills, *Esquire*'s fiction editor, wrote Oppenheimer. McMurtry was particularly incensed by *Texas Quarterly*'s rejection—initially the editors had showed interest in one of his stories and kept it quite a long time before passing on it. "Bastards," McMurtry complained to his agent. His anger at the editors was rather like his mourning for his dog Putnam when he was mostly grieving the state of his marriage—a displacement of his true feelings. He was furious at himself for getting boxed in with a teaching job he didn't want and a pregnancy he wasn't prepared for, all of which impinged upon his concentration. It wasn't short stories he aspired to write. Still, in spite of the editors' rejections, the stories signaled progress. "Breeding Darrell," about a slow-witted boy cared for by the owner of a small-town pool hall, and "There Will Be Peace in Korea," about a pair of old high school buddies, rivals for the same girl, enjoying a final night out together before one of them leaves for military duty: these would become centerpieces in *The Last Picture Show.* All he would have to do is take one of the last lines in "There Will Be Peace in Korea"—"A lot of things happened when me and Bud and Laveta was in high school"—and spin it out.

W HAT'S A SONIC BOOM AMONG FRIENDS? Well, it's somewhat startling, but very solid assurance of protection. It's an unspoken pledge that the safety of you and your family is the prime concern of the day-to-day business of the U.S. Air Force."

This ad appeared in the *Amarillo Globe-News* around the time McMurtry drove into the Texas Panhandle near the town of Claude, thirty miles southeast of Amarillo, on a hot June day in 1962 to witness a staging of mass cattle vaccinations. He had driven across cloud-shadowed plains from Fort Worth, under massive blue thunderheads, rolling south, past road signs declaring "Rattlesnakes. Exit Now," "The Big Texan Steak Ranch. 72-ounce steak. You'll be glad you waited," and "Amarillo. We Like Where We Are." In the wide, dusty streets of Amarillo, under swaying traffic lights clicking at no one, green to yellow to red, stray newspaper pages skipped across the asphalt, wrapping misshapen tumbleweeds.

The sonic boom ad celebrated the tenth anniversary of the siting of a Strategic Air Command base here. Within a few more years, Amarillo's Pantex Plant would become the final assembly spot for all nuclear weapons manufactured in the United States—about four a day, or fifteen hundred warheads per year. Many of the locals working on bomb components at the plant were fundamentalist Christians, eagerly awaiting the world's end, when the Kingdom of Heaven would appear on Earth. In the meantime, B-52s from Oklahoma City's Tinker Air Force Base occasionally landed on a long, straight stretch of I-40 nearby, refueled, resupplied, and took to the air again to protect America from the growing Soviet threat.

This was the new Cold War Texas, redrawing the map of the state McMurtry had known, on which he could pinpoint, in this same area near Amarillo, the spot where, in the late nineteenth century, the sad last running of the buffalo occurred in the Panhandle. It was a single buffalo, begged from Old Man Goodnight on his famous ranch by a small, ragged band of Comanches who'd slipped away from their reservation in the Indian Territory. They showed up one day riding old, emaciated horses, wearing tattered feathers and scraps of white man's clothing. They asked Goodnight to release an animal to them. He complied out of compassion, giving them a ropy young bull, assuming they'd take it back to the reservation and eat it. Instead, they let it loose and chased it across the plains—to the extent that their horses could run—the way their ancestors had once pursued millions of animals here. They killed the bull with lances and arrows, just to taste the lost old ritual, then sat silently on their exhausted mounts staring at the dead animal, reckoning with their longing and the staggering absence of what once was. A chilly wind from the north ruffled the rags of their clothing.

McMurtry's uncles had told him that story. Now, near where the bull had died, a blue-eyed movie star spun a white Cadillac in circles under rows of obscenely bright lights. Hollywood arrived in McMurtry's life at around the time his child did, and it was Hollywood that had tugged him toward the Panhandle.

One cold, snowy day in January he had been teaching the Ramayana in his World Literature class at TCU to a bunch of farm kids and kids from the oil patch, worrying about the hundreds of ungraded papers stacked on his office desk and wondering if his department head would somehow learn about the unscheduled time off he took every so often to write or go book scouting in Louisiana. At the end of the day, as he was sitting down to a supper of meat loaf, he received a call from a man named Lloyd Anderson, a Paramount location scout. Anderson said he'd just arrived in Fort Worth and wanted to take McMurtry to dinner. Leggett's "straw in the wind"— the rumor of movie interest in *Horseman, Pass By*—had swirled around for months in the form of options by a respected screenwriting team, Irving Ravetch and Harriet Frank Jr. They'd bought exclusive rights to the novel, six months at a time for $1,000 every six months, while they wrote a screenplay. Suddenly the straw became a bale of hay and then a whole damn field. Paramount Studios green-lighted the movie for one simple reason: they had the guarantee of a star. Paul Newman had read McMurtry's novel and wanted to play the part of Hud (rewritten to suit him).

Anderson took McMurtry to a nice restaurant and bought him a huge steak. The man wore an immaculately pressed pinstripe suit. He said he was going to snoop around Texas for a suitable film site. Of course, the title would have to be changed: "They're thinking of calling it *Wild Desire*," he said.

McMurtry suggested *Coitus on Horseback,* but that didn't fly. He *did* manage to sell the studio on using his cousin Alfred's cattle in the film at five dollars a head. Alfred had a ranch in the little Panhandle town of Clarendon. Anderson looked at Clarendon and at Archer City, too, freezing his hands and nose in an icy norther over the course of a couple of days. Finally, he settled on an abandoned ranch outside of Claude (population 895), close to the old Goodnight ranch perched near the rim of Palo Duro Canyon, where Georgia O'Keeffe had once fallen in love with the sky.

The film news boosted McMurtry at a "gloopy" time. Jo was shuttling back and forth between Fort Worth and her parents' house in South Carolina, less for help with her pregnancy than for advice on how to fix her marriage. McMurtry was physically as well as emotionally depleted, picking his way through the "clutter" of anticipatory "baby junk" and suffering a painful swollen prostate following a serious urinary tract infection. Filming on what the studio now called *Hud Bannon Against the World* was scheduled to begin in May. Meanwhile, McMurtry had to figure out what to do about those stacks of student papers—"millions of finals," he complained to Oppenheimer. He stalked the university corridors fiercely wielding his Ping-Pong paddle. Even the news that the Texas Institute of Letters had awarded his book Best First Novel by a Texan failed to lift his mood. The Lord of Perry Lane's over-the-top success with *Cuckoo's Nest*—wild critical acclaim, movie options, play options, a paperback deal—made him feel he'd fallen behind in the literary sweepstakes, with further backsliding inevitable once the child arrived. "Every moment [the baby] stays inside [Jo] is—I feel—a moment gained," he confessed to his agent.

James McMurtry was born on March 18, 1962, in Fort Worth's St. Joseph Hospital—originally the Missouri Pacific Hospital, founded by a railroad magnate in 1883. An order of nuns from San Antonio was recruited as the nursing staff, after which the hospital promptly burned and had to be rebuilt. James came crying into the world on a site of ancient ashes—a suitable premise for one of the wry tunes he would later compose.

"Even as a baby he was a companionable child, interested in whatever was going on around him," Jo said. "He would sit in his plastic sitter-thingie and watch Larry type, fascinated, and would shake his rattle to pick up the rhythm. Jam session."

For some reason, McMurtry and Jo took to calling the baby Podge. Mc-

Murtry showed up bleary-eyed in his classes. He wrote long letters to Oppenheimer professing, "I am no less susceptible to you than I used to be," and telling her the "child is healthy as a pig . . . He is a very bright eyed relaxed child who takes life pretty much in stride. All the same I'm ready for him to be grown up. Fatherhood is too constant at this stage and I am not quite adjusted to the hours." He did not pretend to be "much of a childraiser," especially when Podge manifested his "will of iron."

It was a sign of how swiftly things were moving in McMurtry's life that Leggett wrote him asking for news on the "movie front" and exhorting him, "Courage on the night watch."

A few weeks after James was born, McMurtry received a check from Harper & Brothers for "Author's share of Movie money": $7,938.00," a first installment, along with $6,000 from Popular Library for a paperback release. Hollywood had saved him from the Ramayana. He left Jo with the baby and took a brief vacation to Mexico City (it rained the whole time). He spent $550 trying to secure the only extant copy of the three-volume initial publication of James Jones's *From Here to Eternity*. (The University of Virginia finally outbid everyone else on it.)

In early June, once the semester was over, McMurtry headed toward Amarillo to visit the movie set. In addition to Paul Newman as Hud, veteran actor Melvyn Douglas had been tapped to play Homer, and a young man named Brandon deWilde (who'd played the little boy in *Shane*) would be Lonnie. The character of Halmea, the Black cook, had been written out of the story, replaced by actress Patricia Neal as a no-nonsense housekeeper. The scene of her assault by Hud remained. Apparently it was not okay for a white man to attack a Black woman on-screen, but it was perfectly acceptable for a white man to rape a white woman.

As he passed through Claude just before midnight, streets empty, houses dark, a yellow blinking light illuminating Main Street downtown, McMurtry looked up, he said, and was pleased to see that, for the purposes of filming, the town's name on the water tower had been changed to Thalia, the fictional town in McMurtry's novel. Actually he remembered this wrong. The name on the tower was Vernal, the filmmaker's choice; the Claude High School senior class of 1962 had painted the letters on the metal. In any case, McMurtry's imagination had changed a little piece of the world.

He pulled into the parking lot of the Ramada Inn in Amarillo, where the film crew was staying. Though it was the middle of the night, cars circled the motel, kept at bay by a string of local cops. McMurtry checked in with them. One officer standing by the swimming pool said, "If it was teenagers I could see it." He nodded at the traffic. "But it ain't. It's grown women . . . hopin' Paul Newman will come out and dive off this here divin' board. Somethin' like this comes to town you find out just how crazy the public is."

"You can't stop all these women," another cop mused. "Funny thing is, I grew up in this town and I don't remember there being so many women around."

The following morning, out near the old Goodnight ranch, McMurtry met his first screenwriter, Harriet Frank, bundled up in a great hat and many veils and bandannas against the harsh North Texas wind. She and her partner, Irving Ravetch, "really didn't want me to read the script," McMurtry said. "They saw me as the Author, not as the altogether timid young man I actually was; I believe they felt that if I read the script I would inevitably feel that they were mutilating my book. I might become upset, or even start to berate them. This was unlikely, since I had more or less mutilated the book myself, before I published it."

When McMurtry first arrived on set, the director, Martin Ritt, was preparing a scene in which a cow was to kick Brandon deWilde—actually his stunt double—into a fence. The local cowhands who'd been hired to handle the animals were eager to see this, as they'd taken a mild dislike to both deWilde and his stand-in. DeWilde drove everyone crazy, complaining about all these strange local women who wanted to crawl into his bed; he said he was engaged to be married. He had scruples. The cowhands knew his scruples "were of about the consistency of toilet paper," McMurtry said. As for the stand-in, he was a local boy who'd let moviemaking go to his head. A swift kick by a cow would do him a world of good.

McMurtry admired the way deWilde and Newman looked in their Levi jackets, straw hats, chaps, and spurs. The costuming was authentic, but still they didn't quite resemble cowboys. "De Wilde [*sic*] looked like someone a millionaire oil man might invite to his ranch for a weekend," McMurtry said. "He was enjoying the fantasy that he was a real cowboy, a man of the soil, but he walked like a young executive, and showed no hint of the characteristic slouch most cowboys adopt when they are afoot. On a horse he was even worse." Newman was more observant—he had picked up "the cowboy's habit of cocking one hip higher than the other when he was standing still." He could have passed except for his startlingly blue eyes: "His look was introspected and self-occupied, though not egotistical; he simply looked more curious about himself than most young ranchers look." McMurtry found him personable and intelligent—a passionate reader.

His third day on the set, the filmmakers erected a dehorning gate, a contraption with heavy levers and bars designed to lock an animal's head in place while it received a brand or a vaccination. Naturally, animals tended to thrash wildly when led into the chutes, and it was easy for a gate operator to get his jaw broken by the levers if he didn't know what he was doing. The director was about to let his inexperienced star get seriously hurt until McMurtry suggested it was perhaps not a good idea to let Newman work the gate. This would have been a worse disaster than the buzzard incident of a few days earlier.

A scene had been planned featuring a bunch of buzzards sitting in a dried-up tree, waiting to feast on a dead heifer. The fact that the carcass was clearly a steer and not a heifer (as McMurtry pointed out) wasn't the problem; the problem was that the scene called for Newman to drive up in his Cadillac, hop out, and shoot at the birds to scare them away. The birds were not cooperating. A buzzard handler from Laredo had flown a dozen buzzards by private jet to Amarillo. The plan was to wire the birds' feet to the tree to keep them in place, and then to release them electronically when Newman fired the gun, so they'd lift majestically into open sky. Wires or no, the birds kept trying to flap free of the limbs, paying no attention to the carcass. They fell over and dangled upside down in the tree. A "bird man" had to be flown in from LA to "teach the sulky bastards how to fly," McMurtry said.

Martin Ritt (covered in cowshit, most of the shoot) appeared to be a shattered man, a man who would have done well to read a local travel guide before attempting his filmic folly: "[This] way lay only madness: the madness of the incessant howling wind[;] . . . the madness of the unbroken prairie where a man might wander aimlessly until the blistering sun and the windblown dust finally felled him; the madness of icy snow borne horizontally on the wings of a roaring gale. This was the Texas Panhandle."

By contrast, McMurtry had a fabulous time on set. He particularly enjoyed the lunches of chicken, ribs, and ham, along with the potato salad and pinto beans with chili peppers served by the 110-man crew of caterer Walter Jetton, who would later move to the White House to barbecue for Lyndon Johnson. McMurtry got a kick out of listening to the camera operators and sound men brag, between takes, about their sexual exploits in Hollywood. They were like Archer City high school kids. They thought they'd be rolling in clover once they returned to Los Angeles wearing their new Texas gear. McMurtry knew LA women would simply see them as jerks in cowboy shirts.

"I love the movie set milieu. Fascinating," he told Oppenheimer. "In fact I think Hollywood may be the place for me. It certainly cuts the university." He admitted he thought he was a spendthrift and only movie money might manage to accommodate his tastes. He praised Paul Newman and Martin Ritt. "But," he said, "I think it will be a lousy movie."

He didn't know what he'd do, but returning to the university was out of the question. He and Jo thought of moving back to Denton (where they'd once been innocent and happy) or going back to Archer City (cowboying, disagreeable though it was, beat teaching). "I dig moviemaking," he told Oppenheimer. "I think I could knock out hack novels if I had to, write movie scripts or TV if I had to, or do any kind of hack writing circumstances require. And believe me I will hack like mad . . . if it comes down to hacking or going back to teaching."

August found him, Jo, and James in San Francisco. Jo had loved the city's beauty, and McMurtry thought it a good use of his movie money to see if moving back to California might improve the chances of righting their marriage.

"San Francisco that fall hadn't changed much," Jo recalled. "Many of the . . . people [we had known] were still around. We even lived in the same house—stopped in to say hello to the landlord, and it turned out he had a vacancy. I'm surprised, looking back, at how easy it was to move around. Rents were low. Landlords didn't bother with a lease—or that was the case with [us]."

But nothing else came easily. Jo had an affair; McMurtry resumed his intimacies with Gus Guthrie and Jane Burton. Though the friendships remained chaste, conducted mostly over the phone late at night, they never-theless pulled him away from Jo, emotionally.

Tensions were high with his agent. Often, he admitted, he was "shame-fully cold and neglectful" toward Oppenheimer. "Primarily I was that way through fear of calamity if I was any other way . . . I had much on my mind, and Podge on my hands a good deal of the time. The time has not yet come, it seems, when I can love you just as a very good friend; feelings of general warmth are still complicated by thinking of you sexually, so that when presented with an opportunity for seeing you, I was frequently at odds with myself. I still don't know what to do about this—I don't think there is anything to do."

The city was its usual self, cold and foggy, fishy-smelling. McMurtry roamed the steep streets wearing a heavy green parka, a Ping-Pong paddle stuffed into his pocket.

Dispiritedly, he moved back to Archer City while Jo took James to South Carolina. "The issue [now is] whether or not to stay married," he wrote Oppenheimer. "Everybody wants me to leave Jo, but I am fairly determined not to, despite our frequent intense difficulties. Because they aren't really difficulties between us, but internal hangups which [with] sufficient doggedness and help Jo may someday resolve . . . [and] we could probably have a good life . . . She's been frightened all of her life and has not yet felt loved or secure enough to start trusting herself and other people. At least part of which is my fault. If this fear can be removed, I believe we will all profit by it; if it can't it will make me very sad."

He worried that he'd never retrieve his wife and child from her parents. Podge wouldn't be raised as a Texan—whether this was a tragedy or a bless-ing, he wasn't sure. Meanwhile, Hazel argued with her son: the trouble was, neither he nor that ridiculously thin girl of his had any religion.

In marathon phone calls, he convinced Jo to reunite with him one more time. He suggested they move to Austin—as beautiful, in its way, as San Francisco, smaller than Houston or Fort Worth, fresh territory with new people they hadn't met and one or two potentially interesting book-stores. O. Henry, who had spent some time in the city, once wrote that early settlers "killed off all the Indians between the [Texas State] lunatic asylum and the river, and laid out Austin. It has been laid out ever since," a randy mix of soap factories, racetracks, cocaine parlors, and saloons. Another of the city's early writers, Mary Lasswell, wrote that Austin "produces a feeling of being in two places at once. Skyscrapers . . . in one block, and a few blocks away an ancient wooden store with a false front high above it bears the crudely lettered words RAW FURS BOUGHT. The frontier past and the urban present . . . are separated by a very short span of time."

The Balcones Fault, an escarpment dividing the Edwards Plateau from the Coastal Plain, ran through Austin, marking, with patchy ridges of chinaberries and sycamores, the spot where the American South met the American West.

When the McMurtrys arrived there in January 1963, the city's now-famous "music scene had not appeared in more than rudimentary form, and the river had not been transformed into a series of lakes," Jo said. "But the city had lots of charm and was easy to get around in. We lived in a pleasant breezy house on Windsor Road." In the evenings they'd take James in his stroller and walk among the oaks along the banks of the Colorado River, watching light from the setting sun sparkle the surface of the water and pitch shadows among the striated sandstone cliffs. At a certain time every night, just at dusk, webs of bats lifted above the water, flying erratically from beneath a wide stone bridge to perk up among the low clouds and the dusty beards of moss draping stooped trees. James laughed with delight as the sky developed seams, rippling with crazy motion.

"Let me tell you something about McMurtry," the late writer Jan Reid said to me one night in Austin. "Until his son and grandson became noted musicians in Austin, he had this thing about the town. He hated it because his wife had done whatever she did, you know, ran off with a poet or whatever. His time here had been very unhappy and he took it out on *everyone*."

During the few months in 1963 that McMurtry and Jo tried to make Austin work for them, their marriage went from bad to worse. Neither of them had a job. They fretted over what to do for money once the movie funds ran out. McMurtry was exhausted from trying to write (often with the baby sitting in his lap as he typed). He confided to Ken Kesey, in a long letter, that he was in the "post-book dog days" when "interior intensity" dropped away precipitously. He wished he had some post holes to dig: the physical activity would help temper the edge.

He was weary, as well, from the emotional strain of his marriage. It wasn't confusion that drained him most days; he feared he saw all too well what lay ahead. "I know a good deal too much about myself," he wrote Dorothea Oppenheimer. "Self-knowledge has never been a problem." To Kesey, he expressed his worry that his married life was not going to get any better, and he praised Faye for being so generous and understanding of her husband's foibles. He said Jo was learning to drive and to play bridge: "Bridge has made her less nervous of society, and driving has made her less likely of staying anywhere long." Her eating problems—exacerbated, he was convinced, by stress—had not improved, and he feared she was often on the verge of a physical, if not a complete emotional, collapse.

He talked her into seeing a therapist and agreed to attend sessions himself. The results, he felt, were mixed. With the analyst's help, Jo was able to state her frustrations with McMurtry over what she saw as his self-denial—the quality he reacted so strongly against in his father but found himself tormented by as well. He admitted to Kesey, "I am ambivalent in marriage, frankly . . . I thought a year ago that I had opened every door in me to [Jo]. I thought, well, she doesn't want in. But perhaps there is a small secret door in the pit of my being that I absolutely won't open, which door being the only one she can get through." As for Jo, McMurtry felt "there [was] something in [her] that has never given," some obstinacy against making the "necessary surrender to the claims other people have on one's selfhood." He feared this trait might impair her nurturing capacities. "There has been tension in her relationship with Podge that is much harder to handle than any tension between her and me," he told Kesey. Her withdrawal from the child (McMurtry believed) made him "smother" Podge in father. Ultimately, he saw his wife as waging "a really massive (and really admirable) rebellion" against her conservative upbringing, one that she had "carried out with considerable integrity, so that really knuckling into marriage is almost an abandonment of barricades she has defended for a good long time now." He understood her need to rebel, even if it caused him anguish—besides which, his greatest anguish "grew out of the bitter realization of how smoothly and coyly life and one's own ignorance traps one in situations which hammer incessantly at one's nature . . . It is nothing to cry about," he concluded, "but to learn from."

His personal anxieties were sharpened by professional pressures—namely, the desire not to fail with his second book, to establish himself as a writer for the long haul. With the exception of Kesey, most of his old Stanford cronies were having little success with their sophomore efforts, and Leggett, he felt, had been much too resistant to *Leaving Cheyenne* in its early stages. His friendship with Kesey buzzed with competitive energy; wryly he wrote: "Noted your paperback [for *Cuckoo's Nest*], which was more attractive than mine. Mine, though, has a more sexual cover, with Pat Neal's bosom for the heteros and Paul Newman, looking like one magazine's Playmate of the Month—even to the bulge in the jeans—for the homos. I trust you've got a Why Hud sticker for your car; they're all over [the place] down here. Very freakish advertising." (In preparing for the upcoming release of the movie *Hud*, Paramount had flooded the nation with bumper stickers reading "Why Hud?" a deliberately mysterious phrase intended to stoke word of mouth. Leggett wrote to tell McMurtry he had seen them in all the subway cars in New York.)

"I suppose it's the bookman in me, or the scholar, or perhaps the ironist, but I get a strange quiver now and then, thinking how odd all our letters are going to look a hundred years from now, solidly bound in brown university press binding, sitting on the shelves of doctoral candidate carrels," McMurtry wrote Kesey. "All these scandals and heartbreaks passing before the eyes of graduate students." The thought amused him, but he *did* have an inkling—or the confidence to believe—that he and Kesey, and perhaps a few more of their peers, had a chance of adding something important to the American literary canon. "I can tell you and mean it that I think you have as much talent as any writer I know," McMurtry wrote his pal.

But already Kesey was making noises about abandoning literature and staging Happenings instead (whatever those were). He had begun to think the world was too absurd for the stately grace of novels. His thinking had changed when his friend Ken Babbs was recruited into the army in 1962 to become one of the first military advisors in Vietnam, flying helicopter sorties over a conflict that made no sense even then. "[I] had no perception of the right or wrong of the situation before I went into Vietnam, but it took about six weeks to realize we were wasting our time there," Babbs told Kesey. So Bob Stone, with his crazy Communist talk—he had been *right,* muttering all that subversive shit on Perry Lane late at night. Now Kesey wanted to shake up the world at a faster pace than he figured fiction writing would allow.

McMurtry tried to keep him fixed on the task at hand: "I do hate to think of you giving up writing, or even to hear you talk about it," he said. "Except for Faye and your kids it's the best thing you have, or are likely to have . . . I don't think you have come anywhere near doing yourself justice as a fiction-writer. If you think you have you are probably listening to your press or your disciples, not your peers." He said Kesey's work had "beautiful things" in it, as well as "holes you can drive a tractor through. If you have any love for writing you can't afford to quit, Ken; you haven't done enough. You haven't told what's happened . . . You've [not] embedded enough of your spirit in a book [so] that [future readers] can respond to it, can feel what a guy Ken Kesey must have been."

Aiming for the long haul, indeed.

Yet he wondered, was he in any position to offer advice? Once more he felt ambivalent, one week complaining to his agent that his editor didn't respect his literary integrity, the next deciding he'd rather just pump out tripe for Hollywood (if it meant not teaching). But no, Hollywood didn't pay enough for all the hassles involved . . .

He dragged his short stories out of a drawer and personally walked them to the offices of *Texas Quarterly* on the University of Texas campus. There he met an attractive young editor named Betty Burkhalter. His interest in her quickly superseded his interest in publishing stories in the magazine, though she took the pages and said she'd have a look. He thanked her and quietly left.

Every day, his brain whirled from migraines to mental storms, spinning out ideas to keep the literary world interested in him. To Leggett he proposed editing an anthology of western short stories. He'd feature some of his friends, Kesey and Grover Lewis, and an obscure young writer he'd met through Oppenheimer named Dave Deck, who was trying to be an American Kafka but was mostly practiced at "sitting at a bar drinking beer," Oppenheimer said. He also floated the notion of doing a book on rodeo. The anthology didn't intrigue Leggett, but he leapt at the rodeo suggestion. This was right up his young author's alley. Immediately, Leggett was ready to offer a contract, to connect McMurtry with professional photographers who'd supply pictures for his text. McMurtry developed an ambitious schedule: over a period of six months, he'd follow the professional rodeo circuit from Laramie, Wyoming, to Calgary to Salinas to Pendleton, Oregon, to San Francisco to LA to Dallas and New York. He'd cover the history of rodeo, its rituals, its cultural legacy, its major stars (Larry Mahan, Casey Tibbs, and the great Todd Whatley, who carried off $9,000 in prize money in 1947).

Before he even hit the road, though, he confessed to Oppenheimer: "I can not be quite sure yet that my real motive for wanting to do a rodeo book is not just wanting to get out and drive to . . . interesting places."

Sure enough, his commitment to the project quickly waned when he encountered the realities of the modern-day circuit. In 1974, he would publish an essay on rodeo suggesting why he never wrote the book. For one thing, it was altogether too jarring to catch a whiff of cowshit while riding up an escalator in Madison Square Garden. This was a scent belonging to prairie and open skies, not to steel and rubber and glass. He might have had a Proustian reverie in New York—remembering tumbling off the edge of the ranch-house porch at the age of three into his first cow pat—if escalators permitted Proustian reveries, but their constant motion and scary flattening steps prevented meditative pleasures. The next disorienting incident was the singing of "America the Beautiful" by a white-hatted, sequined young girl obviously meant to represent American Purity but whose showbiz, sexed-up version of the song suggested she was the Fruited Plain instead—all while a somber little boy waved an American flag in a searing spotlight and slowly approached her as if entreating the Madonna. The girl had entered the arena on a snow-white horse. "If that horse had shown up in a cow camp someone would have summarily whacked him on the head with an axe, it being a well-known Western fact that cattle are deathly afraid of white horses and will instantly gather themselves and dash over the nearest precipice if exposed to one," McMurtry wrote.

And the hot dogs tasted like grout.

As much as Hollywood Westerns, the modern-day rodeo romanticized the restless drifter, the bull rider traveling from city to city, singled out in the white-hot spots as embodying the traditional values of hard work and patriotism when in fact he was akin to a circus performer, a journeyman with few commitments anywhere. The *real* hard workers, the real traditionalists, were the ranchers, the settlers on the edges of what were fast becoming ghost towns in middle America—"men," McMurtry wrote, "who have lived in one place, loved the West and its ideals, and increased only in despair—as the oil industry ruined their grass, as the air and water grew foul, as the land taxes rose so high they could not afford to stock their acreage, as their politics became meaningless, their life styles scorned and then parodied, their children drawn away to the cities and there subverted. In these men one finds a love of the Old and a hatred of the New so passionate and intense it makes the beery rebelliousness of rodeo cowboys seem like half-hearted posturing, which is what it usually is."

Surely he was thinking of his father when he wrote: "Real cattle people are sad now, with something of the sadness of gorillas. Like gorillas they may become truculent and make noises to scare interlopers away, but in reality they are a breed in retreat, with a deeply ingrained sense of their own doom. They would be glad to just get out of the way, if there was only some place that civilization didn't want, but there is no such place." The escalators had covered every polished inch of the available floor space.

Leggett was disappointed when McMurtry told him there would be no rodeo book, but he took the news in stride: "I think if you discover you don't like an idea in a 4000 mile drive, they are 4000 miles well driven. And there is no question but what you should concentrate on fiction."

One morning, on a rural highway back in deep Central Texas, Mc-Murtry was cruising along at about a hundred miles an hour when he came upon "one of those strange, inexplicably remote traffic lights [one is] always encountering in Texas, miles from anywhere." A couple of cowboys were standing by the side of the road, staring at an obviously broken-down pickup. They were suspicious of McMurtry, whose hair had grown rather long on the road, but they accepted a ride from him, anyway, into a gas station in the next town. Climbing into the car, the younger of the two boys shook his head. "Ort not to of tried to go nowhere this mornin', nohow," he said. McMurtry's sentiments, precisely, concerning his four-thousand-mile trek chasing a vague rodeo dream.

Austin was lousy with writers, but few of them had made any headway with New York editors. In 1961, when *The New Yorker* ran a two-piece article on the "Super-American State" of Texas, it didn't turn to a Texan, but to an outside reporter who spent only nine months in and around Dallas, mostly. John Bainbridge wrote: "[T]he so-called American Dream . . . come[s] true . . . in Texas," and "The life-style in Texas is marked by bravado, zest, optimism, and ebullience." He might as well have spent his nine months watching Hollywood Westerns. Any one of two dozen or more writers sitting around Austin's Scholz Garten at night, where artists, journalists, and a few liberal state legislators gathered to debate whether LBJ was the devil incarnate or a secret angel, could have written a more cogent profile of the Lone Star State than Bainbridge had. There was Willie Morris, firebrand journalist, future editor of *Harper's*. Every year he threw a party to announce the winners of his annual Neanderthal Awards, given to the dumbest, most inept Texas congresspeople. The competition was always fierce. "Shoot fire, Willie, I've read *Prowst* and all them," a legislator was overheard at one such party, trailing Morris to impress him with his great intelligence. There was Ronnie Dugger, a rare independent voice in Texas journalism. He edited *The Texas Observer* under the credo "We will serve no group or party but will hew hard to the truth as we find it and the right as we see it"—which pissed off just about everybody in the capitol building. McMurtry admired these men and spent time with them both in the Scholz Garten, and he met a group of writers who called themselves the Mad Dogs. Eventually they'd distinguish themselves as sports reporters or long-form magazine authors: among them, Bud Shrake, Gary Cartwright, and Jay Milner. Milner tooled around Austin in a black 1949 Cadillac hearse he'd bought for seventy-five dollars at a used car lot in Dallas—a good novelistic detail, McMurtry thought. The Mad Dogs prided themselves on being outlaws, of sorts: creative people in an environment where the arts were generally held in low esteem, young urbanites in a place still professing to cling to rural values. "We exaggerated the cadence and flatness of our Texas accents and articulations, especially when in the company of those we somewhat snidely regarded as being on the pompous side," Milner said. Their writings were also stamped by an ironic, stylized Texanness, a break from the seriousness of their forebears Dobie, Webb, and Bedichek. Their reigning hero was a young man named Billy Lee Brammer who had published, in the same year *Horseman, Pass By* appeared, a novel called *The Gay Place,* featuring an unforgettable fictional portrait of Lyndon Johnson, for whom Brammer had worked as an aide in both Texas and Washington, DC. The novel had not been a huge commercial success, but its impact on the Austin literati was immeasurable; unlike the two other notable Texas books of its time—McMurtry's novel and John Graves's *Goodbye to a River*—it did not look to the past. Shrake said that reading *The Gay Place* "was the first time I'd ever realized that you could write about us, and what we were doing, and modern-day Texas, and have anybody in New York publish it . . . Billy Lee, I think, showed a whole generation of us that our lives were actually publishable."

Since writing his book, Brammer had become a rather reluctant mentor to the Mad Dogs. Already he had developed the amphetamine addiction that would lead to his death by overdose in 1978. His self-destructive tendencies weren't helped by his acolytes, offering him every stimulant available just to get near him. McMurtry was not impressed by the Mad Dog scene—it did not escape him that they talked about writing a lot more than they wrote—but Brammer *did* interest him a good deal, not just because he admired *The Gay Place,* but because Brammer, a likable and generous fellow, had become a cult figure the way Grover Lewis and Ken Kesey had. He was yet another example of the warping effects even local literary celebrity could have on a personality not strong enough to resist its lures, none of which were conducive to producing written pages. The difference with Brammer was, he didn't invite disciples. He was astonished to find himself so revered, and not entirely comfortable with the situation. He was struggling to write a second novel in the midst of the high jinks around him, and McMurtry watched him closely as a cautionary tale. One night, Brammer sat alone on the floor in a corner of his house, sipping a longneck Dr Pepper while a party blazed around him. He looked up with a sheepish grin when a friend walked in. Solemnly he asked, "Am I this much fun?"

Hud arrived in the movie houses in mid-April, a year after John Ford's subversive Western *The Man Who Shot Liberty Valance* and seven months before the Kennedy assassination in Dallas. The 1960s as a distinct cultural period were about to come into their own. Eerily, *Liberty Valance* appeared to anticipate some of the confusion surrounding Kennedy's killing and the country's growing anti-government sentiment. Ford seemed to have sniffed something in the air. The movie—about corruption at the heart of democracy—centers on an unscrupulous politician (Jimmy Stewart) whose career flourishes when he is credited with killing a villain (Lee Marvin). The villain was actually shot by a roughhewn cowboy played by John Wayne. The plot involves a lengthy official investigation into the shooting contrasted with what really occurred; a line from the script, "When the legend becomes fact, print the legend," could well have applied to media coverage of JFK and Vietnam.

The nation's always skeptical view of Texas would darken even further after the events of November 22, 1963.

Appearing between *Liberty Valance* and the grassy knoll, Paul Newman as the scoundrel Hud charmed national audiences. Much to the studio's surprise (Paramount executives almost canceled the film, fearing it would bomb), the movie was a critical and commercial hit—"this year's most powerful film," said Bosley Crowther in *The New York Times*, "as wide and profound a contemplation of the human condition as one of the New England plays of Eugene O'Neill . . . [catching] the whole raw-boned atmosphere of a land and environment lying between nature and cheap urbanity, between the vastness of yesterday's open country and the closeness of the claptrap of tomorrow." It was nominated for seven Oscars. Patricia Neal and Melvyn Douglas received acting awards, and James Wong Howe won for his cinematography. In print, McMurtry later disparaged the film for the same reasons he dismissed his novel—too sentimental, he said. But at the time, in letters to friends, he declared himself quite pleased with it.

The filmmakers were profoundly uneasy with the general audience's reaction to the movie. Like John Ford, the makers caught the zeitgeist— but that's not what they were aiming for. Martin Ritt, an Old Left director who'd been blacklisted in 1952 for his apparent Communist leanings, was surprised to hear critics calling *Hud* a genre-busting Western in the mold of *Liberty Valance*. Following McMurtry's novel (as *he'd* read it), he'd intended a social drama warning about the dire consequences of ignoring traditional American values. He meant Homer to be the embodiment of social responsibility and Hud, boozing, womanizing, and scheming, the personification of hateful narcissism, the breakdown of society; as critic Pauline Degenfelder parsed the story: "The outbreak of hoof-and-mouth disease coincides with Hud's ascendancy, suggesting that he is a sick animal and an infection in the state . . . [H]is emblem is the Cadillac, at times suggestive of a hearse, for Hud is death-inducing."

"We felt the country was moving into a kind of self-absorption, indulgence, and greed," said screenwriters Ravetch and Frank: they shaped the character of Hud to reveal the dangers ahead. "[I]t was a terrible shock to . . . us," then, Ravetch admitted, when audiences cheered Hud rather than rebuking him. "Here's a man . . . who tries to rape his housekeeper, who wants to sell his neighbors poisoned cattle, and who stops at nothing to take control of his father's property. And all the time, he's completely unrepentant. Then, at the first screenings, the preview cards asked the audiences, 'Which character did you most admire?' and many of them answered, 'Hud.' We were completely astonished."

Superficially, there was a simple explanation: Paul Newman was so beautiful, so charismatic, that he was irresistible, no matter how badly his character behaved. Too, for the sake of appealing to a general audience,

Ravetch and Frank had knocked off a few of the character's corners (he behaves much worse in McMurtry's novel). But the subtler truth is, young moviegoers embraced Hud as a western variant of the Rebel Without a Cause. McMurtry had transcended regionalism; in an exchange between Homer and Hud, he'd captured the essence of the generation gap: "What the hell do you want? I don't doubt I treated you hard, and I don't doubt I made some mistakes," Homer says. Hud replies, "You're too old to know what I want. You always were." The movie caught the gist of a tension central to the sixties, and the audience sided with Hud. In spouting weary platitudes, Homer was as "prating and tedious as Polonius," Pauline Kael said. When Homer asserts his social conscience, refusing to sell his diseased cattle to unknowing neighbors and "risk startin' a epidemic," Hud responds like Abbie Hoffman damning the System: "Why, this whole country is run on epidemics, where you been?"—meaning tax dodges, price-fixing, graft. The stark imagery of the cattle herded into a pit to be shot, echoing photographs of mass exterminations in Nazi Germany (not so distant to 1960s audiences), reinforced the idea that Hud's rebellion against the Old Ways was perfectly justified.

Among critics, only Pauline Kael seemed to grasp the country's "Divided Heart," and the inevitable reaction to *Hud*: "[It is] just possibly the most completely schizoid movie produced anywhere anytime," she wrote in *Film Quarterly*. "*Hud* is a commercial Hollywood movie that is ostensibly an indictment of materialism . . . But those who made it protected their material interest in the film so well that they turned it into the opposite: a celebration and glorification of materialism—of the man who looks out for himself—which probably appeals to movie audiences just because it confirms their own feelings. This response to *Hud* may be the only time the general audience has understood film-makers better than they understood themselves. Audiences ignored the cant of the makers' liberal, serious intentions, and enjoyed the film for its vital element: the nihilistic 'heel' who wants the good things of life and doesn't give a damn for the general welfare."

Said Martin Ritt: "I got a lot of letters after that picture from kids saying Hud was right. The old man's a jerk . . . And if I'd been near as smart as I thought I was, I would have seen that Haight-Ashbury was right around the corner. The kids were very cynical; they were committed to their own appetites . . . That's why the film did the kind of business it did—the kids loved Hud. That son of a bitch that I hated they loved. So the audience makes a film their own—it depends what's going on at the time in the country."

On the 22nd of May, after a month of increasing franticness, Jo left suddenly," McMurtry reported to Oppenheimer. "She left with a poet, but I can't attach too much consequence to him. If it hadn't been him, it would have been somebody else. I expect his reign will be of fairly short duration, though I could be wrong. Perhaps subliminally she was paying me back for . . . you. Which I realize now was a quite heinous thing to do to a female as insecure and unconfident as Jo is, and probably damaged her more than any single thing I ever did. However, there is no use sinking into remorse at this point. And as I say, I may be wrong about the poet; one doesn't want to under-rate poets."

Jo had flown to Albany, New York, where she had close friends, leaving McMurtry alone with the baby, whom he no longer addressed as Podge. The new circumstances seemed to have brought the child into sharper focus for the young father. The boy was now, indisputably, Jamie. Jo's therapist advised McMurtry to give her time, leave her alone, so as not to push her into a complete breakdown: "Of course I am quite worried about her, and don't think she has much chance of coming through this without some kind of collapse . . . And of course, I simply miss her a great deal. It's strange that two people who do genuinely care for one another as much as Jo and I do could have done such a miserable job of loving. I suppose ignorance was as much to blame as anything."

He felt he no longer had any friends in Texas; he worried about cash; his father had been diagnosed with rheumatoid arthritis and faced the possibility of confinement in a wheelchair. The only bright spot was the movie: "It is better than the book, really, and is only weak where the book was weak."

As a result of the film's success, he received an offer from Rice to teach two classes over a period of nine months for an annual salary of $7,500. It was a good offer, but he couldn't see himself raising Jamie alone in Houston. Plus, he feared if he had that much money, he'd only spend it on books.

To his (rare) delight, he'd discovered the Brick Row Book Shop in Austin, above a drugstore called Faulkner's on the corner of Guadalupe and 24th, one of the few places that dispelled his blues. He'd take Jamie there of an afternoon and browse among the musty shelves while classical music or Fats Waller played on a phonograph in the proprietor's office. The proprietor was a slow human basset hound from Cuero, Texas, named Franklin Gilliam, who'd moved the store from New York in 1954. Gilliam loved spending his mornings drinking tea in his bathrobe and ending his days with martinis and two or three bottles of wine. In between, Brick Row customers often found a note taped to the door: "Back at 3:30." Long lunches and baseball were also among Gilliam's passions.

"You speak my language, white man," he told McMurtry one day when McMurtry brought in a box of books and said he wanted credit, not cash, for them. At Brick Row, he bought his first penny dreadful, nineteenth-century pulp fiction along the lines of *Sweeney Todd, the Demon Barber of Fleet Street.* He brought it home and sealed it off in his part of the Windsor Street house, along with his other books and Jamie's toys. He did so because he had invited Billy Lee Brammer, whose wife had also left him, to live in the other part of the house. McMurtry was not trying to escape Brammer, whom he quite liked, but Brammer's groupies. As a local cultural hero, "he was a natural target for anyone in Austin who was aspiring, frustrated, or bored," McMurtry observed. The sycophants included unloved wives, "proto-hippies with beach balls full of laughing gas . . . bitter young journalists who looked like they had been using themselves for blotters," and UT professors more interested in sleeping with students than securing tenure, among them John Sullivan, a Liverpudlian and a regular at Scholz's. He became a model for McMurtry's character Godwin Lloyd-Jons in his novel *All My Friends Are Going to Be Strangers*—an English prof who refers to undergraduate girls as "fuckists."

McMurtry admired the way Brammer tolerated grasping, needy people "with the courteous and rather melancholy patience with which he would probably face a buffalo herd." He could not have done it himself. Austin, he concluded, was an "adolescent" place, obsessed "with its own pubic hair, and [gripped by] a corresponding uneasy fear that its sexual development might stop just short of adequate." His animosity toward the city only deepened in time. Like John Bainbridge (but with far more expertise), he would soon accept magazine assignments to write about Texas. In *The Atlantic*, in 1975, he said of Austin: "It is a dismal, third-rate university town . . . I don't believe it can claim a single first-rate artistic talent, in any art."

"Billy Lee was wounded by that *Atlantic* piece," Jan Reid recalled. "Absolutely wounded. It was a direct and unprovoked attack on him, and everybody in Austin knew it. People were mortified on his behalf."

Why McMurtry's disdain for Brammer's groupies eventually attached to the man himself was never clear: disappointment, perhaps, that Brammer allowed his talent to become so distracted; competiveness; the fact that both men briefly shared an interest in the same woman while they were living together—a young lady named Janie Butterfield, whom Brammer accused of plagiarizing his notebooks for stories she was writing.

In 2015, McMurtry told me, "I didn't know [Billy Lee] well, but I knew him well enough to know he wasn't going to make it."

With Janie out of the picture, he turned his attention again to Miss Burkhalter at the *Texas Quarterly*. He had never been strictly committed to monogamy, but now, in letters to Kesey, he declared he had absolutely come down on the side of free love: "I hope you never learn to keep it in your pants," he wrote his friend. "I would love to see you get away with a lifetime of irresponsible screwing, & think the good causes would be served if you could." But his bark was fiercer than his bite. On the phone to Betty Burkhalter, he was actually rather shy, asking about the status of his stories, of which there was no news. "In all the rambling I forgot to ask her for the date, but it's just as well," he told Oppenheimer. "I am not very social anyway these days."

He said he was more in love with Jo than ever, feeling guilty, and losing confidence "in [his] ability to make people happy."

And then—of all folks—his roaming pal Kesey cautioned him not to abandon his marriage: "I have always feared divorce," Kesey admitted. "[B]rought up to believe that it was about as sinful a situation as one could get into. Then I got brainwashed and changed my mind. Now I sometimes think I'm changing back . . . I'm sure if you divorce Jo that you can find a woman who will make you a better wife and your son a better mother, but I'm not so sure you can ever find another person who will be so much a part of you." He said he and Faye experienced deeper tensions in their marriage than their friends could ever know, but "I would never dissolve the relationship . . . no more than I would pluck out an offending eyeball."

The sexual revolution was turning out to be a "one step forward, one step back" affair.

McMurtry had no post holes to dig, but he did turn to physical activity to relieve his depression, building a small "fence to protect the traffic from my child," he told Oppenheimer. In July he reported to her that he'd taken the Rice job: "No choice. Move to Houston early August. I'm sure this will finish me on Texas for a long time; next year, if I do get a movie sale or can afford it [he had optioned *Leaving Cheyenne*], I plan to move more or less permanently to a house in the Berkeley hills. I wish I could move there now . . . I don't think writing for money is necessarily the genius-killer it's sometimes made out to be."

And then on September 5, he wrote Oppenheimer a brief, surprising note: "Jo is back. Things have been hectic and sometimes perilous but I much prefer the perils of having her here to the blankness of not, and I think with luck we will all come through finally, if only to old age."

Houston had changed a good bit since 1960," Jo said. "Air conditioning had become almost universal. Houses mostly had window units, chug-chugging but effective, and large buildings were like refrigerators. What people talked about in these cool places, or outdoors when the weather allowed, was often the space program, which preoccupied the town. Then, the Rice campus was close to the hospitals on Main Street, where Dr. DeBakey and Dr. Cooley were getting started on heart transplants and artificial hearts and thus becoming a subject of conversation in the Rice coffee shop. The brand-new Astrodome was a great wonder—one could even watch polo games—and the nearby Warwick Hotel had a transparent elevator that floated up and down outside the building. Anybody could just walk through the lobby and ride the elevator. Then there were the suburban shopping centers, a new idea at the time. And LP albums—the Beatles, Bob Dylan, the Swingle Singers, sometimes live concerts—Peter, Paul, and Mary. Clothes were zippety-zap. In other words, it was now what people think of as the sixties."

The couple rented a two-story brick house on a shady avenue, Quenby Street, near the Rice campus, and offered their garage to Billy Lee Brammer; turning on, dropping out, he was drifting further from the mainstream. "[W]ith the use of many blankets, [he] made himself an air-conditioned cubicle," McMurtry said. Brammer's wife, Nadine, was trying to serve him with divorce papers. The sheriff would come around, looking for him. McMurtry would chat with the sheriff, distracting him, while Brammer hid beneath quilts inside the garage. After a few months, Brammer settled back—into greater and greater obscurity—in Austin. His decline was painful and slow, the snuffing of a talent many observers felt might have produced Texas's version of F. Scott Fitzgerald. In point of fact, if one believed lessons could be learned from the times, the 1960s suggested that if a great novelist was ever to emerge from Texas, the nurturing womb would not be incandescence and fame but the quiet doggedness of a writer like Larry McMurtry.

"I can imagine just how intense the agony must be for all the good people in Texas," Jack Leggett wrote McMurtry on November 29, 1963, following the assassination of John F. Kennedy Jr. McMurtry agreed "it was about the worst," and had "sunk this area, or at least my part of it, into a deep unlocalized gloom." But it was too painful to think about, and (unlike most other Texas writers, who were scrambling to comment) he "wouldn't want to write about it for twenty years or so." Indeed, he was sorely preoccupied with personal affairs. He told Dorothea Oppenheimer he and Jo "were driving [their] analyst crazy." The Waddingtons were still around; the resumption of the friendship was awkward. And, he said, "I loathe teaching."

The school had changed its name from Rice Institute to Rice University in 1960, pumping resources into developing new programs, particularly in the humanities, where it had lagged, and hiring personnel to become a first-rate research institution. The old-guard science teachers considered the literature profs second-class citizens; a siege mentality gripped the English department. Among McMurtry's colleagues were Walter Isle, whom he had known briefly at Stanford, a pioneer in the study of environmental literature, and Gerald O'Grady, a medievalist who fell under the sway of Marshall McLuhan and, with the support of Jean and Dominique de Menil, developed a major film and media center on the campus of Houston's private St. Thomas University. (Rice failed to promote him because he was an outspoken critic of the school's institutional racism.)

One day, O'Grady arranged for a young undergraduate named Mike Evans to meet McMurtry in the English department's faculty lounge. O'Grady believed Evans had literary talent; he should meet a "real novelist." "I met Larry and Jo and James in the lounge and we had lunch," Evans recalled. "I was not awed by him. He didn't look like what you'd think of as a writer." His belt didn't run through all the loops in his pants. "He had this black curly hair in a kind of Texas pompadour. He looked like Buddy Holly. Heavy glasses. I don't remember what we talked about, but I thought he was really cool. What I remember of that lunch was watching James crawl around the floor."

Evans, who was thin and slight, with a sweep of blond bangs across his forehead, was about to spend a year in Cambridge, studying philosophy. When he returned from overseas, he took McMurtry's creative writing class along with his housemates, William Broyles and Greg Curtis. The three boys shared a duplex on Westheimer up the street from Trash and Treasure, where McMurtry often found book bargains. None of them had any particular educational direction when they first applied to Rice. They went because it was free. Swayed by the young new "all-star faculty"— especially by McMurtry, Curtis said—the trio plunged into writing and books and never looked back. Evans was a precocious writer of fiction ("Kind of a phenomenon. He had read more than any other student," according to Curtis); Broyles, from the refinery hub of nearby Baytown, leaned toward journalism and nonfiction; and Curtis, who'd grown up in Kansas City, was "somewhere in between," Broyles said. McMurtry took them all under his wing. And it was a fortuitous time to be young in Houston. "It was still a southern city. The tallest building was the Humble Building, which you can't even see in the skyline now," Broyles said. "It was so accessible, no traffic, no flooding. It still had a postwar feel." He had worked as an usher in Rice Stadium on September 12, 1962, the day John F. Kennedy announced, "We choose to go to the moon," ensuring that, seven years later, "Houston" would be one of the first words uttered from another planetary body.

"I loved Houston. I didn't know I loved it, but I loved it," Curtis said. "It was beginning to stretch out and be more comfortable with its identity. There were writers, there were artists, there were book collectors. And Larry was a key figure in the development of all that."

One late afternoon, McMurtry dropped by the boys' duplex. The floor was littered with pizza boxes and beer cans; grocery carts were stuffed with unwashed clothes. "I have seen undergraduate squalor in San Francisco. I have seen undergraduate squalor on the Lower East Side in New York. But I have never seen undergraduate squalor like this," McMurtry said.

Probably they are hopeless, he thought.

"Larry didn't think you could do much for younger writers except give them a reading list," Evans said. "He handed out a four-page list. Not just fiction, but travel books, anthropology . . . whatever he had found useful or interesting. His class was not particularly productive. He'd bring in stuff to read to us, like Richard Brautigan's [*A Confederate General from*] *Big Sur* or Gogol's 'The Nose.' But mostly he'd tell us about Gogol and how on his deathbed, the physician was trying to reduce the swelling by putting leeches on his nose. Larry said Gogol died whimpering because of the leeches. That was the sort of thing that interested him. And he gave us a bit of literary gossip, about Kesey and others."

"He was mildly discouraging," Curtis recalled. "He didn't come down hard, but it was rare to please him. I'm not sure anyone ever did. You wanted his approval. You thought, *Where am I failing? What can I do?*"

Broyles said, "I went to a KKK rally once and wrote about it. While I was there, I ran into an old high school friend of mine. He took off his hood. You know: 'What are *you* doing here?' I wrote it straight, not as a short story. Larry picked it up and said, 'Well, let's take a look. Your fiction sucks. But if you write nonfiction, you might not starve.' That was the highest compliment I ever got from him."

The boys learned from McMurtry's example, not from his direct mentorship. They watched him closely, to see how a writer moved through the world. "He made it all seem so easy. Very laconic. Very much an observer," Broyles said. "When you're young, you don't know how you're going to go from getting an education to partaking in creativity to having a career, but he seemed to be doing it so effortlessly, and with great discipline. He was not that much older than we were, but he didn't act as if he was above us."

"He wasn't even thirty yet!" Curtis said, marveling. "He was exploring things himself. I was so aware of my own quest that it didn't occur to me that he was on a quest, too. He was so remarkably attuned to the culture."

He'd invite the boys to Quenby Street. Cicadas sang in the grass; they heard the distant sounds of sirens and inhaled the funky bayou smell. The boys would have dinner with McMurtry, Jo, and Jamie. "I thought Jo was fantastic," Broyles said. "Ahead of her time. So free-spirited. Barefoot, a hippie. She would have fit on Kesey's Magic Bus. Larry had this room in the house . . . pool table [he'd traded a book dealer an old car for it], movie posters, French films." A *Casablanca* poster; a poster of W. C. Fields studying a fan of cards in his hand; a picture of the Beatles. A floor-to-ceiling bookcase featuring the Russians and Thomas Hardy. Upstairs, the pornography room: Betty Page bound and gagged, *Sheena, Queen of the Jungle.* "We'd all watch the late movies on TV"—*The Maltese Falcon, The Treasure of the Sierra Madre* (from which Jamie named his pet turtle Fred C. Dobbs)—"and then, at midnight, the station would go off," Broyles recalled. "The jet fighter planes would fly past on the screen and they'd play 'The Star-Spangled Banner.'"

"There was one moment I witnessed," Curtis said. "Larry always wrote on yellow paper. I remember once he showed us this big pile of yellow paper, a novel manuscript, and Jo said something like, 'There's Larry walling himself off from the world with his pile of paper.' It was the only discordant moment I ever saw between them." He thought perhaps it explained the rare night he saw McMurtry indulging in alcohol—two or three rum and Cokes.

Evans was also aware of McMurtry's "tinge of melancholy." His "voice was soft . . . and though he often spoke with amusement, especially when it came to the sexual peccadilloes of his friends, there was an edge of sadness in his talk, an undertone of melancholy, as if the people he was remembering were from a world lost to him," Evans said. "Larry was the most affable of men and could be a merry companion, but I think in his mind he was always alone."

McMurtry was working on a rodeo novel now, using the observations from his travels on the circuit to construct another elegiac fiction, but with a more contemporary setting this time. He was also considering a collection of nonfiction pieces on modern-day Texas—spurred, perhaps, by John Bainbridge's wan example. He was thinking of including a profile of Billy Lee Brammer and his time with LBJ. He wanted to write a meditation on movies and small towns. He'd call *that* piece "The Last Picture Show."

"He had models—European models—for the kind of literary figure he wanted to be," Curtis remembered him saying. "He said his books came from other books."

Money continued to be a worry. Jamie—vivid, verbal—cost more than he had anticipated. McMurtry had tried to interest Ravetch and Frank in composing a screenplay for *Leaving Cheyenne*. They were not compelled by the novel. Discouraged, he urged Oppenheimer and Harper & Row to make some sort of deal with Hollywood: "Movie money is just the kind of unreal money I like to spend," he told his agent. But despite *Hud*'s success nothing developed.

Some relief arrived in the spring when he received a Guggenheim Fellowship, but by then sex had—once again—replaced financial strain as the major source of marital discontent. After all this time, McMurtry still could not accept that physical intimacy did not always remove barriers between two people, allowing them access to the most secret parts of each other and establishing foolproof bonds. Jo teased him for his "clean-cut" approach to lovemaking. He insisted on believing that if they tried hard enough, they'd reach a blissful plateau from which there'd be no return to the gritty world. The burden of this belief muffled spontaneous enjoyment—as did Houston's heat and humidity. Sometimes the couple sprinkled water on the sheets to cool the bed before touching. Torpid and groggy, they'd fall together like a pair of wilted fronds.

One of his descriptions of Houston, from the fiction he was developing out of the rodeo material, imagined the city as an ideal lover: "[I loved] her heat, her dampness, her sumpy smells. She wasn't beautiful, but neither was I. I liked her . . . looseness . . . [that was] her substance, and if she had been cool and dry and odorless I wouldn't have cared to live with her." Houston offered the "kind of gentleness" he never felt with his wife, he wrote, and he imagined walking and stroking "[the city's] shoulder for an hour or two, in the night." Such abstractions were easier to cherish than the day-to-day presence of another human being in a claustrophobic space, expressing needs and irritations.

He feared the sourness of his marriage was causing him to write unpleasantly of Texas and of sex. The novel's "sexual confusion . . . [its] frank talk and . . . ticklish issues" would probably offend the prim folks at Harper's, he said to Oppenheimer; and he couldn't believe how "dreadfully hard" he was being on his home state. "I love Texas, and am surprised at my own venom . . . I shall be hated, disbelieved. I may have to move to California."

Things are hellish. Jo has really almost cracked up, her worst time in years, and despite two hours of analysis a week it is hit or miss yet whether she will have to be hospitalized or not. I fear she may," McMurtry wrote Oppenheimer on March 5, 1964. He was sending her letters every week— sometimes more than one. "I am really I suppose writing to keep sane."

Two weeks later, he reported, "I am afraid Jo is reaching the point where she cannot support much responsibility. I have had no hope for a long time that our marriage could be saved." In his exhaustion, he sounded a familiar cultural note: that of the married man trying to seduce a woman—*Trust me, my marriage is really over.* And he *had* flirted with

Oppenheimer. Occasionally, still, he dropped hints in his letters that he'd like to rendezvous with her in Denver or Dallas.

And she responded, probably much as he hoped: "[Y]ou have nothing to feel guilty about. I mean, one simply can't go on indefinitely protecting people from coping with what psychiatrists call reality . . . American men, in particular, are absolutely smothered by guilt. It is a national phenomenon. I don't know how they get that way, but if you find out anything let me know." "Be good to yourself (but you never will be)," she said.

He did not discuss his own failings in the relationship with Jo—the "sexual confusion" he was writing about so freely in his fiction—nor did he mention how well Jo got along whenever she separated from him. Instead, he concentrated on her need for "heavy therapy" and his stoic bearing under unfair circumstances: "I have been reading the Fitzgerald letters during all this, very gallant documents, and helpful. He had a genius for not feeling sorry for himself and I think has helped me to realize that really nothing is sloppier, weaker, or less justified than self-pity." It is not hard to read this as an indictment of Jo's behavior, a recoil from her refusal to be the stony pioneer woman, the "gallant" figure going silently, uncomplainingly about her morning chores. Nor is it hard to imagine a male therapist in 1964, hoping to project professionalism, siding with a rational-seeming husband against a "free-spirited," sexually frustrated woman suffering stress (perhaps long-term postpartum depression) and trying to avoid staring, as it were, at a patch of yellow wallpaper.

Jo took a place on her own nearby. Jamie stayed with his dad—a "complicated decision but one that made for the least disruption in James's life," Jo said. McMurtry told Oppenheimer, "I have the impulse to write you love letters."

In late March, he flew to California to personally deliver pages to his agent, leaving Jamie with Jo (whom he had just claimed could not accept responsibilities). After he'd returned to Houston, Oppenheimer wrote to tell him she felt guilty about his trip.

In San Francisco, he had been his old ambivalent self.

"I hope you aren't feeling that my trip was a failure because we didn't have a love affair," he answered. "The reason it was so uneasy . . . was principally the worry and discomfort involved in leaving Jamie—I wish I weren't that sort of parent, but clearly I am, and it's not too likely that I'm going to have many fully enjoyable trips until he gets of travelling age." He chalked up "the nervousness when we're together that neither of us can do anything about" to "the fact that we did have a sort of love affair, emotional if never quite physical . . . I regret that we never made love and regret that small layer of nervousness[,] but neither regret diminishes the fondness I have for you or my enjoyment of your company. If I let such regrets cut me off from people I would have been in a state of isolation long ago."

That summer of 1964, "the breeze of the future was about to blow through my quiet street," McMurtry wrote. He was talking about the moment Neal Cassady, Ken Kesey, and the rest of the Merry Pranksters pulled the Magic Bus up Quenby Street.

Kesey had been searching for new ways to hold court ever since Perry Lane had been demolished in the summer of '62. A Menlo Park realtor bought the acreage for $50,000, mailed eviction notices, and sent the bull-dozers in, sparing the Keseys' cottage a little longer than the others only because Faye had just given birth to their son, Jed, and needed time to recover.

The night before the residents were finally forced to leave, Kesey threw a block party, cooking up a pot of venison chili, festooning the courtyard oak with colored ribbons, and dragging a piano from one of the houses into the street so everybody could smash it with axes and set it on fire. "It is the oldest living thing on Perry Lane. Its annihilation is symbolic," Kesey explained.

He and Faye moved into a log cabin in La Honda, an isolated village in the foggy redwood hills between Palo Alto and the Pacific Ocean. There Kesey strung flashing lights and stereo speakers in the trees. He planted dozens of morning glories, having discovered that their seeds possessed psychedelic properties. He'd load a shotgun with the seeds and pepper them into the bank of a hill across the highway to propagate the plants. He summoned his disciples and set about establishing a forested lysergic kingdom. From La Honda, he wrote McMurtry to tell him he was going to *draw*, rather than write, his novels in the future.

For $1,250, Kesey bought a 1939 International Harvester bus from a sales engineer in Atherton, California. The engineer had torn out the bus's interior and installed bunks and a bathroom so he could take his family on vacations. Ed McClanahan said Kesey added a generator and a sound system, instructed his friends to buy Day-Glo paint and plaster the bus with "psychedoodles and psychedribbles," and write the word "Furthur" on it—the spelling was later corrected. On its rear, someone painted "CAUTION: WEIRD LOAD."

Kesey had hit upon the idea of taking a merry band from west to east— reversing the pioneers' trek—spreading the fresh gospel of LSD along America's highways. They left one morning in early June 1964, dressed as cowboys. Ostensibly, the goal was to reach New York for an autograph party in a bookstore, celebrating the publication of Kesey's second novel, *Sometimes a Great Notion* (arguably, the last serious literature he ever wrote). A larger goal was to crash the New York World's Fair. Even better, "What we hoped was that we could stop the coming end of the world," Kesey said. Donning neon masks, blaring Beatles tunes through the speakers, sloshing acid-laced orange juice in fat plastic jugs, they filmed their every move for posterity. "[M]e and Kesey . . . we were trying to move into a new creative expression which was movie making and being part of the movie. This was all a tremendous experiment in the arts," said Ken Babbs. Plus, "We always figured we would be totally successful and make a lot of money out of it."

Faye stayed home to watch the kids. Before Further had completed its cross-country rounds (with frequent hassles from cops, who were too puzzled by the group's short hair, western demeanor, and red, white, and blue clothing to bother to arrest them for anything), most of the other women on the journey—Chloe Scott, Jane Burton (pregnant with Bob Stone's baby), and Cathy Casamo—had gotten off the bus.

Tom Wolfe's 1968 account of the trip, *The Electric Kool-Aid Acid Test,* would transform Kesey and hippie culture into legends, but it would also obscure certain facts and perpetuate feminine stereotypes (*the hysterical woman*)—clichés that may have convinced Jo's therapist she was on the verge of a breakdown. Wolfe wrote that one of the Pranksters on the bus, known to the group as the Beauty Witch (Cathy Casamo)—and with whom they'd all been, or tried to be, casually intimate—leapt out of Further, stark naked, when it pulled into a neighborhood of massive elms and manicured lawns one day in Houston. She embraced McMurtry's son, mistaking him for her own child. Afterward, she was regarded by the rest of the Pranksters as someone who "had completed her trip. She had gone with the flow. She had gone stark raving mad."

In fact, she was high, and addled by the constant abuse of the men on the bus.

McMurtry's account of the Pranksters' visit to Quenby Street, written in 2002, said: "My son James, aged two, was sitting in the yard in his diapers when the bus stopped and a naked lady ran out and grabbed him . . . [B]eing temporarily of a disordered mind, [she] mistook him for her little girl. James, in diapers, had no objection to naked people, and the neighbors, most of them staid Republicans, took this event in stride: it was the Pranksters who were shocked . . . I soon coached [the woman] inside, where she rapidly took seven showers. Neal Cassady came in, said not a word, went to sleep, and didn't stir until the next day, when it was time to leave."

The truth was, McMurtry had been quite anxious about the Pranksters' arrival. They had phoned him from Flatonia, a short drive from Houston, and he had been standing, pacing at the kitchen window, holding Jamie, waiting for them to show. Jo was there that day, to see her boy. "Oh, God!" McMurtry said suddenly.

"What is it?" Jo asked.

"It's them. But what a them."

"What do you mean?"

"It's indescribable. You'll have to see for yourself."

He walked outside carrying Jamie. Casamo, naked (slipping out from underneath a blanket), tripping on acid, shrieked, leapt from the bus onto the curb, and grabbed at the boy.

"Ma'am," McMurtry said. "Ma'am, would you please let go? The boy is crying, ma'am."

On the drive, Casamo, a former waitress from Sausalito who had come under Kesey's spell, had been sorely missing her daughter Caitlin, whom she had left behind in San Francisco with her partner, an actor named Larry Hankin.

That night, the Further crew slept on McMurtry's floor. "Is she going to be okay?" McMurtry nudged Kesey, nodding at Casamo. The following morning, at about ten o'clock, Hankin got a call from one of the Pranksters. "[He said] Cathy had disappeared last night around two A.M. and they couldn't find her and the Pranksters were going to leave town . . . so I better come down and look for her because nobody's going to be here in Houston," Hankin said.

Kesey stayed around long enough to greet Hankin when he arrived, but Hankin wouldn't listen to him. Kesey still insisted on filming everything for his movie. "I didn't believe anything anyone told me. I was just angry," Hankin recalled. "I was there to find Cathy. To me, all the Merry Pranksters were just one big person of interest in Cathy's disappearance." He came to rely on McMurtry. He "calmed me down," Hankin said. "You need a house with a stone foundation and a kitchen table. I clung to Larry McMurtry's every word. At least he gave off an assumption of sanity. He lived in a house with a solid foundation that didn't go anywhere. He's to be trusted. Larry McMurtry was the only voice I allowed myself to listen to."

McMurtry knew a lawyer. Casamo was finally located at a police station, arrested for her erratic behavior and for biting an officer. Then she was transferred to a county asylum. When Hankin and McMurtry went to the station to complain—how could the cops commit a person to a "nervous hospital" for simply resisting arrest?—the police captain opened the slatted blinds on his window, streaming the searing sun. "You Damn Yankees see that?' he said (clearly oblivious to McMurtry's West Texas drawl). "That's Houston, Texas, out there. You're not in the North no more and we do things different down here."

By now, the Pranksters had hightailed it out of the city.

Hankin sat in McMurtry's house for a couple of days, "playing cards with Jo and slowly unravelling," McMurtry later reported to Kesey.

Eventually, his lawyer negotiated Casamo's release. McMurtry, Hankin, and the lawyer went to the asylum to retrieve her. It was "on the outskirts of Houston, a massive gray hospital building out of a Batman comic book," Hankin said. Casamo was silent, scared, and exhausted. Hankin was ordered to get her out of the state of Texas within twenty-four hours or they'd both be arrested. "She was psychotic," a doctor informed him. "She was having psychotic episodes."

"You mean she was angry? What does that mean?"

"It's hard to define in layman's terms. Psychosis is a very general medical term that covers a vast array of mental problems, so it's really difficult to define simply or succinctly."

If Kesey had stuck around, he might have collected enough material for a sequel to *Cuckoo's Nest*.

Before Casamo was allowed to leave, the doctor wanted one more blood sample from her. He'd taken several samples over many days, and she screamed she'd had enough. No more! Hankin rose from his chair to prevent the man from forcing her down the hall, but McMurtry held him back. "Let them take the blood," the lawyer whispered in Hankin's ear. "We've got to get Cathy out of here."

McMurtry drove them home and prepared "a lot of food and wine," Hankin said, but Casamo "just sat on the back porch and petted Larry's dog." For some reason, she seemed angry with Hankin. She ignored him. She said she was going to hitchhike to Pensacola. "I took her for a ride (Jamie was along) and she managed to escape me at a drive-in, though by some determined chasing through the weeds and among box-cars I caught up with her," McMurtry wrote Kesey in August, once Kesey had returned to California. "Back home, while I was making air reservations she got away again, and Jo and [Hankin] went chasing off barefooted after her; finally got her somewhere near Rice." Since she wouldn't talk to Hankin, McMurtry decided he'd better fly with her back to San Francisco. That night, at the airport—the next flight to San Francisco was a red-eye—"I asked her if she was hungry and she said she might eat a grilled cheese sandwich," McMurtry said. "She ate $78 worth." The food seemed to restore her balance and she decided to leave with Hankin, after all. "When her boyfriend straggled up, the picture of woe, she meekly took his hand and got on the plane," McMurtry said.

Meanwhile, Kesey *did* make it to New York, but the World's Fair was already such an insane carnival, the Pranksters' presence barely registered. Besides which, spectacles were replacing spectacles so quickly now in daily life, the New was Old the minute it was born. "The irony is that curved, finned, corporate America as presented by the 1964 World's Fair was over before it began. '64! Things were changing. We didn't know that World's Fairs were a thing of the past," said Robert Stone.

In New York, Kesey met his old Beat hero, Jack Kerouac, but Kerouac, sick from alcohol abuse, had grown increasingly conservative as he'd aged, and was appalled by the Pranksters' appearance as well as their use of the American flag as an art object, streaked with psychedelic colors. Kesey also met Timothy Leary, another LSD guru, but Leary struck him as a stuffy old lecturer, an "Ivy League egghead . . . walking around in robes and talking like [a] comparative religion professor."

In a letter to McMurtry in August, Kesey admitted he'd driven a lot of miles, spent a lot of money, endured a lot of bugbites, and didn't know what he'd accomplished.

McMurtry pronounced the whole episode "a lot of foolishness." He believed it "ruined" his good friend Ken.

The summer of '64 delivered another personal crisis, this time in Archer City. As an older man, McMurtry looked back at that July and claimed a family problem had prompted his sudden return to Northwest Texas; in a rush of emotion, during a six-week period, the trouble, combined with the repressive atmosphere of his old hometown, inspired him to write *The Last Picture Show*. This appealing anecdote did not track with truth.

"If the Panhandle chicken-fried steak was no different from thousands of others, likewise my family crisis," McMurtry said. "All over the world family crises . . . happen, one after another, all the families allowing themselves to be taken completely by surprise by some of the most often repeated actions humans are capable of."

His parents' marriage, never an oasis of calm, had rippled lately with deeper tremors as a result of his rumblings with Jo. His mother continued to insist that if he and Jo had supported their vows with a stronger moral foundation to begin with—the blessings of God—they wouldn't be on such shaky ground. And then, as if startled awake by her advice to her son, she seemed to remember her *own* long-standing dissatisfactions with her husband: his inattention, his roughness, his unrealistic expectations of domestic order. As if her oldest boy's travails weren't enough to upset her, her boy Charlie was now on the cusp of adolescence, becoming aware of girls, and what kind of examples were the men in his family setting? . . . and then, to top it off, crippling arthritis slowed Jeff Mac, making him more dependent on Hazel, less able to carry out *his* chores, piling on her an insurmountable amount of strain.

McMurtry went home to provide his mother emotional support and help with the ranch, and to try to ease the tensions. "The effect of this crisis was to make me even more wary of Archer City than I had already been," he said. "Simply put, it's not a nice town." He didn't blame his parents for behaving as they did; marriage was marriage. He blamed the stunted "culture" of the place for limiting their visions of how to proceed.

All of which easily fed into the themes of *The Last Picture Show*. But the novel did not tumble out of McMurtry in a feverish six-week rush. It had been gestating for quite some time, bubbling into consciousness through cracks in the rodeo book, whenever that material frustrated him. Already he had written two short stories, "Breeding Darrell" and "There Will Be Peace in Korea." He'd stitch them into the novel, with some changes (Miss Burkhalter at *Texas Quarterly* had finally shown some interest in "Korea.") And he provided Oppenheimer with an elaborate outline for the book, along with a list of two dozen characters whose lives he imagined following throughout the narrative. The novel was originally conceived as much longer than the final product. Its scope and structure would change, but in a brief proposal to Oppenheimer, he had distilled its essence:

> [T]he novel examines a crisis in the friendship of two eighteen-year-old boys, Bud Moore and Sonny Crawford. Their friendship has done much to sustain them for otherwise bleak childhoods; the crisis arises due to the small-town rich girl, Laveta Farrow, a young lady of quick but somewhat shallow affections. There is a fight and Sonny loses an eye, but in the end he and Bud resolve the matter and regain one another's friendship: this happens the night before Bud leaves for Korea, and the night, also, of the last picture show in Thalia. A host of minor characters and any number of amazing incidents document the decay of the small town in which the central conflict takes place.

He returned to Houston in late August preoccupied with many matters: Jamie's needs, most immediately; his faltering marriage; his rodeo material; his small-town story idea; and his preparations for teaching again in the fall. ("It's the most physically wearing work I've ever done and is mentally wearing to boot," he told Kesey. "If one could be contemptuous of one's students it would be easy to sluff through the year, but one . . . inevitably begins to care enough about some of them as people not to want to appear a total shithead. To avoid that there's nothing to do but give what you know and feel.")

Despite his friendships with Evans, Curtis, and Broyles, he complained to Oppenheimer, "I don't feel at all in touch with the younger generation, and am terribly surprised actually that there *is* a generation younger than my own."

Campus activism was stirring nationwide. Broyles was head of the Rice Student Association. The association had combined forces with Black students at Houston's Texas Southern University to join an amicus curiae brief supporting the Rice trustees' attempts to overturn the will of the institution's founder. William Marsh Rice's will explicitly stipulated that the school was intended for whites. African Americans and Jews had always been barred from attending classes. In 1961, students and younger faculty had voted to integrate the school, but strong alumni resistance had stalled efforts to do so. Broyles's work on behalf of the student association paid off when a federal court ruled that the trustees did in fact have the power to amend the university's charter. In late '64, Raymond Johnson became the first African American student admitted to Rice, in mathematics. In 1965, the school would start to fully integrate and appoint African Americans to the faculty, beginning with Vivian Ayers. She had been working as an apprentice librarian in the Fondren Library on campus, where McMurtry—who had a key to the library and still often spent many late nights there—got to know her.

Like Jo, she was a native of South Carolina, a member, in 1939, of the last graduating class of the Brainerd Institute in Mount Vernon, a school opened (in a log cabin) in 1886 for the children of freed slaves. The school instilled in her a love of reading: "We recited 'Thanatopsis' and all of the catechism in the seventh grade, and we learned Milton." She conceded that the "Black militants" of the 1960s "would be horrified by what they would call a Eurocentric curriculum," but she continued to revere Shakespeare and she became a poet. In 1952, her collection *Spice of Dawns* was nominated for a Pulitzer Prize, and in 1957, eleven weeks before the launch of Sputnik I, she published *Hawk,* a book-length poetic allegory linking space flight with racial freedom. NASA would later display enlarged reproductions of *Hawk*'s verses in the Lyndon B. Johnson Space Center.

Following the publication of her second book, a Fordham University professor was quoted in the nation's newspapers, calling Ayers "the most exciting, intelligent, and beautiful woman in America." Ayers responded, "I am a poet but not yet a saint."

She had struggled hard for her achievements, escaping an abusive marriage to a prominent doctor. (At one point, in the mid-1950s, *Jet* magazine reported that "a noted poetess and author claims she fired a bullet at the feet of her dentist ex-husband . . . after he allegedly tried to run a house guest from her home.") She raised three children on her own, taking them to Mexico for a spell when, in her view, they were most vulnerable to the effects of American racism.

By the time McMurtry met her, she had become a passionate cultural activist, supporting Black arts in Houston. (Her son Andrew—Tex— would become a jazz musician. Her daughter Debbie Allen would become a famous choreographer and director. Her other daughter, Phylicia Rashad, would devote herself to acting; her best-known role was that of Clair Huxtable in TV's landmark series *The Cosby Show*.) In 1964, Ayers was trying to start a magazine for Black writers in Houston called *Adept,* and she enlisted McMurtry's help as a reader and editor. The project was short-lived, but her friendship with McMurtry grew, to the consternation of her children, especially her son.

"Did we all think he was having an affair with her? Yes," Broyles said. "But perhaps that was our overheated sex-starved twenty-year-old imaginations working. She was a woman of uncommon beauty and sensuality compared to almost all the women on the faculty and the wives of the men. The fact that [she and Larry] had an open friendship [in those days] was something."

In fact, "after Jo left I fell into a brief and rather amusing amour with a Negro lady, a lovely one," McMurtry wrote Oppenheimer. "The lady's name is Vivian and she had the good or ill fortune to be the first Negro staffer hired at Rice in line with their new integration program. I derived a good deal of secret amusement from my knowledge of how well the integration program was succeeding."

Ayers lived in Houston's Sugar Hill neighborhood, in the city's Third Ward, east of downtown, near Texas Southern University. From her, and from Broyles's activism, McMurtry got a quick and up-close civil rights education. He believed Ayers had become sadly "neurotic" from being "put on by white intellectuals for so many years that she [didn't] know whether she [was] going or coming." But his education still had miles to go: glibly, callously, he joked that, while dating Ayers, "I figured it was a toss-up whether I got bombed by my neighbors or knifed by her children (I'm sure they're Black Muslims)."

In the end, though he greatly admired the woman, he was still stuck on Jo. He was not in love with Ayers. "It was an honest experience," he said, "[but] I find it makes me terribly lonely to sleep with someone I do not care for a lot."

Jo had decided to enter graduate school in the English department, beginning that fall. "Larry was very supportive. He paid my way and gave me lots of books; he always knew what I would need for my courses," she said. They continued to live apart but saw each other nearly every day (Jo zipping back and forth, driving a tiny Sunbeam Alpine), spending time together with Jamie.

McMurtry's dream of moving to the Berkeley hills had long since dissipated. Without movie money, without the sale of a new novel, and now with Jo making an uncertain new start, he had no choice but to stay put. "I'm sure I would be better off if I could get completely over Jo, but do not know precisely how to, since she is among the people I care most about; also I have a rather exacerbated sense of responsibility for her," he told Oppenheimer. He feared she would need looking after for a long time.

In the midst of all this motion, he completed a draft of his rodeo novel, variously titled, in his mind, *The Water and the Blood, Sometimes the Matador* ("[No,] the corrida is out, man," Leggett said), or *Lovebreaking*. Neither Leggett nor Oppenheimer responded favorably to the pages. McMurtry pretended not to be devastated by their reactions, but he was shaken.

Leggett expressed no patience with the troubled married couple at the center of events—two spoiled, self-indulgent youngsters, he thought. He felt McMurtry had skimped on the rodeo material, relegating it to the background: "Won't you please try to do a full, sensual job on the rodeo—show us the crowd and its anticipation—every sound and sight of the approach to the arena—an explanation of how the rodeo works . . . I know [that you] are bored with the kind of external details I'm suggesting."

Oppenheimer agreed with him. McMurtry explained to them both: "I am interested almost exclusively in relationships. Setting suffers [as a result], and to keep the interest in relationships from getting too abstract, character description proliferates. Perhaps it is [too] proliferate . . . But I don't see a drastic flaw in the novel as it stands . . . My concern as a novelist is not to explain, or even, necessarily, to <u>understand</u> . . . why and what about . . . a marriage. My concern is <u>to show</u> how it feels to my characters and how it affects them, how it works itself out—not <u>why</u>. Why is for the critics."

To Kesey (who, post-Further, seemed to have shed all pretense of writing), he said: "For me the novel is character creation. Style is nice, plot is nice, structure is okay, social significance is okay, symbolism worms its way in, timeliness is okay too, but unless the characters convince and live the book's got no chance."

Of this *particular* novel he said, "I was worried to really cut loose on [the subject of] destructive relationships for a few years, fearing I would reenact Jo's and mine in an obvious way (I have, but not . . . hurtful[ly]) so I idealized females (Halmea, Molly . . .) and stylized a form of maleness (Hud . . .). Finally [I] couldn't believe in my own females and had to match Hud with someone his size (the girl named Patsy in the new book)."

When Oppenheimer suggested he further refine the material (she found the characters cold), he said, "I took this novel very close to where I set out to take it. No one, of course, is obliged to like where I set out to take it . . . You may think [this] is sort of egomaniacal madness, but I don't think so . . . I recognize [the novel] would not please too many people . . . I think I will undoubtedly write books with wider appeal. But I must keep the right to write books with narrow appeal, or no appeal at all, if it seems necessary or interesting [to me] . . . I would like to have some money for it and would like to have it published but whether I get some or not or whether it is [published] or not I still feel content to have written it and shan't worry overly much about it."

With Leggett's rejection of the novel as it stood, and a lengthy deliberation by Random House, after which its editors passed on the book as well, McMurtry set aside the rodeo material and concentrated on finishing *The Last Picture Show*. His first two novels had been written in the first person, heavy on dialect—narrated by "innocent bumpkins [who seemed] terribly stagy and posed," in Dave Hickey's view: "It makes you wonder about the novelistic convention which requires a writer to divest himself of half his vocabulary and a proportionate amount of brains when he approaches a character less learned than himself. Certainly it is a feat of skill to approximate primitive speech. Whether it is worth doing or not is another question."

"Primitive" or local dialect had long been a literary characteristic of the region. "It has often been noted . . . that Texas is hell on women and horses," Hickey observed. "What hasn't been noted . . . is that there is some retribution, since women and horses are hell on Texas writers."

Initially, McMurtry had composed the rodeo novel in first person, test-driving various narrators. Then, in frustration with the story's lack of energy, he switched it to third, but only by changing pronouns, replacing "I" with "he" or "she," a cosmetic difference signaling no difference at all (a corpse with makeup on its cheeks is still just a corpse). But with *The Last Picture Show*, he was determined to understand third-person point of view, plunging into its nuances and depths, a more flexible and comprehensive vantage point (given the subject matter—the broad culture of a region shaping individual sensibilities). This perspective allowed access to various minds in the story and introduced sarcastic comment without breaking character: "Charlene Duggs, as her name suggests, has only two things to recommend her," says an early version of his free-floating narrator. The freedom of voice made the final writing of *Picture Show*—once he had decided to reduce its scope to the boys' friendship and their romantic rivalry—relatively smooth, accounting, perhaps, for his later belief that the novel had emerged in a rush.

He read portions of the novel in progress aloud to his classes at Rice, a further exercise in streamlining the material: narrative weaknesses—dead spots, draggy passages—tended to jump out unmistakably in public performance. McMurtry had replaced Leggett's formal responses with the facial expressions and body language of his students. Whole sections of the novel fell away as a result: the sexual affairs of a host of minor characters.

Bill Broyles had the sense that McMurtry was standing in front of the class "inventing himself."

Meanwhile, Broyles, Curtis, and Evans went on book-scouting excursions with McMurtry "to parts of Houston I had never seen," Curtis recalled. "He'd take us to Goodwills and to the bookstores on Telegraph Road. He knew every square inch of the city. Riding in the car with Larry . . . he was constantly seeing things, observing stuff I never even thought about. Small details. 'Look at that stairwell outside that house,' he'd say. 'What do you think that's for?' I would never have registered it. Or we'd see a man and a woman talking on the street: 'Oh, he's in trouble. You can tell!' He sought the story behind what he was seeing, and I learned that way of being from him. You know: my presence here has nothing to do with what's happening around me. I'm just here as an observer."

"My book hunting seldom turned up anything of much value, but it kept me in reading matter and also gave me a knowledge of the funkier reaches of Houston," McMurtry said. "[I loved] its steamy, shoddy, falling-down sections. Houston as a city was a series of crumbling, half-silted-over neighborhoods. You could still come upon little drugstores that looked as if they had been free-framed by a *Life* photographer in the thirties. Once, in a district not far from the slum that's called the Bottoms, I came upon a vast wooden boat, so weedy and overgrown with vines and creepers that it was hard to even guess what period it dated from. It sat in the middle of a large, neglected lot, visited only by winos and grackles. Sam Houston could have ridden in that boat, or Cabeza de Vaca."

Sometimes, after a full day scouting, McMurtry would take the boys out to eat, occasionally at a nice new restaurant on Westheimer, La Carafe: "Red-checked tablecloths, candles in wine bottles, wax dripping," Broyles said. "It was the first time I was ever served wine at dinner. They had something called *ex-presso*! It was all new to me in those days." Part of the boys' education. Broyles loved his teacher's stories of buying books for fifty cents apiece, then turning around and selling them for fifty or sixty dollars. "*Oh my god*, I thought. *I could do that!* So once, when I was visiting Greg in Kansas City, we went into an old 1930s bookstore there. I filled two or three boxes with books. I took them down to the counter, thinking, *This old guy*—he's chomping a cigar—*he's going to know how valuable these books are. A Farewell to Arms, The Sun Also Rises*, all classics. But no. He was asking a dollar, two dollars for each. I spent all my money. I drove back to Houston and went straight to Larry, thinking I'd be able to live for a while on what he paid me for the books. 'Well, let's take a look,' he said. 'This one's a reader's copy—I'll give you a quarter for it. This one's a book club edition. I'll give you fifteen cents.' I think I made about twenty dollars. It was a real lesson in bookselling. In flea markets, garage sales, bookstores, Larry was like a really good doctor who knows what you have within five minutes. He'd just reach out and pick the one he wanted."

When the group wasn't dining at La Carafe, trading book stories, "we'd go to a steak house called the Stables or to a seafood restaurant, but mostly we ate hamburgers," Evans recalled. "The bacon cheeseburger had just been invented and we thought that was great! Or we'd eat waffles and pancakes. Larry had a terrible diet. He loved Dr Pepper. He drank it like water."

Usually, Jo and Jamie accompanied the boys at dinner—and for a while, Grover Lewis came along. He moved to Houston, briefly, to work as a copyeditor at the *Houston Chronicle*. He lived in McMurtry's pornography room. "He was really an intimidating figure. Pale, scarred face," Curtis said. "I remember he had these boxes of 33 records . . . I don't know where he got them, but he was legally blind, so he didn't have to pay for them or he got a discount on them or something. He had the soundtracks to some black-and-white exploitation films. Weird stuff. I thought, *Why would anybody want to listen to* this?"

"When he got drunk he would rant," Evans said. "One night he was drunk and ranting and scaring James. Larry told Grover he had to go. Grover moved out. He didn't talk to Larry again."

Being a single parent had gotten no easier. While Jo was busy taking classes, McMurtry had to schedule a tonsillectomy for Jamie at the Texas Medical Center, on the same day (as it turned out) that Denton Cooley was performing the first American heart transplant there: "[W]ith such world-shaking events going on, it took an awfully long time to get anyone to pay attention to my son's bleeding throat."

Jamie was "a beautiful child with enormous dark eyes," Mike Evans recalled. "[H]e was in day school, which gave Larry time for writing and book work, and I think I remember a nice Hispanic woman who would run the vacuum cleaner, fix lunch, see that a nap was taken." In addition to the turtle, Jamie had a pet rabbit. It "lived in a cage in James's room but sometimes escaped and was apt to be found in the kitchen," Evans said. "Larry loved to play with James, listen to him, roughhouse with him on the lawn. In the evenings we might take James for a walk to the little park a few blocks away, where he hauled his basketball with him and tried to get it up to the hoop. Jo was almost always with us." McMurtry, he said, was "indifferent to food; his later attraction to places like Chasen's was for the atmosphere, not the grub." Once, "he tried to roast a Smithfield ham which Jo had brought, but he didn't soak it, so it was all but inedible. When I experimented with some recipes from a gourmet cookbook he was bemused. 'What are we having tonight—braised hummingbird tongues?'"

On occasion, McMurtry still accompanied Jo to South Carolina to take Jamie to see his grandparents. Evans would house-sit while they were gone, sometimes staying in the garage apartment where "Billy Lee's mattress and bean pot" remained. Once, when McMurtry was away in California on a book-scouting trip, Evans moved into the house. "Larry and Jo had a neurotic, affectionate dog, a Shelty named Susie," he said. "One day Jo came over to make sure Susie was all right, and she and I began a romance together."

Over the next few weeks, the affair progressed rapidly and became more and more serious. Evans was drinking heavily, a shade more avidly than the average college-age student.

"Jo and I thought Larry knew [about us], but it turned out he didn't. When he *did* discover us, he didn't suddenly unfriend me or get mad at Jo. He was the most honest person I ever met. He continued to be a good friend."

Curtis recalled, "There was a period when, on Friday or Saturday nights, Mike and Jo, my girlfriend Janice and I, and Larry and James would all have dinner together. After dinner, Larry and James would go and the four of us would stay and play bridge."

After years of agonizing and the many separations, the marriage's end was anticlimactic. "[Our] divorce decree is dated September 13, 1966," Jo said. "[Still,] we saw each other nearly every day." McMurtry continued to pay for her classes at Rice. She never hesitated to call on him whenever she needed him, night or day. "He was always the guy that drove everybody home," she said.

In February 1966, Ken Kesey parked a truck on a coastal bluff near Eureka, California, leaving a note inside the cab: "Ocean, ocean, I'll beat you in the end." Then he vanished. In the following days, a bold headline appeared repeatedly in national newspapers: "LSD GURU SUICIDE!"

By then, Kesey was in Puerto Vallarta, Mexico—he would later move to Mazatlán—having escaped the United States in the trunk of a friend's car to avoid going to jail for marijuana possession. McMurtry was one of the few people who knew where he was; Kesey wrote him letters from his lair, an abandoned pet food factory that Kesey referred to as La Casa Purina. The letters were long and largely incoherent: "I am chancing hell . . . as Sol Almande, Prankster Extraordinaire" in "fink ridden Mexico" . . . "Praytell, could a storm be a-building? Always."

Mountain Girl (aka Carolyn Adams), one of Kesey's lovers—by whom he would have a child, Sunshine—was with him. She noted in a journal one day: "He's working on his wave theory. This morning for breakfast he brewed and drank enough weed to put a horse in orbit. He's been out there [on the beach] for three hours with his eyes closed . . . imagining that he's a piece of kelp or a jellyfish."

He had come to this pass after a frantic period following Further's cross-country journey—a period defined by the Acid Tests, as Kesey called them. The Acid Tests were large gatherings bathed in the flashing strobes of psychedelic light shows (pioneered by expatriate Texans Gary Scanlon, Travis Rivers, and Steve Porterfield), vibrating to the largely improvised rock music of a San Francisco band called the Warlocks, later rechristened the Grateful Dead. The Hells Angels were frequent guests at the parties. The Pranksters would set up two thirty-gallon trash cans, line them with plastic, and fill them with Kool-Aid. Then, using Dixie cups, they'd pour a couple of glass ampules of LSD into one of the cans—about 300 micrograms, or six Dixie cups. Most of the LSD was manufactured by a self-taught chemist named Owsley Stanley III. Wavy Gravy, a journeyman entertainer and a Prankster hanger-on (his real name was Hugh Nanton Romney Jr.), would stand beside the cans and say, "The one on the right is for the kids or kittens, and the one on the left is electric for the tigers."

LSD was still legal then. Pot was not, and Kesey had been busted twice for possession.

So he imagined himself a jellyfish in Mazatlán.

"I tell you Larry, the Pranksters have come a long way since we greeted you in Houstin [*sic*] was it? With a sudden stark naked to drag at your baby's foot . . . a long way indeed."

"[T]he interior of [Kesey's] bus"—driven carefully across the border by Ken Babbs—"was a cornucopia of strange pills, exotic herbs, magic mushrooms, peyote buttons, LSD, uppers, downers, poppers, and of course marijuana," said a former hotel owner in Manzanillo. "On a windless day you could get stoned just strolling past [it]."

Kesey was soon joined by a squad of other Pranksters, including Neal Cassady (who'd die of exposure in Mexico) and Faye, who brought the children, Shannon, Zane, and Jed, along with a "spongey" air of paranoia, Kesey thought. She'd bang on the door of his room when he was inside, on the bed, rolling joints with Mountain Girl, and shout that, in case he was interested, police cars were cruising the beach.

When Greg Curtis graduated from Rice in the spring of '66, he wanted to travel before settling back into graduate school. McMurtry told him where Kesey was. "I went to Mexico and found him and stayed with him for a couple of days," Curtis said. "Faye was there, and Mountain Girl. Kesey was sleeping with both women. I said, 'Larry sent me.' That was my way in. And I remember Faye saying, 'So, you knew Larry at Rice?' 'Yes,' I said. And she got this faraway look in her eyes. She said, 'He's such a wonderful writer.'"

In 1967, Kesey returned to the States to serve six months in prison at the San Mateo County Jail. McMurtry hoped he would calm down now and begin writing novels again. Kesey waved away the suggestion: "If you've made two fairly high mountains why make a third?"

B*ecause you haven't even started,* McMurtry told him in so many words. McMurtry was starting over. Oppenheimer hoped to match *The Last Picture Show* with an editor more in tune than Leggett with McMurtry's personality and development arc. She had left San Francisco to live and work in New York. She approached a small New York publisher called the Dial Press, whose editor in chief, E. L. Doctorow, was also a novelist. His first book, in 1960, *Welcome to Hard Times,* had been a western. Years later, he'd reflect that working at Dial had been "an enormously satisfying time" for him: "We were very busy and very ambitious, and it was an exciting period. For a little house we made a lot of noise." Norman Mailer, James Baldwin, Jules Feiffer, Vance Bourjaily, Thomas Berger, Anne Moody, and Richard Condon were among the authors he worked with. He published one of Abbie Hoffman's first books.

"He is really quite nice and not as scatterbrained as he may seem," Oppenheimer told McMurtry. (One day, Doctorow had phoned McMurtry very early in the morning, oblivious to time zones. Wasn't the whole world keyed to New York?)

One of the editors working for him, William Butterfield Decker, who would also write a western (*The Holdouts* in 1979), got a look at *Picture Show* and wanted it. He had edited Oppenheimer's other important client, Ernest Gaines, and he had been a student of Wallace Stegner's. If these intersections weren't enough, he shared with McMurtry the experience of cowboying. Before attending college, he had been employed on an Arizona ranch owned by the family of Bruce Babbitt, who would become the U.S. secretary of the interior.

Dial offered a $12,500 advance on the novel. There was also immediate talk of movie interest. "I hope you will have much joy out of this. You've really not had much so far in your life, have you. And you deserve lots of it," Oppenheimer wrote McMurtry.

Decker didn't do much editing (nor would McMurtry have allowed him to tinker much with the manuscript). Once McMurtry had decided to reduce the story's focus, he changed little besides a few names (Bud became Duane; Darrell, Billy; Laveta, Jacy). Aside from adopting a satirical tone (naming the driver of a gas truck Fartley, for instance) and employing third-person point of view a la *Middlemarch*—establishing a roving, omniscient narrator privy to the goings-on in the town's every cranny—McMurtry extended his reach by foregrounding the manners of village life, using sex as the determinant around which all human behavior could be measured.

"The novel was a mixture of modes and motives," McMurtry said. "A certain amount of affection [for Archer City] struggled in it, and a certain amount of genuine hatred. Affection lost, and the predominant tone of the novel is rather harshly satiric." As Mark Busby noted, the novel reflected "the growing anti-Texan attitude that was beginning to sweep Texas intellectuals in the mid-1960s as they watched LBJ bare his [appendicitis] scar and drive the country deeper into Vietnam." As such, *The Last Picture Show* resembled Joseph Heller's enormously popular *Catch-22*: both novels were set in earlier decades, but they crackled with 1960s cynicism, earning substantial cult followings as a result.

In *The Last Picture Show*, sex is presented soberly, unsentimentally, as opposed to McMurtry's handling of the subject in *Leaving Cheyenne*. In retrospect, he felt his earlier novel was a form of childish wish fulfillment: "What *Leaving Cheyenne* really offers is a vision of adult life in which sexuality cannot seriously interfere with friendship," he said—a state of affairs he no longer trusted.

As in *Middlemarch*, *Picture Show* pits individuals against society. ("Sometimes Sonny felt like he was the only human creature in the town," the novel begins.) Unlike Lonnie in *Horseman, Pass By*, Sonny cannot slip the social pressures molding him; he must learn to cope with a complex thicket of relationships. The story is loosely episodic but marks Sonny's development with precise regularity. He matures step by step, initiating his first serious sexual engagement with Ruth Popper, the repressed wife of the high school basketball coach; mourning the loss of Sam the Lion, the owner of the pool hall and the picture show, and the closest thing to a mentor Sonny has ever had; and finally reckoning with the accidental death of Billy, a developmentally challenged boy whose welfare has fallen to Sonny following Sam's passing. Charged with the weight of responsibility, Sonny fails to keep the boy safe and is hurled the hard way into adulthood's startling consequences.

(In *Horseman, Pass By*, the town's pool hall owner is called *Lem* the Lion—an old Black man. He is mentioned only in passing. Over time, the character evolved and grew in stature in McMurtry's mind.)

Sonny's first kiss with Ruth occurs roughly a third of the way into the novel, his first sign of growth; Sam dies another third of the way through the book; and Billy is hit by a truck near the story's end.

McMurtry made the autobiographical nature of the novel explicit in the book's dedication, an obviously snide nod to his hometown.

"You can't imagine how horrible it is to be the least bit different from your provincial fellow man," he had once mused about Archer City in a letter to his buddy Mike Kunkel. The letter is dated August 31, 1956, when he was twenty years old, already feeling the "hatred" that would animate his third novel. "I may be burned at the stake any day now," he said. "The [town] folks are bad . . . I am passive, but waiting for an opening in which to thrust [at them] with knife like wit."

Living in the town had driven him to "the verge of schizophrenia," he told Kunk; with their bigotry, narrow-minded snobbery, hypocrisies, and repressed vanities, his fellow citizens, he said, could "shove off for Hell anytime, except a few choice adults" (his father, a model for Sam the Lion; Margaret Ellen Slack; and a high school English teacher).

And yet McMurtry was capable of viewing himself from others' points of view (accounting for his strength as a novelist): "[H]ow could the elders be sure that a bookish and suspiciously observant youngster like myself might not in time disgrace the line? I knew from an early age that I could never meet their standard, and since in those days theirs was the only standard I knew existed I was the more defensive around them," he wrote in *In a Narrow Grave.* "Tolerance was a quality I think no McMurtry ever understood, much less appreciated, and though one or two of them came to understand mercy it was not the family's long suit."

Through his characters Lonnie and Sonny, the young writer examined possible solutions to his social problem: leaving or staying and facing the consequences. He found both options wanting, solidifying—once more—his bone-deep ambivalence. "[I would] like to live where I could do as I see fit without bringing consternation to people who I care for but [who] do not think some of the things I do are fit," he wrote his friend. But he also acknowledged that homesickness was a "very sick sick." And like Thomas Hardy, one of his favorite novelists, he would never trust the "social or intellectual elite[s]," who despised the "common" folk he came from: "I want no part of that kind of brains or that kind of money . . . [C]ulture's only yardstick is character. What profits it to have read a thousand books or to have plowed a thousand fields if it has done nothing but make you look down on those who haven't."

Socially speaking, his dilemma was insoluble—he didn't know where he belonged—and it would dog him all his life. It was this dilemma that gave *The Last Picture Show* its energy, its bite, and its broad perspective.

The sexual desires of the teenagers in 1950s Thalia have been warped by the adults' stoic silence and by community rules designed to keep desires in check. Duane Moore and Sonny Crawford, buddies on the high school football team, hang out in Sam's pool hall, go to the picture show on the weekends to watch old Westerns, and obsess about sex as a cure to the town's bleakness. Sonny befriends Billy, who lives with Sam in the pool hall after his father abandons him. Every day Billy sweeps the billowing dust in the windblown streets, beneath the sole traffic light. He is the only kid in town not overwhelmed by loneliness and hopelessness. He lacks the capacity to know better. Sam, a former cowboy, keeper of the traditional values of duty, hard work, and loyalty, watches over the boy. Sam's opposite is a man named Abilene, an oil-field worker who is selfish, greedy, and beholden to no one. He is a masterful billiards player, keeping a special cue stick in the pool hall, which he handles as if it were a prized Remington rifle. A callous lover, he has been having an ongoing affair with Lois Farrow, once a lively, vibrant girl but now a bitter, disappointed alcoholic, miserable in her marriage. Her daughter Jacy, currently the prettiest girl in town, is dating Duane, but like her mother she craves a better life than Thalia can offer. Her sexual allure is her natural advantage, the one quality she can wield like a weapon to pry whatever she wants from others and perhaps escape the dead ends awaiting her peers. Eventually she dumps Duane for the more socially and economically exciting scene in Wichita Falls. There, rich teens stage weekly skinny-dipping parties and challenge one another to lose their virginity as casually as if they were playing a game of Truth or Dare. Jacy recognizes that her virginity is an impediment to acceptance in the social world she craves, so she seduces Duane, a disappointing experience. Then she beds her mother's lover, who shuns her after getting what he wants from her. Angered and humiliated, determined to be acknowledged (talked about in town, becoming its central bauble), she sets her sights on Sonny. Sonny has begun his unlikely affair with Ruth Popper. Ruth, neglected, abused by her husband, coping with illness, bestows genuine affection on Sonny, enjoying a sexual awakening with him. In turn—though bewildered at finding himself with this older woman, and passive in pursuit—Sonny begins to feel the stirrings of commitment . . . until Jacy seduces him. She convinces him to elope with her, knowing full well that her parents will have the marriage annulled, guaranteeing she'll become the talk of the town.

Duane and Sonny fall out over Jacy; Sonny nearly loses an eye when Duane hits him in the head with a beer bottle. The boys reconcile briefly just before Duane ships out to Korea, seeing no further prospects in Thalia.

Sonny, who has inherited both the pool hall and the care of Billy from Sam the Lion, has failed to nurture either one, just as he failed to keep Jacy. When Billy dies, hit by a cattle truck as he is sweeping the street, Sonny, devastated, seeks solace from Ruth. She is torn between accepting him back or venting her rage at his abandonment of her.

The Last Picture Show was McMurtry's most complex novel to date, an incisive autopsy of his hometown and the contradictory emotions it raised in him. Though it was very much the story of young men growing up in a stunted social environment, the richest, most sympathetic characters in the book were the women. Their chances for fulfillment in Thalia—emotional, sexual, intellectual—are virtually nil, yet unlike the men, who passively accept the *nothing* of their lives, the women are smart enough to recognize and chafe against their predicament. They may be vain and misguided, pursuing happiness through sexual manipulation, but at least they try to make things happen.

The book's episodic nature gave a twist to the standard western story plot, which was almost always triggered by a damsel in distress, requiring rescue by a heroic cowboy. Certainly, Thalia's damsels are deeply distressed, but there are no more cowboys to save them. In dispensing with the hoary, schematic plot, McMurtry offered his women the possibility, however remote, of finding their own creative solutions to the bleakness of their surroundings. Ruth Popper takes enormous emotional risks with young Sonny; Jacy's selfish manipulations are at least attempts at self-reliance.

Establishing a female alternative to familiar (male) story lines, the great short-story writer Grace Paley once wrote: "Every character, real or imagined, deserves the open destiny of life." Beginning with *The Last Picture Show,* McMurtry—often chastised by critics (and by his first editor) for his baggy plots—adopted Paley's "open" approach to fiction and consistently created strong, independent female characters.

Arguably, Jacy Farrow is a stereotyped shrew, a calculating femme fatale, but the novel's omniscient perspective makes it clear that she is fighting the confines of her narrow world with all the power she knows how to muster. Her character has not been corrupted by sex; rather, her healthy sexuality has been warped by society's linking of sex with vanity. Social acceptance is the ultimate form of success in Thalia (along with provoking envy in others). Accordingly, Jacy spends hours at the liver-shaped makeup table in her bedroom, applying powders, rouges, and creams to her face to become more sexually desirable. Sex has become a performance staged for society's approval—or failing that, its regard, even if it takes the shape of gossip. "If the story had got out that she had slept with Abilene on a snooker table, she would have been a legend in Thalia forever, but she couldn't think of any way to publicize it," Jacy muses. "Neither Abilene nor her mother were going to, that was for sure. So the whole thing was just wasted. It was disgusting."

Genevieve, a waitress at the café in town, is remarkably free of vanity, and Sonny cannot stop watching her: "Her cheeks and forehead shone with [sweat]; there were beads on her upper lip and the armpits of her green uniform darkened . . . As always, Sonny found himself strongly affected by her. Sweat, if it was Genevieve's, seemed a very intimate and feminine moisture. Even Jacy"—disguised in her powders and creams—"didn't affect him quite as strongly . . . [B]eside Genevieve, Jacy seemed strongly diminished, and apparently Jacy knew it. She always made Duane take her to the drive-in rather than the café when they ate together."

If Thalia has crushed the women's healthy sexual urges, it appears to have prevented the men from developing any healthy impulses whatsoever. "Is growing up always miserable?" Sonny asks Sam the Lion. "About eighty percent of the time, I guess," Sam replies.

For teenage boys, sex is either a quick release of physical pressure—a nearby heifer will do the trick, since the community frowns upon premarital sex with girls—or an occasion for bragging: the one who got the prettiest girl in town (akin to scoring the winning touchdown). Male role models are scarce. Sam the Lion still lives by the code of the West, standing "tall in the saddle" and trying to "do right," but his code has been reduced to a form of cheap entertainment at the picture show. Abilene, the oilman, has based his life on gambling and financial speculation. For him, rules of any sort have fallen out of date. They are mere romantic shackles. As with Homer Barron, Sam, in his dignity, is admirable up to a point. When the boys in town abuse Billy's innocence, forcing Billy into the arms of a prostitute, traumatizing him, Sam banishes them from his pool hall and picture show: "Scaring an unfortunate creature like Billy when there ain't no reason to scare him is just plain trashy behavior," he says. "I've seen a lifetime of it and I'm tired of putting up with it."

But the Old West has vanished, leaving the code of "doing right" scattered across the chilly High Plains. Sam dies, taking his values with him. And it is the modern commercial form of those values—the transfer of cattle—that kills Billy. Trashy behavior rules the day; the oilman drives a big, expensive Mercury, brandishes his pool cue as if he were a gunslinger, sleeps with, then discards the most vibrant women in town, and owns the ultimate bragging rights.

Though Sonny is drawn to Sam's vision, he lives in a world controlled by men like Abilene. He has not learned the skills it takes to meet Sam's (dying) standards. Men like Sam and Homer Barron claimed they learned the code by working intimately with nature. But Sonny's generation—and that of McMurtry and his peers—couldn't "scrape up enough nature-lore between us to organize a decent picnic," McMurtry believed. Moreover, he says, "I spent more than twenty years in the country and I came away from it far from convinced that the country is a good place to form character, acquire fullness, or lead the Good Life. I have had fine moments of rapport with nature, but I have seen the time, also, when I would have traded a lot of sunsets for a few good books. Sentimentalists are still fond of saying that nature is the best teacher—I have known many Texans that felt that way, and most of them live and die in woeful ignorance."

Yet in *The Last Picture Show*, McMurtry was sentimental enough, even at his most caustic, to propose true sexual intimacy as the path to "fullness"—though a callow youth like Sonny is incapable of recognizing such a possibility. When he first kisses Ruth by a collection of trash cans outside a community dance, he "look[s] over her head, [past] the town," but he can see only "beyond the pastures . . . the lights of an oil derrick, brighter than the cold winter stars." He hasn't the vision to transcend the circumstances trapping him. By contrast, when Ruth "open[s] her eyes for a moment" during the kiss, "she [is] looking straight up, toward the stars."

"Loneliness is like ice," she tells Sonny. "After you've been lonely long enough you don't even recognize you're cold, but you are. The reason I'm so crazy is because nobody cares about me . . . It's my own fault, though—I haven't found the guts to do anything about it."

Yet Ruth struggles mightily to achieve growth and honest expressions of love. Similarly, Genevieve, the café waitress, thoroughly comfortable with her body, and Lois, Jacy's mom, ruefully wise despite (or maybe because of) her world-weariness, maintain the ability to see the stars beyond the pump jacks. If they all wind up embittered, it is not for lack of trying to be better—more than the men can say.

By novel's end, Sonny has betrayed Ruth's trust and consigned her once more to loneliness. But then he comes to her, groveling. At this point, whatever might occur between them, good or ill, lies entirely in Ruth's hands. Does her future growth (and his) depend on her rejecting him, her refusing to accept the trashy behavior she's been subjected to all her life, or does it rather rely on forgiveness, on her risking the possibility that she can touch the decent core she believes she has detected in Sonny? Does it depend on what her mind believes to be true or on what her body knows it needs? Can the two ever be reconciled?

As she stares at her abject lover, instead of "saying something fine . . . something wise or brave or beautiful . . . [that] would be just what Sonny needed to know about life," she gives in to "the rush of her blood . . . the quick pulse inside her," reaches out and "stroke[s] his fingers with hers." "Never you mind, honey," she says. "Honey, never you mind."

McMurtry sent his mother a copy of the book when it was published. ("To Mom and Daddy. You probably won't like it. Love, Larry," he wrote inside.) She tried to read it. She managed about a hundred pages. Then she hid the book away on the top shelf of her bedroom closet. "Larry, honey, is that what we're sending you to Rice for? Those awful words?" she nearly wept to her son on the phone. The novel's relentless focus on sex was bad enough. But then he had used her middle name for the shriveled woman disappointed in marriage!

"Nothing much happens in Larry McMurtry's third novel, 'The Last Picture Show.' But then nothing much happens in Thalia, the small Western town he is writing about," Thomas Lask wrote in a review of the novel in *The New York Times* on December 3, 1966. "Thalia behaves like a geological phenomenon. As soon as a crack appears or something untoward occurs that offends it, it moves inexorably to eradicate it. With nothing to do and nothing to stimulate the mind, sex becomes the common pursuit and the townspeople, youngsters and adults, act out their frustrations, their compulsions, their boredoms and their hates in physical couplings. These are more bestial than exalted or joyous."

He complained that McMurtry was "not exactly a virtuoso at the typewriter. Some of the transitions as he works from one scene to the next are noticeable; some of the writing could be smoother. But he knows his town and its folkways . . . Thalia is pretty hateful, but you are likely to remember it."

On its initial printing, the book sold roughly nine hundred copies in hardback—hardly enough to induce Dial to take a chance on McMurtry's next novel. He faced the very real possibility that his writing career was over and he'd be stuck with teaching the rest of his life. Too, once the heat of writing the novel had subsided—his urge to "lance some of the poisons of small town life"—his old ambivalence returned, and he questioned what he had done. "By the time the book was published, I was aware it was too bitter," he said. "Archer City had not been cruel to me, only honestly indifferent, and my handling of my characters in my book represented a failure of generosity for which I could blame no one but myself."

His regret did not temper the anger of the townsfolk. Many of them saw themselves mistreated in the novel. Oppenheimer's prediction that he might be run out of Texas seemed an imminent possibility. "I read the book," said Junior Wakefield, an old acquaintance of McMurtry's. "I said, 'Goddamn,' said, 'Ol' Larry just sat there and he just . . . while we was [tellin'] all these stories about what we done on the weekends . . . ol' Larry just wrote it all down. He finally made a book out of it. And got rich off it."

"Horseshit," McMurtry responded when told of Wakefield's remarks. "I didn't sit down and listen to the stories . . . I don't think there was a kid in town that *told* any stories. You know, they were all fucking or they were throwing rocks at the teachers' cars or something like that. They weren't sitting there telling wonderful stories that I could store up like a squirrel to use in my novels years later."

"Absolutely, there are Jacy Farrows in Archer City," said a fellow named Sean Alsup. "The kids here *are* different."

"Oh, I think [Celie Slack] might have [had] a touch of [Jacy]," Bobby Stubbs averred. "I was portrayed as Sonny, I think."

When some of the locals published letters in the *Archer County News,* castigating McMurtry and his family and falsely identifying one of the high school English teachers as Ruth Popper, McMurtry wrote to the paper telling the townspeople they could abuse him all they wanted, but they'd better leave his family alone. He challenged citizens to a debate about the town's true nature. He said he'd pay to rent the American Legion Hall. He'd arrive prepared to discuss any book anyone cared to mention, including the Bible, to prove how illiterate and intellectually backward Archer City really was. No one accepted his dare. Years later, the sting had not lessened. Men would gather to drink and talk in the hall of an evening—roustabouts and ranch help. Cigarette smoke swirled around signs for the Rodeo Association and Jimmy Ashton's gun shop, hanging at a tilt on the wall. Beer cans sloshed, tugged two or three at a time from Styrofoam coolers. Eventually someone would mention the McMurtry family. The atmosphere would stiffen. One night, a crusty fellow wearing a white straw hat, dressed a little like Chester in reruns of *Gunsmoke,* said he remembered Larry McMurtry as a kid: "Look[ed] like he just crawled out of a piss-hole."

Another good old boy, big as a bull, wearing worn yellow boots and spurs clacking across the floor like someone beating a rock with a stick, said he'd worked the McMurtry ranch as a teenager, and by god, young Larry "wasn't no cowboy."

12

It was from a a rare-book dealer named C. Dorman David that Mc-Murtry had acquired the pool table in his Quenby Street home, by trading an old car for it. He also traded David several rare editions for a red Mercedes coupe, which he tooled around Rice in, impressing his students and a few prospective girlfriends.

David was the son of a log-thick Louisiana mud driller who made a fortune working with oil companies. The family's wealth meant David could indulge his every whim and never have to face his mistakes. Once his childhood dyslexia was diagnosed and addressed, he developed a fine eye for rare books and historical imprints. He founded and designed a shop called the Bookman on San Felipe Road in Houston, where the family kept its residence—a literary cathedral featuring Oriental rugs, massive mahogany tables, oak doors with smooth brass knobs, rare engravings on the walls, and displays of brass printing plates for old newspaper ads. Robert Altman used the central showroom as the setting for a rich man's library in his film *Brewster McCloud.* The showroom rose two stories high and was illuminated by a vast skylight. It was equipped with a balcony and a wooden catwalk for accessing books otherwise out of reach. A movable pulpit attached to a spiral staircase occupied one corner of the room. The walls of the bathroom were lighted by glass photographic plates from the nineteenth century. Next door, David installed an art gallery for western paintings, run by his sister, Diana. The place was so beautifully austere, it intimidated most customers and kept them from disturbing, much less buying, the books. "At that time there were only two new bookstores in Houston, a city of over a million; there was one other secondhand store, in the Village, a little shopping center near Rice," Mike Evans said. "Texas is not a good place for buying books. The weather is as much of a problem as the habits of Texans, who are not given to reading."

David didn't sweat the challenges. He worked hard at first, charming other book dealers with his Texas drawl, his western jacket, and yellow boots (he was a big man, a champion boxer during his stint in the army). He traveled across the country and even into Mexico seeking rare books, prints, and documents.

He also knew where to find the best drugs. He plunged into heroin addiction. He ran through six wives like a man thumbing through pages in a world atlas. He indulged in buying motorcycles, sports coats, and boots. He loved speeding down Gulf Coast freeways trying to elude the cops; when he failed to give them the slip, his father's money bailed him out. In the mid-1960s, around the time he met McMurtry, he fell asleep at the wheel of his Thunderbird at three o'clock one morning on a book-buying jaunt to Central Texas. He smashed into a farmer's parked pickup. Greg Curtis got the story from him. "He gave the farmer $1,000 and the car and hitchhiked to a hospital in Waco," Curtis said. "As doctors sewed him up, David got on the phone and started trading, winding up with two antique six-shooters. He hired a plane to fly to Austin. Once in the air, blood seeping from his sutures, he pulled out the pistols and shouted, 'Let's go to Cuba!' David's taste, energy, and wealth carried him on a wild ride for almost ten years."

While he went careening across the state, a well-organized band of thieves began robbing Texas libraries, pilfering valuable documents and putting them up for sale. The community of collectors buzzed with rumors that David led the gang. He appeared to encourage the gossip by publishing a lavish book catalogue engraved on the cover with a depiction of a stagecoach holdup. "The Bookman Offers for Sale Texas Books from a Recent Robbery," the title declared.

One day, one of David's former secretaries found him baking paper in his oven at home. Nonchalantly, he said he was trying to make the paper look older, presumably to use in forging ancient-looking documents.

Steadily, his reputation as a book dealer began to slide. Bankruptcy loomed. His mother, Grace, fifty-three in 1966 when McMurtry met her, couldn't bear to watch her son fail. She stepped in to run the bookstore, though she had no experience in the field. What she had was her husband's wealth, a surplus of optimism and confidence, and as her name implied, plenty of style.

She had been born in Mason, Texas, a small Hill Country town, the daughter of a rancher. In 1935, she earned a teaching degree from Texas

Woman's College and seemed destined for a humble life until she met the insanely rich mud driller in Houston. Immediately, she became part of Houston's lively arts scene, studying photography and becoming the first woman admitted into the Houston Camera Club. She was the second person, following Dominique de Menil, to commission Philip Johnson to design a private home in the city. A hit on the social circuit—"I'm Grace David, and I *have* to know you," she'd chirp to strangers at all the best parties—she prompted a *Houston Chronicle* reporter to write of her: "[Grace] may live to be one hundred, but she will never be old."

In the late 1960s, "a lot of young artists gravitated to Houston because of money," McMurtry said. "Houston was a very open town, still is. Everybody that had some pizzazz and energy [was] welcome in Houston." At the time, Grace David and Dominique de Menil were the faces of the city's aesthetic blossoming. Quite simply, the Bookman was the most gorgeous bookstore in the country. Before he flared out, Dorman had installed a humidor room, made of cedar, for rare tobaccos. "For a safe he had a boll of a Louisiana gum tree," McMurtry said. "At some point, a Japanese houseboy enjoyed a brief tenure [at the shop]. His job was to serve sherry, or sake, or whatever."

When Grace took over, she built a penthouse on the property featuring a "wall-sized aquarium, containing hundreds of lovely, mysterious fish," McMurtry said. In addition to books, she collected various rare items: designer tables, totem poles, a Greek cheese board, a Hungarian shepherd's crook.

One of the Bookman's annual Christmas catalogues featured a pre-Columbian clay dog, an early American camera (priced at ninety dollars), a brass boundary marker separating Oklahoma from the Indian Territory, "a . . . Spanish slave whip used on American Indians in Florida (29 in. long, ca. 1620)," and a "document concerning Texas Indians signed by Sam Houston" (possibly one of Dorman's forgeries).

One day, when Dorman was still running the shop—shortly after the store's grand opening—McMurtry walked in. He bought a "signed, limited copy of Dr. Rosenbach's *Early American Children's Books,* for which I paid a pittance," he said. "Dorman chased me down and asked for it back—it was supposed to be part of his reference library, though, as far as I could see, there was no reference library. I reluctantly yielded it up, taking some Tarzan first editions in exchange."

After Dorman fled to Mexico, Grace—"a woman of indomitable spirit," in McMurtry's quick estimation—hired a friend of hers, a former librarian, to help her run the shop. Almost immediately, they were contacted by "the Yount family in Beaumont," McMurtry recalled. "The Younts had been partially responsible for bringing in the Spindletop oilfield, and thus naturally had a mansion containing a huge for-show library—there were something like nineteen sets of de Maupassant alone.

"The Yount books in their thousands were brought to Houston and piled in heaps in the great room of the Bookman. I wandered in, one day, just scouting, and there were Grace and [her friend] Deena, buried beneath piles of books they knew absolutely nothing about. What I saw were two nice ladies who had no idea how to proceed. The library they had acquired, though vast, was nearly worthless."

McMurtry approached Grace, suggesting he help her. "[I] was hired on the spot, and began one of the best friendships of my life, with Grace . . . a woman who faced many disappointments with a powerful spirit," he said. (Her philosophy was that life "should be about holding each other's hands and leading each other through the tough times, and then holding each other's hands and laughing together as the problems get solved.")

McMurtry managed the Bookman for two and a half years while continuing to teach at Rice. He hired Greg Curtis as a shipping clerk and factotum. He made buying trips to the Seven Gables Bookshop, Scribner's, the Gotham Book Mart ("Wise Men Fish Here"), and Dauber & Pine (all now defunct) in New York.

As the shops closed one by one over the years, he considered New York a ghost town.

One day he learned that the Larry Edmunds Bookshop in Hollywood was reducing its stock to clear more shelf space. He knew the place well from his California days; for ten dollars, he had once sold the proprietor a copy of Mrs. D. W. Griffith's *My Life in Movies* for which he had paid only a buck.

He swooped in and bought Edmunds' entire inventory for the Bookman—seven thousand volumes. The owner later had second thoughts about letting herself be sweet-talked into the deal: "I'm not sure [she] . . . has ever forgiven me for that cultural rape," McMurtry admitted.

Back in Houston, he needed help cataloguing the Edmunds haul. "He offered me $40 a week," said Mike Evans. "[He] provided me with copies of John Carter's *ABC for Book Collectors,* McKerrow's [*An Introduction to*] *Bibliography for Literary Students,* a shelf of catalogues from other dealers, and turned me loose. He would show up for an hour or so, read the mail, price some books, and check on what I was doing. We put out two catalogues at the end of the summer and two more in the fall. They sold well enough for Grace to want us to keep going."

Grace "never liked being more than a step from a telephone; at one point the Bookman had nineteen," McMurtry said. Years later, Houstonians in the know would speculate that Grace David was the inspiration for McMurtry's character Aurora Greenway in *Terms of Endearment* (1975)—the elegant manner, the optimism, the stylish fashions, the love of art (notoriously, Aurora cherishes a prized Renoir hanging in her bedroom where only her lovers can see it).

Evans didn't buy the rumor: Grace was much more down-home Texas than the New Haven–born Aurora, he said. And in fact, Aurora was a complex amalgam of several powerful women in McMurtry's life, augmented by his imagination. But he never denied Grace's part in the character's creation. Coyly, he said, "Grace was lovely and she was complicated. She may have been complicated in a different way than Mrs. Greenway."

Of Aurora, he wrote, "Despite forty-nine years that seemed to her to have consisted largely of irritation and disappointment, she still almost always managed to look pleased with herself"—Grace David to a tee. He *did* dedicate *The Evening Star* (1992), the sequel to *Terms of Endearment,* to Grace.

Although the sixties are remembered as a time of violent protest and counterculture revolution, life on Quenby was serene," Mike Evans said. "There was little protest in Houston, aside from a police riot at Texas Southern University, not much of a hippie or style scene. Civil rights was obviously the right way to go and the war was obviously the wrong way; they did not call us to action."

Instead, of an evening, he and McMurtry would sit at McMurtry's kitchen table, Evans sipping a beer, McMurtry a Dr Pepper, while Jo played with Jamie in the living room. They'd discuss books—the European classics, of course, but also "books that had missed the canon—lost novels, as [Larry] called them, like Julian Claman's *The Aging Boy,* and *Weeds* by Edith Summers Kelley." McMurtry explained the importance of pornography to Evans (he had been called upon to testify as an expert witness in the obscenity trials of several local magazine dealers). "He argued that pornography serves for the education of the young and the stimulation of the old and shouldn't be criminalized," Evans said. "His interest in it was almost clinical"—though, interestingly, "[b]efore James got to the age when he might be educated, the pornography collection disappeared."

McMurtry had met an aspiring writer named Max Crawford—born in Blanco Canyon, raised in Floydada, Texas, a former Stegner Fellow. Crawford came to Houston for a while, to work on a novel he was then calling *The Penis of Jesus.* Retitled *The Backslider,* it would finally be published in 1976. "Max was a great companion—ebullient, funny, profane. We often took him book scouting," Evans said. "In the summer of 1967 Larry took Max and me on a buying trip to California. This was not only to acquire stock, but to introduce me to the California dealers . . . We hit the bookshops . . . visited the poet and sometime book scout David Meltzer and his beautiful wife in North Beach, and spent a hilarious evening with Gus Guthrie . . . She was working [then] in the music business in Memphis and was in California to promote a little-known guitar player who was coming out with a great song; she recited its opening lines to us in the car: 'It's knowing that your door is always open and your path is free to walk, that makes me keep my sleeping bag rolled up and stashed behind your couch.' We thought it sounded pretty good."

Watching McMurtry laugh with Guthrie and Crawford, Evans decided "the key to Larry's range of friendships was that he liked to be entertained and he was nonjudgmental. He did not forgive cruelty or exploitation, and he would cut the cruel or the exploitative right out of his life. For the rest he was forbearing, perhaps seeing us the way he saw the characters in his novels. He did not like stupidity or craziness—but he took them in stride—we are all stupid or crazy sometimes . . . He rarely argued. If you said something with which he disagreed, he would tuck that away as just another thing about you, like your taste in ice cream."

While in California, "Max and I joined an antiwar march in LA, but Larry preferred to spend the day reading," Evans said. Back in Houston, Mc-

Murtry still avoided most of the sixties ferment—"I did . . . a lunch-counter sit-in . . . It was the right thing to do, although I don't think it made anyone in Houston either more or less racist," he said. He preferred to hide in the aisles of the Bookman. "The music touched [him] a little," Evans said. "Larry had a couple of Johnny Cash and Bob Dylan albums, Jo played folk songs on her guitar, and she and James were Beatles fans . . . When the Rolling Stones rolled into town, though, we passed. Larry was an early subscriber to the magazine *Rolling Stone,* but mainly for cultural criticism. We did watch the '68 Democratic convention with horror, like most of the country. Larry and I both admired Norman Mailer's *Armies of the Night.* However, I can't remember Larry ever discussing politics. The revolutionary sixties were another country."

Instead, it was books, books, more books. "He was fascinated by psychology and anthropology—Freud, Erik Erikson, Claude Lévi-Strauss, Robert Ardrey," Evans said. "Man as a killer ape was easy to accept in Texas."

The mud driller liked to hit. His marriage to Grace had always been tempestuous. He didn't like the fact that, while he was out golfing every day, his wife and children spent his money freely on stuff he didn't give a damn about. "Henry sober was a nice man; Henry drunk was to be avoided, as Grace was well aware," McMurtry said. "She kept a bicycle by her bed, in case she needed to flee; she also saw to it that there were about a dozen doors between her bedroom and Henry's—once, at least, she locked herself out of all twelve." There was a small moving company in town "that made a sufficient career" of periodically hauling Grace and her things out of the house.

McMurtry wrote many letters to her. Though they worked together, he often found it easier to communicate through writing. The letters suggest they engaged in a sort of love affair, similar to his relationship with Dorothea Oppenheimer: whether or not the affair tilted into the physical, it was nevertheless intensely emotional. "I love you, and you know it," he wrote her, "but God knows you have no business coping with a bookshop . . . [B]ooky people irritate the hell out of you. You have a great sense of life, a great feeling for life, but your instincts aren't literary and I have

noticed often that booky people make you defensive, especially so unless
I am between you and them . . . Your temperament is a great deal more
open than any business."

On one occasion, as he was considering leaving the Bookman because
his work there was interfering with his writing, he wrote Grace:"I do love
the Bookman and do love you and really did give both of you my best for
as long as I could, considering the improbably complex circumstances of
both our lives . . . [O]nce I knew that the only thing to do with you was
to love you, I should have quit working for you and let nothing pass between us but such gifts of the spirit as we might naturally have given one
another. We should not have been employer and employee . . . There is a
lot about giving that I am only beginning to learn, but I do know that it
sometimes takes a fine eye to distinguish giving from selling. When two
people are fond of one another it is very difficult indeed to detect the moment at which giving becomes selling. All I really know about my time at
the Bookman is that I loved it when I felt I was giving and I began to feel
wrong about it when I began to feel I was selling."

One day in 1968, "Dorman wandered over to his mother's with some
excellent Texana," McMurtry said. "Letters from Sam Houston, Stephen
F. Austin, and the like, most of them addressed to the commandant of the
port of Galveston. These documents were of the first importance, dealing . . . with the Texans' effort to free themselves from Mexico." Grace paid
$200,000 for the lot of them.

Mike Evans researched the documents' provenance, priced them as very
valuable indeed, but discovered that they already belonged to the Rosenberg
Library in Galveston. "[W]e simply could not sell those documents," Mc-
Murtry knew. "At my insistence they were put in a safe-deposit box—about
ten years passed before the matter was concluded, to the extent that it could
be said to be concluded. I'm not sure it was ever really settled."

He tried to convince Grace it was time to close the Bookman, much
as he loved it—"I'm quite sure that it can never make you a living," he
wrote her. It was a shop with no real customers, bleeding money, and it was
further poisoning the already toxic relationships among members of the
David family. Now Dorman had threatened to criminalize the operation
(as he had probably done many times in the past, though no one knew for
sure). The store "is, of course, one of the most beautiful physical bookshops

in the country—no doubt of that," McMurtry wrote Grace. "[B]ut I fear that in bookshops, as in women, physical beauty isn't everything, nor even, perhaps, the most satisfying element."

He argued that Grace was too "private" a person to be a public businesswoman. Her nerves were clearly fraying. And he was ceasing to be a writer. The commercial failure of *The Last Picture Show* ate away at him. "I am not so good a novelist as to be able to afford so attractive an avocation as the bookshop offers," he wrote. "I have long, I fear, used books as an escape from something. Once it was from Jo—lately it has been from [my] novel, from the difficult task of going beyond my adolescent experience in fiction and trying to make something of my adult experience . . . The bookshop is a lovely, pleasant, relaxing, convivial place . . . Unfortunately good writers are made in empty rooms with typewriters in them." He concluded that "half the bookshops in the country are managed by failed novelists with bad consciences. I had rather not join them."

L arry is a writer, and it's kind of like being a critter," Dave Hickey said. "If you leave a cow alone, he'll eat grass. If you leave Larry alone, he'll write books. When he's in public, he may say hello and goodbye, but otherwise he is just resting, getting ready to go write."

A few years after McMurtry quit the bookshop, Dorman David held an auction at Houston's storied Warwick Hotel, near the Rice campus—its spacious lobby was decked out with Romanesque statues. Among other items for sale, Dorman offered a letter written by Stephen F. Austin from a Mexican prison, military orders from Sam Houston composed at San Jacinto, and a letter from Jim Bowie declining Austin's offer of a command post in the Texas Revolution. All the state's leading collectors attended the auction. All of them wondered, skeptically, where these amazing documents had come from—but no one said anything publicly, at the time, and the auction proceeded without a hitch, everyone glancing nervously around the room, waiting for a sudden burst of law enforcement.

Afterward, a dealer named John Jenkins, who had bought an item from Dorman at the auction, returned it, writing him: "I still have doubts about the provenance of this large group of documents that you have come up with. Ten or twelve of the items in your sale were listed in [state libraries]. I

hope you will have the good sense to check out your sources very carefully
before buying any more."

In the next year, as his heroin habit ballooned, Dorman no longer tried
very hard to hide his trail as a forger. He enlisted a British company to man-
ufacture paper to the specifications used in Texas during the revolution. He
told Greg Curtis he made his own ink. "He lit a candle, then held a bag over
it," Curtis said. "With its oxygen limited, the candle began to smoke. David
scraped the carbon from the smoke off the inside of the bag. He mixed the
carbon with boiled linseed oil, working the mixture with a butter knife on a
sheet of glass until he had a substance that would pass for period ink."

Dorman's days as a bookseller, long threatened, finally ended following
a raid on his house one humid summer night by two Texas Rangers, two
detectives from the Houston Police Department, and an assistant district
attorney. A state archivist identified, from items seized in the raid, three
documents that belonged to the state of Texas. Dorman was indicted for
receiving stolen property. He swore he had bought the items without
knowing they'd been pilfered, and there was no proof to the contrary.
Shortly before the case went to trial, charges were dismissed. But collectors
no longer trusted him, and he was through.

Grace David's marriage to the mud driller ended in 1973, when she was
sixty years old, having barely "survived Henry" and his physical abuse—"it
was, for a while, a near thing," McMurtry said. He knew of at least three
occasions when Henry had tried to kill her, "and he almost succeeded the
last time. He strangled her while their . . . daughter was having an art
opening" in the gallery next to the bookstore. Grace moved to England for
ten years, and finally settled in Santa Barbara, California, dying at the age
of ninety-seven. She and McMurtry remained lifelong friends.

Her son seemed to have inherited her stubborn optimism and indomita-
bility. After his humiliating failure as a bookman, after multiple convictions
for drug possession, after hitting rock bottom, Dorman crowed, "You know,
I think all of you owe me something. Because of me everyone is having to
look at Texas history a lot more closely."

In March 1967, Ken Kesey returned to Houston to visit McMurtry and
to stake what turned out to be the Merry Pranksters' last stand. He and
McMurtry had kept in touch, though McMurtry was less and less interested

in Kesey's silly antics now that Kesey had effectively stopped writing Mc-Murtry's concern was for Faye—she was forced to muster as much forbearance as Lady Bird Johnson in the face of her husband's mercurial behavior and crazy plans (though Kesey had very little to do with planning).

In the spring of '67, Kesey was feeling restless in his La Honda compound, so he cranked up Further, repainted it yellow, blue, and red, gathered a few adventurous pals, and hit the road, leaving Faye to mind the home fires.

By 1967, Houston was far savvier about psychedelics than it had been in 1964. As Patrick Lundberg, a chronicler of the sixties and the author of *The Acid Archives,* wrote: "[It] could be argued that, along with California, Texas was the pioneering US state for a non-academic psychedelic culture. Experiments with peyote and morning glory seeds began among college students in the early 1960s . . . and early batches of non-pharmaceutical LSD were common in hip circles. All of the elements of an underground culture were in place."

At McMurtry's suggestion, Billy Lee Brammer had gone to spend some time with Kesey at La Honda. Brammer was on the run from creditors, his ex-wife, narcs, and publishers whose advance money he had frittered away on meth with no intention of ever writing anything. McMurtry figured the men would hit it off; indeed, Kesey was stunned by Brammer's capacity for ingesting mind-altering handfuls of stuff, even greater than his own. Brammer returned to Austin inspired by the Head Prankster. He went all over town, exhorting his friends to close their eyes and stick out their tongues. He'd pop a pill into their mouth. Susan Walker, wife of country singer Jerry Jeff Walker, swore she thought Billy Lee had single-handedly turned Austin on to LSD—for sure, she said, he had indoctrinated Janis Joplin before she left Texas for San Francisco.

Austin also gave rise to the nation's first psychedelic rock group, the 13th Floor Elevators. In Houston, another experimental band, the Red Krayola, staged performances more accurately coined as Happenings, along the lines of John Cage extravaganzas. Their members included Frederick Barthelme, younger brother of Donald, who had by now burst out of Texas to shake up the staid *New Yorker* magazine on an almost weekly basis with imaginative short stories reminiscent of Kafka and Beckett, but in a category all their own. The Red Krayola implicitly encouraged hallucinogenic states of mind.

In sum, Kesey arrived in Houston to a congenial atmosphere (improbably, acid remained legal in Texas for a while after California outlawed it). Still, because of his pot arrests, and because McMurtry was unenthusiastic about his high jinks, Kesey was a little more muted than usual.

The Pranksters piled into McMurtry's quiet house on Quenby. "[They] were still beautiful, but they were far from fresh," McMurtry said. "They looked mushed, crushed, smushed, as bedraggled as World War I aviators who had just managed to get their Sopwith Camels safely on the ground . . . At this juncture the ideal of companionship seemed to be cracking under the strain of travel—and of Ken's celebrity."

One of McMurtry's graduate students, who attended a party at his house, said the Pranksters were "kind of spooky and impossible to talk to . . . they just play[ed] games and compile[d] scrapbooks and constantly repaint[ed] the bus."

One of the Pranksters, knowing McMurtry was a book collector, tried to convince him that the most important volume in the world was "a weighty piece of metaphysical (in the bad sense) slush called *The Urantia Book*," McMurtry remembered. The manuscript "was said to have been deposited in a Chicago bank vault by an alien."

McMurtry "had given James a small log fort for his [fifth] birthday; it was set up in the back yard. Soon birthday party guests and Prankster children, of which there seemed to be a good number, merged in a wild melee," he said. "The confusion was so great that when I took the party guests home I forgot a little boy; he was found, hours later, sitting quietly in the darkened fort. In the morning I came down to find another little boy sitting on my kitchen counter, digging Cheerios out of a box and eating them by the fistful. For a moment I feared I had forgotten yet another party guest, but this little boy was young Jed Kesey, who offered me a Cheerio."

The Houston visit was the Pranksters' last hurrah together. Shortly afterward, along with Jane Burton, McMurtry drove to California to see how Faye was faring at La Honda. "Jane said we should take food, so we took a carful, which was immediately inhaled," he said. "Faye hurried out to warn me to keep a close eye on my car—people had begun to cannibalize any vehicle that moved in hopes of getting one of the several rusting hulks scattered around running again. Ken was in a work shack, editing the many thousands of feet of bus film. Mountain Girl (later, as Mrs. Jerry Garcia, the matriarch of the Grateful Dead) was much in evidence; though it might be more accurate to say that much of Mountain Girl was in evidence. She was scantily clad."

After that, Kesey went away to serve his prison sentence in San Mateo. Upon his release, he retired with Faye and their children to a sixty-four-acre farm in Pleasant Hill, Oregon, in the fertile Willamette Valley about fifteen miles southeast of Eugene. He parked Further in the woods, near a wetland, where creepers and vines overtook it. He and Faye baled hay, chopped trees, milked cows, and raised their kids together. "[T]he farm was loaded with lots of loaded people trying to take care of lots of land without much more than optimism and dope to go on," Kesey said. That first year, they endured an unusually cold Oregon winter—gas froze in the fuel lines of cars; water stoppered in the faucets.

Faye tried—often in vain—to stir her husband into taking care of their cows. One morning she pointed to one of the animals and told him the cow was pregnant: "She's secreting, her hips are distended, and listen to her complain out there." Kesey didn't believe her until the moment the cow delivered. On another occasion, Faye told him they had to thin their herd. Hamburger, their hulking bull, was impregnating too many of the cows.

"What can we do?" Kesey asked Faye.

"Pen [him] up, or auction him off, or sell him, or—"

"Or what?'

"Or eat him."

"I guess it ain't all free love and frolic," Kesey said to the bull, mourning his own past.

The couple paid a local slaughterhouse to dispatch Hamburger with a .30-.30, and thus began "what in Prankster mythos [was] called the time of Hamburger's Revenge," McMurtry said. "Hamburger got eaten, after which there was disorder in the heavens, with Lear-like confusions and alarums."

Kesey couldn't sustain any piece of writing because he still couldn't convince himself literature held any power. He drew crowds and hangers-on to the farm any way he could, trying Faye's patience. He'd stage impromptu performances in the back pastures. In one field, he built what he called the Thunder Machine, a contraption with no function, composed of old bicycle wheels, car parts, a still for making moonshine, and a slideless trombone: a manifestation, perhaps, of the wreck of the sixties.

One night, Kesey drove his car across a railroad track in Springfield, Oregon, just as a train was passing. He was not badly hurt in the collision, nor was his daughter Shannon and their dog Pretzel, but his son Jed appeared to be dead. "Ken, through a combination of will, prayer, and mouth-to-mouth resuscitation, coaxed Jed back from the Shadows," McMurtry said.

But then, in 1984, Jed died in a van accident: the van had been carrying members of the University of Oregon's wrestling team to a meet. Kesey's always erratic behavior unraveled even further. Friends thought he was manic-depressive. He spent most of the rest of his years in a fog of nostalgia, endlessly editing footage from Further's 1964 trek across the continent. He *did* manage to publish a few more books, finally, pale efforts compared to his first two novels. "People aren't reading novels anymore," he said in 1986. "Novels just won't do it. A writer has to keep up with the times. Rock 'n' roll and video. That's where the future is."

Just months before he made this statement, his old pal McMurtry had won the Pulitzer Prize for his novel *Lonesome Dove,* and would soon see it turned into one of the most popular miniseries in television history, making him a wealthy man.

McMurtry's days at the Bookman had stalled his work on the rodeo novel to such an extent that he feared he was not a novelist at all anymore—at best, he'd become a part-time essayist. He gathered the essays he'd written on Texas and asked Oppenheimer to pitch the collection to Dial. He was calling it *The Cowboy's Lament* (after toying with *The Cowboy in the Suburbs*).

Oppenheimer asked him to run the manuscript by her first. In early January 1968, she sent him two and a half pages of objections to the essays. ("I don't believe you [here]," "This section . . . is disappointing.") McMurtry was furious and hurt.

She followed up in a letter on February 12: "[W]hat most bothers me about THE COWBOY's LAMENT [is that in your] novels you find all the things you talk about [in the essays]: the sadness of parting . . . the death of the old way of life and how it moves you; the rural and soil traditions competing with the urban traditions for the allegiance of the young; and especially the PASSION. In COWBOY'S LAMENT . . . there is no passion. Only a sort of dry amusement and an underlying irritation [with Texas]. The irritation seems to hit its peak in the chapter on cities and especially the part about Austin . . . I think in this book you are arguing with yourself."

Doctorow agreed and rejected the book.

After a heated phone call, in which he pressed the volume's merits on Oppenheimer, McMurtry dashed off a three-page single-spaced letter to her, defending himself vigorously: "[T]he editor's remark that he didn't feel this book would do anything for me irritates the hell out of me because of all that is implicit in it. The masterpiece syndrome, you might call it." A case in point was William Styron, he said; Styron had been ruined by the "compulsion to produce successive masterpieces." As a result, *The Confessions of Nat Turner* was "terribly inflated and empty." "I probably will write 30 books in my life. I can't produce a constantly ascending stairstep of increasingly complex and thunderous novels. So I want to take off and write an essay, or an essayistic book . . . I didn't say it was going to be profound or a major statement. I meant it to be suggestive and engaging and written in damn good prose. You don't expect . . . to agree with the author on every point, you read it because you like his style and enjoy the play of his mind.

"The book, nonetheless, is part of my canon. I don't mean to stick it away in a drawer and pretend I only write novels. I wanted to write it and now I want to publish it . . . I just think of my work as organic and don't like to deny a part of it because it happens to be imperfect. It would be like denying a love because it wasn't perfect. I think a writer who means to stick with writing for a lifetime simply has to have the courage of his mistakes or he's probably not ever going to learn enough to write the masterpieces."

He railed against the publishing world's provincialism; against the appetite among readers (especially in New York) for Texas stereotypes a la John Bainbridge and J. Frank Dobie; against the love of profit undermining the nurturing of youthful talent ("I don't mind them thinking about their sales, that's legitimate. I resent them thinking they have to think about my reputation because that's in my hands and they either have to trust me over the long stretch or they have to kiss me goodbye").

This rejection reopened the wound of *Lovebreaking* (the rodeo novel) and Leggett's dismissal of *it*: "[I]t truly saddens me that I didn't go on and get it published, because it really belonged in there, between <u>Cheyenne</u> and the <u>Last Picture Show</u>," McMurtry told Oppenheimer. "Sure it was flawed in some ways, but it was a damned interesting flawed novel and there are some beautiful things in it I will have to cut away to write it as I now want it."

He said he would publish the essay collection privately.

As for the tension the book had caused between him and his agent, he said it would grieve him terribly if a permanent rift opened in their relationship. He admitted her reaction to the essays continued to puzzle him; he couldn't understand why she didn't see the originality of the book: "Anyhow, of course, I love you, and don't let it worry you so much."

Bill Wittliff, born in South Texas in 1940, became, like McMurtry, a collector of texts when he was a teenager. He tried to sneak into an Elvis Presley concert in San Antonio. He crawled through a back window in the auditorium which turned out to be a portal into Presley's dressing room. Startled and then amused by the boy's explanation that he'd traveled a long distance and couldn't get in, Presley wrote a note on a paper towel telling the security guards to seat Wittliff in the arena. Wittliff kept and later framed the paper towel—"because it was my way of telling myself that I mattered," he said.

His father was a "toilet-hugging drunk" (though Wittliff convinced his schoolmates his dad was a war hero, killed in World War II), and his mother scraped by as a twenty-four-hour switchboard operator, earning thirty dollars a month. The boy led an aimless existence until J. Frank Dobie's folklore collection, *Tales of Old-Time Texas*—a gift from his aunt—"set [him] on fire. Until that moment it never occurred to me that books and writing could come out of your own experience, your own soil," he said. His mother saved some money so he could go to college. At the University of Texas, he majored in journalism, but he didn't want to learn to type. He showed up in class each day wearing his arm in a sling. What he excelled at was poker.

In 1963, he married his college sweetheart, Sally Bowers, and went to work as a production manager for Southern Methodist University Press in Dallas. Already, in addition to his love of writing and his passion for collecting historical artifacts and documents, he had begun to pursue photography, and he developed a fine eye for book design. Sitting at their kitchen table one night, he and Sally decided to use his poker winnings to start a small publishing house, the Encino Press. "Starting the Encino Press was a way of being involved with books without being at risk personally," he said. "Later, when I got more confident [with my writing], I was willing to take my clothes off and lay down on the table. Which is what it is when you're writing and really going for it." He would design the limited edition books. They would concern Texas and Texas history, and be aimed at collectors. Wittliff was determined that his first author would be J. Frank Dobie. Charmed by the young man's passion and knowledge, Dobie gave him a story, royalty-free.

The Wittliffs moved to Austin, eventually landing in an old two-story house at Sixth and South Lamar once occupied by O. Henry. From there they issued beautifully produced and designed editions, including books by John Graves, *The Narrative of Robert Hancock Hunter,* which was about a soldier in the Texas Revolution, *Cooking and Curing with Mexican Herbs,* and rodeo histories. Over time, the press would win more than a hundred literary and design awards.

Graves often visited the house on South Lamar, to advise the Wittliffs on possible titles. He looked like a "peach farmer, wearing khakis," said Joe Holley, a young graduate of Abilene Christian College who worked for the Wittliffs unloading trucks, proofreading, and copyediting. "Reading with Bill was my education," he said. He devoured Graves and Willie Morris. One day in 1968, Wittliff handed him a manuscript of essays by Larry McMurtry. "He was writing about stuff I knew about and was turning it into art," Holley said. Like many other young writers who'd discovered Mc-Murtry's prose, "I thought it was close to what I might be able to do some-day." (Holley would become a celebrated and accomplished journalist.)

McMurtry had turned to the Encino Press after the rejection from Dial. He told his friends he'd given up on New York. Publishers there would never understand him, and it was too much trouble to try to educate them. He'd retitled the essay collection *In a Narrow Grave* after the ballad "The Dying Cowboy" ("By my father's grave there let mine be . . . In a narrow grave just six by three . . ."). The book was the beginning of a long and bountiful partnership between McMurtry and Bill Wittliff.

"*In a Narrow Grave* . . . had all these four-letter words [in it]," Wittliff said. "And it jumped some of the Texas heroes, some of my heroes. Ooh, man, once or twice a week somebody called my office and chewed my ass out [about that book]."

In his "irritated" and "fine, dry, literary 18th century style" (Dorothea Oppenheimer said), McMurtry had eviscerated southwestern literature, dismissing Dobie, Webb, and Bedichek as men of "inhibited reflection"; he trash-talked Texas cities ("Midland . . . a new oiltown, a community of some 70,000 nervous people located many many miles from anywhere amid the desolate West Texas plain . . . [has an] unpleasantness quotient [that is] very high"); he mocked American celebrity culture ("The Texas writer who really wants to get famous has only to work up his autobiography in such a way that it will (1) explain the [Kennedy] assassination and (2) make it possible for President Johnson to be impeached. If he can do that, his name is made. *The New York Review of Books* will beat a path to his door, particularly if his door happens to be somewhere in Manhattan . . . [H]e may even meet Susan Sontag").

But McMurtry's cynicism was leavened by his elegiac sensibility: "In Austin, I was walking down Travis Street toward noon of a summer day, on my way to visit a bookshop, when I saw Mr. Dobie starting up the hill below me," he wrote. "He had a book in his hand . . . As he approached I debated speaking, but the day was broiling, I was carrying my young son, and Mr. Dobie was obviously concentrating on getting up the hill and into the shade. He didn't look up and I said nothing, but when I crossed the street at the foot of the hill I saw him at the top, his Stetson pushed back and his white hair fallen on his brow, resting a moment by a parking meter. Though I did not know him and . . . did not care for his books I felt that catch in the heart that always comes when I see that one of the Old Ones of this land will soon be gone, no more to ride the river nor follow the Longhorn cow."

Contrary to Oppenheimer's objections, the fact that the book laid out a long-running self-argument was what made it so fascinating: McMurtry openly discussing, without sentiment or deference to anyone, his love-hate for the places and forces shaping him. Critic Tom Pilkington noted that the "essay is not a form that most Texas writers find congenial. Like the people from whom they spring, they are apparently too impatient and too inclined toward action . . . to feel at home in such a leisurely, introspective genre." He praised McMurtry's humor, wit, and insight: "He seems very sure of himself, and his comments have an air of crisp authority. Occasionally he is almost cocky . . . One reason, I think, that he can write about his native state with absolute certainty . . . is because he has been tested severely; he has been able to look upon Texas in the harsh light of day, to see all her warts and wrinkles and to love her still." Dave Hickey wrote: "Here is an honorable and self-effacing novelist who has chosen to publish an honest set of personal essays about Texas, and to publish it *in* Texas . . . [W]hat is most delightful about this book is McMurtry's voice, educated, indirect and full of surprising turns and modulation that are simply not in his novels."

In a Narrow Grave was "the best-designed book I will ever have," McMurtry said. "Bill Wittliff was reaching his peak as a book designer just about then." The volume also had the most tortured printing history of any of McMurtry's books.

Wittliff ordered 2,250 copies of it. Along with Joe Holley, Betty Greene, wife of Texas author A. C. Greene, was assisting the Wittliffs as a proofreader. She noticed over sixty errors in the first copies returned from the printer, the most egregious of which was the word "sky*crap*ers" instead of "skyscrapers" (emphasis mine). *Crap indeed,* Greene thought. How could the book go through three sets of proofs and still contain so many typos? Wittliff told conflicting stories. He said he had to use a new printer because his regular printer refused to publish McMurtry's "cuss words." The printer fouled up the text. Wittliff also said the first typographer he approached was "unwilling to 'contribute to moral decay' and refused to set type for that language." So Wittliff turned to a "Mexican typesetter" who "took it upon himself" to "reset type during the slicking process if the slugs were too high or too low."

Wittliff swore that 845 copies of *In a Narrow Grave* had already been bound before anyone noticed the errors. He said McMurtry kept five of them, Encino stored away eight, and all the rest were destroyed before Encino reprinted the book with corrections.

McMurtry never corroborated this story. He said he believed Wittliff was too cheap to pulp that many books. Ultimately, the press had to cop to its sloppiness (and McMurtry himself was a notoriously poor proofreader).

Over the years, rare-book dealers have debated how many copies of the first edition still exist: "[R]eportedly all but 15 of the error-riddled first issue were destroyed," one dealer claimed. Another said, "Supposedly 12 copies of the first edition survived a fire," but that version of events appeared to refer to a warehouse disaster *before* McMurtry's manuscript made its way to Wittliff. The confusion and competing stories have increased the book's value. In 2016, Heritage Auctions sold a set of page proofs containing the "skycrapers" error for $2,750. And occasionally a "skycrapers" volume will still surface in a bookshop or auction house, highly coveted by collectors.

I could have fallen for Larry, but I was really smart not to," Babette Fraser said. "We did have some romantic involvement, but it wasn't extensive. He didn't really like to be in one place. Larry had to be off roaming, even when he was living in Houston. He had the enjoyment of moving on the highway, even at night, the sense of openness, space."

Hollywood was one of the places he'd light out for, when he got a break from teaching. Through the LA talent agency Ziegler-Ross-Tennant, Dorothea Oppenheimer had sold a movie option for *The Last Picture Show* for $7,500 to a young, on-the-make film producer named Steve Friedman. Friedman's first check bounced. And then nothing happened. (Bill Tennant, of the talent agency, would help produce *Easy Rider* and *Rosemary's Baby*, and he would be called upon to identify Sharon Tate and other victims of Charles Manson's gang after the murders.)

As McMurtry waited for a star to step in to get *Picture Show* made, the way Paul Newman had jump-started *Hud, he* was being approached for screenwriting jobs. After the success of *Hud*, he was seen in LA as a man who could deliver surefire Westerns. The only problem was, he had never laid eyes on a screenplay, much less learned how to write one. Producer Alan Pakula had summoned him to Hollywood to discuss turning a book called *Spawn of Evil*—a history of Mississippi outlaws—into a movie. After touring the Warner Bros. lot, and glimpsing Natalie Wood sitting in a chair "looking very very bored" on the soundstage where *Inside Daisy Clover* was being filmed, McMurtry sat on a couch in Pakula's office sipping a Dr Pepper during a lengthy story conference. He gathered it would be his task to stretch the eleven pages of the book that actually interested Pakula (or maybe the only pages he'd read) into a full-length motion picture. "[M]y imagination doesn't really work unless a typewriter is sitting directly in front of me—I am all but incapable of conceiving stories abstractly," he said, so he was no help when Pakula pitched "ideas" at him. "[I]t is a charming thing to watch," when "moviemakers have 'ideas,'" McMurtry said. "The delight these 'ideas' occasion, when they finally appear, approximates what an ardent 89-year-old lover might feel upon discovering that he has an erection. Unfortunately, the promise of these 'ideas' (like that of not a few erections) is something that is often appreciated only by the possessor."

Pakula sent him back to Houston to write a treatment, and not knowing that a treatment was simply a summary of the story, usually about twenty pages long, McMurtry produced five hundred pages of "swamp chases, tavern brawls, and slave revolts." The results "disappeared forever into Burbank." But he learned that a writer gets paid—in this case, $3,000—whether or not the movie in question ever gets made. In a bookshop on Hollywood Boulevard, he found a Xeroxed copy of Frank and Ravetch's script for *Hud* and purchased it for forty dollars. By studying it, he taught himself to write movie scripts. He continued to receive projects from LA, including a proposed adaptation of John Barth's first novel, *The Floating Opera*. None of the movies made it to the screen, but McMurtry was happy to pocket the money. And he liked Hollywood. It was mercifully free of the foggy marine layer that had kept him so gloomy in San Francisco. He stayed in the Roosevelt Hotel, where Faulkner had spent time drinking during his tenure in California. McMurtry would leave story conferences and hang out in the open-till-midnight bookstores on Hollywood Boulevard. One afternoon, departing a movie lot, he saw a gruff man with the arrogant air of a producer shove a young woman through a narrow doorway, slap her, call her a bitch and a terrible actress, and swear she was through. The incident did not lessen his pleasure in Hollywood's generally sunny atmosphere, but it taught him not to overvalue the industry into which he was being invited.

The main thing was the drive. Houston to Wichita Falls on US 287, cutting over to Texas Highway 86 West, past the Midway Drive-In, a holdover from the fifties (popcorn and pajamas in the front seats of cars, with metal speakers hanging in the windows, big as saddlebags), all the way to Clovis, New Mexico, and then—depending on his mood—swinging by Billy the Kid's grave in Fort Sumner (not much to see, really, just a rough, chalky stone), darting up to the red-dirt canyons, the adobe casitas, near Abiquiu ("Wild Choke Cherry Place" in the Tewa language). From there, he could skim the borders of Georgia O'Keeffe's Ghost Ranch and hit I-40 or catch the remnants of the old Okie road, Route 66, heading for the teepee-shaped cabins of San Bernadino's Wigwam Motel, ending up at the crumbling edge of the continent at the Santa Monica Pier. Either way, as he passed through the middle of Arizona—the Petrified Forest—he'd stop to stare at the yellow blossoms of the creosote bushes or the green-white flowers of desert sage. He'd breathe in the bitter turpentine odor of shaggy sage leaves after a mild rainfall, redolent of camphor, terpenoids, and other pungent oils.

Over time, though, as LA beckoned him, his roaming habits changed. As much as he loved driving long distances, especially in the wide-open West, he appreciated it when Hollywood picked up his expense tab, and he developed a fondness for first-class air travel.

Back in Houston, he asked Babette Fraser out. She was a tall, dark-haired Texas girl who'd just returned to the States from a stint studying in England. She wanted to take a creative writing class at Rice; she asked McMurtry if she could audit his course. He handed her a reading list and wanted to know how many of the books on it she had read. "The canon according to Larry," she said. "I told him I had read a number of the books, though I really hadn't read as many as I checked. I probably overestimated by about a third, listing books I'd just heard of. Anyway, he was impressed."

McMurtry didn't attract her at first. "Everybody wore jeans, but no-body turned up the cuffs. Larry turned his up. How uncool can you be?" But he *was* driving the red coupe he'd taken from Dorman David, and he was a wicked Ping-Pong player, having improved his skills by testing them against the Chinese mathematicians and Hungarian pilots (exchange students) he'd met at Rice.

"Larry had no problem dating students," Fraser said. Soon she was play-ing tennis with him every afternoon. "One night we had a barbecue dinner together—nothing green was in sight—but most of our dates were after-noon dates," Fraser said. "We'd take James to the park, where he'd play on the jungle gym. We talked books. He gave me a copy of *Anna Karenina*. He was fascinating. He had a sense of humor and erudition—and he didn't *look* like he had it. At that time, some of the professors affected an urbane quality. Larry was twice as erudite as any of them were. He'd read every-thing and thought about it. In those days, he smiled a good deal." Many years later, when she'd run into him occasionally at Texas literary functions, she'd sense a deep melancholy in him, "but I didn't get those sad notes at all when he was young. If I had been spending the night, I would have seen it. I have tended toward depression, and I would have resonated with that. But ours were afternoon dates."

She learned that he was "seeing about five people" while he was dating her, including Carol Flake Chapman, who would one day work for *Vanity Fair*, *The New Yorker*, and many other magazines, and Lili Milani, who became a renowned architect.

Fraser didn't approve of Ken Kesey and the Pranksters in the spring of '67 when they arrived in Houston. She found them loud and dull.

"One night Larry picked me up at my house and met my mother," she recalled. "She was a bit like Aurora in *Terms of Endearment*, and I have always wondered if he used part of her in the book . . . My daddy had died a year earlier. When Larry walked into the house, he went right over and sat down in the Daddy Chair, a leather La-Z-Boy with an ottoman. He put his feet up. Mother, appalled, told me later, 'You don't need to have anything to do with that young man.'"

At one point, in late 1967, Greg Curtis became aware that McMurtry was seeing a new woman and "he had a telephone in his house whose number only she knew. Larry taped a sign to the phone that said 'No one but me is to answer this phone EVER.'"

"Larry's tinge of melancholy may have helped make him [so] attractive to women. He was not a womanizer, though—he was a serial romancer," Mike Evans said. Evans thought McMurtry met "the lovely Marcia Carter" at "James's day school. She had a daughter James's age named Ceci. Larry had a theory that the way to approach a woman with a daughter was to make up to the daughter, which would awaken feelings of jealousy in the mother or at least get her attention. I don't know if that's what worked with Marcia, but something did . . . An English major who had written a thesis on Muriel Spark, she had come to Houston with her journalist husband Philip Carter, who was the Houston bureau chief for *Newsweek*."

Marcia Spruce McGhee was born on January 20, 1940. Her father, George Crews McGhee, born in Waco and educated at the University of Oklahoma, was a geophysicist, eventually a top-ranking State Department official, and an ambassador to West Germany during the Cold War. Working for his father-in-law, Dallas businessman Everette Lee DeGolyer, he discovered one of the country's major oil fields, the West Tepetate in

Louisiana, and became a wealthy man before the age of thirty. His knowledge of oil production and his association with DeGolyer made him an invaluable government consultant. After the war he joined the State Department. In 1947, when Marcia was seven, Harry Truman tapped McGhee to be the coordinator for U.S. aid to Greece and Turkey. He was also charged with mapping a refugee program for Palestinians displaced by the founding of Israel. In 1949, he became the assistant U.S. secretary of state for Near Eastern and African affairs, the first man to hold the position.

Everette DeGolyer had been a staff member of both the Petroleum Administration for War and the atomic energy committee on raw materials. He did a stint with the Office of Strategic Services, the forerunner of the CIA. He was a prolific writer and public speaker, publishing several books on geology, law, science, literature, and southwestern history. He amassed an enormous personal book collection and helped establish important research libraries at Southern Methodist University, the University of Texas, and the University of Oklahoma. Marcia was especially fond of his wife, Nell, who showered her with gifts.

In fact, Marcia's youth can be traced in a series of thank-you notes to her grandmother (known affectionately as Birdy), archived now in the DeGolyer Library at SMU—expressions of pleasure at the latest bracelet, scarf, chocolate box, or engraved silverware to arrive in the mail from Birdy's home in Dallas to wherever Marcia happened to be staying with her family—in their house in Washington, DC, or on their farm in Middleburg, Virginia, or at an outpost in Greece or Turkey, or on vacation in Europe.

Between the listings of goods, glimpses of Marcia's life emerge: playing with the ducks on the farm, worrying about her weight, missing radio and TV while living in Turkey (M&M's weren't available at the American PX, she complained), distrusting the Turkish people (the boys were arrogant, the old men untidy, the women dour), chafing against her high school English teacher for insisting she write metered poetry, marveling at the many boys who wanted to date her.

She was sixteen when Everette DeGolyer killed himself with a single gunshot, despondent over his deteriorating eyesight and his inability to read.

She attended the Madeira School, a private all-girls boarding school on a 376-acre campus minutes from the center of DC. She went to Vassar, where she fretted about not having anything to do "socially," dated several boys (one "simple," one "mushy," one "plain"), enjoyed the sights and shows of New York, and once she'd met Philip Carter, a budding southern journalist, sneaking off to see him in New Orleans.

She was funny, confident, dazzlingly beautiful with short brown hair. Just out of college, she wasn't sure what she wanted to do with her life, but she knew she needed intellectual stimulation and an "old and musty— like old books" atmosphere. She returned to school for a while, at George Washington, to study philosophy and literature.

Philip Dutartre Carter, the young man she married in September 1962, was the son of Hodding Carter II (known to his family as "Big"), a legendary journalist, author, and publisher in Greenville, Mississippi. Big won a Pulitzer Prize for his editorials denouncing racism. He waged decades-long civil rights battles with the Klan. He once told the entire Mississippi state legislature to "go to Hell, collectively or singly."

Philip, along with his brothers Tommy and Hodding III, grew up hearing anonymous telephone threats made against their father for his courageous stands on race. (Even Walker Percy's father, Will, who had financed Carter's paper and generally approved of his crusading, thought he went too far sometimes—there was nothing wrong, Will Percy insisted, with having a Black manservant bringing you juice and coffee in the mornings.)

Philip watched his father load his twelve-gauge of an evening and sit on the front porch or among the bushes next to the driveway, waiting for trouble. "Guns were an enormous part of our lives," he said. "We were always fantasizing about violence." As kids, he and Tommy would play with their father's pistol, removing five out of six cartridges from the chamber, pointing the gun at the ground and pulling the trigger. Years later, Philip was medically disqualified from military service because he'd accidentally shot himself in the foot while hunting. And in 1964, nineteen-year-old Tommy would shoot himself in the head, fooling around with a gun after a late-night party, playing Russian roulette.

Philip attended a private Episcopalian high school in Alexandria, Virginia, before losing a few years, along with his brother Hodding, to partying and drinking. "There seemed to be a very civilized and purposeful attention to getting falling-down drunk, like after a war when the officers don't know what to do with themselves," said a friend. Not only did the brothers have Tommy's tragedy to face, they had Big's shadow to escape. Finally Philip realized he couldn't outrun his father's legacy. He followed the old man into journalism, writing for the *New York Herald Tribune, The Washington Post,* and *Newsweek.* Hodding went to Princeton, served in the Marine Corps, worked as a newspaper reporter, and then as a Democratic Party activist, eventually becoming Jimmy Carter's assistant secretary of state for public affairs, and a spokesperson for the State Department during the Iran hostage crisis.

Marcia's letters to Birdy concerning the early years of her marriage to Philip sing his praises as a junior star reporter, his princely behavior, and the idyllic life she was sure to share with him. He agreed with her that he should finish college, so he enrolled in Tulane and the couple moved to New Orleans. They got a typical French Quarter apartment with a wrought-iron balcony overlooking a quiet garden; Marcia furnished it with a hope chest from Birdy and a big brass bed. She entertained guests, using the fine, heavy silverware from her grandmother. She vacationed in the Netherlands, in Florence and Venice, living in "Embassy splendor." She feared her life was too easy. She remained on guard, she said, against becoming a "frivolous" wife.

One night, her mother- and father-in-law came to the Quarter for a quiet dinner in the apartment. Through an open window they heard a car backfire in the street. Old fears and old habits prompted Hodding to yell, "Hit the floor! Get your gun!" Horrified, Marcia sat upright in her chair as the Carter family went down, and Philip crawled across the floor toward the balcony, wielding his weapon.

Lingering family tensions weren't reserved for the Carters. Marcia made a major faux pas one spring when she failed to send a prompt thank-you note to Birdy following the gift of a pair of earrings. Birdy wrote to say she was angry and traumatized that her generosity had not been acknowledged right away, and Marcia—a twenty-seven-year-old married woman—sounded as abject and frightened as a child in her lengthy reply, apologizing profusely for her thoughtlessness. Her nervousness revealed the strict social pressures she had negotiated all her life.

Her daughter was born in 1963. Soon LBJ and the space program, shooting for the moon, made Houston a powerful magnet for journalists, and Philip was drawn there. The move was hard on Marcia. Often Philip left her alone with Ceci, flying to the LBJ ranch to cover the president's press conferences. Fitfully, he tried writing a book on Johnson's boyhood. The old family newspaper in Mississippi was becoming a strain on him: his mother didn't know what to do with it; it needed a good managing editor to maintain Big's progressive legacy. (Finally, the Carter family sold the paper for $18 million to Freedom Newspapers, a far-right-wing chain based in Santa Ana, California.)

With Philip feeling busy, tense, and distracted much of the time, Marcia and Ceci spent lengthy stretches in DC, or at "Farmer's Delight," the family farm in Middleburg. Marcia's letters to Birdy began to swell with laments about her naiveté, her careless and thoughtless approach to marriage, the turmoil she was experiencing. She feared she had disappointed her grandmother with her immature behavior and deprived her daughter of a peaceful home. She mentioned the couple's strenuous efforts to solve their problems, to close the growing distance between them.

In late '67 and early '68, McMurtry's phone calls and letters to Dorothea Oppenheimer frequently mentioned his romance with an astonishing woman with whom he shared a passion for books and the joys and aggravations of raising a child. Oppenheimer wished him luck and expressed her concern when she learned the woman was married.

"Larry said Marcia was his great passion," Babette Fraser remembered. "Like Anna Karenina—you only get one of those in your life."

Jamie, six, didn't pay much attention to his father's girlfriends. Nor did he care much for books. They were always lying around—something to line the walls with. The radio was a lot more interesting.

"[My dad and I] didn't have a washing machine, so we'd go to the laundromat every Sunday," he recalled. "It was in a strip mall, and we'd wait for our clothes and go over and play the jukebox. Three songs for a quarter. We'd listen to Hank Williams sing 'Cold Cold Heart' and then 'Gates of Eden' and 'Like a Rolling Stone' by Dylan. A great mix of music. We also spent a lot of time at this little beer-joint-drive-in over in Richmond, outside of Houston. They had a great jukebox too. With those tableside jukebox machines. We'd play Merle's 'Working Man Blues' and 'Radiator Man from Wasco,' and soak up the country."

Listening to music was much more fun than reading—and not nearly as much work as writing, Jamie figured, observing his father at the typewriter.

One day a driller driving his pickup south down Texas 6, near the current intersection of I-10 and Westheimer, noticed a young man sitting in a weedy field pecking at a typewriter. The fellow parked his truck and approached the young man, to see if he was all right. "What are you doing?" he asked. "Writing a novel," Larry McMurtry answered. "Okay," the fellow said. "Good, I guess." He shook the young man's hand, returned to his pickup, and drove away.

Meanwhile, in "the spring of 1968, Max [Crawford] and I had started a little magazine, *The Redneck Review*," Mike Evans said. "For our first issue Larry gave us a chapter from [a novel he was writing] . . . his love letter to Rice graduate school." This was the rodeo novel he'd been revising since before *The Last Picture Show*; it had become an epic of the modern American West, with glimpses of the rodeo circuit, of Hollywood, and of urban student life. McMurtry considered it his first attempt at an *adult* novel, free of childhood reminiscences and nostalgia. "One night [Larry] got a call from Michael Korda at Simon & Schuster," Evans continued. "Korda had picked up a copy of the *Redneck* at the Gotham Book Mart, where I had sent a dozen copies, and he had read Larry's chapter and wanted to publish the novel."

Korda remembered his introduction to McMurtry slightly differently. He had recently become editor in chief at S&S, following Robert Gottlieb's departure for Knopf. He said Oppenheimer called him up one day, pitching a young writer from Texas, a major talent who'd not yet had the luck of good sales, despite the very successful movie made from his first novel.

Korda was a sophisticated gentleman, born in London, educated in France, Switzerland, finally at Oxford. As a member of the Royal Air Force, he'd done intelligence work in Germany. When he was a young man, he fell hard for the myth of the American West. His mother was an actress and his father, a Hungarian, was a film production designer; when the couple split, his mother remarried and moved to Dallas with Korda's stepfather, a hotel manager. His dad went to Hollywood. In Texas and in California, and at ski resorts in the Rockies—old miners' camps, where his father took him on vacation—Korda learned to ride horses. The animals became an integral "part of [his] life," he said. Oppenheimer's news of a writer who knew the West like the back of his hand intrigued him, though he dreaded dealing with the agent, "an Olympic-level kvetch," he said of her, fiercely loyal to her clients. "Shy, retiring, and always apologetic . . . Dorothea shied away from conflict, but she more than made up for that by sheer stubbornness and patience," Korda explained. Still, "once she knew that you shared her enthusiasm for an author's work, she was fair and never asked for the impossible." She was a formidable "woman endowed with extraordinary taste, courage, [and] humor in the face of adversity."

She gave Korda an earful about how "East Coast reviewers just didn't get McMurtry." (Though, to be fair, he had been generally well received—just not as *warmly* as she wished.) "It was, she thought, a question of urban prejudice—they simply couldn't take seriously a novelist who had been born in Archer City, Texas, was raised as a cowhand, and wrote about life in Texas." Korda conceded there was a good deal of truth in this. "[T]he prevailing tone of American fiction at the time was urban, Jewish, and Eastern—the West was seen, in the eyes of the literati, as 'a colossal mistake' (to quote Freud's famous remark about America)," he said. Moreover, "publishers, by and large, lived in New York City (except for the few who lived then in Boston and Philadelphia) and most of them were 'progressive' in a mild way, 'liberal' in the sense that New York City itself was liberal. Book readers, the review media, the publishing industry as a whole, were, seen from west of the Hudson, people who believed in certain liberal values." This did not automatically exclude McMurtry from their radar: his fiction was neither screamingly liberal nor conservative—but his focus on the past and certain (largely white) American traditions tended to puzzle eastern book people, or else it left them cold.

In the late 1950s, when Korda had first joined Simon & Schuster, the publisher felt moribund to him, caught in a postwar malaise, pushing cocktail-party stories, stories of soulless, gray-suited Organization Men. But then a Harvard-educated Democrat was elected to serve in the White House, a man who actually read books "and surrounded himself with 'progressive' figures from academia," Korda said. At that point, "many in publishing were feeling that 'all's right with the world.'" At S&S, Robert Gottlieb's marathon sessions with Joseph Heller editing the *Catch-22* manuscript became legendary: Korda would pass by Gottlieb's office and see strands of Heller's novel "endlessly retyped, look[ing] at every stage like a jigsaw puzzle as [Joe and Gottlieb] labored over it, bits and pieces of it taped to every available surface in Gottlieb's cramped office. *That*, I thought, is editing." The result was one of the most popular and enduring books of the 1960s, an era-defining novel sitting atop the rubble of the war in Vietnam.

By the time Dorothea Oppenheimer approached Korda about Larry McMurtry—Kennedy long dead, Johnson mired in Southeast Asia, Nixon high-stepping to power—the decade had darkened considerably. Gottlieb had left Simon & Schuster, taking Heller with him. Korda needed a big score to boost S&S's fortunes. Given the eastern bias against him, McMurtry was a long shot, Korda thought—but the man knew horses, and that was good enough for him! He asked Oppenheimer to send him a section of McMurtry's manuscript. "I read it [over]night, and it was love at first sight," Korda said. "I found it difficult to believe that any reader, even a *Times* reviewer, could dislike the heroine, Patsy Carpenter, around whose marriage to a young graduate student the whole book revolves. As for rodeo, here it was. If the American public wanted the *Moby-Dick* of rodeo, McMurtry had provided it." Korda resolved to fly to Houston to meet the young author.

An elegant, slender, thin-faced man—able to "adapt to any social habitat, high or low, not excluding the Hungarian revolution," McMurtry said— Korda had chosen to wear jeans, cowboy boots, and a silver bolo tie featuring a cow's skull, to impress the Texan. He stood nervously in the lobby of the Warwick Hotel, beneath a massive chandelier just inside the doorway reflecting sunlight from the fountain outside. Peering among statues of nude women, hands hiding their pudenda, and bouquets of lilies lining the walls, he saw no one who looked either literary or range-roughened. Remarkably (he thought), Houston was full of handsome men in Brooks Brothers suits and lovely, bejeweled women, just as in any other cosmopolitan center.

Finally, a "very tall, lean, serious-looking fellow, dressed in a sports jacket" emerged from the crowd and asked if he was Michael Korda. "He did not, at first glance, look like a Texan to me," Korda admitted. "He wore glasses and had a thick head of black hair, emphasizing his pallor." With him was Babette Fraser, who had a tough time suppressing her laughter at the New Yorker's rustic getup.

Korda was further surprised when McMurtry only muttered, "Uh-huh . . . uh-huh . . ." when the editor praised him, telling him he "was already an unusual phenomenon in American writing . . . with a remarkable ability to write about women and an absolutely sure eye for the bleak landscape of small-town Texas." (In later years, Korda would only half jokingly refer to McMurtry as the "Flaubert of the Plains.") He was stunned to learn that McMurtry's "own interest in rodeo was rather less than mine. He had seen plenty of rodeo in his life, and he could take it or leave it alone. He did not share my enthusiasm for horses, either . . . So far as he was concerned, he had seen as much of horses as he ever wanted." The men *did* begin to bond when they discussed their young sons, both about the same age.

McMurtry and Fraser took Korda to an Italian restaurant just off Telephone Road, notorious, then, for its whorehouses and bar violence. (McMurtry said he had based a scene in his new novel on a newspaper clipping he'd found about a man who'd shot up a beer joint because there weren't enough beans in his chili.) Now *this* was Texas! Korda enjoyed himself immensely. From that first meal, he realized that McMurtry would not accept editorial advice from anyone. Korda decided, there at the table, to have the good sense not to offer any such advice: "I returned to New York as [Larry's] publisher, carrying with me a carton of Diet Dr Pepper, to which [he] had converted me and which was at that time unobtainable in the Northeast."

McMurtry was calling his novel *Country of the Horn,* hoping to evoke both the image of cattle and a sense of erotic heat, and he intended to dedicate it to Marcia Carter, "the woman with whom I found the unemptiable Horn."

Marcia wrote to Birdy that she didn't believe her marriage to Philip could survive. She'd found a wonderful new friend with whom she shared many interests and who offered her unqualified moral support.

"I have had a hard day," McMurtry wrote Oppenheimer at one point. "We were discovered last night—her husband broke into a lock box and found all my letters. Much chaos and confusion just now, it may work out and may not. I'm hoping."

Oppenheimer sent her best wishes, along with a warning: "[N]ever, never write letters that might reveal something. That is a very old rule. I mean in a situation of this kind."

Soon thereafter—in the spring of 1969—Marcia told her grandmother the marriage was over. She didn't know what she would do. At the same time, Jo was set to graduate with her doctorate from Rice. In December, in New York, at the Modern Language Association conference, where prospective college teachers sought jobs, she had lined up fourteen interviews for positions at various institutions across the country. She didn't know where she'd end up, but her professional need to move "was worrisome for her relationship with James," Mike Evans said.

As a graduation present, McMurtry gave Jo a complete set of the Oxford English Dictionary, "a princely gift," Evans noted, and an expensive one.

As if these potential changes weren't enough to give McMurtry migraines, the fact that he had just received tenure from Rice made him itchy—job security, yes, but also a life sentence, if one chose to see it that way. "I was beginning to feel I needed out of Houston," he said. "It was time for me to decide if I was going to be a novelist or a professor . . . and if I was going to be a writer, going East was the thing to do . . . [It] made more sense than teaching the same old classes year after year."

Besides, a lot of his old pals had left. The Waddingtons were living in Wisconsin now. McMurtry missed them despite the turbulence he had caused the relationship, romancing Linda. Even his beloved coupe was gone now, or at least no longer whole. Mike Evans had wrecked it. McMurtry knew the boy couldn't afford to pay for it, so he didn't even suggest he pony up for repairs.

The decision to leave was made easier by Korda's enthusiasm for the new novel, an infusion of cash from Dell for the paperback rights to *The Last Picture Show*, and by continuing movement on the movie front. "That Michael Korda is a dynamo and is stirring up a lot of publicity on THE COUNTRY OF THE HORN," Oppenheimer wrote McMurtry when she sent him the nearly eight-thousand-dollar signing advance from Simon & Schuster. "At this rate it should sell a million copies."

Simon & Schuster also purchased the rights to reprint *In a Narrow Grave* in a mass market edition.

"The savage lusts of adolescent innocence . . . The explosive boredom of a dusty Texas town," gushed the cover of Dell's *The Last Picture Show*, alongside a sepia drawing of a nearly nude woman nuzzling a tall bare-chested man. The publisher was aiming to sell thousands of copies of the novel to horny teenagers thumbing through drugstore book racks. It paid McMurtry $14,000 for the chance to do so.

Throughout the spring, summer, and fall of 1969, while McMurtry's life was becoming more and more unsettled, Oppenheimer informed him of fast-moving action in Hollywood: in June, Steve Friedman was trying to sell *Picture Show* to a "third party," potentially securing $15,000 for McMurtry plus a share of future profits. Meanwhile, Friedman owed McMurtry nearly $25,000 to maintain the option. In August, Oppenheimer told McMurtry that Friedman had "sold THE LAST PICTURE SHOW to Bert Schneider, who produced EASY RIDER . . . [T]hey are using a different screenplay, thank God." Then, in October, she passed along the news that, through Schneider's outfit, a director named Peter Bogdanovich had stepped into the project. "It all sounds rather fuzzy to me," she confessed. "I know nothing about Bogdonavich [*sic*] except that he has been maneuvering to get ahold of TLPS for a long time so if nothing else he is at least persistent. I don't trust any of these types."

Temporarily encouraged by these developments, McMurtry took a leave of absence from Rice. Jo received a teaching offer from Westhampton College at the University of Richmond, not far from her birthplace; by "a lucky chance," Mike Evans said, the offer coincided with Marcia Carter deciding "she wanted to move to Washington, DC, near her family farm in the horse country of northern Virginia." McMurtry could follow his new love back east, and his son's mother would still be close.

With Marcia Carter, he'd finally found a world he fit. Despite her jet-setting childhood and her eastern social ties, she remained Texan enough, with family in Dallas, to be familiar to him. She understood *his* background (including his fondness for guns). At the same time, through her father and grandfather, she'd developed a passion for books and reading—to her way of thinking (unlike the McMurtry family), the literary life, the life of the mind, was in no way a betrayal of the values of hard work and simple philosophies of living. Marcia was patient, smart, and kind. Additionally, as he'd grown accustomed to traveling first class on Hollywood's dime, he appreciated her taste for the finer things. He'd found the complete package in her, and she felt the same about him.

It charmed him, how such a confident woman, quick at making pronouncements to others about how to live their lives, could sink so swiftly, on the spur of the moment, into a mass of insecurities. He believed she needed his pragmatism and calm.

He'd left Houston before. This felt like a bigger, more permanent break. He'd often told his students they wouldn't turn to sand if they crossed the Texas border, but now he wasn't sure he had the courage of his convictions. Lying awake at night he'd imagine speaking to his twelve-year-old self, telling him, "Try not to get hurt working the cattle" because there was so much more to life beyond the ranch. Now the ranch seemed comfy and safe.

Late in the afternoons he took long walks along Buffalo Bayou, inhaling Houston's rubber-and-brine, cabbage-rot odor, sweetened by the fragrances of rose and hyacinth blossoms; in the muddy water, he could identify people's castoffs, thrown from car windows or carted down here at night to be discarded—toaster ovens, pants and shoes, tire irons and hammers, busted guitars; he stood under the spreading, angel-like wings of Spanish moss dripping from rust-colored oaks creaking mildly in the wind; he sped along the Gulf Coast Freeway, aching to drink up the clouds spinning overhead; he went to double features at the River Oaks, imagining how he'd rewrite the scripts. He was about to rewrite his life, and he was right: though he'd return to Houston many times, he'd never live there again.

"Are you ok? And where are you?" Oppenheimer wrote him care of the Rice English Department on August 29, 1969. "I called your house and a nice young man"—probably Evans—"answered and said you had moved out with some of the furniture and he was staying there temporarily . . . I also called the Rice English Department secretary today and she said she was waiting to get your address . . . It's a funny feeling not knowing where you might be . . . In case you don't know it, I'm a worrier."

"He told me he was moving and wrote me a letter," said Babette Fraser. "He told me, 'Don't contact me in Washington.' He didn't want Marcia to get word of all his activities in Houston, though how she couldn't know was beyond me. But I stayed away as Larry asked."

Oppenheimer warned him, "I think you are living dangerously . . . You've been on the move since I've known you, come to think of it."

She knew how he was with women: generous and impulsive. "Be careful," she said.

PART TWO

Country Bypasses

14

"Larry hated Washington," Marcia Carter said. "He doesn't like the people, doesn't like the trees, doesn't like the closed-in feeling. He just doesn't transplant well."

In Waterford, Virginia, forty miles northwest of DC, nestled close to Carter's family farm in Middleburg, he rented a quaint old farmhouse with Jamie and a basset puppy named Franklin. McMurtry's new home was thirty-five miles from Willa Cather's birthplace—he'd reversed the course of his fellow western scribe. Immediately, he was afflicted with a severe case of "forest claustrophobia." "I felt gloomy [there] without knowing why," he said. "[I]t was only after many drives home to Texas that the reason finally became clear. I began to notice that once I crossed the Mississippi at Memphis and began to proceed across the delta, the Arkansas flats, my spirits would suddenly lift. The sky had quickly opened up, become a Western sky, with Western horizons beneath it. Coming into the openness, time after time, brought relief and indeed a kind of exhilaration. This lifting (and a corresponding lowering as I drove back east), occurred many times; I began to understand it bespoke a kind of sky longing."

The entire hamlet of Waterford was about to be officially declared a National Historic Landmark for its fine examples of Colonial and redbrick Federal houses. Built along the Catoctin Creek in Loudoun County, near the Blue Ridge Mountains, it was founded by Quakers in the 1730s and became the home of mill workers and Irish shoemakers. The courthouse, built in 1811 after the first courthouse had fallen into disrepair, was a site of multiple slave auctions as well as a secret gathering place, at night, for workers in the Underground Railroad. Three public lynchings occurred in Loudoun County following the Civil War, and in 1908 a Confederate memorial was erected in town under the auspices of the United Daughters of the Confederacy—the "Silent Sentinel," a bronze soldier cocking his musket.

Every October, a massive Civil War reenactment was the centerpiece of the Waterford Fair. The costumed recruits would dash across the countryside—a splendid expanse, along the creek, of green fields, wetlands, and marshes, with the smell of burning leaves in the air. Cattails and sumacs, herons and hawks. When spring came around, rabbits bounded plentifully among tall stalks of swaying grass, and occasionally a citizen would see a fox or even a lone coyote prowling among the gray and white houses in town.

It was the kind of pert village Marcia Carter was well accustomed to, having spent long childhood summers with her family at the farm. McMurtry and his boy felt alien there. Still, for Jamie, more and more attuned to the radio, the move from Houston provided some advantages. In a way, "[b]eing around Waterford was actually really good," he said. "I got exposed to a little bit of bluegrass, which I never learned to play all that well, but I got to hear bluegrass played by the people who'd actually done the things that were described in the song. Like plowing the field, and this, that and the other. There's a one-room schoolhouse in Lucketts, which [was] over the hill from us on Route 15, between Leesburg and Point of Rocks. They'd have bluegrass every Saturday night. They had a local house band and they usually had a road act, the Potomac Valley Boys or Country Gentlemen, something like that."

Private schools were another fact of Carter's world that McMurtry had a tough time accepting. She encouraged him to give Jamie the best education possible, and he agreed, but (after Jamie's short stint in the Loudoun Country Day School), he was distinctly uneasy sending his boy to Maret in the heart of DC, an expensive college-preparatory school founded by three French nuns. On the weekends, Jamie stayed with his mother in Richmond, two hours south of Waterford—a stone's throw for the road-loving McMurtry.

"In Richmond Jo and I married, and Larry seemed fine with that," Mike Evans said. "He picked up James after [our wedding] ceremony and in our apartment found my collection of his books, which he proceeded to inscribe." Jamie spent vacations, as well as the weekends, with Evans and Jo. "I would take him camping and fishing—two activities that had no appeal for Larry," Evans said. He also took the boy to concerts: Johnny Cash at the Richmond Coliseum, Kris Kristofferson. "I wanted to be Johnny Cash," James said. "I didn't know where songs came from . . . Then during [the] Kristofferson show I was close enough so I could see how much fun they were having. That's what I wanted to do." He had no idea what Kristofferson was singing, "but I liked the way the words ran together, so maybe that had something to do with me wanting to be a songwriter." McMurtry bought him a guitar and Jo taught him a few chords. At the age of seven, he'd retreat to his room with the instrument. "It was his escape from a great many things—homework and whatever pressures he may have had when he was growing up," McMurtry said. "I'm not musically very sensitive, [but] I did realize [right away] that he was a very good guitar player."

At the University of Richmond, Jo began a steady, productive, and rewarding career that would eventually span nearly forty years, teaching and writing, specializing in Shakespeare, Spenser, and Thackeray. Her marriage to Evans would end in an amicable divorce after a dozen years. She produced several books, introducing students to Shakespeare's plays, to Victorian literature, and to English-language fiction in general.

She and McMurtry had married young, bringing idealistic expectations to the state of holy matrimony, trusting the hope of commitment to erase all of life's uncertainties and provide inexhaustible delight. Despite the difficulties they had witnessed in their parents' relationships, they could not know (or could not believe) that the tyrannies of daily life and aging would be insurmountable to any but the strongest partnerships, rooted in the deepest wells of forgiveness. They had met, as most couples meet, unprepared, and they could not withstand their lack of readiness. But they taught each other tolerance, if not forbearance; patience, if not complete acceptance. They remained friends, perhaps the most challenging achievement of all under the circumstances.

In the years ahead, "I was often in Larry's territory but I didn't see that much of [him]," Jo told me. "My connections were with James, his teachers, his friends, his friends' parents, while Larry was busy with his many-faceted life." Always, she cheered "every bit of success that came his way."

Waterford was not McMurtry's only residence during his years in Virginia. He also rented houses in McLean, Leesburg, and different spots in Waterford. He lived part time in Georgetown—with Carter and then on his own. He moved back and forth from city to country, collecting so many speeding tickets that, at one point, his license was suspended. "[H]e explained to the judge that he was writing in his mind and sometimes just got excited," Evans said.

Already—now that he'd left Texas—his episodic existence had begun.

He appreciated the countryside's beauty, the white wooden fences, the sleek golden-brown ponies grazing in sloping summer fields. On the farm roads, sputtering tractors slowed traffic to a crawl, so drivers had no choice but to take in the pleasant surroundings, the polleny smell. But he slumped in his car whenever he pulled into the parking lot of a small-town Safeway or fast-food joint. There, amid a plethora of Swanson TV dinners, Spaghet-tiOs, Cap'n Crunch, and Big Macs—all of which McMurtry himself quite enjoyed—people maneuvered around one another on the sizzling asphalt, clutching their torn, sticky bags, apparently thinking of nothing, smiling, in a daze, at no one. (Jeff Mac would have said these easterners had lost their purpose in life because they'd lost touch with hard work on the land.)

The suburbs ringing DC's perimeter were distinguishable only by the number of massage parlors and TV repair shops they offered.

McMurtry's love of roads came to a crashing halt in the tangle of DC's inner-city freeways, whose designers seemed to have missed the crucial step of connecting them. Befuddled tourists from Iowa and North Da-kota, sweating in their wide-body Oldsmobiles or Winnebagos, squinted through their windshields hoping the Washington Monument would sud-denly appear to them; then, as they lost their bearings altogether, they seemed resigned to marveling at the splendid on-ramps in our nation's capital, surely the best on-ramps in the world.

Georgetown struck McMurtry as a fortress constructed for the preser-vation of caviar. The light delicacy glistened in silver tureens. Carter intro-duced him to salon life, where wealthy women known simply as hostesses or (in whispered gossip) as Potomac party girls threw lavish dinner soi-rees for politicians, lobbyists, soft-handed diplomats (priding themselves on their inoffensiveness), pale civil servants, and even paler congressional aides, lawyers, and journalists. Invariably, the journalists affected an attitude of boredom at the low company they were keeping—while feeling secretly pleased to be included at all—exhibiting just enough motor skills to toss back glasses of wine. They spoke slowly and pretentiously, like members of the old British Raj. Guests at these parties practiced a remarkable bal-ancing act, maintaining their elegant demeanor while indulging voracious appetites. In fact, McMurtry had never seen hungrier people, but they didn't seem to enjoy eating. Their insatiable cravings appeared to be the product of unfulfilled ambitions and stress: food was consumed quickly and cleanly to fill a variety of emotional gaps. Couscous, fried rice, lamb, coq au vin, smoked salmon, shrimp. Quail eggs and honey-soaked bacon. More often than not, McMurtry longed to slip away to grab a Big Mac in the nondescript suburbs.

Among the hottest hostesses in Georgetown—women to whose parties *everyone* sought an invitation—were Katharine Graham, who ruled *The Washington Post*; painter Polly Kraft, a "power doyenne" who saw her parties (rather too optimistically) as a "way of communicating, [getting] Republicans and Democrats all together in one room"; Evangeline Bruce— like Carter, the daughter of a diplomat—whose social events prompted Jacqueline Kennedy Onassis to compliment "the bright path [she] cut through an age where so few people have grace and imagination and the virtues of another time"; and Barbara Howar, who was just as likely to do the Frug in a miniskirt in the middle of a room as to sit quietly sipping vodka by a fireplace, discussing world affairs with a United Nations envoy.

"The French would say that a salon is like-minded people getting together to converse on literature, art, history, and politics," Bruce explained. "The tone has to be light, humorous, witty, and, the more elusive the reference, the more prized. [Sadly,] in Washington we don't go in for elusive statements. We are not particularly well-read and therefore even the deft allusions are lost."

McMurtry would have put it another way: "The higher a monkey climbs, the more it shows its ass."

Accompanying Carter to endless rounds of dinners, he felt a bit like a rodeo clown on the arm of a homecoming queen. Some nights, he believed she was happy to be showing off his rough edges to her peers, like a woman exhibiting an exotic plains animal. Such women had long ago ascended "the sheer, ice-covered face of American society, a peak I had never so much as glimpsed," says his character Jack McGriff in *Cadillac Jack,* a 1982 novel filled with McMurtry's caustic observations of Washington. "It was as if [my companion] had decided to try out the concept—or at least the image—of us as a couple." His gangly lope and his West Texas drawl proved an intriguing contrast to the pasty DC lifers, as long as he didn't embarrass everyone by scooping his hands into the celery dip or failing to polish his boots. Ever since the Days of Lyndon, Washingtonians had been wary of Texas vulgarians . . . LBJ's aides Harry McPherson and Billy

Lee Brammer, who used to sneak Johnson's booze from his Senate office at night, and who wrote his LBJ book while flying on Dexedrine and Dr Pepper . . . journalists Willie Morris and Larry L. King, who reportedly got into a fistfight over Howar at one of her parties, brawling all the way out into 31st Street . . .

McMurtry thought that Carter, always dazzling—faint freckles speckling her bare shoulders, her hair a smooth maple cascade—counted on him to complement her elegance at these stately Georgetown affairs: not *too rough,* just charmingly *unwashed.* From the first, though, as he watched his hostesses display impressive genius, planning seating arrangements, perfectly blending "age and beauty, brains and egos," it was apparent to anyone observing him that he would never be part of the in-crowd. He simply didn't understand the fine art of networking. He freely admitted his incompetence. "I immediately lose the phone numbers of almost everyone I know of any importance," he confessed.

Fairly early in McMurtry's Washington novel, Jack's social-climbing girlfriend begins to despair of her Texas beau, who cannot hack the Georgetown circuit. By taking up with him, she says, she had made the terrible mistake of "fuck[ing] down." Carter was far too classy to ever say such a thing to McMurtry, but on certain evenings—say, the night he heard "a famous Washington hostess" say of another writer (while putting books firmly in their place), "Good God . . . I'd rather fuck him than read him"—he couldn't help but suspect that Carter doubted her aspirations for him.

Every morning, in Washington, bus exhaust lingered over everyone, smudging the streets gray, blurring distant streetlights, turning the city into a bad pointillistic painting and leaving a trace of ash in the air. Harry McPherson once said political power emanated from the residents here like an overwhelming deodorant, casting a flat, pervasive odor as unmistakable as cordite.

McMurtry always cherished an anecdote he'd heard about Katherine Anne Porter, another Texas transplant to the East: she'd expressed her opinion of her surroundings by buying a black coffin to use as a coffee table.

These wise old expats were right: this was no place for a plains boy to settle.

Yet his departure from Texas, long in coming, had been inevitable. Just before he'd moved, his younger brother Charlie had gotten married in Archer City. Charlie was a freshman at Tarleton State College in Stephenville, Texas, and his bride, Sandra, was a senior at Archer City High School. Everybody arriving for the ceremony at the Baptist church knew these kids were too young to be married. Misery awaited them (though Sandra would eventually give birth to a son, Todd Wayne, an open-road enthusiast who'd come to share his dad's passion for motorcycles). But that's what you did in Archer City—you played the few moves left to you by an absence of options.

McMurtry's first three novels had thoroughly explored that empty inheritance; in his labors over what he'd long called his rodeo novel, he'd been trying to extend this early theme and follow a generation of characters who'd escaped their bare environs for the cities. One of his struggles with the novel had been his inability to identify what the cities had to offer his characters in place of the lives they'd fled. He'd loved Houston, but damned if people there seemed just as unhappy, on the whole, as the folks he'd grown up with.

"I doubt . . . that I have any business setting a novel in any city, Texan or otherwise, for . . . [cities] have apparently failed to seed my imagination with those pregnant images from which a living and well-voiced fiction might grow," he had admitted in *In a Narrow Grave*.

But he began to think that Washington was perhaps the perfect place to finally finish the book. In true exile, now, estranged from his origins in ways he'd never quite been in Houston, he experienced the profound alienation of urban life. Perhaps his task as a novelist was not to emphasize the contrast between rural and urban, but simply to trace the journey from one to the other, a movement marked by desperation. His theme was not renewal or even change. It was exodus.

In the fall of 1969, he completed the final draft of what would become his fourth novel, the first in an exodus cycle, *Moving On*. The title was the only editorial suggestion he accepted. Michael Korda told him *The Country of the Horn* didn't "sound . . . like a bestseller." McMurtry offered *Patsy Carpenter*, the main character's name. Korda didn't think so. On a trip to New York to meet with his editor, McMurtry was introduced to Korda's wife, Casey, a Bennington girl, at the couple's Sutton Place apartment. She suggested *Movin' On,* after a cute country song she'd heard on the radio. McMurtry wasn't crazy about it, but he agreed.

"*Moving On* was not the Great American Novel, but for a time I thought it was," he said. It was his homegrown version of a European novel of manners, his *Madame Bovary,* with pinches of black humor, absurdism, and metafiction tossed in—these were the current rage in American fiction. It also contained long passages of surface detail devoid of any psychological depth, anticipating the minimalism of the late 1970s and early 1980s, in the work of such writers as Ann Beattie and Raymond Carver.

"Is Patsy Carpenter worth 794 pages? Patsy is young, pretty, recently married, financially secure and psychologically adrift on a sea of qualms in the American Southwest, circa now. She reads a lot, she cries a lot, she worries a lot about her sex life. But the several years we spend with Patsy seem like just that . . . several years," began John Leonard's review of the novel in *The New York Times* on June 10, 1970. Almost every subsequent review also harped on the book's length, as well as its wealth of details, which most reviewers found tedious.

Never a consciously political novelist, McMurtry nevertheless anchored his story in the social torpor of the late 1960s. As the book opens, "at the beginning of the evening" (twilight in America), Patsy is reading Joseph Heller's *Catch-22,* a favorite among young readers opposed to the war in Vietnam. A short while later, she and her husband, Jim, drive toward the Texas Panhandle, once the site of grand cattle drives, now the home of the Danang Training Center, where soldiers bound for Vietnam practice landing helicopters in low scrub brush. Underscoring the fact that Patsy's generation is aimless—caught between the discarded values of the past and the hippie extremism of those just a few years younger—the training center sits near an old, abandoned drive-in movie theater, the kind of place that played cheap Westerns, Hollywood's unintentional parodies of frontier traditions. On the marquee, local kids have spelled HORS SHIT with the only letters remaining—a commentary on the crap culture Patsy and her peers have inherited.

Later in the novel, after a scene in which the antiwar song "Ruby, Don't Take Your Love to Town" ("that old crazy Asian war") is mentioned, Patsy has "a strong sense of being involved along with everyone else in the ruin of something. What was being ruined scarcely mattered: a civilization, a generation, or only the summer, or only an evening, or perhaps only themselves. What seemed important was that they were all in it together. No one seemed unhappy, and yet no one was likely to be spared."

The worlds explored in *Moving On*—the rodeo circuit, the university, Hollywood—have all been ruined by America's Vietnam Syndrome: they pretend to uphold the values they have in fact betrayed. Just as the nation, in fighting the war, undermined human rights and democracy, the very justifications it offered for its actions, the rodeo merely pantomimes ranch life; bull riding and barrel racing are just costumed Kabuki. The university turns scholarship into a series of careerist moves designed not to foster literary insight but to slot mediocre minds into professional positions. Hollywood peddles illusions—spectacles of violence packaged as high-minded parables decrying the corruption it sells.

Similarly, in *All My Friends Are Going to Be Strangers,* a companion volume to *Moving On,* written in just weeks after he'd finished the earlier novel, McMurtry paints the publishing industry as a promoter of schlock inflated by fatuous praise.

Starting with *Moving On,* his exodus cycle portrayed not only rural existence but the nation's elemental principles as a relic of modern life: it is truly the beginning of the end.

Disparate worlds are held together in *Moving On* by a uniquely American glue: unearned wealth. Jim Carpenter is a rich boy freed of the need to work, able to indulge his whims. A spoiled dilettante, he decides he wants to be a photographer. He buys expensive equipment and follows the rodeo, hoping to capture dramatic scenes. When that doesn't work, he returns to school in Houston, buying expensive books and declaring himself a budding scholar. When he shows no more aptitude with texts than he did with cameras, he drops out and ends up working for IBM in California.

His wife, Patsy, the novel's focus, follows Jim through his transient fevers, becoming more and more displaced, believing, then losing faith in, an elusive happiness, wondering if it lies in marital companionship or sexual fulfillment or friendship or motherhood, in the city or in the country. Visiting Jim's uncle, Roger Wagonner, an old cowboy, a scrap of the nineteenth century about to perish (the Homer Bannon and Sam the Lion of this novel), she experiences, at his ranch, "a cleanness and clarity that were tangible; everything in sight was very distinct," as opposed to the "foggy, mushy nights" in Houston, "melt[ing] everything together." But she can never be a ranch girl. Wagonner's way of life has disappeared. She is only familiar with his frontier manners through movies and books. Fog and mush are all she has.

She reads the heavy volumes that Jim and his fellow graduate students lug home from the library—psychology texts praised for their insight into human nature: "She skipped from book to book, always with the sense that the next chapter or the next page might reveal to her why she was in trouble and tell her what she might do to get out . . . and yet, as it turned out, nothing she came to was precisely applicable, or even helpful. She still fought with Jim, yearned to be out of trouble, slept with Hank"—a Vietnam veteran, a friend of Jim's, whose wartime experiences have left him passive and indifferent.

Patsy feels herself to be "two women in the same skin . . . women of differing minds and differing hearts," almost schizophrenic. She longs for emotional fulfillment but settles instead for quick sexual pleasure—apparently, the only gratification available in a compromised world: "Her days lost all consistency; pleasure and distress, desire and shame beset her by turns, and she never knew in the morning which skin she would wear in the afternoon." As in *Leaving Cheyenne* and *The Last Picture Show,* sex is a destructive element. "It was the question of consummation that was breaking them apart," Patsy thinks of her affair with Hank. She is happy to hold hands and kiss, to bask in companionship—"she [can't] understand why it wasn't enough for him." When they *do* make love, he becomes "hard to handle," the friendship less satisfying. With Jim, too, the gentle joy of "kissing had got lost somewhere . . . It was a pity, she felt, and it was almost as if sex had destroyed it."

Like his wife, Jim searches fruitlessly for what he believes will be the *making* of him. His travels misplace him among the likes of Sonny Shanks, a world champion rodeo cowboy, a serial womanizer who seduces his victims in the back of his tricked-up hearse; Pete Tatum, a sad and aging rodeo clown; and Peewee Rankin, a young wannabe rodeo star who ends up driving a kiddie train in a Houston park. Through Shanks, the subject of a hagiographic movie about his cowboy adventures, Jim stumbles into Hollywood's tinsel milieu, meeting Joe Percy, a jaded screenwriter with no real love for his work.

Back in Houston, Jim aspires to teach like his arrogant professor William Duffin. In none of these worlds does Jim belong—he incurs a series of physical injuries from his awkwardness around people he has no business knowing. But even if he *did* belong, none of the worlds are worth grasping: Duffin is more of a predator than a scholar, setting sexual traps for his students; Percy is a purveyor of fairy tales, puffing up the already inflated reputation of Sonny Shanks; and Shanks is a fraudulent cowboy. Fittingly, he dies in a car crash on a Hollywood freeway, crushed by speed in the land of illusion.

As for Patsy and Jim, they never come close to reaching a plateau of contentment. They simply move on.

If McMurtry put all his childhood and adolescence into his first three books, he stuffed *Moving On,* his *adult* novel, with everything he'd known since leaving Idiot Ridge. He gave aspects of himself to several of his characters: Duffin is a book collector; Patsy's lover Hank comes from a rural background (and he has flown helicopters like Kesey's buddy, Babbs); Jim is a restless traveler, a harried expectant father; Joe Percy is an indifferent screenwriter; Danny Deck, mentioned briefly, is a novelist with a nostalgic Texas book to his credit.

Flap and Emma Horton, pals of Patsy and Jim, parents of two small boys, are clearly modeled on Ray and Linda Waddington. Emma emerges as the warmest, most motherly figure in the book, accepting all her friends unconditionally. As for Patsy, "that was Marcia Carter," Babette Fraser believed. "Many of Marcia's attributes that he talked about to me, he gave to that character . . . That book came out of what was going on with her at the time. Nothing is as rich as thwarted love . . ." Of course, McMurtry had drafted early sections of the book before he'd met Carter: Jo was Patsy's *initial* inspiration. Carter rounded out the picture. "[A]ll the women I then knew cried practically all the time," McMurtry said later, after his "women friends," having "discovered their not so latent feminism," objected to his "lachrymose heroine."

McMurtry was not just indulging himself when he included autobiographical elements in the book; he took matters a step further, adding a metafictional layer. At one point Patsy tells Hank he's not as sexy as Paul Newman: "I saw *Hud*." In a Houston park, she meets a little boy named James, whose "parents [she] knew slightly." She reads *One Flew Over the*

Cuckoo's Nest and makes a dispirited visit to Perry Lane. By slipping his ghost presence into his novel, McMurtry calls the reader's attention to the act of reading, to the question of fact versus fiction (the Vietnam Syndrome again—what is true and what is a lie?). He specifically foregrounds reading in a lengthy book about people seeking life's meaning. Is reading the problem or the solution? It can spread myths or it can usefully inform.

Moving On gives us 794 pages of what seem to be Patsy Carpenter's every gesture, every thought and emotion, and yet, because the author deliberately chooses to avoid psychological depth, concentrating instead on the surface details, how well do we know her? Where does meaning reside? In the explanations (do we *trust* the explanations—of our lovers, of our government?) or in the glittering textures at the ends of our fingertips?

And what is the novelist's responsibility?

McMurtry had been arguing this question with John Leggett, Dorothea Oppenheimer, E. L. Doctorow, and Michael Korda for years. And judging by the public response to the novel, he would have to continue arguing it with reviewers and critics. An "obese catastrophe," one reviewer called *Moving On*. Another said it was "constructed like tumbleweed"; it was as if "Hemingway had decided to write a Sears Roebuck catalogue." McMurtry's shallow world view could be summed up as "All about Sex in Texas," one writer complained, and an irate reader in Dallas told the *Atlantic Monthly* editors that McMurtry's view of the Lone Star State was "about five coon-ass miles southwest of reality."

In *The Texas Observer,* Donald Barthelme's younger brother, Steven, a developing short-story writer, attacked McMurtry for writing a bloated novel that was "quite simply ugly and dull." McMurtry responded: "I am indifferent to structure, but I find texture absorbing . . . [and it] is absurd to chide the author of a long novel for a lack of interest in economy. If economy interested me I would have written a short book. In fact I find economy a fucking bore, whether it be literary, sexual, or monetary. It bespeaks the tight-ass . . . it may be a virtue in homeowners and a word beloved of pedagogues, but it's hardly the mistress for a novelist."

Some of McMurtry's more sympathetic readers admitted they were simply nostalgic for his pastoral subjects. The lack of what they considered natural detail in *Moving On,* particularly in the Houston sections, struck these readers as a failing (as if city life did *not* consist of natural detail).

Elroy Bode admitted, "I frankly miss the Old McMurtry . . . He has apparently given up the technique of having a narrator who uses the speech patterns and vernacular of McMurtry's Panhandle home territory, and has decided to write from the point of view of a rather detached novelist of manners. I believe that this change has been unfortunate, for it was a voice full of country poetry that spoke to us so well in his first books." Presumably, Bode's *us* was Texas readers from rural backgrounds, who felt betrayed by McMurtry's desire to leave behind the limited vocabulary of prairie folk.

The problem was, his vocabulary meandered erratically now. In a lengthy critique, Kerry Ahearn pointed out: "There is the high-toned [diction], to convey humor and condescension . . . And the low-toned, to capture the racy rhythms of street talk . . . [and the] subdued, ungracious, matter-of-fact style." Worse, McMurtry had an irritating "penchant for repetition": "[A]t least twenty times McMurtry records that [Patsy] gets up and puts on her bra and panties; the garments appear so often as to imply a fetish," Ahearn said.

McMurtry was caught between city asphalt and the soil; his dislocation affected every aspect of his novel, from subject to style to vocabulary to narrative pacing. Once upon a time, he had written that "country traditions were still very strong" in Texas; the "city will win . . . the allegiance of the young," but as "the cowboys leave the range and learn to accommodate themselves to the suburbs, defeats that are tragic in quality must occur and may be recorded." Sumptuous fiction could yet be wrung from rural settings. But now he'd changed his mind. Novelists, he said, "exploit a given region, suck what thematic riches they can from it, and then, if they are able, move on to whatever regions promise yet more riches . . . I suddenly began to notice that where place was concerned, I was sucking air."

What kind of novel, then, could he write? If *Moving On* wasn't quite it—wasn't *quite* the Great American Novel he'd hoped it would be—nevertheless, even its fiercest critics recognized that McMurtry was a serious talent moving thoughtfully toward his own, very idiosyncratic literary reckoning. "[E]ven though *Moving On* is interminable and tedious in many places, it's the closest anyone in Texas has come to doing a Trollope number about the petty miseries of graduate student life, and for some readers, like myself, it's strangely addictive," Don Graham wrote. John

Leonard, after questioning whether Patsy Carpenter was worth the pages devoted to her, praised McMurtry's "good ear. These people talk the way people actually talk . . . McMurtry also has a marvelous eye for locale."

He is a pure pleasure to read and "Patsy is real," Leonard said. *Moving On* was a "novel of monumental honesty, consisting of insights as undeniable as this morning's weather. Attention must be paid."

I'm not interested in young men; I never have been," McMurtry said. He knew all he needed to know about young men—after all, he *was* one. He said he'd rather write what he *didn't* know, in other people. "Insofar as I have been interested in men at all I'm interested in old men, like Sam [the Lion] or Roger [Wagonner] . . . but young men . . . are almost without exception my dullest and least vivid characters. If there's an exception it's Danny . . . as far as I'm concerned, [he] is the first interesting young male I've done." He was speaking of Danny Deck, the protagonist of *All My Friends Are Going to Be Strangers,* the novel he plunged into immediately after finishing *Moving On.* "I [still] had a good deal of narrative momentum going," he said. "I felt something like Hemingway mentioned feeling in *A Moveable Feast,* when, in Spain, he wrote two stories in one day and was being prodded by a cheeky waiter to write a third. What Hemingway, in that regard, called Juice I call narrative momentum. I was on a kind of fatigue high, which I thought I could probably sustain long enough to write a good short book . . . Thus I sailed into *All My Friends* . . . which I wrote in about five weeks."

Deck, author of a "simple novel" called *The Restless Grass* "about a good old man whose one son has gone bad," narrates the story of his alienation from his graduate school friends after his book publication; he tells the story of his disastrous marriage, his disappointing flirtation with Hollywood, his increasing isolation, and finally his disappearance—in the end, he seems to be speaking from beyond the grave like a Beckett character who wishes to stop talking but keeps chattering away ("I can't go on, I'll go on"). Clearly, he was McMurtry's alter ego.

And just as clearly, the novel was a prequel of sorts to *Moving On,* its events occurring earlier than the events in its predecessor (Danny's disappearance is mentioned briefly in *Moving On*). It features some of the same characters. Danny has a warm, sad affair with his friend Emma Horton, the only person who appears to understand him. Emma is the bridge between the novels.

All My Friends was an exuberant burst of energy: wry, sardonic, vivid, enormously fun to read—and it signaled a major crisis of spirit for Larry McMurtry.

"I had ceased to like my own prose," he said. In spite of his lingering momentum, he was at the beginning of "a kind of work trauma that probably afflicts most writers who write prolifically . . . My own feeling was that my fiction had somehow lost all freshness. I knew that fallow periods were normal in the literary life. But still, I seemed unable to take my own in stride."

His uneasiness signaled a deeper problem. Writing itself had become an almost unbearable burden, even though it provided McMurtry with his most basic approach to the world. Whereas his earlier characters—reflecting his own concerns—found themselves adrift, belonging nowhere because the traditions, professions, and places they'd inherited had all dried up and the cities were not fulfilling enough to replace them, Danny's dislocation pierces further: his vocation, his sturdiest defense against loneliness, has too effectively walled him in. It has become the biggest barrier between him and others, removing him from life rather than immersing him in a profounder understanding of it, as it appeared to promise at the beginning. Danny's friendships become strained when he earns a publishing contract—his friends cannot overcome their jealousy of his success. Trust becomes difficult to establish in intimate relationships—Danny's partners fear he will *use* them for material ("[Writers] ought to be imprisoned. They're all thieves," a literature professor hisses at him). Daily responsibility becomes hard to maintain—it interferes with the life of the mind (the repetitive demands of fatherhood are particularly stressful, in this regard). Finally, the financial lure of Hollywood, while irresistible, becomes a source of self-loathing, distorting the initial goal of producing great literature. (Danny meets a producer in LA who keeps, as a pet, a twenty-pound rat.)

Worst of all is the writer's self-consciousness: the experience of being imprisoned in the skull. "All I had was in my head—images, and the memory of images," Danny says.

"Being a writer sooner or later causes you to reflect on what you are doing and creates a kind of ambivalence," McMurtry told an interviewer soon after the novel's publication. "You get to wondering what it is doing to you, sitting in a corner with a machine, projecting your emotions [into fictional characters]." On another occasion, he lamented: "It is true that the better you write the worse you live. The more of yourself you take out of real relationships and project into fantasy relationships, the more the real relationships suffer. The popular theory is that writing grows out of neurosis, but it doesn't cure it; if anything, it drives it deeper and makes it nearer to being a psychosis. I do not think that real writing is a purgative . . . I do not think that writing, or any art pursued seriously is necessarily a health-producing activity."

His despair over writing was combined with his conviction that he had mined his material as thoroughly as he could. A Homer Bannon/Sam the Lion figure appears in *All My Friends*: Danny's ninety-two-year-old Uncle Laredo, overseer of a camel ranch called the Hacienda of the Bitter Waters. He is a grotesque parody of McMurtry's earlier men of the range. "It seems to me I've taken these Western figures as far as I can take them, and that . . . Roger Wagonner [in *Moving On*] . . . is the best I have to say about the old Westerner," McMurtry said. "The treatment of the old man of the West [in *All My Friends*], which I think is the last time I am going to do such a figure, is an ironic and rather savage treatment which takes all the glamor and all the romance out of him and he is presented really as a mean old son-of-a-bitch." The scene at the Bitter Waters becomes absurd when one of Laredo's ranch hands, crazy with loneliness and hatred of the barren earth, drops his pants and humps post holes in the dirt—a pointed image for McMurtry at this stage of his career: the Texas novelist exploiting his landscape for scarcer and scarcer rewards.

"Texas was there, beyond the sunrise, looming," Danny muses late in the book, returning to his home state after an extended period away from it. But his relationship to the place has changed. "It was the sky that was Texas, the sky that welcomed me back. The land I didn't care for all that much—it was bleak and monotonous and full of ugly little towns. The sky was what I had been missing, and seeing it again in its morning brightness made me realize suddenly why I hadn't been myself for many months. It had such depth and such spaciousness and such incredible compass, it took so much in and circled one with such a tremendous generous space that it

McMurtry as an infant, 1936

Jeff Mac with baby
McMurtry, 1936

McMurtry with his grandparents
Louisa and William and other
"McMurtry quail" at the ranch,
c. 1940

McMurtry in high school, 1953

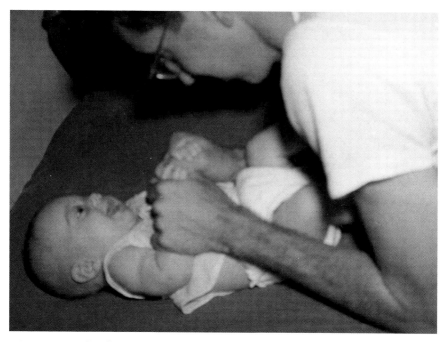

McMurtry with infant James, 1962

Paul Newman
in *Hud,* 1963

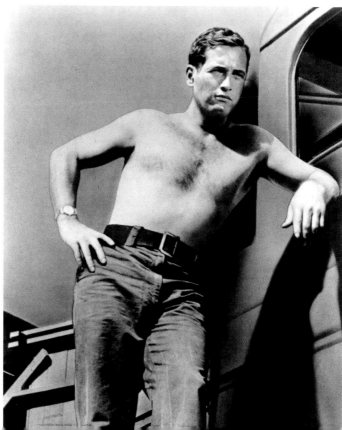

McMurtry with James, Mike Evans, and Jo (in background with dog), 1968

McMurtry with James in a Houston diner, 1968

McMurtry playing pool
with Mike Evans in his
Houston house (James
in foreground), 1968

McMurtry in
front of The
Bookman, 1968

McMurtry in his personal library, Houston, 1968

McMurtry, 1968

McMurtry
teaching at
Rice, mid
1960s

Cybill Shepherd in *The Last Picture Show,* 1971

Debra Winger and Shirley MacLaine in *Terms of Endearment*, 1983

McMurtry and other guests with Ronald Reagan at the White House, 1985

Robert Duvall and Tommy Lee Jones in *Lonesome Dove,* 1989

McMurtry with Sara and Diana Ossana at Swifty Lazar's Oscar party, 1993

Heath Ledger and Jake Gyllenhall in *Brokeback Mountain*, 2005

McMurtry and Diana Ossana with their Oscar for *Brokeback Mountain,* 2006

Booked Up, Archer City, c. 2015

McMurtry in Booked Up, Archer City, 2015

McMurtry receiving National Humanities Medal from President Obama, 2015

McMurtry with Faye Kesey at their wedding, 2011

was impossible not to feel more intensely with it above you." Of course, the passage reflected McMurtry's own sky deprivation, living in Washington, but it also revealed the impasse he had reached in his writing: a novelist rooted in place who no longer cares for the land or the stories of the people in the "ugly little towns" has lost his way; a man aching to be swallowed by the sky is yearning for spiritual renewal.

McMurtry's ambivalence about what he was doing was apparent in the novel's uneven registers. Alongside searing parodies of life in the Old West were straight-faced allusions to mythic hero quests. In his restlessness, Danny constantly encounters water—rivers, flash floods—and experiences terrifying instances of baptism; he considers "Odysseus' visit to the underworld . . . the spirits that came out of the fog . . . and approached the pool of blood at Odysseus' feet . . . It seemed to me I was in such a fog," he says. "The spirits of the dead ought to be moving in it." Often serious in tone, the novel kept throwing up its hands, as if to say this whole enterprise "falls somewhere between silliness and the outright ridiculous" (as McMurtry had once remarked of any attempt to sustain tradition beyond its time).

Like most McMurtry characters, Danny seeks—and fails to find—solace in sex. Erotically, he is too "clean cut" for his impatient wife. His strongest intimacies are with Emma Horton and Jill Peel, an artist and movie production designer he meets in LA. Betrayal spoils both relationships. "My fate seemed to be to meet women it was impossible not to love, but whom it was impossible to love right," Danny laments. Emma is married to his friend Flap—his coupling with her, full of genuine tenderness, cannot withstand the weight of guilt: "Emma and I couldn't talk. My life had gotten that awry. Even Emma, I couldn't talk to . . . It meant I was totally cut apart from people." From Jill, he steals the idea for his second novel, the story of a baby bed passed from couple to couple. He decides to call it *The Man Who Never Learned,* McMurtry's own working title for *his* book.

Once again in a McMurtry novel, sex is the largest hurdle to happiness. "Why does everyone want sex, anyway? I can't even know anyone without sex messing things up," Jill complains when Danny first meets her. "Despite all the good times we had Jill and I developed a mutual, internal sadness. Sex caused it," Danny says. "It wouldn't work for us, so it worked against us."

Having lost both Emma and Jill and faith in his own artistic vision, Danny heads for the little town of Roma, Texas, near the Texas-Mexico border, ostensibly in search of historical meaning, a reconnection with the past, but it is not to be had: Roma was where the Hollywood epic *Viva Zapata!* was filmed—a false history, just another contribution to a world of illusion.

At the end of his tether, Danny wades into the Rio Grande clutching the manuscript of his second novel. "[T]he flowing of rivers [was] more interesting than making black marks on paper," he says. "The marks didn't have faces, and I had forgotten the faces that had been in my mind when I wrote them. Jill had a face. Emma had a face. My words didn't. They didn't flow like rivers, either. They had no little towns on their banks—little towns full of whores, people, goats. I didn't know what I was doing, spending so much time with paper . . . What a waste of me."

He wrestles the manuscript into the water, drowning the pages one by one, a symbolic suicide: "I had never felt such black, unforgiving hatred of anything as I felt for the pages in my hands," he says. Because of those pages, he had missed "the door to the ordinary places . . . the door to Emma's kitchen . . . There would never be an Emma's kitchen for me . . . I would live in the other places, among the exiled."

The novel's last glimpse of Danny freezes him in a placeless blank: "I [couldn't] see the great scenes anymore, the Old Man riding, the Old Woman standing on the ridge, the wild scenes from the past . . . It was always a borderland I had lived on, it seemed to me, a thin little strip between the country of the normal and the country of the strange. Perhaps my true country was the borderland, anyway."

Reviewers greeted the book cautiously. Even if they didn't know anything about McMurtry's life, a novelist writing about a novelist invited speculation, and some reviewers didn't know what to make of what looked to be an extended suicide note. Would the author ever write again—or, indeed, go on living? "It is a desperate and intimidating work and you are liable to finish it with relief and then pick it up several days later to see if the man really said what he did," Jim Harrison wrote in *The New York Times*. "The scenes are . . . a mixture of the tragic and pathetic," he noted. "McMurtry's development of his character is harrowing . . . [and] the novel end[s] in a galvanic shriek."

Yet, as ever, the reviews praised McMurtry's scene-setting, his vivid

characterizations, and his ear for dialogue. He continued to be recognized
as a serious writer tackling significant themes. Writing in *Publishers Weekly,*
Barbara Bannon said: "McMurtry is coming to terms in his own special
way with much that has gone wrong in this country and the dubious possibilities of its ever being quite right again."

The author had a stronger ego, more discipline, and a sharper habit
of self-reflection than his creation; he wasn't about to stop writing or self-
destruct, but that didn't mean his disillusionment with making novels
wasn't acute, and getting worse.

Professional recognition didn't help matters: in the summer of 1970
he was invited to a literary conference at Hollins College near Roanoke,
Virginia, at which "a campus full of nubile young rich girls" romped with a
cadre of "obnoxious" middle-aged writers, he said. The poet James Dickey
arrived "in the company of . . . a former stripper whose stage name was
the Miami Hurricane." Very little literary discussion ensued. Disgusted,
McMurtry left early—"I [took] my money and was gone." He learned
he'd much rather fraternize with book dealers and readers than with other
writers.

Even the money to be made from his books was disappointing, at times
humiliating. Oppenhiemer's letters to him became halfhearted account-
ings of less-than-hoped-for advances and admissions that sales were lower
than expected. Yet this was the bargain he had struck: he'd wanted to be a
writer; a writer needed a publisher.

In 1964, his old teacher, Wallace Stegner, had published an essay called
"Born a Square: The Westerner's Dilemma," in which he'd insisted that the
corrupt standards of the East Coast literary establishment were anathema
to the values of the western writer, making it hard for a westerner to maintain his identity. The writer, shaped by the people and land of his region,
receives his "invitation from the great world" in the form of a publishing
contract, Stegner said; surrounded by now-jealous friends, or by those
who simply do not understand his ambitions, he begins to feel that his
old world is too narrow, so he moves east to become part of the literary
in-crowd; he quickly finds that he is out of place, out of sync with the
values of those who comprise his world now, like the "obnoxious" writers
at the Hollins conference. As a westerner, he has been taught not to be a
quitter. He continues working, compromising his subjects for greater sums

of money, unable to adapt to his new surroundings but also certain that his old material, disdained by his eastern acquaintances, is "unusable." He has become an "orphan."

Critic Barbara Granzow was the first to notice that Danny Deck "fits Stegner's definition so well . . . that one might think McMurtry created him primarily to give specificity to Stegner's generalization." Whether or not McMurtry had read the essay, he had come to embody Stegner's stages of alienation. The result, as Emma tells Danny: "You can't take care of yourself. You just look like you can."

Sitting in Washington and rural Virginia, hating his prose, itching to shake off the dust of Texas or traveling to New York to meet his editor, he tried to reckon with his strange circumstance: that of being an exile, an orphan, doomed to roam the spaces in between.

15

On a daily basis, the news in Washington was a mix of interchangeable stories: car wrecks, plane delays, drug busts, legislative failures, going-out-of-business notices, births, deaths, sex scandals. Switch the names, fill in the blanks, run the details all over again. But the want ads at the back of the newspapers—*they* revealed the true variety of human existence: what people longed for, kept, discarded, grasped. Barbecue grills, mattresses, musical instruments, hutches, coins, pet snakes, surfboards, sewing machines, porcelain dolls, libraries. It was the mind of the collector that documented the comedy and tragedy of life on earth and gave them whatever importance they had.

McMurtry's happiest moments in DC were at the flea markets and auction houses, browsing among old books, furniture, weavings, and garments. Marcia Carter shared his fascination with the "relationship people have with their objects"—it was perhaps the couple's strongest bond. "[She] bought a great Buffalo Bill poster, and some Apache basketry that is very valuable now. I [got] a Sumatran village drum . . . and a great Maori war club, not to mention half of the last buffalo killed in Arizona territory," McMurtry said. "I secured a fine skull collection from a dealer . . . who had acquired the skulls when the anatomy lab closed at Penn." Among the bones were those of a saber-toothed tiger, a rhinoceros, and a gorilla. In later years, his goddaughter Sara Ossana would admire his Balinese bed and a "museum-worthy Ethiopian triptych . . . apparently acquired by an American ambassador in the early 20th Century from Haile Selassie depicting the burial story of a rich merchant." McMurtry chose these items "willy-nilly," he said, while searching for books. He called himself "an accumulator" rather than a collector.

One of his favorite browsing spots was the Georgetown Flea Market, held each Sunday in a "raffish splash of color" in the parking lot of Hardy Middle School. He and Carter also frequented the Harris Auction Galleries in Baltimore, pausing, while in the city, to eat crab cakes for lunch.

Occasionally, they'd find bargains on French furniture at Weschler's auction house, across the street from the "hideous" FBI building. "[I] can get irrationally competitive at auctions," McMurtry said. "Besides the stirring up of one's innate competitiveness, there is also the thrill of immediacy . . . no small thrill." Carter shared his spirit for winning bids. She wasn't just slumming when she accompanied him to dusty warehouses and dimly lit book nooks. She had a genuine "craving for books," McMurtry said. When she'd gone to Vassar she'd begun "to come into New York and go to some bookstores, and the famous Margie Cohn of House of Books, Limited saw her."

Cohn was an "explosive" woman: "I believe she once flung a copy of *Three Stories and Ten Poems* at someone: her husband, who was Hemingway's first bibliographer; one of her husband's mistresses; or Edmund Wilson. The record is not clear, but the book is currently worth maybe $75,000," McMurtry recalled.

When Cohn encountered Carter, "She knew a rich girl when she saw one," McMurtry said. "She began to cultivate Marcia and sell her very good books." In 1970, Carter purchased a "perfect copy" of *Mrs. Dalloway* from the old woman—and sold it years later for $10,000.

McMurtry and Carter would go book scouting together to the St. Joseph's Ladies Auxiliary Thrift Shop in DC. On one occasion the writer Calvin Trillin came along to observe them, amazed when McMurtry told him "we would have to spend the night on the sidewalk to guarantee being first in line, and Marcia cheerfully agreed to participate to the extent of lending me a pillow." When a scout of McMurtry's acquaintance arrived shortly afterward toting a shopping bag, McMurtry ribbed him, "You're late." He informed Trillin where to find "sleepers"— "books that through carelessness or ignorance have been priced with the herd of popular novels and book-club editions instead of being cut out for special attention." Often, they got lost among the "writers of the Harlem Renaissance and American radical fiction." Cookbooks were also hot items.

When the thrift shop opened early in the morning, McMurtry stalked inside, "confident that what the other browsers [might take] to be a dusty old industrial pamphlet he [would] recognize as the first published book of Thomas Wolfe." As he poked among tables and shelves, he would occasionally stop a person carrying a box of books to the cashier's desk and ask, "Can I help you with that, ma'am?", seizing the opportunity to peek into the box. He didn't head for the rare-book room right away, certain it was a "death trap." The real gems would be hidden, unidentified, among piles of clutter. "At 10:30, McMurtry stashed his shopping bags, both full, against a pillar and threw his coat over them, planning to cull them later in the afternoon. Then he went out for a Coke," Trillin said. The major find that day was a cookbook for $75.00 that he was certain he could unload for two or three hundred dollars.

McMurtry always remembered with exquisite fondness snatching his first copy of *Evergreen Review,* issue 2, introducing the San Francisco poetry scene, at a sidewalk newsstand on Commerce Street in Dallas. It mattered where you bought a book. The conditions of purchase clung to the yellowed pages. He remembered happily his first tentative forays as a bookseller in the early 1960s, before going to work for Grace David. He'd gone into business then simply by typing up lists of titles under the heading *Dust Bowl Books*: a volume of prophecies by the Abbot of Fiore, published in Venice in 1589; a Black Sun Press edition of James Joyce's poems, printed in 1935. He remembered the joy these volumes had brought collectors, and he imagined dealing books again, an idea that appealed to Carter as well. It was something they could do together, to bridge their temperamental differences—differences they were discovering as they negotiated the Georgetown social circuit.

DC's great rare-book shop at the time was W. H. Lowdermilk & Company, originally founded in 1872. DC had always had a literate middle-class population—and a largely transient one: government employees shuffled in and out of the city with each election cycle. Estates were constantly shedding and acquiring books.

But when McMurtry arrived in Washington, Lowdermilk's was facing savage challenges: the expansion of the subway system downtown, properties changing hands, rising rents. Furthermore, the quality of the city's public schools had declined and movies and TV were eating into reading time: widespread middle-class literacy was no longer a given. As McMurtry and Carter contemplated opening a bookstore (*how serious are you?* they asked each other), they wondered if such a venture could prosper these days, and they kept a close watch on Lowdermilk's.

Carter made him the T-shirt that had *Minor Regional Novelist* written on it. Sometimes he wore it to social gatherings, among the eastern reviewers it was meant to skewer.

If accumulating books and rare objects at flea markets made DC tolerable, teaching nearly sunk him. Money from his novels and from movie options on *The Last Picture Show* was not enough to keep him afloat as comfortably as he wished to live—especially as he darted about, buying skulls—so he accepted part-time teaching positions at George Mason and American University. He also commuted back to Rice for a term. His Rice students had never much challenged him—except for a handful— but they were pleasant people to be around. The Washington kids were a different breed. Generally, they came from greater wealth; with money came a firm sense of privilege. In their view (McMurtry perceived), education was not a necessity or an opportunity, but a product along the lines of an automobile or a house: a down payment (usually made by Dad) on a future already assured. Such a view made the teacher not a mentor but a salesperson serving the consumer—the student. If the consumer did not like the product (that is to say, did not want to read a book for class), the consumer could not be forced to do so. The customer was always right.

Money or no money, faced with a stream of spoiled, incurious, and unprepared children, McMurtry left academia for good.

I think we quarreled [on the phone] because you were trying to find some work to do to justify your commission and there really was no work to do," McMurtry wrote Oppenheimer in early 1970. Oppenheimer seemed nervous about losing him as a client: for the time being, he was secure with Michael Korda at Simon & Schuster, and Peter Bogdanovich was determined to film *The Last Picture Show.* McMurtry's business affairs were in place. If he still fretted about finances, he nevertheless felt there was little for Oppenheimer to do. "I am sorry to have seemed so brutal . . . but in examining my honest feelings [I] do find that it seems ridiculous to me to have a movie agent . . . Movies are a separate branch of life to me and one in which middlemen are just in the way." Wisely or not, he was negotiating now directly with Bogdanovich and his representatives.

Oppenheimer pleaded with him to keep communicating with her. "If you write me a letter I promise I won't sell it to anyone ever," she wrote. She sounded desperately possessive of him, counseling him against giving too many interviews: "[Y]our appearance is keeping a lot of other industries going [publishers, filmmakers, TV, radio, magazines] and helping them to sell their product. As for you, largely, it diminishes you . . . I don't think Nabokov has ever been publicly interviewed, I mean on the air, and come to think of it it may be a certain mysteriousness about what kind of person he is that intrigues people." The bottom line: only speak to "someone who really understands what you are trying to do, in your writing." Her meaning was clear. *She* was that someone.

Meanwhile, Marcia Carter had pulled McMurtry into another new sphere for him—the political. She had joined the reelection campaign of U.S. Representative Allard K. Lowenstein, from the 5th Congressional District in Nassau County, New York. Lowenstein had risen to prominence in 1968 when, as one of the organizers of the Dump Johnson Movement, he had helped rally support for Senator Eugene McCarthy. When Johnson refused to seek reelection, Lowenstein claimed victory for the liberal cause: "We did it without a major name, money, or the mass media. We showed that the system is not so resistant to change, but that it is badly corroded."

Now, in pursuing his *own* reelection to the House, he had formed another "dump" movement—this time against Richard Nixon and his aggressive Vietnam policies. He mobilized his followers to register millions of voters under twenty-five.

As a volunteer in his Washington office, Carter met a young man named John Curtis, a former Peace Corps volunteer in Borneo and an avid book collector. He had been a literature major at Harvard. He had done his honors thesis on Ford Madox Ford. He was serving as Lowenstein's administrative assistant.

Convinced that McMurtry would like him, Carter introduced the men, and soon the three of them were fixtures at the parties Curtis threw at his house for Lowenstein and his followers. McMurtry didn't join the campaign in any appreciable way, but "he was incredible," Curtis said. "By face recognition, he'd remember everyone's names. He could pick out the congressman's coat from a pile and bring it to him. He was really brilliant, far more than I could ever be." Not only could he teach others savvy political skills, but he could run for office himself, Curtis thought.

Lowenstein's campaign had sputtered from the start: the voter registration drive was not proceeding as successfully as everyone hoped, and New York's Republican-controlled state legislature was busy trying to gerrymander the congressman's district, replacing a liberal region with a more conservative one, making it harder for him to consolidate a base. Discouraged, disconsolate, Curtis and Carter leapt when, one day, McMurtry suggested a distraction from their work: a quick trip to Archer City, Texas. Something very strange was happening there.

Polly Platt would always dispute her husband's account of how *The Last Picture Show* got made and how it came to be shot in Archer City. She had married Peter Bogdanovich, the son of a Serb immigrant, a painter, in 1962 when they were both twenty-three. From the first, they behaved together more like a professional team than an amorous couple. A lonely and precocious child, Bogdanovich absorbed American movies and got a job as a film programmer at the Museum of Modern Art when he was barely in his twenties. He wrote a monograph on Orson Welles for the museum. Platt was an army brat, the daughter of an alcoholic and a mentally ill mother. Her mother used to beat her. Her father was involved in the postwar humanitarian trials in Germany—she spent a good portion of her childhood in a war zone. "I started fantasizing that I had these incredible powers, that I could rebuild all the broken buildings," she said. She had a serious brush with polio. She became a debutante in Boston and escaped her parents with an early marriage, but then her husband died in a car accident after they'd had a fight. She moved to Pittsburgh to study scenic design for the theater but was discouraged by her professors at Carnegie Mellon because she was a woman. She went into costume design instead—a more acceptable line of work for a young female, she was told.

She got pregnant by a man who didn't love her and gave the child up for adoption.

When she met Bogdanovich in New York, she was distinctly different from the women he had known. She had spent some time in Arizona with her husband; she had fallen in love with the tough, informal manner of desert folk and took to wearing faded jeans, rawhide Navajo boots, concho belts, and blue work shirts. The pants and boots accentuated her lanky frame and her height; her straight blond hair, cut short, seemed dyed by the sun. She wore no bras or panties because she didn't like having extra clothing to wash. Bogdanovich had never met anyone like her. He was used to dating girls with short bob haircuts and pillbox hats: the Jackie Kennedy look. He was a gangly kid himself, awkward, shy, most comfortable in stylish suits. His black hair was immaculately trimmed, swept back, above a pair of thick black glasses. He didn't find Platt sexy, exactly, but her directness and easy sensuality overcame his tentativeness, made him bolder, more confident (to her, he was "Holden Caulfield ice-skating at Rockefeller Plaza with wholesome young girls in knee socks"). They married at New York's City Hall and moved into a small apartment in Manhattan, where she did costume designs for off-Broadway shows and he wrote about the movies. She helped him interview filmmakers. They saw cheap movies in Times Square and survived on Canada Dry and Fudgsicles.

Harold Hayes, an *Esquire* editor, sent Bogdanovich to California to write stories on Hollywood. "I watched Hawks do *El Dorado,* Hitchcock do *The Birds* . . . I learned how to direct by watching these guys," Bogdanovich said. Platt's dispute with him about the genesis of *The Last Picture Show* began on the set of John Ford's film *Cheyenne Autumn,* which Ford was shooting in Monument Valley. Bogdanovich later said he found and read McMurtry's book on his own, but Platt always insisted that in Monument Valley the actor Sal Mineo gave her a tattered paperback by Larry McMurtry—the cover suggested soft-core porn—gushing about what a great movie it would make.

Bogdanovich and Platt would argue as well about who discovered the sexy young woman who eventually starred in the film, but in any case, none of it would have mattered if Hollywood had not just undergone a sea change, making it possible to film McMurtry's book in ways that would not have been feasible just a few years before.

The movies had been losing money for well over a decade; the "[film] industry started dying from being too bulky, toothless, and dated—just like all those other saurians of a few aeons ago," said critic John Simon. Predictable Westerns, cop procedurals, and quaint bedroom farces did not speak to the Day-Glo, tear-gassed sixties. Then in 1969, Dennis Hopper,

Peter Fonda, Terry Southern, and Jack Nicholson grossed over $19 million off a $375,000 production budget for *Easy Rider,* a slapdash cinematic fuck-you to law-and-order America. *Easy Rider* "changed everything," wrote film historian Jon Lewis. Its box office success, "despite and because of its (B-movie) mode of production, its obvious nod to the youth culture and its counterculture sensibilities prompted the predictable industry response: panic." Columbia Pictures had acquired the film's distribution rights from a company called Raybert, run by producers Bert Schneider and Bob Rafelson, but Columbia's executives knew that a film like *Easy Rider* "would never have been optioned, developed, or produced in-house and that the studio had no one under contract prepared or equipped to follow up on the film," Lewis wrote. Across the board, movie studios scrambled to overcome their inertia and move past business-as-usual: they'd no longer require a Paul Newman to guarantee a film's financing; if Hopper and Fonda could succeed without a bankable star (Nicholson's career had not yet taken off in '69), well, okay—let's put cameras in the hands of these kids and see what they can do.

Perhaps Joan Didion put it best—like McMurtry, she was a serious novelist drawn to Hollywood's quirky inner workings as much as its money: "[in the] summer and fall of '69 . . . every studio in town was narcotized by *Easy Rider's* grosses and all that was needed to get a picture off the ground was the suggestion of a $750,000 budget . . . a nonunion crew, and this terrific 22-year-old kid director . . . [Suddenly] all the creative 24-year-old producers [were using] up the leases on their office space at Warner Brothers by sitting out there in the dull Burbank sunlight smoking dope before lunch and running one another's unreleased pictures after lunch."

The Raybert production outfit had now morphed into BBS (Bob Rafelson, Bert Scheieder, and Steve Blauner). Columbia made a deal with them, paying them to produce more *Easy Riders.* In short order, BBS would make the Monkees' *Head, Five Easy Pieces, Drive, He Said,* and *The King of Marvin Gardens.* And from Steve Friedman they secured the right to film *The Last Picture Show.*

These guys weren't exactly counterculture, but they were activist liberals in the grand Hollywood tradition, raising money to pay the legal fees of Daniel Ellsberg and Abbie Hoffman (whom Schneider had helped jump bail). They also gave Black Panther leader Huey Newton sanctuary in Blauner's Bel Air mansion, before helping him escape to Cuba in an operation worthy of a big-screen thriller. And they were committed to making personal films on low budgets.

When they learned that Peter Bogdanovich was hankering to adapt *Picture Show* (even though Orson Welles had told him "it was a dirty movie and he shouldn't direct it"), they asked to speak with him. Bogdanovich had become eager to switch careers, from writing about movies to creating them. The B movie maker Roger Corman, impressed with his articles, asked him to cowrite and codirect a film called *The Wild Angels,* starring Peter Fonda. "I went from getting the laundry to directing the picture in three weeks," Bogdanovich said. Then, with Corman's money, he made a low-budget film called *Targets,* based loosely on the story of mass murderer Charles Whitman, who fired on luckless passersby from a tower on the campus of the University of Texas. *Targets* caught the eye of the BBS team—they thought it was a lousy movie, but the script had its smart moments, and the costuming and design were notable. Bogdanovich seemed to have the goods.

What the team didn't know was the extent to which Polly Platt had contributed to the script and to keeping the finances straight. She had been fully responsible for the costuming and design. "Polly was a very strong driving force behind Peter," said Paul Lewis, the film's unit production manager. "She did not let his ego get in the way . . . She would say, 'Don't be an asshole about things,' and he would respect and listen to her."

"He's the locomotive, I'm the tracks," Platt said.

But already it was clear to her that in Hollywood, as at Carnegie Mellon, men would always get the credit; professional women were shoved into the shadows. One night, over dinner at a restaurant on Ventura Boulevard, Howard Hawks leaned across Platt, ignoring her completely, and addressed Bogdanovich while eyeing Sherry Lansing, seated across from them; Lansing was a lovely actress who had just starred in Hawks's *Rio Lobo.* "If you really want to be a director, this is the kind of girl you should be with," Hawks advised the young man.

Riding the adrenaline of his ambitions, and despite the fact that Platt had just given birth to their first child, a daughter named Antonia, Bogdanovich began to believe his wife was a potential liability to his future in LA. She didn't fit socially, always making gaffes. One night, when Hawks

complained about the antiwar demonstrators at the Chicago Democratic
Convention in 1968—"If I was in charge, I'd arrest them all, cut their hair
off. Shoot 'em!"—Platt responded, "You know, Howard, they have a point.
We have no business in Vietnam." Bogdanovich dropped his head in his
hands. Platt looked at him, disgusted. "I think that was the day I stopped
loving Peter," she said later.

"Polly could be very abrasive. Very loud. Jumping in with her opinions
when they weren't asked for," Bogdanovich said. "There were a lot of dark
areas in Polly's life that I didn't really understand. It was never really a very
romantic relationship. It was more that we enjoyed working together. I
was very young, didn't really know the difference between love, in love,
sympathy, compatibility. I don't think I knew what I was getting into."

Given these dynamics, and their mutual talents and ambitions, they
inevitably clashed at work. Just as they argued over who first discovered
McMurtry's book—Platt certainly *read* it first, all the way through; Bogdanovich was appalled when he realized he'd committed to making a
movie about teenage lust in Texas—they quarreled over who first saw Cybill Shepherd's face on the cover of *Glamour* at a supermarket near their
house in Van Nuys. They *did* agree on Shepherd's allure: "She had funny
little spit curls, she was very impertinent, and Southern-looking, blue eyes.
She looked like she had a sexual chip on her shoulder, as if she were daring
you to try something," Platt said.

BBS green-lighted the project (as long as Bogdanovich could "get some
nudity" into the script, Schneider said). The company flew McMurtry to
LA to meet with Bogdanovich and Platt at their little house on Saticoy
Street, overlooking a quiet valley. Right away, he entered into negotiations
with Bogdanovich about cowriting the screenplay. Since low budgets and
efficiency were priorities, Bogdanovich hoped to skirt some of the rules of
the screenwriters' guild; it wasn't clear whether McMurtry would get credit
for his work on the script, since he wasn't a guild member. He didn't care as
long as he got paid—2½ percent of the film's net profit (contingent upon
his working on the screenplay during actual production)—and as long as
he had serious input on the story.

"I did not find [Peter] responsive to what [*The Last Picture Show*] was,
and I didn't think he would have found it himself," McMurtry said. "Polly
was much more likely to do an American story with American characters.

She had a singular instinct about who to go after for the roles, too." He felt her commitment to the material sprang from the fact that its bleakness was "akin to her own autobiography."

"Everything that's in the book, the taking off of the bra, hanging it on the car mirror, the hands that were cold and the girl who would only let him touch her tits, just barely getting your hand up this girl's leg, were experiences I'd had as a young woman," Platt said. "There were parts of a woman's body that were completely off limits in America. These were things it was just impossible to show in Hollywood films, whereas in European films, like *Blow-Up*, you saw pubic hair." She thought McMurtry's honesty and BBS's production approach might make it possible to "[film] the book in America the way the French would have made it, where these weird American sexual mores could be investigated."

McMurtry met the couple's daughter (they seemed "pretty married to me," he said); he enjoyed a fine Mexican meal with them. The next night, he met them and Bert Schneider for dinner at Chasen's: "[I]t did nothing to familiarize us with one another, if that was its purpose," McMurtry said. "Peter and Polly, I believe, concluded . . . that I was a strange and troublesome creature, but held their peace."

They all trooped over to the Columbia studios to hammer out story ideas. "It was immediately clear to them that I knew nothing about writing screenplays, and just as immediately clear to me that they knew nothing about Texas." They found Texas "exotic and exciting; while I, having lived in the state thirty-odd years, had begun to find it boring . . . I had also begun to be dissatisfied with the ways in which I imagined it," McMurtry said. Bogdanovich chewed his way through a packet of toothpicks, an attempt to quit smoking. He said he wanted to remain as faithful as possible to the book. McMurtry had soured on his novel and believed that, unless major changes were made to the plot, it would result in a silly melodrama. Platt remembered him becoming quite grumpy when she expressed her admiration for his scenes. In particular, he felt that "despite [his] efforts at savage satire, [he] had still somehow romanticized the place and the people." He saw the book as a missed opportunity: "I had wasted so much time . . . on those uninteresting kids. The novel, I suddenly saw plainly, was . . . about middle-aged courtship in a small town," he said. "While Peter was working out his fascination with youth, I was beginning to develop mine with middle age."

After several such meetings, they'd gotten nowhere—in other words, "we had . . . normal script conference[s]," McMurtry remarked.

While in Hollywood, he received a call from Marcia Carter: Lowdermilk's was going down. On February 2, 1970, he caught a red-eye out of LA and arrived just in time for the auction.

The building's owners had served the store managers formal notice to move, to make way for another subway line. The managers searched futilely for an alternative site downtown; finally, they decided to liquidate the business. "Old Choice and Rare Books. 150,000 Volumes, 200 Paintings, 1000 Prints, Mezzotints, Engravings at Auction," read the notice.

The store had "the task of disposing of some half million [items] in a short amount of time . . . Marcia and I went into the auction flying blind," McMurtry said. A dealer who usually "dealt in high-end erotica" bought "the one lot we coveted most: several issues of the famous literary magazine *The Little Review,* all of them heaped on a shelf on the third floor" (*The Little Review* had once bravely published several installments of James Joyce's *Ulysses*). McMurtry glimpsed his fellow Texan, John Jenkins, at the sale. "[H]e turned out to be the biggest buyer . . . sinking a good deal of money into government documents . . . He was so busy bidding that I don't think we ever spoke." McMurtry and Carter came away with some 1,500 volumes, including several biographies. "Getting our purchases out of Lowdermilk's was . . . a nightmare," McMurtry recalled. "There was only one service elevator, and it was always crammed, mostly with government documents bound for the Jenkins Company. I lugged most of our boxes down and stuffed them in my car," huffing from too much dust.

He and Carter stored the books in their respective dwellings until such time as they could rent a space to set up shop. It seemed they had decided to open a bookstore.

Immediately, McMurtry flew back to LA, for more script conferences with Bogdanovich and Platt. Then came a day when Bogdanovich asked to meet him in Texas, to scout locations for the film. McMurtry flew into Dallas. "Where you wanna go? You wanna go north or south? You wanna go to Archer City?" he asked his companions as they collected their luggage in the airport. "Well, let's go there last," Bogdanovich said. "Let's see everything else." He'd thought "probably Archer City wouldn't . . . be right. I thought, 'That'd be his hometown. Why would that be right?' So we spent

a couple of days driving around Texas . . . [Larry] loves to drive around . . ."
In Austin, they had dinner with Bill and Sally Wittliff. Wittliff made noises
about wanting to get into the movie business someday. "[Finally] we said,
'Let's fly back to Dallas and drive up to Archer City,' Bogdanovich recalled.
"And the minute we drove into town, the minute I could see that stoplight
blinking at me . . . I said, 'This is it.' And Larry of course said, 'Well, it
oughta be. It's the town I wrote about.'"

The couple was so stunned by the "emptiness in front of the (burned-
out) Royal Theater . . . I had to push them out of the street to keep them
from getting run over by oncoming traffic," McMurtry said.

Platt remembered, "I was asleep in the back seat listening to Larry
and Peter in the front talking about the movie, and I would sort of go to
sleep and wake up and listen to their murmuring voices. It was very, very
special. And we got into the town—it was a stormy, rainy, sleety March—
and the town was as gray and ugly as you've ever seen. There were tumbleweeds blowing through the [streets]; [everything] was closed down." She
"couldn't believe that Larry McMurtry ever grew up in a town like that . . .
I had read all of Larry's books by then [and] it did not seem possible that
anybody with that gift could have survived that town . . . [But] it was [the]
town that incubated that talent . . . What else was there to do?"

As McMurtry stared at the city limits sign, pocked with bullet holes,
listening to Platt and Bogdanovich discuss his characters' motivations, he
realized they only saw the town as an "extension of [his] imagination";
they couldn't accept "that real people could ever have lived there." Their
notions of behavior in such a place were purely "diagrammatic." "I felt that
a novelist might, after all, be of some use in the creation of a movie script,
if only as the guardian of valid motivation," he said.

He had grown a beard while snowed in for a week in Virginia—a third
strike against him, after writing "dirty" books and leaving Texas, as far as his
family was concerned. "[W]e went into the McMurtry house, and Jeff Mc-
Murtry, Larry's father, instead of saying hello to Larry—Larry said, 'This is
Polly and Peter,' and Hazel was all friendly and everything, and she gave us a
pecan pie," Platt said. "[But then] Jeff McMurtry just came right over to me
and was looking at Larry, and instead of saying 'How do you do?' or 'Nice
to meet you' or the usual Texas thing, he said, 'You know what?'—he was
looking at Larry—'You pour kerosene on him, and I'll light the match.'"

Platt managed to ease tensions by charming the old man and quickly "becom[ing] one of his favorites," McMurtry said, "or enough of [a favorite] to receive lectures on the hardships of pioneer life."

A day or so later, McMurtry returned to Virginia, his collaborators repaired to LA, and for weeks, by airmail every day, they traded pages. McMurtry shaved off his beard—having been told by a lady acquaintance that he looked like a Harvard professor. He began to fill the gaps of his cinematic knowledge by catching Bergman, Fellini, Truffaut, and Renoir films at DC's many theaters. Bert Schneider was unhappy that he wouldn't move to California, but he wasn't about to take Jamie out of school or abandon the nascent bookstore plans. Besides, though he liked LA and was amused by the movie industry, he had already spent enough time in Hollywood to know that being there was like "working in a city filled with immensely attractive children. The people, who have all the power and all the money and a portion of the charm, also have the patience spans of two-year-olds."

Schneider insisted on massive cuts to the evolving script—the film was starting to swell into a three-hour epic, and he didn't have the budget for that. In the end, the restrictions strengthened the story's tragic power, increasing the sense of claustrophobia by limiting the movie's focus to just a few people and places.

McMurtry understood now that *The Last Picture Show* was "exactly the kind of novel from which good movies are made—that is, a flatly written book with strong characterizations and a sense of period and place . . . [the kind of book] that offer[s] a director no stylistic resistance whatsoever. Towering classics have a style, and adapting them is like attempting to translate poetry, only more difficult."

Three weeks before shooting began in Archer City in October 1970, Polly Platt gave birth to a second daughter, Alexandria. Bogdanovich's parents, living now in Phoenix for the climate's good effects on his father's health, agreed to watch the kids while the couple spent the next ten weeks making their movie.

McMurtry visited the set twice—in October and again in December. It was on that first visit that he brought along Marcia Carter and John Curtis, to take their minds off Allard Lowenstein's failing congressional campaign.

The high sky above the stock tanks and oil rigs was nearly brazen in its blueness. The autumn winds sliced across the grasses, stirring up dust, freezing the young cast members in their "scanty clothing," Platt recalled. "[W]e needed to shoot summer sequences . . . [but] we started . . . in October." So the "climate was hostile . . . [O]nly people in Texas know what I'm talking about, that wind coming down, right across the plains, flat, flat, flat."

Ben Johnson was the only veteran actor in the crew, a regular character actor in John Ford and Howard Hawks Westerns. His weathered face and gravelly voice brought gravitas to the role of Sam the Lion, but he refused the part at first. "Nah, Pete, there's too many words. Also, it's kind of a dirty picture and I couldn't show it to my mother," he told Bogdanovich. The director called John Ford and asked him to apply some pressure. Ford told Johnson, "What do you want to do, play Duke's sidekick your whole life?" Johnson finally agreed to the role, saying, later, it was easy for him because, growing up, he'd "seen those old cowboys outgrow their usefulness, get old and try to retire and move to town. Well, it never works . . . So that's the way I created my character."

Bogdanovich chose young Jeff Bridges for the part of Duane because of Bridges's likeability—Duane might disgust audiences, especially after injuring his friend Sonny in a fight, if the actor inhabiting him didn't radiate natural appeal to begin with. Timothy Bottoms, a reserved, brooding, uneasy young man, was tapped to transfer his personal qualities to Sonny. "If you ask my honest opinion, Tim's the movie," said Sam Bottoms, Timothy's brother. He played the role of Billy, the disabled kid under Sam the Lion's care. "It's all coming from Sonny. I think Larry is Sonny. He doesn't want to admit it. Larry's Sonny, in an introverted, sort of twisted way. Shy."

Cloris Leachman and Ellen Burstyn played the town's bitter middle-aged women. The roles came naturally to them. "[Cloris and I] were both going through divorces. So we were always talking about that and crying and carrying on in our Texas accents," Burstyn said.

"[Archer City] is a very hard-bitten place; you felt the lives, living there. It's so painful," Leachman recalled. "I mean it's so, what do they call it? Quiet desperation. Everybody knows everybody . . . When we were shooting in the main part of town, there was [a restaurant] . . . the Golden Rooster; we would always go in there, and while we'd be waiting, Ellen and me, a woman we met . . . would sit with us. And one day she was just beside herself. She finally burst into tears and said that she was married and everything . . . and she was crying uncontrollably. And we were consoling her and feeling very sorry, and she said, 'No, not my husband; my lover.' I mean, we were in the middle of *Last Picture Show* without even realizing it."

For the crucial role of Jacy, Bogdanovich cast Cybill Shepherd, the only woman he'd considered after seeing her face in *Glamour*. A Memphis-born fashion model, Shepherd overwhelmed Bogdanovich with a "kind of offhand, destructive quality" when she auditioned for him in his room at the Essex House hotel in New York. "I had just had breakfast, and I was sitting on the couch with the coffee table in front of me and the remains of my breakfast—you know, sometimes they put a flower in a little vase, a rose? So she sat on the floor on the other side of the coffee table, and we're talking, and she kind of offhandedly was fiddling with that little flower. And the way she did it, I thought, 'Well, that's kind of the way she plays with guys, just kind of offhandedly.' And that little gesture [assured] me . . . that she could do this part."

"I didn't think I was like Jacy at all, but the reality is I was a *lot* like Jacy," Shepherd admitted, years later. "Just in the sense of having men fall in love with me and then breaking their hearts. I did a lot of that."

When the film crew arrived in Archer City, the locals greeted them with quiet suspicion. R. J. Walsh, the owner of the Mobil station, said, "Most of our people have never been out of Texas and they have heard a lot about California—all the trials and the kidnappings and all them Tate murders coming out of there."

Bogdanovich was quoted in *The New York Times* as saying, "[This is] a savage, brutal place. The faces of people in Texas are so old, the land and the weather brutalizes them." His attitude did not endear him to the townsfolk. "I don't know Peter Bogdanovich from shit from shinola," one disgusted oil worker said. "With a name like that, I knew he wasn't from Wichita Falls."

Letters appeared in the *Archer County News,* stopping just short of linking the filming with the work of the devil: "I, for one, feel that Archer City will come out of this with a sickness in it's [*sic*] stomach and a certain misgiving about the support the City is lending to the further degradation and decay of the morals and attitudes we foist upon our youth in this Country . . . Wake up, Small Town America. You are all that is left of dignity and decency."

The paper's publisher, Joe Smith, wrote: "I do not endorse or purchase dirty or obscene books, nor do I attend or endorse dirty movies . . . I must admit I have read only a few excerpts from the book and from what I read the book 'stinks.'"

Initially, of course, McMurtry's mother had fully agreed with these sentiments. "I could kill you," she'd said to her son about the book. "With your education and your choice of words you couldn't think of anything else to say?" But as filming began, and the town turned venomous toward the family, her hackles rose (tinted, as per local custom, with light blue rinse). "I didn't understand the criticism because Larry had been nice to all of 'em. All of us had, and we'd lived here always," Hazel said. "And I couldn't see 'em being that ugly to us and our son when they knew he was intelligent, probably more so than most of 'em that were writing the pieces in the paper and saying things about the picture and about the book . . . dern it, I'm *still* mad [thinking about it]."

It didn't matter what anyone said; as the production moved forward, the accuracy of McMurtry's town portrait became obvious to everyone. Though he'd been writing about the 1950s, much remained the same twenty years later. Richard Hill, a sixteen-year-old high school junior recently arrested for drinking beer and driving around the courthouse in reverse, told a reporter, "There ain't nothing else to do except go wild." Loyd Catlett, a local who'd landed a part in the film as an extra and as an informal dialect coach, complained to members of the cast, "There's flat nothing to do around these parts but fistfight and fuck, and ah ain't even got a girlfriend. Sometimes ah feel lower than whale shit." The paper reported that nine of the twenty girls in the recent Archer City High School graduating class had been pregnant the day they'd received their diplomas (one reason for this was the town's only doctor: he refused to educate his patients about birth control).

"When we were . . . shooting, somebody would nudge me and say, 'Look, there's the real Duane,'" Bridges said. "A lot of these characters were still walking around."

While on the set, McMurtry got to see a different side of Polly Platt: the pro in motion, fidgeting with the costumes until every button was perfect, aligning the camera shots (by offering detailed suggestions to Bogdanovich, most of which he took). Orson Welles had convinced them to shoot in black-and-white because the script was "an actor's script, it's all about the

performances . . . [and black-and-white is] the actor's friend. *Every* performance looks better in black-and-white." Besides, it captured the bleakness
and the period better than sharp color. Platt instinctively understood how
each scene should look. The dailies proved her right. "You might have a
gas station [in a scene], like the Texaco station. I remember [Polly] taking
out the E, so you'd just see T-XACO," Bridges said. "It was very subtle, but
something about the design—you felt like it had *happened.*"

She had a sure touch with actors, as well, doing their makeup and hair,
putting them at ease. "She was Mom. She was *everything*," Timothy Bottoms said. She even soothed Grover Lewis's jitters—McMurtry's estranged
old buddy had been hanging around, covering the shoot for *Rolling Stone*
(McMurtry was not happy to see him). Bogdanovich saw Lewis's ravaged
face and thought he'd be perfect for the part of Sonny's alcoholic father. As
Platt aged him with makeup and grayed his hair one day, she said, "Oh,
fantastic, great! . . . [Y]ou look lunchier than Dennis Weaver in *Touch of
Evil.* Just don't wander out in the streets without a keeper. I don't want
you getting arrested."

McMurtry was not just impressed with her skills. He was attracted by
her pageboy haircut and her gamine look, and intrigued by her complex
demeanor: "amazingly tough and totally vulnerable at precisely the same
moment—so that she can either kill you or burst into tears," director
James L. Brooks once said of her.

In Texas, she had plenty of opportunity to express every facet of her
personality: it had become a poorly kept secret on the set of *The Last Picture
Show* that the loneliness and sexual acting-out in the story had spilled over
into the lives of the filmmakers. On location, "[c]ast and crew conspire in
an implicit acceptance and discretion about the phenomenon of musical
beds, about who is seen emerging from which star's trailer or which grip's
room at the Motel 6," Shepherd said. "The set is like an office Christmas party, where indiscretions are absolved when the party's over . . . It's
a dreamscape of sorts, basically free of familial and adult responsibilities. I
was twenty years old when I entered that world [in Archer City], mischie-
vous and recklessly self-absorbed." She said she was aroused the entire ten
weeks. She "dated" Jeff Bridges "for, like, half a minute." Timothy Bottoms
said gloomily, "[W]e all wanted to see her. Naked. I never saw her naked."
And then one afternoon, "We were in Olney, Texas, and we were sitting in

the theater—you know, 'cause the picture show in Archer City had burned down, we used the interior of Olney," Shepherd said. "So Peter and I are sitting in that theater, and we're talking and stuff . . . And he said to me, 'I can't decide who I'd rather sleep with, you or Jacy.'"

"Cybill shot the shit out of his heart, man. After that, he was a goner," Bridges said.

Bogdanovich confessed to Platt—as if she were a pal who'd understand and commiserate with him—that he was feeling old and he'd never had a starlet before. He'd sneak into Shepherd's room at the Ramada Inn in Wichita Falls or into her dressing room on the set, on the second floor of an old hotel above a seedy hamburger shop.

To avoid running into them one night in the restaurant of Wichita Falls's Trade Winds motel, Platt crawled under tables toward the door, so she wouldn't be seen.

"I felt ugly," she said. "I'd just given birth . . . and wasn't much good in the sex department. For god's sake, I was still bleeding . . . [I was] winding myself in sheets to stop my mother's milk from flowing." She told herself she was a pro; the movie was as much hers as her husband's, and she was not going to jeopardize her stake in it. "I just pretended it wasn't happening, all of it. My thought was 'The only drama is what goes on in front of the camera.'" She did Shepherd's hair every day, cutting and styling it. "I was tempted [to harm her], but Cybill was irresistible," she said. "I thought about it—I thought if I was a man and a beautiful girl like that was making a pass at me, I don't know what I would do. I could see why Peter was so head over heels in love with her."

McMurtry said, "Polly later told me that somewhere, somehow she knew she was creating her own successor in Cybill." Her daily makeup session with the actress, turning the girl into a teenage dream, "was moving Peter further and further away from her."

When Bogdanovich's father died of a stroke in Arizona, Bogdanovich turned to Shepherd for comfort. Platt refused to attend the funeral because she could face neither her mother-in-law nor her children under the circumstances.

McMurtry urged her to force her husband to choose between Shepherd and her. The couple's tensions only mounted. By McMurtry's second visit to the set, Bogdanovich had essentially left his marriage (though the full unraveling would take many months). When McMurtry pulled into town and was sitting still at the stoplight, Platt ran up to his car to tell him the sad news. Then she scurried off again to resume her many jobs on the set.

"Later in the day I finally met Cybill," McMurtry said. "In fact we sat in the car on the bridge over the Red River near Burkburnett, Texas," while a scene was being readied. "As I recall, we held hands, a sign . . . that Cybill was feeling shaky, as well she might have been. She was young and in a bleak place, making her first film. It was a cold day and she may or may not have just broken up . . . the director's marriage. She would have held hands with a mule, but, no mule being available, she held hands with me."

On still another cold, bleak day—drinking Dixie cups of coffee and brandy to brace themselves—the crew shot the scene of Sam the Lion's funeral in the Archer City cemetery, a "neatly tended tract with a few knobby trees jutting up here and there, form[ing] a strong, stark tableau, so devoid of ornament that each stone and plant and ruptured fissure of the land . . . subtly forc[es] the eye out to the horizon and up to the sky," Grover Lewis wrote for *Rolling Stone.* The boneyard's most imposing structure belonged to the Taylor family—the old man whose second-floor light McMurtry used to watch as a boy, imagining the weary fellow reading in bed, just as he was. "It's Boot Hill, son. The last roundup, motherfuckers," yelled one of the technicians just before the cameras rolled. His voice echoed and died in the wind above the modest markers of the McMurtry family, Louisa F. (1859–1946) and William J. (1858–1940).

Soon thereafter, the men and women of Hollywood packed up cameras, lights, and a few wrecked lives and abandoned the plains of Texas.

Once Al Lowenstein had been gerrymandered out of office, John Curtis didn't know what to do with himself. "I think Larry and Marcia felt sad for me because we had lost the election, and my wife didn't want me to be involved with politics anymore," Curtis said. So McMurtry invited him to join the book venture. "We found the space simply by walking around Georgetown and seeing if there were empty places," Curtis recalled. "It was very amateur, in a way." On the corner of 31st and M, they located a former apartment building, with space for rent at $120 a month. "It was near the post office, which was convenient. All of us put in the money," Curtis said. They had about $1,000 in capital and the 1,500 volumes they'd purchased at the Lowdermilk sale. McMurtry donated a few volumes of Trollope. Slowly they'd expand to fill the rest of the three-story brick building. It had once contained nine small apartments. The rooms would soon be stacked, floor to ceiling, with books.

"The bookstore wasn't really, when we started it, full time for any of us. I'd always had an interest in architecture. My job was to design the bookshelves. It was just a small little walk-in, at first," Curtis said. "It was very loose and open, our way of doing business. Someone would take the shop. Marcia was there a lot. Bill Matheson of the Library of Congress lived nearby, and he'd often stop in. And various people would come to see Larry, especially the scouts he had known. There were always a few fools who'd drop in, and that didn't please him."

Curtis gave the store its name: "I called it Booked Up, because Marcia was always booked up, socially."

It was not a propitious time to open a shop. In addition to Lowdermilk's in DC, venerable stores were vanishing all over the country, victims of declining reading habits and soaring real estate values. Additionally, the opening was bittersweet for McMurtry because Carter had met a nice man named Robin Hill, an Australian painter, well-known in his home country as an arts writer and wildlife watercolorist. "[He] came from Australia to have a show of his paintings at a Middleburg art gallery," Carter said. She found him fascinating. "He had intended to be here for only two weeks, but . . ."

Soon he had replaced McMurtry on Carter's arm at the hostesses' gatherings, much more at ease in the social milieu. Carter was ebullient. She spoke of fashioning a studio for him on Foxcroft Road in Middleburg, near her family's old farm.

A month after the bookstore unlocked its doors, McMurtry wrote Grace David: "[O]pened a little bookshop, very tiny but very nice. I'm not entirely sure why I did. Marcia and I have not made it and I will have to begin, at the very least, a phased withdrawal sometime soon—I suppose since I failed to replace her family I wanted to leave her at least a bookshop." Also, he said, he wanted to free himself of "several thousand books. I like the book trade but am not all that rabid to possess books myself, anymore." This would prove not to be true.

He and Carter remained close. Without drama, the two of them made the transition from lovers to friends and business partners. Ruefully, Mc-Murtry figured he had repeated an old mistake: believing irrationally—narcissistically—that he was responsible not for a woman's happiness, but rather for her vague sense that life was usually disappointing (who could deny it?). At least the absence of sex took the pressure off the partnership and eased the social demands. And few things in life were sweeter than a flirtatious friendship.

It actually helped him that other stores kept failing—he stayed busy pilfering collapsing businesses, such as the Park Book Shop on 19th Street, run by a woman named Amalya Reifsneider. "She got elephantiasis and her legs swole up something horrible," McMurtry said. "She couldn't get off the second floor and she got fleeced by various people. Since she couldn't go up and down, she couldn't see what was not there anymore. People took stuff she didn't know they were taking." He coveted her historical memoirs by "upper-class ladies," full of "juicy descriptions of long-ago scandals in foreign courts."

In time, he filled Booked Up's shelves with treasures from over one hundred and fifty private libraries, the contents of which would have gone to Lowdermilk's had it still existed. Objects he and Carter had purchased at flea markets and auctions furnished the small space, trimmed with warm wood. Of an evening, he'd sit in a leather chair in the shop, contemplating what he'd done. Buying books at estate sales—libraries of the dead—was like summoning the minds of ghosts, gathered by ghosts. He'd surrounded himself with cabinets and trunks once cherished by those long gone, solid pieces that would easily outlast him and his loves.

16

"Please don't call them used," Marcia Carter would say, standing beside a rolling ladder and a red velvet swing braided with Italian tassels. The ladder fronted a row of shelves bearing, among other volumes, *Blackstone's Commentaries,* a compendium of eighteenth-century British laws selling for $6,000. "All these books are treasures," including, she'd insist, *So You Want to Be an Airline Stewardess* ($15) and *A Book of Toasts* from 1923 ($10, or make an offer). "I put out what interests me and catches my eye."

She quickly got to know her regular customers. "Oh, there goes Yolanda," she said to McMurtry one day, glimpsing a woman passing on the sidewalk. "We can sell her the Eleanor Roosevelt." John Curtis, dressed "like a tennis pro," according to one visitor, puttered around the shop, replacing lightbulbs. He would soon leave for Williamsburg—his wife landed an academic job there—where he'd open another store.

McMurtry, restless behind the counter in his jeans and loose maroon sweaters, sipping iced tea thoughtfully from a paper cup, wondered what to make of himself. He still felt a compulsion to write, "but I had written a lot, and it was no longer exactly a passion." He still loved to read, but he had "burned out as a reader of fiction," after reviewing so many novels for newspapers. He seemed to be a bookseller now, but his zeal was for scouting, hitting the road for the hunt: "Scouts are the seed carriers, a vital link to the food chain of bookselling," he said.

Most of all, he'd slouch in the shop of an afternoon, craving Peanut Patties. He hadn't had one since the last time he was in Texas.

If he got particularly bored, he'd roam the store, reshelving books, often at random, just to see how a pair of volumes might look side by side from across the room. Occasionally, scouting his own inventory, he'd discover a book he hadn't known was there, and more rarely, he'd reconsider the price of an item. He'd once nearly made a major blunder with a book called *The Fiend's Delight* by Dod Grile; he was about to price it at fifteen dollars when he learned, by happenstance, that Dod Grile was the pseudonym of Ambrose Bierce. *The Fiend's Delight* was Bierce's first book.

One day he plucked *Mr. Zouch: Superman* by Anthony Powell from his shelf: it was an American edition of Powell's novel *From a View to a Death*, retitled abysmally by some addled publicist. McMurtry was shocked to see that he or Carter or Curtis, in a hurry one day, had priced it at $7.50. He bumped it up to $350 and sold it that very afternoon.

He rarely hid his boredom. He'd stare out the windows, aware of how many bookstores in the eight-by-four-block corridor near them, from F to K Streets, from 9th to 17th, had shuttered in the last ten years: at least eight that he knew of. Gloomy, he'd turn at the wary approach of a customer. One day, a young man indicated he wished to buy an English travel book but felt it was overpriced at $150. McMurtry, eating a chicken-and-mayonnaise sandwich, just shrugged. The young man went ahead and paid for the book. McMurtry wrote up the invoice without a word, and continued munching his bread, spilling crumbs on the counter. The young man slipped away. "[T]he atmosphere in Booked Up was chilly, if not frigid, and certainly off-putting to casual browsers," said Alan Bisbort, the owner of a small bookstore. "Not once did anyone who worked at Booked Up acknowledge my existence, except when I reached for a book on an upper shelf and I detected a pained wincing sound at my back."

A sign on the wall said smokers lit up "on penalty of death."

The treatment visitors received was dictated by McMurtry's moods, changeable by the hour. If he'd had a good writing morning, he could be quite helpful, if not overly friendly, to his customers, many of whom recognized that what appeared to be rudeness was merely shyness, his natural taciturnity. Kenneth Turan, a *Washington Post* writer who would one day become a prominent movie critic, wandered into the shop one afternoon and came across a copy of James M. Cain's *The Postman Always Rings Twice*, inscribed by Cain to Lana Turner, who'd starred in the 1946 film of the book. The volume cost $900. Turan told McMurtry he absolutely had to have the book but couldn't afford the "nosebleed" price. After a few minutes, McMurtry offered him a one-time-only half-price "enthusiasm discount."

What especially irked McMurtry was the fact that, sitting just a few blocks from the White House and Capitol Hill, Booked Up's stock rarely attracted the interest of the nation's leaders. As Bisbort put it, "[T]he heaviest lifters . . . the politicians . . . and their power-tripping staffers, were known for throwing money around at bars, strip joints and whorehouses, but certainly not at bookshops. They were too cheap to even buy the bestsellers they desired. Instead, Congressional lackeys would pester the overworked staff at the Library of Congress to buy extra copies of the latest Grisham or Clancy or Grafton to 'loan' them (which they then would never return)."

McMurtry recalled selling "only one real book" to a member of Congress: "Senator Charles Mathias of Maryland bought a very fine edition of Gibbon's *The Decline and Fall of the Roman Empire* from us, and he read it. Otherwise, the only sale we made to a member of Congress was a $4 book on cartooning that we sold to Bob Eckhardt of Texas, who aspired to be a cartoonist." Eckhardt was one of the post-vulgarian Texans in town, now married to Nadine Brammer (Billy Lee's ex-wife), and an acquaintance of McMurtry's at Georgetown gatherings. Wearing a red bow tie, he'd ride to Capitol Hill on his bike, equipped with a loud rubber horn and a basket full of booze. "Gary Hart, pre-and-post Donna Rice [a reference to one of Washington's many sex scandals], often browsed, but I don't recall that he bought," McMurtry said. Gilbert Harrison, *The New Republic*'s editor, was an avid early customer.

Discouraged by the absence of literary intelligence among the nation's top officials, McMurtry was happy to escape the store on scouting trips or to flea markets and auctions, often in Carter's pleasant company. Their friendship flourished now that their love affair was over. Together, they "bought an excellent library from a crusty retired diplomat with a younger and very beautiful wife," McMurtry recalled. "In a room on a lower floor of his house, there were at least a million dollars' worth of bird books, but these belonged to the diplomat's former wife. We weren't allowed to touch them. Still, we bought a carful of very nice books—though I remember with longing the one we didn't get: a beautiful copy of T. E. Lawrence's *Seven Pillars of Wisdom,* worth $50,000 today."

Teddy Roosevelt's daughter, Alice Roosevelt Longworth, widow of a former Speaker of the House and "something of a social terror in Washington," McMurtry said, offered to sell a few of her books from the house she shared with her granddaughter, a woman named Joanna Sturm. "[We] didn't actually enter her house," McMurtry said. "The books were brought down and piled under a porte-cochère, and Sturm handled the transaction. The books were excellent, and the transaction suited us fine. When Mrs. L. died, the remaining books passed into Sturm's possession . . . One day, [she] walked into the bookshop and asked if we'd like to buy any more of Granny's books . . . [Apparently] Joanna wanted to buy a BMW motorcycle, which cost about $7,500. We happily gave her that amount, and I spent a day rummaging under stairwells and in closets in Mrs. Longworth's house until I had a carful more of her books."

One day McMurtry got a call from a College Park resident, a man whose name he thought was Kane, spelled K-A-N-E. The fellow said he had some books to sell. "I went and discovered a grouchy old man watching the World Series on what was probably the world's oldest functioning TV set," McMurtry said. The house was disappointingly void of interesting items—just sets of biographical dictionaries and *Who's Who*. McMurtry was about to leave when he glimpsed a few boxes tucked beneath the dining room table. The man said McMurtry could take a look, and he discovered stacks of manuscripts and movie scripts by James M. Cain— the slumping old grouch fidgeting in front of the television. Cain grunted that he was willing to sell the lot of them. "This one's okay," he murmured, pawing through the yellowed scripts. "This one got made."

McMurtry's longest scouting trip was to England—his first visit to Europe—alongside Carter, an experienced world traveler since earliest childhood. In London, they visited Cecil Court, a renowned booksellers' street, but were disappointed by the fare. In Cheltenham, they bought forty-five books by Virginia Woolf's father, Leslie Stephen. McMurtry was pleased to see that Booked Up's atmosphere stacked up well with the quaint shops in London's foggy back streets, with their lavish volumes of equestrian arts displayed behind leaded windows, or museum catalogues of glass collectibles splayed on oak podiums under amber lights.

Back home, refreshed by his travels, he made an effort at genial salesmanship—a mask lasting all of a week. Trying to make small talk with customers, he'd say things like, "I had an expensive education, but I learned most of what I know in secondhand bookshops."

One day, a homeless little girl who'd cut her foot on a broken wine bottle in the street hobbled through the door: one of the surprises of "street-level book selling in an urban setting," he said. McMurtry called a doctor and got her patched up. After that, she'd hang around the store. She turned out to be a descendant of Button Gwinnett, one of the signers of the Declaration of Independence.

On another muggy afternoon, a matronly woman wearing a thick red coat entered the store, carrying a green shopping bag and walking a well-groomed dog named Cricket on a leash. She was looking for an out-of-print book by Groucho Marx. "We don't have it," McMurtry informed her. Well then, how about something by Winston Churchill? "Too bad," he said. Sniffing, the woman pointed Cricket toward the door. "Well, thank you," McMurtry called after her. "See my movie." She clearly had no idea, and no interest in, what he was talking about.

The Last Picture Show premiered at the New York Film Festival on October 22, 1971. After the screening, Cybill Shepherd's mother, appalled by the nudity and convinced the film was smut, approached Bogdanovich and said, "Better luck next time."

Writing in *Newsweek,* Jack Kroll said, "[*The Last Picture Show*] is not merely the best American movie of a rather dreary year; it is the most impressive work by a young American director since *Citizen Kane.*" *Cue* chimed in, calling the movie "nothing short of a contemporary American classic." Pauline Kael said, "Bogdanovich is so plain and uncondescending in his re-creation of what it means to be a high school athlete, of what a country dance hall is like, of the necking in cars and movie houses, and of the desolation that follows high school graduation that the movie becomes a lovingly exact history of American small-town life." She praised McMurtry's contribution to the script, for which he did, in the end, receive official credit as a member of the guild: "McMurtry also wrote *Horseman, Pass By,* on which the movie *Hud* was based, and this new movie is set in the same dust-and-oil Texas. But *Hud* was written by Hollywood pros, cast with star personalities, and directed for 'meaning' and charge. This time, the author did the script together with the director, and McMurtry's storytelling sense and his feeling for authenticity have been retained. The dialogue is so natural an emanation of the characters that you're hardly aware of it as dialogue." (Boganovich said McMurtry had "written the best regional dialogue of anyone since Mark Twain.")

Kael added, "McMurtry's truth is a small one, but Bogdanovich has been faithful to it: the nostalgia of *The Last Picture Show* reflects the need to come to terms with one's own past."

The movie received eight Academy Award nominations, including one for Best Adapted Screenplay (McMurtry and Bogdanovich), Best Picture, Best Director, and Best Cinematography (Robert Surtees). Ben Johnson, Cloris Leachman, Ellen Burstyn, and Jeff Bridges were all nominated as supporting actors. Polly Platt's enormous contributions to the film were ignored. (She was barred from receiving production or design credit because, as a woman, she had never even been considered for membership in the Art Directors Guild.)

At the 44th Academy Awards ceremony in LA's Dorothy Chandler Pavilion, Tennessee Williams, befuddled and bumbling onstage, announced the Adapted Screenplay nominees, calling the script's cowriter "McMurdee." Ernest Tidyman, an old screenwriting hand, won for *The French Connection.* Bogdanovich lost the Best Director award to William Friedkin. He "sat in his tux looking like a Serbian martyr—the only survivor of the Field of Blackbirds, perhaps," McMurtry said. Ben Johnson and Cloris Leachman won the acting awards. With the exception of the ever-gracious Johnson, who thanked "Mr. Peter Bogdanovich['s] . . . lovely wife Polly," Platt's name was erased from all discussions of *The Last Picture Show.*

The movie would gross over $20 million worldwide. In an era when American kids were being shot at on college campuses by National Guard troops, a nostalgic movie about 1950s teenagers, filmed in the timelessness of black-and-white, touched a nerve. The movie's success convinced McMurtry "more than ever that we live in a zombie-state these days; people respond to *The Last Picture Show* partly because it reminds them of how it was in the days when they felt."

The movie contained just enough "counterculture" elements to hold strong appeal for youthful audiences—the focus on sex, the anomie associated with European avant-garde cinema. At times the story approaches the surreal, as when Sonny guns his pickup to escape the town but can't get past the city limits sign, as if a supernatural force were holding him back.

Some critics accused Bogdanovich of softening McMurtry's brutal vision of small towns. In the novel, the "last picture show" is a run-of-the-mill trifle called *The Kid from Texas,* and watching it "[doesn't] help" Sonny and Duane overcome their hopelessness: "It would have taken *Winchester*

'73 or *Red River* or some big picture like that to have crowded out the memories [of Jacy] the boys kept having." Instead, Bogdanovich chose, as *his* last picture show, Hawks's *Red River,* starring John Wayne on a cattle drive, exhorting his hands to "drive 'em on to Missouri!" Sonny and Duane leave the theater after the film, flushed with warmth for the town, for the movies, for each other. It is by far a more sentimental and mythic moment than McMurtry would have allowed, but he came to feel it was right for the film, like the movie's ending, which Bogdanovich fought for: Bert Schneider wanted to end with the cattle truck smashing Billy in the street, rather than the talky scene where Ruth Popper admonishes, then seems to forgive Sonny. "Peter . . . coming to the material without the corruption of having lived it, was gentler to everyone than I had been," McMurtry admitted. "[T]he film is extraordinary in this day and time for the sheer *feeling* which it releases . . . [Ruth] finds the fact that she can feel more important than anything that has happened . . . It leaves us, not just with a movie about defeat, but with a movie about living-in-spite-of-or-in-the-teeth-of-defeat, a superb thing for any work of art to try to be about."

L*iving-in-spite-of-or-in-the-teeth-of-defeat* was Polly Platt's whole existence. For a while, she continued to work with Bogdanovich, at his request, but the marriage was over. (Film historians have been quick to note that Bogdanovich's movies ceased to be commercial or artistic successes once Platt quit collaborating with him.)

Regarding the marriage, the final straw for her came one "rainy night in Van Nuys," she said. "Peter was staying out to one, two, three in the morning; supposedly he was cutting [*The Last Picture Show*], but I was pretty sure he was seeing Cybill." Antonia had the flu. She was vomiting. Platt's pediatrician recommended an enema. "It was two in the morning," Platt said. "I realized to go get the medication, I would have to wake [Alexandria] up, put them both in the car, and drive to get it. There was no one to stay home with the children." She realized with a shock that she was completely "alone in the world . . . All our fancy friends who were famous were not the type of friends I could call in the middle of the night to babysit my children while I went to get a prescription."

The one person she *could* call was Larry McMurtry. He'd listen to her cry for hours. He was across the country, in DC, suddenly in demand on the Georgetown dinner party circuit because of the movie. Forget Marcia and her elegant painter! Where's that lanky writer in his cowboy boots? Barbara Howar, Evangeline Bruce . . . they'd call to invite him, telling him to be sure to wear his Levi's. Lone Star dust was as dear now in Washington as a pound of caviar. Ben Bradlee will be there, David Halberstam, I. F. Stone . . . they all want to meet you . . .

He gave an interview to Tom Shales of *The Washington Post.* McMurtry mentioned he'd been missing Peanut Patties. The power of the press: "I was soon deluged with at least a hundred Peanut Patties, all sent from Texas by well-meaning fans," he said.

Book collectors came to his shop lugging sacks stuffed with his first editions, seeking autographs. A while back, he'd sold some of his personal books to a dealer, who'd spent time erasing McMurtry's name from the inner covers. Now that dealer could kick himself: McMurtry's signature was worth saddlebags full of dough.

"In three months my fame ended," he reflected. Bigger movies and splashy scandals came along to edge his name out of the swirl of gossip—this was, after all, the Washington of Watergate, of Nixon's eighteen-and-a-half-minute tape gap: the fun was just beginning, and if some of the salon guests would soon be facing prison . . . well, McMurtry figured, what was a salon without a scoundrel or two?

It was just as well the movie fervor had subsided when it did; the fawning was becoming cloying. To escape it, he'd drive to Los Angeles, leaving Jamie with his mother. Platt was trying to work again, to take her mind off the wreck of her marriage. Bogdanovich was living with Shepherd now. McMurtry would listen to Platt's misery ("All our famous friends [are] Peter's friends now"), take her out and feed her, babysit her girls and do the laundry while she was busy fixing up a film set somewhere. His brief courtship of her would never be free of the traumas Platt had experienced at the hands of her parents, after the death of her first husband, and now, with the collapse of her marriage. It all made for a sad, troubled intimacy.

Platt agreed to work as the production designer on Bogdanovich's film *What's Up, Doc?* She began drinking heavily, and she commenced an affair with a property master named Anthony Wade. ("Big Tony," she called him—he resembled her notion of Paul Bunyan.) The affair enraged Bogdanovich, not least because it was a social gaffe in Hollywood for someone on Platt's level to mingle with the second-class citizens in the technical crews.

McMurtry had not given up on her. He suggested they take the kids—Jamie, too—to Antigua for a Christmas vacation, at the end of 1972. Right before they left, she agreed to an interview with director Robert Altman in New York; he was looking for a production designer for his movie *Thieves Like Us*. McMurtry looked after Platt's daughters in a room at the Sherry-Netherland while Platt met Altman in his suite. Immediately, the director tried to seduce her—with her children sitting right next door. She laughed at him and flew off with her writer chum to the stormy Caribbean.

It was a melancholy trip. It rained the entire time and the mosquitoes were relentless. The children were testy. Antonia argued fiercely with her mother—she forgave neither of her parents for the family's breakup. "I loved being with Larry and his very shy young son," Platt said. "But I realized how deep a fissure this separation from Peter, the father of my children, was to be."

She said, "The most poetic day was watching a lone Antiguan boy ride his black stallion right into the sea at sunset, driving the horse deep, deep into the Caribbean . . . until the horse was swimming with the boy holding on to his mane. They emerged shiny with the water and happy as two young creatures could be. I looked at Larry and . . . he said that he loved me."

"I *was* in love with Polly," McMurtry affirmed. "Unfortunately, she had just fallen in love with Big Tony. She spent all her time phoning [him]."

Afterward, both of them saddened, a little wistful, Platt and McMurtry went their separate ways. They remained close friends. She would inspirit at least three of his books, *All My Friends Are Going to Be Strangers* and *Somebody's Darling*, in which she served as the model for Jill Peel, and *Terms of Endearment*, in which her arguments with Antonia informed the book's central relationship.

Eventually, Platt married Big Tony. Following the disappointments with her and Marcia Carter, McMurtry never again spoke of major life-altering passions. No more *Anna Karenina* romances. It seemed that what people most wanted in life was what they were forced to live without.

If he had once been "a bruised optimist, convinced that he could love one woman forever" under the right circumstances, he was no longer so sanguine. From now on, he said, when "he yearn[ed], he yearn[ed] for individuals, not for a home."

Billy Lee, do you reckon people who don't appreciate chicken-fried steak with cream gravy can do justice to McMurtry on film?" Larry L. King asked his friend, Bill Brammer.

"Naw," Brammer answered. "No way. I bet they don't even drink Dr Pepper."

The two writers were standing around Austin's Chariot Inn, at McMurtry's invitation, watching a film crew wolf down soggy tacos and lament the lack of bagels. The crew had gathered to make the third film from a McMurtry novel, *Leaving Cheyenne*. The movie was tentatively titled *The Wild and the Sweet*; it would be released as *Lovin' Molly* in 1974, and it would not fare as well, commercially or critically, as *Hud* or *The Last Picture Show*.

The great period of auteurism, nurturing films like *Picture Show*, would not come to an end until the return of the blockbuster (*Star Wars*, *Jaws*) and the financial debacle, in 1980, of Michael Cimino's bloated Western, *Heaven's Gate*. But already Hollywood—sensing that *Easy Rider* was, after all, a one-off rather than a moneymaking trendsetter—was re-seizing control from the kid directors and returning it to the producers. As Joan Didion said, "[T]he game [was] back on, development money available, the deal dependent only upon the truly beautiful story and the right elements," the right elements being stars and pots of money.

McMurtry knew that the timing had been just right on *The Last Picture Show*—a few months earlier, Peter Bogdanovich couldn't have gotten the job; a year or so later, he wouldn't have wanted it.

Lovin' Molly was a slick Hollywood package, put together to capitalize on *Picture Show*'s popularity. The producer and screenwriter, Steve Friedman, didn't know and didn't care about the differences between ranching and farming, grassy plains and lush green swamps ("Is that Vietnam, or Missouri?" McMurtry blurted one day, watching the dailies). Hammers and post-hole diggers were all the same to him ("So who's gonna know?" Friedman said. "How many moviegoers ever saw a fence made?"). Director

Sidney Lumet dressed his stars, Beau Bridges and Tony Perkins, in clod-hoppers and what appeared to be bib overalls. They looked like Mr. Green Jeans on *Captain Kangaroo.*

"You know what your book's about?" Lumet gushed at McMurtry one day. "Larry, it's about . . . well, it's about . . . *the glory of no reward!*"

"Hm," McMurtry responded.

He watched, chagrined, as a makeup artist—no Polly Platt—tried to turn Tony Perkins into an elderly man; he "appeared to be about two years older than Christianity," said Larry L. King. "McMurtry took one look and grunted like somebody had poked him in the ribs with a pitchfork."

Later, in New York, watching a rough-cut screening of the movie with a test audience, McMurtry kept sinking in his seat: "It's not so bad if you only see the top half of the screen." Afterward, he said, "Lumet apparently shot the thing in track shoes—zip, zip, zip. People . . . kept laughing in all the wrong places, and some walked out. Near the interminable end, I realized a woman behind me had been crying for twenty minutes. I wondered what kind of woman would cry at such a film. When I risked a look behind me, it was my agent."

He had bigger worries than the fact that a bunch of Hollywood bozos was botching his material—he'd never cared much, anyway, about what moviemakers did to his books. The books were over and done with, and the movies—with the exception of *Picture Show*—weren't his concern.

Before visiting a fake Texas on the *Lovin' Molly* set in the little town of Bastrop, he'd paid a visit to Archer City, where the *real* Texas was quite a bit rougher. As he told his pals Larry L. and Billy Lee, as they sat up late one night in a Bastrop motel room, he'd dropped by the old family ranch one day and watched his father attempt to rope and rescue a frightened mother cow from a ditch. Jeff Mac was stiff and frail. "He was butted in the head, nearly tore off his ear, and he got hooked in the leg," McMurtry said. "Took him half an hour, but he finally got that old cow out of there. Then he made it back to the house, poured blood out of his boot—and passed out looking happier than I've seen him in thirty years."

He'd told the story for gentle laughs. Then the conversation swung back to the klutzy film crew, "unable to distinguish asses from elbows." Their idealized West insulted men like Jeff Mac. But the cow incident was no laughing matter to McMurtry. The death throes of cowboying had been breaking his father's body as well as his spirit, and taken Hazel down with him. The ranch hadn't felt right this time. Some kind of page had been turned. And ever since Hollywood had come to town, his parents could no longer count on Archer City to respond with (its version of) friendly support. He'd left home feeling sad, more concerned for his folks than he could remember.

Hazel figured she'd just about had enough. Jeff Mac had been slowing for years, his back stoved up so much, he was nearly crippled some mornings. Most of the chores around the house—the ranch, too—had fallen to her. This had long been the case. She was worn to the bone. To make matters worse, he'd barely spoken to her in forty years except to ask what's for supper.

By some miracle—clearly, she'd caught him in a moment of painful agony—she got him to assent to a meeting with a marriage counselor in Wichita Falls. But then they both agreed that if folks in Archer City found out, there'd be no end of talk, so they canceled.

On the phone, Hazel told her son she was thinking of moving out, maybe taking a long trip to Hawaii. Was he really hearing this? In her whole life, she'd rarely been farther than thirty miles into Oklahoma by car . . . to the Grand Canyon, once, and to South Dakota in the 1950s . . . the choking restriction of her days filled him with gloom.

His parents' forty-second wedding anniversary was approaching. McMurtry suggested they celebrate by taking a vacation together, visiting him back east. When the occasion finally arrived, he flew to Texas to make the trip with them; otherwise, he knew they'd bail at the last minute. It was his mother's first travel by air. His father had once taken a brief ride in a biplane in 1928.

"The night before the trip my parents had a tremendous fight—it was, I believe, over some pajamas that either had or had not been packed," McMurtry said.

Jeff Mac appreciated the tall grasses of Virginia, but DC soured him. Hazel, too. She couldn't abide the absence of lawns in Georgetown. The bookstore impressed neither one of them: titles no one had heard of, priced so high you'd be afraid to touch them. McMurtry explained that one mediocre book could destroy the integrity of an entire store. Why didn't he display his own books, his mother wanted to know (though she still wondered how he ever got the silly things published)? He said he wasn't in the business of selling his novels; writing them was trouble enough.

When his father glimpsed the Department of Agriculture downtown, he launched into a red-faced snit—the place was worthless, he said, it had eaten his taxes for years and offered nothing in return. Those idiots didn't deserve such a big building.

McMurtry's editor, Michael Korda, was in town. He offered to take them all to dinner at the restaurant atop the Kennedy Center. Hazel insisted that locating a restaurant close to the clouds was a dangerous idea: probably the altitude would spoil the food somehow.

"The next day the two of them, Hazel and Jeff, flew home, separated, and never traveled together again," McMurtry said.

His aging parents would likely amass huge medical expenses in the months to come, and Jamie would soon be headed for an expensive boarding school, Woodberry Forest, in Madison County. (Neither McMurtry nor his boy embraced this idea, but most of Jamie's friends would be enrolling there, so it seemed the decision was made.) The movie money had arrived at a good time, and though he was no longer a star attraction at Georgetown affairs, his stock had risen on college campuses as a result of *The Last Picture Show*; he welcomed the surprisingly extravagant speaker fees.

Texas schools courted him eagerly (though he tended to speak in a monotone). He traveled to Austin, Dallas, Houston, San Marcos, Midland-Odessa. Joe Holley, teaching at Dallas College's Mountain View campus in the early 1970s, remembered him coming to lecture "and he had this beautiful young woman with him. I didn't know who she was, but I thought, *This must be the life.*"

At Southwest Texas State University in 1974, he told an audience that his first two novels were "country" and "sentimental," and he had "used up the basic materials and impressions of [his] youth and adolescence." The committee in charge of speakers must have wondered why it had invited this has-been. He said he had been offered a chance to write a screenplay based on a magazine article entitled "Urban Cowboy," about suburban youngsters in Houston working dead-end jobs, dreaming of cowboy life, flocking to a bar named Gilley's at night and riding a mechanical bull. McMurtry was not inclined to tackle the script. "It seems to me that it's a kind of sad story and . . . it's really *The Last Picture Show* taken one step further. It is what happens to the boys in *The Last Picture Show* after they have gone to Houston and got jobs in the chemical plant and have wished that somehow there was a way to get back to better times before the death of the old cowboy." As such, the material seemed tailor-made for Mc-Murtry, a natural evolution of his exodus tale, into which he could offer great insight. But he felt the story was "pathetic rather than tragic." The movie, eventually written by James Bridges and Aaron Latham, starring John Travolta and Debra Winger, would play to enormous success. Mc-Murtry was simply tired of Texas.

He could be a vexing guest, particularly in his home state. In 1975, SMU booked him to headline its first annual Literary Festival. He was set to arrive at the DFW airport in the afternoon before his evening lecture. Two students were dispatched to meet him, settle him at his hotel, and take him to dinner. The plane landed. No writer. No word on whether he had missed his flight or turned up ill or canceled. The terrified students drove back to campus and sheepishly told their teachers they had failed to deliver the goods, they didn't know what had happened, and the festival would be spoiled. (I was one of those students.) Ten minutes before the lecture was scheduled to start, with the auditorium at full capacity, McMurtry showed up backstage, casually saying hello and asking for a glass of water. He said he hadn't needed a student escort; he knew Dallas and he loved to drive. He'd caught an earlier flight, rented a car, and spent a pleasant afternoon roaming the freeways. He just hadn't told anyone.

Whenever he made the college circuit in Texas, he'd stop by Archer City. He saw, quite clearly, that his father was failing. "When arthritis and fatigue slowed him to the point where he couldn't move fast enough to get out of the way of a gate or a running animal, the ranchers he had worked with much of his life became reluctant to call him to help them work cattle, for fear he would injure himself," McMurtry said. "[H]e had been a highly respected man and they were reluctant to relegate him to an old man's chores." Jeff Mac couldn't ignore the fact that his neighbors were right. He became embittered. He wondered what his life had been worth.

When McMurtry told him he'd earned the love of his children and he'd kept his good name for over seventy years, he'd perk up some. He'd say the luckiest thing had been the two or three good horses he'd owned. But then the wind would blow through the brittle grass outside his window—*all flesh is grass*—and he'd turn somber again.

He'd see the yearly handbook of the Department of Agriculture sitting in his mailbox, a thick catalogue of articles blaming the range-cattle business for defiling prairie ecosystems; he'd yell about "creeping socialism," big-city bureaucrats sticking their noses where they didn't belong.

He'd gaze across his acres to the land of his nearest neighbor, an oilman named J. S. Birdwell, and mumble that he was jealous: this rich fellow could afford to bulldoze the mesquite off his land. Birdwell's pastures, "separated from ours only by a wire fence . . . looked like a paradise while ours looked like a hell," McMurtry said. "[O]ur grass was clearly less robust and less varied than his. The reason was obvious: we had mesquite and he didn't."

Jeff Mac complained he'd been hamstrung all his life by his sense of duty: while his brothers left home and modestly prospered in the Panhandle, he'd stayed behind to tend the land and care for his elders. Now here he sat, at the end of his days, tangled in mesquite.

"On the last day of my father's life . . . he slowly drove around the hill down at the home place where his parents, William Jefferson and Louisa Francis, had stopped some ninety years before, enticed by water, by [a] fine seeping spring," McMurtry said. "The next morning my father lay down in the kitchen and died. The hired man who found him and woke my son [who was visiting] merely said, 'Jeff's gone.'" He was seventy-seven years old.

Afterward, McMurtry's mother, in "four or five conversations over [a] few weeks" let loose "a lifetime of worry, fear, uncertainty, nervousness, panic, and pain about sex," McMurtry said. It "all poured out, not the kind of stories one had expected to hear from a prudish, overly proper parent."

As he was driving her home from a cataract operation in Wichita Falls one day, she told him that his father's personality had changed after he'd had a vasectomy in his mid-fifties following the unexpected birth of their youngest boy, Charlie. Jeff Mac was frequently moody after that, Hazel said, convinced that since he was no longer able to sire children, she would take up with a younger man and wheedle him out of his money and land.

She said she'd been happier about sex when she was younger and didn't know she was supposed to have orgasms, too. It was all a lot of hoo-ha, once she knew the truth. "Suddenly, while waiting for a light to change on Taft Boulevard . . . we were flung back into Victorianism—to the 'Lie back and think of England' mode of wifely behavior, in which sex was a male pleasure only, one in which women were not expected, much less encouraged, to respond. (And anyway, [what] would my mother have to think of: Abilene?)" McMurtry wondered.

Up to this point, Hazel "had never said a word . . . about anyone's sex life, much less her own; but once she started, she seemed unable to stop," he said.

She soon "took up with an elderly fellow named Roger," a man McMurtry didn't know well, "who, conveniently, had a very bad back—so bad, in her view, that he had no business even thinking about an activity as risky as sex." When he died, "my mother stopped having anything to do with men."

For the rest of his life, McMurtry would frequently hear his father's voice in his head: *The land was yours, if you could just hold it.* He'd remember—or dream about—Jeff Mac picking up an ax, a spade, a grubbing hoe, or a can of kerosene, and going after the mesquite in the fields in his hopeless quest to eradicate it. He'd drive it back a few yards, for a short while. Then the winds came. Another drought. The land shriveled up. Cold dawns, Jeff Mac groaning his way out of bed, from underneath a pile of homemade cotton quilts . . . a weary glance out the window . . .

The mesquite had won again.

17

A city of ruins, of the dead, softened by early morning sunlight slanting past the chalky stones of buildings in downtown Rome, through the silvery-black tops of olive trees and a shimmering haze of car exhaust. The streets smelled of grapes and fig, of cocoa biscuits laid out on platters in front of open-air bakeries, of sugar pasticcini, wood-fired ovens, and *parfum* from card samples in the glass-fronted cosmetics shops. The perfume sailed above the odors of deep black tea from the breakfast cafés and the oleander blossoms lining the sidewalks. If it had stormed the night before, which it often did, the lingering smell of rain weighted the air, and the memory of lightning remained vivid, carrying its *own* almost-secret tint, a moist, powdery flash of a scent so faint it might not have been real.

Feral cats curled among the chipped blocks of the Largo di Torre Argentina or scampered after rats. Jamie was amused by them, and just as intrigued by the bent old women, the *gattare,* the cat ladies dressed in black who ran a shelter for the animals beneath a concrete ledge at the ruin's edge.

McMurtry and his boy were in Rome because Peter Bogdanovich had cast Jamie to play Cybill Shepherd's kid brother in his film adaptation of Henry James's novella *Daisy Miller.* The casting came at a fortuitous moment for McMurtry; he'd been itching to get out of Washington for a few months, to go *somewhere,* a change of scene to jump-start his imagination. He booked a room in a San Antonio hotel, intending to hunker down there to start a new novel, but after a week, he was restless again and returned to DC. Then word came from Bogdanovich: he'd remembered Jamie's long, intense face from his time in Texas and thought it perfect for the obnoxious, prematurely world-weary Randolph, Daisy Miller's sibling.

So now McMurtry was in Rome, free during the day while Jamie, "much pampered by the stout Italian ladies who got him dressed," was busy on the set. Before leaving the States, McMurtry's friends had assured him there were plenty of typewriters in Italy, so he didn't bring one with him. The problem was, the typewriters in Italy "had a rather different keyboard than what I was used to . . . We stayed at the Hilton and I spent most of my days pecking away at my story on an old machine, in which the Z appeared where I had been used to finding an A, or possibly the E," he said. After committing countless typos in the mornings, in which his characters suddenly burst into gibberish, he'd wander the city in the afternoon, into mazes of cobblestone streets, stopping for a chilly Prosecco on the Piazza Navona (where he glimpsed Andy Warhol, licking a gelato), then sitting on the lip of the Trevi Fountain, cool droplets splashing his back, in the shadow of the building in which Keats had wasted away. He wasn't getting as much writing done as he'd hoped, but he was immensely charmed by Rome. At a leisurely pace, he was rereading Balzac, George Eliot, Jane Austen.

After a few weeks in the Eternal City, the film crew shifted its location to Vevey, Switzerland, near Lake Geneva, where James had drafted chapters of *Daisy Miller* in the late 1870s. There, Cybill Shepherd's high-pitched voice carried crisply in the thin mountain air. After filming was completed, McMurtry would say he never ran into Shepherd while traveling in Europe, but in truth, he spent a good bit of time with her, especially at the grand and towering Hotel des Trois Couronnes. Ever since *The Last Picture Show,* her love affair with Bogdanovich had filled the Hollywood tabloids; critics accused Bogdanovich of making *Daisy Miller* just to show off his no-talent girlfriend. She could not understand the hostility directed their way (though they might have thought twice about leaving a press junket one afternoon to go make love, very audibly, in the next room). One day Cary Grant, the couple's good friend, advised Bogdanovich, "Stop telling people you're so in love and so happy." "Why?" "Because people are not in love and not happy." "I thought all the world loves a lover." "Don't kid yourself," Grant snapped.

McMurtry had not approved of the way Bogdanovich left Polly Platt, nor could he disagree with critics who insisted Shepherd was in over her head in the role of James's heroine, projecting superficiality rather than reckless innocence, but he also thought it unfair that the tabloid writers gave her no credit for intelligence or serious ambition. On more than one public occasion, he saw her withdraw rather than engage in a conversation for which she believed she'd be ridiculed later. He wrote her a letter, lamenting "the silence of a woman who won't give her voice and heart to the world because she had concluded that the world would not hear it or understand it or love it. I felt such a silence in you."

On another occasion he was moved to write: "You have brought joy and fragrance to my life. Your human fragrance is as complex as your new perfume: partly dry, light, of the brain; partly wet, deep, of the heart and loins . . . Of course, when you love someone very much, you have a natural fear that they will stop loving you. It's part of what makes the whole business of need-desire-attachment-freedom-dependence so complicated. Love is so easily bruised and ruined, or, even more often, simply worn out and lost in the repetitiousness of life. I often have these fears where you are concerned, and yet mostly I have a deep trust in us."

In Switzerland she was immensely grateful for his attention. It was like the time he'd sat in the car with her near Burkburnett, Texas, holding her hand while she talked out her fears. They spoke of working together in the future, of cowriting a screenplay.

Later, in her memoir, she would write, "[He] sat with me in the lobby of the Hotel Trois Couronnes, rubbing my feet and reading aloud the gruesome 'Crazy Jane' love poems by Yeats. He was, physically, one of the least attractive men imaginable, but as a friend he was everything I wanted: a renaissance cowboy, an earthy intellectual . . . who could take pleasure in a dive that served two-dollar tacos. He became my touchstone in life, and for a brief time our collaboration became sexual."

Meanwhile, the film crew was well aware of her erotic collaboration with their director during a ten-day fog delay in Vevey. The couple would disappear into a room while the cameras sat idle and the budget ballooned. Jamie, bored, perked up when McMurtry bought him some fishing gear and took him to Lake Geneva. Jamie hauled in several perch and enjoyed the arguments of the old Swiss men who disagreed over who'd caught the biggest fish. He was less thrilled when his father walked him the short distance to the French border, to look at the Montreux Palace, where Vladimir and Vera Nabokov were rumored to be staying.

Occasionally Bogdanovich emerged from his afternoon trysts to discuss Westerns with McMurtry. "Ever since [I'd] known Peter . . . [he'd] been talking about making a Western," McMurtry said. Soon after wrapping *The Last Picture Show,* he'd invited McMurtry to Miami, where Shepherd was shooting a movie, so they could hole up together at the Fontainebleau and hash out a script. "I will never forget the incongruity of Larry and me sitting on a balcony at the Fontainebleau, overlooking the Olympic-sized swimming pool where Cybill [was] doing laps, and Larry saying to me, 'So what kind of Western do you want to make?'" Bogdanovich said.

Bogdanovich cared less about the story than about getting John Wayne, Jimmy Stewart, and Henry Fonda to star in it: a vehicle to "serve as a kind of homage to three men who had achieved so much in the Western film," McMurtry said. "It would, in a way, [Peter] hoped . . . top their achievements off."

"I said it needed to be a trek: they start somewhere, they go somewhere," Bogdanovich said. "We didn't want to do cattle because that was *Red River*. Larry suggested horses. Fine. And he said we might as well start at the Rio Grande and go north."

Bogdanovich would improvise, pacing the room, acting out unmoored snippets of dialogue while McMurtry typed. "Larry said they could have a pig farm, that would be funny," Bogdanovich recalled. "We named [one character] Augustus, because we liked the way Jimmy Stewart would say, 'Augush-tush' . . . And Cybill had a cut on her lip from running into a barbed wire fence as a child. So I said let's emphasize that. Let's have someone say, 'Where'd you get the scar?' and she could respond, 'Somebody bit me.' Things like that went into the plot."

The cowboy heroes were has-beens, on a last adventure. "It was definitely about the end of that era," Bogdanovich said. "One of the first things Jimmy's character goes into is how long it takes to pee when you're older."

For months, the men traded pages through the mail, McMurtry writing, Bogdanovich cutting or amending; eventually a script emerged, variously titled *West of the Brazos, Palo Duro,* and finally *Streets of Laredo.* "The draft was welcomed by the studio"—Warner Bros. But the three actors turned it down. "Eventually Stewart and Fonda came around because they weren't working that much. Wayne was working right up until he dropped, but he didn't like it, and wouldn't do it." Why would he? He "wanted the last adventure to be a wild success, not a dim moral victory," a melancholy farewell to the whole genre of Westerns.

Now, in Switzerland, Bogdanovich was feeling wistful about the script. It was just languishing over at the studio. The thought of it drove him crazy. He still wanted to make a Western. McMurtry was hankering to make something—another novel—but it wasn't quite coming. His head throbbed with the complex rhythms of Henry James and George Eliot.

One morning, on the movie set, Bogdanovich shot a scene in which Jamie's character, Randolph, said to a fellow traveler, "You live in Europe? Why? What happened?"

The lines struck a chord with McMurtry. He was feeling restless again.

Jamie recalled, "[One day] my dad said, 'I've got to get back to the States. My characters won't talk to me here.'"

She did as she pleased" was *Daisy Miller*'s tag line in promos for the movie. Daisy is Jacy in the Swiss Riviera, flirtatious, manipulative, head-strong, but with this difference: she is an innocent, incapable of grasping the consequences of her actions. After a careless night out with a suitor, strolling through the empty Roman Colosseum in the moonlight, she dies of malaria.

The tragic story of a young woman chafing against the strict conventions of bourgeois matrons appealed to McMurtry, and dovetailed with some of the story elements he'd already arranged in his developing novel. Mothers and daughters: Grace David and Diane, Polly Platt and Antonia—it fascinated him, the friction generated by these energetic young women and their vital mothers. And of course Platt was on his mind . . . the set of *Daisy Miller* was a European reunion of *The Last Picture Show* crew: besides Peter and Cybill, Cloris Leachman and Eileen Brennan both had prominent roles in the film. And Barry Brown, who played a young suitor smitten by Daisy, had worked with Jeff Bridges on his previous movie. Bridges's spirit was strong on the set.

The only one missing was Polly.

The last time McMurtry had seen her she was drinking too much. ("Peter was fundamental to my sickness," she said. "I [will] never understand men and their incessant need to seduce women.") And she was fighting fiercely with her oldest daughter, whom she called "unmanageable."

On his Italian typewriters (his characters slurring sudden Zs), McMurtry had begun sketching a prickly relationship between a self-reliant woman, battered by cascading circumstances, and her confused but resilient young daughter.

"[Larry] knew me and I was not exactly an easy kid, even before I was a teenager," said Antonia Bogdanovich. "Me and my mom . . . [we] had an interesting dynamic . . . There was a lot of tension, but there was a lot of sense of humor . . . My mom was really tough, but I was, too . . . I was unafraid of her and everybody else was intimidated by her."

Her sister Alexandria said, "What I was told by my mom was that [Aurora] was based on her. I think it flattered her—I mean, she told me *he* [McMurtry] told her that."

Just as he neither denied nor confirmed that Aurora had a pinch of Grace David in her, McMurtry averred, "I wouldn't say [Platt and her daughter] had nothing at all to do with *Terms.*"

More broadly, as he listened each day to Peter Bogdanovich try to comprehend the mixture of vulnerability and independence in Daisy Miller (*and* Cybill Shepherd), he was trying, not for the first time, to fathom the "mulish, resigned silence" of the women he'd known growing up, a muteness "like the muteness of an empty skillet, without resonance and without depth . . . the last defense of women who had long since given up on curiosity and the imagination of men." His mother's late-life independent streak had startled him. He said he was beginning to "think I became a novelist only because I couldn't resist trying to imagine what Texas women would say if they talked. The men's speech one could pick up anywhere, in the barbershop, the feedstore, anywhere. But"—until his mother opened up (like Aurora Greenway)—"the women's talk had to be imagined, which meant attempting to compensate for the self-reductions that were so evident in life."

From his women friends, he'd learned that his two most popular female characters tended to be Ruth Popper in *The Last Picture Show* and Emma Horton in *Moving On* and *All My Friends Are Going to Be Strangers.* He thought this was so because both characters were "domestic victims, worn down by husbands whose sensitivity never approaches theirs." But he noticed it was "middle-aged women who identify with [Ruth and Emma]; young women are now rather contemptuous of them for not simply walking out." He thought Patsy Carpenter was more like the new generation of women he was coming to know: "[W]hen her men finally prove too stolid and inflexible, unable to respond when she tries to nudge their lives into larger spiritual spaces, she does walk out."

In the end, Emma, though young, belonged with McMurtry's old cowboys in the sense that she was mired in the values of a dying life—*stand by your man*. Since elegy was McMurtry's gold, it was no surprise that he had returned to Emma in the new novel.

As for Emma's mother, not only did he draw on the regal Grace David, the tough Polly Platt, and his own stoic mother to create a composite portrait, he used a glimpse he'd got of Elizabeth Taylor one day in Rome, in the Hilton Hotel after he'd emerged from a morning of writing in his room. Taylor was filming a forgettable television movie in the hotel, along with her soon-to-be ex-husband Richard Burton. On his way to lunch, McMurtry stumbled into a mass of film cables in a narrow hallway, looked up, and saw the woman he'd long fantasized about, down from the screen, the most beautiful woman in the world.

She *did* have an impressive bearing in real life, and the most strikingly gorgeous violet eyes, but it wasn't her physical beauty that most dazzled him in Rome that day. By this time, he'd read a great deal about her life in the same Hollywood tabloids that were giving his friends Peter and Cybill such a hard time; he knew she'd not had smooth sailing in her marriages or her career, and yet here she was, still working, and with Burton, expertly balancing the personal and professional, "making no difficulties for anybody," as far as he could see. "Husband management," he thought, "may be a feminist skill." It was her dignity and forthrightness that gave her beauty such strength. Aurora Greenway had just acquired a new dimension.

He had already given his character the aphoristic speech patterns of a James or Jane Austen figure—"The success of a marriage invariably depends on the woman"; "Disgrace abounds . . . but good dinner parties are rare"—as well as the preternatural social perception of Virginia Woolf's Clarissa Dalloway. Like Elizabeth Taylor managing her mates, she balances a motley assortment of old and middle-aged suitors.

Unlike Daisy Miller, Emma Horton largely accepts her lot in life, bowing to her mother's wishes despite their awful arguments, refusing to leave her indifferent husband—and yet in some ways, she, too, does as she pleases, initiating an affair with her friend Danny Deck, and remaining, like Daisy, clueless as to the consequences. Perhaps her greatest tension with her mother stems from the fact that she "had learned something about heat from life in Houston. Heat was an aid to suspension, and there were times when suspension was an aid to life. When she really didn't know what to do with herself, she had learned to do nothing at all. It was not an approach her mother would have approved of."

Undignified and dumpy, Emma does not pretend to control her life. She lets circumstances fall on her like piles of dirty laundry. Aurora, in her zeal to wield power over everything she sees, is a collector—of artworks and men (whose degrees of intimacy with her she tightly manages). The two cherished paintings in her bedroom, a Renoir depicting "women in hats standing near some tulips" and a "stark" Klee, "a few lines that angle . . . sharply and never quite [meet]," define the two sides of life as Aurora views them: shapely order, pleasing to the eye and heart, and chaos, spiky and threatening. The former must always check the latter.

Similar to McMurtry's earlier novels, *Terms of Endearment* was episodic, a series of mostly comic scenes in which Aurora's men fail to win her full affection. A growing preoccupation with slapstick and satire, first evident in *The Last Picture Show,* more developed in *All My Friends Are Going to Be Strangers,* was realized in the minor characters: the ne'er-do-well husband of Aurora's maid, who chases her down one night by crashing his potato chip truck into a dance hall, and Vernon, an almost catatonic oilman in pursuit of Aurora's hand. He lives in his car on the roof of a parking garage in downtown Houston, another of McMurtry's Old Men of the West, pushed to ludicrous extremes, lost in the new urban Texas.

What held the novel together—loosely—was McMurtry's irresistibly readable prose and the mother-daughter bond, poignantly revealed to be the only stay against paralyzing fear: "Suddenly, to Aurora's terror [one night], life seemed to bolt straight from her grip. Something flung her heart violently, and she felt alone . . . [N]othing was certain, she was older . . . She had no way to see how things would end. In her terror she flung out her arms and caught her daughter."

As the final volume in a trilogy of books about Houston, *Terms of Endearment* offered a capstone to McMurtry's exodus cycle. "It is tempting to see Aurora as the embodiment of Houston, a city vested with the trappings of wealth, whatever is shiny and new and extravagant," wrote critic Ernestine P. Sewell. "Overall it is a verdant and lush place—all surface, some say—its people exuberant with the joy of following their dreams and sadly unmindful of human suffering until brought face to face with it. Aurora/Houston, so desirable, opens her arms, if not her heart, to all who come to her, and she accepts their worship as her due."

And McMurtry made no secret of the fact that in Emma's slovenly, welcoming warmth, her shambolic environs, he saw the funky Houston he so loved. She was what "women are at their best," in his view: "[My] vision of the normal and the good."

As such, as part of a cycle's finale, as well as in her role as a female version of the Old Cowboy, Emma faces a foreordained fate. Reviewers balked at the novel's last sixty pages, in which Emma, living in Nebraska with her husband Flap, suddenly takes ill and dies of cancer. "[T]he ending—a real tear jerker—dangles from the rest of the novel like a broken tail," Robert Towers complained in *The New York Times*. Not only did the story line seem tacked on from another book, the tone of the novel switched from comedy to tragedy without any warning. Yet McMurtry always felt he knew where the story had to go. "I consider it a process of discovery, writing a novel. But I always start with an ending," he said. "I get tremendous surprises. People pop in that I had not expected, who aren't in the final scene perhaps, totally surprising characters. Sometimes novels zig to the left or zig to the right as I go through them, but I've always ended up at the final scene. I've never missed. So far I've always ended up with exactly what I thought I'd end up with, although not always with exactly the kind of book I thought I'd have."

Too, it was now possible, after six novels, to see that McMurtry's sense of realism in fiction had nothing to do with traceable structure or straightforward time management. A minor character in one novel would appear as the major character in the next one, before or after the time frame of the previous story—completely shattering any notion of progress or change, or indeed, any perception that McMurtry was writing discrete books. His novels had to be seen as one long stream. "One of the prime abilities for a novelist is . . . moving people from generation to generation, or at least decade to decade. Consequently it is very appealing to be able to take a character and carry him through more than one book," he said, and, "Narrative is not, finally, memorable; one forgets stories and even outcomes and remembers moments, just as in life one forgets years, even decades, and remembers— moments."

The final sixty pages of *Terms of Endearment* contained McMurtry's strongest moments yet. Emma, dying, calls her boys, Tommy and Teddy, to her hospital bed to give them a final hug. "Tommy, be sweet," she says. "Be sweet, please. Don't keep pretending you dislike me. That's silly." Grudgingly, Tommy answers, "I *like* you." "I know that, but for the last year or two you've been pretending you hate me," Emma says. "[Someday,] you're going to remember that you love me. I imagine you'll wish you could tell me that you've changed your mind, but you won't be able to, so I'm telling you now. I already know you love me, just so you won't be in doubt about that later. Okay?" "Okay," Tommy says.

Afterward, Aurora leads the boys from the hospital, along with some friends of the family:

> Tommy felt like he wanted to run back upstairs to his mother, but instead Teddy was babbling something about cub scouts and he suddenly said bitterly that he had never been a scout because his mother had been too lazy to be a den mother. He didn't mean to say lazy, or to say anything bad, or even to speak. It just slipped out, and to everyone's horror his grandmother turned and slapped him so hard that he fell down. It astonished everyone . . . and before Tommy could help himself he burst into tears. Watching his face finally open was a great relief to Aurora, and before he could run away she grabbed him and hugged him as he went on crying helplessly.

McMurtry admitted he felt great emptiness once Emma died. She had been his companion for nearly ten years, through three novels. The loss of his favorite character exacerbated his disillusionment with writing in general.

When he thought about the script he'd composed with Bogdanovich, he could sometimes feel the juices flowing again, the excitement of contrariness, of countering his own instincts to be a chronicler of modern urban Texas. What if he *did* "inch backwards rather than forwards, to try to deal with the time in Texas in which the Old West really ended?" He had always been leery of western clichés; he was wary of writing outside his own time, but then, the Old West *was* his time, through his father, his uncles—just as much as the present. He understood that even thinking these things meant he was trying to grasp his father's life—not its meaning, necessarily, but its human entirety. And remembering his father made him keenly aware of "[his] own long descent toward the country [he wouldn't] be back from."

For now, *contemplating* a story about the Old West seemed safer than actually writing it.

In the meantime, he entered a nearly ten-year period in which he felt nothing but "cool distaste" for *all* his work, old and new.

I n all likelihood, the old cowboy in the White House was not a man his father would have respected: a movie gunslinger, an unconvincing one, Ronald Reagan had appeared in dozens of Westerns, among them *Cattle Queen of Montana, Law and Order, Santa Fe Trail,* and *The Last Outpost.* He was a faux John Wayne. And even John Wayne was not the real thing.

On the occasion of a state dinner at the White House, in early November 1985, a sparkling affair in honor of the Prince and Princess of Wales, President Reagan's deputy chief of staff, Michael Deaver, told McMurtry that the president had stayed up all night recently reading a novel called *Lords of the Plain* by McMurtry's buddy Max Crawford. It was clear that the president felt it was a shame the book hadn't been published when he was still in the movies, so he could adapt it to the screen, playing a heroic cavalryman bravely murdering Indians. It was also clear to McMurtry that the reason he had received an invitation to the White House was because the president's staff had been unable to locate Max Crawford. As a writer of modern-day Westerns, McMurtry was the next best thing. It was up to *him* to convince the president he still rode tall in the saddle.

In the ten years since he had killed off Emma Horton, McMurtry had trudged through a "literary gloom," compulsively writing, as always, five pages a day, but hating those five pages, considering it a tyranny that he had to keep reading the same author over and over—himself. He had produced three novels in that decade: *Somebody's Darling* (1978), *Cadillac Jack* (1982), and *The Desert Rose* (1983). Some of his critics lumped these books together as "The Trash Trilogy," referring to their subject matter: the "glitzy but uncentered worlds of Hollywood and Las Vegas and the trash and garbage through which Cadillac Jack [a collector of odds and ends] . . . sifts," wrote Mark Busby. McMurtry himself called this period his weakest as a writer, though he always evinced a fondness for *The Desert Rose.*

In any case, he felt like an impostor at the state dinner, among social royalty (Princess Diana, Brooke Astor), the cultural elite (William F. Buckley Jr., J. Carter Brown, the director of the National Gallery of Art), actors (Peter Ustinov, Clint Eastwood, John Travolta), and creative artists (Mikhail Baryshnikov, Helen Frankenthaler). "From the first it was apparent that the evening was going to echo the Marx Brothers," McMurtry said. He ordered a taxi: "My driver was Afghan, probably one of the few drivers in Washington who had never heard of the White House." The car passed a throng of "mounted policemen, Princess-watchers, and protesters" along Pennsylvania Avenue; when the driver spotted the royal motorcade, he shouted, "There they go!" and inexplicably he gave chase, an eerie precursor to the reckless traffic event that would one day kill the princess. Finally, McMurtry persuaded the man to drop him at the East Gate of the White House, where Mounties and Marines glanced indifferently at his invitation.

Once inside, among women horrified to be caught wearing gowns similar to those of other women, and men asking each other anxiously, "Do you expect to dance with the princess?" he realized he was socially "off"— even more than usual—but since this was his "customary state," he was comfortable enough and decided to roll with the evening. (The president, he noted from across a room, was only about "80% on," which seemed "more than adequate" for the occasion.) No one appeared to know when, or even if, it was proper to sit. Where was the royal couple? Were they still on their feet? If they were several rooms away, it was probably okay to take a seat.

J. Carter Brown approached McMurtry and said he had been in Montana the previous summer, and everyone there was reading his books. Presumably this was intended as a compliment, but he'd made it sound as though the citizens of Montana were laboring strenuously under a state mandate to read Larry McMurtry.

At dinner—"lobster mousse with a little crabmeat, a chicken breast, some green beans and brown rice, a little sherbet"—McMurtry watched Diana. Her startling blue eyes reminded him of the first time he'd seen Paul Newman on the set of *Hud*, twenty-five years earlier.

The president raised his glass to toast Her Royal Highness and— definitely not "on"—called her "Princess David." Diana looked flustered. Prince Charles made a short, gracious speech, but forgot to return the toast—a deliberate slip, McMurtry decided, to balance the president's gaffe. He was a "professional" prince, very good at his job.

Few of the anxious men got to dance for any length of time with the princess. John Travolta, fresh from his success with the disco movie *Saturday Night Fever*, took the most spins with her, and she kept pace with him exuberantly. "The gloomy Baryshnikov"—the only real dancer at the affair—"did not dance," McMurtry noticed. (Observing the dazzling Travolta, he may have wished he had accepted the screenplay assignment for *Urban Cowboy*.)

The evening ended with someone suggesting they all keep drinking at the Hay-Adams Hotel. It had been a splendid event, the usual farce, but McMurtry, ever alert to elegiac chills in the air, had noticed a changing of the guard: the hostesses of old were aging, vanishing, declining to appear as often as they used to appear in public. At the White House, he thought, "the absence of Evangeline Bruce seemed to presage an era of instability in international affairs."

By 1985, he had become a Washington fixture, though he still felt out of sorts there. He had befriended the journalist Joseph Alsop, whose strict social rule was "One diplomatic couple at a dinner is sufficient. Any more is ruinous to the conversation." And he had come to know and like the writer Leon Wieseltier, the child of Polish Holocaust survivors, "part Maimonides, part Oscar Wilde," in the estimation of journalist Sam Tanenhaus. "Wieseltier frequented A-list gatherings presided over by Katharine Graham; Susan Mary Alsop . . . Polly Kraft . . . and one or two others who ruled the city's social arrangements and provided vivid links to the nation's patrician past."

McMurtry began "dining regularly . . . in good restaurants, and he was gaining weight, developing a belly and plump cheeks," Mike Evans, Jamie's stepfather, said. "Back in Houston he had rarely worn blue jeans or boots, but out of the state it was jeans and boots everywhere."

In rural Virginia, he spent time with a man named Sam Adams, a numbers nerd who had crunched information for the CIA. Adams lived on a farm and raised a few cows, mostly as a hobby. He, his wife Eleanor, and his son Clayton often spent weekends with McMurtry. Clayton met Jamie at the Loudoun Country Day School and they became best friends. Evans took the boys camping to Shenandoah Park and fishing on Lake Anna. "Clayton was also a musician," Evans said. "He played guitar and had a rock group of his own." He and Jamie spent hours together flat-picking.

Disseminating data from Vietnam, Adams had come to believe that the conflict's casualty numbers were being deliberately faked by General William Westmoreland or by the White House to suggest that America was making more progress than it was in the war. And Adams had said so publicly.

He was a simple man: he believed truth was truth, and he had suffered mightily for his clash with officialdom. Eventually he ended up demoted at work, divorced, and broken. He retreated to his farm to raise pigs and cows and to try to write a book. In 1988, he'd die of an apparent heart attack before he finished his memoir, though McMurtry believed he never would have completed it, anyway: too many false starts and stops. "I saw Sam as being rather like some of the great explorers of the South American forest—Colonel Fawcett perhaps—battling the murk of American intelligence; it was a noble exploration," McMurtry said.

Wieseltier also had a devil of a time finishing projects: he was easily tempted by America's celebrity culture, women, and cocaine, and by the money and glitter of Condé Nast, which paid him handsomely to write ephemera.

He found himself squarely in the center—of society, politics, publishing—aware of the center's "parochialism," far "greater than that of the provinces. In the provinces, they keep an eye on the center, but in the center they just gaze lovingly at themselves with both eyes," he realized. It was not a healthy circumstance for getting good work done. His friend McMurtry, a child of the provinces, was an interesting case. "Larry was respected but not well understood" by the center, Wieseltier observed. And he saw it was not a bad position from which to operate.

One day McMurtry offered him a furnished room above Booked Up and urged him to retreat there, quietly, to write each day. Wieseltier piled books and journals on a desk in the room, alongside a bottle of whiskey and a framed photograph of Georges Bataille for literary inspiration. He greatly appreciated his friend's generosity. The only problem was: "It was a little demoralizing working there on the third floor while Larry was churning out one book after the other on the second."

"The novels got darker," Mike Evans said. "When I mentioned to him that *Somebody's Darling* seemed depressing, he answered that he didn't care much for it himself, but that was the book he wrote that year."

Claiming he was wearier than ever of the "mental and emotive inartic-ulateness" he found in Texas, convinced that he had sufficiently lamented the death of the cowboy, McMurtry concentrated on other frontiers—Hollywood, Washington, Las Vegas. Sick of reading his own sentences, he kept writing them, anyway, "determined to hang in there," he said, "be-cause I really had no place else to hang." He freely admitted that money, more than literary passion, motivated him during this period—he needed the $25,000 advance for *Cadillac Jack* to help pay his high Virginia taxes; Universal Studios was willing to pay him a hefty sum, and even provided him with hundreds of pages of research material, if he'd consider writing a showgirl story for the screen (this became the genesis of *The Desert Rose*). His lack of full commitment to the subjects of these books was apparent in the skimpy details (his Hollywood was a run of clichés, lotus-eaters gliding along snakelike freeways); his disinterest was evident in the scornful satire (his hapless Washingtonians bore names such as Khaki Descartes and Bris-ling Bowker); his haste manifested itself in the flat voices. He admitted that just because he'd developed an ear for the way folks spoke in these places, he hadn't necessarily acquired insight into what the people were like.

McMurtry's heart wasn't really in skewering Hollywood's superficiality or being the Evelyn Waugh of Washington; in both *Somebody's Darling* and *Cadillac Jack,* his actual concern was the value and fragility of friendship: "[It] . . . is ruinable," Joe Percy laments. "Friendship can be destroyed as quickly and as absolutely as love." It was "the little roads that lead people up to and then away from one another" that captivated McMurtry.

Significantly, both novels conclude that what we think we most want to escape is in fact inescapable. "There's no getting away from cowboys, no place I've ever been," says a minor character in *Somebody's Darling.* "Texas is the ultimate last resort . . . It's always a good idea to go to Texas, if you can't think of anything else to do." Not surprisingly, road trips to the Lone Star State provide the books' most vital paragraphs.

If his fiction seemed to call for a return to Texas, beneath its stubborn refusal to admit it, he did not in life relent from bashing his home state.

In 1981, Susan Freudenheim, who had graduated with an art history degree from the New York University Institute of Fine Arts, was working as a curator at the Fort Worth Art Museum. (She would go on to be an arts editor at the *Los Angeles Times* and the executive director of Jewish World

Watch, an activist organization fighting genocide.) She invited McMurtry to give a lecture at the museum. Before his speech that night, he told her it was "about the horrors of Western writing"; it was "going to cause some controversy."

Later, charmed by McMurtry, she defended him, saying only (and rather mildly), "[his speech] caused a certain amount of backlash."

Ronnie Dugger, the editor of *The Texas Observer*, had just hired Joe Holley to fill in for him while he finished writing a book about LBJ. He heard the scuttlebutt concerning McMurtry's speech; he figured Holley would need a few issues to get his feet wet, so, to buy him time, "what if we get McMurtry, who's a cynic, and give him an entire issue to stir up trouble."

The resulting article, adapted from the speech, published in the *Observer* on October 23, 1981, was called "Ever a Bridegroom: Reflections on the Failure of Texas Literature." (McMurtry had misunderstood the term *bridegroom*—he'd meant to suggest the groom's perpetual runner-up.) In the piece, "he went back and machine-gunned everybody he hadn't taken out in *Narrow Grave*," Don Graham said. "It was like the Germans in World War II retracing the field for anyone still living. He went through the whole catalog of Texas writers and said they were too sentimental and romantic, that they should stop writing about the past."

"Texas has produced no major writers or major books," McMurtry declared. He charged his fellow literati with "intellectual laziness . . . [offering] a limited, shallow, self-repetitious literature which has so far failed completely to do justice to the complexities of life in the state." The sole exceptions, he said, were the poet Vassar Millar, who possessed a "high gift wedded to long-sustained . . . rigorous application," and Donald Barthelme, a "high-risk modernist . . . a trapeze artist . . . [whose] perfect stories accumulate slowly, usually one or two a year . . . an impressive achievement."

James Ward Lee summed up his fellow writers' reaction: "For some years now, Larry McMurtry has . . . felt the urge to befoul the nest that fledged him. When he is having one of his fits, he usually sets out to destroy the Holy Trinity of Dobie, Bedichek, and Webb before moving on to attack on an even broader front."

Barthelme had the sharpest—most whimsical—reply: "Larry McMurtry implied Texas had no literature that you didn't have to tie a pork

chop to its head to get the dawg to read it . . . The response from the
Texas literary community was striking . . . Four writers in Abilene stopped
drinking, cold turkey . . . Larry King considered taking the veil . . . Laura
Furman called up Rainer Maria Rilke in heaven and asked him what to do
next . . . [Yet] one must ask: What has Nevada done for literature lately?
Who's the Alaskan Tennyson? . . . We've done at least as well as Rhode
Island, we're pushing Wyoming to the wall. . . ."

Soon enough, McMurtry's peers would have another reason to feel
embittered by him: as he was composing his speech, insisting that Lone
Star lit must turn away from the grizzled Old West toward the cities, he
was also pursuing his idea—born of his desire to understand his father—of
writing a novel about a nineteenth-century cattle drive. He had gone so
far as to buy back from Warner Bros., for $35,000, his script for *Streets of
Laredo.* He was busy changing the story, adapting it to fiction. "I picked
it up and laid it back down three times," he said. "I started it and stopped
to write *Cadillac Jack,* and then again to write *Desert Rose,* and then I left
it for another year or two. I didn't have a title."

The Desert Rose took him utterly by surprise. It began as a Hollywood
assignment. Researchers hired by Universal Studios had gone to Las Vegas,
at a producer's behest, to interview showgirls for a possible script about life
on the strip. The producer sent the interviews to McMurtry and asked if he'd
write a screenplay. At that point, he had "some twelve hundred pages . . . in
hand" on the cattle drive novel. "My characters seemed to be moving at an
ox-like pace up the great plains. They still had a thousand miles to go . . . [I]
was growing a little bored with their slow trek . . . I needed a vacation."

The Vegas interviews contained the gist of a novel. From the thorough
research, he learned that showgirls, large, busty women who'd been hired
to parade around onstage, were being replaced by smaller, lither dancers.
"I have always been attracted to dying crafts," he said after studying the
transcripts. "It became clear that the showgirls were the cowboys of Las
Vegas; there were fewer and fewer jobs and they faced bleak futures, some
with grace, and some without it . . . I also like mother-daughter stories.
Why not a mother-daughter story [I thought] in which the daughter re-
places the mother on her own stage, in the show in which she had been a
star for some years?"

McMurtry took only three weeks to write *The Desert Rose*. It seemed to come to him, rather than being forced *through* him, and unlike the reviewers—one of whom called the novel "brain-sphinctering"—he always regarded *The Desert Rose* with affection. He credited it with renewing his interest in writing, mainly because Harmony, the main character, in spite of many troubles, remains an optimist, unusual in a McMurtry novel. She "graced [his] life," he said.

Summarizing most critics' reactions to "The Trash Trilogy," Clay Reynolds wrote: "As a young writer with many stories yet to tell, McMurtry has decisions to make about his future . . . He must reflect on the feeling he attributes to Jack, a feeling that Texas is calling him home . . . He must learn to recognize . . . that wherever he hangs his hat, home will always be Texas . . . 'Come Home Larry, All Is Forgiven!'"

Polly Platt was not in a forgiving mood—even though her ex-husband's girlfriend had just been shot to death and he was mourning. Bogdanovich had broken up with Shepherd. (Her inner Jacy Farrow, selfish, manipulative, cold, had finally worn him down, Platt figured.) He'd fallen in love with Dorothy Stratten, a former Playboy Playmate. Stratten's ex, unable to handle her rejection of him, had asked to meet with her, then repeatedly raped her and shot her in the face. Immediately afterward, he called Platt, demanding to know, "Where's Peter Bogdanovich? Where's Peter Bogdanovich?"

That was the end of it, Platt said: "Peter had always justified his behavior by trying to find fault with me, and he had a very good partner in that. I would always agree that it was my fault. But my family had never had a murder in it. I cut the cord." In his sorrow, Bogdanovich traumatized her children, for whom she still bore most of the responsibility. He'd call and say it was Dorothy's birthday—he wanted his girls to visit her grave with him. Then he became infatuated with Stratten's younger sister when she was still a minor. Eventually, he married her. Platt could no longer speak to him—about anything—without screaming into the telephone.

All this she laid on McMurtry, in lengthy phone calls. Or she'd complain about the studios, thwarting her attempts (over money, they claimed) to write a screenplay of *All My Friends Are Going to Be Strangers*.

Now she was calling to say she'd just been dropped from the production of *Terms of Endearment*—again, because of costs. (She knew it was really because she had clashed with the screenwriter, Michael Leeson, and the director, James L. Brooks.) The truth is, she thought she should have been the producer, director, and writer all along. No one understood McMurtry's material better than she did—after all, some of it was based on her: when Aurora slaps her daughter, that's *me*, she wrote in an unpublished memoir.

But Paramount had given the project to Brooks. Recognizing her "genius," he had recruited her to be his production designer. She'd undermined herself: *she* was the one who'd arranged Brooks's meeting with McMurtry; *she's* the one who'd been able to handle Debra Winger, when everyone wanted her for the role of Emma Horton. At dinner one night, Winger, who was "trying to seduce [Brooks], emptied her glass of red wine all over my head," Platt said. "I retaliated by pouring a pitcher of water over hers."

But now, in the middle of production in steamy Houston, Platt had been fired.

McMurtry listened to her rant. He didn't really care about the movie. He'd had nothing to do with it (aside from buying back his rights to his own character, Emma—she'd been sold as part of a movie option for *All My Friends Are Going to Be Strangers*. McMurtry paid to reclaim her; now *Terms* could proceed). His expectations for the movie were exceedingly low. The days of *The Last Picture Show* were gone. Once again, only a bankable star could get a picture made. *Terms* had received a green light from Paramount only because Jack Nicholson had agreed to play Aurora's astronaut lover, a character not even in the book. Brooks had written the role (originally for Burt Reynolds) so the movie might have a chance.

McMurtry gave Platt all the time she needed on the phone—he knew Big Tony was dying. Tony had a rare illness, akin to lupus. He wouldn't take care of himself. "You're killing me," Platt told her husband. "He fought the disease by neglecting it," she said. He would die shortly after *Terms of Endearment* opened in theaters.

Soon after Paramount banned Platt from the set, Brooks begged to get her back. She was the only one who could reason with Debra Winger. One day, Winger got a pimple on her face and threatened to end the production, Brooks said. Shirley MacLaine, playing Aurora, didn't know what to make of her costar. MacLaine appeared on the set one morning "wearing all my leftover movie-star fur coats," to try to capture the essence of Aurora, and "there was Debra dressed in combat boots and a miniskirt . . . I thought, 'Oh my goodness.'" Winger tried to tell her where to stand, once, before filming a scene. MacLaine snapped, "I know my marks when I see them." Winger replied, "Good. How's this for a mark?" She lifted her skirt, glanced over her shoulder, and farted in MacLaine's face.

The good news for the movie was that, inadvertently, the actresses were finding the perfect mother-daughter tension for the story; the bad news was, morale was plummeting among the crew. Brooks knew he needed Platt back. "Polly was brilliant at her craft," McMurtry said. "Smart and decisive. One of the reasons she worked so well with James Brooks was that he had a difficult time making decisions. Polly was very decisive—a plus when in production on a film." She returned and righted the ship.

As it turned out, what was jarring in the novel worked beautifully on screen, thanks to the strength of the performances. Additionally, in the roller-coaster years of McMurtry's tenure in Washington, from Nixon to Ford to Carter to Reagan, Americans had grown accustomed to watching slapstick embrace tragedy on their home screens. The contrast was no longer so startling—*and,* as McMurtry had argued with his editors all along, it *was* true to daily experience. "A wonderful mix of humor and heartbreak," Leonard Maltin wrote of the film. The movie was nominated for eleven Oscars.

On April 9, 1984, at the 56th Academy Awards ceremony in Los Angeles, MacLaine and Nicholson won acting honors for their performances in *Terms.* The movie was also celebrated for Best Adapted Screenplay and Best Director. It won Best Picture. Platt was nominated for production design; though she didn't win, McMurtry was pleased to hear Brooks acknowledge, from the stage, that she had made "an enormous contribution" to the film.

She called McMurtry that night, three sheets to the wind, to complain about rampant sexism in the industry.

At one point, Brooks had considered Diane Keaton for the role of Emma Horton. Keaton was best known for playing Woody Allen's impulsive, insecure, and endearing girlfriend in *Annie Hall* (1977), for which she won the Best Actress Oscar. She admitted that the flighty, neurotic woman in the film was based on her (or Allen's perception of who she was).

McMurtry got to know her when she expressed interest in cowriting a screenplay of *Somebody's Darling* with him. Perhaps she'd play Jill Peel in the film. She said she could easily relate to Peel's experience of not being taken seriously enough by Hollywood. Together, over a period of years, she and McMurtry worked on various drafts of the script. No movie was ever made. They'd meet in Van Nuys, where Keaton's grandmother, Mary Hall, lived, or Washington, or New York. McMurtry was naturally drawn to her exuberant beauty. She *was* his Emma, reborn—everything good in women, he thought.

But even more than her beauty, her sad moods, swift to descend, intrigued him. He thought of her as existing purely in black and white ("other colors seem omitted," he once wrote about her). She could dim or brighten her lights on a whim—a metaphor he often used when speaking of her. "We met [once] in Washington and worked on [the] screenplay," he said. "[T]he sky was gray and ugly; that plus my own dourness reduced Diane to a state of low definition. I am always dour at the beginning of a film project and frequently dour at the end of one, too." McMurtry took her that day to a Kandinsky exhibit at the National Gallery, and suddenly "I saw her snap into full definition," he said. "At the sight of Kandinsky's horses, Diane switched on her brights . . . No one had noticed her when we walked in; within five minutes everyone had noticed her and was looking at her, rather than the Kandinskys."

On another day, he met her outside the Madison Hotel in DC. "She was rummaging in a bag big enough to hold a caribou, which contained a camera heavy enough to stun the caribou with, should that be necessary," he said. "Diane was sad, her sparkle subdued. That being the case I took her at once to a somewhat grotty antique mall in Alexandria, Virginia, and plunged her right into . . . the world of goods. The tactic worked. In minutes she had switched her brights back on. She bought a couple of items whose . . . beauty eluded everyone but herself. On the way back to Washington she told me she hoped to be complicated, someday. Someday?"

In addition to a love of flea markets, the two of them shared the delight of hitting the road. ("If I could I'd wander all over the United States

LARRY McMURTRY   311

for an indefinite period of time. I'd seek out warmth," Keaton once said.)
McMurtry took her to Ponder, Texas. She introduced him to her grammy,
with whom he fell in love. "I was a farmer, you know," Grammy Hall told
him. "I should have stayed a farmer."

Keaton often played the clown in movies—her comic timing was
spot-on. But like all true clowns, McMurtry thought, she was hiding a
deep melancholy which he glimpsed only in splinters. What it was about,
he didn't know. She admitted to him she'd always felt insecure about her
looks, her intelligence; she feared if she didn't have smart men writing
scripts for her, she'd be a mediocre actress. She didn't tell him she'd once
suffered, severely, from bulimia, often eating, for dinner, a bucket of Kentucky Fried Chicken along with a couple of TV dinners, chips and blue
cheese, a pound of peanut brittle, and a bottle of 7UP—then purging
herself to stay slender. Even so, she hated her body. Lingering hints of her
old disorder may have reminded McMurtry of Jo's early problems.

In 1986, he interviewed Keaton for a profile he planned to write of
her. He intended to publish it privately for book collectors. He worked on
the profile as hard as he worked on his novels, taking it through numerous
drafts, winnowing it until very little of the original material remained.
The final version, "A Walk in Pasadena with Di-Annie and Mary Alice,"
eventually appeared in his movie book, *Film Flam* (1987). It focused on a
long walk he took one day with Keaton and her grandmother. The original
opening section, cut from the essay, concerned Keaton's romances.

He expressed worry that her opposing impulses—joy and sadness—
could lead her astray. "My own suspicion, as a concerned friend, is that
white is slipping across the board, in the color-scheme of Diane's life"—
leading her toward the black, he wrote. He couched his uneasiness in an
elaborate allegory, comparing her lovers to cars: "[T]hose who can read the
signs are emphatic in their belief that her new love is the black Wagoneer.
The white Volkswagen van of which she was enamored for so long . . . has
slipped precipitously in her affections."

The allegory was labored, which probably accounted for its absence
in the final draft. But perhaps McMurtry cut it for another reason: in
describing the Volkswagen van, he seemed to indicate himself. He said
Keaton had accompanied the van (just as she had accompanied him), "all

over the West, throwing it extravagant kisses, rushing back to it in parking
lots from Los Angeles to Albuquerque."

L os Angeles, Albuquerque, and Van Nuys were just a few of McMurtry's
    ports of call in the 1980s. He got to know most of the nation's major
freeways, its back roads, its country bypasses. As the decade began, he drove
with James to Montana and up and down the eastern slope of the Rockies,
looking at colleges. James was James now, no longer little Jamie, now that
he was set to graduate from Woodberry Forest. He'd never felt part of the
school; he remained shy and withdrawn, but he'd branched out to play
Fagin in a school production of *Oliver!* and he began to write songs after a
roommate introduced him to the music of John Prine. He'd spent a spring
term abroad in Spain, loved it, and wanted to return there the summer
before starting college. He settled on the University of Arizona in Tucson,
"having decided that Rice is too tidy for him, or something," McMurtry
wrote Grace David. "He is unbelievably big and hasn't cut his hair in about
3 years." James was dating a woman twenty years his senior, McMurtry
said; this gave Dad cause for worry, bemusement, and hope that his son was
learning useful life lessons. Just before school started in the fall, the woman
"dumped" James, but he was "okay," McMurtry reported. "[H]e's picked up
excellent survival skills." In no time, he'd fallen in love with a schoolteacher
in Tucson—also twenty years his senior.

   With his son out of the house, McMurtry no longer saw any reason to
live in Virginia. He moved into an apartment above Booked Up, "and also,
unfortunately, above the discos of M Street, which pushed out their rowdy
clientele about two a.m.," he said. "I finally got a 'white noise' machine,
which, if set on 'waterfall,' more or less held its own with the revelers."

   His brother Charlie had been staying in the old family ranch house
outside Archer City. He decided to move out, so McMurtry reclaimed
it for periodic retreats whenever life in Washington and/or Hollywood
became too hectic. "I will be moving the contents of my Virginia house
down there . . . in two painful stages," he told David. He fixed up the
ranch, giving it a new coat of white paint, and set his typewriter on a big
wooden table in the dining room, just inside a pair of wide double doors.

   "Writing lots of screenplays," he wrote David: decent work, if not
overly stimulating. Doing a screenplay was like making "an elaborate no-

tation," he said—it wasn't really writing. And working with most of the producers and directors he met in LA was "not much more exciting than mowing lawns."

Whenever he drove to Los Angeles, he'd stay at the Chateau Marmont ("not so much a hotel as a storehouse for antique TV sets"). Or he'd register at the Beverly Wilshire (where he watched guests arrive in their "Mercedeses, Cadillacs, Lincolns, and Rollses . . . all of them bright as babies and with their leather upholstery smelling like it had just come off a pure-bred goat"). He'd visit Diane Keaton in her angular glassy house not far from Laurel Canyon, where the actor Ramon Novarro had been murdered by a pair of hustlers. The Black Dahlia murders had also taken place near there, in a house that looked like a Mayan temple. LA could be spooky, but many of its neighborhoods also had that Lost World feel; they stoked his imagination. In drafty houses on dry, sloping hillsides where early celebrities once lived and loved—Bette Davis, Preston Sturges, Howard Hughes—hippies had moved in, paying cheap rents in now-dilapidated mansions; entire rock and roll bands camped out in empty rooms. After a while, rents rose again; gentrification took over, the hippies moved out, replaced by California-centric cults: self-help groups, nonprofit religions. Synanon. Scientology. Culture as a jigsaw puzzle, spelling out, in big bold letters, "Real Estate."

McMurtry got a place in Santa Monica. He rented a quaint guest cottage in back of a large Sherman Oaks estate.

On his way back to Washington from LA, he'd often stop in Houston. "I must say I still like it," he wrote Grace David. "It still seems to me an interesting city and I love those new buildings out in the Galleria area, particularly that new sky scraper."

He now felt a dutiful responsibility to many places, as he did to many women. Washington claimed him because of the bookstore and his business partner, Marcia Carter. LA was a workplace, Tucson the home of his son. Archer City was a (still vexing) refuge, and the family seat, for better or worse.

"You never know where I'll be," he told David. "I recently made a trip that went D.C.—Memphis [to see Cybill Shepherd]—Tucson [to see James]—L.A.—Tucson—Dallas—Albuquerque [to see the family of his new friend, the writer Leslie Marmon Silko]—L.A.—Tucson—Archer City—D.C."

In DC, he'd resume following his motley band of characters up the trail in his cattle drive story.

And that was his life now, much of the year. He admitted to friends he ate trash whenever he was home writing. And also whenever he drove cross-country.

"I have been poorly," he wrote Grace David at the beginning of 1985. "I travel all the time now and have so many environments it's hard to say which one is doing me in. I sort of . . . have something that's a combination of flu, asthma, allergies, and walking pneumonia. Somewhat weakening."

He added, "My doctors say my whole life is a bad habit. Probably is."

PART THREE

The Heart

19

I sing about life. I am happy, but life is sad." So says a minor character in *Lonesome Dove*.

On May 7, 1987, after *Lonesome Dove* had stayed on *The New York Times* bestseller list for almost two years, Dorothea Oppenheimer died of pancreatic cancer. She was sixty-eight years old. She had languished for three years, while pretending she wasn't as ill as she was. "She remained to the end a high-born Mitteleuropa woman," McMurtry said. "[She] had quality, even in [her] dusty apartment on York Avenue [in Manhattan], and unto the hour of her death . . . a wonderful if eccentric woman who got through life on an intricate balance of beauty and bravura."

McMurtry hadn't needed her professionally for many years, and their personal connection suffered as a result. In one of her last substantial communications with him, in the early 1970s, she said: "Ideally (for me) I would like to act as [your] agent, but if there is no need for an agent, then there is no reason I should." She asked him to please send her any screenplays he worked on before they were finalized, but he rarely did. She couldn't keep up with his travels. She was often confused as to when he was coming to New York and when she might see him. On one occasion, she said she hoped to catch up with him, but she pleaded with him not to visit when her client Thomas Sanchez was in town—he was arriving to drop off a new novel with her "and has no money and no place to stay." Until she could no longer get out of bed, she nurtured her writers the way a mother would. *If* they'd let her.

"She just didn't get Hollywood and, for that matter, Hollywood didn't get her, despite all the émigrés who lived there," McMurtry said. "I took over all the Hollywood deals . . . and attempted to translate them for Dorothea, but it seldom worked smoothly." She'd farm the contracts out to the William Morris Agency, but this always caused delays, and McMurtry concluded it wasn't worth the trouble to call her.

Oppenheimer's passing affected him little, on a daily basis: his life had moved on since their first contact in the early 1960s; hers hadn't, much.

But occasionally the flutter of a woman's dress, a perfume trace, or a distant laugh would remind him of her and of how much he had loved her.

Irving Paul Lazar was the only man in America "who could step off an airplane anywhere in the world with his hands in his pockets," S. J. Perelman once wrote, by which he meant the man had style. He was at ease anywhere.

And *anywhere* was precisely where he wanted the freedom to go. An aggressive talent agent, he was no respecter of other agents' clients: he'd nose his way into anyone's business, whether he knew them or not; broker deals for people, whether they knew it or not; and then approach them as if he'd done them a huge favor. Ergo, they *had* to work with him, he said (whether the deals were legal or not).

"Everybody who matters has two agents: his own and Irving Lazar," a Hollywood insider once remarked.

One of the places Lazar felt at ease was in Dorothea Oppenheimer's dusty New York apartment as she lay dying. He had met McMurtry in Hollywood, saw an opportunity, and inveigled his way into McMurtry's life. But he genuinely shared Oppenheimer's "tastes and attitudes," McMurtry said. "Irving, with uncustomary discretion, quietly [took over] the work of agenting me. He treated Dorothea with . . . distinguished courtesy." He admired her for going out "with her courage intact." As a result, a "dying, impoverished European woman got the credit—then minimal—for selling *Lonesome Dove*."

Lazar, born in Brooklyn in 1907, the son of a Russian Jewish egg salesman (and loan shark), learned to be tough, self-reliant, and nattily dressed from neighborhood gangsters Legs Diamond and Greasy Thumb Guzik. He attended law school and went to work mediating bankruptcy cases. One day, after representing a down-and-out vaudeville juggler, he realized he could make more money in showbiz by calling on his old neighborhood contacts in mob-owned speakeasies. He booked musical acts in strip joints along West 52nd Street, among "people who were perfectly willing to have him beaten up or killed—and, in fact, he was beaten up, and even stabbed, in the course of business, yet he never felt intimidated," Michael Korda said.

He moved on and up, negotiating contracts for East Coast playwrights in demand as Hollywood screenwriters: Cole Porter, Noël Coward, Moss Hart.

In the 1940s, the lure of Tinseltown drew him west. He "understood instinctively that the prevailing ethos of West Coast movie people was then (as it is now) fear and envy of New York. New York was where the money came from; it was where the *owners* of the studios were—the bosses to whom men like Mayer and Zanuck actually reported," Korda said. "New York was, above all, where talent, ideas, culture, and fashions came from, and in the days when it took nearly four days to cross the country a person arriving from New York was greeted like a traveller from St. Petersburg arriving in some remote provincial town in nineteenth-century Russia."

Lazar "quickly established himself as the connection between New York and Hollywood."

Korda met him in 1958 when he had just begun working as an editorial assistant at Simon & Schuster. Lazar phoned him one day: "Meet me for lunch, my dear boy. . . . I'm not doing any business with your shop, and I want to know why . . . I do lots of business [elsewhere]. I don't know why I'm not doing any fucking business with Simon & Schuster."

Charming impatience was a major key to Lazar's success. "Sometimes I wake up in the morning and there's nothing doing, so I decide to *make something happen by lunch,*" he said.

He'd call Korda early in the day. "Lazar here. What's cookin', kiddo? What have we got going?" Then he'd make a series of rapid-fire sales pitches, throwing out names of clients who might or might not actually *be* his clients, and who might or might not know he was talking them up. Celebrity bios were big with him: "How about Cary Grant? . . . Cary could write a great book. Give me, oh, say, a million, and he's yours, I won't even mention him to anybody else . . . Greg Peck, how about him? Gene Kelly? I saw Gene last night, give me a million right now and he's yours." If Korda suggested he'd have to think about it, Lazar cut him off, kvetching—obviously, this thickheaded "kiddo" was not interested. He'd take his business elsewhere.

Humphrey Bogart gave him the nickname "Swifty" after Lazar closed three deals for him in one day.

In the 1960s, when the Hollywood studio system began to look shaky,

Lazar moved even more forcefully into the book business. "He changed the rules so quickly that they simply ceased to exist," Korda said.

> Unbeknownst to anyone, Lazar . . . unintentionally created a kind
> of international literary Ponzi scheme, in which he would demand a
> huge sum from an American publisher but promise to "lay off" a large
> percentage of it with the proceeds from foreign rights. He would then
> sell the British rights . . . to [publisher George] Weidenfeld, say, who
> would in turn "lay off" what he had promised to pay by selling the
> first-serial rights to one of the Sunday papers. Lazar had come up with
> a way of producing record-breaking sums for his authors at no apparent
> risk to anyone—until too many other people started to do it. Perhaps
> more important, as the world economy took a downturn, publishers
> all over the world found themselves being acquired by the kind of big
> companies in which there were people who made a profession of looking
> at the numbers and reading a balance sheet—something that had not
> until then been considered a necessary skill in book publishing. Lazar
> went on to make some of his biggest and juiciest deals in the brave new
> world of austerity and number-crunching—selling Cher's book for an
> enormous sum, for example, and coming close to making six-million-
> dollar deals for Madonna and Barbra Streisand.

When McMurtry was first starting out, he wouldn't have earned a second glance from Lazar. "To build a writer's career is a nightmare," Lazar said. "[You have to] concentrate on finding a few good clients who are well established and make a lot of money. They'll still be a pain in the ass, but they'll be worth it."

Truman Capote and Vladimir Nabokov were the kinds of writers he went for—often in the news for the public scandals they stirred up as much as for their literary prowess. "Not for him the contemplative hour with Horace or Virgil," McMurtry quipped. Fresh off the Oscar buzz for *Terms of Endearment*, preparing to deliver a nearly nine-hundred-page western epic to Michael Korda, which Korda was sure would give "McMurtry the attention and reviews he had deserved right from the beginning," McMurtry was exactly the kind of established client Swifty sought. And McMurtry's motherly, loving agent was dying.

"For years, once [Irving] became my agent, I waited for some chance statement that would indicate that he had read at least a page or two of the many books he agented for me," McMurtry said. "[T]he statement never came."

Until a mass shooting at its Robb Elementary School in the spring of 2022, Uvalde, Texas, eighty-five miles west of San Antonio, was best known for being the home of Franklin D. Roosevelt's vice president, John Nance Garner. "[T]he vice presidency is not worth a bucket of warm spit," the laconic Garner is supposed to have said of his achievement.

In mid-April 1986, McMurtry was staying in the Holiday Inn in Uvalde. He had been invited to lecture at a small college there—the first speaker the school had ever had. "Welcome to Larry McMurtry, Author of *Terms of Endearment*," read the Holiday Inn marquee. During a half-hour lunch break on his campus visit, McMurtry learned he had just been awarded the Pulitzer Prize for *Lonesome Dove*. The next day, someone told him the hotel had updated the marquee. He stepped outside, expecting hearty congratulations. The sign read: "Catfish Special, $3.99."

Every year, Swifty Lazar threw an Oscar party, along with his wife, Mary, a former model (a Coca-Cola girl) he'd met in 1962. She was his rock—the one who "made the apologies" when he overstepped his bounds with clients and potential business partners. The parties began "as a relatively informal and modest event—a moveable feast," Korda said.

> By the nineteen-eighties, the Oscar party had moved permanently to Hollywood, and it soon became something at once more formal and more formidable—a kind of *hommage* to Lazar, as well as a potent demonstration of his power to attract both the old guard and the new. Nobody else in Hollywood was powerful enough to bridge these two worlds—or old enough, come to that. An invitation to the Oscar party became the most sought-after ticket in Hollywood, reaching the point where it was once rumored that the Academy had contemplated changing the time of the award ceremony, so as not to incur Lazar's wrath by creating a stream of late arrivals to his party.

Lazar said, "I only invite friends and a handful of people I don't know but happen to admire. Can I help it that most of my friends happen to be stars and that the newcomers often arrive clutching Oscars?"

McMurtry felt he had no business in such a world. Lazar worked hard to convince him otherwise. McMurtry was "far too modest," Lazar believed. He had "never received more than $25,000 for a book before he came to me. It wasn't in his nature to ask for more money. He also didn't like to accept a dime until he finished a book." His father's ethos: don't take compensation until you've done an honest day's work. "I couldn't allow that," Lazar said.

"Simon & Schuster had published all of Larry's novels"—excluding the first three—"so when I sent over the manuscript of *Lonesome Dove,* I asked Michael Korda, the editor-in-chief, for an advance of $500,000. Michael liked the book a lot, but he didn't think he could pay more than $200,000 for it. After some negotiations, he went to $250,000—and wouldn't go higher. I decided to go elsewhere. I offered the book to five other publishing houses. They all wanted the book, but $250,000 seemed to be everybody's favorite number; no house would pay more. So, feeling like a fool, I crawled back to Michael and accepted the $250,000.

"While McMurtry was writing his next book, Simon & Schuster offered him a $500,000 advance. Now it was Larry's turn to be difficult. Once again, he announced that he didn't want *any* money until he had finished the manuscript; this time, however, I convinced him that this was childish behavior and that I should grab some cash.

"Within three years, I had his price up to $2 million a book."

Meanwhile, Lazar had begun shopping the *Lonesome Dove* movie option.

Suzanne de Passe, thirty-six years old, a daughter of Harlem, was the president of Motown Records' TV and film division. She had introduced Berry Gordy Jr. to the Jackson 5. She'd been nominated for an Oscar for writing the screenplay for Diana Ross's *Lady Sings the Blues.* One day she was vacationing at a swanky spa in Tucson, Arizona. There she met Gloria Steinem, who was traveling with Mort Zuckerman, a media tycoon and an acquaintance of McMurtry's from the East Coast salons. Steinem told de Passe that McMurtry was in Tucson, staying with Leslie Marmon Silko, a Laguna Pueblo novelist. Silko had recently moved to town from Albuquerque. Steinem invited de Passe to dinner at a Mexican restaurant with McMurtry, and they hit it off.

Weeks later, in Los Angeles, de Passe took him to lunch. She asked him, "What do you have kicking around that hasn't been produced yet?" McMurtry answered, "Well, I've got a book coming out in June, but you wouldn't be interested. It's a Western." "Au contraire!" de Passe answered, laughing. "I am a horsewoman, and I love Westerns. When I was a young girl I watched Gene Autry and Johnny Mack Brown and Hopalong Cassidy on Saturday mornings, and I always wore a little fringed skirt and pearl-handled pistols when I made my grandfather take me from Harlem to the rodeo at Madison Square Garden." McMurtry offered to have Lazar send the manuscript over so she could have a read.

The next day a flatbed dolly arrived at her office carrying several boxes packed with 1,800 double-spaced pages of *Lonesome Dove*. She took a box home each night. Before she'd even finished reading the novel, she called Lazar, asking if she could option it. "He said, '$50,000.' Not cheap," she recalled. "But he did give me eighteen months, instead of a year, and that's because he knew something I didn't: *Lonesome Dove* had already been passed on by every studio and network."

A friend informed her, "I don't know how to tell you this, but Swifty just took you. That's why he's called Swifty."

One day McMurtry told de Passe, "You know what? I'm all written out on *Lonesome Dove*." He had no interest in doing a screenplay, he announced. He moved on to his next novel. De Passe appeared to be stuck with a turkey. Then Lazar called to tell her McMurtry had won the Pulitzer. "The world changed," she said. "I went from goat to goddess."

She had already decided, after preliminary discussions with Peter Bogdanovich, John Huston, and John Milius, all of whom passed on the project, that *Lonesome Dove* needed to be more than a two- or three-hour movie. She was thinking television miniseries.

She met with Peter Frankovich, the head of CBS's miniseries department, and talked him into giving her six hours to tell the story (later, he agreed to eight). Through her agent, she heard about Bill Wittliff, who, the agent said, would make an excellent screenwriter for the project. He was a Texan and a friend of McMurtry's.

Since publishing *In a Narrow Grave* back in 1968, Wittliff had shut down the Encino Press, but he'd stayed busy with various projects, including photography (a book of portraits of La Frontera on the Texas-Mexico border), archive building (bringing together rare books and manuscripts to celebrate Texas writers, forming the Southwestern Writers Collection), and penning screenplays. "I never had any totally conscious plan about where my life would go," he said. "I just sort of go where the wind blows me." He'd always had a hankering to write. As a boy he'd sent ideas to *Playhouse 90, Robert Montgomery Presents,* and *Kraft Television Theatre,* "basically variations of the same theme: three junior high or high school boys play hooky from school, which I just happened to be doing at the time, and each time they would end up doing something good for the world. They'd capture a bunch of cattle rustlers or they'd free a brilliant scientist who'd been kidnapped by Russians. Needless to say, none of my submissions were accepted." Neither were his offerings to *Reader's Digest* (including a wholly made-up account of his intimate friendship with Lyndon Johnson).

On a whim, in the early 1970s, he began a screenplay based on a story his grandfather had told him. He'd never even seen a screenplay. His friend, journalist Bud Shrake, liked the story and sent it to his agent. The script made it into the hands of the producers of *The French Connection.* They bought it and the movie, *Barbarosa,* starring Willie Nelson, eventually opened to mild acclaim. As a result of the film's visibility, Wittliff was assigned by a studio to revise the script for *The Black Stallion.* He moved on to write *Raggedy Man,* about his mother's life as a small-town telephone operator; *Country,* starring Jessica Lange and Sam Shepard; and another Willie Nelson vehicle, *Honeysuckle Rose.*

Now Suzanne de Passe was asking him to adapt *Lonesome Dove* for the small screen. "There were so many reasons this thing should not have gotten made," Wittliff said. "At that time, there was nothing deader than the Western, except the miniseries. And this would be both." He argued with CBS executives about the length of each scene. "Can't we get them on the trail faster?" the suits would ask. Wittliff told them, "No. You have to get to know these people before you'll be willing to ride with them."

CBS complained that cows cost too much. "Bill, listen to this," a money man told him one day. "What if they start that drive and right away there's a storm and the cattle get scattered? You're the writer; why not let the cows go and have [Captain] Call say, 'Let's just keep going.' Then you have all those guys going to Montana, doing all that stuff, but we don't have to pay for the cattle."

"Or, here's a thought," Wittliff replied dryly. "[W]hy don't we just forget the cattle and get a herd of Angora goats? They can be the first guys to drive a herd of goats to Montana."

"Yeah, goats!"

"No, that's a joke," Wittliff had to explain.

The network had provided $16 million for the production; a multinational company called Quintex Entertainment kicked in another $4.5 million. De Passe suddenly found herself the only female (and the sole African American) in a fierce pecking order of producers and staff. Polly Platt could have told her a thing or two. It was de Passe's movie, but it concerned macho behavior (a subject her colleagues knew *all* about), and the shoot was physically demanding. Taking these factors into consideration and gauging the egos she was coddling, she realized she had to relinquish some of the day-to-day controls for the project to proceed smoothly. It agonized her, but in "letting go, I became more a part of it than I thought I would," she said. "To produce something of this size took a village—a village of men."

Almost from the start, McMurtry had distanced himself from the production. He was busy writing his next book—plus, the financial package had not been entirely to his benefit. "It would be nice to say that Irving was a superb agent, but that would be far from the truth," he admitted. "[H]is carelessness cost me millions. Though he claimed to be a lawyer, in fact law bored him. Thus when Quintex . . . went bankrupt, Irving did not bother to follow the proceedings, costing me millions in royalties . . . I figure [I missed getting] at least $15 million [on *Lonesome Dove*], a sum that would always be useful. But I loved him anyway."

I t all comes out of *Don Quixote*. It is the visionary and the practical man. Gus and Call," McMurtry said.

"Gus is about affection as much as achievement. He is immensely lovable, performing meaningless acts of gallantry just to . . . [be] darling," said novelist Carolyn See, who taught the book to generations of college students. "And Call is such a pain in the ass. He's just awful. But that's why [*Lonesome Dove* is] an American story. If we didn't have the Captain Calls, we wouldn't have skyscrapers or the Golden Gate Bridge or the Pentagon."

The book came from other sources, too. As critic Don Graham pointed out, Teddy Blue's trail-driving account, *We Pointed Them North,* was immensely important to *Lonesome Dove,* not only for details, but also for its "carefree banter and rollicksome" prose. (At one point, Blue says, "[B]efore we left, my girl took one of her stockings off and tied it around my arm, you know, like the knights of old, and I wore *that* to the mouth of the Musselshell." The line could have popped from a page of the novel.)

McMurtry consulted a two-volume oral history originally produced in the 1920s entitled *The Trail Drivers of Texas,* containing accounts of fearsome natural disasters bedeviling cattlemen (dust storms, snakebites, floods, lightning): "There was no timber on our side of the river, and when the hail began pelting the boys and myself made a break for the wagon for shelter. We were all naked, and the hail came down so furiously that within a short time it was about two inches deep on the ground."

The friendship of Charles Goodnight and Oliver Loving, who pioneered one of the first cattle trails out of Texas into New Mexico, profoundly influenced McMurtry's story. The men's relationship was vividly described in J. Evetts Haley's biography, *Charles Goodnight: Cowman & Plainsman* (1936). In particular, McMurtry drew upon Loving's request of Goodnight, after he was severely wounded in a skirmish with Comanches, to take his body home to Weatherford, Texas, for burial. As Haley recounted it: "[T]he cowboys gather[ed] scattered oil cans, beat them out, soldered them together, and made an immense tin casket. They placed the rough wooden one inside, packed several inches of powdered charcoal around it, sealed the tin lid . . . crated the whole in lumber . . . and carefully loaded the casket in [the wagon] . . . [W]ith six big mules strung out in the harness . . . the strangest and most touching funeral cavalcade in the history of the cow country took the Goodnight and Loving Trail that led to Loving's home."

McMurtry's version: "Before [Call] reached Kansas, word had filtered ahead of him that a man was carrying a body home to Texas. The plain was filled with herds, for it was full summer. Cowboys spread the word, soldiers spread it. Several times he met trappers, coming east from the Rockies, or buffalo hunters who were finding no buffalo. The Indians heard—Pawnee and Arapahoe and Ogallala Sioux. Sometimes he would ride past parties of braves, their horses fat on spring grass, come to watch his journey. Some were curious enough to approach him, even to question him. Why did he not bury the *compañero*? Was he a holy man whose spirit must have a special place? No, Call answered. Not a holy man. Beyond that he couldn't explain."

Famously, Goodnight and Loving were accompanied by a trusted African American companion—just as Gus and Call are. His name was Bose Ikard. When Ikard died, Goodnight erected a marker, saying, "served with me four years . . . never shirked a duty or disobeyed an order, rode with me in many stampedes, participated in three engagements with Comanches, splendid behavior."

When Call buries his buddy Deets, "I did copy the words Goodnight put on Bose Ikard's monument in Weatherford," McMurtry said. As for the book's episodic plot, aside from throwing a series of obstacles in the cowboys' path, from homesickness to storms to renegade Indians, McMurtry needed only this guidance from J. Evetts Haley: "All along that trail were graves."

In one of the novel's subplots, an Arkansas sheriff named July Johnson, along with his hapless deputy Roscoe, pursues Johnson's runaway wife. She has fled to find a rascal she loves, a man called Dee. These names—July, Roscoe, Dee—and a similar story line appear in a 1968 Dean Martin movie, *Bandolero!*, suggesting—no surprise—that another source for McMurtry's novel was the generic Hollywood cowboy, whose myth he hoped to deflate. Perhaps McMurtry doctored an early draft of the *Bandolero!* script—credited to James Lee Barrett—but if so, he never copped to it. (And *Lonesome Dove* was very likely not the first Old West novel he attempted. In 1965—as he was still struggling to earn money as a writer—a Young Adult novel appeared from a small publisher, the New York Graphic Society. It was entitled *Daughter of the Tejas*. It was about a twelve-year-old girl pursuing her mother's kidnappers. Rare-book dealers have long suspected that "Ophelia Ray" was a pseudonym for McMurtry. In autographed copies of the book, to children and elementary school classes, the handwriting looks suspiciously like McMurtry's, and a few copies of the book *do* exist signed by him directly. In an edition I own, Ophelia has written, "The Indians in this book are friendly Indians—I hope you will enjoy.")

One of McMurtry's aims in *Lonesome Dove* was to pierce the romantic image of the trail-riding cowboy. "I don't think these myths do justice to the richness and fullness of human possibility," he insisted. "The idea that men are men and women are women and horses are best of all is not a myth that makes for the best sort of domestic life."

The protagonists of *Lonesome Dove* arrive in Texas in the 1840s, when tales of the Alamo—another myth in the making—were on everyone's lips, but now, the narrative says, "the battle had been mostly forgotten." So much for *Remember the Alamo!*

On the trail, Gus says, "If a thousand Comanches had cornered us in some gully and wiped us out, like the Sioux just done Custer, they'd write songs about us for a hundred years." To which Call, mindful of manufactured history, replies, "I doubt there was ever a thousand Comanches in one bunch . . . If there had been they would have taken Washington, D.C."

McMurtry establishes Gus and Call as former Texas Rangers who have outlived their usefulness now that Texas's Native population has been subdued (hence Call's desire to drive cattle to Montana, to do one last thing on a grand scale). McMurtry had long derided Texas literature's soft treatment of the Rangers, beginning with Walter Prescott Webb. McMurtry could not abide Webb's romance or racial arrogance: "His own facts about the Rangers contradict again and again his characterization of them as 'quiet, deliberate, gentle' men." In fact, McMurtry said, "any Mexican unlucky enough to be caught [by the Rangers] was tortured until he coughed up information, then summarily hung. Mexicans found with cattle were shot." Once, according to Webb, a Ranger captain

crossed the Rio Grande to attack a ranch near Las Cuevas, where some 250 Mexican soldiers were assembled. Unfortunately the Rangers dashed into the wrong ranch and found a number of men working at the woodpile, cutting wood while their wives cooked breakfast. The Rangers shot them down, then realized their mistake and went on to the right ranch. Whether apologies were offered to the wives of the slain woodchoppers is not recorded. Webb is aware that [these] methods might conceivably be criticized, but he satisfies himself with the remark that "Affairs on the border cannot be judged by standards that hold elsewhere."

Why they can't is a question apologists for the Rangers have yet to answer. Torture is torture, whether inflicted in Germany, Algiers, or along the Nueces Strip.

In *Lonesome Dove,* McMurtry intended to be anything *but* an apologist for the Texas Rangers. Call is a cold, seemingly unemotional man, with no understanding of women (for him, "the pleasure [of sexual intimacy] was soon drowned in embarrassment and a feeling of sadness"). He refuses to acknowledge his own son. Gus, for all his "lovable" qualities, has a hair-trigger temper if he thinks he's been slighted. The cattle Call drives to Montana are stolen from Mexico. The ex-Rangers serve as judge and jury on the plains, hanging fellows, including one of their old comrades, when they feel the men have violated their code.

Yet witty dialogue, humorous incidents, and moments of tenderness, especially between Gus and a former prostitute, Lorena, who gets caught up in the drive and suffers a series of hardships, soften the men's portraits. McMurtry could not shake the tone of respect he heard in his uncles' voices when they told him stories of the old cowboys.

Added to this elegiac view was his conviction, also learned from his uncles and his father, that, for most of us, "our emotional experience remains largely unexplored, and therein lie the dramas, poems, and novels. An ideal place to start, it seems to me, is with the relations of the sexes."

Lonesome Dove is an amalgam of these two poles: losing one's world before getting a chance to live in it, and wrestling with the unspoken emotions (specifically, fear of intimacy) making it possible for that world to exist.

Both themes come to a head in the narrative when Gus has died—a victim of his buddy's Quixotic ambitions. Grieving, Clara, the woman Gus wanted to marry, admonishes Call, "I'm sorry you and Gus McCrae ever met. All you two done was ruin one another, not to mention those close to you. A . . . reason I didn't marry him was because I didn't want to fight you for him every day of my life. You men and your promises: they're just excuses to do what you plan to do all along, which is leave. You think you've always done right—that's your ugly pride . . . But you never did right and it would be a sad woman that needed anything from you. You're a vain coward, for all your fighting. I despised you then, for what you were, and I despise you now."

Clara speaks here for McMurtry's mother and grandmothers, and for every other woman he knew growing up.

Like those silent women, he had struggled mightily to find the right words for the story he often thought he was born to write. For several years, he had tried and failed, tried and failed to gain traction on his Western. Then one day the title came to him and he was able to finish the book. "Titles are really important to me," he said. "The title helps explain the book to me or to prepare me for the book or something. So I was coming from a restaurant over north of Fort Worth one day and I saw this old church bus sitting over by the side of the road and it said 'Lonesome Dove Baptist Church' and I immediately realized that was my title. Now the real Lonesome Dove was . . . a church and a cemetery . . . If you go back to the Dallas airport you'll cross Dove Road just before you get to the airport and the . . . church and the cemetery [are] just north of [there] . . ."

The fictitious Lonesome Dove is a small settlement—little more than a whorehouse and a saloon—near the Texas-Mexico border, where Augustus McCrae and Woodrow Call, retired Texas Rangers, run a moribund cattle and horse ranch, the Hat Creek outfit. Occasionally they raid Mexican ranches for horses and cows. Gus likes to drink and watch his pigs; Call is constantly looking for ways to keep busy at some arduous task or another. Their faithful old scout, Deets, remains with them, and they've hired a few inexperienced hands. Call's boy, Newt, is "really the Lonesome Dove," McMurtry said. "He's the one that's lonesome, because he's not acknowledged by his father." His mother, now dead, was a prostitute, and Call will barely mention her name, no matter how insistently Gus prods him to recognize the past.

One day, Jake Spoon, an old Ranger buddy who's fallen to gambling and who is now on the run after accidentally killing a man, rides into Lonesome Dove, telling stories he's heard about fortunes to be made raising cattle in Montana. The idea seizes Call as a grand adventure to cap his life; Gus views it as the folly it is, but goes along for the chance to see his old love, Clara. She's living in Nebraska. The Hat Creek gang steals several hundred head of cattle and sets off across the plains, where many of the men, including Gus and Deets, will perish along the way. Lorena, Lonesome Dove's prostitute, talks Jake Spoon into bringing her along; she dreams of branching off and starting a new life in San Francisco. Instead, she gets kidnapped by Blue Duck, a Comanchero, a half-breed Native, an old nemesis of the Rangers. Several men rape her until Gus manages to rescue her—McMurtry's graphic nod to the damsel in distress driving many old Westerns.

The novel ends with Call returning to Texas, honoring Gus's request to bury him there. A young man he meets along the way says to him, "Captain. They say you were the most famous Ranger . . . They say you're a man of vision." "Yes, a hell of a vision," Call answers bitterly—a line McMurtry borrowed from Charles Goodnight, as reported in J. Frank Dobie's *Cow People*. (Goodnight also admitted to Dobie, "My life has been mostly a failure.")

Gus is central to each of the novel's threads—the trail-driving adventure and the meditation on men and women. Quoting poetry and Latin, courting love, and dreaming with a bottle of whiskey in his lap, he appears to be the romantic idealist, Quixote to Call's pragmatic Sancho Panza. But as with Johnny and Gid in *Leaving Cheyenne,* the men's dynamic is more nuanced than that. Gus sees through Call's misguided quest to reach Montana. And his closeness with women suggests a more layered understanding of life's complexities than Call appears capable of grasping. In the end, who *really* tilts at windmills?

Cowboying is no more viable now than Rangering, and Gus knows it. His remarks along the trail are wistful, sprinkled with the ironies of experience and wisdom. "The dern people are making towns everywhere. It's our fault, you know," Gus tells his friend. "Does it ever occur to you that everything we did was probably a mistake? Just look at it from a nature standpoint. If you've got enough snakes around the place you won't be overrun with rats or varmints. The way I see it, the Indians . . . have the same job to do. Leave 'em be and you won't constantly be having to ride around these dern settlements . . . Me and you done our work too well. We killed off most of the people that made this country interesting to begin with."

As for women: early in his acquaintance with Lorena, he badgers her almost daily for a "poke" (his way of asking for sex). But his genuine concern for her after she has been traumatized makes her take him seriously as a potential life partner. She sees his true loyal character. And his devotion to Clara, beyond any possibility of physical intimacy, regardless of distance or time, best expresses McMurtry's vision of men and women at their finest.

Lorena, fearing Gus will leave her if she doesn't offer him sex, insists that he sleep with her. He agrees, but only to hold her tightly and ease her anxieties. As a younger writer—the author of the cynical *Last Picture Show*, say—McMurtry would have considered such a scene sentimental. Now, as a middle-aged divorcé, blessed and abandoned by love, he saw it as stone-cold realism.

Writing in *Studies in American Indian Literatures,* the Choctaw scholar D. L. Birchfield was flummoxed by *Lonesome Dove*: "How can it be that [McMurtry,] the foremost critic of Texas letters, a person who is quite likely the state's most talented novelist, can write a novel glorifying two mid-nineteenth-century Texas Rangers? . . . How can it be that such a choice of heroes can be so taken to the heart of the American public that the book should receive the Pulitzer Prize in literature and become a tremendously successful television miniseries? . . . How can an author such as Larry McMurtry, who is sensitive to racially prejudicial material in Texas literature regarding Blacks and Hispanics, be callous where the sensitivities of Native American people are concerned? Yet it is McMurtry who has given us *Lonesome Dove*."

Sherman Alexie, a Spokane–Coeur d'Alene Native American, a prominent novelist, poet, and short-story writer, agreed that McMurtry's portrayal of Blue Duck in the novel was offensively stereotyped. He didn't say that, as a man of European descent, McMurtry shouldn't write about Native Americans, but he did say "we should be talking about these books, written about Indians by non-Indians, honestly and accurately. I mean, they're outsider books. They're colonial books . . . Larry McMurtry's books are colonial literature. These are books by members of the privileged, of the powerful, writing about the culture that has been colonized . . . so when McMurtry does what he does, he thinks he's being democratic, but he's actually being colonial."

Perhaps McMurtry's description of Blue Duck as a Comanchero was intended to deflect objections of this kind. And he insisted that the "book

[was] permeated with criticism of the West from start to finish . . . But people are nostalgic for the Old West, even though it was actually a terrible culture . . . Exterminated the Indians. Ruined the landscape. We killed the right animal, the buffalo, and brought in the wrong animal, wetland cattle. And it didn't work." Yet his statement that "people are nostalgic for the Old West" raised the question, *Which* people? Certainly not the descendants of those who were slaughtered.

While claiming the freedom of the fiction writer to invent whatever he wanted, McMurtry also prided himself on historical accuracy. He took the name of his villain from a real figure, Bluford Duck, a Cherokee horse thief, bank robber, and murderer, and a lover of the legendary bandit Belle Starr. Bluford Duck's grave can be found in Catoosa, Oklahoma. Yet historical truths do not always make for the best aesthetic decisions. McMurtry's Blue Duck is pure evil, grotesquely comic in his one-dimensionality. As such, he is closer to an old dime-novel caricature than a historical personage— another point McMurtry mustered in his favor: parodying such figures was part of *Lonesome Dove*'s aims, he said. Besides which, Native culture was not the book's subject. That would be another novel entirely, *Lonesome Duck,* perhaps—one that his friend Leslie Silko was much better equipped to write.

Still, McMurtry expressed grave disappointment that most readers elevated Gus and Call to heroic status, that *Lonesome Dove* had failed to dissipate the romance of the West. As Don Graham said, "*The Godfather* was supposed to de-mythologize the mob, too, but we all wanted to be gangsters after we saw it, right?"

While writing the book, McMurtry had not fully shed his own nostalgia—inherited from his father. For better or worse, his nostalgia gave the story much of its power. "If Larry McMurtry's vision of the West" had been more objective, Birchfield reflected, "the popular myth [he] retold might have become a cautionary tale. It might have told us that we must step outside the ethnocentricty of our culture and examine the methods by which we gain fame, and if they are grounded in squalor, so shall our souls be."

The barrancas, mesas, and mountains near Abiquiu, New Mexico, fifty-three miles northwest of Santa Fe, served as Montana during the filming of the miniseries. The "Wild Choke Cherry Place," Tewa settlers named the land in 1742; it became the starting point of the Old Spanish Trail in the 1800s and later a Genízaro settlement, Genízaros being Natives of various tribes once held as slaves and servants of the Spanish. The residue of this long history seemed to hang in the region's heavy air.

Lonesome Dust, the film's cast and crew called the production. The particles they breathed and wore on their clothes certainly added to the look and feel of authenticity captured in every scene.

There seemed to be magic in the atmosphere as well. "It really felt at times like the movie gods were telling us, 'It doesn't matter what you do, you're not going to fuck this up,'" Bill Wittliff said. "In Larry's book, there's a blizzard. Well, we have to shoot that in June, so we've got airplane motors and potato flakes, because that's how you make a snowstorm." But then the pale, high Abiquiu sky grew blue and bluer still before hazing to a solid scrim of white. "[T]he special effects guys are prepared to make a blizzard . . . [and a] freak blizzard has come through."

The snow "was gone in five hours because it was so late in the season," actor D. B. Sweeney recalled, "but the net effect was to add about seven hundred and fifty miles to the cattle drive because you really felt like you had gotten to the Montana cold."

On another day, "the lead steer swam into the middle of [a] river and started circling, and the rest of the cattle followed and couldn't get out," Wittliff said. "I thought, 'My God, we're going to lose the whole herd.' Suddenly [all the actors] became real cowboys. The cast and wranglers jumped on their horses, piled into the water, and turned the herd. We weren't even filming."

Such moments brought gravity and grit to the production, which was also aided by brilliant camera work, managing to make 350 Mexican Corriente cattle appear to be a herd of 2,000. The director, Simon Wincer, a native Australian, understood that McMurtry's novel had become a sacred text in Texas, and he took his task of translating it to the screen very seriously. "[It's] as epic as they come," he said. "When I came to Texas I realized it was like remaking the Bible."

Shooting began in March 1988 in Austin, moved to Del Rio in April, then on to New Mexico, wrapping after eighty-eight days. The cast— Robert Duvall as Gus and Tommy Lee Jones, a native Texan, as Call— seemed as tailor-made for their roles as Wittliff was to write the script.

Duvall appeared to have realigned every bone in his body, said Stephen Harrigan, writing for *Texas Monthly*, in order to become "a rangy, hollow-cheeked cowman with decidedly bowed legs."

Anjelica Huston delivered a fine performance as Gus's old flame, despite learning that "Larry McMurtry wasn't keen on me, which kind of broke my heart. I think he wanted Cybill Shepherd or Diane Keaton."

The eight-hour show aired on CBS beginning on February 5, 1989, becoming the highest-rated miniseries of its time. *Newsweek* claimed it "proves what television can achieve when it forgets it's only television," and *Time* said it offered "the most vividly rendered old West in TV history." Duvall's and Jones's amiable performances further enhanced the heroic picture of Gus and Call, ensuring, yet again, that *Lonesome Dove* would add to, rather than detract from, western myth.

Wittliff's script had focused on adventure—a montage near the end of the show replayed all the deaths along the trail, giving the surviving Call an air of tragic dignity, like a weary general returning, wounded but undaunted, from war. By contrast, the novel ended with the story of the old bartender in Lonesome Dove: he immolates himself in the saloon, grieving after Lorena leaves to follow the cattle drive. It is a deflationary moment, revealing the dark side of adventure: the emptiness uncovered by ignoring intimate bonds and riding off into the sunset; the domestic yearning buried deep within the cowboy's stoicism, unacknowledged and inert.

After its airing, the miniseries went on to become the biggest-selling Western on DVD. Meanwhile, in addition to the Pulitzer Prize, the book won the Spur Award of the Western Writers of America and a Texas Institute of Letters Prize. It had sold over 300,000 copies in hardback, won accolades from critics ("a culmination of Larry McMurtry's career as a novelist," said Clay Reynolds), and catapulted McMurtry into a publishing phenomenon, one of the most sought-after writers in the country.

"The reviewers were beginning to feel a degree of guilt over the way they had reviewed Larry in the past," Michael Korda believed. "That was doubled by the dawning recognition that, with his bookshop, he was involved in the cause of books, and even if he did grow up in Archer City, he was a bona fide intellectual and literary person."

"I have a view about great art, whether it's stories, poetry, music, whatever," Bill Wittliff said. "None of it tells you anything new; it merely reminds you of something you already know but forgot you knew. And that's what Larry did. You start reading *Lonesome Dove,* and you feel you already know these people. They're already in you. They've always been in you."

McMurtry remained unconvinced: "I thought I had written about a harsh time and some pretty harsh people. But, to the public at large, I had produced something nearer to an idealization; instead of a poor man's *Inferno,* filled with violence, faithlessness, and betrayal, I had actually delivered a kind of *Gone with the Wind* of the West, a turnabout I'll be mulling over for a long, long time."

He said, "*Gone with the Wind* is not a despicable book. It is also not a great book. And that is what I feel about *Lonesome Dove.*"

he huge popularity of *Lonesome Dove* rapidly gained me at least five imposters," McMurtry said. They "were middle-aged bullshitters, none of them attractive. One, who hailed from Green Valley, Arizona, liked to hang out at filling stations in south Tucson, attempting to entice promising girls with a part in his new film, a sequel of course to . . . *Lonesome Dove*."

He once had to call the mother of a young woman in Houston to tell her the man her daughter was about to marry was not the real Larry McMurtry. "The mother was indignant," he said. "Indignant at my unwillingness to become their son-in-law."

It took years to escape his phantom self. Once, walking into the executive air terminal at Houston's Hobby Airport, he noticed the startled faces of the pilots who were scheduled to fly him to the *Lonesome Dove* movie set. "Is something the matter?" McMurtry asked.

"It's just that you don't look like yourself," one of the pilots said.

"How would you know? We've never met."

"Oh yes," the other man said. "We had drinks with you two nights ago, in Cabo San Lucas."

McMurtry's lifelong ambivalence—about almost *everything*—made him an ideal target for impostors. In any given twenty-four-hour period, he could sound like two different people. Even as he publicly declared *Lonesome Dove* the mediocre equivalent of *Gone with the Wind* and insisted he never gave the book a second thought once he'd finished it, in private he spread a different story. "He told me, 'I will never write a better book than this one,'" said Michael Wallis. "And I personally don't think he did."

Then there was the problem of *finding* Larry McMurtry. Hunkered in his apartment above Booked Up? No—someone had heard he'd rented a Cadillac and driven west until he'd gotten tired of driving; then he'd ditched the car at a midwestern airport and flown to New York. Or maybe he was back in Santa Monica working on another screenplay. (He always had one going—like that nifty item *The Murder of Mary Phagan,* a five-part television miniseries, starring Jack Lemmon, about a Jewish man in Georgia who'd claimed he was falsely accused of killing a young factory girl; McMurtry had earned near-unanimous praise for the crime and courtroom drama—"a powerful, gripping, conscientious piece of work," *The Washington Post* called it.) He could write anywhere, though. He was spending a lot of time in Tucson these days. His boy was still at the University of Arizona. And hadn't he fixed up his old family homestead in Texas? (Its mailbox was full of bullet holes, he'd said—the local teens used it for target practice—stuffed with years-old flyers and nests of scorpions and spiders.) God knows why he'd want to go back there.

When he *was* in Georgetown, he threw himself into book buying. As if to emphasize that the book trade was more important to him than writing, he tucked away the laminated Academy Award nomination for *The Last Picture Show* script in the bookstore's bathroom. He and Marcia Carter continued to work splendidly as a team—and they needed each other. Their dealings with Janet Auchincloss, Jacqueline Kennedy Onassis's mother, was a case in point. When Auchincloss's husband died, she donated his private library to Yale University. What Yale didn't want, she offered to Booked Up, which was located two blocks from where she lived. But there was a snag. In DC's insulated social circles, "Marcia was, in a small way, a person Mrs. A. knew socially, and Mrs. A. could simply not accept that a person she knew socially was 'in trade,'" McMurtry said. She could not possibly associate with Carter, under these circumstances. "This was the 1980s, but Janet Auchincloss, for one, was simply not going to acknowledge that the rules had changed. And that seemed to be that." In the end, the fact that Marcia's business partner was "in trade" (he was nobody, anyway, right?) was apparently okay. McMurtry "filled the car with books, wrote the check, and beat it out of there." As he did so, Janet Auchincloss "was nowhere to be seen."

Washington's restrictive bubble was often his excuse for getting away—or for inviting women friends to come see him in the city. Another trick to finding him on any given day was figuring out who he was spending time with. His old friend Susan Freudenheim was a frequent companion. It appalled her that the culture birds in Washington and New

York did not seem to know whom they had in their midst. "People do not always recognize . . . the intellectual heft of Larry," she said. "People don't put him in the same category as a *New Yorker* essayist. But he is."

He had more damned discipline and stamina than all his critics put together, she said: "He operates on a different plane than everyone else." Once, when she was in town, "He dropped me off at the apartment, said he'd be back to pick me up in an hour because he had to write a book review for *The New York Times*, and was back exactly in an hour with the review done," she said, astonished.

Beverly Lowry, a young Houston novelist, often came to visit. She stayed in McMurtry's apartment above Booked Up, among his collection of mouse and human skulls, tomes on the history of printing, and esoteric videos such as Werner Herzog's *Aguirre, the Wrath of God*. "I'd never known a man who talked about the emotional life—about falling in love—so openly, and with such self-deprecating humor," Lowry recalled. "I was startled by it, but also comforted, and very comfortable. You just don't expect that—especially in a guy from the Southwest."

Soon after moving east, McMurtry had befriended another woman, Maureen Orth (to whom he'd dedicated *Lonesome Dove*—"At long last, a book, I hope, commensurate with your qualities," he wrote her). He'd met her one day in the bookstore. She was looking for "a cowboy book for my then boyfriend," she said. A native of the Bay Area in California, Orth was a freelance writer, with bylines in *Newsweek, New York, New West, Vanity Fair,* the *Times,* the *Post,* and *The Wall Street Journal.* Eventually, she married TV journalist Tim Russert, whom she met at the 1980 Democratic National Convention.

She claimed she had never been romantically involved with McMurtry, but he was, she said, "a man who completely knows my heart, who gives me lovely presents for no reason, who sends my mother flowers every Christmas, who has written me over a hundred wise and witty letters, who will patiently listen to seven different leads to a story I might write, who told me first that I had finally found the right man to marry." He "loved, respected, and appreciated women more than any man I ever knew," she said. "Through the years there became a small circle of us—women Larry cultivated and cared for, but didn't necessarily sleep with. He was willing to wait, he said, for years to see if anything might spark, and meanwhile he would keep . . . being a prince while we got our hearts chewed up by less worthy boys. 'If I thought a love affair would give me six months of intense pleasure but that this woman I had a real affinity for would not be in my life ten years from now,' he once told me, 'I would walk around the love affair if there was one to be walked around. I would go for the long-term friendship.'"

He gave her his manuscripts to read before he published them because she was "normal," he informed her. She'd give him "an honest reaction." In turn, he was the "shoulder I cried on," she said—often in early morning phone calls, waking him up. "I always wondered why women put up with men, to tell you the truth," he confessed to her once. "My experience with women, the bottom line, is that very few start off with much confidence. It's an acquired characteristic, if they ever acquire it. Many of them acquire it only to a certain depth and beneath that is a bottomless insecurity."

He admitted to her that he "did not have very much Don Juanism," but he was like most males, for whom it was hard not to "make conventional assumptions about women, that you can just grab them, and you can sleep with them, and then they'll be with you from then on if you want them." Men were every bit as insecure as women—if they didn't sleep with a woman they spent time with, they figured people would assume something was wrong with them.

If he'd learned anything at all, it was that possessiveness was poison. The "freest relationships are apt to last the longest [and] I don't like losing people out of my life," he told Orth. "Perhaps it's a need for security, or curiosity. Every person has a story . . . You respond to the potential and the contradictions. Most people are to some degree a mixture of creative and self-destructive impulses; you always like to see how the mix works itself out."

His back-to-back road trips had intrigued him as to the differences between urban and small-town girls, their daily rhythms, their balances between career and personal concerns. And, he said, in all his friendships with women "there has been a sexual aura, which I think is in most friendships. Sometimes it remains an aura forever, and the desire is never consummated. Sometimes it's consummated years later."

He continued his long-distance intimacies with Cybill Shepherd and Diane Keaton (to whom he'd also dedicated novels), driving to see them, phoning them, sending them letters, flowers, cards. Shepherd would come visit, riding her bike around Georgetown, hanging out in his bookstore. "I can confide in him. He was never jealous of me. He loves women. He just adores women. He's like the Pied Piper of women. And we share a love of Dr Pepper," she said. He always told her *she* was *Lonesome Dove*'s Lorena. "When we talk, we don't usually talk very long, and we say I love you. Always and always." They had a brief falling-out, after she'd divorced her second husband. (It always unnerved him to see her picture in the tabloids.) He felt she was too cavalier about marriage and children, and he couldn't protect her from her own "recklessness." But they soon made up. He "is one of my treasures," Shepherd insisted. "It's a continuing love story."

In fact, she said, "I've realized that he is actually the love of my life." Pressed, once, by a Memphis newspaper reporter to explain what she meant by this—*You mean romantic love?*—she replied, "Deeper than that."

Diane Keaton was less reckless than Shepherd, more like the young Jo, never sure she knew what she was doing, personally or professionally, a mass of anxieties concerning her appearance, her social etiquette, or her knowledge. (She *hated* to be beaten at Trivial Pursuit, and McMurtry would often throw a game rather than invite her ominous glare.)

She confessed her profoundest insecurities to him: her fears that she was shallow in wanting to be a star, loved by millions of people she didn't know; her worries that she'd never paid enough attention to her troubled brother, Randy, an aspiring poet who could never pull his work together.

She loved working on the screenplay of *Somebody's Darling* with Mc-Murtry, even though the film never got made. He encouraged her to do more writing on her own.

Once, in the fall of 1989, she called him and asked if he'd come spend the afternoon with her in New York. They could go see the new movie *New York Stories,* she said—a trio of short films in which Martin Scorsese, Francis Ford Coppola, and Woody Allen had each directed parts. McMurtry didn't tell her he'd already seen it. Two nights before, he'd been invited to the White House, along with a few other writers and artists, to spend an "informal" evening with George H. W. and Barbara Bush—the Texans were back in town! (George was more Yalie than wildcatter, but the DC regulars were already muttering, again, about those awful *vulgarians.*) The "informal" evenings were Barbara's idea. George didn't have an informal bone in his body. The White House entertainment that night was *New York Stories,* after which the president asked if anyone could explain it to him. No one knew what to say. After all, "it was not exactly Hegel," Mc-Murtry thought.

It was much more pleasant to watch the film in New York, sitting next to Diane Keaton, though McMurtry tensed a bit, knowing that sitting near them in the theater were Woody Allen's parents (whom Keaton had warmly greeted). He knew that Allen's segment of the film featured a botched magic trick resulting in the giant head of Allen's mother hovering over Manhattan, complaining about her son's failures. McMurtry was mildly surprised to see that the woman had no apparent reaction to the story, even as the rest of the audience chuckled.

Afterward, he and Keaton went to her apartment to meet some of her friends. After the others left, she decided to change for dinner. "I watched night settle over Central Park," McMurtry recalled. "Then something tilted, and it tilted downward. She changed clothes four or five times . . . Diane is a beautiful woman . . . She looks good in anything. Or so I had thought, until, finally, she emerged in a bowler hat and a brown suit that made her look square, and not square as in uncool, but square as in 'not a rectangle but a square.' It was as if she had searched not only her own closets but all of Central Park West and found the one outfit that did not become her. Why? As we waited in sudden misery for the elevator she turned to me and said in a tone to pierce the heart: 'I look like a clown.' It was scary, not silly, and it wasn't about the clothes. What she couldn't find was anyone to be: and forced to a choice, she chose the Clown. In so doing she humbled herself, and would scarcely look at me."

The moment revealed another bond between them: a cold current of melancholy, the sadness of the observer—the actor, the writer—whose task (whose fate?) is to capture (not to correct, not to castigate) the off-kilter world.

"Three weeks later, Red Skelton walked into my bookshop in DC," McMurtry said. "He was a thoughtful book collector who came in when he could. Only this time he was weeping: there were tears on his cheeks. He didn't mention them, I didn't mention them. They could have been allergies, but I doubt it. He wasn't moaning and groaning but there were tears. He was careful not to drip on the books. I think it was the sadness of the Clown inside. There's nothing the fondest friend can do about the pain of clowns"—he was thinking of Keaton. "[P]ain, after all, is where their job starts."

Long-distance intimacies . . . guaranteeing, almost certainly, abiding friendships rather than sexual fidelity; continual longing shrouded in fantasy and memory. McMurtry cherished these emotions and their accompanying physical sensations (sometimes a literal ache) as much as the erotic touch. Maybe more so.

"[N]ot only did I not see these women very often, I rarely even talked directly to them anymore," says his alter ego Danny Deck, revived for *Some Can Whistle* (1989), his sequel to *All My Friends Are Going to Be Strangers*. "Most of the time I now talked to their message machines, a new and seductive form of communication . . . I had become a kind of Proust of the message machine"—McMurtry described *himself* this way—"leaving elegant, finely modulated monologues on the . . . machines of distinguished, or at least distinctive, women in New York, California."

He gathered women as he collected books, and for much the same reason: so as not to feel bereft. "If I'm a connoisseur of anything, it's the female voice," Deck says. "Through the years . . . the voices of women have been my wine: my claret, my Chardonnay, my Chablis." He loved nothing better than discovering "a new wine . . . with depth and color, bite, clarity, body."

McMurtry liked to revisit women at various periods of their lives, just as he revisited the characters in his novels, so as not to lose them (even when, like Emma Horton, they died).

But as he'd explained to Maureen Orth, the key to collecting was to possess lovingly, without turning possessive—hence, the frequent travel, the moving away, the letting go. The security of feeling surrounded by what he loved was inextricable from the emptiness, trailing him like a thunderhead since childhood, prompting the *need* for security. The library and the road. The hug of close quarters and the openness of space.

As he roved between coasts, he "would present his American Express card at the desks of the Hertz company, choosing not a Mercedes, Volvo, or Oldsmobile—rather a Cadillac or a Lincoln," Jan Reid wrote of him in a magazine profile at the height of his nomadism. "McMurtry as a fat cat nouveau riche. He would park [the cars] for days with the meter running—instruct the Hertz folks to get him a new one when the floor-board got trashy."

He'd stuff his dirty clothes into a Federal Express box and ship them back to his house.

He knew he was spoiled (he could just imagine what his father would say). It was easy to laugh at the foibles of his colleagues in the entertainment world, who believed success wasn't worth anything if it didn't buy them "immunity from the common ills of mankind." But he admitted he was just the same. He'd gotten used to privilege.

Traveling as far west as he could go, he'd pause on the edge of the continent to watch America tumble willy-nilly into the sea. He would become an excited kid again fresh from the picture show, gawking at the real-life stars he met—Muhammad Ali stepping onto an elevator with him at the Beverly Wilshire Hotel, Zeppo Marx, who lived above the Café of the Pink Turtle, slipping into a corner booth to order a sandwich. After a few days in LA, sitting through pointless story conferences, he felt his longing for the road return.

In the late eighties or early nineties, he confessed to his friend Max Crawford that his restlessness was exhausting him: "I can't be taking too many more of these trips," he wrote. But then he sang again the virtues of travel: "I drove last week from AC [Archer City] to Roswell and back . . . it was 85 [degrees] and the cotton looked great as I passed the Floydada cut off. Hope it continues."

More and more, he spent time again in Archer City, as a familiar stop-off between his work on the East and West Coasts; as a writing retreat, safe from impostors and movie executives; and as a devoted son and uncle. "I'm trying to decide whether to put Mom in a drug hospital," he wrote Grace David in 1986. "She's a total addict, uppers and downers which she takes indiscriminately. I don't know. She's eighty. She might as well have drugs if we could just get her consistent."

The burned-out shell of the Royal Theater greeted him whenever he pulled into town, its ticket window shattered, the marquee crumbling, resembling a set of buffalo bones straight out of *Lonesome Dove,* the roof blown off, and inside, the seats and projector long gone. The courthouse square was always deserted; the lone traffic light still whipped around like a paper lantern in the stiff northern winds. Sonny and Duane might come walking around the corner any minute.

Yet in spite of appearances, Archer City had undergone surprising changes in the intervening years. In 1973 and 1974, when the Organization of the Petroleum Exporting Countries raised oil prices worldwide, increasing tenfold the value of a barrel of crude, Archer City boomed and just kept booming throughout the seventies. American wealth shifted to the Sun Belt. Political power accrued to the oil patch states—Texas, Louisiana, and Oklahoma. Nor had Archer City escaped the seismic shocks of the civil rights movement, antiwar demonstrations, feminism, and what the media called the sexual revolution. The Baptists who'd objected so strongly to *The Last Picture Show* were still prominent in the area, but as one observer put it, the "Baptists don't always win" anymore. In 1975, Archer City voted, 334 to 295, to legalize the sale of liquor in town. In celebration, "the street was absolutely littered with beer cans," McMurtry said. "It was a wonderful scene—riotous drunkenness."

In place of the old pool hall, the Archer City Recreation Center offered Pac-Man and Asteroids Deluxe. The Golden Rooster Café had been replaced by a spiffy new Dairy Queen. Dish antennas crammed finely trimmed backyards alongside hot tubs and small swimming pools. KTRN, once Sonny's go-to station for Hank Williams, now broadcast ski reports from New Mexico and Colorado. In a town of less than 1,900 residents, there were at least ten, maybe as many as fifteen, millionaires. According to a *New York Times* report, "Deposits at the First State Bank" in Archer City "stood at just under $3 million in 1970. In December 1980 they had ballooned to $14 million, and by February 1982, had leaped to more than $18 million."

McMurtry's sister, Sue Deen, noted that divorce was no longer frowned upon locally. First, the kids who'd gotten hitched just out of high school and realized their mistake hosted breakup parties. Then the couples in their thirties and forties who realized they no longer had to tolerate each other caused a second wave of splits. It was not unusual anymore for couples to live together before marriage, and "people may sleep together a time or two, you know, and then they're still friends," Deen said.

McMurtry's old mentor, Margaret Ellen Slack, said that in the old days, women like Ruth Popper "had to put up with whatever because they had children and no way to make a living. Now"—with the boom—"they have more options."

McMurtry's brother-in-law, Carlton Deen, was the face of the new Archer City aristocrat. Like Duane in *The Last Picture Show,* he'd been a high school football player and a roughneck in the oil fields. But with the boom, he was grossing over $2 million a year, prompting McMurtry to joke about writing a *Picture Show* sequel entitled *Duane Gets Rich.*

Deen's politics reflected strange new American complexities—neither right nor left, liberal nor conservative; rather, a complicated stew of convictions and beliefs, the traditions of his upbringing mixed with fresh experiences, still unsettled. Distrustful of big government, fearful of creeping socialism and the erosion of the free-enterprise system, he was also, he said, "radicalized" by Vietnam. He'd served in the military and known buddies killed in what he came to believe was a wasted cause. He sympathized with youthful protesters. In basic training at Fort Hood, he'd met Black men for the first time and learned racial tolerance, he said, something he'd not been taught in Archer City. Now he wished for a more diverse community.

His wife, the former Rodeo Queen, wore colorful, suggestive T-shirts and considered herself a "quasi hippie."

McMurtry was amused by all this, but by the time he renovated the old family home, the boom had started to fade. Archer City had not quite returned to its old black-and-white self, but its edges were getting ragged again. McMurtry didn't care about that; he was seeking readerly solitude, respite from the world. "I learned early that the kink in my attachment to Archer County, and West Texas in general, was that the place was bookless," he said. "This problem kept me elsewhere for thirty years or so of my life, but I solved it eventually by bringing . . . books to this little town—20,000" to begin with. He shelved them in spaces where he'd read the very first volumes his cousin Robert Hilburn brought him. Then in 1987, to make even more room, be bought an empty building downtown and opened the Blue Pig Book Store (named for Gus's favorite animal in *Lonesome Dove*). His sister Sue managed it. It sat just down the street from where his other sister, Judy McLemore, had opened her realty business. McLemore was grateful to get her brother back in the family fold for as many days as she could during the year. She appreciated his attentiveness to their mother. When Hazel had to be moved to an assisted care facility in Wichita Falls, he brightened her room with his literary and movie awards. He was the "kindest, most generous" man she had ever known, McLemore said, and he was "born with an unimaginable amount of brain power, almost too smart for his own good . . . He told me once he wasn't afraid to die; he was just afraid that he wouldn't get all the books read that he needed to get read. I told him, 'Larry, you have been reading since you were four. Surely you have most of them read.' He replied, 'No, I'm not even close.'"

She was surprised and irritated when some of the townsfolk reacted to McMurtry's increased presence with petulance, still steaming about the town's presentation in *Picture Show*. They were just jealous, McLemore thought. He was living a good life; he "never sought things. They just came" to him. People couldn't stand that.

The grumbling grew louder in 1989, when he bought the only mansion in town, Old Man Taylor's big brick house—the house he'd watched from his bedroom as a child, waiting to see the second-floor light that meant the old man was sitting up, reading; the house in whose basement he'd glimpsed (and coveted) a huge shiny Cadillac. He'd wanted it *all* back then and he wanted it now: every book in the world, every car, every space where he could read and pump out five pages a day, trying to fill (futilely, he knew) the hollow gaps in his makeup.

When he bought the Taylor place, he was surprised to find that among the furnishings left behind were very few books. Maybe he'd been wrong as a child—perhaps Mr. Taylor *wasn't* a fellow reader, after all. Or maybe he'd sold all his books before he'd died. McMurtry hired a pair of contractors and some workmen (a "couple of local depressives," he wrote Max Crawford) to renovate the house. He called it Versailles. He began moving even more books into town and sat at his typewriter in the house's warm dining room every morning, at a large oak table facing the wide French doors.

In the years ahead, he would buy more buildings in Archer City—an empty storefront, an abandoned Ford dealership. This didn't sit well with some of the locals. "The mentality of the city is that Larry is buying up all the buildings and filling them with books, and what do we need books for?" said Abby Abernathy, a businessman in town.

"I'm a polarizing figure," McMurtry admitted. "I don't want to be the focus of any town. I don't want to be the person everybody reacts to. They need another villain, or another hero."

Fortunately, he had his growing family to attend to. "The love of my life now is my dynamic 7 year old niece Mitzi and my main ambition is to sit around and watch her grow up," he wrote Grace David. Mitzi was McLemore's daughter. "She is astonishing and we have been mighty close since she was two. A stormy relationship, however. Recently she defied me by getting a pixie haircut, which I hate, so I retaliated by buying her a stunning Adolfo wig, which she has to wear in my company. She is one of those natural stars that life flings up, unfairly, from time to time. I have 6 other perfectly nice nieces and nephews but Mitzi is so amazing that it's hard to pay proper attention to the rest of them. I gave her her first fur coat when she was 5."

The "rest of them," including Mitzi's brother Matt and Todd Wayne, McMurtry's brother's son, never felt neglected by their uncle. "He was really cool. He always encouraged you to learn and experience different things," Matt told me. "He'd say, 'Read read read. There's a big world outside of Archer City.'" He played tennis with his nephews ("'I'm just an old jump-baller,' he'd say. He'd put this really funky spin on the ball") and he taught Matt the meaning of the word "xenophobe." "Don't be one," he warned.

"My first trip to Washington, DC, when I was in the seventh grade . . . We stayed in his apartment above the bookstore," Matt said. "I got to do this every other year, sort of a work/play deal, moving books around, Big City life. One particular time, he flew me up with Cazimir, Leslie Silko's son. He took us to New York. We stayed in a real nice hotel, the Pierre. Talk about country coming to town. He insisted we get some nicer clothes, then he took us to Petrossian, the caviar restaurant. The cool thing was, before that we had to pick up Diane Keaton from her condo. It overlooked Central Park. We picked her up and Carol Kane. I think the Petrossian had just opened. Larry said something like, 'New York is finally sophisticated enough for a restaurant like this.'"

While he was stretching the kids' horizons, he continued to test his ability to stay in Archer City (Lord knew, it had been a lifelong struggle). "I like it fine in Archer County and only wish my life were simplified to the point where I could be here more," he wrote Grace David. "I manage about 10 days a month and have been very regular except in the most hectic months of the spring when the book business is best [in DC] . . . I use the ranch house as a place to sort of rest, read the mail, refuel my energies, and catch up on minor journalistic chores . . . I think I could live here successfully full time. I don't know if I'd get bored or not. I'm so over worked as it is I think it would take me awhile to get bored. Also since movie chores take me to Hollywood or NY frequently I think that would satisfy what little need I have to travel."

But then the old ambivalence kicked in. "I'm an urban person. I'm not a natural small-town person," he told another friend, Evan Smith. His sentiments made the Grace David letter sound like the work of an impostor. "Even if you discount the fact that I have to deal with my family and have to deal with being the focus of too much local attention, there's nothing to eat." There was the Onion Grill, with its garish poster of Buffalo Bill Cody on the wall, but that hardly fit the bill. "It's one hundred miles to a good restaurant. There's one in Fort Worth, the Chop House, right across the street from the Renaissance Worthington. [I'll] go down, have a good meal, spend the night at the hotel, and go back. That [gets] to seem weird . . . I don't eat a $100 meal every night, but I'd like the option . . . I really struggle with this problem. I don't cook. I can grill fish; I can boil an egg; I can do rudimentary cookery. But I'm very social. I like to go out at night. I like to sit in a nice room and look at beautiful women. I don't want to just sit on my back porch drinking scotch, and there isn't much more to do in Archer City."

In 1999, the *Los Angeles Times* reported that the desert Southwest had become so swollen with humanity, doctors had coined a new term, Valley Fever, for illnesses caused by pathogens in the dirt stirred by continuous activity: fatigue, fungus in the bones or brain. The cost to the state of Arizona had topped $20 million. "Everybody who lives here has a health problem," one citizen said.

McMurtry was no exception. In addition to the fatigue and muscle aches symptomatic of Valley Fever, accompanying massive migraines starting at four-thirty every afternoon, he suffered uncontrollable sneezing and coughing caused by an outbreak of cedar fever in Tucson. It turned out, he was terribly allergic to cedar trees and to juniper.

Nevertheless, he found Tucson "particularly pleasant" much of the time. Aside from the presence of his son (now "involved with his 3rd 43 year old lady," he wrote his friend Grace, "but this one, at least, is not a dope dealer"), one of its attractions was a little Italian restaurant he'd adopted. He ate there every night when he was in town. "I'm very much a creature of habit," he said. "I sit at the same table six nights a week. I'd eat there seven nights, but they're closed on Sunday."

Also in Tucson was his friend Leslie Silko. He lived with her off and on. They'd met in August 1981 at a writers' workshop sponsored by the English department at the University of Texas at El Paso. "We worked with the students for a week at a 'rustic' old dude ranch in the Davis Mountains near Marfa," Silko said. "Afterwards, Larry was driving to Tucson to visit James—so instead of flying back from El Paso, I caught a ride with Larry."

In addition to being fellow novelists (with a love of Hermes typewriters), they bonded over their need for sunshine, their mutual migraines, and their lifelong feeling of never quite belonging anywhere (Silko was of mixed Laguna-Cherokee-Chicana-Anglo background). Silko's headaches got so bad she went to a neurologist to see if there was a cure. There wasn't.

Born in Albuquerque in 1948—"the year of the supernova in the Mixed Spiral galaxy," she said, indicating her primal sense of connection with natural forces—she spent her first year as an infant in an old stucco Santa Fe Railroad depot where her grandparents lived, near the Laguna reservation by the San José River. Wrecked trains were her first play sites (derailments were frequent occurrences). On one occasion, her family collected enough canned hams from a wreck to feed the Laguna pueblo for five years. Though she cherished Laguna customs, especially its nonlinear storytelling tradition, her family did not join tribal rituals because of its mixed heritage.

As a child, she watched her father, Lee Marmon, the tribal treasurer, work with the pueblo's attorneys to assemble witnesses before the Indian Claims Commission. They argued for Native rights to six million acres of land near the Upper San José River. The experience gave Silko a taste for activism—and much later, a searing understanding of injustice when, after two decades, and following a judgment in the pueblo's favor, courts refused to grant the land to its rightful owners, offering, instead, a meager cash settlement of twenty-five cents per acre.

As a girl, she saw the elders who'd returned from World War II shoved off their reservations when the U.S. government launched an extensive drive to remove people from their homes and to politically terminate their tribes. The government wanted to mine uranium on the land.

Because she could speak English, she moved ahead of her peers in school. Eventually, she attended classes at Highland High School, off-reservation, and at the University of New Mexico. She turned to books, she said, because "there were no beloved grandparents or aunts to tell me stories."

She published her first short story in 1969, the same year Vine Deloria Jr.'s *Custer Died for Your Sins* appeared. *Custer* was the first modern "Indian Manifesto." Silko viewed her art as part of Deloria's vision, aimed at creating a world in which "U.S. history ceases to be fabricated for the glory of the white man."

Following two failed early marriages and the birth of two children, Robert and Cazimir, Silko astonished the literary world with her first novel, *Ceremony* (1977), about an aimless Laguna man reconnecting with his past, a book "ris[ing] near to greatness," McMurtry said. In 1991, she published *Almanac of the Dead*. McMurtry called it "a long swim across time and history," decrying "the theft, by the invading Europeans, of the native people's long-accumulated and reverently guarded wisdom about the natural world." Here finally was a woman telling the story of the West from a needed perspective unavailable to him.

Personally, he loved her playfulness and impish humor, her quiet, thoughtful stare as she listened to others. Her rich dark hair was like a bonnet, and she had a movie-star mole above her lip.

In 1978, when she moved from Albuquerque to Tucson, she settled into a house constructed in the twenties on West Camino del Cerro, near a sandy arroyo "crisscrossed with bird and animal tracks that make the trail humans have used for thousands of years," she said. From the arroyo she collected crystal quartz and turquoise pieces and placed them around her rooms. She tacked blankets inside the windows and arranged a series of large birdcages throughout the house where they could catch the outside light. She had a flock of macaws, among them an old bird named Sandino who'd lost a leg to an owl. She also kept a pet rattlesnake, a pit bull, and six mastiffs. Here McMurtry stayed, inhaling the feathery, furry scents, listening to Silko try to explain her perceptions of the material world: "If gravity is distributed in this Universe unevenly, then there are places here on Earth where the gravity is weaker or stronger, where even light may speed up or slow down," she said. "Parallel planes or worlds may be visible briefly at certain points . . . from time to time." McMurtry couldn't see them, but he firmly believed his girlfriend could.

He'd watch her stand in the wind yelling at developers, whose bull-dozers went roaring through the arroyos, or he'd sit patiently as she railed against stupid cowboys like Ronald Reagan. Men like him, she said, were hell-bent on smothering her people in smallpox blankets.

McMurtry loved her father, a skilled photographer, and he gave her boys money and advice. Briefly, between cruises across America's high-ways, he opened stores in Houston, Dallas, and Tucson—mostly as a way of easing Booked Up's clutter. But the stores also gave him opportunities to employ needy friends, such as Ray Isle, the son of his old teaching col-league, Walter, and Silko's son Robert, who was trying hard to steer clear of drugs. The stores didn't last long, but they served their generous purpose.

Few things in life pleased him more than embarking on a collaborative project with a lady friend. Just as he'd written screenplays with Cybill Shepherd and Diane Keaton, he did three drafts of a script called *Honkey-tonk Sue* with Silko. The story was based on a comic strip by Bob Boze Bell about a rollicking heartbreaker, the "Queen of Country Swing" ("See Sue take on Mr. Disco and make him look like a dork"). In the screenplay, the heroine whips bad boys in C&W bars and fights off evil dam developers in the Grand Canyon. Briefly, Columbia Studios expressed interest in the movie, and Goldie Hawn said she might like to star, but the project never came off. Besides, McMurtry said, Silko was a genius, and it wasn't really possible to collaborate successfully with a talent so grand.

On warm evening walks with the dogs, he discovered that Tucson was a city of murals: Tlaloc, the Aztec rain god, emerging over a water fountain with fierce orange eyes, gazing from the wall of the El Rio Neighborhood Center; President Benito Juárez of Mexico grinning from the side of the Hair Trend Salon on South 12th; the Mexican revolutionary Padre Miguel Hidalgo y Costilla watching strollers on Ajo Way from the back of a Circle K convenience store.

Amazed, he witnessed Silko adding to the colorful store of images. It all began because "I was having trouble," she explained. In moving from New Mexico, she had gone from "the high mountain plateau country into the Sonoran Desert," and she was leaving an unhappy marriage. It was a tough adjustment. At first, "I was in the hills alone a lot and started to feel very sad about how people treated snakes," she said. She related to the snakes. "I started to pay attention to them . . . how forgiving they are, how they really don't want to hide or harm things—you know, they only eat when they're hungry." One day, unable to concentrate on her writing, "I left my typewriter and all my notes and went outside" to the side of a building on Stone Avenue in downtown Tucson, and "painted a great big snake" on the wall, she said. "I . . . said to myself, 'I think I'll just paint for a while, and maybe it will let my mind settle so I can gather myself.'" The snake had "skulls on its stomach, and then it [had] this slogan in my broken Spanish, 'The people are cold, the people are hungry, the rich have stolen the land, the rich have stolen freedom.' The last line is, 'The people demand justice, otherwise revolution.'"

In short order, Silko's mural became an inspiration to the local Latinx and Native communities—until a T-shirt magnate bought the building and painted it out, replacing the snake with the University of Arizona's wildcat mascot, to lure college students into his shop.

It wasn't easy, but Silko encouraged McMurtry to venture beyond his favorite Italian restaurant to try some of the city's other cuisine. One night she took him to a place called Mr. Catfish, whose specialty was not hard to guess. It was an all-you-can-eat joint. Some mutual friends of theirs were sitting at a large table alongside a strikingly tall, long-haired blonde. McMurtry noticed her immediately. She had the high, wide cheeks of a painter's model—more like the subject of a Modigliani than a wall mural. Her name was Diana Lynn Ossana. She worked at a local law firm, writing briefs and trial prep.

McMurtry and Silko joined the table. Ossana couldn't believe it. Surely this wasn't the *real* Larry McMurtry? "I had just finished [reading] *Lonesome Dove*," she said. "It was intimidating. I couldn't imagine what I would have to say that would be interesting to this man."

"Meanwhile," McMurtry said, "I was in awe of this silent, beautiful woman sitting at the end of the table."

He had discovered a fine new wine.

On subsequent trips to Tucson, back and forth between LA, DC, and Archer City, he began to spend time with Ossana. "He would see me in Tucson three or four days a month, but we would talk five and six times a day on the phone," she said. "Larry [had] many women friends . . . and he talked to them on a regular basis on the phone. It was his life." In Tucson, he still stayed with Silko, but he was grateful for any excuse to escape the screeching macaws, especially when his migraines floored him. Ossana had been a serious reader and moviegoer all her life. McMurtry could talk to her. "Larry is a very private person, and when I met him, he had his life very compartmentalized," she said. "When he's in town being your friend, you feel like you're the only friend in his life."

He intrigued her but she was wary. Their friendship developed slowly, over a period of months. "Things evolved," Ossana said. "We just kept getting closer and closer."

"When I first met Larry, he was involved with about five or six different women," she recalled. "He was quite the ladies' man. I was always really puzzled. One day I said to him, 'So all of these women are your girlfriends?' And he said, 'Yes.' And I said, 'Well, do they know about one another?' He said, 'Nooo . . .'"

James seemed to be following his example. When he wasn't wooing women twice his age, he stayed busy writing songs.

McMurtry discussed his son openly and affectionately in long letters to another thrilling woman he'd met—Susan Sontag. "I've been feeling not knowing you as a lack in my life for some time," he wrote her in December 1988. In New York one evening, they'd been billed together with a number of other writers at a benefit reading for PEN (Poets, Essayists, Novelists), an organization announcing itself as "standing at the intersection of literature and human rights to protect free expression in the United States and worldwide." Sontag had long been an active member and was serving as PEN's president. "I thought it was of some interest that you and I were the only two readers who actually read from books, physical books, as opposed to photocopies," McMurtry said in his letter. "As a bookseller . . . I'm just always mildly heartened when I see someone who likes to hold a book."

After the reading, they ate caviar at Petrossian and got to know each other. Like him, Sontag had single-parented a son: an immediate bond.

"You certainly raised a gifted (and likable) man and I think I did too though until a few months ago I wouldn't bet I had even raised a survivor," he wrote her six months after the reading. "[T]he anxiety of wondering for the last ten years if James would make it, not necessarily to art just to more or less happy life, has had a kind of distancing effect on me . . . He has a girlfriend but I'm not sure they live together. James is a kind of solitary like me, if a friendly one, and I don't know if he and his girlfriend weekend together or exactly what they do. It's a charged area and frankly I can't figure out what I hope he does."

What James had done in Tucson was spend four years in school not really going to school. At one point, he took time off to play a bit part in the *Lonesome Dove* miniseries, as a young cowboy afraid to enter a whorehouse.

He did take some creative writing courses at the University of Arizona, but decided (not for the first time) that "writing prose seems to be . . . a chore."

He joined some other dropout players for shows in pubs and bars. His first paying gig was in the Riverside Lounge in Benson, a bend in the road founded as a railroad junction forty-five miles southeast of Tucson. The lounge was an annex to the Elks Club. He played backup guitar to "an old gal fiddler" he'd met who'd put together a band.

Finally, he stopped pretending to be a student and migrated to Talkeetna, Alaska, to play for not enough tips in a roadside diner. When his father told him the ranch house in Archer City needed repainting, James drifted back to Texas. At the old homestead, he said, "I looked at the bullet holes in the mailbox and the moon, and got [a] song right away." He was writing more and more these days, scribbling fragments of lyrics on scraps of paper and setting them to melodies he'd pick out on the guitar. In 1986, he'd worked the Kerrville Folk Festival, seventy miles west of San Antonio, and met the legendary songwriter Guy Clark. The meeting moved him to write still more, and the following year, he was one of six winners of the festival's young songwriters contest. Encouraged, he thought he'd try his luck in Nashville, pitching songs to established performers.

Some time back, his father had been recruited by the singer John Cougar Mellencamp to write a screenplay about a wayward country musician. The movie, eventually titled *Falling from Grace*, took nearly ten years to pull off, during which time Mellencamp stayed in touch with McMurtry.

He'd met James on a couple of occasions and always thought of him as a kid; when James gave his dad a four-song demo cassette and asked him to pass it to Mellencamp—maybe the man could help him in Nashville—the singer's first thought was "Oh God, what's this?" Three months passed. Reluctantly, one day, he finally slipped the tape into a tape deck. He only heard one and a half songs before calling McMurtry's DC apartment. He got the machine: "Larry, have your son call me." James just happened to be staying in the apartment and heard the message. He phoned the next day. "I like your songs. Do you have enough songs for a record?" Mellencamp asked. James had a lot of tunes, but he figured most of them weren't album-worthy. "Can you write enough by February?" Mellencamp pressed him. "I said, 'Yes, I can.' I had no idea if I could actually do it," James remembered. "It looked like the door was open and it might not ever open again. 'Yes, sir, I can do it!'"

Mellencamp offered to produce the record for Columbia. James went back to Texas and stared at the mailbox some more. He wrote a song called "Too Long in the Wasteland," about a man returning to a small town he's always hoped to escape. "I'm Not from Here" came next, about a drifter who's never known where he belonged. The songs' protagonists reflected his father's deepest currents—ripples running through James as well. The album, *Too Long in the Wasteland,* appeared in 1989. The cover featured James standing in a dirt road on Idiot Ridge, the wind whipping his long, tangled hair. Sales were slow, but the critics loved it. "[L]andscape . . . frames the personalities of [the songs'] people, making enemies out of neighbors, loners out of lovers, and pull-together friends out of strangers," Alanna Nash wrote in *Stereo Review.* "His songs [are] brown and bare and windswept," Karen Schoemer said in *The New York Times.* They come from the deep "tradition of men picking up guitars and singing about what's on their minds," a tradition "thicker than pavement across American cultural history."

Larry McMurtry was another big fan. "James's best songs are so good that I don't think my best novels really come up to them," he said. "One element of music is poetry, and poetry is a lot harder than fiction. A lyric is the hardest form. You have to concentrate and squeeze those words. I respect James a lot for having found his own art and done it so well," especially since "it's harder for a second-generation artist than a first-generation artist . . . It's hard to emerge from the shadow of a successful parent in any walk of life, and it seems to me particularly hard in the arts. Those who are wise, I think, generally don't stay in the same art."

One of James's songs, in particular, "Angeline," about a failed farmer and his dismal marriage, struck McMurtry as "a mini-novel. It startled me because it's so much like the mood of some of my books and yet it's in just a few verses. It's made me go back and look at my early books again, to see if the feel for small-town situations is pretty similar." He was twenty-seven years old when he wrote *The Last Picture Show*, just as James was when he wrote "Angeline."

James never agreed when reviewers said—inevitably—that he'd inherited his father's storytelling gene. But he did concede, "We may have gotten [our material] from the same source . . . my grandmother was a pretty good storyteller. Everybody told stories back then. That's what we did. We may have lost that in the era of TV."

A second album, *Candyland*, in 1992, grew his audience. "[M]ore people," he'd mutter, looking out past the spots from the edge of a stage in the back of a bar. *More people* was good. But: "I'm not really a people person."

He toured with Kinky Friedman and got a regular Wednesday night gig at Austin's Continental Club. "Why doesn't James like me?" Jon Dee Graham, another Continental musician, asked a friend one night. "He's said maybe nine words to me . . . and we play together every week!"

"Nine? Wow. He *really* likes you," the friend answered.

Like his father, James never inflated his success. "I used to think I was an artist," he'd announce to a rowdy bar crowd, watching golden pitchers float across the room. "Come to find out I'm a beer salesman." Then he'd remind the audience to tip the bartenders and waitresses.

And the albums kept coming, better each time, if more and more somber. "I tend to look at the dark cloud behind the silver lining," he admitted.

His central "theme is that tragedy and life are inseparable," McMurtry wrote Grace David proudly. "'Just life,' James says."

The Dairy Queen in Archer City was not the kind of place to get a hundred-dollar meal or to watch beautiful women, but it did serve sundaes so creamy thick you could float down the muddy Red River on them, locals swore, and it dispensed cups of Lime Dr Pepper big as mufflers. Whenever he was in town, McMurtry liked to go there midmorning, order a cheeseburger, watch the other diners pick their teeth, and sit and read at a corner table—before the day's temperature topped a hundred and the place became unbearable. As early as 1980, on trips back home, he claimed his spot in the DQ. He took to studying Walter Benjamin there, particularly his essay "The Storyteller," written the year McMurtry was born. Benjamin was a German Jewish philosopher who committed suicide on the French-Spanish border while trying to escape the Nazis. He was only forty-eight when he died. "The Storyteller" laid bare his conviction that oral narrative and practical memory had grown obsolete by the mid-twentieth century: "[T]he storyteller is a man who has counsel for his readers. But if today 'having counsel' is beginning to have an old-fashioned ring to it it is because the communicability of experience is decreasing," Benjamin wrote. Western life, dominated now by technology and specialized professions, had grown faster-paced, glutted with too much information; people had less in common with one another than in the past, he said; they no longer took the time to gather in communal settings, listening to and telling stories—nor did their stories offer enough shared experience to pass into broad knowledge. In Benjamin's view, the novel was a form of modern technology undermining oral narrative: "The birthplace of the novel is the solitary individual, who is . . . himself uncounselled, and cannot counsel others." And now—in McMurtry's time—the novel was also dying, in the opinion of many writers and critics, watching the encroachment of the screen in all corners of life.

McMurtry was well aware that Benjamin was in a position to bemoan the loss of culture because he'd *known* a culture to begin with: the richness of Europe and Europe's long history. One could scrabble for a local past and argue that "the first [American] cowboys were Victorians," McMurtry mused. One could stress that the "values of the old queen traveled West, along with many of her subjects; several of the largest ranches in the West were established with English money." But these facts still did not imbue West Texas with history or culture on a par with the objects of Benjamin's grief. So "[m]y question to Walter Benjamin would be, what kind of stories arise in a place where nothing has ever happened except, of course, the vagaries and vicissitudes of individual life?" McMurtry wrote. "It was these vagaries and vicissitudes, individual in texture yet common to humanity, that usually got discussed on the porch after supper, a dribble of family history usually involving accidents, injuries, bad choices, good choices, mistakes made with horses, misjudgments of neighbors, and the like."

The day he first picked up "The Storyteller" in the Dairy Queen (it was 116 degrees) was the same day Archer City held a historical pageant in the rodeo arena, celebrating the county's last few decades. McMurtry went despite the sweltering heat because as a novelist, he figured the "county's historical materials were *my* materials": "I wanted to know (*a*) what had happened in the county that was worth remembering, and (*b*) . . . did anyone still living remember it? The answers . . . were (*a*) nothing, and (*b*) no one . . ."

Unless the "vagaries and vicissitudes of individual life"—the stuff of novels—counted.

The novelist and the orator *did* share one bond: "Death is the sanctity . . . of everything the storyteller can tell," Benjamin wrote. "He has borrowed his authority from death."

"[S]o it certainly seemed in Archer County, because all anyone could remember with any precision was the local deaths," McMurtry said. "Three boys were killed in a car wreck in 1954. A cowboy drowned in the Little Wichita River in 1956. A roughneck was blown off an oil rig in 1958; and so on. Sudden death, particularly death on the highway—as much a part of that culture as football—lodged in people's memories, whereas about almost everything else they were vague."

He'd begun circling back to Archer City in the 1980s and early 1990s just in time to participate in the town's deepest life by joining its rituals of death. His elders, his parents' generation, were leaving the earth one by one. One hot summer day, he was asked to serve as an honorary pallbearer at the funeral of Margaret Ellen Slack, local painter and poet, the woman he'd considered his first mentor. At the ceremony, in the First United Methodist Church, he read aloud one of her poems to commemorate the encouragement she'd given him when he was little. If anyone in town ever came close to understanding him, it was Margaret Slack. Now she was gone.

In the church, he greeted her daughter, his old friend Celie. She'd traveled far since leaving Archer City. She'd survived an unhappy marriage but never quite gotten her footing, despite her work in academia and publishing. In life and in work, she had been almost as restless as McMurtry, but without his aesthetic focus. They had been two outliers in a bleak, bookless town. Like all lonely children, they had always wanted to come home, but their home had never *served* as a home. (In 1997—with McMurtry's blessing—she would write a memoir entitled *Whatever Happened to Jacy Farrow?*, accepting her role as the model for Jacy.)

She worried about her father now that her mother was gone, and wondered if she should return to Archer City.

"What I think is that you shouldn't be making those kinds of decisions in the emotional state you're in," McMurtry told her. "And furthermore, I want to tell you that if you lived here, you would go crazy within two weeks because there is nothing around here to eat."

She laughed, but he meant it.

The following day, after Celie had flown away again, he went back to Dairy Queen for a cheeseburger. He'd taken to wearing caftans and very large polo shirts to hide his growing girth. His regular musings on "The Storyteller" would eventually result in a book, *Walter Benjamin at the Dairy Queen* (1999), one of several small volumes of nonfiction he would publish in the last thirty years of his career. With the exception of three thin memoirs (*Books, Literary Life,* and *Hollywood*) they would be among his finest achievements, pulsing with the flexible, intelligent, and energetic voice Dave Hickey had praised in the essays collected in *In a Narrow Grave. Film Flam* (1987) brought together various pieces he had written for *American Film* magazine; *Sacagawea's Nickname* (2001) was a compendium of his pieces on the American West written for *The New York Review of Books.* He had become one of the *Review*'s house intellectuals, along with Joan Didion, Joyce Carol Oates, Deborah Eisenberg, Garry Wills, and others. In its pages, he examined an astonishing variety of topics: music, movies, politics, bookselling, history, travel, women. In 1999, he published a short biography of Crazy Horse. He wrote a history of massacres in the American West—*Oh What a Slaughter* (2005)—and a meditation on "the Beginnings of Superstardom in America" in *The Colonel and Little Missie,* about Buffalo Bill and Annie Oakley's Wild West Shows (2005). He wrote a book called *Roads: Driving America's Great Highways* (2000) and a travelogue entitled *Paradise* (2001). His energy was matched only by his roaming curiosity.

And always he'd retreat to Archer City. While sitting in the Dairy Queen, sipping his Lime Dr Pepper, not only did he reread Walter Benjamin several times; he also jotted notes about the town's changes during the oil boom—all the new Jacuzzis and exercise gyms, the municipal tennis courts. The "west edge of town was so flat and ugly that a tennis net could legitimately count as an addition to the skyline," he wrote. Then he noted how the town had changed again because of the bust—those same sterile gyms and tennis courts sat empty now, the exercise craze having faded with the spirit of entrepreneurship.

He began to consider more seriously his *Duane Gets Rich* idea, revisiting the town of Thalia in a merciless satiric novel ("wicked," he told Grace David). It would focus—as all novels must, he thought—on the "vagaries and vicissitudes of individual life," which some writers, like Walter Benjamin, thought too shallow for stories. McMurtry's experiences in Archer City over a lifetime had taught him that vicissitudes were all most people ever had.

Early in *Texasville,* the novel he wound up writing (his first since winning the Pulitzer Prize), the narrator says of Duane Moore, "He spent hours replaying old conversations in his head, or reliving past events. If they had been important conversations or crucial events, the habit might have been understandable, but they weren't. They were just ordinary conversations . . ."

Life as it was lived.

In *Texasville,* a deflationary, antiheroic story after the epic *Lonesome Dove* (*this is what the pioneers fought for?*), the teenagers from *The Last Picture Show* are now in their late forties, early fifties. Duane has gotten rich drilling oil wells, though he is worried about losing money in the bust. Estranged from his children, he doesn't even try to give them fatherly advice, the way

Homer Bannon and Sam the Lion would have done. Lester Marlow, who once took Jacy skinny-dipping in Wichita Falls, is now the bank president, in danger of going to prison on fraud charges. Sonny runs the Quick-Sack store and owns several buildings downtown; he is slowly losing his mental capacities and blames the town for making him crazy. He sits in the burned-out movie theater imagining he is watching a picture show. He seems never to have recovered from the traumas of losing Jacy, losing his eye in the fight with Duane, and getting shot in the elbow by Coach Popper (after the coach discovered Sonny's affair with his wife). Ruth, working now as Duane's secretary, believes Sonny is just waiting to die. Jacy returns to Thalia after her son is killed in an accident on an Italian movie set. For years, Jacy has pursued a mediocre career as a B movie actress in a series of forgettable Italian films. Her return to Texas signals a desire to reconnect with her past, but as in all of McMurtry's work, the past can offer no solace for it has been mythologized and commodified. The events in *Texasville* (such as they are) take place in 1986, on the eve of the 150th anniversary of Texas independence. The town plans a centennial festival to celebrate the county's history; the festival's centerpiece will be a small-scale replica of the first settlement.

A similar cheap replica already exists in Duane's backyard: a doghouse in the shape of a pioneer log cabin. Indifferent to his material riches, bored with his marriage to a woman who expresses her deepest feelings through T-shirt slogans, Duane sits in his hot tub shooting up the doghouse with a .44 Magnum—about as active as he ever gets.

Despite its length, the novel is itself a small-scale replica of its predecessor. McMurtry seemed determined to underscore the fact that nostalgia (for the past, for beloved works of art, for fictional characters fondly remembered) is doomed to end in disappointment. Readers, and moviegoers, would always remember Jacy as the nubile girl jumping naked into a pool. In *Texasville*, she first reappears as a middle-aged woman swimming in a lake, her tired beauty marred by ugly marks left on her face by a pair of goggles.

In *The Last Picture Show*, McMurtry's satire had illuminated social hypocrisies: the homophobia of those who drove the high school English teacher from his job, mistaking his effeminate gestures; the high-mindedness of those who tormented the preacher's son in his sexual confusion (he kidnaps a little girl but does not touch her). In the new novel, the English teacher runs a grocery store in Thalia and spends his evenings cruising bars, "hoping to meet an equally lonely recruit from the nearby air base." The preacher's son has become a spokesperson for the "pedophilic community" and edits a newspaper called *Child's Play.* In negating the whole point of his earlier commentary (as if satirizing his own novel), McMurtry appeared to deny literature's power to elucidate anything: reading novels is just one more nostalgic exercise destined for failure.

Though his prose is energetic and humorous, an air of resignation hangs over the entire enterprise, as in John Steinbeck's sour 1961 novel about American corruption, *The Winter of Our Discontent.* McMurtry updated Steinbeck for the Reagan years. Nothing much happens in *Texasville* (six chapters are devoted to a meaningless discussion in a Dairy Queen). The characters don't evolve. They are stuck in the glut of useless goods that America has become. People are barely described; apparently, McMurtry assumed readers would imagine the actors' faces from the Bogdanovich film. The novel is dedicated to Cybill Shepherd. In a review of the book, Louise Erdrich noted that "'Texasville' often reads like a movie script, all dialogue and situation. The individual scenes are sharp, spare, full of longhorn humor and color, but motivation is sketchy, rarely described, clued by action rather than reflection."

In interviews, McMurtry frequently mentioned that whenever he wrote a novel now, he paused to consider which young bankable actors could play his characters in a movie, and if he could think of none, he would change his characters to fit Hollywood's realities. Such comments sounded like further attempts to disabuse his readers from clinging to nostalgic notions of the Novel as High Art.

Famously, Graham Greene split his fictions between "novels" and "entertainments." "The entertainments . . . are distinct from the novels because as the name implies they do not carry a message," he told *The Paris Review.*

Following *Texasville,* McMurtry would write a series of prequels and sequels to his earlier books, alternating between contemporary stories and historical narratives. The books did not divide as easily as Greene's into novels and entertainments; the more serious efforts always contained farcical humor, and the lighter ones always had a grim undertow. Time did not break easily between present and past; McMurtry's work had become one long river of narrative in which characters—contemporary and historic—nudged one another, directly and indirectly, like pebbles and splinters of wood caught in currents they couldn't control, and none of which, McMurtry seemed to suggest, was to be taken all that seriously.

After all these years, he still felt he had never been taken seriously by his literary peers, either in Texas or New York. "[I]n the main, I attract . . . no reviews," he complained. "After ten books I got a few paragraphs in *Newsweek,* and *The New York Times.*" Astonishingly (to him), the "lack of interest in my books continues to this day . . . Should I be bitter about the literary establishment's long disinterest in me? I shouldn't, and mostly I'm not, though I do admit to the occasional moment of irritation. Any writer with much self-respect would feel a twinge of annoyance at the inequalities of the critical marketplace." Anyway, he said, "In the long run we'll all be dead."

The irony was, McMurtry was his own harshest critic: "Time will sort us out, determine who was really good from who was mediocre. This does not mean that I think I'm very likely to make the high-end cut," he said. "Little of my work in fiction is pedestrian, but, on the other hand, none of it is really great."

It was okay for *him* to denounce his work, but no one else had the right to be dismissive.

At the Texas Institute of Letters' fiftieth-anniversary party at the Adolphus Hotel in Dallas in 1986, McMurtry won the TIL Award for Best Book of Fiction for *Lonesome Dove.* On that same occasion, Donald Barthelme was honored for Continuing Excellence in Texas Letters. Barthelme proposed designing a T-shirt for Texas writers to wear, proclaiming the difficulties of literary life on the frontier: across the chest, the T-shirt would read "NOT TOO BAD," and on the back it would say, "NOT GOOD ENOUGH." McMurtry wholeheartedly agreed. He almost seemed embarrassed to receive the award that night (as if he could hear his father's voice saying writing wasn't really *work*), while conveying the impression that of course he deserved it. "What always impressed me about Larry was that odd combination of graciousness and frostiness," said Stephen

Harrigan, a young Texas novelist to whom McMurtry had been warmly encouraging.

A few months after the award ceremony, the TIL held another event, this one in San Antonio's Gunter Hotel, near the Alamo. The board asked McMurtry to deliver the keynote address. "It was one of the most deflating speeches I've ever heard," Harrigan told me. "Basically he said, 'I'm so tired of *Lonesome Dove* and so tired of people who keep telling me how much they love it.' He was clearly done with it. Later a friend of mine—a writer and herpetologist named Alan Tennant—went up to Larry because he wanted to talk to him about the water moccasin scene in *Lonesome Dove*." (At one point in the novel, the cattle stir up a nest of water moccasins in a river; the snakes swarm and kill a young cowboy.) "I knew what Alan was going to say—that water moccasins don't swarm and attack like that. Alan naively thought that Larry would be grateful for this friendly bit of criticism, but what he got instead was a stone-cold stare." (In fact, it was true that moccasins don't gather in a nest. They are ovoviviparous, the mother carrying the eggs within her, rarely more than five at a time. Once an infant breaks from its sac, it slips off on its own.)

McMurtry felt he was a prophet ignored in his own land, and he believed he fared no better in New York. But Barbara Epstein at *The New York Review of Books* had taken him in; after the success of *Lonesome Dove*, PEN—encouraged by his new friend Susan Sontag, among others—invited him to become its new president. Until then, he said, "I might as well have been living on Uranus, as far as PEN was concerned. I had . . . won a Pulitzer Prize, but it made no difference . . . I didn't have a single friend in the New York literary world." Of course, he hadn't tried very hard to make friends in New York . . . and besides, his complaints about PEN weren't entirely true. In the wake of glasnost, Karen Kennerly, the executive director of PEN American Center, had asked him to join a reading at the Folger Library in honor of Joseph Brodsky and other Russian writers. He toured a few of the Russians through the crowded aisles of Booked Up. Grateful to him and pleased with his performance at the Folger, Kennerly asked him to join a reading at the United Nations—the event at which he and Sontag were the only two book-bearing writers.

Soon thereafter, George Braziller, a distinguished New York publisher, asked McMurtry if he would serve a two-year term as PEN's president. He would be the first non–New Yorker to hold the post since Booth Tarkington, in PEN's earliest days. It was true that Braziller approached McMurtry about the position because "crowds of famous writers were not rushing down to Prince Street [PEN's headquarters] to offer up their freedoms in order to take what might be considered a thankless job," McMurtry said. But it was also true that he accepted not out of any great commitment to the organization, but because it gave him an excuse to spend more time getting to know New York City—from a suite in the Pierre Hotel.

Kennerly visited him in DC to brief him on the "labyrinth of projects and committees" under PEN's umbrella, and he had lunch with Donald Barthelme in New York to discuss the organization. Barthelme had once been an ardent PEN supporter, active in its free speech campaigns, but he was sick now with the throat cancer that would kill him in 1989, and his energy and interest in life were flagging. The men, who had barely spoken before, except glancingly at TIL meetings, spent a pleasant afternoon together. In "Ever a Bridegroom," McMurtry had questioned whether Barthelme considered himself a Texan, since he wrote so little about the place—at least directly. Talking with him, McMurtry learned that Barthelme had strong, affectionate ties to Houston; he was sorry he had ever doubted the man's Lone Star credentials. The two of them laughed together at the silliness of Texas's literary wars. Critic Don Graham had recently claimed that novelists who moved to Texas from elsewhere to write about the state were merely poseurs, "fern-bar writers," he called them. "Did he mean faggot homosexual queer pansy fairies?" Barthelme quipped. "And if so, why didn't he say so?" McMurtry chuckled and shook his head.

As president of PEN American Center, McMurtry defended the organization's prison program, an initiative in which writers educated inmates and encouraged them to write their life stories. After Norman Mailer had lobbied for a prisoner, Jack Henry Abbott, to be paroled, and Abbott went out and killed a man, PEN came under public fire for coddling hardened criminals. In 1989, several members of the executive board called for a vote to dissolve the initiative. "You can kill this program," McMurtry announced in one of his first meetings as president, "but you can't do it on my watch." The vote was canceled.

Most of his public energy as president was spent defending Salman Rushdie after the publication, first in Britain in September 1988, and then in the United States in late February 1989, of *The Satanic Verses.* Iran's spiritual leader, the Ayatollah Khomeini, declared the novel blasphemous and issued a fatwa—a death threat—against Rushdie. Anyone promoting the novel courted danger. America's largest bookstore chains—B. Dalton, Barnes & Noble—pulled the book from their shelves. PEN decried their cowardice. On February 28, 1989, Cody's Books in Berkeley was pipe-bombed for carrying the book. No one was hurt in the blast, but the Rushdie affair had become serious business. Selling books was now a life-and-death matter.

The employees at Cody's voted to continue stocking the novel. Meanwhile, Rushdie went into hiding. (In 2022, believing the threat was over, he was almost stabbed to death onstage in Chautauqua, New York.) McMurtry wrote letters, delivered speeches, and gave readings in support of courageous independent booksellers. On June 2, 1990, he flew to London to speak on "Censorship and the Individual Talent" at a Writers' Day event. "The possibility of giving offense is intrinsic to the task we undertake," he said. He told the story of a journalist who'd run afoul of the Baptist Church in Waco, Texas, in the 1890s. The incident ended in a shootout between the journalist and a Bible thumper in which the men killed each other. Censorship always begins as a local affair, McMurtry insisted: "[L]ocal school-boards may have done more practical censorship than any other group."

Though "the censor may always be with us, he will eventually lose," he concluded. "Censors win many skirmishes but, in the long run, language well-used always wins its war. Note I say language, not writers—such victory as writers enjoy is often apt to arrive unnoticed while the writer's attention is entirely absorbed by . . . images or metaphors." In the end, "Franco went where Lorca is, Stalin soon joined Mandelstam. The words of the writers delight and touch us still, and will touch and delight our children and their children. No censor can claim as much."

Behind the scenes at PEN, McMurtry wasted much time trying to corral his "brattish" board. The members were as temperamental and sulky as his sister Sue back in Archer City, who'd quit the Blue Pig in a snit with another employee there. The board reminded him of his local carpenters, who argued pettily over the renovations at the old Taylor house.

PEN members quarreled over fundraising efforts and political correctness. Often McMurtry wished to throttle his holier-than-thou comrades.

He had to compose dreary reports on PEN's International Congressional meetings. In June 1990, after one such meeting, he wrote dismissively: "The Congress report is rapidly taking on the aspects of an exhausted genre . . . Everyone who could possibly be elected, appointed, approved, promoted, or reaffirmed was elected, appointed, approved, promoted, or reaffirmed."

His work on behalf of the organization was rapidly becoming "unap-petizing," he complained to Sontag. "PEN flops around like a dying fish"; "[S]eeing what they have to deal with, who will want to be president next?"

His friendship with her was the best benefit of his New York business. At dinner, at Petrossian, "Susan drank pepper vodka and ate a lot of fish eggs," he said. "Between us we may have hastened the demise of the stur-geon in various seas, though of course the Russian mob helped."

To Sontag, he referred to himself as "the West Texas Gogol."

In lengthy letters, he continued to compare child-rearing notes with her. James had met a talented mosaicist and tile-maker from Austin named Elena Eidelberg, and he planned to marry her in August 1989. McMurtry described the wedding arrangements to Sontag. He admitted how much he dreaded having to drive with his mother from Archer City to Austin. Hazel, he said, was "fearful of *all* forms of transport and indeed of life itself." Sure enough, "my mother went into her usual pre-trip fit," McMurtry informed Sontag on August 18. "She claims to have had three heart attacks yesterday afternoon, which means she got real upset three times . . . So she managed in a few short hours, during which she was demanding ambulances and attention, to alienate both my sisters and my brother to the point where they refuse to take her to the wedding." They all left for Austin early, Hazel screaming after them that they were leaving her to die alone.

In the end, McMurtry was glad she hadn't come: she "would have dropped dead at the sight of [James], he was unrepentant anti-bourgeois down to not shaving or even tucking his shirt tail in, though he did take off his hat for the ceremony itself." The bride, of "Balkan-Andean-Jewish-Gypsy-Romanian-Peruvian" descent, wore a simple white cotton dress and flowers in her thick dark hair. A female justice of the peace pronounced them husband and wife in front of a small crowd in Austin's Campground Ranch Park. "[I]t was wrenching," McMurtry reported. "[N]o one was ever more glad to see a child grow grown than myself, but there was still surprising sadness in it . . . The bride's sad little Bessarabian father couldn't stop trembling or crying. Her jolly little Peruvian mom didn't bat an eye . . . James's mother . . . was horrified by James's post-scruffiness . . . although she had just come from running a marathon (her obsession of the last ten years) and looked quite a bit older than her own mother. I was most annoyed at my siblings, who had waited like sheep at the motel for me to lead [them] to this not-obscure site."

He concluded: "I suppose I felt an element of removal yesterday, James removing himself from me. He got a rave [for his music] in the Times this morning, an astonishing tribute, and part of my sense yesterday was that he's unaware of just how much he's already separated himself from his old buddies and school chums, too many of whom already look at him from depths of self-disappointment. He's risen clear of failure and will now get to learn about the loneliness of success."

The "loneliness of success" was a favorite topic of Sontag's; much of her correspondence with McMurtry concerned her legacy. She pressed him to bring his book-dealing expertise to the matter of her papers, her letters and manuscripts. She wanted to sell them to the best possible archive and demanded a good price for them. McMurtry negotiated on her behalf with several institutions, including the Harry Ransom Center at the University of Texas in Austin. At one point, he estimated her papers to be worth around $300,000. (Ultimately, she sold them to UCLA for approximately $1.1 million, funds obtained from an anonymous donor.)

In contrast to her businesslike letters to McMurtry, his letters to her describe how much he valued her friendship, how much he would love for her to visit him in Washington or Texas. ("You [could] stay in the big room on the third floor [above Booked Up], the one with the videos in it. They're a mixed lot. I have migraines most nights and combat them with cheap European *policier* movies; I have good films too but am rarely in the mood for Bergman or Godard while having a migraine.")

He tried enticing her to accompany him on visits to intriguing collectors he knew, such as Larry Mooney, "the greatest living morbidity collector." He told Sontag he had once taken Diane Keaton to Mooney's place in Alexandria, just outside DC. Keaton "has fairly unusual tastes," he said, "and was at the time photographing stuffed animals of which Larry has many, most of them stuffed freak animals, [like] two-headed squirrels . . .

He has or did have a great number of penitiente figures, a collection focused on stigmata, as well as many human fragments such as the pickled leg of a gangster. Larry Mooney is as far as I care to go in the morbidity direction."

He did coax Sontag to Archer City on two occasions, promising Texas color. He ordered chicken gizzards for her at a Wichita Falls honky-tonk called the Bar L (she loved them), and he took her to a dusty stock car race on the outskirts of Archer City, to which she responded only, "Oh, wow!"

"I miss you very much and think of you daily, often, a lot," he wrote her once.

He had always longed to have New York literary friends; unfortunately, Sontag was too self-absorbed to be a decent long-term pal. She once snapped at McMurtry, "Don't ever do that again," without explaining what he had done to upset her. On another occasion, when he was delayed on a flight to New York from Washington, she "decimated" heaps of fish eggs at Petrossian, grew tired of waiting for him, and left, instructing the maître d' that Mr. McMurtry would soon arrive to take care of the damages. It seemed that, in New York, what it meant to have a literary buddy was getting stiffed on pricy bills.

A s with all his women friends, he used Sontag as a confidante. "As a novelist, I've reached the age of self-parody," he told her. "I can't seem to write a sentence, create a character, or think a thought that doesn't seem like a parody of an earlier sentence, character, or thought. It's an eerie sensation and not comfortable . . . I feel I ought to have already written the Last Novel and am wondering what the process is for choking this fictionalizing off."

Yet he had started a new book. He wrote Sontag: "I'm proceeding, but with gloom—it's evident to me that I'm competing with myself now, and losing. I'll never be able to do the end-of-the-west story with the authority that I brought to it in *Lonesome Dove,* the last few hundred pages particularly. Sometimes I think I really finished my work with *Texasville* and what's left is just making a living, more or less respectably. This is novel fourteen— what I feel is how hard it is to really escape the novelistic archetypes . . . the Don and Sancho . . . And book after book hinges on confused, deflected, denied, or invented parenthood. On the other hand, there's not much that's more interesting to try." (He didn't add that many of his novels included dead or unacknowledged children—emotionally, the position *he'd* occupied in his family by refusing to follow his father's path.)

In February 1990, he told his friend, "I'm smoking on through this poignant story impelled by my normal early-part-of-the-year panic about income tax. At least half of my fiction has been written in the first three months of the year thanks to this panic." He said he no longer bothered sending his new novels to pals; he knew they were tired of trying to keep up with him. "I live mostly with a sense of my own ignorance and am always surprised to discover that I once knew something."

After *Texasville,* he composed, in quick succession, two historical westerns, *Anything for Billy* (1988) and *Buffalo Girls* (1990), hoping to accomplish what he hadn't managed with *Lonesome Dove,* the destruction of Western Romance. In *Anything for Billy,* a dime novelist named Ben Sippy creates heroic narratives around a failed cowboy, a Billy the Kid–like character. Sentimentally, and with a dash of cynicism, Sippy inflates the myth of the West; his initials, B.S., reflect McMurtry's attitude toward the western fiction that made his name.

Buffalo Girls tells the story of Buffalo Bill Cody's western pageant, the literal commodification of cowboying, but its real interest lies in its variety of narrative perspectives, interrogating the uses of storytelling, exposing the many ways facts become obscured by legend and myth. The novel shifts among omniscient third-person sections, epistolary segments, featuring Calamity Jane's letters to an invented daughter, and a series of free indirect passages conveying the interior point of view of a long-suffering Native man, No Ears. The various angles of vision clash, making it impossible to determine western realities. No Ears suspects "white people simply had no serious interest in truth."

Ultimately, the novel's power is blunted by McMurtry's indeterminate tone: are we meant to take these characters seriously or to see them as parodies of historical figures?

McMurtry recognized that his attempts to "subvert the western myth with irony and parody" got "no better results" in *Anything for Billy* and *Buffalo Girls* than they did in *Lonesome Dove*: "Readers don't want to know and can't be made to see how difficult and destructive life in the Old West really was. Lies about the West are more important to them than truths."

During this period, while running PEN, he also published a contemporary novel, *Some Can Whistle* (1989). He inscribed a copy of the book to Sontag; he said it featured his character Danny Deck "debating with himself about novel-writing and parenthood." Deck is now a wealthy middle-aged overweight television writer suffering from terrible migraines and living in retreat from the world near Thalia. (The novel connects many of McMurtry's disparate narratives—Deck, whose true loves were Emma Horton and Jill Peel, knows Jack McGriff, Jacy Farrow, and Duane Moore.) "I was a loner and a loser who had pretty much failed at everything: at the novel, at screenwriting, at marriage, and over and over again, at romance. I had never enjoyed one day of normal domestic life, and I knew perfectly well I probably never would," Deck says of himself before receiving a telephone call, out of the blue, from a grown daughter he has never met. *Some Can Whistle* traces his path to reacquaintance with the girl, the shock of his plunge into raucous family life, and his sudden return to loneliness when his daughter is taken from him by her former lover, a Billy the Kid–like killer.

The novel is most effective, even touching, in lyrical passages describing Deck's abiding love for Houston, and in a lengthy, elegiac coda extolling the "brainy, sexual whistle of youth and health, tunes that those who once could whistle . . . lose [with age] but never forget." Still, the book's violent climax, poorly prepared for and sketchily engineered, erases any chance of emotional satisfaction. Its strange awkwardness recalls Mark Twain's polemic against Fenimore Cooper's literary offenses. Inexplicably, in *Some Can Whistle,* an appealing character is slaughtered by a stray bullet from the author.

On October 8, 1990, McMurtry wrote Sontag that he had just seen Peter Bogdanovich's film adaptation of *Texasville.* Against great odds, Bogdanovich had managed to reunite the cast and most of the crew of *The Last Picture Show,* including Polly Platt (though she did not directly work on the film). He took them to Archer City for the shoot.

Lightning did not strike twice. McMurtry disliked the film. (So did most critics and moviegoers—it earned only $2 million on an $18 million budget.) "[T]here's a really good movie in it but it was lost in the editing," McMurtry told Sontag. "[Bogdanovich] as usual destroyed his own film . . . Now I feel guilt for not working on the stupid movie . . . He can never resist American trivia but he can sure resist American emotion." (As Mc-Murtry had done in his novel.) "I felt very sad, seeing the movie, very sad."

At the time, he had fallen out with Cybill Shepherd over her reck-less marriages, but it was her performance in the film that most touched him. "I must say I felt a little guilty about her," he told Sontag. "I'm now puzzled as to why I broke with her when I did, since she wasn't just then behaving any worse than she has behaved for the whole twenty years I've been her friend. I'm forced to consider that probably her absolute selfish-ness still wasn't quite enough reason to stop loving her, if I have."

In mid-October 1989, when McMurtry's sister, Sue, watched the film crew roll into town, she recalled, "When Larry said he was writing a sequel to *The Last Picture Show*, he kinda grinned, and I said, 'Oh my God, I don't think we can stand another one!'" The locals' reaction to Hollywood was "a lot different this time," she said. "The area needs money. Also, a lot more people are intrigued this time with the fame that comes with it. Suddenly I have a lot of friends and a lot of relatives I didn't know I had." They were all hoping she'd get them parts as extras in the movie.

In 1971, Shepherd and Jeff Bridges received salaries in the range of $5,000 to $50,000. This time around, Shepherd's contract specified $1.5 million; Bridges earned a little more. Nineteen years earlier, they had stayed in a Ramada Inn and a Days Inn motel in Wichita Falls; now, Shepherd rented a private house and Bridges had taken over an entire suite at the Sheraton. "[T]here was no attention focused on the filming of the first pic-ture," Bogdanovich reflected. "Our emotions were raw, but we were allowed privacy. On this picture, everyone is well-known, including me, who has become somewhat notorious."

He said the most difficult thing about returning to Archer City was "confronting everything that has happened in my own life. I expect . . . my own ghost to walk around the corner and say, 'Hey, things have changed since you were thirty-one, haven't they, bub?'"

"[A]ll of a sudden [it's] twenty years ago," Bridges said, amazed. Shep-herd just buried her face in her hands when she saw the town again.

"[I]t's rare in one's career to be given the opportunity to go back in time and recapture something that's important," Bogdanovich said quietly. "And to approach it from another angle, to find a new way of looking at the same thing."

But the picture almost never got made. The major studios turned it down, citing the book's lack of narrative threads. Bogdanovich was forced to piece together independent financing from Cine-Source and an outfit named Nelson Entertainment. His reputation had suffered in Hollywood after several screen misfires and the bad publicity surrounding his affairs with Shepherd and Dorothy Stratten. In 1985 he had declared bankruptcy. He said he felt a strong kinship with the messy people in *Texasville*.

Shepherd, too, was known now as troublesome to work with, often clashing with her costars. She admitted, along with Bogdanovich, that she had many regrets about her life since *The Last Picture Show*.

Meanwhile, Polly Platt's career had soared: she'd worked on the production design of Barbra Streisand's *A Star Is Born*, co-produced Louis Malle's *Pretty Baby*, received the Oscar nomination for *Terms of Endearment*, and produced two other successful movies, *Say Anything* and *War of the Roses*. Still, she struggled with alcohol; she had never moved past her painful break with Bogdanovich and the death of Big Tony.

At McMurtry's suggestion, she agreed to meet with Shepherd and the women tried to be friends.

In Archer City, in the 105-degree heat, there was "some tension" on the set, Bogdanovich admitted, "but there was also great love. We were sort of like the people in the movie—a few bumps here and there, but we all got along and everyone survived."

The town's initial friendliness toward the film crew dissipated as the production ground on, the humidity increased, and daily temperatures spiked. On the day hundreds of people lined up for cattle calls, hoping to be hired as extras, a pair of thieves took advantage of the chaos to bind and gag two post office clerks. They stole forty dollars, a stack of money orders, and some stamps.

"I don't give a shit about movie stars," a local roughneck complained one day, standing in the wind on a street corner near the old Fina station. "We live on a road a block away—they came through the town in their big semi trucks, rattle our whole house, knock shit off the walls, and do they give a fuck? No. *Last Picture Show* was fine . . . they used my granny's house [for that one]. Cybill Shepherd and them—they were nothin' then. But now they're a big star and you can't get within ten feet of 'em."

One afternoon Polly Platt noticed McMurtry standing near the edge of the set as the crew arranged a short scene at the Dairy Queen. As always, the sight of him comforted her. She approached him. He smiled slyly. "What are *you* doing here?" he asked.

"Healing old wounds," she said.

"Nice trick if you can do it," he replied.

Ceil Cleveland (née Slack) also stood on the movie's sidelines. She watched Shepherd portray her. Beside her was Bobby Stubbs, on whom (he believed) the character Sonny was based. "As we talked, it was sometimes hard to separate ourselves from the lives depicted on celluloid," Cleveland said. For several days, they waited together on the film's perimeter. A short time later, while Cleveland was still grieving for her mother, Stubbs died of a heart attack.

One night, during the filming, Cleveland sat with Stubbs in the back seat of his car. He placed a hand on her cheek and gave her a gentle kiss. "I always dreamed of doing that," he told her. "I thought you'd never let me."

"He smelled of leather and tobacco—Texas-men smells I'd almost forgotten," Cleveland said. "An act of completion. For one moment, forty years' worth of simple affection was expressed in a simple way. It had never happened before; it would not happen again. But it was perfect for this moment: two fifty-something longtime friends acknowledging an old possibility that would never be fulfilled."

Stubbs slipped off the tiny silver pin, shaped like a saddle, holding his bolo tie in place. He set it in her palm. "For the first girl I ever loved," he said.

22

McMurtry was so relieved when his term as PEN president ended, he thought he might never travel east again—though, of course, this was only what he told himself in moments of profound weariness. He still had the bookstore in DC to look in on. But he feared he was "getting too delicate for life in the crowded East," he wrote Susan Sontag. "[C]rowds bug me, noise bugs me. I'm developing Proustian tics." He'd become "addicted to peace and my space here now" in—of all places—goddamn Archer City! Ceil's sister, Mary Slack Webb, cooked for him, leaving chicken and pies on the porch of the old Taylor house.

And down the road in Austin, he had a new grandson, Curtis Eduardo McMurtry (Eduardo was Elena's father's name). He doted on the boy. "He's like a tiny holy man," he told Grace David. "His focus [is] not yet on the things of this world." Already the baby showed a pronounced fascination with music.

Aside from the bad food, the only downsides to spending most of the year in Archer City were that Hazel had had a stroke—she was rude, impatient, and often incoherent with him and his siblings—and when he *did* travel back east, he found his house broken into. He didn't mind the smashed windows and shattered air conditioner, so much; it was the theft of the vintage Dr Pepper bottles he couldn't get past.

The local Baptists, who'd treated him with suspicion ever since *The Last Picture Show,* made him feel unwelcome, but as he told his friend Max Crawford, "the Baptists . . . will all get killed in car wrecks or hunting accidents if you give them some time. [I'll] give them some time."

He was writing a new novel, tentatively titled *Old Women Remember.* It would morph into a sequel to *Terms of Endearment.* He would call it *The Evening Star.* As with *Some Can Whistle,* he seemed to be resurrecting characters from his earlier books only to kill them off and be done with them once and for all. But there *was* a new aspect to the sequels—an often slapstick celebration of family life and squalor, springing from his deer-in-the-headlights appreciation of his nieces and nephews in Archer City, of his grandson in Austin, of his friend Diana Ossana's domestic situation in Tucson. She, too, had a passel of nieces and nephews, and a teenage daughter, Sara, living with her—not to mention seven dogs. Slapstick was unavoidable.

Ossana gave him a photograph of Diana Rigg, his unattainable cinema crush (besides Elizabeth Taylor). He hung it above his writing table in Archer City: an inspirational muse as he extended the story of Aurora Greenway.

One day, in the early fall of 1991, he had written five to ten pages in the morning, read in the afternoon, and at dusk moved some books from his ranch house to his mansion in town. Weary behind the wheel of his rented Lincoln, he turned onto a country lane, "and this Holstein suddenly sidled across the road and I hit her and killed her," he said. The cow flipped into his windshield, blotting out the setting sun, then slid off the hood into a thicket of shoulder-high Johnson grass. He wasn't hurt; the car hadn't sustained noticeable damage. Cars hit cattle all the time on the county's gravel roads. He didn't give the matter a lot of thought. He went home and sat on his porch.

The next morning, "I was coughing and felt crappy," he said. He figured it was dust asthma, from moving books the day before. On his way to breakfast in Windthorst, he noticed his airbag light: it was blinking. "I had forgotten that I even had an airbag. I had hit a two-thousand-pound cow and it hadn't come out, so why was it blinking now?" He turned the Lincoln toward a repair shop in Wichita Falls. On the way, he stopped at his internist's to see if he could get some medicine for the cough. The doctor "didn't think I looked too good, so he gave me an EKG and said, 'Oh my God, you're having a heart attack.'"

The doctor ordered an ambulance, "but I was in a room so tiny they couldn't get the stretcher in," McMurtry said. "They wouldn't let me step out of the room, so they had to dismantle the stretcher. I could have easily died of all the things that happened while they were trying to save me. Then on the way to the hospital, the ambulance drivers became so excited when they found out they were hauling the author of *Lonesome Dove* that they drove straight off a very high curb." The IV bags trembled above his head and the needles stung his arm.

During an angiogram, he saw the tidy interior of his heart, pumping away on a four-inch television screen. It looked to him like a jittery tortoise suffering from delirium tremens. Doctors told him he had blockages in at least three major arteries—he needed immediate bypass surgery. A hundred years earlier, his ancestors, building their first shelters on Idiot Ridge, would never have let sawbones cut into their flesh unless their physical pain was unbearable. Now, thanks to complex technology, he'd been given a mild warning. He decided to interpret it broadly: *immediate bypass surgery* meant sometime in the next six months, he figured (against his doctors' advice). He had to finish his novel first.

The Evening Star covers forty years in the life of Aurora Greenway following the death of her daughter, Emma. Emma's three children, Tommy, Teddy, and Melanie, lost their way when they lost their mother; they have grown up troubled. Aurora has little influence on their behavior. Tommy is serving time in Huntsville for accidentally shooting his girlfriend. Teddy, mentally unstable, is stuck working at a 7-Eleven. Melanie clings to a ne'er-do-well boyfriend, a wannabe actor who has gotten her pregnant and refuses to commit to her. As in *Terms of Endearment,* Aurora flirts incessantly with her elderly suitors. She initiates a fling with her psychiatrist, a younger man, the son of a Las Vegas showgirl much like Harmony in *The Desert Rose.* Aurora fears she has wasted her years. "She had . . . merely lived," she thinks, "partaking rather fully of the human experience, and yet doing nothing with it." Of such vagaries in the life of a wealthy Houston matron McMurtry hoped once more to make a long and satisfying novel. Its pages offered a compendium of daily minutia; his first editor, John Leggett, would have insisted it did not rise to the level of novelistic material. Most reviewers resisted the approach. *The Evening Star* reflected "an author's boredom with his own most popular creatures," Thomas R. Edwards wrote in *The New York Review of Books.*

Yet the novel's ending reminded readers of McMurtry's literary charm when he *did* rouse his energies (and tapped into his mortal fears, projecting his coming absence into the minds of his family's children). Aurora, wordless after suffering a stroke, bequeaths her love of music to her baby grandson Henry. She plays Brahms's *Requiem* to him, causing him to gaze (like a tiny holy man) into her eyes and see "the Other Place," a place without language, without people, without materiality—a place he cannot recall, before he was born; a place Aurora, on her deathbed, is bound for. (Critic

Roger Walton Jones noted that this was the first time McMurtry had ever asserted "a spiritual realm from which all are born and all return.") Looking at Aurora, Henry makes "an indecisive sound—a sound part laugh and part cry. He wanted something, but didn't know what." Twenty-four years later, Henry, having lost his conscious memories of Aurora, attends a musical performance and hears an orchestra play Brahms's *Requiem*. His chest heaves. He drops his face into his hands and weeps: "the music had taken him to another place—to an old place in his memory, to a place so old that he could not really even find the memory, or put a picture to it, or a face. He just had the emptying sense that he had once had someone or something very important: something or someone that he could not even remember, except as a loss—something or someone that he would never have again."

McMurtry knew that had he been born a generation earlier, he would have been a dead man: bypass surgery had only been performed since 1962. Dwight Harken, a young U.S. Army surgeon in World War II, was one of the first men to try emergency heart procedures. His first subjects all died.

Throughout the final writing stages of *The Evening Star,* McMurtry stayed in touch with his doctor, researched the nature of the operation, and considered the best places to have it done. Statistics pointed to Johns Hopkins as the smartest choice.

In an old medical text he'd collected, he read that an anesthesiologist once said that the quality of a patient's sighing while anesthetized was of crucial importance. That was good, he thought: he was a world-class sigher.

He flew to Baltimore for a series of stress tests. He learned that he hadn't really had a heart attack—that is, "if the definition of a heart attack is that part of your heart muscle dies," he told Sontag. "I have an undamaged heart, although clearly not a heart that's getting adequate blood distribution under stress." Doctors told him that if he didn't have the surgery, he'd feel fine right up until the instant he keeled over. He took some convincing. He knew they were right, but he feared slowing down. "If I can't be an overworking overachiever, then where's the salt and the savor?" he wrote Sontag. "I like to overwork and I don't think I'd make a good contemplative."

Finally, he relented. At Johns Hopkins, on December 2, 1991, he underwent quadruple bypass surgery. Dr. Bruce Rietz was the surgeon, Dr. Stephen

Achuff the attending cardiologist. They placed him on a heart-lung machine, which breathed for him and pumped his blood while the doctors stopped his heart, removed it from inside his chest cavity, and packed it in ice, lowering it to a temperature of about 28 degrees C. Four hours later, after bypassing the blockages by rerouting mammary arteries and harvesting saphenous veins from his legs, they shocked his heart back into rhythm.

His "physical recovery involved no pain and little serious discomfort," he said. In rather breezy letters to Grace David and Susan Sontag, he said he was "healed and fine" and experiencing only "the most minor soreness—what you might feel if you were very lightly rear-ended."

He rested for ten days in his Georgetown apartment, then went to Texas for Christmas, avoiding his mother as much as possible—talk about stress. He traveled to Tucson for the month of January, taking with him five volumes of Virginia Woolf's *Diaries* and the twelve-volume Chatto & Windus edition of Proust. He stayed at the Arizona Inn, a quaint, family-run, casita-style hotel, open since the thirties. Leslie Silko had been spending a lot of time with Gus Blaisdell, owner of a bookstore in Albuquerque. McMurtry braved her screeching macaws to sit in her house with Gus and listen to her tell a harrowing story of being stopped by the Arizona Border Patrol. Agents had flagged her car one evening, forced her to step out of the car and stand and be sniffed by a drug dog. Silko could not stop talking about the "awful feeling of menace and violence about to break loose" by the road that night, of the agents' racism and dismissive attitudes toward her, of the "police state" America had become.

Far more relaxing were his visits with Diana Ossana. The house was hectic with rowdy nephews and nieces, but he'd developed a natural give-and-take with Ossana. They could almost complete each other's sentences. "We're kind of like Sancho and the Don," she said. "But we trade places, depending on the conversation."

At the end of January, McMurtry left Tucson "to resume what I assumed would be my normal life," he said. But by "the middle of February I knew that something was wrong. I was pursuing all my normal activities: running rare book shops (in DC and Texas), writing, lecturing, doing a little screen work." But in March he stopped doing anything. "I felt that I had become an outline; then I felt that someone was erasing the outline and that I was simply vanishing—evaporating. I had been reading three newspapers a day and leading a type-A East Coast life; I had just finished being president of an international writer's organization for two years. All that soon came to feel as if it belonged to another person's biography: the biography . . . of the person I had been before the operation. But I had ceased to be that person; I acted him or impersonated him as best I could, for the benefit of loved ones."

A couple who'd retired from the oil patch to run a small restaurant called Cottage Tea & Antiques sent covered dishes to his house to make sure he ate right.

He slept only three hours a night. He'd wake each morning at precisely three-fifteen and not be able to go back to sleep: "I felt as if I were holding up the ceiling . . . by an act of unrelenting will. The ceiling was Death," he said.

Consciousness: the sense of self, the voice chattering at us in our heads, the apparent awareness of a presence, a spirit, a soul inside us, distinct from our bodies and the electrical firings in our brains. Scientists and philosophers fall all over themselves trying to explain, define, or locate consciousness. It is like searching for darkness with a flashlight.

For survivors of heart bypass surgery, the likes of which McMurtry experienced, there is only one essential question: what happened to my *self* during the four hours that my heart, stone still, lay in a cooler of ice outside my torn chest?

"[A]ccording to current medical knowledge, it is impossible to experience consciousness when the heart has stopped beating," writes cardiologist Pim van Lommel.

"I have felt largely posthumous since [my] operation," McMurtry said. "My old psyche, or old self, was shattered—now it whirls around me in fragments . . . The heart-lung machine allows for biologic survival, but my own feeling is that the *person,* as opposed to the body, dies anyway . . . For a certain period of time one is technically alive but in another, powerful sense, dead. Then one is jump-started back into life, but the Faustian Bargain has been made: you're there, but not as *yourself.* That self, that personality, lies back beyond the time when you were on the pump. That gap, in my case at least, has proven unclosable."

In the evenings, before the stars appeared, he'd sit, unmoving, on his porch in Archer City as the yellow sky turned blue, then bluer still before washing out into jagged streaks of whitish gray. All the color, all the content, was draining from his world.

Diana Ossana wanted to quit her job. Preparing trial materials for smug lawyers in a personal injury firm was like writing dialogue for others to speak. They took full credit for it. Surely the books she read as a girl in St. Louis had prepared her for more than this.

She was an unusually empathetic child—so much so that her mother worried about it. "I [grew up] observing people. I've always been an observer, much less of a participant. I'm much more comfortable watching, and I'm very intuitive about people," Ossana said. "I remember when I was a little girl . . . I got my third-grade report card, and I always made really good grades. I was a real nerd; I was quiet so I studied all the time. But [my mother] got the report card from my teacher and she . . . was upset. She said that the teacher said that I got along really well with the other students, but I had this tendency to gravitate toward the lost children, the children that got made fun of or the ones that were sad, and she felt this might not serve me well when I grew up. My mother said . . . 'Now, you know, you need to make better friends.'"

Her instinct for locating sadness would help her enormously with Larry McMurtry.

As a girl in St. Louis, she lived in the library—reading *everything*, from Dickens to Harlan Ellison sci-fi adventures (she particularly loved biographies)—and in the Fox Theater, a five-balcony movie palace screening a wide array of films, from 007 to *The Day of the Triffids* to *Who's Afraid of Virginia Woolf?* "My first real experience with film" as an art form "was *Hud*," she said.

At home, she'd stay up watching George Raft movies on *The Late Show*. She liked gangster stories; she came from an Italian American background and didn't mind the stereotypes. They were fun on-screen.

She wanted to go west for college and majored in English and political science at Eastern New Mexico University. She married young— Michael John Ossana, a carpenter and a pilot from Paterson, New Jersey. "He [went] to Vietnam and came back damaged mentally and he never recovered," she said. For years she struggled to understand his torment and was helped by the "amazing movies of the seventies." His agonized reaction to *The Deer Hunter* opened her eyes. The war trauma experienced by the Christopher Walken character was "so similar to what my husband had been through . . . We divorced a couple of years later. He was the love of my life, and that's my great tragedy, you know, that I lost him."

They remained friends at a distance, sharing time with their daughter Sara. Eventually he moved to Colorado. Sara lived with her mother in Tucson, where Ossana had settled, landing the job in the law office at $700 a month.

Her first literary experience came through the firm. The retired Mafia don Joe Bonanno "had come to Tucson . . . from New York to sort of hide out," Ossana explained. He was a client of one of the lawyers she worked for. "Mr. B would come into the office and talk to me because he knew I was Italian . . . and he'd start bringing me flowers whenever he'd come . . . We talked about [*The Godfather* films] and I realized . . . I think Mario Puzo must have been influenced by Mr. B."

Her boss was so dazzled by his celebrity client, he couldn't stop bragging to friends. Word got around that Bonanno was living in Arizona. One day the man came to the office with a lavish spray of flowers, said to Ossana, "Sweetheart, your boss has a big mouth," and fired the flustered lawyer. Six months later, Bonanno called Ossana and said, "Sweetheart, I am going to write my autobiography and I need somebody to type it for me. And there's nobody I trust, but I trust you, because I know you won't divulge any of this." He said he'd pay her in cash—$2,000, nearly three months' salary for her—but she'd have to do all the typing at his house; he didn't want any pages leaving his possession. He wrote every day in longhand on a yellow legal pad, asked a ghostwriter to translate his Sicilian into English, then gave the pages to Ossana. He trundled down the steps to his basement—*nobody* owned a basement in Tucson! There, he grabbed stacks of cash for her. At the time, Ossana had a roommate who'd look after Sara while Ossana worked at Mr. B's. Sometimes the roommate called to check in. Mr. B nodded at the receiver. He said, "Sweetheart, you know they're listening."

"He was always sweet to me," Ossana said. She saw him years later, shuffling down a street. He was ninety years old (it was the last time she would meet him). "Mr. B, you look terrific," she said.

"Ah, that's 'cause they say I commit a crime every day."

One day McMurtry showed up at her door. He looked terrible. "I [had] ceased to be able to be alone," he said. "The need for close affections and domestic support became imperative." The postoperative depression had forced him to stop moving. (This is a common malady among heart patients, though knowing this doesn't help the suffering individual.) "It just so happened that I stopped at Diana's kitchen table," he said.

"He was falling apart. It was a scary thing to see," Ossana said. Without asking any questions, she let him stay in her house "because he seemed to be comfortable there, and [I] waited, hoping that this would subside."

Sara, fifteen, was bright and chatty, active on the girl's basketball team and in her school's arts programs, but even her energy couldn't spark the sullen guest. Ossana would leave him in the mornings sitting on her white couch staring silently out the window at the Catalina Mountains, drop her daughter off at school, go to work, and come home in the late afternoons to find McMurtry still staring out the window. He tried Zoloft and Prozac with little success. He tried cranial massage. He still couldn't sleep. He had no memory of being splayed across a surgeon's table like a filleted steak, but at night he could almost feel his tissues and muscles throbbing with the unreleased trauma of it. He had a frequent sensation of "heaviness behind my eyes, as if my eyelids were weighted down by little sandbags," he said.

To Ossana's amazement, he hadn't lost the habit of writing fiction every day, "but it came rapidly and impersonally: my pages were like faxes I received from my former self," he said.

"I was in the rhythm of writing a book every fall so what could I have done if I didn't? Just lie there and take antidepressants and stare out the window? I wanted to get to the wound, and I did . . . I knew that I was changed. I knew that other person wasn't ever going to come back, and I wanted to write about it." He set his blocky Hermes on Ossana's kitchen counter, typed for ninety minutes each morning, then retreated to the couch for the rest of the day.

To his publisher's delight, he'd begun a sequel to *Lonesome Dove,* a book called *Streets of Laredo*. Simon & Schuster wanted the manuscript delivered on computer discs, something McMurtry didn't know how to do and wasn't going to bother to learn. Ossana began entering his pages into her computer. "As I was doing it we would talk about [the book] a lot. He came to trust me and my judgment," she said. But she found what she was reading disconcerting. It was unrelentingly bleak.

Streets of Laredo takes place twenty years after Woodrow Call has returned Gus's body to Texas. Call is on his own, having outlived his time. Riding through the unromantic West, he suffers multiple gunshot wounds, finally losing an arm and a leg. "He would have to live, but without himself," Ossana read one day. "He felt he had left himself faraway, back down the weeks, in the spot west of Fort Stockton where he had been wounded . . . He could remember the person he had been, but he could not become that person again."

As she retyped this passage into her computer, she began to weep: "For about ten minutes I couldn't see clearly. I couldn't even type. I kept thinking that it was Larry. This is really how he feels about himself. It was just horribly sad."

The novel ends with Call a cripple, looked after by women and children.

When he finished the book and she had delivered the discs to his publisher, he claimed a spot on the white couch, stared at the Catalinas, and simply stopped moving. Ossana figured he would die if he didn't write every day. But he was no longer writing. No longer reading.

One evening, Sara pulled her mother into the bathroom and closed the door. "Mama," she said softly, "I love Larry, but it hurts me to look at him because he's so sad. When I do, I just want to cry."

ilm studios sent him dozens of screenplay requests, but he kept "bat-ting them away," Ossana said. John McTiernan and Steven Spielberg called him, trying to recruit him for projects, but he refused. He wouldn't leave the house. "It was like his essence leaked away," Ossana said. Over a year passed. Then one day producer Jerry Weintraub con-tacted him on behalf of Warner Bros., suggesting he write a script about the Depression-era Oklahoma outlaw Charles "Pretty Boy" Floyd. He said no at first—his literary muscle had atrophied—but Ossana recognized an opportunity. She knew that McMurtry had always been "fascinated with the difference between mythology and reality. There was a lot of that within the Pretty Boy Floyd story." She quit her job at the law firm. On her own, she researched Floyd. (McMurtry knew nothing about him—he'd thought he was a boxer.) Floyd was a penny-ante bank robber, out of work with a pregnant wife when he began his brief crime spree. After J. Edgar Hoover's G-men killed John Dillinger outside the Biograph movie house in Chicago in 1934, Hoover needed a new Public Enemy No. 1 to stoke the media's ro-manticizing of the FBI. The obvious candidates, mob bosses such as Meyer Lansky, Dutch Schultz, and Lucky Luciano, were too cozy with politicians and labor unions. Hoover knew better than to interfere with corrupt bed-fellows at the heart of the American political system. It was much safer to go after a lone hack whose reputation for violence could be inflated in the press. Pretty Boy perfectly matched Hoover's needs. He became the new top rogue. Eventually, G-men gunned him down in an Ohio cornfield.

Ossana shared her research with McMurtry and nudged him to take the screenplay assignment. "I wanted to get Larry back into writing. I felt not only would it be a loss to the world, but Larry needed to come back to life," she said.

He humored her, saying he'd think about it. He studied the material and complained, "I can't make this character sympathetic." "I was getting sort of desperate for him to snap out of it by then," Ossana said. Then "I could see something sparkling in his eyes. Sure enough, he said, 'I'll write it, but only if you write it with me.'"

He absolutely knew he couldn't do it without her. He'd gotten rusty, lost confidence. He'd always considered himself a "first-stage-of-the-rocket screenwriter. I do two drafts because I can't do more than two drafts of anything, and I get some characters in there that are good enough to show to a studio. I can get characters on paper that major actors want to play, but I have no sense of structure." That's where Ossana came in. "Diana tends to worry the material in a way that's good." He would give her "a five-page segment and she would expand and refine it," give it shape, typing it into the computer. The collaboration was easy—as in conversation, they completed each other's sentences.

Jerry Katzman, the William Morris president who'd soon represent McMurtry's movie work, observed that Ossana got "his juices going and [kept] him wanting to write and keep writing."

McMurtry was starting to take short walks now and make curmudgeonly pronouncements about the world's sorry state. Sara (for whom he now officially served as godfather) said he'd become "a database with opinions."

Ultimately, Warner Bros. did not follow up on the script, but when Ossana and McMurtry finished the screenplay "we still had a certain amount of momentum as collaborators," he said. "[W]e didn't feel we were through with Charlie Floyd."

He began drafting a novel about the outlaw, writing ten pages each morning, then passing them on to Ossana for fine-tuning. She added details, filling out his framework. "I was very worried about our styles merging at first, but [it] just happened without anyone noticing . . . and sort of got lost in the daily activity," McMurtry said. He was moved by the stateliness of her sentences, which he felt balanced his slang and bawdy humor. "I realized . . . that my instinctive choice to try to persuade her to be my partner was correct, because there was something in that prose that I didn't have in *my* prose."

When they'd completed a first draft and sat down to review it together, "I was excited because some of it Larry hadn't seen," Ossana said. "We were reading and he says, 'You know we're going to cut at least a hundred pages of this.' I was aghast. I said, 'No, we're not. Over my dead body.' And we didn't cut a thing, maybe three or four words in the whole book."

Their novel depended heavily on Michael Wallis's biography of Floyd, published two years earlier. "Larry and Diana's novel—I didn't like that book at all," Wallis told me. "It had scenes that were like burlesque. I know it was fiction, but I was seeing things in it that were wrong that didn't have to be. It just seemed sloppy. I remember them appreciating how I was able to present the story without making Floyd sound mythical, while at the same time honoring his complexity. They didn't manage to do that. Our relationship got kind of sticky. My book came out first. Larry loved it. He loved this line I have, which they used to begin their novel: 'He would be thirty years old forever.' My book was optioned several times by the movies—with the movies, I just don't believe it till it happens. What Larry and Diana tried to do was put a deal together with both our books. They obviously needed me. It went back and forth and I thought maybe the movie would go because of Larry, but it didn't."

Critically, the novel didn't fare well, either. The *Los Angeles Times* dismissed the "rather inert quality" of its prose, and Sidney Zion, writing in *The New York Times,* bluntly asked, "What is a guy like Larry McMurtry doing on a thing like this? He is a distinguished novelist," but this joint effort, he said, "was flatter than a Depression pancake."

The disappointing response didn't discourage the writing team. McMurtry was stirring again and Ossana was determined to keep his heartbeat going. In 1997, they collaborated on a second novel, *Zeke and Ned,* partly based on the real-life drama of Ned Christie, a Cherokee statesman in the Indian Territory, accused of killing a United States marshal. For five years, he eluded U.S. lawmen. After he was finally cornered and shot, he became a folk hero among the Cherokee.

The *Los Angeles Times* complimented the novel's "slow, leisurely" pace, like a "yarn spun over a campfire with plenty of whiskey on hand and nobody in a rush to get anyplace quick," while acknowledging that the characters were not "finely wrought"; there was "little" in the book "[to] enlighten . . . a reader about the Cherokee people." *The New York Times* complained that "Mr. McMurtry and Ms. Ossana . . . can't seem to move their story beyond television mini-series terrain." The novel suffered from a "grating folksiness," the reviewer said.

One reason their partnership encountered stiff resistance was the "conservative" nature of the book business, McMurtry believed. "[I]f you try to do something different like a collaborative novel, you've got to expect trouble. Diana was naive about how mean the New York publishing world can be."

But in fact she had initially suggested they leave her name off the cover of *Pretty Boy Floyd*. "I didn't want to deal with Hollywood, I didn't want to deal with the press, I didn't want to deal with all the things that go along with it," she said. "I just wanted to write, that's all." Far from being naive, she knew she'd be accused of "riding on Larry's coattails"—mooching off "the icon."

McMurtry insisted she get credit. She did the research, she wrote half the book. "Everybody [at Simon & Schuster] was horrified," he said.

She was either McMurtry's Yoko Ono or his Eliza Doolittle, depending on whom you listened to in New York. "It was so odd to me that people should care about me," she said. "I don't have the need or the desire for all that attention."

Journalists did not know how to refer to her. She was frequently listed as McMurtry's "companion."

"There's bound to be speculation that she's the girlfriend," McMurtry said. "It's always assumed that it's romantic, whether it is or not."

When *asked* if it was romantic, Ossana replied, "Well, I love Larry."

Certainly, McMurtry's friends wondered, and often worried, about her, questioning her motives in the relationship. "She's a force of nature," Beverly Lowry said.

"Everyone was suspicious of Diana," Susan Freudenheim acknowledged. "Early on, everyone thought she was a gold digger. There were conversations along those lines, and I didn't really know her . . . There was worry that she was taking advantage of him. *I* think he was romantic with Diana. He was very much taken with her."

"I don't know, he may have felt that way about me," Ossana said. But she insisted, "The reason [we] lasted was that it didn't turn into that."

To friends and acquaintances, they never represented themselves as a traditional couple.

McMurtry's final word on the subject: "Call it an *amitié amoureuse*. That's all one can say." (In France, an *amitié amoureuse* is a romantic friendship, an unmarried couple not always living together but deeply involved in each other's families; sex can be central or peripheral to the relationship, depending on age, health, needs, and time of life.)

Meanwhile, their writing partnership continued to strengthen, branching out into more screenplays. When they announced they were writing a screen version of the 1950s television sitcom *Father Knows Best,* observers again assumed Ossana must be leading him astray. "*Father Freakin' Knows Best? . . . How much are they getting?*" the *Los Angeles Times* characterized publishers' skeptical reaction. Ossana and McMurtry flew to Hollywood to discuss the script with executives at Universal Studios, who were delighted, but disbelieving, to land McMurtry. "I think they [saw] it as somehow beneath him. But Larry sees screenwriting as being a gun for hire," Ossana said.

"One thing the Universal people said to [him] that really annoyed him," she recalled. "They asked, 'Why would you, Larry McMurtry, want to write this?' I felt him tense up and the air get thick."

"I'm very annoyed by people presuming to know what I would and would not like to write," he explained.

No one expected Swifty Lazar, eighty-six, to host his annual Oscar party following the death of his wife Mary from bone cancer the previous spring—especially since he was on dialysis. He admitted to friends that he was lost without Mary, but in early March, there he was at Spago, hobbling around in a sweatshirt, white trousers, and sneakers, arranging the seating plan with his assistants. "I want to give good seats to the people I've known and liked for a long time," he said, even if it meant sticking some A-list stars in a tiny corner, blocked from view by large potted plants. One of the assistants asked him, "Where are you going to sit?" "I have no intention of sitting down," he replied.

At six P.M. on the night of March 29, 1993, limos motored slowly along Canon Drive in Beverly Hills, arriving at the restaurant just in time for the Academy Awards' opening ceremonies, beamed from the Dorothy Chandler Pavilion onto nine different television screens arrayed around Spago. McMurtry showed up with Ossana and Sara—he'd introduced Lazar to them on an earlier occasion, on vacation in London. The old man was taken with Sara. He especially loved the "world-class haircut she had [just] given herself," McMurtry said. At Spago's, Lazar winked at Sara and gave her a cigar. (George Burns, with whom McMurtry's party was seated along with Jimmy Stewart at the "geriatric table," would do the same.)

They all sat down to their Alaskan salmon with horseradish crust. Much later in the evening, when the awards ceremony was finished, Elizabeth Taylor appeared at the party, floating among tables in an elegant white gown, her thick hair a perfect black hayrick. For McMurtry, the moment was fantasy come to life. Hours earlier, Taylor had shimmered on the jumpy television screen above his table, accepting the Jean Hersholt Humanitarian Award for her AIDS activism. Now here she stood in the (splendid) flesh. She sat at his table briefly, "perhaps to say hello to Mr. Stewart or the more or less mummified George Burns," McMurtry said. "I stood up and complimented her on [her] fine AIDS speech. As I did, the writer Harold Brodkey, himself then dying of AIDS, showed up at my elbow . . . For a moment we two writers, as well as many people in the room, were simply transfixed by the beauty of Elizabeth Taylor's eyes. Those eyes had a glory all their own: violet eyes with amber lights. Hard to think clearly about the yeses and nos of feminism when you're looking into the best eyes in Hollywood."

(He was also aware that the evening was "sort of the end of the Old Hollywood, a Hollywood where stars were still more important than agents.")

The chance to speak to Elizabeth Taylor was the best thing Swifty had done for him in quite some time. The old man had been slipping, sloppier than usual in the storm of his family's health crises. McMurtry had been forced to hire a pair of high-powered lawyers, Robert Thorne of Loeb & Loeb and Greg Redlitz, to double-check every deal Lazar made just to make sure they were legit.

After Mary's death, Lazar started shedding possessions, giving away silver, cigarette boxes, paintings (a charming little Matisse)—the only problem was, he'd promise the same items to multiple groups of friends. Confused, everyone argued. His business affairs took similarly chaotic turns.

For McMurtry, the last straw was Lazar's promise to him that he'd sold *Dead Man's Walk,* a *Lonesome Dove* prequel, to famous film producer Robert Halmi Sr. for $5 million. This was "such happy news that I dashed off a letter to Senior, as the old rogue was called; he was at his estate in Kenya, where he probably came close to dying of shock," McMurtry said. "No such sale had occurred."

After the Oscar party, Lazar felt he had nothing but emptiness and physical pain to look forward to. He decided to quit dialysis. He died on December 27, 1993.

In the months before his passing, McMurtry and Ossana visited him often in Los Angeles. The last time they saw him, "he rose out of sedation and talked lucidly and lovingly, for almost an hour, about Bogart and Hemingway," McMurtry said. "He spoke about Bogart's death, and Hemingway's torment. But then he began to reminisce about their good times—he ceased to talk about them as if they were dead and spoke as he might speak of people who were traveling, people whom he would probably see again, as it might be, when he was passing through Paris, or lunching at '21.'"

There are already new areas of the business that we're moving Diana and Larry into," Jerry Katzman said, announcing the pair's signing by the William Morris Agency. The agency would take over their motion picture and television projects. Andrew Wylie, known for his cutthroat dealmaking, assumed McMurtry's literary representation. Almost immediately, Wylie tried to shake up the cozy arrangement McMurtry had brokered with Simon & Schuster for nearly twenty years. He knew that McMurtry was one of the few fiction writers in the country enjoying celebrity name recognition; he figured they could both be making a lot more money. He put word out that McMurtry "was willing to entertain bids from other publishers." He intended to sell the author's next four books for $21.5 million.

"Wylie's inquiries seemed curious, in part because the perception in the book industry is that Simon & Schuster has done more than a respectable job with McMurtry over the years. Several publishers speculated that the hard-bargaining Wylie—who recently took on McMurtry after the death of the author's long-time agent, Irving 'Swifty' Lazar—was trying to make a big splash for and with his new client," Sarah Lyall reported in The New York Times.

Michael Korda let it be known that S&S still wanted to publish McMurtry, but not at Wylie's price. Other publishers failed to step up. In the end, McMurtry stayed with Korda, inking a deal guaranteeing $10 million for the next four books.

It was not a landscape Dorothea Oppenheimer would have recognized.

These changes in representation accompanied dizzying developments in the business of pop culture. Though McMurtry half joked about writing solely for money now—"I worry about where the next million dollars is going to come from," he said—he understood that ballooning production costs and fat, agent-driven deals, along with demographic shifts in New York and Hollywood, meant that what he had to offer was increasingly considered passé. His "name had little pull" now, he believed, particularly in the film world. "My books had belched out several winners—*The Last Picture Show, Terms of Endearment,* and *Lonesome Dove*—but none of them were then *current*—and it takes little acquaintance with Hollywood to learn that *current* is critical."

On visits to LA, he was dismayed to observe that "the executives at the various studios where [Diana and I] might be hired or fired were becoming younger and younger; more and more of them seemed to be female . . . Since we were mainly at the studios to pitch Westerns, it was a little disconcerting to find that the executives who were to relay our pitch had never heard of such Westerns as *The Searchers* or *Red River* . . . status or not, we counted for zilch in the world of feature films."

The proof of this seemed evident in the box-office failure of *The Evening Star,* in which Shirley MacLaine reprised her role as Aurora Greenway. Polly Platt had been asked to produce the film. In life, "I really wanted to be [Aurora]," Platt said. After all, hadn't McMurtry originally based aspects of the character on her? Regarding the sequel, Platt admired the aging woman's fortitude. "The only reason I made *The Evening Star* was because I was getting older myself and I was fascinated by the vigor and incredible strength of the character . . . She's just indomitable. She never gives up. She doesn't fall prey to depression, alcoholism, any of the things I fell prey to in my life."

She had read somewhere that "*Terms of Endearment* every year is one of the most rented videos around Mother's Day. So lots of people are still eager to see it again and again, even after all this time. It's still fresh in their minds." But the sequel's director, Robert Harling, was a first-timer, inexperienced and intimidated by the daunting task of trying to match the first film's success. From the beginning, he ignored Platt on the set. "He did not trust me and would not listen to me," she said. More to the point, he insisted on putting *his* stamp on the project, refusing to collaborate lest his contribution be overshadowed by anyone else. He knew that Platt had been a major reason for the first film's glow; his insecurity kept her marginalized. Frustrated and angry, she collected her salary and avoided the set—until the day Jack Nicholson flew to Houston to shoot his small cameo as Aurora's old lover. Nicholson's brief appearance in the film was the main reason the studio had agreed to finance the project. "I'm coming for you," he told Platt on the phone, and he refused to leave his trailer until he knew she was around.

Even his powerful screen charisma was not enough to secure *The Evening Star* a niche in a market now dominated by special effects extravaganzas. And probably nothing could have kept the movie from becoming, in Platt's words, "a tragedy," undermined by a difficult director with no feel for his material. *The Evening Star* was the last major Hollywood film Platt worked on as a producer.

Like McMurtry, she felt passed over by a rapidly evolving industry. She spent years writing the screenplay for *All My Friends Are Going to Be Strangers,* which she saw as a "haunting tale of the misery of being an artist." "On the weekends I drank wine and worked on the adaptation," she said. At various points, Ethan Hawke and Robert Downey Jr. wanted to play Danny Deck. Dennis Hopper said he'd like to direct. Then Platt insisted *she* would take the helm. But the financing never came through. In the 1990s, a quiet film about an unhappy writer, directed by a woman, was a no-sale.

Thwarted and lonely—her children were grown, living on their own—she drank. She'd appear at studio meetings carrying a six-pack of beer. People became afraid to work with her. (That was *another* change in Hollywood—it was full of health nuts now!)

She went into a slow decline, occasionally phoning McMurtry with her troubles, moving in and out of sobriety, until after falling down a flight of stairs and finding herself unable to zip her clothes, she was diagnosed with ALS. "She lost her agency, lost her voice, and lost her life," Karina Longworth summed matters up on the Hollywood podcast *You Must Remember This.* Platt died in Brooklyn in 2011. McMurtry would never shake the belief that the past had killed her as much as the horrible disease—the past and the cruelty of Hollywood. Asked by an interviewer in 2017, "If you could bring back to life one deceased person, who would it be?" McMurtry answered, without hesitation, "Polly Platt, because she was interesting and lovable."

In the mid-1990s, as Platt was struggling to make feature films, McMurtry and Ossana turned to "new areas of . . . business"—namely, writing and producing for television. "The advantage we had, when we started to be TV writers, was of course *Lonesome Dove,*" McMurtry said.

Based on *Dove's* success, they convinced executives at CBS and ABC to air sequels and prequels to the Gus and Call saga. The stories came from the novels McMurtry produced in quick succession after his revitalization: *Dead Man's Walk* (1995) and *Comanche Moon* (1997). These prequels followed the *Lonesome Dove* finale, *Streets of Laredo* (1993), which was also made into a miniseries.

Streets came first as a television event, airing in three parts on CBS in 1995. It starred James Garner as Woodrow Call in his declining years. It also featured Sam Shepard, Sissy Spacek, Randy Quaid, and Ned Beatty. McMurtry's name may have meant zilch in the world of feature films, but in television, he commanded big budgets, all-star casts, and ample airtime. In fact, the show's full title was *Larry McMurtry's "Streets of Laredo."* The miniseries earned ecstatic reviews, though *The New York Times* echoed literary critics' gripes about the McMurtry-Ossana partnership—the storytelling tended to "meander," said the reviewer, and much of the dialogue fell "curiously flat." Also, the violence was gratuitous, featuring, he said, "innumerable bloody shootings . . . a suicide, a hanging, a leg amputation, a body left naked by a stream and a huge sow shot between the eyes."

This last point guaranteed trouble for the next miniseries, *Dead Man's Walk,* broadcast by ABC over two nights in May 1996. Network censors and U.S. senators, grousing about the ill effects of media violence on America's youth, prompted McMurtry to remark, "I think the members of Congress should be ashamed of themselves. They can't even keep the Government open." He produced forty pages of notes for ABC, defending the story's shootings, stabbings, and tortures as historically accurate and therefore dramatically necessary: "We've had to do it item by item, bullet by bullet. This was the most violent era in Texas history. This wasn't Switzerland in the 1840s."

On balance, he got what he wanted. "He gets away with things nobody else gets away with on television," said Frank Q. Dobbs, a coproducer. ("Apparently you can slice and dice people all you want as long as it happened in a previous century," quipped critic Tom Shales.)

McMurtry was much more hands-on with this $20 million production than he had been with *Streets of Laredo*. He was listed, along with Ossana, as executive producer, overseeing casting, location scouting, costume design, and prop selection. He advised the director, Yves Simoneau, on the dusty set during the fifty days of shooting. "I did it because I had a partner," he said, standing one day next to an ocotillo cactus in the middle of the Chihuahuan Desert. "Otherwise I would never have stepped on the set."

"So it's my fault we're here," Ossana muttered.

"Yes. It's your fault."

In fact, she did most of the heavy lifting, keeping order on the set, calming anxious execs on the telephone. Even so, a *New York Times* reporter, covering the shoot, saw fit only to describe her physical appearance—"overalls and blond bangs." He dismissed her as "play[ing] the eager grad student to Mr. McMurtry's slightly aloof professor."

McMurtry would stand behind the director's chair, watching scenes being filmed, and comment. He didn't like the actors' fake Texas accents. The script supervisor tried to make excuses. "The kids were up all night drinking at the Starlight," she'd say, indicating the actors. "We had a problem even getting them here."

Behind McMurtry's back, some of the cast complained that his persnicketiness made everything twice as hard as it needed to be. "You can't let anything slip by," he said. "You can't control it all like words on a page. There, you're just working with sentences, not a 230-member crew. It's much more frustrating . . ."

Which is why Ossana took charge of the next production, *Comanche Moon*. It didn't air until 2008, on CBS. Westerns were becoming prohibitively expensive to make. *Comanche Moon* was the least successful of the *Lonesome Dove* series, deemed "tedious" by Brian Lowry, writing in *Variety*, "at times cartoonishly bad." By then, McMurtry had declared himself sick to death of Gus and Call, and of the nineteenth century in general.

The public had also grown weary of the franchise: another *Lonesome*

Dove sequel and a regular series based on the novel had aired, without McMurtry's involvement or blessing.

Read chronologically (not in order of their composition), the four-novel series stands as McMurtry's most searching investigation of the history of the Old West. The adventures of Gus and Call trace the nation's expansion westward, capitalism's evolution and spread, the resettlement or extermination of Indigenous peoples, and the erosion of the Great Plains, with dire consequences for natural life, individual rights, and democratic order.

In *Dead Man's Walk,* set in the 1840s, Gus and Call, young Texas Rangers, embark on a greedy and foolish venture (based on real events) to capture Santa Fe and annex territory east of the Rio Grande for Texas. The Rangers are depicted as reckless drunkards, often under the command of self-serving soldiers of fortune. Their expedition fails, they barely escape a wily Comanche stalker named Buffalo Hump, and are eventually captured by Mexican soldiers. The soldiers force them to walk the *Jornada del Muerto* (the "Dead Man's Walk") all the way to El Paso. Those who outlast the journey are then blindfolded and ordered to draw beans from a jar. A black bean means execution by firing squad; a white bean earns the poor sod a reprieve. Gus and Call survive. They are allowed to return to Austin, by no means heroes, except for their ability to endure physical hardships.

Comanche Moon resumes their story in their middle years as Rangers. Tasked by the Texas governor to quell Native activity so white settlers (and the flow of money) can proceed unimpeded, they flail about on half-finished missions, unable to prevent Buffalo Hump and his warriors from sacking the city of Austin. Gus and Call avoid the Civil War—they have no loyalty to the Union. (They had managed to skip the Alamo skirmish as well.) Meanwhile, the old Comanche order is dying. Buffalo Hump always fought for his people's cause; not so his half-breed son Blue Duck, an outcast from the tribe. Blue Duck wages war on white settlements purely for personal gain. Remorselessly, he murders his father, signaling an end to ethical fighting on the plains, revealing the spread of dysfunction among Native peoples under siege, and commencing the rise of senseless slaughter.

Lonesome Dove finds Gus and Call much older, in retirement, running a small cattle company, using stolen horses and herds, near the Texas-Mexico

border. Post–Civil War, the Comanches have mostly been tamed, though
renegades such as Blue Duck remain on the loose—another sign of the
Rangers' failure. In no sense can Gus and Call claim to have been successful, except—once again—as hearty survivors. Gus has lost the only woman
he ever loved by being unfaithful and unwilling to settle down, Call has
refused to acknowledge his son by a prostitute he's shunned. Restless, bored,
unable to accept that he has outlived his usefulness, he impulsively decides
to steal a herd of cattle and run it up to Montana. Gus goes along because
he has nothing else to do. True to their lifelong pattern, they lose many men
along the way and essentially relinquish their goal before they have achieved
it. Gus dies, ambushed by Natives, and Call returns to Texas, once more at
sixes and sevens.

In *Streets of Laredo,* Call hires himself out as a bounty hunter, tracking a
Mexican bandit named Joey Garza. Garza has replaced the Comanches as an
irritant in the forward march of white capital, attacking railroads and inter-
rupting the free flow of goods across the country. Once again, Call is tasked
with making the plains safe for "civilization." His former ventures, including
Montana's Hat Creek Cattle Company, have collapsed. His son, Newt, has
been killed by a wild horse Call gave him. Call is a ruined relic, with nothing
to show for the life he chose over domestic contentment. In his showdown
with Garza, he is so seriously wounded that Lorena (the former saloon girl
his old buddy Gus rescued from Blue Duck) must cut off his leg to save him.
Lorena is married now to one of Call's former cattlemen. Call winds up dependent on Lorena and the many children in her house—at the mercy of the
quiet domestic order he avoided all his life.

Despite McMurtry's relentless emphasis on the men's failures, readers
viewed Gus and Call as romantic, even admirable figures in the tradition
of lone, stoic cowboys. Countless books and movies had engraved the
archetype too firmly in the public mind. McMurtry's energetic writing,
humorous dialogue, and eye for detail were irresistible. Though none of
the other three novels matched the richness of *Lonesome Dove's* prose, in
just a few words McMurtry could describe a landscape in such a way as to
provoke uncanny awe and suspense.

Critics admired his fealty to the historical record; in each of the volumes, the weaving of his fictional characters into actual events was seam-
less. And if we consider the novels back-to-back, it is possible to recognize

nuances in his depictions of Natives that were easy to miss the first time through.

In all of the books, Comanches are described as fearsome—"Whipped they might be, but as long as there was one free Comanche with a horse and a gun it would be foolish to take them lightly," reads the *Lonesome Dove* narrative. But it soon becomes clear that this statement cannot be taken at face value. This is in fact the Comanche of popular white imagination. By embedding the portrait so thoroughly in the novel's narrative voice— fluid throughout, roaming among many points of view in a free indirect manner—McMurtry acknowledges how completely the Comanches have been typecast in the dominant culture's popular accounts. He makes the reader complicit in accepting the bias. Thereafter, almost every encounter between Caucasians and Natives belies the stereotype. Most of the Natives are starving; white marauders have destroyed their way of life. One of Call's cowboys fears running into a "huge Indian getting ready to poke him with something sharp," but then he admits that "[m]ost of the Indians he had actually seen had all been scrawny little men." In another scene, Call's son, Newt, fears the approach of a band of Comanches, but they are peaceful. Up close, Newt is shocked "at how thin and poor they looked. The old man who was their leader was just skin and bones . . . one of his eyes was milky and white. Their ponies were as thin as they were. They had no saddles, just saddle blankets, and only one had a gun, an old carbine."

Blue Duck, a ruthless sociopath, is the exception, but he is explicitly identified as a renegade, shunned by his own tribe as much as by white men. And several of the white men in the story are just as violent as he is.

The other novels in the series do not avoid the *savage Indian* trope as carefully as *Lonesome Dove*. In graphic detail, the narratives depict several instances of Native torture techniques. Yet, here again, McMurtry's voice is more supple than it seems. The descriptions of skull bashings, disembow- elings, and scalpings are so over-the-top, even a casual reader recognizes that the words mime the lurid qualities of pulp fiction. Once more, we are reminded it is all too easy to fall into the trap of flatly accepting familiar narratives.

Because of his dealings in rare books and his knowledge of books in general, McMurtry knew all about captivity narratives. They became the basis of late-nineteenth-century dime novels—among the young republic's most popular entertainments. The first widely distributed captivity narrative was Mary Rowlandson's 1682 account, modestly titled *The Sovereignty and Goodness of God, Together, with the Faithfulness of his Promises Displayed; Being a Narrative of the Captivity and Restauration of Mrs. Mary Rowlandson, Commended by Her, to All that Desire to Know the Lords Doings to, and Dealings with Her.* The story recounts the capture of a good Puritan woman by "athiesticall, proud, wild, cruel, barbarous, bruitish . . . diabolicall creatures . . . the worst of the heathen." Eventually (by God's grace) Mrs. Rowlandson is rescued, and her community realizes that the Indians are merely the Lord's instruments, warning the Puritans not to stray from righteous paths.

McMurtry's scenes of Native torture in *Dead Man's Walk* and *Comanche Moon* echo the captivity accounts. In addition to sailing in and out of his characters' minds, his narrative enters various historical texts, assuming their contradictory biases, just as it assumes the characters' conflicting attitudes. The voice constantly moves among various angles of perception, providing not an *account* of history, but a deep *meditation* on it.

Whether McMurtry's (often clashing) ambitions entirely succeed in the *Lonesome Dove* series is open to question. Even when he most explicitly mocks Native clichés, he approaches the subject with an ethnocentric bias. As Edward Said wrote in *Orientalism,* identifying the narrative strategies Westerners have often used to assert their superiority over the Orient, "[T]he Westerner [places himself] in a whole series of possible relationships with the Orient without ever losing . . . the relative upper hand."

Nevertheless, with this massive project—over three thousand pages of continuous narrative, reminiscent of Fenimore Cooper's Leatherstocking Tales—McMurtry had made a powerful argument for the novel's continuing relevance as a cultural touchstone, a locus of thought and discussion about the very meaning of America. When placed in the context of his contemporary narratives, the *Lonesome Dove* novels reverberated beyond their immediate historical referents. Danny Deck could be seen as a spiritual brother of Gus and Call, a mythologized persona in the public mind—A Successful Author—who was in fact an abject failure in his life. Homer Bannon, Sam the Lion, Roger Wagonner from *Moving On,* and Uncle Laredo in *All My Friends Are Going to Be Strangers* were the useless relics left by the shattering of the open range's economy. Hud, the rodeo star Sonny Shanks, and the boyfriend who kills Deck's daughter are the lingering shadows of renegades like Blue Duck and Billy the Kid, stuck in an outmoded gunslinger mentality. The Old West left more than physical and emotional detritus when it (never quite) vanished—it planted ineradicable pathological elements deep in the country's soul: such was McMurtry's view. Whatever its flaws, the *Lonesome Dove* series was unmistakably the work of a major American novelist with a unique and comprehensive vision.

You don't always get better as a writer—you get old, you get tired, you exhaust an original gift. But in books you're dealing in knowledge. The older you get, the better you get. It's almost the opposite of being a writer," McMurtry said.

Now that the other aspects of his business affairs—the screenplays, the novels—had been taken care of following his heart episode, what was left was his life as a bookseller. The checkerboard of high-stakes Georgetown real estate was about to knock him and Marcia Carter out of the game.

Carter had been running the DC store on her own during McMurtry's convalescence and absence. She had bought much of the inventory of the Heritage Book Shop in Los Angeles, modern literary volumes priced at $500 or less. She made them a centerpiece at Booked Up. When McMurtry returned to active book trading, in the mid-nineties, he helped her negotiate a buy of Vilhjalmur Stefansson's personal library. Stefansson had been a great Arctic explorer and he owned several rare travel volumes, as well as a comprehensive Inuit grammar.

Booked Up had expanded over the years, but the store's rental space was about to shrink. The building's owners sold it to developers, who'd soon bring in a Pottery Barn and a spa. Booked Up moved back across 31st Street, near the tiny space it had first occupied. McMurtry whittled down its inventory to about 5,000 books, making it into more of a specialty shop. He shipped close to 300,000 volumes to Archer City, filling the old Ford dealership. Then he stored books inside three other buildings he'd bought in town, separated by a flat four-lane highway (certain death for wandering armadillos). He renamed the Blue Pig Booked Up, constructed shelves inside the buildings, and turned the buildings into annexes—Booked Up Two, Three, and Four. To their stock, he added mass purchases from Serendipity Books in Berkeley and Riverrun in Hastings-on-Hudson, New York.

There were a few famous book towns in the world: the village of Redu in Belgium, Bredevoort in Holland, Montolieu and Bécherel in France, and most notably Hay-on-Wye in Wales—entire communities devoted to the selling of books, biblio-cities drawing readers and tourists from across the globe. McMurtry spoke openly now of making Archer City such a place, the most unlikely Texas transformation since Ann Richards had gone from being a falling-down drunk to becoming governor of the state. As one observer put it, "McMurtry sounds a little like . . . Noah, building his ark and filling it with books."

Marcia Carter, who would struggle to keep the DC store open for another four years, said, "It's wonderful what [Larry's] doing there. He thinks on a Texas scale."

Mostly he split his time now between Tucson and Archer City. Occasionally he'd go to Hollywood for movie work. In Tucson, he bought a modest house across the street from Diana Ossana, in the Oracle Foothills Estates. He'd stay with her, then retreat to his own space when he needed solitude or wanted to phone his other lady friends, nurturing his "not-quite-relationships." Diane Keaton called him often, rehearsing, like an actress learning her lines, the latest traumas in her life.

He'd recovered from his depression enough to argue rather frequently with Ossana—about screenplays, food, domestic arrangements. Sometimes he'd get in such a huff, they'd communicate for days only by sending letters back and forth between their neighboring homes. Or she'd turn her phone off for a week. "[H]e would be frantic," she said. "That's one thing he can't stand."

She traveled with him to Archer City and stayed with him in the mansion. He'd painted the walls white, restored the original hardwood floors and the massive oak stairway, and placed a glass-topped table made of animal bones in the center of the dining room. He claimed he was renovating the house the way he'd been "renovating the cowboy" in his historical novels. His personal library consisted of about 20,000 volumes. He turned an outdoor carriage house into a study. He transformed the house's attic into a children's library for his nieces and nephews and for Curtis.

He made regular trips into Wichita Falls to purchase stuffed animals or battery-powered ray guns for his grandson.

Whenever he was back in Tucson, the Texas house sat empty or he'd offer it as a place for his friends to stay. Sometimes items disappeared from the house—including four hundred dollars' worth of steaks from a deep freeze. McMurtry argued with his sisters: they were convinced his no-good writer guests were the thieves. McMurtry blamed bored "Archerites."

He had problems with some of the local kids he'd hired to staff Booked Up. They took advantage of his lax management style, his general disorganization. For a while, one teenage employee dealt drugs from a company van. Another got caught running a business scam out of the store involving an industrial screw company. He'd installed a hidden camera in a bathroom to spy on girls.

McMurtry spent much of his time with an adding machine at his kitchen table, trying to figure out how much had been stolen from him. He lifted and unloaded almost every box himself. The one aspect of writing he'd never gotten used to was its sedentary nature. It wasn't physical labor, at least not as his father had seen it. He liked manual work. He'd arrive at the main building in the mornings, wearing a nice blue cotton shirt, khaki pants, New Balance sneakers, and a sweater wrapped around his neck; by the end of the day, customers might see him wheezing, shirtless, in a back room, bent over dusty yellowed tomes. In certain places, the store smelled of mildew, cat urine (a calico named Colette roamed the aisles), and brown rainwater seeping in from the sidewalks outside.

At one point, Mike Evans came from Virginia to help him with the pricing. Evans was divorced from Jo but they remained close, and he kept in frequent touch with James. Side by side, he and McMurtry crawled up shaky stepladders, pulled books from the shelves, and penciled numbers inside brittle flyleaves. They'd been pricing items for so many years now, few types of books had escaped their attention, and they didn't need to consult any catalogues to estimate a volume's value. McMurtry recalled how his heart surgeons had possessed "the eyes of assassins." A rare-book dealer needed the same quality, he thought.

He paid Evans $3,000 a month and let him stay at the ranch house. "I'd go running in the mornings, be around books all day, look at the stars at night," Evans said. "It was like health camp." He'd given up drinking and felt reborn.

Booked Up's offerings—mostly scattershot—ranged from Dashiell Hammett mysteries to *H is for Heroin* to *Caterpillars and Their Moths.* Dance, theater, the arts. A slender volume called *Who Stole Feminism?* leaned against *Origins of Hydraulic Mining in California.* An illegally printed paperback copy of J. D. Salinger's uncollected fiction shared shelf space with vintage Olympic Press erotica and *Soma: The Divine Mushroom of Immortality.* A collection of Ezra Pound's typed letters from 1934, worth $2,500, lay open on a table, the startling, garbled sentences shouting from the page: "Dear sir and incidentally gorrdamnit—This is heinous! . . . the scum of Judea in the treasury . . ."

On one tall wall, a Barry Goldwater for President poster ("In your heart you know he's right") slumped above a wrinkled T-shirt proclaiming: "A woman's love is like the morning dew. It's just as apt to fall on a horse turd as it is on a rose." On another wall a wanted poster for H. Rap Brown curled above a delicate first edition of Edith Wharton's *Italian Villas and Their Gardens,* lying open on a pale wooden shelf.

Some of McMurtry's younger employees talked him into displaying his own books in a glass case, but he wanted nothing to do with selling them. One glance around the store placed his achievement in perspective, he thought: "Say you were looking for minor writers of the 1855-to-1950 period. Well, there would be thousands of them. And you would just know, you would get this feeling as you went down the row, that none of these books was ever going to be read again. They'd all started out bright with hope, and somebody had really invested some energy in them, maybe even had a public, and now they were just dead. Never to come again."

One day he was surprised to find texts he'd once owned as a Rice student turn up in a batch of books he'd bought, his name scribbled inside. On another occasion, he came across several of his novels, inscribed to friends. He figured his friends must have gotten divorced or otherwise fallen on hard times, needing to jettison their books.

His sister Sue helped him in the store. "He's pretty calm now," she observed. "He seems to like it here and seems more settled."

"I spent a lot of time in New York, Washington, and LA . . . I took the measure of several powerful places. But it just got to be where the homing instinct came over me," he reflected. "It's kind of a normal pattern—you go out into the world and then bring what you want of the world back home with you."

Of course, Archer City would never be Shangri-la. An "evil woman" ran the Dairy Queen now, he said—she owned a chain of twenty-seven DQs all across Texas. She'd turned this one into a shrine to him to lure literary tourists, displaying his book covers on the slick tiled walls, taping his standard breakfast order to the side of the cash register for everyone to see.

He still had to drive to Wichita Falls to get a decent meal. These days, he particularly liked a hole-in-the-wall Mexican joint called Sevi's, though the waitress there tended to argue with him, convinced that the beef enchilada plate, his favorite, was too much food for an elderly man: "I'll make you something smaller."

Local community leaders—Archer County judge Gary Beesinger, married to the local librarian; businessman Abby Abernathy—were delighted that McMurtry was trying to make the town a destination spot for book lovers. They wanted to build on his efforts, restoring the Royal movie theater, opening hotels and cafés to take advantage of their local celebrity's drawing power. McMurtry was skeptical; when asked to support an Archer City overhaul, he was "as indifferent as a butter churn," his friend Ceil remarked.

"The old folks don't read his novels and the young people just know him as the frail guy who buys milk at the grocery store," said Ceil's sister, Mary Slack Webb. Still, Webb, a former diagnostician with the Archer City schools, was keen to siphon what she could from McMurtry's presence. She and Ceil opened the Lonesome Dove Inn in the town's former fourteen-patient hospital on Main Street, a Colonial-style building constructed in 1927. (Archer City no longer had a doctor—just a nurse practitioner.) Each guest room at the inn was named for a McMurtry novel. The Terms of Endearment Suite, the bridal quarters, offered a king-size bed and a private bath equipped with miniature bars of Dove soap. The common room, sporting a large television and VCR, was called The Last Picture Show. On request, Webb would pack picnic lunches for people who wished to take their food to one of the Booked Up annexes and munch a beef sandwich before scanning the shelves.

Down the street from the inn, the Spur Hotel—"We only have enough business to stay open on Thursdays, Fridays, and Saturdays"—featured a stuffed bobcat and wild turkey in the lobby, various-sized antlers on the breakfast room's walls, and McMurtry books on end tables beside the rooms' narrow beds.

The Texasville Café served catfish and steak—unless they ran out of everything.

Susan Sontag, visiting, remarked that her friend seemed to be living in his own theme park: the Mickey Mouse of McMurtryville.

24

Almost every day, as the twentieth century drew to a close and the media warned of apocalypse, the approaching panic of Y2K, when the world's computers would implode and crash the technology on which we all depended (*not me,* McMurtry could rightly say, *I still do all my invoices by hand*), he drove to the Presbyterian Manor in Wichita Falls to watch his mother die. His path took him by the city's ratty outskirts, the hourly rates motels, the gravel side streets glinting with used needles. The neighborhoods were depressing, but no more so than the nursing home, the pills in paper cups, the former men and women (they weren't much of anything, anymore) parked in the hallways in their wheelchairs like old sticks of furniture to be shoved around so the janitors could mop the shit and vomit off the floors; his mother, dim and sad, unaware, clinging to a "low, almost vegetable form of life." Did she even know he had come to visit? Was there any *self* left of her? Wasn't she now like he was when he lay stretched on a chilly table, his heart packed in ice? Or maybe she *could* sense him, and it would be best to stay away, so she'd feel free to leave this world she so clearly had no use for anymore.

Often he'd drive to Wichita Falls three times a day—once to see his mother, once to copy manuscript pages at the Xerox store, and once to eat dinner. He'd thought of buying his own copy machine, but then everyone in Archer City would drop by, wanting to use it.

Some days, making the trip to see his mother, he felt like checking into a room in one of the grotty motels rather than returning to Archer City, a room where the tap water in the bathroom barely eked out, and the brown curtains, on a broken rod, wouldn't close, and no one would know where he was, so no one could ask him for anything. No decisions to be made. He'd lie on a bed so creased and worn it felt like a hammock and stare out the dusty window at the meth dealers and runaways and whores and whoever else washed up in places like this, almost as broken as the old relics curled in their sheets in Presbyterian Manor.

Don't do this to yourself, he could say. *You have a nice big house in Archer*

City—the most comfortable spot in the county. You have your family. But the old
Archer City "gloop" was closing in on him again, as it always did, no matter
how hard he tried to reconcile himself to the place, to tell himself he was glad
to be back. His sister Sue . . . what did she want, really? Working in *his* bookstore, her horizons no more distant than the red light blinking in the middle
of town (why did he always think of it as a *red* light?) His brother Charlie,
unmoored, it seemed, teaching intro lit now at San Angelo State, his welding
business having gone down the drain. Well. At least Charlie had his boy Todd
nearby, and they enjoyed riding together, weekends, on their motorbikes.

McMurtry decided to go away for a while. Quiet and alone. To think
about his folks, his birthplace, his love for it, his hatred of it, his inability
to escape it once and for all. He wouldn't check into a dirty motel room.
His instincts were healthier than that. Instead, he booked a ticket to Ta-
hiti and the Marquesas Islands, a part of the world he'd always heard was
paradise, as far from Archer City as he could get.

His sisters and his brother didn't want him to leave. Their mother
would die while he was away, they warned him. He wasn't sure if this was
a good or a bad thing.

Immediately, arriving at the airport in Dallas, he felt twin sadnesses:
an ache for his mother, remembering how small her trips had been, all
her life, both in distance and ambition: for god's sake, she'd barely made
it to Oklahoma. And of all the possible choices, he had planned a trip to
the *sea.* What was he thinking? The first time he ever saw vast waters was
when Jeff Mac and Hazel accompanied him to the Gulf Coast when they
all drove to Houston to look at Rice: it was the moment he'd made his big
move away from his folks. The break. And he'd never really gone back, no
matter how many times he returned to Archer City.

Afterward, what did he recall most about his visit to paradise? Not
the stories of artists—Herman Melville, Paul Gauguin—who'd taken
inspiration from the islands. Not the splendid orange sunsets over the
mist-draped sea. Not the Muzak version of "Streets of Laredo" repeating
endlessly in a beach restaurant. Not even all the American women reminding him of his mother, bossy and picky, hiding their irrational panic about
travel behind their irascibility.

No, what he remembered was his feeling of isolation, his apartness
from others, as the waves unfolded beneath their pleasure boat, weaving

among rocky bays. His *self* remained somewhere else; he had *still* not re-covered from his surgery. He never would. And he remembered how un-easy other people looked at the sight of him scribbling in a notebook on the boat's deck. Clearly, writing was a deeply suspicious activity.

He'd hoped the time away from home would enable him to slow down, to reflect on his parents, his childhood. But his observing eye was too fo-cused on the present, on the specifics of its vivid surroundings. It refused to turn inward (though lately his left eyelid had begun to droop; he was lucky to make any observations at all).

At least he never got seasick. He figured this was true because he'd been brought up swaying on the backs of unruly ponies. That was about as reflective as he was able to get.

In the evenings, in shoreline hotels, he'd line up behind others at pay phones beneath the glaring moon, its light striated on the foamy crests of blue-black waves. He called his sisters. His mother was still alive. Maybe that's why his mind was determined to stay in the present.

He left paradise early one morning on Air France Flight 071. At LAX, he transferred to a red-eye to Texas and landed at DFW an hour before dawn. As the plane made its descent, he glanced out the window to see a breast-like moon hovering over the vast, blowing waves of West Texas dirt.

In the airports, he had been seriously moved by the sight of excited children holding their parents' hands, running around (but never too far from their folks, always glancing back to make sure they were there), un-able to cap their lust for adventure. He'd never seen such sweetness, he thought—not even in paradise.

He rented a Lincoln to drive home. The moon had vanished into streaks of pink daylight by the time he'd passed Decatur and pulled into the crowded parking lot of the Village Kitchen in Jacksboro. After a big breakfast of greasy eggs and bacon, he drove past the ranch house where Jeff Mac and Hazel had filled his earliest days with incomprehensible yelling. He slowed but didn't stop. He passed a storage shed he rented on the edge of Archer City, packed with collectible Barbie dolls and G.I. Joes he'd somehow picked up along the way (he'd need to find a buyer for them soon; time to scale back his *stuff*). He swung by his bookshop to check the stacked-up mail. It would probably do him good to lift a few boxes and shake off his travel fatigue, but he didn't have the energy for it. He headed for Wichita Falls, past the moldy motels.

"Hi Mom, I'm back," he said softly. Hazel's room was dark. Her eyes were unfocused. Or maybe they had turned inward. Her hand did not return his squeeze. Still, he thought perhaps she had been waiting to see (or feel or sense) him one last time. Twenty-four hours later, she died.

Soon after Aulds Funeral Home interred his mother in the Archer City cemetery, on February 23, 2000, he got a call from James, informing him that James and Elena were divorcing. Curtis was nearly ten. McMurtry felt a pain in his chest, but it wasn't physical. Ossana, sitting in the room with him, watched his face go white. The explanations weren't entirely clear—were they *ever* clear when men and women parted? The musician's life on the road. Too much time apart. McMurtry remembered the children in the airports, gripping their parents' hands. The aching sweetness of it. Ossana noticed his cheeks were wet. It was the first time she'd ever seen him cry.

In fact, he was usually *too* dry-eyed these days. He tended not to blink much (a condition he sometimes blamed for his migraines). Somehow his eyelid had gotten lazy.

"I hope my left eye doesn't fall out before dinner," he'd say.

"It's drooping," Ossana would answer, too concerned to joke about it—especially since doctors had insisted he'd need surgery to correct the problem. They called it ptosis, possibly a natural by-product of aging, when the levator muscle responsible for lifting the eyelid gets stretched or some damage occurs to the muscle. Either that, or it was a symptom of myasthenia gravis, indicating an underlying condition interfering with the communication between neurons and muscles—Parkinson's, for example. The persistence of migraines was not a good sign, in this regard.

Neither was surgery, which did little to alleviate the sag.

As it turned out, the world's computers did not blink and go dark when the century ticked over, but clearly nothing else was going to stay the same. The years ahead would bring sober reckonings.

On November 15, 2004, Susan Sontag entered Memorial Sloan Kettering in Manhattan, her body pocked with more cancer than it could manage. She would survive for little over a month. It was the worst possible development, one that would occur more and more, McMurtry knew: the death of a girlfriend. He had last spoken to her when she was recovering from an earlier related illness, a uterine sarcoma, in Presbyterian Hospital. He did what he could do, then. He offered his love and goodbyes. He sent a plate of caviar to her hospital room.

"Tired of fiction, more tired of film," he wrote Max Crawford. To friends and acquaintances, even journalists, he'd pronounce, "I've written enough fiction." No one believed him. It was exactly like the time he'd declared the western dead, then turned around and written the finest series of westerns since the nineteenth century. And sure enough, the books kept coming.

"[Larry's] views . . . were in constant flux. He would say something one moment then change his mind the next. I guess in some ways [he was] a constant storyteller and moving target. I think my mother would call that 'being a contrarian' for his own amusement," Sara Ossana said.

His latest novels certainly seemed born of a contrarian impulse. The "pleasures" of his earlier books are "largely undone" by their grim sequels, Verlyn Klinkenborg complained in *The New York Times*. In *Duane's Depressed* (1999), a psychiatrist tells a patient, "You're cutting all ties, aren't you?" and that seemed to be the case with McMurtry. The books' regular appearances gave the impression of energy and industry, but their thin textures bespoke exhaustion and compulsion—a desire to kick them out and be done with them—and they resembled, more than a little, lengthy obituaries.

As with *The Evening Star* and *Some Can Whistle*, *The Late Child* (1995) revisited characters only to snuff them or leave them stranded. In this instance, Harmony, the aging Las Vegas showgirl from *The Desert Rose* who lost her job to Pepper, her coldly ambitious daughter, learns that Pepper has died of AIDS in New York City. *The Late Child* follows Harmony through wild, long, implausible road trips as she tries, rather vainly, to cope with her grief. "Mr. McMurtry's career as a serious novelist is becoming checkered fast," Klinkenborg grumbled. "Still you keep reading, because he has written novels good enough . . . to make you wonder why the rest are no better than they are."

Reviewing *The Late Child* in the *Los Angeles Times,* David Ulin wrote: "One of the things I've always found compelling about Larry McMurtry is the breadth of his literary vision, the way his characters reappear from book to book with all the serendipity of life. Particularly in his early work, McMurtry constructs a universe as fully realized as William Faulkner's Yoknapatawpha County, in which individual books are not so much separate as part of some larger progression that seems to exist beyond the page." Unfortunately, Ulin said, "in recent years . . . McMurtry has narrowed the scope of his writing, turning his back on these more fluid associations to write a series of specific sequels," revealing a writer who has "chosen to reexamine old themes because he [feels] he ha[s] nothing new to say."

Ulin had identified the problem, but his analysis was too mild. The books actually sounded angry (anger masked as outrageous, jeering humor): attempts to subvert the earlier work—as if the contrarian McMurtry was intentionally erasing his career.

His late style was not a culmination or fulfillment of his initial promise; it was a declaration of uneasiness with what he had done.

Beginning with *Texasville,* the sequels had coincided with his recommitment to Archer City, his return to the place he'd lived before he'd become known as a writer, in the shadow of a lost self, his father's son, a boy who could literally smell, in the folds of his father's shirts, the work his father insisted he do. His father's work smelled stiffly of leather, sweat, scorched hides, and animal oils.

His own shirts, the shirts he wore writing novels, didn't smell like that. They didn't smell like much of anything; they might have been the shirts of a man who hadn't done a lick of work in his life.

Was it coincidence that he began to mutter, "I've written enough fiction," as he threw himself into lifting heavy boxes in the swelling Texas heat, sweating so much he had to take his shirt off at the end of the day? He became fond of saying he was a book herder.

And yet he never stopped writing. Long ago, he had made a commitment to literature. His father had ingrained too much work ethic in him to permit him to ever abandon his commitments.

For all the undercurrents of exhaustion rippling through his sentences, there was also, in the back-to-back sequels, an urgency to wrap up unfinished business, to locate his *characters'* selves one final time—before burying them.

He was like a displaced child who'd once needed imaginary friends to approve of him. But then he'd outgrown these characters (or thought it was time to try). Without losing fondness for them, he nevertheless felt compelled to reject them in order to move ahead. And once their continuing possibilities had been eliminated, they became more thoroughly, more silently, a fixed and permanent part of him, of who he had been.

In *Duane's Depressed,* which the publisher called the capstone to the *Last Picture Show* trilogy (it *wouldn't* be the end), readers learn that Jacy Farrow has died, and Sonny Crawford dies in the course of events. "So those two stories are ended," Duane Moore says—almost a relief. A story's end does not signal its abandonment. The story becomes easier to carry then, a whole package, definable, easier to grasp.

Aging, of course, accounted for McMurtry's push to get things done. But something deep in the body and spirit beyond any rational explanation—the essence of life he had always chased in his fiction—could only be approached indirectly, which is why fiction was the ideal medium for examining human acts. Working on novels, he reaffirmed his belief that nothing important could really be explained; it could only be experienced in the daily clutter of *stuff* that fiction was so good at cataloguing.

To even attempt to explain, "to say something simplistic, such as . . . it was time for a change, would not be stating the matter accurately," he wrote in *Duane's Depressed.* "It wasn't that it was *time* for a change, particularly; it was that he had just *changed . . .* He didn't become a different man, but . . . he found himself in a different life. He hadn't given any forethought to [it]."

And just as critics and reviewers thought they had explained Larry McMurtry—he had become a tired writer, they said, cranking out sequels for money or out of weary habit—he wrote his finest contemporary novel in *Duane's Depressed.*

Gone was the harsh mocking of small-town life, the long slapstick sequences depicting the chaos of families, the sexcapades, the clever dialogue for dialogue's sake. For the first time since his earliest novels and certain sections of *Lonesome Dove,* he engaged in long, reflective passages and lyrical landscape descriptions. The prose was patient, laced with poetic repetitions and Hemingwayesque phrases linked with strings of conjunctions.

"Thunder had rumbled all afternoon," McMurtry wrote. "[Duane] closed the book [he'd been reading] and took it with him outside. He wanted to sit a minute in his lawn chair. When the shower broke, the raindrops were at first hot too, but they soon cooled. As the rain began to fall harder he rose and took the . . . book back inside . . . then he took his clothes off and went back to the lawn chair for a few minutes, letting the cool rain pelt him. It had been a sweaty day—it was nice to be showered by the fresh-smelling rain before he went to bed."

Little actually occurs in the book, beyond Duane Moore deciding one day he no longer wants to drive his pickup, run his oil business, or live with his family. No explanations; just change. The book's achievement lies in its probing of a sixtyish man's depression—McMurtry admitted Duane was a stand-in for him here—his fear of aging, his wistful backward glances. If the material was familiar, McMurtry's straightforward, unsentimental treatment of it lifted it out of the everyday: "As he watched the river . . . the river the cattlemen dreaded because of its quicksands, the river the Indians fought to keep and failed to keep, the river young Texas couples once crossed in order to get married quickly, before their parents could catch them and stop them—he had come to the edge of his country, and it felt as if he had suddenly come to the edge of his life. He had gone as far as he could go with the work he knew, with the people he knew, with the family he had helped create . . . Mixed in the sudden pain was the feeling that he had arrived at the far edge of himself . . . [His death] might not be a near thing; he might live another twenty years, or even thirty—but it lay directly ahead, the next big event, the one thing he still had to accomplish."

Duane gardens. He reads (*Lonesome Dove* is one of his favorites, and he struggles through Proust). He cultivates nonsexual friendships with women. The novel offers no startling revelations about how to cope with grief or sadness or aging. It offers what a novel can, a rich, full experience of an individual mind. "[McMurtry] proves again that he is as clear-eyed a writer as anyone in the business," Robert Houston wrote in *The New York Times*. "He understands counterpoint wonderfully, knows when to balance pathos with humor, irony with admiration . . . 'Duane's Depressed' is a worthy end to an important trilogy, one that captures vividly and movingly nearly half a century of life in a great swath of America."

He often felt frail—and would feel frailer still—but he had not lost his curiosity about the world, nor had he lost his love for driving. Between bouts of writing, he made frequent trips to Austin to see his grandson, and sometimes drove farther south and east just for the hell of it, along the lovely rivers of the Hill Country or into the old German communities or the woodlands north of Houston. In the early nineties, he had traveled for his nonfiction (which he pursued with more zeal than fiction, these days), gathering material for pieces he published in *Harper's* or *The New Republic* or *The New York Review of Books*. The rise of domestic terrorism had preoccupied him for a while, occurring, as it did, most often in his part of the world: the ATF/FBI siege of the Branch Davidian compound near Waco in '93; the Oklahoma City bombing two years later.

He remembered cruising down to Waco just days after seventy-two people, including children, burned to death in an old structure made into a religious shrine. The FBI and the ATF had attacked it with tanks, on the pretext that the godly group inside was illegally turning semiautomatic assault rifles into "full auto," something that happened every day in every back shed "here in the Fifty Caliber Belt," McMurtry said. The whole point of assault rifles was that they were easily converted into full auto in just a few minutes. Everyone knew that—including the FBI, who simply wanted to make an example of the religious leader, David Koresh, a man, McMurtry learned, who "mainly liked to preach, fuck, and play the guitar, in which preferences he was hardly unique in the annals of dipshit gurus." Still, families had sacrificed their material possessions to follow him; they were practicing a faith, as so many American subcultures had done throughout the country's history in this land of religious freedom. But the FBI decided to pull a tough-on-crime publicity stunt and go after them. Seventy-two people died.

Since "death is . . . always reported in numbers" now ("CNN alone wraps us in the griefs of the world twice every hour," McMurtry pointed out), many Americans no longer even registered such tragedies or absorbed the fact that death was always a singular experience, profoundly altering the immediate survivors.

But Timothy McVeigh was watching. Calculating. He sat for days in his truck near the roadblocks surrounding the charred Davidian compound, right where McMurtry pulled up less than a week later, hoping to get closer to the ashes. The highway patrolmen wouldn't let him near the crime scene, though they were happy to pose for photos with the author of *Lonesome Dove*.

He wasn't a reporter. He had no startling scoops to offer, to explain what had happened, what *would* happen in Oklahoma City, or to illuminate the pathologies in American culture that made such things possible. Nothing important could be explained. A novelist in his bones, he could only provide the heartbreaking details of daily life testifying to human experience: the sheet unfurled from a window of the flaming compound in the assault's sixth hour, not asking for political considerations or offering surrender, but reading WE WANT OUR PHONES FIXED, "not quite so eloquent as the letter Colonel Travis wrote while besieged in the Alamo," McMurtry said, "but not without its poignancy"; the handwritten sign in the Triangle Grocery down the road from the tragedy, offering "Hand-Made Sandwiches" and "Ammunition for Shotguns, Rifles, and Pistols"; the hawkers selling T-shirts featuring David Koresh's face in the crosshairs of a scope sight, displayed on card tables in the parking lot of the Egg Roll House Chinese Restaurant; the government officials, Attorney General Janet Reno and FBI director William Sessions, barking tactics to Waco from a communications bunker in Washington, DC, a windowless, metal-sheathed room suggesting they feared "lightning bolts from the young Messiah in Texas"; the Sleepy Hollow Pet Cemetery near the Davidians' last stand, lamenting the passing of "Buster, Not Just a Dog, He was Family," "Cougar, My Friend," "Peanut," "Cricket," "Honey Bun," almost identical to sentiments carved into the gravestones of those who perished in the Branch Davidian fire.

His curiosity about the world—and longing for lost selves—took him to the pine woods of western Oregon, on occasion. A couple of times, before Ken died, he drove out to visit the Keseys on their farm in Pleasant Hill. Faye was always happy to see him. Her hair was gray now, but she wore it longer than she had as a younger woman. It was quite becoming. Her smile remained gentle and demure after all these years.

He felt self-conscious, standing there with his drooping eyelid.

They had been kids together, in some far-off realm.

They'd walk and talk through tangled grass fields, past grazing goats and llamas and the tin-roofed barn, a wooden "University of Oregon Wrestling" sign on the house's front porch. Desuetude had claimed what was left of the bus, Further, parked in a swampy back pasture and smothered in blackberry vines.

McMurtry last visited Kesey five years before the millennium, when his goddaughter was visiting the Pacific Northwest to look at colleges. He had taken Sara and Diana to meet the Merry Prankster (the history of those days meant little to Sara, though she found Kesey's stories "awesome"). He showed them a homemade film called *Twister*—a bunch of silly old men dressed like the characters in *The Wizard of Oz,* dancing and singing "They Called the Wind Maria" . . . another poorly conceived project Kesey would never finish. It saddened McMurtry that his last visit with the man had instilled only regret over a giant wasted talent. It seemed emblematic of much of their generation, a valediction for the discarded century.

Since that visit, Faye now had two graves to tend: Kesey, dead of liver cancer in 2001, and lying next to him, his young son Jed, whom McMurtry remembered eating Cheerios in his Houston kitchen years ago. McMurtry pictured Faye now, standing in the grass, folding her arms on her chest, a mother trying to hug her absent child.

Faye had had a wearisome time of it since Kesey's passing. It was hard being the Famous Widow, especially as she'd long since lost patience with the pranks—the sleeping around, the inebriated escapades—for which Kesey would always be celebrated.

There was the memorial show for him at the McDonald Theater in downtown Eugene in the fall of 2001, in which Dave Frohnmayer, the University of Oregon president, had eulogized Oregon's literary light. Mason Williams sang the Grateful Dead's "And We Bid You Goodnight." Seven hundred and fifty people crammed the theater's seats and hundreds more stood on the streets outside. Afterward, a band of honorary Pranksters spent three days on the farm digging a hole for Kesey's colorful coffin, adorned with swirls of paint.

Faye contended with pushy tourists—the morbid and the literary—wanting to find the grave. She parried with journalists and biographers combing through her husband's textual bones. She addressed lawsuits brought by failed screenwriters claiming Kesey had swiped their intellectual property (who could prove anything? the man never signed a contract!). She negotiated with the University of Oregon concerning Kesey's manuscripts. Kesey fans raised $400,000 toward the university's purchase of the papers, $10,000 of which came from Eugene's Voodoo Doughnuts; the shop contributed fifty cents from every sale toward the cause. The school kicked in another million dollars. Faye witnessed the planning and construction of a statue in downtown Eugene—Kesey reading to a pack of kids.

As if overseeing all this wasn't enough, McMurtry thought, she had to endure Oregon's mist and rain in a claustrophobic valley where nary a horizon emerged. Yet endure she did. She always had, even when her forbearance for Kesey's recklessness ran out. McMurtry remembered when she had "finally detonated, and a just thunder was heard far across the land." It was around the time the couple retreated to the farm. Eventually she chased away the "[c]ourtiers and the groupies . . . [But the] marriage went on." In spite of everything, Faye remained as loyal to her husband as McMurtry had remained to Archer City. Clearly they were cut from the same cloth.

He had half a mind to drive back up to that dripping farm and take her away from the gloom.

On daily walks in Tucson, he would pass Susan Sontag's childhood home on Drachman Street, a boxy, flattish house with a free-standing single-car garage where Sontag spent thirteen lonely, asthmatic years before her family moved to Los Angeles in the 1940s and she "launched her ascent of the great universities of America and Europe," McMurtry said, "[moving] quickly and always upward" into the highest reaches of intellectual life. When he'd first gotten to know Tucson and learned that Sontag had been raised there, he sought the house and sent her a handful of pictures, showing her how little the place had changed. "Hope these photographs are not too much of a shock to you—your child-hood home looks as if it's waiting for your return," he wrote her. "It's empty and hasn't been spruced up in a while; still, the little tree abounds in fruit and the area is really rather prime now."

She had always refused his invitations to come to Arizona. She never wanted to see it again. Since her passing, he wished more than ever that she'd return to the city and pay him a visit—young again, eager to read every book in the world. The empty house was a melancholy reminder that the new century was only going to strip him further of the people he loved. He could not stave off depression. Earth was becoming a ghost globe, an alien planet, increasingly inhospitable. He couldn't breathe its air.

Not that Tucson was a particularly unpleasant spot to practice purga-torial existence. Arizona had its problems: stringent immigration laws; use-less ugly fences facing Mexico (don't get Leslie Silko started on the Border Patrol!). McMurtry found he couldn't joke with his neighbors about how Anglos were the real illegals in the state. "After all," he'd tell them, "we stole Arizona, along with the rest of the Southwest, in 1848, when the Treaty of Guadalupe Hidalgo was signed in Texas." They didn't want to hear it, even in jest. They were mostly "elderly, wealthy, and Eastern," and their attitude was, "The nice Mexican who works in your garden . . . coexist[s] with the bad Mexican who steals your plasma TV." And it was true that his quiet suburban street in the Catalina foothills had recently become a target of burglars so efficient (moving up from the city's southern barrios) "they might be called home invasion squads."

Still, the Book Stop on Fourth Avenue, with its inventory of 25,000 volumes, along with the children's bookshop, Mrs. Tiggy-Winkles, and the Mad Hatter over on Campbell (whose owner once threw McMurtry out for excessive browsing), made life good. The annual Tucson Festival of Books on the University of Arizona campus was an activity well worth supporting, he thought.

In sum, Tucson was, in the words of his young friend Mark Jude Poirier, "a really ugly city in a beautiful setting . . . full of interesting characters." Not bad, on balance.

McMurtry had met Poirier through Sara, who'd dated Poirier's brother for a while. Poirier had gone off to the Iowa Writers' Workshop, Johns Hopkins, Georgetown, and Stanford. His literary precociousness—and his apparent desire to impress every academic institution in the country—reminded McMurtry of the young Sontag. But Poirier was having trouble finishing a novel he'd long fought. Impressed with his talent, McMurtry and Ossana encouraged him.

Meanwhile, his clear-eyed view of his hometown had helped McMurtry accept the place with a touch of grace. McMurtry liked his arrangement with Ossana, living separately, living together, but always partnered up. Ossana worked with McMurtry in her house surrounded by dozens of unused screenplays they'd begun (a version of *Fear and Loathing in Las Vegas,* an aborted Bogdanovich project called *The Lady in the Moon*), and proposed adaptations of McMurtry books. (Terry Gilliam wanted to make *Anything for Billy,* and Terrence Malick had been approached to do *The Desert Rose,* possibly with Nora Ephron directing. Neither film got made.)

In the late mornings or early afternoons, McMurtry would take a walk, often with one or more of Ossana's dogs. He'd pass Sontag's house, its little fruit tree filled with the stutter trill of vermilion flycatchers or the chatter of cactus wrens. Down the street, finches pierced the air with sharp cheeps, and Gila woodpeckers hammered palo verde trees or pecked at dry dog food left in plastic bowls on deserted back patios.

The sounds were completely different in Archer City, regardless of the time of year: always the *chuff-chuff* of distant oil rigs, metallic echoes on

the wind (a smell of sulfur and gas), and the occasional boom-shrieks of
fighter jets from the Air Force base in Wichita Falls. McMurtry and Ossana
would unpack their bags in the tawny brick house, check to see if golfers
on the course nearby (where the old country club had been) had broken
any windows with errant hooks, and settle in. Over time, McMurtry had
given the house the flavor of a museum as well as a library: primitive oils of
buxom nudes filled the front room ("The claim is that they're from a bor-
dello," McMurtry explained), near a large painting of a cow stampede. A
grand piano reflected afternoon sunlight in the high-ceilinged living room,
from tall picture windows left curtainless, framing the soaring sky above
the plains. "Sunset is the magic time here. I can see deep into the West,"
McMurtry said. To the south, he could gaze into the Cross Timbers, the
tree belt marking the lower border of Texas's Great Plains.

He'd moved the bone table into the entrance hall, beneath a row of
antlers on the wall. Upstairs, his canopied Balinese bed.

He made daily walks into town, where he owned four out of the ten
buildings in Archer City's core. A visiting journalist from the *Architectural
Digest* wrote:

> There is something hallucinatory about Archer City: Like the Great
> Nature Theatre of Oklahoma conjured up in Kafka's *Amerika* or the
> virtually infinite library described in Elias Canetti's *Auto-da-Fé*, it seems
> to exist more in the realm of literature than in reality. In the landscape
> of the town, with its corner filling stations, scrubby farms and lone oil
> wells standing out against the horizon, a bookshop where you can find
> a rare first edition of Cyril Connolly's *Enemies of Promise* or Evelyn
> Waugh's biography of Father Ronald Knox seems utterly incongruous.
> Yet there's something heroic about it; a hundred years from now the
> book town Larry McMurtry created on the Texas prairie will be a
> legend, as mythic in its own, quintessentially American way as Sylvia
> Beach's Shakespeare & Company was in the Paris of the twenties.

"What I have in Archer City now is a kind of anthology of bookshops
past," McMurtry said. "Remnants of twenty-two bookshops now reside
there, with, I hope, many more to come. I still believe that books are the

fuel of genius. Leaving a million or so in Archer City is as good a legacy as I can think of for that region and indeed for the West."

In the late 1990s, somewhat aggravated by Mark Jude Poirier's inability to finish his novel, Ossana had suggested he come live with them part of the year in Archer City. He could work in Booked Up during the day and spend his evenings moving his fiction forward. Her tactic succeeded. "I went out there and just worked on my books and read tons," Poirier said. "I turned out *Goats,*" a highly acclaimed coming-of-age novel set in Tucson, "and *Naked Pueblo,*" a collection of short stories.

Thus it was, in Archer City in 1997, that Poirier handed Ossana a copy of the October 13 issue of *The New Yorker.* He said, "There's a story in here that I think you ought to read."

"I have insomnia. I can't sleep. It's a chronic problem I've had since I was a child, so [one night] I picked up the story," Ossana said. "[I]t's funny, when I first started reading it, I read the first column, and it was beautiful prose, but it was a Western and I had been writing Westerns, working on Westerns, for several years, and I said, 'I don't want to read this.' I put it down, but I was still pretty wound up and I said, 'Oh fine, I'll read it.'"

The story was Annie Proulx's "Brokeback Mountain," about a pair of young sheepherders in Wyoming named Jack Twist and Ennis Del Mar. Cold and lonely one night on the mountain, they initiate a homoerotic dalliance that turns into a lifelong love affair. Suffering guilt, shame, and fear, the inevitable disruptions of their family lives, they carry on in secret until Jack is killed in an accident or a homophobic beating—it is never clear—and Ennis is left to ponder what might have been had they found a way to openly celebrate their love.

"If I recall the feelings that I had when I put the magazine down, in retrospect I think what it tapped into was my own, sort of, sadness," Ossana said. "The humanity in it [touched me] . . . it tapped into my own well of grief over lost loves, or what might have been." She thought of it as a simple love story and felt great compassion for the characters.

"I was very anxious to get [Larry] to join me in writing [a] movie, and he's so stubborn. Trying to get him to read this story was a challenge," she said. She ambushed him in the kitchen one afternoon, when he'd walked in from the bookstore. "You know, he didn't want to read it because he doesn't read short fiction, because he can't write it. He had all these excuses. I said, 'Just humor me and read the thing.' So he went upstairs and read it, and when he came downstairs he didn't say anything, which, for Larry, is a big deal. If he's dismissive about something right away he'll say, 'I hate it, it was awful, never mind,' but he didn't say anything, so I was thinking, 'Yes, this has affected him.' [I'd] known this man for twenty-three years . . . and it's really the first time, and the last time since, that he's agreed with me right away about something. I said, 'Do you think we could write a script?' and he said, 'Sure,' and I was thinking, 'My God, what happened?'"

That evening, "I asked Larry how he would feel if any staunch *Lonesome Dove* fans turned against him for being involved with a film that subverts the myth of the American West and its iconic heroes. He replied that he'd never given it a thought. I told him good, I figured as much, I just needed to hear you say the words."

They wrote Proulx a single-page fan letter, saying, "We admired your story. Would you consider optioning it to us to write a script?" About a week later they got a letter from her: "Well, I don't really see a movie here, but have at it."

Proulx's story had begun to take shape one night in a cowboy bar in upstate Wyoming. "I had noticed an older ranch hand, maybe in his late sixties, obviously short on the world's luxury goods," Proulx said. "Although spruced up for Friday night, his clothes were a little ragged, boots stained and worn. I had seen him around, working cows, helping with sheep, taking orders from a ranch manager. He was thin and lean, muscular in a stringy kind of way. He leaned against the back wall and his eyes were fastened not on the dozens of handsome and flashing women in the room but on the young cowboys playing pool. Maybe he was following the game, maybe he knew the players, maybe one was his son or nephew, but there was something in his expression, a kind of bitter longing, that made me wonder if he was country gay. Then I began to consider what it might have been like for him . . . for any ill-informed, confused, not-sure-of-what-he-was-feeling youth growing up in homophobic rural Wyoming. A few weeks later I listened to the vicious rant of an elderly bar-café owner who was incensed that two 'homos' had come in the night before and ordered dinner. She said that if her bar regulars had been there (it was dart tournaments night) things would have gone badly for them."

Initially she hesitated, writing the story, because "I was an aging female writer, married too many times, and though I have a few gay friends, there were things I was not sure about." Then when McMurtry and Ossana contacted her, "I simply did not think this story could be a film: it was too sexually explicit for presumed mainstream tastes, the general topic of homophobia was a hot potato unless gingerly skirted, and given Hollywood actors' reluctance to play gay men (though many gay men have brilliantly played straight guys), it would likely be difficult to find a good cast, not to say a director. It was only because I trusted Larry's and Diana's writing skills, film experience and, especially, Larry's incomparable knowledge of the West's mores and language that I signed the contract."

McMurtry and Ossana spent three months writing the script. First they converted the "long bones" of Proulx's story into screenplay format, thirty-five pages in length, Ossana said. Then they looked for moments in the story to "enrich," gaps to fill, adding details and texture to the men's domestic lives.

The story had stunned McMurtry. He wished he had written it. It was "a story that had been sitting there all my life," he said, "waiting in patient distance for someone to write it. Now Annie . . . [had] written it, in spare, wire-fence prose . . . congruent with the landscape itself."

He saw, clearly, how Ennis and Jack slotted into the "strong, long American tradition of doomed young men: *The Great Gatsby, The Sun Also Rises, Miss Lonelyhearts,*" as well as intimate literary pairs such as Ishmael and Queequeg and Huck and Jim.

Of course, McMurtry's own body of work had always explored the intricacies of sex. "[T]he Code of the West carried with it an extremely strong prohibition against overtly homosexual action—so strong indeed that most of us did not really believe in homosexuality as a physical possibility until we reached college age," he wrote. "I witnessed a good deal of youthful homoerotic exhibitionism, but nothing more clear cut than that, and I can recall only two occasions on which there was group masturbation, both on afternoons when it was too hot to play baseball."

In the *Brokeback* screenplay, McMurtry and Ossana stressed that in many regions, the Code of the West had not substantially changed: the men's wives, upset by their husbands' behavior, were contemporary echoes of Clara from *Lonesome Dove,* angry about Gus's lifelong attachment to

Call: "All you two done was ruin one another, not to mention those close to you."

And McMurtry insisted on making explicit the link between repressed sexuality and violence, a reality "evident on the front page of almost every Texas newspaper every day," he said. He had written about this in *The Last Picture Show,* imbuing Coach Popper with rage. He had written about it in *Horseman, Pass By.* Much like Hud, McMurtry's Ennis has turned his violence "inward, on himself and his family," so puzzled is he by his smothering social climate.

The novelist in McMurtry seized on the story's key lines—as when Ennis, thinking of Jack after parting, "felt like someone was pulling his guts out hand over hand a yard at a time"—while the scriptwriter knew how to translate Ennis's turmoil into a powerful visual correlative: following the men's first sex, "ENNIS rides [across a field] . . . and discovers a shredded sheep, clearly the victim of a coyote pack. A look of shame washes across ENNIS's face."

In the story, Ennis finds work on a "highway crew." In the screenplay, roads are predictable grids made to tame the wilderness. They stand in strict contrast to the secretive wanderings in the woods of Ennis and Jack hoping to fill untamable needs. That Ennis paves roads (while longing to escape them) suggests his ongoing struggle.

Proulx was delighted by the script. Like McMurtry, she believed nothing important could be explained; fiction's job was to immerse the reader or the viewer in an experience. The "accumulation of very small details gives the film authenticity and authority," she said of the screenplay. "Ennis's dirty fingernails in a love scene, the old highway sign ENTERING WYOMING not seen here for decades, the slight paunch Jack develops as he ages . . . Ennis and Jack sharing a joint instead of a cigarette in the 1970s . . . the speckled enamel coffeepot, all accumulate and convince us of the truth of the story. People may doubt that young men fall in love up on the snowy heights, but no one disbelieves the speckled coffeepot, and if the coffeepot is true, so is the other."

Seven years would pass before *Brokeback Mountain* became a viable possibility. "I pretty much gave up on the whole idea," Proulx said. "It wasn't going to happen, because there were no producers or directors who understood the rural West, the rural anything. Old story."

It didn't even help that the screenwriters were willing to put up a chunk of their own money, an almost unheard-of proposition.

At first, "the biggest obstacle was getting the Ennis character cast," Ossana said. "There were several major, young film actors [interested], but when push came to shove their representatives just dissuaded them from it. Because they would hang on to the script for three or four months, and they wanted to do it, wanted to do it, thought it was the most amazing script they'd ever read, blah, blah, blah, blah, blah. But when it came to signing the contract they would just back away."

Brad Pitt, Matt Damon, Joaquin Phoenix, Leonardo DiCaprio, and Josh Hartnett were among the actors approached. Mark Wahlberg said, "I read fifteen pages of the script and got a little creeped out. It was very graphic, descriptive—the spitting on the hand, getting ready to do the thing . . . it's just not my deal."

When the film's first option ran out, producer James Schamus bought it for $5,000 and "sent it to four or five different directors," Ossana said. "The only director who expressed any interest was Joel Schumacher and, as it turns out, I think he pretty much just wanted to meet Larry, which he never got to do. Larry was disgusted with him because he didn't make any movement forward with it."

"Diana, don't worry," McMurtry assured her. "It'll find its way."

Meanwhile, they had watched Ang Lee's *Crouching Tiger, Hidden Dragon,* and thought *here* was a director who knew how to shoot vast landscapes. Sara had brought the actor Heath Ledger to her mother's attention—"You really ought to look at his work." She did, and she made McMurtry sit through half of the overheated race drama *Monster's Ball* at home, until he snapped, "I don't want to watch anymore, just turn it off." He stood. He'd hated the movie, but Ledger's performance impressed him. "That young man's Ennis," he said, and walked upstairs.

Schamus's studio, Focus Features, thought Ledger "wasn't macho enough," Ossana recalled, but she fought for him. When the actor saw the screenplay, he said, "It's the most beautiful script I've ever read in my life, and I would've rowed a boat halfway around the world . . . to be in this movie."

After scratching his blockbuster itch by making *The Hulk,* Lee also came aboard.

Filming began in Calgary, Alberta, in the late spring of 2004: twenty-six different locations, forty-two shooting days. McMurtry stayed in Tucson to write. Ossana flew to Calgary to oversee production. "I shared my trailer set with three guys, and it was tough, and I got pneumonia while we were making the film, but I suffered through that and kept going," she said. "[Moose Mountain,] the place where we filmed . . . those scenes, no one had ever filmed there before. The road was forty-five minutes in. It was a two-hour drive and then you had to go forty-five minutes in, four-wheeling, but you could only go *in,* or *out,* because the clearing was so narrow." Sara joined her on the set as an unpaid intern and as an assistant to the production designer. The story had become important to her, personally. About a year after her mother and godfather had completed the screenplay, Matthew Shepard, a gay University of Wyoming student, was pistol-whipped and left to die by two men just outside of Laramie. Sara happened to be attending the university at the time on a basketball scholarship. "[T]hey found Matthew's body tied to a fence not five minutes from her apartment," Ossana said. "I flew to Wyoming to be with her."

Brokeback had sprung to life.

Ossana kept a copy of Proulx's story beside her on the set. "Whenever I would feel exhausted or overwhelmed, I would center myself by rereading her story," she said.

One day Ang Lee spent several hours trying to film a flock of sheep drinking from a slow-moving brook. Ossana called McMurtry to give him an update. She mentioned the sheep. Exasperated, McMurtry said, "Hasn't anyone told him sheep won't drink from a brook? They'll only drink from still water." How did Hollywood *ever* get Westerns made?

James McMurtry provided a song for the soundtrack. Shooting wrapped in August 2004.

During the long editing process, McMurtry saw a second cut of the film in Los Angeles. "Larry is such an odd fellow," Ossana said. "He's very humble and unassuming, and he doesn't grasp the weight his words carry when he speaks, so he just says what he thinks, very direct. That's a little scary in Hollywood. So when we all went to the screening of the second cut, we got there and nobody said anything; they were very nervous. And Larry was just himself. He sat down by himself sort of in the middle of the theater and I sat way over on one side. We saw the film and the lights came on, and I looked over at him and there were tears coming down this man's face." It was the second time she'd ever seen him cry. "So we knew we had something special."

Months later, they watched a final cut of the film with a group of close friends and family in Tucson's Loft Cinema. "I was not at all prepared for the emotional tidal wave that swept over me," Ossana remembered. "[T]here I sat, having lived with these characters for over eight years—they had been more real to me at times than the corporeal—and I felt as if I were being introduced to them for the first time. After the credits rolled and the lights came up, everyone just sat there. The women were crying; the men were silent. No one spoke until we wandered outside."

On December 18, 2005, *Variety* announced the film's release date, saying, "'Moving,' 'haunting,' and 'disturbing' are words often used to describe this potent, spare story."

The film played to good critical and commercial success, grossing $178 million (off a $14 million budget). It earned eight Oscar nominations, including nods for Best Picture, Best Director, acting accolades for Heath Ledger and Jake Gyllenhaal, Best Original Score for Gustavo Santaolalla, and Best Adapted Screenplay.

McMurtry and Ossana were feted for their work, featured prominently in industry publications. *Backstage* listed them as husband and wife (and mistook Archer City for Austin). Warren Beatty let them know he didn't think there was a false note in *Brokeback Mountain*.

Gratified by the movie's reception, McMurtry dropped his curmudgeonly demeanor—briefly—sounding almost optimistic in interviews, despite the recent passage of Proposition 2 in Texas. It declared, "Marriage in this state shall consist only of the union of one man and one woman." Following the vote, Governor Rick Perry had crowed, "If there is some other state that has a more lenient view than Texas, then maybe that's a better place for them to live."

"If the governor wants to say foolish things, I can't stop him," McMurtry said. "And it's too bad about the proposition. But that's not forever. Five years from now, Governor Perry won't be there." He said he was hopeful for a flowering of tolerance, and he believed *Brokeback Mountain* would change a few minds. "I'm from the plains of Texas—the part that connects with the Midwest and with the Rocky Mountains. I think there's more decency in the great American middle class than most homophobic legislation would indicate . . . I'm not going to give up on the capacity of Texans to deal with controversy in a fair and compassionate way." (This was *Larry McMurtry*?) "I know what I'm confident of. And I'm totally confident. The right wing will not win on this issue."

As had been true throughout his career, his views were more welcome in Hollywood than in his hometown. "You know about that McMurtry? You know about his gay cowboy movie?" someone yelled across Archer City's American Legion Hall one night. Disgusted nods of assent came from the ranch help, the oil-field workers, the Wade's Well Service drivers, and a woman who worked over at the chicken processing plant in Olney. Almost in unison, they shook their heads over moist cans of Miller Lite. Wild horses couldn't drag them to that goddamn movie. Not even Charlie McMurtry, home briefly from his teaching stint in San Angelo, would see it, he said. Charlie was from the good side of the McMurtry family, the bar crowd said. He always combed his hair and wore a crease in his jeans. A fellow slapped his back. How the hell could he be related to that Larry? Even Charlie couldn't figure it out.

In 2006, Hollywood's interminably long awards season began in January and stretched until early March, culminating in the Academy Awards ceremony in the Kodak Theatre. Publicists insisted that Ossana submit to teams of beauty technicians prior to each show (she rarely wore makeup at home). She bristled "while strangers prodded and picked at me like monkeys with their young." McMurtry paced in the background, muttering to anyone who'd listen that his partner's "natural looks [were] hard to improve upon."

He confounded interviewers, offering clipped responses to their questions. When asked what he'd thought of the *Lonesome Dove* miniseries, he said he'd never watched it all the way through. He had neither the time nor the interest.

At the Critics' Choice Awards, held at the Santa Monica Civic Center, organizers told McMurtry to expect a huge protest, but only one lonely man showed up, waving a small sign: "No homos on the range."

Then came the Los Angeles Film Critics Awards. "Five and half hours sitting at a table, listening to every journalist in Los Angeles who had ever written a film review," Ossana said. "Most of them were obviously hacks," McMurtry added. And the food was bad.

The Golden Globes, sponsored by a league of foreign journalists, followed soon thereafter. Ossana almost skipped the evening: "It was the hair person's fault. My daughter Sara had given her specific instructions on how to do my hair, since I'm clueless in that regard. When the woman was finished, I experienced one of the very few meltdowns I've had in my life. I looked like Shirley Temple." She sobbed and told McMurtry to leave for the ceremony without her. Eventually Sara coaxed her out of the room. The couple won in the Best Adapted Screenplay category—a good indicator of how the Oscar vote might go. Accepting the award, McMurtry thanked his typewriter, then promptly disappeared for a lengthy spell in the men's room. Publicists, interviewers, and hosts searched frantically for him, enlisting the aid of Harrison Ford.

He also disappeared into the loo at the Writers Guild Awards, right before a presenter announced Ossana and McMurtry as winners. Panicked, Ossana flipped raspberry sorbet onto her shirt. She "looked like [she'd] tried to commit hari-kari," McMurtry remarked. The presenter ignored the spreading stain when she met Ossana onstage.

At the Directors Guild Awards, McMurtry began to wonder, "If it feels this bad to attend these affairs and win, what must it feel like to be here and lose?"

Ossana accused him of having the "attention span of a gnat. Unless the stage is lined with beautiful women, you have no interest at all in what's happening up there."

On the night of March 5, arriving at the Kodak Theatre for the walk up the red carpet, McMurtry said he felt "a little like Captain Cook must have felt walking ashore in the Society Islands just before he was bludgeoned to death." Annie Proulx noticed a purple tinge to the red carpet from the glare of a nearby SCIENTOLOGY sign blazing on a building.

Ossana wore a sleeveless blue gown from the Italian fashion line M Siamo—"I was loyal to my heritage," she said. McMurtry wore a tuxedo coat, a bow tie, and blue jeans. He told Ossana he'd lost his tuxedo trousers, but she knew that wasn't true. He was simply determined to remain comfortable during the lengthy ceremony. It was bad enough being squeezed into the auditorium, stuck for hours listening to gasbags, fretting about your bladder.

Crash, an LA crime drama, a pointed "message" film concerning U.S. race relations, won Best Picture that year. Jack Nicholson made the announcement; McMurtry thought he mouthed the word *fuck* when he opened the envelope. Nicholson had told him he was pulling for *Brokeback Mountain.* "We lost because ours was a rural story," McMurtry reasoned. "America is so urban now, people can't truly grasp the reality of rural life anymore."

Annie Proulx was furious about the result. "If you are looking for smart judging based on merit, skip the Academy Awards," she groused. "Roughly 6,000 film industry voters, most in the Los Angeles area, many living cloistered lives behind wrought-iron gates or in deluxe rest homes, out of touch not only with the shifting larger culture and the yeasty ferment that is America these days, but also out of touch with their own segregated city, decide which films are good."

Yet Ang Lee became the first non-Caucasian to win Best Director. And McMurtry and Ossana took home Oscars for Best Adapted Screenplay. Ossana felt McMurtry "deserved to be up there more than anyone in that theatre" because "films derived from [his] writing [had] gotten thirteen Oscars and thirty-four Oscar nominations."

When Dustin Hoffman announced their names from the stage, Mc-Murtry turned to his partner, grinning like a child, but she was already up from her chair, spanning the aisle, deadly serious. Shoulders back, head high. She was regal. She didn't look behind her. McMurtry trailed her at a distance. He nearly stumbled on the stage steps, and Hoffman moved to lend him a hand if necessary.

"The duty of art is to send light into the darkness of men's hearts," Ossana said, gripping her statue. She thanked her "good friend Mark Poirier" for bringing Proulx's story to her attention. "Thank you to my writing partner Larry," she added, "and thank you for giving this award to him as well."

When she'd finished speaking, the couple's allotted time was up and a backstage gofer was gesturing crazily, trying to shoo them from the stage. McMurtry ignored him and approached the microphone. He praised Ossana's "smarts, guts, drive, good judgment, tenacity, loyalty, and generosity. That's the kind of virtues you need in the rough strife of moviemaking." He announced his love for and pride in his son James and grandson Curtis. "Finally, I'm gonna thank all the booksellers of the world," he said. Audience members glanced around, puzzled. They would have been even more perplexed if they'd ever seen McMurtry lifting boxes in the aisles of Booked Up in the godforsaken town of Archer City, Texas. This man who'd just snatched their coveted trophy, wearing faded blue jeans, didn't seem to belong to *their* tribe. "Remember that *Brokeback Mountain* was a book before it was a movie," McMurtry went on. "From the humblest paperback exchange to the masters of the great bookshops of the world—all are contributors to the survival of the culture of the book, a wonderful culture which we mustn't lose."

26

Polly Platt—soon to be one of his ghosts—had once said of Mc-Murtry, "There's something about him that's such a mystery—he's the unknowable man."

Diana and Sara left the Kodak Theatre following the Academy Awards ceremony to celebrate; the unknowable man, determined to share no more of himself that evening, handed his Oscar to Sara and said he was returning to Santa Monica, to the Casa del Mar Hotel, and to bed. His personal publicist, a woman named Amanda Lundberg, walked him to his limo. It was only after Lundberg had disappeared into the dark that he realized the car was waiting for Diana and Sara. They had all come together. He'd have to get back on his own. He figured he'd stroll partway up Hollywood Boulevard, then catch a cab to blessèd slumber.

It was a risk for an old man to be walking alone so late, but he used to walk this street all the time when he and Jo had first come to California in the early 1960s. Back then, he couldn't have known who he'd become, how often he'd return to Hollywood, whom he'd meet, and what he'd achieve. Over the years, as a lark, he'd enjoyed visiting fortune-tellers in various cities, asking them to reveal who he was. (His favorite was a "French woman in Tucson who kept a rather ill-tempered goose by her side as she worked.") The seers always hedged their bets, assuring him he'd become neither rich nor poor. If someone had told him he'd one day play tennis with Barbra Streisand on the private court of famous film producer Robert Evans, and that she'd be such an intense competitor, he'd spend the next half hour throwing up, he'd have been impressed.

But his celebrity encounters did not make him who he was, any more than the Oscar he'd fondled earlier this evening. As he moved east up the boulevard, he found he could not concentrate on the cinema legends he'd known or—to be honest—desperately fled when he'd left the theater tonight. The *self* he feared he'd lost on the operating table remained elusive.

Here he was, a seventy-year-old man shuffling past Musso & Frank, feeling inside more like the twenty-five-year-old he was when he first strolled this street. The self was a palimpsest, layers of time, memories laid upon memories like pages in a novel, and who he *really* was, when the wind riffled those fragile leaves, was anyone's guess. It all depended on where you put your finger in the book.

It used to take him twenty minutes to walk as far as he had. Now it took forty.

The Hollywood Walk of Fame: more lost selves. Louis Armstrong, Patsy Cline, Bogie, the effervescent Marilyn . . .

Madame Tussauds, busy casting the past in a pale rigor mortis, gussied up and posed handsomely, the way we'd always hoped it would look.

But the real ghosts were the quiet spirits of the bookstores, more than fifteen of them along this stretch of road and on adjacent streets, now long gone, except for Larry Edmunds. The shops had stayed open most of the night, and he had wandered their narrow aisles until stumbling into the first light of dawn.

He recalled the Heritage. Over there, the Pickwick . . . He turned to see . . .

And then, unbidden, another layer fell on his *Leaves of Grass*.

Houston. 1968 or '69. James was five or six. Little Jamie.

He remembered he had been driving a Ford Sedan down Greenbriar Drive. A big square "For Sale" sign stuck in a dying lawn in front of a modest house caught his eye; in his usual way, back then, he wondered what the story was. Had a young couple lived in the house? Had they gotten divorced? Or was there a death? He'd taken his eye off the road just for a second or two, but it was enough: he slammed into a delivery truck stopped at a red light. Jamie, in back, hurtled forward, hitting his nose on the seat. Fortunately, they'd been traveling at only some five miles an hour. Jamie's head throbbed, but his nose didn't bleed.

The driver of the delivery truck was a young Black man wearing a white T-shirt. He had done nothing wrong but seemed inordinately nervous. A Houston cop, dressed in brown and with a glum demeanor to match, pulled up, took out a ticket book, and glared at the truck driver. McMurtry said, "No, sir, it was my fault." He assured the cop the ticket should go to him. No matter how many times he confessed his error, the officer wouldn't stop staring angrily at the deliveryman, whose fear grew more and more palpable. In the end, McMurtry couldn't remember whether he'd been issued a ticket. He'd not thought of the incident since, and in fact hadn't worried much about it then, since no one was seriously hurt and they all went their separate ways.

Why did this minor affair nudge his memory tonight?

In retrospect, he understood that the truck driver knew things Mc-Murtry didn't know then. He was a Black man passing through a white neighborhood, so it didn't matter if he was innocent. Watching the cop's face, the man knew the whole situation was about to teeter into nastiness, and it's a wonder it didn't.

Now, standing alone and a little cold on Hollywood Boulevard, Mc-Murtry felt like both his younger self *and* the Black man, ignorant and wise all at once, embittered by experience, waiting there anxiously on a busy city street.

Certain forms of knowledge existed beyond a young man's confidence, a novelist's imagination, a fortune-teller's skills . . . or an old man's meanderings once completed in half the time.

This trembling figure, the truck driver, standing in his mind like a wax effigy in the dark . . . he seemed to demonstrate the self's tenacity, its deep instinct toward self-preservation. Then, just as quickly as he had arrived, sweating, the driver wavered and disappeared. What remained in McMurtry's head was him at twenty-five, his desire to make seventy; the seventy-year-old's gentle reach from the future to cradle the younger man. Tonight, in the extinguished lights of the bookstores they'd both cherished, they had met here on the street, young and old, the innocent and the worn, as if they'd long known each other. As if they crossed paths all the time, trading secrets, sharing knowledge.

The lights went out in Larry Edmunds, the lone bookstore remaining on the block. Closing time.

At Hollywood and Vine he flagged a cab. It took him to Casa del Mar. While the ghost of Swifty Lazar toasted Bogie at some ethereal Oscar bash, vibrating to the music of actual celebrations the length and breadth of the city, McMurtry ate a cheeseburger and went to bed.

He was weepy these days. Old age depression was different from a young man's black moods. Youthful depression was like a cloudburst, often sudden and intense. It was all-encompassing, difficult to see through or wade past. As an older man, he fell into a funk like a golfer strolling casually across a sloping smooth green and then stumbling into a sand trap, unable to extricate himself. The quick collapses took him by surprise. He could live with the aches better than he had as a youth (they were so familiar by now), but they were no less debilitating. Doctors spoke of chronic versus situational depression. He couldn't separate the two. Life was a situational affair, and it was chronic until it wasn't.

Two years after winning an Oscar, he was back in Los Angeles. He had hoped the Oscar would bring producers to him, rather than the other way around. He didn't want to be dragged to LA anymore. Flying was a pain in the ass now. The security lines, exposing everyone's irritability . . .

Ossana got tired of hearing him complain. "I'm funnier the grouchier I get," he told her. She did not agree.

This time he'd come to LA to receive the Los Angeles Public Library's Literary Award. At a dinner banquet downtown, Diane Lane, Jake Gyllenhaal, and Jeff Bridges praised him as an unstoppable creative force and a bringer of truths. Diane Keaton read a passage from *Terms of Endearment*. She gave him a print of a photo she'd taken of a pair of taxidermied conjoined sheep, which they'd found together, years ago, in Larry Mooney's morbidity collection. She handed him the award.

He rose slowly, wearing his comfy jeans and boots, and a "wide red tie that surely dated from the Carter administration," one observer wrote. He spoke haltingly of the death of the book. Dutton's Books, one of LA's largest independent bookstores, had permanently closed its doors, just that day. McMurtry said that, in 1963, when he'd first arrived in Los Angeles, there were 115 secondhand bookstores between Long Beach and Van Nuys. All gone. He said he could still name seventy-five of them. He started to list a few. He choked up after the first three. "Even thinking about them makes me cry," he apologized. "It makes me very sad to come here now."

He attempted to read a stanza from a Philip Larkin poem about the end of Western culture. He faltered again.

The following afternoon, in a public discussion at the Central Library, he repeated his belief that book culture was dying. "I fear for libraries," he said. "The computers are marching into libraries now and the books are being sent away."

Computers "can't bring us love, endow us with grace . . . they can't exempt us from death."

"The great majority [of people] don't read anymore, and what in my childhood was a democratic pleasure, open to anyone who could get a library card, [has become a] mandarin pleasure," he said.

He knew that children still loved to read—in Archer City, he had just culled over eight hundred children's books from Booked Up's shelves and donated them to a nearby play school. "However, there is a point at which technology seduces [children] toward a more and more broken narrative."

He mentioned his grandson Curtis, seventeen now, a budding musician like his father. "Curtis was a big, big reader . . . like me, meticulous about reading. And yet I don't think that Curtis is reading now." He paused. His hands shook. "I don't know if Curtis will come back." Or if there would be anything for him to return to.

"I don't think [books] are going to be there much longer," he concluded.

A few months later, in Houston, delivering the Friends of Fondren Library Distinguished Guest Lecture at Rice University, he reiterated that the "tsunami of technology: iPod, iPhone, Blackberries, [and] computers" was destroying children's reading abilities. He wept again.

He said he once believed book culture would last forever. He was sadder but wiser now. "It will never come back," he said.

He spent most of the year in Tucson now. About once a month, for two or three days, he'd check on his bookstore in Archer City. He'd left the buildings in the capable hands of local managers, a sprightly group of women led by Khristal Collins, who'd worked in the store since she was a teenager. A visiting journalist, in town one day to do a feature on McMurtry's business, described Collins as having "internalized some of the store's suffusing stillness . . . [S]he was patient and gracious and helpful, but said no more than she had to, and after showing me into the main room of the first building, she left soundlessly, before I realized she'd gone."

She'd hung a guide to Booked Up's holdings on the side of a shelf in the second building: "*Q: How are the books arranged?* A: Erratically/Impressionistically/Whimsically/Open to Interpretation."

In the afternoons, McMurtry liked to sit in the main building, reading to the children of his employees. In Tucson, he scanned *The New York Times, The Washington Post,* and *The Wall Street Journal* every morning; here, there was only the *Archer County News*: "Having hog problems? We will trap your property or keep them run off with dogs." He much preferred Dr. Seuss, rocking calmly with a child in his lap.

Sometimes James came to town. He split his time between Austin and the ranch house. From the ranch house porch he could see a new wind farm across the grass fields, the whirling blades silhouetted against the horizon, next to the skeleton ribs of skinny oil rigs. His boy lived in Austin, playing guitar in various "teenage bands," he told McMurtry. Soon Curtis would be off to Sarah Lawrence College, to study music composition and contemporary chamber music.

Unless James was around, McMurtry kept himself scarce, avoiding most customers and newspaper folks. Donna Marney, the manager of Allsup's convenience store, just down the street from the original Booked Up, was amazed where "people come from to go to these stores. New York—way out of state. I'm thinking, 'My God!'" The locals were just like *her*: "I'm not a reader and I don't have the time."

In search of supper, on his way to Wichita Falls, McMurtry passed little fires on the prairie—scamps cooking meth. The drug had become the county's scourge. Rig workers doing twenty- or thirty-hour shifts had always needed some kind of boost; speed was nothing new in this part of the world. But the meth heads were crazy, desperate to fund their habits and schemes, resulting in the theft of a lot of oil-field equipment. Between the fires and the Walmart Supercenters rimming the outskirts of Wichita Falls, sucking all the local business their way, poor old Archer City felt under siege. In fact, aside from McMurtry's stores, it looked like a ghost town again. On Main Street, there were three gas pumps, but no full service. Businessman Abby Abernathy had led a drive to bring more tourists to town, piggybacking on McMurtry's book trade; he'd even succeeded in reopening the Royal Theater, turning it into a live performance venue, but the townsfolk gave it little support. It was struggling again. Abernathy gave up and moved to Wichita Falls. "I did everything I could do," he said. "I gave them all I had . . . There's some really good people here, but many are suspicious of change . . . [and] they don't understand what [Larry] created."

"He's what's keeping the town alive right now," said Mary Webb, over at the Lonesome Dove Inn. "Other than that, I don't know why anyone would want to come to Archer City."

But McMurtry wasn't keen on playing to tourists. Serious book lovers were one thing. Tourism . . . it just meant pawed-over stock and smelly, plugged-up bathrooms.

So he spent more and more of each passing year in Tucson—kept there, in part, by his cataracts. Over time, they afflicted both eyes, impairing his reading.

"He's been a bear. Extremely irritable," Ossana told people.

Surgeries—eight months apart—didn't seem to help, at least not immediately.

Blessedly, Ossana's household was pleasant and manageable, single-storied with a low flat roof. He could stand at the glass-plated door and soak up the light. It was a "house of many creatures," he said, a sisterhood of dogs and a haven for a black rescue bunny, Beauty, who spent her days quietly nibbling lettuce leaves next to Ossana's bed.

Soon the house burbled with kids. It was one of the surprising pleasures of his old age that he was surrounded by children—those of his employees in Archer City and Sara's two kids, a girl and a boy, along with their buddies in Tucson.

Sara had met her husband, Mathew Provost, a filmmaker, on the set of *Brokeback Mountain*. Together, they established an independent film company. After playing basketball for the University of Wyoming, Sara had gone to Rice and then to the Rhode Island School of Design, graduating with a master's in interior architecture. She cofounded a hand-crafted furniture company (she had always been impressed by the fineries McMurtry had collected, and her father was a carpenter); eventually, she would devote herself to designing assisted living homes, after seeing her father through his last days in hospice care.

Surrounded by family and friends at dinner, McMurtry would hold forth on any number of topics. Their friend Skip Hollandsworth recalled one two-day visit to Tucson in which McMurtry's "restless, roving intellect" ran him over. "During my time with him, he talked about the personal lives of European leaders during World War I, a Siberian leper colony . . . presidential campaign[s], concussions among professional football players . . . the problems with air travel, his love of Dr Pepper and Fritos, the geoglyphs that can be found in the Atacama Desert of Chile, and a rodeo performer he once knew whose boot was ripped off during a bull ride, then sent flying through the air until it clobbered a spectator sitting in the bleachers."

Ossana recalled an evening "when my whole family was here for dinner . . . Larry started talking about early twentieth-century authors and he ended up talking about women and inverted nipples. We just sat there, our mouths open, wondering how his brain works."

The older the violin, the sweeter the music," Gus remarks in *Lonesome Dove,* but the older McMurtry got, the more he wondered how the *world's* brain worked—if it worked at all. He'd strain his eyes over his Hermes typewriter (whose ribbons he had more and more trouble changing with his trembling fingers), pounding out cries of the heart for *The New York Review of Books.*

The GOP, he wrote, had "become the party of stale air," its candidates resembling statues, parade floats, or mannequins. Republicans legislated by "sound bite." Among the worst of the lot was Texas governor Rick Perry, a "slicked up trashmouth . . . whose only salient principle seems to be that all attention is good." McMurtry was aghast when Perry announced that Texas would "leave" the Union "if Washington continues to thumb their nose" at us, and when he declared climate change a fraud even as the worst wildfires in Texas's history threatened Austin's city limits.

In January 2011, when Representative Gabrielle Giffords of Arizona was shot in the head outside a Safeway in Tucson, at a constituent meeting in which six people died, including a nine-year-old girl, McMurtry struggled to understand the claims of those who argued that reasonable gun regulations would threaten the First and Second Amendments.

But when had America *ever* been reasonable about guns?

"More people died outside that Safeway on a Saturday morning . . . right up the road from where I write . . . than died in the famous and endlessly re-enacted shootout at the O.K. Corral in Tombstone, also not very far down the road," he wrote. He had met Gabby Giffords; once, on a flight from Dallas, they'd had a grand time together, talking movies. He'd found her "lively, and full of sass," a levelheaded populist. He shopped all the time at that Safeway. It carried his favorite detergent. He owned several guns; he used to like to hunt. Suddenly, each of these facts had become integers in a series of equations for or against gun control, abstracted into rants about rights, oppressions, greedy leaders, and extremists, none of which made much sense when returned to their real-world particulars—a smart, lively woman; a neighborhood grocery store; a hobby requiring discipline; a poorly treated mental illness.

It would take more than a local fortune-teller and her irritable goose to envision a happy future for a nation so determined to break itself into a thousand little pieces.

And how could he recover *his* self (again, again) if he couldn't spend long hours reading? Reading not for information or even pleasure—but for security, the safety and familiarity of it. The print in most books hurt his eyes now.

There *was* one volume he came across, Pekka Hämäläinen's *The Comanche Empire*, that intrigued him.

Revisionist western historians, such as Professor Hämäläinen, dominated academia now. They rejected the old narrative—that, in the nineteenth century, white settlements in the American West were triumphalist, overcoming incredible hardships of economics, weather, and indigenous violence to establish an orderly foothold in the wilderness. The revisionists preferred a different story, describing European expansionism as an unmitigated disaster, destroying Native populations, the environment, and humane relationships among white families.

McMurtry didn't disagree with these upstarts—essentially, he was one of them—but he didn't appreciate inflexibility. For instance, he'd never bought his uncles' view that the Comanches were simply murderous devils unworthy of in-depth study; nor did he buy Professor Hämäläinen's assertion that before the Europeans' arrival, the Comanches had "created a centralized multilevel political system, a flourishing market economy, and a graded social organization that was flexible enough to sustain and survive the burdens of their external ambitions"—in short, a colonial empire, though it was not, Hämäläinen admitted, "a rigid structure held together by a single central authority, nor was it an entity that could be displayed on a map, a solid block with clear cut borders."

What? McMurtry thought. "How can the Comanche empire be centralized and multilevel on one page while lacking a central authority on the next?" Apparently, the revisionists liked to keep and eat their cake, too. (Though he was also willing to admit that his "prairie-born way of thinking about Comanches" may have blinded him some, and he readily conceded that traditional historians, such as Roy Bedichek, Bernard DeVoto, and Wallace Stegner were all too willing to give white settlers a pass.)

Patricia Limerick, one of the leading revisionists, later summarized the *real* difference between McMurtry and her camp: he was an elegist, needing to grieve a lost way of life, susceptible to the idea of a vanishing frontier, while she was an ongoing champion of reparations. Righting old injustices. She had a political agenda to attend to. He had mourning to do. Aside from this, they agreed entirely on the actual historical events. "If we were to conceive of the activity of speaking forcefully about sorrow, loss, and disappointment in Western history as a horse race, Larry McMurtry had crossed the finish line while I was still saddling up," she wrote warmly, in an appreciation of him after he died.

(Most recently, the elegist in him was particularly haunted by the fact that when he and Diana Ossana produced the *Comanche Moon* miniseries, they'd hoped to find young Comanches to hire as extras, riding bareback in an attack scene. "[W]e were regarded with astonishment by the Comanche youth," he said. "Ride bareback? Us? Young Comanches nowadays ride pickups, and maybe now and then a tractor . . .")

In any case, quibbling with the revisionists gave him plenty of energy to pore through pages in spite of the pain in his eyes.

McMurtry always felt that if he could capture the rhythm of a strong narrative voice, he could write as fast as he could type: the work was in his fingers and mind more than in his eyes.

No tardy recovery from cataract surgery was going to prevent him from achieving his daily ten-page quota. He began at seven-thirty each morning. An hour and a half later, he'd be done.

As a matter of fact, he'd honed this lifelong routine, getting it almost down to the minute, in the months *before* his eye operations. Such discipline carried him through his vision fog.

And as usual, it had produced a raft of books.

In 2000, he'd published *Boone's Lick*. The novel told the rather sparse story of Mary Margaret Cecil and her clan, journeying from Boone's Lick,

Missouri, to what would later be the state of Wyoming, right after the Civil War. Related in screenplay-ready dialogue, the episodic tale balanced farce with random violence (the drama lay in the journey itself, rather than in the excuse for the journey). Most reviewers dismissed it as minor McMurtry.

The actor Tom Hanks read the novel one summer on a camping trip in Idaho and thought it would make a successful movie; McMurtry and Ossana obliged him with a screenplay, but this was yet another project fated to burn in development hell.

Boone's Lick was followed quickly by *The Berrybender Narratives*, a quartet of novels—*Sin Killer, The Wandering Hill, By Sorrow's River,* and *Folly and Glory*—published between 2002 and 2004. They concerned the misadventures of a wealthy British family roaming the U.S. West, starting in the 1830s, in search of wild game. McMurtry had long been fascinated by the fact that American westerns had always been popular in Europe—maybe more so than in the United States. (Rudolf Muus, a Norwegian, wrote over five hundred westerns, bested by the Frenchman George Fronval, weighing in with more than six hundred tales. By contrast, Zane Grey managed only seventy-eight.)

The *Berrybender* books also drew upon McMurtry's love of the Lewis and Clark journals, several passages of which provided fodder for key scenes and even memorable phrasings in his novels. (In the narrative, women's privates are referred to as "the battery of Venus," a direct lift of Captain Clark's description of Wahkiakum women wearing bark clothing.) Once more, the journey is all; incidents tilt toward farce. Life, the novels insisted, is an uninterrupted sequence of arbitrary violence—interspersed, intermittently, with clever dialogue.

As in the past, McMurtry seemed determined to undermine his earlier work with self-parody—specifically, here, the *Lonesome Dove* quartet. Reviewing *By Sorrow's River* in *The New York Times,* Verlyn Klinkenborg said "the Berrybender version of the American West" was no more real than "Harry Potter's England."

McMurtry had also broken a rule he'd set for himself—not to write past his family's memory. The *Lonesome Dove* novels fell more or less within his great-grandparents' lifetimes; he felt he could claim the events of those days as legitimate scraps of his family lore. The *Berrybender* books took him further back, into less intimate territory.

Texas critic Don Graham, usually a McMurtry champion, was dismayed by the results (though the novels' energy and humor will likely earn them more favorable critical assessment someday). Graham wrote that "boredom is the essence of the *Berrybender* saga." The books read like television comedy scripts, he said, full of "munchkins, munchies, and milquetoast males"—"It's as though McMurtry took the worst of James Fenimore Cooper and married it to the worst of Jane Austen." The "laugh track" was the only missing element.

McMurtry did not please critics when he published another western just two years after completing *The Berrybender Narratives*. *Telegraph Days*, an episodic account of a spunky lady journalist mingling with the likes of Buffalo Bill, Wild Bill Hickok, Wyatt Earp, and George Custer, seemed "unedited" and "clunky," according to *The New York Times*.

Dwight Garner, one of the *Times*' most prominent book critics, felt so exasperated with McMurtry, he declared that "Mr. McMurtry . . . hasn't made it easy [for us]. He writes so much that supply outstrips demand. A lot of his stuff verges on being—how to put this?—typed rather than written. He's published more guff, over the past 50 years, than just about any other major (semimajor? majorish?) American writer. It's not just that Mr. McMurtry has written his share of not-good novels . . . He also tends to muddy the memories of his best ones . . . by writing sequels to them."

Yet—as before—just when McMurtry seemed to have outworn his welcome, he surprised readers with a vital, funny book, *Loop Group* (2004), his first contemporary novel in years. It was about a middle-aged woman named Maggie Clary searching for love and sex following a hysterectomy. Like McMurtry's heart surgery, the hysterectomy has left Maggie feeling the loss of her essential self. With her friend Connie, she sets off on a road trip—what would a McMurtry novel be without a long journey?—hoping to scare up adventure. The novel was notable not for its story line or structure, but for the accuracy and affection with which McMurtry observed Maggie, Connie, and Maggie's three grown daughters.

"She had been a caregiver too long," Maggie realizes one day. "[S]uddenly life had taken an unexpected turn—the caregiver needed care."

Writing in *The New York Times*, Liesl Schillinger pointed out that "the book's primary classification in the Library of Congress catalog is: 'Middle-aged women—Fiction.'" Generally, the "heroines of popular fiction tend to be much, much younger," she observed, "but when you think about it, middle-aged women have never fared particularly well, even in serious literature . . . Clearly, more sincere praise of the mature woman is overdue. And McMurtry's adulation is more than sincere, it's heated." *Loop Group* struck her as "heroic."

Janet Maslin went further: "The Chick Lit genre has many mothers. It also has a father: Larry McMurtry, whose 'Terms of Endearment' anticipated the kind of headstrong, dizzy, happily self-interested heroine who has since become so familiar." She welcomed Maggie Clary, McMurtry's latest smart and appealing "Old Chick," a feisty woman determined not to "fade away."

The McMurtry novels of the early 2000s, none of them destined to rest among his best, challenged his longtime readers and highlighted a pattern in his career: even when each new book seemed weaker than the last, his growing body of work came to look more and more impressive. Individually, some of the novels disappointed; collectively, they expressed a unique American vision, Faulknerian in its dense social webbing.

"He's too good," Norman Mailer said. "If I start reading him, I start writing like him."

Critic Benjamin Moser wrote:"Every great writer has his failures. The bad books are inextricable from the good ones. The great writer isn't the one whose every utterance is crafted and workshopped and polished. When you read through a writer's work, you see that the successes depend upon the failures; they come out of them. The failures suggest the problems; the successes solve them. And that's why the great writer is the one who dares to fuck up."

When McMurtry read his comments, he wrote Moser: "That's the best piece anyone's ever written about me."

Contemporary or historical, what bound the novels together was Mc-Murtry's sensibility, his eye for America's dying subcultures, for the ghosts they unleashed, and for the viral erosion stirred by their demise, threatening the health of culture as a whole.

27

One day in early March 2011, McMurtry called Faye Kesey, up in Oregon. Would you like to come visit me in Tucson? he asked. And take a look at Archer City?

She said sure, she'd always wanted to see his bookstore.

So she flew out. "It got romantic quickly," Ossana said. Faye was seventy-six, McMurtry seventy-four. For some time now, McMurtry liked to joke that he and Ossana "sound[ed] like an old married couple," bickering constantly. But the thing with Faye . . . it was much different from the old-shoe friendship that he and Ossana had settled into and his long-distance phone partnerships with women. For one thing, "Faye didn't like to be on the phone," McMurtry complained. She'd hardly say a word. And she "didn't know his reputation" as a serial caller.

Later, Faye said the romance "was very unexpected," though it's true they'd long been curious about each other. "Actually, I thought he might be very ill and that he wanted to see old friends before he was going to die." What was "partly in the back of my mind . . . I know Ken had wished he'd talked to people. He had gone downhill so fast," she said.

McMurtry admitted he'd called Faye, thinking, "I was going to die soon. I thought she probably wanted to be helpful."

"That's a bunch of malarkey," Ossana remarked whenever McMurtry uttered such things. "You invited her down here . . . who knows what was in your head."

Things heated up when "I realized he wasn't about to die," Faye said.

She made three trips to see him in March. On the third visit, when she arrived at DFW, he proposed marriage to her. "I got off the plane and we walked to the Hyatt Hotel . . . we had gotten a room," Faye recalled. The next day he bought her a ring at a Zales jewelry store in downtown Wichita Falls.

They had known each other most of their lives (though they'd seen each other rarely), and what they didn't know, whatever differences lay between them, was quickly dispatched in the accelerated time frame of their status as elders. Faye, a teetotaling Baptist, asked him if he believed in God and he said no. Okay, she said.

He liked her slight frame, her unwavering smile, the way she stood half a head shorter than he. She had wonderfully big feet.

Faye called to tell her children the news; they "were pretty surprised." McMurtry informed Ossana in a letter. When he called James, James was driving; he almost ran off the road. "Dad hasn't been married in fifty years. What the hell?" he thought. Then he figured, "At their age . . . do they want to dillydally around or get right to it? Who can blame them? This is what he wants to do."

On April 29, 2011, at the Archer County courthouse, a justice of the peace pronounced them husband and wife. Karren Winter, the county clerk, said they were "very sweet. It was really good to see Larry look so happy. They were just the sweetest couple coming in to get their marriage license."

"I promise I'll always be interesting," McMurtry said in his vows.

Two months later, on June 21, they held a public celebration at the big house in Archer City. Dozens of friends and family members were invited—not without stirring tension. McMurtry's sisters didn't know what to make of the marriage. His brother Charlie was standoffish; he was staunchly anti-Obama, and he and McMurtry tended to avoid each other so as not to get into political scrapes. McMurtrys gathered in a swelling herd from all across the plains.

Faye's boy, Zane, came from Oregon. Diane Keaton flew in for the party, as did Maureen Orth, Susan Freudenheim, Andrew Wylie, and Leon Wieseltier. Laurence McGilvery, McMurtry's old bookselling buddy from the Perry Lane days, said he "was the person who knew Faye the longest, aside from her family." Marcia Carter arrived; she became "my encyclopedia to all things Texas," McGilvery said. "We were all in the house the night before—a couple hundred people," he remembered. "We were up on the balcony. There was a big storm. It wasn't raining, but we could hear thunder and see rain and lightning in the distance."

The next day, before the festivities started, McMurtry learned that his nephew Todd Wayne, his brother Charlie's boy, had been killed on the road the night before as he was winding his way to Archer City. He'd been struck by lightning, maneuvering his motorbike on the slick back roads.

Naturally, the news cast a pall on the proceedings, but by the time everyone tramped over to Booked Up to toast the brave couple, McMurtry and Faye were beaming, she in a dark sweater and a nearly ankle-length polka-dotted dress, he in baggy pants snagged by red suspenders, his eyeglasses draped on a cord around his neck beneath a shock of shaggy gray hair.

As James would later write of an old couple, in a song called "Canola Fields," they had cashed in on a more-than-thirty-year crush: a pleasure denied callow youth.

Oftentimes, "Larry was kind of a prick" before his heart surgery, Ossana said. Then he'd mellowed. Faye gentled him even more.

The three of them quickly settled into a Tolstoyan arrangement, McMurtry said—a feeble old man surrounded by women, including, whenever she was in town, Sara and her daughter, Sofia Camilla. Ossana's brother and her nieces and nephews completed the picture. McMurtry couldn't climb stairs anymore. He and Faye shared a back bedroom in Ossana's house, a queen-size bed topped with a white comforter, a sofa and a small desk, end tables packed with medications. Manila folders and typing paper sat next to McMurtry's Hermes, beside a box of tissues and a bottle of Advil.

The couches in the living room were covered with plastic to keep the dogs from soiling them. A platoon of maids came regularly, vacuuming around loose scripts, segments of scripts—*The Johnson County War*, *Rambling Rose*, sent by Oprah's production company; the story of Britt Johnson, a Black ranch foreman whose family was carried off by Comanches—and tatters of scripts nibbled at by Ossana's voracious bunny.

Faye developed a "good relationship" with Tucson's stores, McMurtry said. (She didn't do badly with the Wichita Falls Sears outlet, either, procuring a new television and washing machine for the Archer City house.)

McMurtry enjoyed his daily routine: shaving, breakfast, ten pages at the typewriter, walking with Faye and the dogs, picking Ossana's nephews and nieces up from school, dinner, then an episode of *Downton Abbey*, *The Sopranos*, or *Everybody Loves Raymond* (one of whose stars, Doris Roberts, he knew, had been married to the late Texas writer William Goyen).

His left eye drooped again.

His fingers shook.

Then he had a mild heart attack.

L ike a giant rat, the internet had eaten the bottom out of the antiquarian bookselling trade in two specific ways. First, dealers stopped scouting for books because everything they wanted was posted online (never mind the treasures they didn't *know* they needed, awaiting them on the road— the whole reason for scouting in the first place). Second, when the dot-com bubble burst, snowbirds—retired couples from the upper Midwest who'd formerly wintered in the Sun Belt, spending loads of money in bookstores to while away the hours—could no longer afford their annual pilgrimages.

"Book prices dropped dramatically," Laurence McGilvery said. "What once went for fifty dollars went for less than ten."

Yearly, McMurtry was losing over $100,000 in his store. "Miraculous birth! Visit the newly born book town of Archer City, Texas, and help the endless migration of good books continue," he'd proclaimed in ads printed in bibliophile magazines when he first opened the shop. But Archer City had not developed into West Texas's version of Hay-on-Wye. No other dealers had come prospecting there. He thought about shutting down. In February 2005, he'd even posted a notice on the main building: "I . . . need a sabbatical. I will soon enter my seventieth year . . . The books will stay right where they are. They can slumber in their majesty until the next turn of the wheel. Thank you for your participation in the life of Booked Up."

News spread swiftly on the wires that McMurtry was done; many of his colleagues urged him to continue the good fight. Weeks later, he posted another notice on the door: "It's nice to be missed before we're even gone . . . Several caravans of book people have declared their intention to come this summer, including two ladies from Tibet! If the world book community takes up the challenge and decides to save us of course we will allow ourselves to be saved. If the world book community lags we may adopt the hunting-lease concept (used by area ranchers, meaning [w]e might open on demand for groups)." This was followed, shortly thereafter, by a web page announcement; McMurtry had agreed to let Khristal Collins establish an online presence for the store: "The economic crisis that forced us to consider closing . . . has mostly passed. To a large extent it was a crisis felt by hundreds of antiquarian booksellers in America. Many closed. We, fortunately, won't have to . . . We are sorry for the alarm, but things did look discouraging for a while. Profound change has come to the antiquarian book business in the last few years. When and if it will stop nobody knows, but Booked Up, for now and we hope for a long time to come, is still in the game."

The economic crisis had been—and remained—real enough, but the closing/not closing confusion was as much a product of McMurtry's lifelong ambivalence as the trade slump. And it was a manifestation of his flickering unpredictable depression.

Booked Up limped along until his heart attack. Soon after marrying Faye, he also noticed his memory was slipping, sometimes rather alarmingly. A friend told him he'd read that the great Colombian author Gabriel García Márquez was suffering from Alzheimer's. "I don't know if [my problem] is as serious as his case," McMurtry said. "But sometimes I can't remember things from the day before, or earlier the same day." The heart attack caused him to acknowledge that "it's [getting] toward the end of my life." He had to face the fact that James and Curtis were smart boys, but they didn't share his passion for reading. His book collection was "a potential liability for my heirs," he confided to friends. "They don't know the book world . . . They have got their own concerns." Something had to be done. Nothing as dire as threatening to close again, but scaling back, perhaps. Finally he decided to empty three of the four buildings (leaving the properties to James, to do with as he wished), and to operate Booked Up solely out of the original main building.

He'd hold an auction to disperse the stock—thinning the herd. He'd call it "The Last Book Sale."

In the summer of 2012, he contacted the "cracker-jack team" of Addison & Sarova, auctioneers from Macon, Georgia, to oversee the proceedings. He scheduled the two-day event for mid-August.

"It's bittersweet," Faye admitted. "It's like anything at the end of life—kind of like leaving your family behind."

"In a summer when the shoreline temperature in the Little Arkansas River reached 98 degrees—bad news for catfish—should I really have attempted to bring a bunch of citified northerners into the heart of the heat, which peaked locally at 116? Well, yes. It's just weather," McMurtry said. Aside from culling upward of 300,000 books, he was curious to know, "Are there still young people piling up books in their garages, hoping to have a shop someday? I didn't know. Calling for the auction was a way to find out."

So it was, on a broiling Friday afternoon, that phalanxes of Mercedes-Benzes and sleek new Lexuses pulled up and parked in front of the Archer County courthouse, next to dirt-smeared pickups sporting naked-lady mud flaps. One hundred and fifty bidders officially registered for the auction, but hundreds more came, many of them Larry McMurtry fans, just to watch the spectacle. The Royal Theater screened *The Last Picture Show* on Friday night. Before the movie began, McMurtry picked up a microphone and muttered his appreciation to everyone for coming. Then he vanished. As the attendees watched the film, "an atmosphere of *coolness* began to pervade," said Kurt Zimmerman, a book collector, "coolness in the sense of knowing that this was a place to *be,* a special event, one that everyone in attendance had cautiously hoped for as they rolled into this tiny one-stoplight town."

That night, the Royal served barbecue with all the fixings along with truckloads of Shiner Bock beer. The Lonesome Dove Inn and the Spur Hotel were booked to the max (self-serve—keys waiting in envelopes on the desks). There was a run on toilet paper in town. All the U-Hauls were rented. The door to the dairy case in Allsup's convenience store nearly broke—it made a "Moo" sound when it opened; naturally, the novelty of this had to be experienced over and over. More than one customer observed the Jacy-like flirtiness of the blond waitress in the Wildcat Café (where you could get a chicken-fried steak as big as your plate).

The following day, James and Curtis performed music sets in the main building, James's story-songs sounding like condensed versions of his father's novels ("I'm a fiction writer," he said). Curtis had begun making a name for himself in Austin. James joked that there had only been a brief moment in his life when he wasn't known as either his father's son or his son's father.

The bidding commenced in Building No. 4. Air conditioners strained to keep everyone cool. Beer and water flowed, free. McMurtry spent most of his time in the main building, sipping Dr Pepper in a folding chair, speaking to old acquaintances and book dealers who'd come to see him.

Mike Evans and Greg Curtis stopped by. "We had a good time together . . . But it was sad, too," Evans said. He was shocked to see McMurtry's drooping eye, and to realize, in fact, that his face was partially paralyzed, from the onset of Parkinson's. McMurtry told Evans he had congestive heart disease; he took eighteen pills a day. "I think I suspected that this would be the last time I would see him, because . . . I told him that he had always stood in my mind as a model: be kind, be honest, and do the best you can with what you have. He waved a hand at me, embarrassed, but I'm glad I said it," Evans acknowledged.

McMurtry had organized the auction perversely. Instead of separating rare books from more commonly available editions, he bundled them together in groups of two hundred, to be sold as single packages. His "approach of mixing rare books and shelf filler into large auction lots meant that most buyers were returning home with a lot of dead weight, commercially speaking," one attendee complained.

Still, a few young collectors found books they hoped would seed new stores; one Austin couple dreamed of opening a shop with "free same-day bike delivery." An anonymous West Texas rancher, a "self-made wildcatter" with a love of reading sent a proxy in his place to bid for as much as he could get, spending close to $20,000. A heavily tattooed woman from Tyler, Texas, convinced that, in the future, books would simply be novelty items, bought a stack to sell in a booth she owned in a Dallas marketplace. She traded in oddities such as "tattooed furniture and skateboard decks."

The most impressive sale of the first day went to Tom Congalton, owner of Between the Covers Rare Books in New Jersey. For $2,750 he purchased a six-inch typescript, roughly bound, of some twenty-nine erotic stories commissioned in the 1940s by Oklahoma oilman Roy Melisander Johnson. Johnson, elected to the Oklahoma Hall of Fame in 1953, praised by Oklahoma Supreme Court Justice Robert A. Hefner Sr. as a man "great in mind, heart and soul, a devoted husband and a wise and affectionate father," was also, according to porn writer Gershon Legman, a connoisseur of smut, a man of "jaded virility" who "could only erect his oil derrick once per story, leaving him constantly wanting more." So Johnson approached book dealers—Ben Abramson of Chicago's Argus Book Shop, Stanley Rose of the Satyr Book Shop in Los Angeles, and Legman (selling erotica under the pseudonym Rudolph Bernays). He instructed them to offer writers one dollar per page to compose hard-core drama for him. None of the stories were signed, but Anaïs Nin was one of the first steady contributors to Johnson's collection. Other writers in the stable included Henry Miller, Jack Hanley, and Robert De Niro Sr., father of the actor.

McMurtry had owned the typescripts for over two decades. Seeing them on the auction block, he remembered his encounters through the years with Gershon Legman. Legman had left the United States in the early 1950s after being accused of distributing porn. He had once edited a little magazine called *Neurotica,* and copies of his first book, *Oragenitalism, Part I: Cunnilinctus*, were seized and destroyed by New York police.

McMurtry admired Legman's self-published anti-censorship polemic *Love and Death* (1949), and he knew that Legman owned a vast collection of sex doggerel—"what in my high school days were called fuck books," McMurtry said. He was eager to study Legman's collection. Shortly after opening Booked Up in Georgetown, he'd flown to Paris and then driven to Nice and Valbonne to meet him. Ultimately, Legman refused to sell him much of value, but he did convince McMurtry that his memoir in progress, *Peregrine Penis,* encompassing several volumes, would be the finest erotic autobiography since Casanova's teasers. He pressed several hundred pages on McMurtry, who took them to Nice and skimmed them in the "not-particularly-comfortable hotel" where Chekhov finished *The Three Sisters.* What the hell? McMurtry thought. If nothing else, the book would be a curiosity, and maybe a valuable one. He agreed to subsidize the writing of *Peregrine Penis.* Then Legman had a stroke. He died in 1999.

When Tom Congalton bought the erotic typescripts, waving his wooden paddle in the air at the auction in the swirling heat of Building No. 4, McMurtry popped the cap on another Dr Pepper and said goodbye to a rarity he'd long prized but now had no earthly use for.

Didn't that just about sum it up?

The auction's second day was dominated by representatives from some of the nation's major stores: the Midtown Scholar in Harrisburg, Pennsylvania; Powell's Books in Portland, Oregon, whose lackeys carried away 450 boxes; and Between the Covers, claiming more than 500 boxes of mixed goods. A couple from a smaller shop, the Full Nelson in Magnolia, Arkansas, filled 157 containers. "Power to the young dealers!" McMurtry said.

Jon Guetschow of Powell's said he didn't understand why McMurtry had decided to hold an auction rather than utilize the internet: "He could have made a lot more money, and I'm surprised there's nobody in his circle who stopped and did that for him. I don't want to criticize the host . . . this was a really cool occasion. It just doesn't seem like the way to sell books anymore, or buy them."

As the crowds thinned, McMurtry said goodbye to his friends. He glimpsed Cheryl Beesinger, the local librarian. He had once asked her which signed book she would most like to own. "Other than one of yours?" she asked. "Yes," he said. She answered, "*To Kill a Mockingbird.*" He laughed. "Wouldn't we all, wouldn't we all?" he said.

He declared himself pleased with the last two days. He'd made around $200,000, though profit had never been the point. Fiction was the only genre that didn't sell. In fact, one buyer had culled the fiction from the stacks he'd bought and dumped the books in front of the library.

It was also hard to ignore the demographic: mostly white and old. "There isn't the next generation [here]. I hoped there'd be more people my age. I'm really kind of disappointed," said forty-two-year-old Eddy Nix, who'd come from Wisconsin, representing Driftless Books.

George Getschow, a writing instructor at the University of North Texas, said, "You can't spend a lifetime collecting books and dealing with books without feeling melancholy about this. Right now Larry is pleased. He is surrounded by book buyers and people of his ilk who talk about books and who care about books . . . But I just think in a couple of weeks it will be a difficult passage for him to see these three stores shut down. This was his dream, to turn Archer City into a book town . . . Now this is the end of the dream. There is just no way around it."

Cliff Byrd, a lifelong citizen of the town, feared Archer City would vanish along with "The Last Book Sale": "The oil business is gone, most of the wells have dried up. The ranching business is gone. A few ranchers are handing down land through families, but they don't contribute a lot to the economy. They used to buy vehicles, but there's no longer a dealership here. I see no new business."

Journalist Michael Agresta, covering the sale for *The Atlantic,* summed up the weekend: "The proceedings had the aspect of a living wake, and the constant *Last Picture Show* references brought to mind the character of Sam the Lion, whose death towards the end of the novel leaves his three businesses on the square—the café, the pool hall, and the picture show—in danger of closing."

McMurtry had another heart attack, in Tucson, in July 2013. "[It] took a lot of strength out of me . . . I had a slow time recovering," he admitted.

His health crisis accounted in part for the glancing treatment he gave General George Custer in his biography of the man, published that year. Too, Simon & Schuster had pressured him to turn it into a coffee table book, filled with illustrations, rather than a rigorous history. The book did not turn out as McMurtry intended, increasing his disillusionment with S&S. His dissatisfaction had been growing since *The Berrybender Narratives.* He felt his publisher had grown "tired" of him, dumping the Berrybender novels on the market with insufficient support.

His heart attack kept him off the road. He couldn't get to Archer City. As a consequence, he finally acceded to the need, long urged on him by Khristal Collins, to sell books on the internet. To his surprise, China proved a quick and steady customer. "We had a lot of good porcelain books. Sold every one of them to China," he marveled. "I mean, these were thousand-dollar books. They're not cheap. I guess they are really serious about porcelain in China."

When he finally *did* feel like traveling again, he didn't go far—just a few blocks, down to Tucson's La Paloma Hotel, one of the city's grand old hospitality lodges. There, in the Cottonwood Room, Bob Boze Bell, the executive editor of *True West* magazine, gave McMurtry and Diana Ossana the magazine's first True Westerner Award. *True West* had been publishing for sixty years, covering topics of general interest in the West. The award, Bell explained, was meant to celebrate people who had been "hugely influential on conversations of the West." He also admitted, "Larry McMurtry bugs the hell out of me. He set out to 'demystify' the West and strip it bare—what kind of respect is that?" Nevertheless, he recognized the value of McMurtry's penchant for "fan[ning] the flames and promot[ing] national discussion" of the region.

"He wasn't doing too well that night," Michael Wallis said. Wallis had come for the ceremony. "He didn't look great. *Diana* looked great. I couldn't hear him very well. He'd mumble. He was very taken aback—the men were all decked out in Stetson hats and boots. He was wearing something like Hush Puppies. He felt very embarrassed by this. Diana had on these glorious boots which cost her $2,500 or something."

Despite his frailty, McMurtry enjoyed the evening—his first outing since the heart attack. It was "low key" with "little fanfare," he said appreciatively. Bell gave him a little bronze statue of a cowboy fashioned in the style of J. R. Williams's old comic strip figures—the strip his father had enjoyed reading so much at the breakfast table in the ranch house.

"He was very self-effacing," Wallis said. "All evening he shined the light on Diana: 'This should be *her* award.'"

Less than two years later, he was stuffed into a suit and a red tie and asked to attend another ceremony—this time at the White House, as one of ten recipients of the 2014 National Humanities Medal, honoring an individual or organization whose work has "deepened the nation's understanding of the human experience, broadened citizens' engagement with history and literature or helped preserve and expand Americans' access to cultural resources," according to the National Endowment for the Humanities.

On the morning of September 10, 2015, he sat in the White House's East Room along with Annie Dillard, Jhumpa Lahiri, Tobias Wolff, Stephen King, actress Sally Field, and others, including architects and scientists, suffering through the half-hour ritual. President Obama received an enormous ovation when he took his place behind the podium. He quipped, "I always do pretty good with writers and scientists. That's sort of my crew." He said he loved this annual event, "when truly extraordinary artists and innovators and thinkers are recognized for their brilliance while the rest of us look on and feel totally inadequate."

He quoted Emily Dickinson: "Truth is such a rare thing, it is delightful to tell it." Then he spotlighted McMurtry as a prime reason for the gathering: "[Today] we celebrate writers like Larry McMurtry, who grew up on a Texas ranch without books but went on to pen a multitude of memoirs and essays, more than thirty novels, and cowrote screenplays for films like *Brokeback Mountain.* He wrote about the Texas he knew from his own life, and then the Old West as he heard it through the stories of his grandfathers—on his grandfather's porch. And in *Lonesome Dove,* the story of two ex–Texas Rangers in the nineteenth century, readers found out something essential about their own souls, even if they'd never been out West or been on a ranch."

As each recipient's name was called, the crowd applauded, the recipient took the stage, and President Obama bestowed the award. McMurtry rarely applauded. He rubbed his hands on his pants. His palms were sweating. Nothing was required of him in the way of speechmaking; he simply feared he might not be able to stand—a justifiable worry, as it turned out; when he heard his name, he teetered once or twice in rising from his chair. A uniformed Marine, assisting the president onstage, walked over, grasped McMurtry's upper arm, and helped him move. McMurtry sagged a bit. He tried to smile but didn't quite manage it. President Obama draped the heavy circular medal, dangling from a long red sash, around his neck, found the writer's trembling hand, and turned him toward the towering Marine, to be escorted off the stage.

As the ceremony concluded, Obama invited his guests to enjoy the White House and to stick around for a "wonderful reception." McMurtry absented himself quickly. Michael Lindenberger, then a reporter from *The Dallas Morning News,* had scheduled an interview with him after the reception, but when "an aide called to say he had no energy for our . . . chat, I wasn't surprised."

Barbara Phillips, owner of the *Archer County News*, had traveled from West Texas to cover the hometown boy. She was disappointed that she didn't get to speak much with him, but insisted that everyone back home was "excited about us coming out here . . . Many of us support him, and I see a new momentum going his way. Some [townsfolk] don't even know who he is, probably. But those who are more educated and have read a lot are just really proud of what he has done."

It was just as well he had little energy, he mused, removing his medal—he didn't want to poke around DC, anyway. It wasn't the city he had known. He had lived here before he'd died beneath the surgeon's scalpel. In Georgetown, before he'd died, *his* M Street had been quaintly lined with bookstores and boutique shops, restaurants, scrappy vendors. Now Nike, Patagonia, and other mega-chain stores hulked above the sidewalks where the sellers of trinkets used to spread their wares. He didn't want to see it. He wanted to sleep. He didn't want anyone explaining the changes to him, trying to reorient him so he could get his bearings. He *had* his bearings; he had just enough energy left to know who he was: the last bookman, gently wiping printer's ink off his hands.

28

His road trips were over. From his earliest days—precocious reader that he was—he knew that America's first roadways were its rivers. The Susquehanna, the Delaware, the St. Lawrence, the Monongahela, the Hudson, the Ohio, the Columbia, the Arkansas, and most of all, the Missouri-Mississippi. Stations of the Cross. The Missouri took Lewis and Clark a fair distance toward the West. "When I lay abed as a boy in our ranch house, listening to . . . trucks growl their way up Highway 281, the sound of those motors came to seem as organic as the sounds of the various birds and animals who were apt to make noises in the night," he said, a shoreline symphony as he drifted past . . . or as the world drifted past him.

He would spend much of his life a nomad, hoping to catch promising currents somewhere. And at the end of the day, his fellow scribbler Nelson Algren would neatly encapsulate nomadic wisdom: "Never eat at a place called Mom's, never play cards with a man named Doc, and never sleep with a woman whose problems are worse than your own."

Once he floated in a rented Lincoln down Interstate 35 from Duluth, Minnesota, to Oklahoma City, one of the nation's great migration routes, past F. Scott Fitzgerald's birthplace—the man who'd said there were no second acts in American life, an adage McMurtry had thoroughly disproved. As he drove, "a skim-milk light . . . spread itself over the forests and fields" where ice fisherman cast their lines. The mornings were crisply cold; a smell of drying wheat thickened the air, dull as wet cardboard.

South of the Twin Cities, where starving Sioux once fought U.S. soldiers, hoping for a simple distribution of food to their people (it never came), America's farmlands began, a site of bitter harvests by the time McMurtry made his journey, at the twentieth century's close. Now the farmers were just like the Sioux—starved by men who organized what lamely passed for centralized government. "The killings that resulted in *In Cold Blood* took place in Kansas, which is also where Timothy McVeigh made the bomb that took out 168 people and ruined at least a thousand lives," McMurtry observed from the road. Violence was endemic here. "The term 'going postal,' which means to blow one's stack and murder as many people as possible, we owe to a postal worker in Oklahoma, who went postal and killed fourteen people . . . It may be that the Midwest," with its fierce battles over tough hardscrabble, "produces a distinct kind of disappointment, which, in some, becomes a murderous resentment."

These killing plains dumped him finally into the West Texas grasslands veering toward his home in Archer City, where the trouble took stubborn root and grew. Here, "generations of . . . farmers [had] to cope not only with the slow failure of their farms but with a sense that they [had] failed their ancestors as well."

It was a lingering sadness he inhaled with his very first breath in the Wichita Falls General Hospital.

His uncles had tried to warn him about the world. Jeff Dobbs, related to him by marriage, had retired to the Oklahoma backwoods to grow peanuts and read the Gospels when McMurtry got to know him as a boy. After forty years of argumentative marriage, Dobbs's wife, Minta, got hit by a truck on a farm road one day. She was killed instantly. It "was an awful tragidy . . . my car was a total loss too. Things like that will just hoppen though. It is lonesome dreary," Dobbs wrote McMurtry a week after the accident. At the time, McMurtry had just entered graduate school. Lest the foolish young man believe that books could help him in life, Dobbs snickered, "What does PhD stand for? to me its post-hole digger, guess that would be about what it would stand for with all other old Texas cowpokes."

McMurtry's uncle Johnny, hanging on in the wind-slapped Panhandle crook of muddy old Clarendon, married late in life, taking an elderly bride at the age of sixty-five, after losing his voice box to cigarettes and his hip to a rolling, out-of-gear pickup running him down. The day after his wedding, Johnny enlisted his wife Ida to help cull a herd of cattle he'd bought in western Louisiana. Shortly thereafter, he got crushed by several hundred-pound sacks of cattle feed, toppling from a barn loft.

What further evidence did McMurtry need that he should grab what he could *while* he could? The world didn't wait. The world didn't sort. It was just the fucking world.

But all his life, McMurtry wandered. And wandered some more. As if he might find different answers somewhere. Another vision.

Now the heart was weak. The mind was soft. The wandering was over. In fiction, too.

For him, it had always been the novel, a "forgiving form," Diana Ossana said. "It's easier to meander around in a novel" than in a short story or a poem. "Larry basically [remains] a wanderer."

Yet even before his Parkinson's and his heart disease worsened, he was telling friends, "If I could not write another word of fiction and make a living, I would. But I can't . . . It's kind of embarrassing."

No, Ossana said. That was not the case. Not at all. She knew the truth. Despite his growing difficulties, "Larry is like an old cowboy who has to get up in the morning and do some chores," she said. "He has to get up and write. I don't think he would know what to do with himself if he didn't have something to write."

Okay: "I *might* have one more novel left in me," he admitted.

He kicked out *When the Light Goes* in 2007 and *Rhino Ranch* in 2009, both additions to *The Last Picture Show* series, Duane Moore's twilight years—the phase of life when resignation and happiness become almost indistinguishable. Neither novel enhanced the McMurtry canon; *Rhino Ranch* in particular reads like a painful draft composed by a man who once knew, but has forgotten, how to write fiction.

"Larry McMurtry closed the book on Duane Moore . . . with 'Duane's Depressed' . . . Yet life, and book contracts, go on," John Leland wrote cynically in a review of *When the Light Goes* in *The New York Times*. "Why not bring Duane back for a light sex frolic—say, something that begins with 'stiffening nipples' and proceeds from there?" McMurtry was a "top-shelf writer" engaged here "in a low-stakes diversion," Leland wrote. "No brain cells appear to have been harmed in the writing . . . of this playfully smutty book."

Smutty it was—uncharacteristically—featuring a "marathon [sex] session that defies the laws of gerontology, if not physics," Leland said. In the novel, sex (always desperately approached) tends to reduce everyone—young and old—to their most primitive selves, causing them to behave in ways McMurtry had not prepared the reader to accept, eroding the affection we may have once felt for his characters. As with many of his previous sequels, *When the Light Goes* seemed to be another puzzling exercise in literary self-destruction. Its ostensible subject? Duane "growing lonelier and older, as the people he had lived his life with continued to die."

Rhino Ranch found Duane still wondering what to do with himself as his arteries clog and the world becomes more and more unrecognizable to him. (For instance, a wealthy young philanthropist hopes to save African rhinos by breeding them in West Texas, an activity only vaguely comprehensible to Duane.) The novel he inhabits drifts like a river topping its banks, most of its chapters dribbling into silt. Finally, as if McMurtry just grew tired one morning of living with this character for over forty years, he wrote: "Duane Moore quietly keeled over dead while laying a trot line." End of story.

"An old Mississippi mule trader by the name of Ray Lum was fond of saying, 'You live and learn. Then you die and forget it all.' That about sums up the feeling the reader is left with at the end of Larry McMurtry's elegiac 'Rhino Ranch,'" Tim Gautreaux wrote in *The Washington Post.*

McMurtry could still write powerfully of loss, and occasionally a serious purpose could be sensed beneath the comic sex romps. Duane desires intimacy, but he resists out of fear, uncertainty, or revulsion. He becomes an erotic Everyman. He is a test case—sometimes the boorish aggressor, then the passive partner, forced to surrender (increasingly, as he ages, he prefers "woman-superior" arrangements). He is McMurtry's imagined surrogate, exploring the variety of people sex had revealed him to be over the years.

But mostly the final Thalia novels bespoke exhaustion. After *Rhino Ranch,* McMurtry insisted once more, "I'm about at the end. I can write certain things. I don't think I can write fiction anymore. Not too many great novels are written by people over seventy-five. Hardly any. Maybe Tolstoy."

Then, in 2014, he surprised everyone with another novel, a quiet little triumph called *The Last Kind Words Saloon.* It was another takedown of Old West mythology, a send-up of the themes that had made *Lonesome Dove* so popular, but this time the effort came wrapped in affection and smiling humor, a gentle wink that said it was still okay to like *Lonesome Dove.*

Why had he changed his mind about giving up fiction? "Oh, I don't know," he said. "The title is ripped off from a very legendary blues song called the 'Last Kind Words Blues.' There was just a piece in *The New York Times Magazine* about that record, that song. There were only two copies of it for a long time. It was recorded in Wisconsin. I liked the title. So I decided to see if I could make something with it, and I did. It was just an accident."

He came close to self-publishing the book. He sensed Simon & Schuster didn't want it. Michael Korda had retired and McMurtry didn't click with the new regime. "They seemed to be having trouble getting past *Lonesome Dove,* which made them a lot of money," he said. I'd always been a midlist writer. I was a midlist writer for ten books. *Lonesome Dove* was the only book that lifted me out of the midlist, and in a way it warped my career."

Instead of self-publishing *The Last Kind Words Saloon,* McMurtry asked Andrew Wylie to shop it around. Robert Weil at Liveright, an imprint of W. W. Norton, bought it, saying, "Larry is like Charles Dickens. He shows it's okay to write a lot, and it's still literature."

McMurtry called the novel "a ballad in prose whose characters are afloat in time; their legends and their lives rarely match." He went on, "I had the great director John Ford in mind when I wrote this book; he famously said that when you had to choose between history and legend, print the legend. And so I've done"—neglecting to add that he'd chosen the most *deflationary* legend possible.

The Last Kind Words Saloon tells the story of Wyatt Earp, Doc Holliday, and the shootout at the O.K. Corral. It follows the trail rides of cattleman Charles Goodnight and tabloid journalist Nellie Courtright. It begins in a town called Long Grass, a nowhere place, befitting a tall tale. Long Grass is "nearly in Kansas, but not quite. It's nearly in New Mexico, too, but not quite. Some have even suggested that we might be in Texas," Wyatt says. "It depends on your notion of where Texas stops," Doc adds. The men have achieved the reputation, established by the yellow press, of being fierce gunslingers, but they laugh and admit they couldn't hit the side of a barn with their bullets. Mostly they sit around and drink in front of a ragged saloon. As the novel opens, somebody's hat goes blowing down a dusty street. Idly, they wonder whose it is. Doc takes a couple of shots at it and misses. Then he asks Wyatt his opinion of women. Wyatt admits his wife Jessie is "about all the female I can handle, and it ain't a hundred percent that I can handle her. Why do you ask?"

"Just to be making conversation," Doc answers.

In an admiring review in *The New York Review of Books,* Joyce Carol Oates wrote, "It's as if Vladimir and Estragon of Beckett's *Waiting for Godot* have been transformed into two aging gunslingers trading wise-cracks and platitudes in an existentially barren western landscape, waiting for a redemption that never comes."

Wyatt and Doc stumble toward their destiny—which is to be remembered as key players in the corral shootout, an event squeezed, in the novel, to less than a page and a half, and presented as a "damn waste of time." "You fool, you could have been killed," Wyatt's wife yells at him. "Yes, but I wasn't, let go," he responds.

"So much for legend," Oates wrote.

Meanwhile, Charles Goodnight gets rich running cattle. Then he grows old and stupid and gets swindled out of his land.

These grim vaudeville high jinks are rounded out by renegade Indians who think "[t]orturing whites [is] a splendid way to spend the afternoon." Political correctness is no more a concern of McMurtry's here than fealty to western history.

At novel's end, we learn that the heroes' exploits have been chronicled by Nellie Courtright, the tabloid writer. She rescues the saloon sign, "Last Kind Words," picking it out of Wyatt's dump heap when she visits him in San Pedro, California. He has gone there to retire, in ill health, haunted by foggy memories. He "lived in a dilapidated little bungalow," Nellie reports, with a "yard filled with junk: old tires, some buckets, a saddle, tools of various kinds, a wheelbarrow, and the like." She's sorry she came. "There was nothing to be had" anymore from faded Old West figures.

Oates called *The Last Kind Words Saloon* a "radically-distilled . . . dark postmodern comedy . . . subversive" in its "merciless" irony. As such—unlikely as it seemed—it resembled the final novel of McMurtry's contemporary, his fellow Texan Donald Barthelme. *The King,* Barthelme's posthumously published elegy, was another historical mash-up, featuring Winston Churchill and King Arthur, structured in Beckett-like dialogues. Like *The Last Kind Words Saloon,* the novel reduced history to a mild slap-stick routine. It took a pair of Texans to work through their jaded attitudes toward inflated western myths to come out on the other side, laughing, shaking their heads. "Things yet to come will make us sadder still!" Barthelme wrote, bitterly blithe—a sentiment McMurtry wholly embraced.

At first he refused to do any press or make public appearances on behalf of *The Last Kind Words Saloon*. He didn't feel up to it, physically. But he had a new publisher to please. And "I want this book to have every chance to do well," he said. "Plus, I want some money."

So he wandered up to Dallas in the spring, with Ossana, to appear onstage at the Dallas Museum of Art for a discussion of the new novel in the context of his career. Skip Hollandsworth was the moderator. McMurtry began by pointing out that "my partner [Diana] is becoming more and more famous all the time. She's wearing black tonight, which may or may not be sinister."

Clearly at ease with Hollandsworth, an old friend, he replied, "That was just a tactic," when Hollandsworth asked him how he could say he was finished writing fiction, then publish another novel. "I have to earn a living, after all. There comes a time when writing another western is the quickest way."

He'd claimed he didn't really give a damn about Wyatt Earp. He'd written the book as a tribute to the nineteenth-century parodist Max Beerbohm (a Barthelme fave)—whom people should go out and read.

Hollandsworth didn't buy it. He insisted that McMurtry was obsessed with making fiction and telling stories of the Old West. McMurtry refused to take the bait. "You can read [the new novel] at a stoplight," was all he'd say.

Was his writing energy in danger of flagging? "Not my energy exactly . . . it's some force . . . something . . . I'm not *totally* flagging . . . [but] I don't think I feel an urgency . . ."

Regarding death's stealthy approach, "I'm a little wistful, sure," he said. "I think most old folks find some wistfulness creeping in."

Ossana was the evening's color commentator, providing background: "Larry's bark is highly misleading," she said (after admitting they argued all the time). "He's one of the kindest, most humane writers I've ever encountered . . . underneath that exterior beats one of the loveliest, most compassionate writers you will ever meet"—though it was true, she said, that in spite of his reputation for "doing women really well" in his fiction, he was "just as clueless as the next guy in real life."

"That's her theory," McMurtry muttered.

Several months later, he and Ossana appeared onstage again, this time at the Miami Book Fair International, at the Chapman Conference Center, for an evening with his new editor, Robert Weil. Weil did not have the easy rapport with McMurtry that Skip Hollandsworth enjoyed; nervously, he kept urging McMurtry to hold his microphone closer to his mouth so the audience could decipher his mumbling. Only a few months had passed since Dallas, but McMurtry's voice was significantly weaker than before. He sagged in his chair. Weil kept noting how vital McMurtry seemed. His remarks only emphasized the degree to which he was indulging in wishful thinking.

"We speak of great world writers like Tolstoy, and I would contend that Larry McMurtry is on that level, a great American writer," Weil pronounced. "*Lonesome Dove* is America's *War and Peace,* in that it just chronicles a world that no other American writer of the twentieth century has chronicled so well." As he spoke, Ossana shot a glance at McMurtry, barely able to stifle her laughter. She knew what was coming.

"Actually, *Lonesome Dove* . . . is the West's *Gone with the Wind,*" he said, a line he loved to repeat. "It's not Tolstoy."

"I humbly disagree," Weil offered.

"It's touch and go, Bob," McMurtry answered.

He was happiest talking about Faye. "I come out of a female-centered society, although it didn't look like it," he said. "I mean, the images of the cowboy were everywhere, but it was the women that seemed to make things work . . . [Now] I spend my life with women as much as I can manage. It seems a sensible thing to do. They're a lot more fun than men, and a lot more instinctive than men, also . . . Faye has come into our lives, which is a huge benefit . . . and children and dogs, and it all seems normal to me. As normal as I care to be."

Old age comes on apace to ravage all the clime," McMurtry recited often now—a quote from the eighteenth-century Scottish poet James Beattie. "And old age is doing what it can to ravage me."

"The depression that had always stalked him came back with a vengeance, sending him to hospitals and electroshock therapy. James made frequent trips from Austin to Tucson, and Diana and Faye were there to care for him. But the days were darker and the writing stopped," Mike Evans said.

The joke around Hollywood was that Jack Nicholson, in the film version of Ken Kesey's *One Flew Over the Cuckoo's Nest,* did for electroconvulsive therapy what *Jaws* had done for sharks. In the movie, a vengeful nurse in a mental care facility punishes Nicholson's unruly character with brutal shocks to the brain.

In reality, electroconvulsive therapy—inducing mild seizures in a patient with timed electric impulses, stimulating brain activity—was often an effective treatment for clinical depression. McMurtry knew that in the early days of experimentation, some patients suffered violent whole-body contractions, breaking bones and dislocating joints. In one of the first attempted procedures, in 1938, two Italian doctors wired a patient's head with electrodes obtained from a pig slaughterhouse.

But doctors assured him that these days, with the employment of general anesthesia, IVs, oxygen masks, and careful monitoring of blood pressure, a patient's body simply tensed for a moment, then relaxed. The procedure took five to ten minutes.

McMurtry's short-term memory, already faulty, slipped further after treatments. Sometimes the trouble corrected itself after a few weeks. Frequent headaches—a lifelong problem—plagued him, along with nausea. His mumbling grew worse.

Faye drove him to Archer City from time to time so he could look in on the much-diminished bookstore. After McMurtry died, Evans met James at Booked Up to appraise the stock. "For some time [Larry] had worked to no good end," he discovered. "The prices often didn't make sense. Condition was ignored, editions might be wrongly identified. He had lost touch with reality."

McMurtry knew one thing for certain: "What's happening to me is that my cronies are dying."

Jo wasn't dying, but she had moved into an assisted living facility in Lexington, Virginia.

In the summer of 2019, McMurtry heard that Bill Wittliff had suffered a fatal heart attack just one day after celebrating his fifty-sixth wedding anniversary. Twice, Wittliff had played major roles in McMurtry's career, publishing his first book of essays when nobody else would take it and guiding the *Lonesome Dove* television miniseries to its phenomenal success.

Then, in January 2021, Ceil Cleveland, his first important female friend, the model for Jacy Farrow, passed away, four days after her eighty-fifth birthday. "There's nobody to talk to," McMurtry lamented.

Diane Keaton *had* insisted he learn to email her; they stayed in touch almost daily. Ossana bought him a MacBook. She encouraged him to dictate stories to her so she could post them on a blog site, an easy way to communicate with his readers. He let the MacBook sit for six months, and then "made a cautious approach to the keyboard, as one might approach a wary woman," he said. "[T]hough I work at it every day, we are not yet on familiar terms. But maybe, if time allows, I'll improve."

He doubted that time would allow.

I am in no way a spiritual person . . . I am a realist, an atheist, and I have no thoughts or opinions about spirituality or the after life, or what inspiration the stars may hold . . . I wasn't much for stargazing as a child or as an adult. I was mainly focused on what kinds of lives people in other places were experiencing," McMurtry told Benito Vila by email, in what was perhaps his last interview on record. Vila wrote for a website called *Please Kill Me,* devoted to cultural criticism. Initially, he found McMurtry's contact information in order to reach Faye, to interview her about the Merry Pranksters. "I am sorry, I do not act as an intermediary between my wife and others," McMurtry responded. Then Vila decided McMurtry would be a good interview subject and asked if he'd consent to answer a few questions. McMurtry replied, "I'm sorry I'm only on this medium occasionally. It depends upon when my writing partner Diana can get on the computer with me. I'm computer illiterate . . . I don't do phone interviews anymore. You can post questions here that you'd like answered and I'll see if I can answer." Months passed before he popped up again. "I apologize for the delay," he wrote finally. "We've had two challenging months here."

By then, near the beginning of 2021, the coronavirus pandemic had exacted an enormous toll on the world's health, particularly in the United States, so politically divided that even scientific data and the efficacy of vaccines were subjects no one could discuss rationally. People were dying needlessly in every American city. McMurtry, reading the news, was dismayed. He made one final comment to Vila before signing off email: "It appears that the pandemic has caused people, for some odd reason, to re-ignite the philosophy of 'rugged individualism.' It's an archaic philosophy that won't apply to the modern world . . . Whether people believe it or not and whether they like it or not, we are all connected."

He dreamed of houses filled with books, endless corridors lined with shelves, the pages still uncut in some of the dusty volumes, never opened.

Many times, he'd been asked what people should read. *The Europeans,* he'd always reply. *The Russians.* Proust. George Eliot. Tolstoy. Everything anyone needed could be found in *War and Peace.*

Critics loved to play the game: If you were to update "Ever a Bridegroom," what would you say today about the state of Texas literature? How would you rate your own contribution?

He refused to answer, but that didn't stop the critics from speculating. They crowed about fresh young talents sprouting in Texas: Stephen Harrigan, Benjamin Alire Sáenz, Lawrence Wright, Ben Fountain. But where were the women? The people of color? And did any of these writers *really* excite national audiences?

Don Graham didn't think so. "There is a fair amount of interesting regional writing from these parts, but there is very little, for example, that makes it into American Lit anthologies or that reaches a wider audience," he wrote. By and large, after all these years, he still agreed "with McMurtry's general assessment of Texas writing." It had a long way to go.

More interesting, with respect to the national literary culture, were the views of those, such as American Lit professor Robert Brinkmeyer, that the West had become the site of national reckoning. Brinkmeyer observed that writers from the South, long considered the cradle of one of America's richest literary traditions—steeped in slavery and the Civil War, America's DNA—were turning to the West now. They did so to trace the past's bloody consequences. He noted that Cormac McCarthy's *The Crossing,* part of McCarthy's Border Trilogy, ended with the atomic blast, "the twentieth century's most frightening image of uncertainty and anxiety"; in McCarthy's *Cities of the Plain,* "the military-industrial complex appears on the verge of completely engulfing the West and its way of life." McCarthy implied that these developments resulted from traditional southern notions of heroism and individualism. They were leaving ever-deepening scars on the American West, and in the American psyche.

A provocative thesis; however accurate, it spoke to the enduring power of western myth, which McMurtry could never escape—and then he stopped trying. As he lay dying, the cinematic Western was having yet another resurgence, this time in the hands of female directors (working in numbers unheard of when Polly Platt and Diana Ossana were young): Kelly Reichardt, Mouly Surya, Nia DaCosta, Emelie Mahdavian. Chloé Zhao with *Nomadland*. Jane Campion with *The Power of the Dog*. These filmmakers depicted the American West from the "headspace of women," Mahdavian said. "I felt as a woman . . . who loved the land that I had just as much insight as John Wayne."

In films and in books, no one of his era had wrestled with the American West as assiduously as Larry McMurtry. Few males of his generation had been praised so consistently for portraying complex women in fiction. Yet he knew better than anyone that the legacies of western life and gender politics were still evolving; no literary reputation based on these subjects could rest secure.

Sherman Alexie was not the first, nor would he be the last, reader to dismiss McMurtry's work as the privileged prattling of a white colonialist.

And in the #MeToo era, more and more writers would question, along with Diana Finlay Hendricks, whether a "focus on strong women . . . and interest in opinionated, forceful and dominant female characters" was enough to make McMurtry "a mid-twentieth century pioneer in American feminist literature." (The question arose just as *The Atlantic* cut its ties with his old buddy, Leon Wieseltier, over allegations of inappropriate behavior with women in the workplace.) Indeed, some critics would insist that as a man, McMurtry had no business writing about women at all. "There is a kind of writing that has a laser focus on a woman's anatomy, her breasts, her calves, her shoulders, as though they were the expressive medium, as though they were what amounted to her personality," said writer/bookseller Madeleine Watts. McMurtry was guilty of this sort of prose, she charged. Furthermore, none of his women "are possessed of authentic sexuality, not really, and if they do feel desirous of sex [McMurtry] can't untangle it from a desire for money, security, or attention. It's a light-touch misogyny which runs through many mid-century American writers, like Saul Bellow, Philip Roth, John Updike." The usual suspects. Watts aired her accusation less than a month after McMurtry died. The scalpels were out. The postmortems weren't waiting—nor were the tributes, both personal and professional.

"We're talking about one of the greatest men who ever lived," said Cybill Shepherd.

"He cast a big shadow across the landscape," Lawrence Wright agreed.

Benjamin Moser called his books "masterpieces. His characters were so vivid, his plots so intriguing, his language both so natural and so refined, that I came to regard him, book by book, with something approaching awe . . . I'm not a crier, and those books made me cry."

Before he died, Bill Wittliff said, "Larry took us out of our literary adolescence to a beginning maturity."

On April 22, 2021, the 87th Texas Legislature passed a resolution stating, "WHEREAS, The death of acclaimed author Larry McMurtry . . . has brought a great loss to American literature and deep sorrow to his fellow Texans . . . and . . . WHEREAS, Mr. McMurtry found acclaim with his first novel . . . and . . . WHEREAS, For two years, Mr. McMurtry promoted freedom of expression as the president of PEN America . . . and . . . WHEREAS . . . Mr. McMurtry decided to pursue his dream of turning Archer City into an American version of Hay-on-Wye . . . and WHEREAS, Larry McMurtry possessed a singular ability to distill, without sentimentality, the complexities and contradictions of the Texas spirit, enthralling millions of people with his gifts as a storyteller, and although he is sadly missed by his family and friends, his works will continue to beguile generations of people in the years to come; therefore be it RE-SOLVED, That the Senate of the State of Texas, 87th Legislature, hereby pay tribute to the life and legacy of Larry McMurtry."

As usual, the contrarian in him tried to squeeze in the final word. In one of his last interviews, he said he really was what his old T-shirt once proclaimed him to be: "I *am* a minor regional novelist. You should not let *minor* put you off a book." *Minor* fed the great stream of literature, he said, providing tributaries to the thrusting, ongoing current. "Very few writers in any generation are *not* minor. To make it to *minor* puts you in the company of Trollope in the nineteenth century . . . and a jillion others . . .

In the last generation, I try to think of anyone I think is really major. In the generation of Mailer and Roth and Bellow [the usual suspects] . . . I think *all* those guys are minor. The one person I think is not minor is Flannery O'Connor. I think she was a true genius, painful genius . . . But there's nothing wrong with being minor. If you're in the show, still writing books . . . it's fine if you're minor. I'm glad I got that high. Not everybody does."

He didn't think his life was worthy of a movie, but he conceded, "There'll be some kind of biography."

In the end, he said, "What I have hoped to be, all my mature life, is a man of letters . . . I believe I now am one."

Blue movies, blue moods, blue china serving his favorite beluga caviar, blues ballads loping to country beats, blue runnels of lightning shooting along the horns of cattle, blue streaks of eastern sky at dawn . . . the range of hues in McMurtryville.

In the waning days of March 2021, in Diana Ossana's house, when he knew his heart was going out, he had the names of women on his lips. Jo. Diane. Cybill. Susan. Maureen. He wanted to say goodbye on the phone.

Polly . . . Dorothea . . . Grace . . .

James and Curtis were with him. So was Sara. Diana and Faye. Three dogs.

He made arrangements to be cremated with Martin Oaks Cemetery and Crematory in Lewisville, Texas.

"Larry didn't go to the big cattle drive in the sky. He's prowling for rare books at the big garage and estate sales in the sky," Leslie Silko said.

"He was my friend for thirty-five years. There is no one like him, and there will never be anyone like him," Ossana reflected. She said, "I keep walking through my house and remembering so many things he did, where he'd sit, typing at the counter, staring out at the mountains for hours at a time. I know I'll survive, but at the same time, I don't know how I'll survive. This feels like someone is sawing off one of my limbs."

At least she had work to do. She and McMurtry had written a final script together, *Good Joe Bell*, about the anguished father of a murdered gay son. Mark Wahlberg was about to turn it into a movie: the return to the screen of McMurtry-Ossana, fifteen years after *Brokeback Mountain*.

McMurtry had also left behind a partial manuscript, a memoir of friendship, *62 Women,* doing what he swore he'd never do. "I'm not going to write about women," he'd insisted. "Why would I? Remember what Tolstoy said. He said he'd tell the truth about women when he had one foot in the grave, and then he'd jump in."

McMurtry's sister, Judy McLemore, didn't care about the work. She was just grateful that her brother had benefited from the kind ministrations of Faye at the end, "a very polite and good Christian woman."

Faye moved back to Oregon, to be near her farm and the graves of her first husband and son.

Three months after his father died on March 25, James released his finest album to date, *The Horses and the Hounds*—songs about rueful old age.

"The rules of happiness are as strict as the rules of sorrow; indeed, perhaps more strict," McMurtry had written. "The two states have different densities, I've come to think. The lives of happy people are dense with their own doings—crowded, active, thick—urban, I would almost say. But the sorrowing are nomads, on a plain with few landmarks and no boundaries; sorrow's horizons are vague and its demands few . . . I lived on the plain."

ACKNOWLEDGMENTS

I did not ask to write an authorized biography, but without the generosity of the McMurtry family, I would not have pursued this project. I am grateful to Faye Kesey McMurtry for the use of archival materials and to James McMurtry for his permission to reprint images and for his otherwise easygoing attitude about such matters. Jo McMurtry was extraordinarily gracious in offering me stories of her life with Larry. Matt McLemore in Archer City shared many warm memories of his uncle.

In a grace note, Diana Ossana was more forgiving of a biographer's bad timing than he deserved.

Larry McMurtry was very kind to me on occasion, first when I was an aspiring young writer in Dallas and later when I asked for his insights while completing my biography of Billy Lee Brammer. McMurtry found ways to be a teacher, though the formal profession didn't suit him.

Gregory Curtis and William Broyles gave me needed encouragement and engaged in splendid candid conversations with me, providing firm foundations for this book. Mike Evans was a catalyst for so much here—the book couldn't have been written without his deep knowledge and patient cooperation. Skip Hollandsworth served as a sort of midwife to the early drafts; he shared with me numerous notes, unpublished interviews, and observations from his many years as a reporter covering Texas topics, including Larry McMurtry. He gave me the gift of his experience and material, prompting me to think I could write this book, after all.

I've been blessed with the long support and friendship of Colleen Mohyde of the Colleen Mohyde Agency and Michael Homler, my editor at St. Martin's Press. Without them, this book would not have happened and would not have been such a pleasure.

Henry Kaufman provided splendid legal advice, good humor, and welcome encouragement. Many thanks, too, to Cassidy Graham and John Morrone for moving the project forward, and to Nancy Inglis for her copyediting.

I've been fortunate, in a literary life spanning nearly five decades now, to meet and speak with many of the principals in these pages, including Ken Babbs, Donald Barthelme, Rust Hills, Karen Kennerly, Ken Kesey, Wallace Stegner, and Calvin Trillin. Their stories have enriched the story I have to tell.

In addition to those listed above, the following people took the time to respond, often at length, to my questions, comments, requests, and visits. I am grateful for their contributions, some of which I gathered over a period of years—and a few of these good people are now no longer with us. Like the subject of this book, they valued making a record of events while there was still time. Any misinterpretations of facts or circumstances within these pages are mine, not theirs:

Cheryl Beesinger, Madison Smartt Bell, Betsy Berry, Shelby Brammer, Sidney Brammer, Dorothy Browne, Mark Busby, Gary Cartwright, John Curtis, Steve Davis, Ronnie Dugger, Nadine Eckhardt, Michael Granberry, Babette Fraser Hale, Stephen Harrigan, Dave Hickey, Joe Holley, Ray Isle, Beverly Lowry, Libby Lumpkin, Ed McClanahan, Laurence McGilvery, Sara Ossana, Jan Reid, Al Reinert, Leslie Marmon Silko, Dirk Van Nouhuys, Katy Vine, Ray Waddington, Jerry Jeff Walker, Susan Walker, Michael Wallis, Sally Wittliff, and Jim Wolpman.

My thanks to Richard Watson at the Harry Ransom Research Center at the University of Texas at Austin, Steve Davis and Katharine Salzmann at the Wittliff Collections at Texas State University, Norie Guthrie and Dara Flinn at the Fondren Library at Rice University, Julie Grob and Christian Kelleher of Special Collections at the University of Houston, Meagan May of Special Collections at the University of North Texas, J. Weston Marshall of the Southwest Collection at Texas Tech University, Christina Jensen of the DeGolyer Library at Southern Methodist University, and Molly Haigh of Special Collections at UCLA. The dispatch and efficiency with which they met my research needs, some of them during the difficult pandemic period, was truly impressive.

Elizabeth Seramur was my angel of the image, helping me collect and secure photographs. For additional permission to reprint images, I am indebted to Sarah Wylie VanMeter, representing the James Baker Hall Estate, and to others listed in the inserts. I am grateful to *Southwest Review* for permission to reprint lines from "For Erwin Smith, Cowboy Photographer" from the Winter 1960 issue (45, no. 1).

Jon Lewis and Kerry Ahearn, colleagues at Oregon State University, have taught me much about McMurtry and the movies. For their sustaining friendship during the writing of this book, I also thank Jon Sandor and Maryann Wasiolek, Geri, Richard and Sally Sandor and the rest of the Sandor family, Ted Leeson and Betty Campbell, Kathy Brisker, Creighton and Deborah Lindsay, David Turkel and Elena Passarello, Martha Lewis, Sue and Larry Rodgers, Bob and Mary Jo Nye, Kevin and Amy Clark, Suzanne Berne, and the Corvallis Sessioners. For being there at the finish line, gratitude to Debra Vetter, Anne Daugherty, and Barb and Ernie Martinez. Thanks to Sue Jones for her encouragement. To Hannah and Arlo Mullin and to Joey and Charlie Vetter, my deepest love. Finally, without Marjorie Sandor, my fellow rhythmist in the Infectious Unit, nothing happens, nothing matters.

BOOKS BY LARRY McMURTRY

(in order of publication, per the Library of Congress)

Horseman, Pass By (Harper & Brothers, 1961)
Leaving Cheyenne (Harper & Row, 1963)
The Last Picture Show (Dial Press, 1966)
In a Narrow Grave: Essays on Texas (Simon & Schuster, 1968)
Moving On: A Novel (Simon & Schuster, 1970)
All My Friends Are Going to Be Strangers: A Novel (Simon & Schuster, 1972)
It's Always We Rambled: An Essay on Rodeo (Frank Hallman, 1974)
Somebody's Darling: A Novel (Simon & Schuster, 1978)
Cadillac Jack: A Novel (Simon & Schuster, 1982)
The Desert Rose: A Novel (Simon & Schuster, 1983)
Lonesome Dove: A Novel (Simon & Schuster, 1985)
Film Flam: Essays on Hollywood (Simon & Schuster, 1987)
Texasville: A Novel (Simon & Schuster, 1987)
Anything for Billy: A Novel (Simon & Schuster, 1988)
Some Can Whistle: A Novel (Simon & Schuster, 1989)
Buffalo Girls: A Novel (Simon & Schuster, 1990)
The Evening Star: A Novel (Simon & Schuster, 1992)
Streets of Laredo: A Novel (Simon & Schuster, 1993)
Pretty Boy Floyd: A Novel (with Diana Ossana; Simon & Schuster, 1994)
Dead Man's Walk: A Novel (Simon & Schuster, 1995)
The Late Child: A Novel (Simon & Schuster, 1995)
Comanche Moon: A Novel (Simon & Schuster, 1997)
Zeke and Ned: A Novel (with Diana Ossana; Simon & Schuster, 1997)
Crazy Horse (Viking, 1999)
Duane's Depressed: A Novel (Simon & Schuster, 1999)
Walter Benjamin at the Dairy Queen (Simon & Schuster, 1999)
Boone's Lick: A Novel (Simon & Schuster, 2000)

Roads: Driving America's Great Highways (Simon & Schuster, 2000)

Still Wild: Short Fiction of the American West, 1950 to the Present
     (Simon & Schuster, 2000)

Paradise (Simon & Schuster, 2001)

Sacagawea's Nickname: Essays on the American West (New York Review
     of Books, 2001)

Sin Killer: A Novel (Simon & Schuster, 2002)

The Wandering Hill: A Novel (Simon & Schuster, 2003)

By Sorrow's River: A Novel (Simon & Schuster, 2003)

Folly and Glory: A Novel (Simon & Schuster, 2004)

Loop Group: A Novel (Simon & Schuster, 2004)

*The Colonel and Little Missie: Buffalo Bill, Annie Oakley, and the
     Beginnings of Superstardom in America* (Simon & Schuster, 2005)

Oh What a Slaughter: Massacres in the American West, 1846–1890
     (Simon & Schuster, 2005)

Telegraph Days: A Novel (Simon & Schuster, 2006)

When the Light Goes: A Novel (Simon & Schuster, 2007)

Books: A Memoir (Simon & Schuster, 2008)

Literary Life: A Second Memoir (Simon & Schuster, 2009)

Rhino Ranch: A Novel (Simon & Schuster, 2009)

Hollywood: A Third Memoir (Simon & Schuster, 2010)

The Berrybender Narratives (Simon & Schuster, 2011)

Custer (Simon & Schuster, 2012)

The Last Kind Words Saloon: A Novel (Liveright, 2014)

Thalia: A Texas Trilogy (Liveright, 2017)

NOTES

EPIGRAPH

ix *The gold song:* Willa Cather, "Spanish Johnny," *Cather: Stories, Poems and Other Writings,* ed. Sharon O'Brien (New York: Library of America, 1992), 799.

CHAPTER 1

3 *the River Oaks Theater:* For a brief history of Houston's River Oaks Theater, see Ramona L. Hopkins, "The River Oaks Theater: Saved from the Wrecking Ball?" in *Houston History* 9, no. 3 (July 29, 2012), 34–38.

3 *"lovingly dedicated to my hometown":* Larry McMurtry, *The Last Picture Show* (New York: Simon & Schuster, 1989 [1966]), dedication page.

3 *"He wanted to keep":* Ibid., 18.

4 *Nationally, box office revenue:* Cary Darling, "Why Houston Needs the River Oaks Theatre," *Houston Chronicle,* February 28, 2021, https://preview.houstonchronicle.com /movies-tv/essay-why-houston-needs-the-river-oaks-theatre-15980172.

5 *"Houston was my first city":* Larry McMurtry, *Walter Benjamin at the Dairy Queen* (New York: Simon & Schuster, 1999), 66.

5 *"The tradition I was born into":* Mark Horowitz, "Larry McMurtry's Dream Job," *New York Times,* December 7, 1997, https://archive.nytimes.com/www.nytimes.com/books/97 /12/07/home/article2.html?_r=2.

5 *"The bookshops are a form":* Joe Holley, "Larry McMurtry, Award-Winning Novelist Who Pierced Myths of His Native Texas, Dies at 84," *Washington Post,* March 26, https://www .washingtonpost.com/local/obituaries/larry-mcmurtry-dead/2021/03/26/953c4660 -ae09–11e7-a908-a3470754bbb9_story.html.

5 *"I would sit really near":* Darling, "Why Houston Needs the River Oaks Theatre."

6 *"I'm drawn to stories":* Staff writers, "Larry McMurtry: Last Posts from a Vanishing Frontier," [London] *Times,* February 19, 2011, https://www.thetimes.co.uk/article/larry -mcmurtry-last-posts-from-a-vanishing-frontier-mt95q5j7ffj.

6 *"American bleakness":* David Streitfeld, "The Yellowed Prose of Texas," *Washington Post,* April 6, 1999, https://www.washingtonpost.com/archive/lifestyle/1999/04/06/the -yellowed-prose-of-texas/98598edd-b6a6–4c85–9a3e-fc72a836a5e7/.

6 *"One of the things":* Walter Benjamin at the Dairy Queen, 22–23.

6 *"I can't escape":* Horowitz, "Larry McMurtry's Dream Job."

6 *Minor Regional Novelist:* Malcolm Jones, "The Ghost Writer at Home on the Range," *Newsweek,* August 1, 1993, https://www.newsweek.com/ghost-writer-home-range -192576.

6 *"Being a writer":* David L. Ulin, "The Son Rises with the Saga of a Texas Family," *Los Angeles Times,* June 14, 2013, http://www.latimes.com/books/jacketcopy/la-ca-ic-phillip -meyer-the-son-20130616-story.html.

6 *"Larry straddles":* "Larry McMurtry: Last Posts from a Vanishing Frontier."

7 *"men and women of letters":* William Zinsser, "Men of Letters," *The American Scholar,* October 1, 2010, https://theamericanscholar.org/men-of-letters.

7 *"When I was a boy":* Larry McMurtry, *Roads* (New York: Simon & Schuster/Touchstone, 2001), 205.

7 *"Knowing Larry":* Dave Hickey in conversation with the author, May 18, 2021.

7 *"long, long stretch":* Roads, 150–51.

7 *"more and more like a ghost":* Holley, "Larry McMurtry, Award-Winning Novelist."

8 *"Prose must accord":* Amy Laura Hall, "Men Without Guns: A Tribute to Larry Mc-Murtry," *Religion Dispatches,* May 3, 2021, https://religiondispatches.org/men-without-guns-a-tribute-to-larry-mcmurtry.

8 *"Larry was an elusive idea":* Raven Jordan, "Dallas Writers Have Been Searching for Larry McMurtry's Ghost Years Before His Death," *Dallas Observer,* March 30, 2021, https://dallasobserver.com/arts/dallas-writers-recall-their-early pilgrimages-in-search-of-the-mythical-larry-mcmurtry-12000328.

8 *"as soon as something's ended":* Douglas A. Jeffrey, "Larry McMurtry and the American West," *Claremont Review of Books* 7, no. 2 (Spring 2007), https://claremontreviewofbooks.com/larry-mcmurtry-and-the-american-west.

8 *"My women friends":* Steve Davis, email to the author, May 5, 2021.

8 *D. L. Birchfield:* D. L. Birchfield, "*Lonesome Dove*: The Bluing of a Texas-American Myth," *Studies in American Indian Literatures* 7, series 2 (Summer 1995), 45–64.

8 *Alexander Lalrinzama:* Alexander Lalrinzama, *Critiquing the Representation of Native Americans in Selected Narratives of Louis L'Amour and Larry McMurtry,* unpublished dissertation, Mizoram University, April 2019: mzuir/inflibnet.ac.in/bitstream/123456789/900/1/ALEXANDER%20LALRINZAMA%20Eng.pdf, 38–99.

9 *"an irresponsible white man's adventure":* This and subsequent quotes from Larry Mc-Murtry are from Jeffrey, "Larry McMurtry and the American West."

CHAPTER 2

10 *"I knew as I was growing up":* James Bryant, interview with McMurtry in Tucson for the Antiquarian Booksellers' Association of America, January 8, 2014, youtube.com/watch?v=6NQyeRc0d_1.

10 *As late as the 1980s:* See Robert M. Adams, "The Bard of Wichita Falls," *The New York Review of Books,* August 13, 1987, http://nybooks.com/articles/1987/08/13/the-bard-of-wichita-falls/.

10 *several hundred acres once owned by Mark Twain:* See Barbara Schmidt, "Livy, Will You Buy Me a Home in Texas?" www.twainquotes.com/TexasLand.html.

11 *The name can be traced:* George F. Black, *The Surnames of Scotland: Their Origin, Meaning, and History* (New York: New Public Library, 1946).

11 *"The Indians, believing the Great Spirit":* Myra Madison McMurtry, "The McMurtry Family," *Register of Kentucky State Historical Society* 5, no. 15 (September 1907), 65.

11 *"huge deformity of waters":* Larry McMurtry, "Life on the Missouri," *The New York Review of Books,* November 15, 2001, http://nybooks.com/articles/2001/11/15/life-on-the-missouri/.

11 *"death song":* Leta Byrne Gage, *Archer County Through Ninety-Eight Years,* unpublished master's degree thesis, North Texas State College, Denton, Texas, 1957, 12.

11 *"If you kill me":* Ibid., 14.

12 *"My grandparents":* Larry McMurtry, "The Southwest as the Cradle of the Novelist," *The American Southwest: Cradle of Literary Art,* ed. Robert W. Walts (San Marcos, TX: Southwest Texas State University, 1979), 27–28.

12 *"she'd had one at her back door":* Sue McMurtry Dean, "The McMurtry Family," *Archer*

County, Texas, Centennial Family History Book and Program (Archer City, Texas: McCrain Publishing Company, 1980), 95.

12 *"Cowboys are romantics"*: Larry McMurtry, "Take My Saddle from the Wall: A Valediction," in *In a Narrow Grave: Essays on Texas* (New York: Simon & Schuster, 1968), 149.

13 *"my 9 cowboy uncles"*: Larry McMurtry, letter to Max Crawford, January 20, 1985, Max Crawford Papers, Southwest Collection/Special Collections Library, Texas Tech University.

13 *"sobriety settlement"*: Clarendon, Texas, *Texas Online*, web.archive.org/web /20080509165409/http://texas-on-line.com/graphic/clarendon.htm.

13 *"people lean west"*: Richard Manning, *Grassland: The History, Biology, Politics, and Promise of the American Prairie* (New York: Penguin Books, 1995), 15.

13 *At that time, Archer County*: Except where noted, facts in this paragraph are gleaned from Gage, *Archer County Through Ninety-Eight Years*, 2, 36, 41, 49, 57.

14 *brand-new sandstone jailhouse*: John Egan, "Famed Texas Town Is Selling Its Historic Jail Beginning at Just $5,000," *Culturemap/Austin*, https://culturemap.com/news/real-estate /01–24–20-historic-jail-archer-city-for-sale-5K-larry-mcmurtry-bids#slide=0.

14 *"People had more religion"*: Gage, *Archer County Through Ninety-Eight Years*, 60.

15 *"soiled dove"*: Larry McMurtry, *Paradise* (New York: Simon & Schuster, 2001), 36.

15 *"To the end of his days"*: *Walter Benjamin at the Dairy Queen*, 47.

15 *"My parents, like the Tolstoys"*: Ibid., 48.

16 *"Oklahoma"*: *Roads*, 205.

16 *"At some point in her childhood"*: *Paradise*, 42.

16 *she issued William an ultimatum*: "Take My Saddle from the Wall: A Valediction," 143.

16 *Great Drift*: Gage, *Archer County Through Ninety-Eight Years*, 42.

17 *Aridity*: For a full discussion of the environmental conditions of the Southwest, see Ross Calvin, *Sky Determines: An Interpretation of the Southwest* (Albuquerque: University of New Mexico Press, 1948). I have drawn upon Calvin for background information.

17 *The plains on which McMurtry dreamed*: I have drawn upon Richard Manning's *Grassland: The History, Biology, Politics, and Promise of the American Prairie* (New York: Penguin, 1995) for information about the geological formation and the culture and history of the Great Plains.

18 *"Grass is worthless"*: Ibid., 117.

18 *"The American West as we know it"*: Larry McMurtry, *Sacagawea's Nickname: Essays on the American West* (New York: New York Review of Books, 2001), 169.

18 *The earliest drives out of Texas*: See Mary G. Ramos, "Cattle Drives Started in Earnest after the Civil War," *Texas Almanac* (Texas State Historical Association), https://texasalmanac .com/topics/agriculture/cattle-drives-started-in-earnest-after-the-civil-war.

19 *"I believe the grassland"*: Manning, *Grassland*, 9.

20 *"so big and slow"*: *Roads*, 180.

21 *"wasn't particularly mean"*: "Take My Saddle from the Wall: A Valediction," 158.

21 *"To me [that life] was hollow"*: Lynn Neary, "Larry McMurtry Loves the West, but Knocks the Cowboy Off His High Horse," National Public Radio, May 7, 2014. http://www.npr .org/2014/05/07/310422556/larry-mcmurtry-loves-the-west-but-knocks-the-cowboy-off -his-high-horse.

21 *"I [now] regard ranching"*: Scott Kraft, "The Loner," *Los Angeles Times*, December 15, 2002, https://www.latimes.com/la-tm-mcmurtrydec15-story.html.

21 *"Lacking a tail"*: Manning, *Grassland*, 51.

21 *"[I was] . . . conscious"*: "The Yellowed Prose of Texas."

21 *"A huge sky"*: *Walter Benjamin at the Dairy Queen,* 71.

22 *"I have looked at many places"*: *Roads,* 189.

22 *"No sabe"*: Larry McMurtry, "A Look at the Lost Frontier," *In a Narrow Grave: Essays on Texas,* 83.

22 *On another cattle-buying jaunt*: *Roads,* 52.

23 *Closer to home*: *Walter Benjamin at the Dairy Queen,* 26.

23 *"Dutchmen"*: Ibid., 26.

23 *One day when McMurtry was ten*: *Roads,* 184.

23 *He would frequently see*: *Walter Benjamin at the Dairy Queen,* 19.

24 *"character"*: Ibid., 190.

24 *Self-denial*: *Paradise,* 25.

24 *"My father could no more be optimistic"*: Larry McMurtry, letter to Ken Kesey, November 10, 1961, Ken Kesey Papers, University of Oregon Libraries, Special Collections and University Archives.

24 *"Now, Lyndon"*: Ronnie Dugger, *The Politician: The Life and Times of Lyndon Johnson* (New York: Norton, 1982), 212.

24 *"set aside their corrugated washboards"*: Ibid., 213.

25 *"in the company of older farm children"*: Larry McMurtry, *Books: A Memoir* (New York: Simon & Schuster, 2008), 7.

25 *Will Taylor*: See *Walter Benjamin at the Dairy Queen,* 119.

26 *climbed the windmill*: *Books,* 5.

26 *If he could get his paws*: See Larry McMurtry, "For Susan [Sontag], A Memento," unpublished, December 1989, Susan Sontag Archives, Library Special Collections, Charles E. Young Research Library, UCLA.

26 *His only quiet times*: Larry McMurtry, "True Westerners," Flash & Filigree (blog), https://flashandfiligree.com/2013/03/14/true-westerners/.

26 *"McMurtry Means Beef"*: *Books,* 2.

26 *"[I] formed my consciousness"*: "The Southwest as the Cradle of the Novelist," 30.

26 *"When the conflict of the generations"*: Ibid., 31.

27 *Robert Hilburn*: See *Walter Benjamin at the Dairy Queen,* 97; see also *Books,* 6–7.

27 *"stability I could always depend on"*: *Walter Benjamin at the Dairy Queen,* 97.

27 *"What I don't remember"*: *Books,* 8.

27 *"It was like he was starved"*: Bill Broyles in conversation with the author, May 26, 2021.

CHAPTER 3

29 *"I am one of the few American writers"*: Larry McMurtry, cited in Benjamin Moser, "Saboteur in Texas," *The New York Review of Books,* May 27, 2004, http://www.nybooks.com/articles/2004/05/27/saboteur-in-texas/.

29 *"one long snore"*: Ceil Cleveland, *Whatever Happened to Jacy Farrow?* (Denton, TX: University of North Texas Press, 1997), 26.

29 *"the same early mentor"*: Ibid., xviii–xix.

30 shit, piss, *and* goddamn: Larry McMurtry, "Eros in Archer County," in *In a Narrow Grave: Essays on Texas* (New York: Simon & Schuster, 1968), 58–59.

30 *"The movies could never get it right"*: Larry McMurtry Speaking and Q & A at Texas State 1974, vimeo.com/106627001.

30 *"driven across the screen"*: Larry McMurtry, "Cowboys, Movies, Myths, & Cadillacs: An Excursus on Ritual Forms in the Western Movie," in *In a Narrow Grave: Essays on Texas,* 22.

31 *"believed the main message"*: Larry McMurtry Speaking and Q & A.

31 *"heroes and heroines"*: Roads, 185.

32 *"Two of us liked horses"*: Thomas Swick, "Book Rancher McMurtry Rides Herd Over Words," *Chicago Tribune*, May 23, 2001, https://www.chicagotribune.com/sns-archer -city-story.html.

32 *"I am agnostic"*: Larry McMurtry, "An Abridged Autobiography," North Texas State College, Larry McMurtry Collection, Special Collections, University of North Texas University.

33 *"The Spit and Whittle Club"*: "Fred Walsh (1912–2001)," Find a Grave Memorial, https://www.findagrave.com/memorial/61453379/fred-walsh.

33 *"stimulated by knowing"*: George Hickenlooper, *Picture This: The Times of Peter Bog-danovich in Archer City, Texas* (Nelson Entertainment, 1989), dailymotion.com/video /xqdjx9.

33 *Mr. Tee-Hee-Hee*: Cleveland, *Whatever Happened to Jacy Farrow?*, 7.

33 *Comic books, men's magazines*: Books, 11,16, 25.

34 *"armpit" publications*: Adam Parfrey, *It's a Man's World: Men's Adventure Magazines, the Postwar Pulps* (Los Angeles: Feral House, 2003), 15.

34 *the word* nympho: Ibid., 18.

34 *"girl pinching" or "animal nibbler"*: Ibid., 14, 13.

34 *"Redman's Trail of Death"*: This and subsequent quotes in this paragraph are from Parfrey, *It's a Man's World*, 54–55.

35 *"I had no purpose in mind"*: "Eros in Archer County," 58.

35 *"Ssh"*: Ibid.

36 *"frigid"*: Larry McMurtry, letter to Mike Kunkel, 1956, Larry McMurtry Papers, Special Collections, University of Houston Library.

36 *"In . . . school"*: "An Abridged Autobiography."

36 *"constant and will never change"*: McMurtry to Mike Kunkel.

37 *Slack remembered*: Cleveland, *Whatever Happened to Jacy Farrow?*, 35–36.

37 *"Be prepared!"* Ibid., 49.

37 *"stepping just a little too high"*: Ibid., 25

37 *McMurtry's young cousin*: See Daniel Kusner, "CAN'T QUIT—EVER: McMurtry Promises That 'Brokeback' Will Stem the Trend of Texas Homophobia," March 19, 2018, www.danielkusner.com/blog/mcmurtry-promises-that-brokeback-will-save-texas.

37 *"Last Saturday morning"*: Archer County News 44, no. 23 (May 22, 1958), 1.

38 *"Charlie Spraggins"*: Archer County News 35, no. 10 (March 3, 1949), 1.

38 *"You Can't Be First"*: McMurtry used this detail in a characterization of his sister in *Texas-ville*, according to Skip Hollandsworth in unpublished notes for a profile of McMurtry, given to the author, June 2021.

38 *sad cowboy reunions*: See In a Narrow Grave: Essays on Texas, 151, 158, 164, 170; see also *Walter Benjamin at the Dairy Queen*, 88.

38 *"How you doin', Larry?"*: "A Look at the Lost Frontier," in *In a Narrow Grave: Essays on Texas*, 87.

39 *"I had a nice, manageable boyfriend"*: Cleveland, *Whatever Happened to Jacy Farrow?*, 40.

39 *"The things I loved most to do"*: Ibid.

39 *"While I have talked a good deal"*: Larry McMurtry, letter to Ken Kesey, February 21, 1961, University of Oregon Libraries, Special Collections and University Archives.

39 *"We probably derived a more realistic view"*: "Eros in Archer County," 73.

40 *"Most West Texas husbands"*: Ibid., 69.

40 *"roughly as neurotic as Kafka"*: Caroline Fraser, "Pretty in the Sunlight," *The New York*

Review of Books, October 4, 2001, http://www.nybooks.com/articles/2001/10/04/pretty
-in-the-sunlight/.

40 *"men see women":* Cleveland, *Whatever Happened to Jacy Farrow?,* xv.

40 *"Boys [to me]":* Ibid., xviii.

40 *"seemed so dumb":* Ibid., 33.

40 *"kidney shaped dressing table":* Ibid., 8.

40 *"Most of the boys":* "Eros in Archer County," 64.

40 *"through a fluke":* Paradise, 32.

41 *"went home determined to rot":* "Eros in Archer County," 64.

41 *he found an abandoned book:* See *Sacagawea's Nickname,* 62.

41 *"reading a few of Angie Debo's sinewy sentences":* Ibid., 63–64.

42 *"in my own damn bed!":* Cleveland, *Whatever Happened to Jacy Farrow?,* 51.

42 *"Larry can read a whole book":* Matt McLemore in conversation with the author, July 2, 2021.

42 Don Quixote *seized his attention: Walter Benjamin at the Dairy Queen,* 113.

42 *"I [long] pondered":* Books, 11.

42 *The 1954* Wildcat: Archer City High School, *The Wildcat,* 1954, Portal to Texas History,
texashistory.unt.edu/ark:/67531/metapth11573821/?q=larry%mcmurtry, 21, 79, 86, 98.

42 *"as popular as you can be":* Scott Kraft, "The Loner," *Los Angeles Times,* December 15,
2002, https://www.latimes.com/la-tm-mcmurtrydec15-story.html.

43 *"I was already several Miss Somethings":* Cleveland, *Whatever Happened to Jacy Farrow?,* 34.

43 *"The 4-H boys":* Archer County News 35, no. 10 (March 3, 1949), 1.

43 *In 1953:* Archer County News 39, no. 16 (April 9, 1953), 1.

43 *an all-expenses-paid trip:* For details about the 1953 4-H Club Congress in Chicago, see
Guy Noble, "A Delegate Never Forgets His Experience at the 4-H Club Congress in
Chicago," National 4-H Club Congress in Chicago, Draft Copy, November 2017, 5–6,
70–71.

44 *"horses, dangerous devil-may-care stampedes":* "An Abridged Autobiography."

44 *"hyperbole":* "Eros in Archer County," 67.

45 *"He would just say":* Hickenlooper, *Picture This.*

45 *"was a mischief-maker":* Ibid.

45 *"and invited me down the street":* Ibid.

45 *"I was a kind of special case":* Books, 20.

45 *"gray as dishwater":* Paradise, 29.

46 *his father dismounted:* Ibid., 31.

CHAPTER 4

48 *"I had never read":* Larry McMurtry, *Literary Life* (New York: Simon & Schuster, 2009), 4.

48 *The city was founded on a scam:* For a brief background on Houston's founding, see Joe
Holley, "Allen Brothers: The Wheeling-Dealing Duo Who Turned Mud into Gold,"
Houston Chronicle, May 19, 2016, https://www.houstonchronicle.com/local/history
/Allen-brothers-The-wheeling-dealing-duo-who-7722822.php. Quotes in this chapter
regarding Houston's origins all come from this source.

49 *"I was often the only white person":* Books, 41.

49 *"All three of Houston's main secondhand bookstores":* Books, 41.

49 *Edward Hopkins Cushing:* For a useful history of Houston's bookstores, see Aric Richardson, "The Evolution of Houston Bookstores," *Houston History* 15, no. 1, 38–41, https://
houstonhistorymagazine.org/wp-content/uploads/2018/04/Houston-Book-Stores.pdf.

49 *"One reason I'm comfortable":* Books, 43.

50 *"schizophrenic"*: Larry McMurtry, letter to Mike Kunkel, July 5, 1956, Larry McMurtry Collection, Special Collections, University of Houston Library.

50 *"I read omnivorously"*: "An Abridged Autobiography."

50 *"dreadfully homesick"*: Ibid.

50 *"vastly overrated aggregation"*: Letter to Mike Kunkel, December 3, 1955.

51 *"I hope I get famous"*: Letter to Mike Kunkel, October 20, 1955.

51 *"I couldn't stand the thought"*: Letter to Mike Kunkel, September 30, 1955.

51 *"Well-meaning friends"*: Letter to Mike Kunkel, October 20, 1955.

51 *"been just friends"*: This and subsequent quotes regarding Tissa and Douglas are from letter to Mike Kunkel, December 3, 1955.

51 *"I feel silly"*: Letter to Mike Kunkel, December 3, 1955.

52 *Benjamin Moser*: Benjamin Moser, "Houston and History," *The American Scholar* 73, no. 3 (Summer 2004), 59, 64–65.

52 *"[all] things . . . Texan!"*: Frank D. Welch, *Philip Johnson and Texas* (Austin: University of Texas Press, 2000), 39.

53 *"Archer City is rather a mess"*: Letter to Mike Kunkel, January 14, 1956.

53 *"[Larry] soon joined me"*: Ceil Cleveland, *Whatever Happened to Jacy Farrow?* (Denton, TX: University of North Texas Press, 1997), xii.

53 *"a very foolish thing to do"*: "An Abridged Autobiography."

53 *"kind of gulag operation"*: Grover Lewis, "The Legacy of Huckleberry Finn," *Splendor in the Short Grass: The Grover Lewis Reader,* ed. Jan Reid and W. K. Stratton (Austin: University of Texas Press, 2005), 239.

53 *"freighted toward business"*: Lewis, Ibid., 240.

53 *"I am a pure Caucasian Democrat"*: "An Abridged Autobiography."

54 *"better men than the institution"*: Lewis, "The Legacy of Huckleberry Finn," 245.

54 *"the first man I ever knew"*: Ibid., 237–38.

54 *"world"*: Letter to Mike Kunkel, November 4, 1955.

54 *"the soft white hands of a dentist"*: *Literary Life,* 11.

54 *"some outrageous, absolute judgment"*: Dave Hickey, "Grover Lewis: An Appreciation," *Los Angeles Times,* June 25, 1995, https://www.latimes.com/archives/la-xpm-1995–06–25-bk-16812-story.html.

55 *"Larry—he was a very good person"*: Dave Hickey in conversation with the author, June 8, 2021.

55 *"In 1943"*: Grover Lewis, "Cracker Eden," *Splendor in the Short Grass,* 248.

55 *"We [did it] three or four times running"*: Lewis, "The Legacy of Huckleberry Finn," 239.

55 *"The grass on the low hills"*: Larry McMurtry, "The Untrodden Ways," unpublished short story included with a letter to Mike Kunkel, July 5, 1956.

55 *"Don't be too critical"*: Letter to Mike Kunkel, July 5, 1956.

55 *"You clearly have the ability"*: Letter to Mike Kunkel, November 4, 1955.

56 *"Grover was regarded"*: Katy Vine, "Return to Splendor," *Texas Monthly,* March 2005, https://www.texasmonthly.com/the-culture/return-to-spendor/.

56 *"Grover's stories and poems"*: Ibid.

56 *"McMurtry and I"*: Lewis, "The Legacy of Huckleberry Finn," 240.

56 *"Got your toothbrush?"*: This and ensuing dialogue is from Lewis, "The Legacy of Huckleberry Finn," 241.

56 *"the living tar"*: Lewis, "The Legacy of Huckleberry Finn," 241.

57 *McMurtry later disputed Lewis's memory*: *Literary Life,* 17.

57 *"Larry knew a trick"*: Lewis, "The Legacy of Huckleberry Finn," 240.

57 *"took a rather dim view"*: Ibid.

57 *"young turks"*: This and subsequent quotes in this paragraph are from Lewis, "The Legacy of Huckleberry Finn," 240.

57 *"Mistah LOO-WIS!"*: Lewis, "The Legacy of Huckleberry Finn," 239.

57 *"Grover and his old running-mate"*: Hickey, "Grover Lewis: An Appreciation."

58 *"Boy Scout virtues"*: This and subsequent quotes from McMurtry's undergraduate papers are from the Larry McMurtry Collection, Special Collections, University of North Texas Library.

59 *"I . . . don't think one has to worry"*: Larry McMurtry, letter to Ken Kesey, June 17, 1964, Special Collections and University Archives, University of Oregon Libraries.

59 *"obscurantist school"*: Letter to Mike Kunkel, August 31, 1956.

59 *"A very pleasant little town"*: Jo McMurtry, letter to the author, April 25, 2021.

60 *"sand"*: James McMurtry Facebook post, August 11, 2020, https://nl-nl.facebook.com /JamesMcMurtry/posts/10162311977738682.

60 *"preview of one of the dresses"*: *Florence Morning News,* April 23, 1954, 6.

60 *"Queen of Bohemia"*: Greg Curtis in conversation with the author, May 12, 2021.

60 *"seemed rather quiet"*: Jo McMurtry letter.

61 *"McMurtry and I justified"*: Lewis, "The Legacy of Huckleberry Finn," 242.

61 *McMurtry insisted: Literary Life,* 17.

61 *"college gentlemen"*: Lewis, "The Legacy of Huckleberry Finn," 242.

61 *"Southwest was literally perishing"*: Ibid.

61 *"shape" their writing*: Ibid., 239.

61 *"novel folk-literature"*: Larry McMurtry, "Beiderbecke," *Avesta* 37 (Spring 1957), 14.

62 *"historical"*: Patrick Bennett, "Larry McMurtry: Thalia, Houston, and Hollywood," *Talking with Texas Writers: Twelve Interviews* (College Station, Texas: Texas A&M University Press, 1980), 17.

62 *"The title"*: Lewis, "The Legacy of Huckleberry Finn," 243–44.

62 *McMurtry claimed: Literary Life,* 11.

62 *"BOO!"*: Larry McMurtry, "Credo," *The Coexistence Review,* issue 1, Special Collections, University of North Texas Library.

63 *"beauty"*: Larry McMurtry poem, *The Coexistence Review,* issue 1.

63 *"Let me alone"*: Grover Lewis, "Credo," *The Coexistence Review,* issue 1.

63 *"I would rather be a Communist"*: John Lewis, "Credo," *The Coexistence Review,* issue 1.

63 *"On impulse"*: Lewis, "The Legacy of Huckleberry Finn," 244.

64 *"I swear or affirm"*: Cover, *The Coexistence Review,* issue 2.

64 *"Larry and I started dating"*: Jo McMurtry letter.

64 *"kind thing"*: Larry McMurtry, "Grandad's End," a section from *Horseman, Pass By, The Coexistence Review,* Issue 1.

64 *"Now, four centuries"*: Frederick Jackson Turner, "The Significance of the Frontier in American History," *The Frontier in American History* (New York: Henry Holt, 1920), 38.

65 *"Lead me along the hills"*: Larry McMurtry, "For Erwin Smith, Cowboy Photographer," *Southwest Review* 45, no. 1 (Winter 1960), 73.

65 *"so thrilled": Literary Life,* 35.

66 *"Goat" Mayo:* See J. H. "Goat" Mayo, Texas Rodeo Cowboy Hall of Fame inductees, https://texasrodeocowboy.com/inductees/j-h-goat-mayo.

66 *reportedly the site of Texas's first rodeo:* See Clay Coppedge, "The First Rodeo," *Texas Escapes,* www.texasescapes.com/ClayCoppedge/First-Rodeo.htm. See also "The History of the Texas Rodeo," *The Daytripper,* February 29, 2020, https://thedaytripper.com/the -history-of-the-texas-rodeo/.

66 *The rodeo craze:* See Larry McMurtry, *The Colonel and Little Missie: Buffalo Bill, Annie Oakley, and the Beginnings of Superstardom in America* (New York: Simon & Schuster, 2005), 115.

67 *"Things used to be better around here":* Larry McMurtry, *Horseman, Pass By* (New York: Simon & Schuster/Touchstone, 1992 [1961]), 88.

67 *"Granddad made something good":* Ibid., 148.

67 *"All of them wanted more":* Ibid., 145.

68 *"minute":* Literary Life, 25.

68 *"My time in Houston":* Ibid.

68 *"missed [the city]":* Larry McMurtry, *Some Can Whistle* (Simon & Schuster, 1989), 74.

68 *"old fishy smell":* Ibid., 77.

68 *"city [was] only forty-one feet":* Larry McMurtry, "A Handful of Roses," in *In a Narrow Grave: Essays on Texas,* 125.

69 *"The people in Larry's life":* Jo McMurtry letter.

69 *"The first inkling I had":* Literary Life, 19.

70 *"realistic fiction":* This and subsequent quotes from McMurtry's paper on Elizabethan realism are from the Larry McMurtry Collection, Special Collections, University of North Texas Library.

CHAPTER 5

73 *"She was very friendly":* Ray Waddington in conversation with the author, October 14, 2021.

74 *"as beautiful as any woman on the planet":* Larry McMurtry, "A Life for the Star," *The New York Review of Books,* April 26, 2012, https://nybooks.com/articles/2012/04/26/life-star.

74 *"were the advance guard":* Books, 27.

75 *"brought us that particular interest":* Gloria Leonard, "About Irving Klaw—'An Interview with Paula Klaw' (1980)," *High Society,* October 1980, https://americansuburbx.com/2013/05/interview-about-irving-klaw-with-paula-klaw.html.

75 *Eric Stanton:* See Pierre Perrone, "Obituary: Eric Stanton," *Independent,* June 4, 1999, https://www.independent.co.uk/arts-entertainment/obituary-eric-stanton-1098149.html.

76 *"The time may have come":* In a Narrow Grave: Essays on Texas, xiv.

76 *"No, I am not quite Johnny and Gid":* Larry McMurtry, letter to Ken Kesey, 1962, Special Collections and University Archives, University of Oregon Libraries.

77 *"He just couldn't believe sex":* Larry McMurtry, *Leaving Cheyenne* (New York: Simon & Schuster/Touchstone, 1991 [1962]), 202.

77 *"If I made him sit around":* Ibid., 214.

77 *"[I] am not, alas":* Letter to Kesey, 1962.

77 *"It may just be":* Letter to Kesey, June 16, 1964.

77 *"If you stay loose":* Leaving Cheyenne, 77.

77 *"I never had been able":* Ibid., 175.

78 *"the following are two excerpts":* Editor's Note, *The Rice Mill* (Fall 1958), 5.

79 *"Mexicans were, and still are":* John Phillip Santos, "Américo Paredes vs. J. Frank Dobie," *Texas Monthly,* October 2019, https://www.texasmonthly.com/being-texan/americo-paredes-j-frank-dobie/.

79 *"the university cherished":* Ibid., 90.

79 *"tried to build a Maginot line":* Jason Mellard, *Progressive Country: How the 1970s Transformed the Texan in Popular Culture* (Austin: University of Texas Press, 2013), 94.

79 *"radical":* Ibid.

79 *"a big, shambling, deep-voiced man"*: Ibid., 90.

79 *"bred to mint and bourbon"*: Ibid., 89.

79 *"Forget it"*: Ibid., 94.

80 *"that great Texas liberal"*: Santos, "Américo Paredes vs. J. Frank Dobie."

80 *"There is a cruel streak"*: Ibid.

80 *"there would be nothing left"*: Ibid.

80 *"One notes"; "Just about the truth"*: Ibid.

80 *"shoot the sonofabitch"*: Ibid.

81 "Momma*": See Larry McMurtry's letter to Dorothea Oppenheimer, August 22, 1961, Larry McMurtry Papers, Harry Ransom Humanities Research Center, The University of Texas at Austin.

82 *"Larry and I were married"*: Jo McMurtry letter.

82 *"our marriage reading Proust"*: Books, 49.

83 *"Houston was growing"*: Jo McMurtry letter.

83 *"bright shy white new university"*: Donald Barthelme, "See the Moon?", *Unspeakable Practices, Unnatural Acts* (New York: Farrar, Straus & Giroux, 1968), 161.

83 *"cops who failed to see the virtues"*: Books, 41.

84 *"Frank. This newspaper critic"*: Mark Busby, *Larry McMurtry and the West: An Ambivalent Relationship* (Denton, TX: University of North Texas Press, 1995), 15.

84 *Texas Institute of Letters*: See Karl Killian, "The Texas Institute of Letters," *Texas Monthly*, December 31, 1989, https://www.texasmonthly.com/the-culture/the-texas-institute-of-letters/.

85 *"he always had an instinct"*: Elaine Woo, "John 'Jack' Leggett, mentor of emerging authors, dies at 97," *Los Angeles Times*, January 31, 2015, https://www.latimes.com/local/obituaries/la-me-john-leggett-20150201-story.html.

85 *"He once told me"*: Ibid.

86 *"I had a bedrock of observation"*: Larry McMurtry, Lecture at Texas State, 1983, vimeo.com/111894302.

86 *"Hooray!"*: Jo McMurtry letter.

86 *"I was really fortunate"*: Lecture at Texas State, 1983.

86 *"I would have published it in gibberish"*:

86 *"much evidence"*: John Leggett, letter to Larry McMurtry, April 7, 1960, Special Collections, University of Houston Library.

86 *"There's something awfully appealing"*: Leggett to McMurtry, May 10, 1960.

86 *"allows maximum freedom"*: Ibid.

87 *"genital turns of mind"*: Leggett to McMurtry, August 23, 1960.

87 *"Sex and Lonnie"*: Leggett to McMurtry, June 16, 1960.

87 *"work[ing] with an author"*: Leggett to McMurtry, June 27, 1960.

87 *"Now what disturbs me"*: Leggett to McMurtry, August 31, 1960.

87 *"[T]his is where you and I"*: Ibid.

87 *"How . . . would [you] feel"*: Ibid.

87 *"Minds grow"*: Stanford Creative Writing Program, "History of the Stanford Creative Writing Program," https://creativewriting.stanford.edu/about/history-stanford-creative-writing-program.

87 *"arrived at Stanford"*: Ibid.

87 *"pure luck"*: Ray Waddington in conversation with the author, October 14, 2021.

88 *"He had the most earnest interest in"*: Larry McMurtry, "Ben Jonson's Feud with the Poetasters, 1599–1601," a thesis submitted to the faculty of Rice Institute in partial ful-

fillment of the requirements for the degree of Masters of Arts, Houston, Texas, February 1960, 43.

88 *"satiric spirit"*: Ibid., 1.

88 *"not in a sentimental mood"*: Larry McMurtry Speaking and Q & A at Texas State, 1974.

CHAPTER 6

89 *"In the late fifties"*: Rick Dodgson, *It's All a Kind of Magic: The Young Ken Kesey* (Madison: University of Wisconsin Press, 2013), 81.

89 *"There aren't many crackpots"*: Ibid.

89 *"the last wagon-master"*: Dedication page, *In a Narrow Grave: Essays on Texas.*

89 *"contemplate the heavens"*: Dodgson, *It's All a Kind of Magic,* 80.

90 *"sport"*: Ibid., 54.

90 *"a deep keel"*: David Stanford, "Working with Kesey," in *Spit in the Ocean #7: All About Ken Kesey,* ed. Ed McClanahan (New York: Penguin Books, 2003), 209.

91 *"I was never sympathetic"*: Dodgson, *It's All a Kind of Magic,* 75.

91 *"writing to people"*: Ibid., 76.

91 *"full of the worst and best writing"*: Ibid., 75.

91 *"It was an easy commute"*: Jo McMurtry letter.

92 *"If the world of men"*: David Arnold, "Westword, Bound," *Stanford* magazine, July 2021, https://stanfordmag.org/contents/westword-bound.

92 *"[telling] the world"*: Ibid.

92 *"beautiful short story writer"*: Arts & Letters Live, May 17, 2014, youtube.com/watch?v =rsa1yEvE3Cg.

92 *"Malcolm Cowley"*: Ibid.

92 *"He made it plain"*: Larry McMurtry, "On the Road," *The New York Review of Books,* December 5, 2002, https://nybooks.com/articles/2002/12/05/on-the-road.

93 *"who* was *this lumberjack"*: Ibid.

93 *"It was a pretty brilliant class"*: Malcolm Cowley, "Ken Kesey at Stanford," *Northwest Review* 16, no. 1 (Fall 1976), 1.

93 *"extraordinary character"*: Malcolm Cowley, *The Long Voyage: Selected Letters of Malcolm Cowley, 1915–1987,* ed. Hans Bak (Cambridge: Harvard University Press, 2014), 606.

93 *"wild young man"*: Ibid., 546.

94 *"Be gentle"*: Ken Kesey, "Remember This: Write What You Don't Know," *New York Times,* December 31, 1989, https://www.nytimes.com/1989/12/31/books/remember-this-write -what-you-don-t-know.html.

94 *"Gossip about the great"*: *Walter Benjamin at the Dairy Queen,* 134.

94 *"With his grand white hair"*: James Baker Hall, "Ken," in *Spit in the Ocean #7,* 151.

94 *"brought some of the passions"*: *Walter Benjamin at the Dairy Queen,* 134.

94 *"Jesus, Larry"*: Ibid., 134–35.

94 *"It doesn't bend"*: Hall, "Ken," 151.

95 *"short story remains by its very nature"*: Cathy Brown, "Frank O'Connor and the Lonely Voice," *746 Books,* https://746books.com/2016/03/10/frank-oconnor-and-the-lonely -voice/.

95 *"was very special"*: Jo McMurtry letter.

95 *He tried one day: Books,* 50.

95 *"a pile of local fine printing"*: Ibid.

96 *Last of the Great Scouts:* Ibid., 57.

96 *"I went around with Miles"*: Larry McMurtry, "Splendors and Miseries of Being an Author/Bookseller," https://www.abaa.org/member-articles/splendors-and-miseries-of-being -an-author-bookseller.

96 *"One day he . . . asked me"*: Books, 55.

96 *"The dominant East Bay bookshop"*: Ibid.

97 *"indecent, vulgar"*: Ibid.

97 *"We were all learning"*: Dodgson, *It's All a Kind of Magic,* 164.

97 *"What was really nice"*: Ibid.

97 *"These parties"*: Ibid.

97 *"those mesmerizing dialogues"*: Hall, "Ken," 150.

98 *"oppressive air"*: Dirk Van Nouhuys, email to the author, June 8, 2021.

98 *"empathetic"*: Ibid.

98 *"he seemed as country and as shy"*: Ed McClanahan in conversation with the author, May 24, 2021.

98 *"To enjoy the strength of Ken's friendship"*: "On the Road."

98 *"I wasn't the only one"*: Hall, "Ken," 150.

99 *"[We] disagreed"*: Ken Kesey, "The Day After Superman Died," in *Demon Box* (New York: Viking, 1986), 58.

99 *"So. What has the Good Old Revolution"*: Ibid.

99 *"wild boy from the hills"*: "On the Road."

99 *"There was a lot of the frontiersman"*: Dodgson, *It's All a Kind of Magic,* 89.

99 *"Cold War"*: Hall, "Ken," 150.

99 *"We all came from conservative backgrounds"*: McClanahan conversation.

99 *"As to the politics"*: Van Nouhuys email.

99 *"To me Perry Lane"*: "On the Road."

100 *"One night we decided"*: McClanahan conversation.

100 *"[I] found little about [Cassady]"*: Walter Benjamin at the Dairy Queen, 129.

100 *"I was all turned on"*: Dodgson, *It's All a Kind of Magic,* 115.

100 *"ward"*: Ibid., 116.

101 *"It's called lysergic acid"*: Ibid.

101 *"I knew [then]"*: Ibid., 121.

101 *"It's quarter to one"*: Ibid., 117.

101 *"sneak[ing] nameless pills"*: Hall, "Ken," 150.

101 *"[I]n my staid opinion"*: "On the Road."

101 *"I think I was deceived"*: McClanahan conversation.

102 *"That's what I like"*: Leggett to McMurtry, March 6, 1961.

102 *"carelessness"*: Leggett to McMurtry, November 15, 1960.

102 *"[Hud is] such a prick"*: Leggett to McMurtry, August 23, 1961.

102 *"By god"*: Leggett to McMurtry, March 2, 1961.

102 *"Leggett is a good honest guy"*: This and other quotes from McMurtry's letters to Bill Corrington are from Joyce Corrington, "The Writing and Publication of *And Wait for the Night,*" Books by John William Corrington and Joyce H. Corrington, www.jcorrington .com/2013/07/20/the-writing-and-publication-of-and-wait-for-the-night/.

104 *"big city; She was there"*: Mary Ellen Doyle, *Voices from the Quarter: The Fiction of Ernest J. Gaines* (Baton Rouge: LSU Press, 2003), 21.

104 *"There'll never be"*: Jonathan Yardley, "Porch Talk with Ernest Gaines," *Washington Post Book World,* November 21, 1990, www.washingtonpost.com/archives/lifestyle/1990/11 /21/book-world/220fdl8a-b58a-4034-a5c6-4689499ca3d5/.

104 *"nothing publishable loose"*: Larry McMurtry, letter to Dorothea Oppenheimer, September 26, 1960.

105 *"We'd recently been initiated"*: Madison Smartt Bell, *Child of Light: A Biography of Robert Stone* (New York: Doubleday, 2020), 77.

105 *"We all hallucinated"*: Ibid.

105 *"I don't remember anyone"*: Ibid.

105 *"Everybody was sleeping with everybody"*: Ibid., 76.

105 *"an incredibly supportive group love affair"*: Ibid., 77.

106 *"a lot of feeling; but the one time"*: McMurtry to Kesey, February 21, 1963 (?).

106 *"Did I tell you of the night"*: Ibid.

106 *"[Without] a context for emotion"*: Ibid.

106 *"delight"*: Ibid.

107 *"marital crisis"*: Leggett to McMurtry, October 15, 1962.

107 *"never defined"*: Leggett to McMurtry, July 6, 1964.

107 *"Larry's hung up"*: Kesey to McMurtry, summer 1963.

107 *"uncivilized"*: This and subsequent quotes in this paragraph are from Larry McMurtry, *Moving On* (New York: Simon & Schuster, 1970), 127.

108 *"ethereal"*: Email to the author, June 19, 2021.

108 *"smart, pretty, open"*: Van Nouhuys email.

108 *"passing strange"*: McClanahan conversation.

108 *Kesey spread a story*: Mark Busby in conversation with the author, July 7, 2021; Betsy Berry in conversation with the author, June 19, 2021.

108 *"She threw up a lot"*: Van Nouhuys email.

108 *"the unwobbling pivot"*: "On the Road."

109 *"How could [Bonney]"*: Mervyn Rothstein, "A Texan Who Likes to Deflate the Legends of the Golden West," *New York Times*, November 1, 1988, C17.

109 *"Faye's forbearance"*: "On the Road."

109 *"If you're lucky"*: McMurtry to Kesey, December 18, 1963 (?).

110 *"I dislike Xmas"*: Larry McMurtry, letter to Susan Sontag, December 7, 1989, Susan Sontag Papers, Library Special Collections, Charles E. Young Research Library, UCLA.

110 *"may create some mild bad scene"*: McMurtry to Dorothea Oppenheimer, June 19, 1961.

110 *"I don't love Linda"*: McMurtry to Dorothea Oppenheimer, July 14, 1961.

110 *"I can't kid myself"*: Ibid.

111 *"[By now] you have become"*: McMurtry to Dorothea Oppenheimer, June 11, 1961.

111 *"pelvis-grinding"*: Ibid.

111 *"about the inquisition-like"*: This and all subsequent quotes in this paragraph are from Mary Duncan, "The Tropic of Cancer: Booked for Selling a Book," *Huffington Post*, September 14, 2017, https://www.huffpost.com/entry/the-tropic-of-cancer-booked-for -selling-a-book_b_59a04cb8e4b0cb7715bfd505.

112 *He reported to Kesey*: McMurtry to Ken Kesey, February 21, 1963.

112 *"so obviously not a thing"*: Ibid.

112 *"Just between you and me"*: John Howard Griffin, letter to John Leggett, March 20, 1961, Special Collections, University of Houston Library.

112 *"Reluctant as I am"*: A. B. Guthrie, letter to John Leggett, May 15, 1961.

113 *"The beatnikers"*: Leggett to McMurtry, March 6, 1961.

113 *"[If] we get up close"*: Leggett to McMurtry, June 2, 1961.

113 *"pulse"*: Leggett to McMurtry, June 28, 1961.

113 *"she breathes"*: Leggett to McMurtry, June 19, 1961.

113 *"the reviews are extraordinarily good"*: McMurtry to Dorothea Oppenheimer, June 11, 1961.

113 *"irritating"*: Ibid.

113 *"I feel I've truly come home"*: Ibid.

113 *"Jo's stomach"*: Ibid.

113 *"unleashed"*: This and all other quotes in this paragraph unless otherwise noted are from McMurtry to Dorothea Oppenheimer, June 11, 1961.

114 *"marriage for my generation"*: McMurtry to Dorothea Oppenheimer, July 7, 1961.

114 *"When I look at families"*: McMurtry to Susan Sontag, August 20, 1989.

CHAPTER 7

115 *"follows a conventional structure"*: Mark Busby, *Larry McMurtry and the West: An Ambivalent Relationship* (Denton, TX: University of North Texas Press, 1995). In the following discussions of *Horseman, Pass By* and *Leaving Cheyenne*, I am indebted to Busby's critical insights.

115 *"why [Texas literature]"*: Paul Christensen, "From Cowboys to Curanderas: The Cycle of Texas Literature," *Southwest Review* 73, no. 1 (Winter 1988), 10, https://www.jstor.org/stable/43469983. The following discussion of literature's development in Texas owes much to Christensen's insights.

116 *"Texas isn't as religious"*: Ibid., 28.

116 *Moreover, historian Louis Cowan*: Louis Cowan, "Myth in the Modern World," in ed. Robert O'Connor, *Texas Myths* (College Station, TX: Texas A&M University Press, 1986), 20.

116 *"free thought"*: Christensen, "From Cowboys to Curanderas," 12.

117 *"There have been revolutions"*: Christensen, Ibid., 17.

117 *"I began to feel that poetry and revolution"*: Ibid., 21.

118 *the contemporary Texas novel*: For an extended discussion of this topic, see Roger Walton Jones, *Larry McMurtry and the Victorian Novel* (College Station, TX: Texas A&M University Press, 1994).

118 *"nature [will] always work her own cures"*: Larry McMurtry, *Horseman, Pass By* (New York: Harper & Brothers, 1961), 3.

118 *"What good's oil to me"*: Ibid., 106.

118 *"You thought I should drive"*: Ibid., 78.

119 *"Why, I used to think"*: Ibid.

119 *"Hud, a twentieth-century Westerner"*: In a Narrow Grave: Essays on Texas, 24–25.

119 *"steady shrinkage"*: Ibid., 26.

119 *"I went all over"*: Horseman, Pass By, 148.

119 *"I been keeping 'em"*: Ibid., 52.

120 *"That life died"*: In a Narrow Grave: Essays on Texas, 139–40.

120 *"airplane beacons"*: Horseman, Pass By, 6.

120 *"the music of departure"*: This and all other quotes in this paragraph are from *In a Narrow Grave: Essays on Texas*, xvii.

120 *"The isolation"*: "Horseman, Pass By," *Kirkus*, June 15, 1961, kirkusreviews.com/book-reviews/larry-mcmurtry/horseman-pass-by.

120 *"McMurtry is already well up"*: Charles Poore, "Books of the Times," *New York Times Book Review*, June 10, 1961, 21.

121 *"On the positive side"*: Leggett to McMurtry, February 24, 1961.

121 *"You don't have to deliver"*: Leggett to McMurtry, March 2, 1961.

121 *"I'm skeptical"*: Leggett to McMurtry, May 5, 1961.

121 *"I grow more and more annoyed"*: McMurtry to Dorothea Oppenheimer, June 11, 1961.

122 *"[D]amn it"*: McMurtry to Dorothea Oppenheimer, June 16, 1961.

122 *"I do feel"*: McMurtry to Dorothea Oppenheimer, June 19, 1961.

122 *"unsound notions"*: Dorothea Oppenheimer to McMurtry, June 16, 1961.

122 *"I . . . am most interested"*: Interview published in *Collage,* May 1967, 8, cited in Charles D. Peavy, "Coming of Age in Texas: The Novels of Larry McMurtry," *Western American Literature* 4, no. 3 (1969), 32.

122 *"I've gone over the manuscript"*: Leggett to McMurtry, April 5, 1963.

122 *"The Cheyenne of this book"*: Larry McMurtry, *Leaving Cheyenne* (New York: Harper & Row, 1963), unpaginated note.

123 *"Leaving Cheyenne met"*: McMurtry to Ken Kesey, May 7, 1963.

123 *"Texas emerged from that war"*: Dave Hickey, "Elegy and Exorcism: Texas Talent and General Concerns," in *Taking Stock: A Larry McMurtry Casebook,* ed. Clay Reynolds (Dallas: Southern Methodist University Press, 1989), 129.

124 *"THREE GRAVESTONES"*: *Leaving Cheyenne,* 300.

124 *"The job of the writer"*: Busby, *Larry McMurtry and the West,* 92.

124 *"created effects"*: Lon Tinkle, "Of Fate and Doom in Ranch Country," *Dallas Morning News,* October 13, 1963, Section 1, 24.

124 *"Larry McMurtry's narrative"*: Marshall Sprague, "Texas Triptych," *New York Times Book Review,* October 6, 1963, 39.

CHAPTER 8

125 *"Dallasans . . . are tentative"*: *In a Narrow Grave: Essays on Texas,* 129.

125 *"Neighboring Dallas"*: Jesse Sublett, "Wild Town," *Texas Monthly,* November 1999, https://www.texasmonthly.com/articles/wild-town.

126 *Fort Worth Stockyards:* See "History," Fort Worth Stockyards, https://www.fortworthstockyards.org/history.

126 *Two Minnies:* "Wild Town."

126 *"[T]hings looked . . . cheerful"*: *Leaving Cheyenne,* 63–64.

126 *"Western way of life"*: Waymarking.com, "Larry McMurtry-Fort Worth Stockyards-Fort Worth, TX-Citizen Memorials on Waymarking.com," https://www.waymarking.com/waymarks/WMP9NJ_Larry_McMurtry_Fort_Worth_Stockyards_Fort_Worth_TX.

127 *Its Christian mission:* For the history of Texas Christian University, see TCU, "Mission and History," https://www.tcu.edu/about/mission-history.php.

127 *"the generation of American writers"*: *Walter Benjamin at the Dairy Queen,* 132.

127 *"I got to teach the jocks"*: Arts & Letters Live, May 17, 2014.

127 *"I didn't take Larry's classes"*: Dave Hickey in conversation with the author, June 25, 2021.

128 *"Even if one succeeds"*: *Literary Life,* 71.

128 *"Jo has found"*: McMurtry to Dorothea Oppenheimer, June 16, 1961.

128 *"We both know [Jo] is two people"*: McMurtry to Ken Kesey, May 7, 1963 (?).

128 *"all the pain"*: McMurtry to Dorothea Oppenheimer, July 14, 1961.

128 *Ray Waddington heard a rumor:* Conversation with Ray Waddington, October 14, 2021.

128 *"I feel that I've established"*: McMurtry to Dorothea Oppenheimer, July 14, 1961.

129 *"a straw in the wind"*: Leggett to McMurtry, September 7, 1961.

129 *"56 deluxe units"*: Russell Hill, *Lubbock* (Charleston, SC: Arcadia Publishing, 2011), unpaginated.

130 *"You'll never know"*: This and further quotes concerning Lubbock trip are from McMurtry to Dorothea Oppenheimer, July 14, 1961.

131 *"[L]ast night"*: McMurtry to Dorothea Oppenheimer, July 18, 1961.

131 *"I'm frequently in a frenzy for you"*: McMurtry to Dorothea Oppenheimer, July 20, 1961.

131 *"I'm gloop"*: Ibid.

131 *"I've caused you a lot of misery"*: McMurtry to Dorothea Oppenheimer, August 9, 1961.

131 *"thinking that if I really examine"*: McMurtry to Dorothea Oppenheimer, July 14, 1961.

132 *"I think a writer's needs"*: McMurtry to Ken Kesey, February 21, 1963.

132 *"I'm glad he pulled the trigger"*: McMurtry to Dorothea Oppenheimer, July 14, 1961.

132 *"sometime wife"*: McMurtry to Dorothea Oppenheimer, August 5, 1961.

132 *"One grows numb"*: Ibid.

132 *"I'm afraid this pregnancy"*: McMurtry to Dorothea Oppenheimer, August 7, 1961.

132 *"Getting [Jo] pregnant"*: McMurtry to Dorothea Oppenheimer, August 9, 1961.

132 *"what a jewel"*: McMurtry to Dorothea Oppenheimer, August 11, 1961.

133 *"storm"*: Ibid.

133 *"on the permanent shitlist"*: Ibid.

133 *"I'll probably be more help"*: Ibid.

133 *"was up till dawn"*: McMurtry to Dorothea Oppenheimer, August 25, 1961.

133 *"an incredible yard"*: McMurtry to Dorothea Oppenheimer, September 17, 1961.

134 *"[I've] decided that in the future"*: McMurtry to Dorothea Oppenheimer, August 13, 1961.

134 *"I come closer than anybody"*: McMurtry to Dorothea Oppenheimer, September 3, 1961.

134 *"Larry, I feel I've lost touch"*: Dorothea Oppenheimer to McMurtry, July 18, 1962.

134 *"stern letter"*: McMurtry to Dorothea Oppenheimer, undated, 1962.

134 *"Coming as you do"*: McMurtry to Dorothea Oppenheimer, undated, 1962.

135 *"I seem to have been"*: Ibid.

135 *"Dear, poor Larry"*: Dorothea Oppenheimer to McMurtry, November 29, 1961.

135 *"I'm afraid this is much too dirty"*: Rust Hills note to Dorothea Oppenheimer, undated, 1961, Harry Ransom Humanities Research Center, University of Texas at Austin.

135 *"Bastards"*: McMurtry to Dorothea Oppenheimer, September 11, 1961.

136 *"A lot of things happened"*: Larry McMurtry, "There Will Be Peace in Korea," in *Texas Bound: 19 Texas Stories,* ed. Kay Cattarulla (Dallas: Southern Methodist University Press, 1994), 166–67.

136 *"WHAT'S A SONIC BOOM"*: A. G. Mojtabai, *Blessed Assurance: At Home with the Bomb in Amarillo* (Boston: Houghton Mifflin, 1986), 38.

136 *"Rattlesnakes"*: Details of Amarillo are from my own observations of the area over the years.

136 *It was a single buffalo: In a Narrow Grave: Essays on Texas,* 18–19.

137 *"They're thinking of calling it"*: Ibid., 4.

138 *"clutter"*: McMurtry to Dorothea Oppenheimer, January 20, 1962.

138 *"millions of finals"*: Ibid.

138 *"Every moment"*: McMurtry to Dorothea Oppenheimer, January 31, 1962.

138 *"Even as a baby"*: Jo McMurtry letter.

138 *Podge:* McMurtry to Dorothea Oppenheimer, November 21, 1962.

139 *"I am no less susceptible"*: McMurtry to Dorothea Oppenheimer, February 24, 1962.

139 *"child is healthy"*: McMurtry to Dorothea Oppenheimer, April 4, 1962.

139 *"much of a childraiser"*: McMurtry to Dorothea Oppenheimer, April 27, 1962.

139 *"movie front"*: Leggett to McMurtry, March 15, 1962.

139 *"Courage on the night watch"*: Leggett to McMurtry, April 4, 1962.

139 *"Author's share"*: Leggett to McMurtry, April 12, 1962.

139 *As he passed through Claude:* See *In a Narrow Grave: Essays on Texas,* 6.

139 *Actually he remembered this wrong: Claude News* 72, no. 39, May 17, 1962, 1.

140 *"If it was teenagers"*: In a Narrow Grave: Essays on Texas, 6.

140 *"really didn't want me"*: Larry McMurtry, *Film Flam: Essays on Hollywood* (New York: Simon & Schuster, 1987), 16.

140 *"were of about the consistency"*: In a Narrow Grave: Essays on Texas, 15.

140 *"De Wilde [sic] looked like someone"*: Ibid., 8.

141 *"the cowboy's habit"*: Ibid.

141 *"bird man"*: Ibid., 10–11.

141 *"[This] way lay only madness"*: See *Fodor's Travel Guide, Texas* (New York: McKay, 1974).

142 *"I love the movie set"*: McMurtry to Dorothea Oppenheimer, June 5, 1962.

142 *"I dig movie-making"*: McMurtry to Dorothea Oppenheimer, June 6, 1962.

142 *"I think I could knock out hack novels"*: McMurtry to Dorothea Oppenheimer, June 13, 1962.

142 *"San Francisco that fall"*: Jo McMurtry letter.

143 *"shamefully cold and neglectful"*: McMurtry to Dorothea Oppenheimer, November 21, 1962.

143 *"The issue"*: Ibid.

143 *"killed off all the Indians"*: William Sydney Porter (O. Henry), "Austin: A Brief Glance at Her History and Advantages," *Literary Austin,* ed. Don Graham (Fort Worth: TCU Press, 2007), 3.

144 *"produces a feeling"*: Mary Lasswell in collaboration with Bob Pool, *I'll Take Texas* (Boston: Houghton Mifflin, 1958), quoted in *Literary Austin,* 3.

144 *"music scene"*: Jo McMurtry letter.

CHAPTER 9

145 *"Let me tell you something"*: Jan Reid in conversation with the author, Austin, April 16, 2015.

145 *"post-book dog days"*: McMurtry to Ken Kesey, February 21, 1963.

145 *"I know a good deal too much"*: McMurtry to Dorothea Oppenheimer, July 25, 1963.

145 To Kesey, he expressed: McMurtry to Ken Kesey, February 21, 1963.

145 *"Bridge has made her less nervous"*: McMurtry to Ken Kesey, May 7, 1963.

145 *"I am ambivalent"*: Ibid.

146 *"there [was] something in [her]"*: McMurtry to Ken Kesey, February 21, 1963.

146 *"a really massive"*: Ibid.

146 *"Noted your paperback"*: McMurtry to Ken Kesey, May 7, 1963.

146 *"I suppose it's the bookman in me"*: McMurtry to Ken Kesey, February 21, 1963.

147 *"I can tell you"*: McMurtry to Ken Kesey, May 28, 1963.

147 *"[I] had no perception"*: Andrew Olson, "Ken Babbs," thefountainheads.com, sites.google .com/view/Andrew-olson/ken-babbs.

147 *"I do hate to think of you"*: McMurtry to Ken Kesey, May 28, 1963.

148 There he met an attractive young editor: McMurtry to Dorothea Oppenheimer, April 26, 1963.

148 *"sitting at a bar"*: Dorothea Oppenheimer to McMurtry, January 29, 1962.

148 *"I can not be quite sure yet"*: McMurtry to Dorothea Oppenheimer, June 13, 1962.

148 For one thing, it was altogether too jarring: Larry McMurtry, *It's Always We Rambled: An Essay on Rodeo* (New York: Frank Hallman, 1974), 7–8.

149 *"If that horse"*: Ibid., 22.

149 *"men . . . who have lived in one place"*: Ibid., 19.

149 *"Real cattle people"*: Ibid.

150   *"I think if you discover"*: Leggett to McMurtry, July 25, 1962.

150   *"one of those strange"*: It's Always We Rambled, 24.

150   *"Ort not to of tried"*: Ibid.

150   *"[T]he so-called American Dream"*: John Bainbridge, "The Super-American State," *The New Yorker,* March 11, 1961, 47.

150   *"The life-style"*: Ibid.

150   *"Shoot fire"*: Jay Dunston Milner, *Confessions of a Maddog: A Romp through the High-Flying Texas Music and Literary Era of the Fifties to the Seventies* (Denton, TX: University of North Texas Press, 1998), 68.

150   *"We will serve no group"*: Gary A. Keith, *Eckhardt: There Once Was a Congressman from Texas* (Austin: University of Texas Press, 2007), 125.

151   *"We exaggerated the cadence"*: Clay Smith, "Notes on Mad Dogs: On Being Young, Talented, and Slightly Insane in Old Austin," *Austin Chronicle,* January 26, 2001, https://www.austinchronicle.com/books/2001-01-21/80284.

151   *"was the first time I'd ever realized"*: Ibid.

152   *"Am I this much fun?"*: Milner, *Confessions of a Maddog,* 72.

152   *"When the legend becomes fact"*: See Brandon Soderberg, "Subversive Western 'The Man Who Shot Liberty Valence' at the Senator," *Baltimore Sun,* April 8, 2015, https://baltimoresun.com/citypaper/bcpnews-subversive-western-the-man-who-shot-liberty-valence-at-the-senator-20150407-story.html.

152   *"this year's most powerful film"*: Bosley Crowther, "Screen: 'Hud' Chronicles a Selfish, Snarling Heel: Newman in Title Role of Western in 60's," *New York Times,* May 29, 1963, https://www.nytimes.com/1963/05/29/archives/screen-hud-chronicles-a-selfish-snarling-heel-newman-in-title-role.html.

153   *Pauline Degenfelder:* Randall Spinks. "'You Don't Know the Story': *Horseman, Pass By* and the Misprision of *Hud,*" *Bright Lights Film Journal,* April 25, 2021, https://brightlightsfilm.com/you-dont-know-the-story-horseman-pass-by-and-the-misprision-of-hud/.

153   *"We felt the country"*: Ibid.

153   *"[I]t was a terrible shock to us"*: William Baer, "Hud: A Conversation with Irving Ravetch and Harriet Frank, Jr.," *Michigan Quarterly Review* 42, no. 2 (Spring 2003), https://quod.lib.umich.edu/cgi/text/text-idx?cc=mqr;c=mqrarchive;idno=act2080.0042.201;g=mqrg;rgn=main;view=text;xc=1.

154   *"What the hell do you want?"*: See Spinks, "'You Don't Know the Story.'"

154   *"prating and tedious"*: Pauline Kael, "*Hud,* Deep in the Divided Heart of Hollywood," *Film Quarterly* 17, no. 4 (Summer 1964), 15–17.

154   *"risk startin'; Why, this whole country"*: Spinks, "'You Don't Know the Story.'"

154   *"Divided Heart; [It is] just possibly"*: Kael, "*Hud,* Deep in the Divided Heart of Hollywood," 15.

154   *"I got a lot of letters"*: Spinks, "'You Don't Know the Story.'"

155   *"On the 22nd of May"*: McMurtry to Dorothea Oppenheimer, June 21, 1963.

155   *"Of course"*: Ibid.

155   *"It is better than the book"*: Ibid.

156   *classical music or Fats Waller:* Sidney Brammer, "Not All of Me Will Die: Remembering Joe Watson," *Austin Chronicle,* October 23, 2010, https://www.austinchronicle.com/daily/books/2010-10-23/not-all-of-me-will-die-remembering-joe-watson/.

156   *"Back at 3:30"*: Bruce E. McKinney, "John Crichton: A Career in the Rare Book Trade," *Rare Book Hub,* November 2020, https://www.rarebookhub.com/articles/2895?id=2895.

156 *"You speak my language":* Mike Evans, "Larry," an unpublished memoir sent to the author, September 27, 2021.

156 *"he was a natural target":* In a Narrow Grave: Essays on Texas, 134.

156 *"fuckists":* Larry McMurtry, *All My Friends Are Going to Be Strangers* (New York: Simon & Schuster, 1972), 7.

156 *"with the courteous":* In a Narrow Grave: Essays on Texas, 134.

156 *"adolescent":* Ibid.

156 *"It is a dismal":* Larry McMurtry, "The Texas Moon, and Elsewhere," *The Atlantic,* March 1975, 29.

157 *"Billy Lee":* Conversation with Jan Reid.

157 *"I didn't know [Billy Lee]":* Larry McMurtry, letter to the author, January 22, 2015.

157 *"I hope you never learn to keep it":* McMurtry to Ken Kesey, February 21, 1963.

157 *"In all the rambling":* McMurtry to Dorothea Oppenheimer, July 25, 1963.

157 *"in [his] ability":* McMurtry to Dorothea Oppenheimer, July 11, 1963.

157 *"I have always feared divorce":* Ken Kesey to McMurtry, summer 1963.

158 *"fence to protect the traffic":* McMurtry to Dorothea Oppenheimer, April 2, 1963.

158 *"No choice":* McMurtry to Dorothea Oppenheimer, July 11, 1963.

158 *"Jo is back":* McMurtry to Dorothea Oppenheimer, September 5, 1963.

CHAPTER 10

159 *"Houston had changed":* Jo McMurtry letter.

159 *"[W]ith the use of many blankets":* Literary Life, 64.

160 *"I can imagine":* Leggett to McMurtry, November 29, 1963.

160 *"it was about the worst":* McMurtry to Dorothea Oppenheimer, December 5, 1963.

160 *"were driving; I loathe teaching":* McMurtry to Dorothea Oppenheimer, November 20, 1963.

160 *"real novelist":* This and subsequent quotes from Mike Evans, unless otherwise noted; Mike Evans conversation with the author, May 14, 2021.

161 *"all-star faculty":* This and subsequent quotes from Greg Curtis; Greg Curtis conversation with the author, May 12, 2021.

161 *"somewhere in between":* This and subsequent quotes from Bill Broyles; Bill Broyles conversation with the author, May 26, 2021.

163 *"tinge of melancholy":* Quotes from Mike Evans, "Larry," an unpublished memoir sent to the author, September 27, 2021.

163 *"Movie money":* McMurtry to Dorothea Oppenheimer, undated, November 1963.

164 *"clean-cut":* A character clearly based, in part, on Jo expresses this sentiment about her husband in *All My Friends Are Going to Be Strangers,* 36.

164 *"[I loved] her heat":* Ibid., 63.

164 *"sexual confusion":* McMurtry to Dorothea Oppenheimer, undated, April 1964.

164 *"dreadfully hard":* McMurtry to Dorothea Oppenheimer, March 18, 1964.

164 *"[T]hings are hellish":* McMurtry to Dorothea Oppenheimer, March 5, 1964.

164 *"I am afraid Jo is reaching the point":* McMurtry to Dorothea Oppenheimer, March 18, 1964.

165 *"[Y]ou have nothing to feel guilty about":* Dorothea Oppenheimer to McMurtry, June 26, 1963.

165 *"Be good to yourself":* Dorothea Oppenheimer to McMurtry, August 22, 1963.

165 *"heavy therapy; I have been reading":* McMurtry to Dorothea Oppenheimer, March 18, 1964.

165 *"complicated decision":* Jo McMurtry letter.

165 *"I hope you aren't feeling":* McMurtry to Dorothea Oppenheimer, March 25, 1964.

166 *"the breeze of the future":* "On the Road."

166 *"It is the oldest living thing":* Rick Dodgson, *It's All a Kind of Magic: The Young Ken Kesey* (Madison: University of Wisconsin Press, 2013), 173.

167 *"psychedoodles":* Madison Smartt Bell, *Child of Light: A Biography of Robert Stone* (New York: Doubleday, 2020), 93.

167 *"What we hoped":* Stephen Ehret, "The Magic Bus, Ken Kesey, Neal Cassady, Cathy Casamo, and the Merry Pranksters," www.cathryncasamo.com/themagicbus1.htm.

167 *"[M]e and Kesey":* Ibid.

168 *"had completed her trip":* Tom Wolfe, *The Electric Kool-Aid Acid Test* (New York: Macmillan, 2008 [1968]), 86.

168 *"My son James":* "On the Road," *The New York Review of Books,* December 5, 2002.

168 *"Oh, God!":* This and subsequent dialogue from Ehret, "The Magic Bus." All further details of the Pranksters' visit to Houston, unless otherwise noted, are from Ehret.

169 *"nervous hospital":* McMurtry to Ken Kesey, August 9, 1964.

169 *"playing cards with Jo":* Ibid.

170 *"I took her for a ride":* Ibid.

170 *"The irony is":* Bell, *Child of Light,* 96.

171 *"Ivy League egghead":* Ehret, "The Magic Bus."

171 *In a letter to McMurtry:* Ken Kesey to McMurtry, August 1, 1964.

171 *"a lot of foolishness":* Dave Walker, "The Acid Test as Literature," *Phoenix New Times,* November 28, 1990, https://phoenixnewtimes.comnews/the-acid-test-as-literature-6412080.

171 *"If the Panhandle":* Literary Life, 67.

171 *"The effect of this crisis":* Ibid.

172 *"[T]he novel examines":* The Last Picture Show proposal and outline, McMurtry to Dorothea Oppenheimer, January 24, 1965.

172 *"It's the most physically wearing work":* McMurtry to Ken Kesey, November 10, 1961 (?).

173 *"I don't feel at all in touch":* McMurtry to Dorothea Oppenheimer, undated, November 1964.

173 *"We recited":* Roberta Hershenson, "Faraway School Close to Mount Vernon Woman," *New York Times,* May 1, 2002, https://www.nytimes.com/2002/05/01/nyregion/faraway -school-close-to-mount-vernon-woman.html.

174 *"the most exciting; I am a poet":* Shane Savoy, "Texas Poet Sues Dentist Husband for Divorce," *Jet,* April 22, 1954.

174 *"a noted poetess":* Shane Savoy, "Texas Poetess Shoots at Dentist Ex-Hubby," *Jet,* November 8, 1956.

174 *"Did we all think":* Conversation with Bill Broyles.

174 *"after Jo left":* McMurtry to Dorothea Oppenheimer, undated, November 1964.

175 *"neurotic; I figured; It was an honest experience":* McMurtry to Dorothea Oppenheimer, undated, November 1964.

175 *"Larry was very supportive":* Jo McMurtry letter.

175 *"I'm sure I would be better off":* McMurtry to Dorothea Oppenheimer, undated, November 1964.

175 *"[No,] the corrida; Won't you please":* Leggett to McMurtry, July 6, 1964.

176 *"I am interested":* McMurtry to Dorothea Oppenheimer, January 12, 1965.

176 *"For me the novel":* McMurtry to Ken Kesey, February 21, 1963.

176 *"I was worried":* McMurtry to Ken Kesey, June 18, 1964.

176 *"I took this novel":* McMurtry to Dorothea Oppenheimer, January 12, 1965.

CHAPTER 11

177 *"innocent bumpkins":* Dave Hickey, "McMurtry's Elegant Essays," in ed. Clay Reynolds, *Taking Stock: A Larry McMurtry Casebook* (Dallas: Southern Methodist University Press, 1989), 101.

177 *"It has often been noted":* Ibid.

177 *"Charlene Duggs": The Last Picture Show* proposal and outline.

178 *"inventing himself":* Conversation with William Broyles.

178 *"to parts of Houston":* Conversation with Greg Curtis.

178 *"My book hunting": Walter Benjamin at the Dairy Queen,* 163.

178 *"Red-checked tablecloths":* Conversation with William Broyles.

179 *"we'd go to a steak house":* Conversation with Mike Evans.

179 *"He was really an intimidating figure":* Conversation with Greg Curtis.

179 *"When he got drunk":* Conversation with Mike Evans.

180 *"[W]ith such world-shaking events": Literary Life,* 31.

180 *"a beautiful child":* This and subsequent quotes in this paragraph are from Mike Evans, "Larry," an unpublished memoir sent to the author, September 27, 2021.

180 *"Billy Lee's mattress":* Conversation with Mike Evans.

180 *"Jo and I":* Conversation with Mike Evans.

180 *"There was a period when":* Conversation with Greg Curtis.

181 *"[Our] divorce decree":* Jo McMurtry letter.

181 *"He was always the guy":* Conversation with Mike Evans.

181 *"Ocean, ocean":* Lawrence Downes, "In Mexico, on the Lam with Ken Kesey," *New York Times,* March 23, 2008, https://www.nytimes.com/2008/03/23/travel/23Kesey.html.

181 *"LSD GURU":* Ibid.

181 *"I am chancing hell":* Ken Kesey to McMurtry, undated, 1966.

181 *"He's working on his wave theory":* Downes, "In Mexico, on the Lam with Ken Kesey."

182 *"The one on the right":* Cecilia Rasmussen, "Merrily Tripping into Los Angeles' Colorful Past," *Los Angeles Times,* April 10, 1995, https://www.latimes.com/archives/la-xpm-1995–04–10-me-53008-story.html.

182 *"I tell you Larry":* Ken Kesey to McMurtry, undated, 1964.

182 *"[T]he interior":* Downes, "In Mexico, on the Lam with Ken Kesey."

182 *"spongey":* Kesey to McMurtry, undated, 1964.

182 *"I went to Mexico":* Conversation with Greg Curtis.

182 *"If you've made": Literary Life,* 22.

183 *"an enormously satisfying time":* John F. Barker, "PW Interview: E. L. Doctorow, 1975," *Conversations with E. L. Doctorow* (Oxford: University of Mississippi Press, 1999), 3.

183 *"He is really quite nice":* Dorothea Oppenheimer to McMurtry, September 16, 1966.

183 *"I hope you will have much joy":* Dorothea Oppenheimer to McMurtry, August 25, 1966.

183 *"The novel was a mixture":* McMurtry cited in Mark Busby, *Larry McMurtry and the West: An Ambivalent Relationship* (Denton, TX: University of North Texas Press, 1995), 97–98.

184 *"the growing anti-Texan attitude":* Ibid., 98.

184 *"What* Leaving Cheyenne *really offers":* McMurtry cited in Raymond L. Neinstein, "The Ghost Country," in *Taking Stock: A Larry McMurtry Casebook,* 141.

184 *"Sometimes Sonny felt like": The Last Picture Show,* 1.

184 *"You can't imagine":* McMurtry to Mike Kunkel, August 31, 1956.

185 *"the verge of schizophrenia"*: McMurtry to Mike Kunkel, January 24, 1956.

185 *"[H]ow could the elders"*: In a Narrow Grave: Essays on Texas, 158–59.

185 *"[I would] like to live"*: McMurtry to Mike Kunkel, November 11, 1956.

185 *"social or intellectual elite[s]; I want no part"*: McMurtry to Mike Kunkel, December 3, 1955.

187 *"Every character"*: Grace Paley, "A Conversation with My Father," *Enormous Changes at the Last Minute: Stories* (New York: Farrar, Straus & Giroux, 1974), 162.

188 *"If the story had got out"*: The Last Picture Show, 223.

188 *"Her cheeks and forehead"*: Ibid., 30–31.

188 *"Is growing up"*: Ibid., 154.

189 *"Scaring an unfortunate creature"*: Ibid., 112.

189 *"scrape up enough; I spent more"*: In a Narrow Grave: Essays on Texas, 36.

189 *"look[s] over her head"*: The Last Picture Show, 99.

189 *"open[s] her eyes"*: Ibid., 100.

189 *"Loneliness is like ice"*: Ibid., 126.

190 *"saying something fine"*: Ibid., 280.

190 *"To Mom and Daddy"*: Thomas Curwen, "Larry McMurtry, Author of 'Lonesome Dove' and 'The Last Picture Show,' Dies," *Los Angeles Times,* March 26, 2021, https://latimes.com/obituaries/story/2021-03-26/larry-mcmurtry-author-of-lonesome-dove-and-the-last-picture-show-dies-at-84.

190 *"Larry, honey"*: George Hickenlooper, *Picture This: The Times of Peter Bogdanovich in Archer City, Texas* (Nelson Entertainment, 1989), dailymotion.com/video/xqdjx9.

190 *"Nothing much happens"*: Thomas Lask, "The Last Picture Show," *New York Times,* December 3, 1966, https:// https://www.nytimes.com/books/97/12/07/home/mcmurtry-show,html.

191 *"lance some of the poisons; By the time"*: Jan Reid, "Return of the Native Son," *Texas Monthly,* February 1993, https://texasmonthly.com/arts-entertainment/profile-return-of-the-native-son/.

191 *"I read the book"*: This and subsequent quotes from Archer City citizens in Hickenlooper, *Picture This.*

192 *"Look[ed] like he just"*: Paul Knight, "Broken Brotherhood," *Center and Main,* October 15, 2013, http://centerandmain.org/broken-brotherhood/.

CHAPTER 12

193 *"At that time"*: Mike Evans, "Larry," an unpublished memoir sent to the author, September 27, 2021.

195 *"I'm Grace David"*: Ann Todhunter Brode, "Grace David, 1913–2010," *Santa Barbara Independent,* October 14, 2010, https://independent.com/2010/10/14/grace-david-1913–2010.

195 *"[Grace] may live"*: Ibid.

195 *"a lot of young artists"*: Erin Mulvaney, "In Houston History, Socialite, Store Owner Served as Inspiration for Classic Character," *Houston Chronicle,* July 29, 2015, https://chron.com/business/real-estate/article/A-piece-of-houston-history-Socialite-store-6412429.php.

195 *"For a safe"*: Books, 74.

195 *"wall-sized aquarium"*: Mulvaney, "In Houston History, Socialite, Store Owner."

195 One of the Bookman's: Norie Guthrie, "What's in Woodson," The Bookman Christmas Catalog, December 12, 2017, woodsononline.wordpress.com/2017/12/12/the-bookman-christmas-catalog.

195 *"signed, limited copy"*: Books, 75.

196 *"a woman"*: Mulvaney, "In Houston History, Socialite, Store Owner."

196 *"the Yount family"*: Books, 76.

196 *"[I] was hired on the spot"*: Ibid.

196 *"should be about holding"*: Brode, "Grace David, 1913–2010."

196 *"I'm not sure"*: Books, 76–77.

196 *"He offered me $40"*: Evans, "Larry."

197 *"never liked being more than a step"*: Books, 77.

197 *Evans didn't buy the rumor*: Conversation with Mike Evans.

197 *"Grace was lovely"*: Mulvaney, "In Houston History, Socialite, Store Owner."

197 *"Despite forty-nine years"*: Ibid.

197 *"Although the sixties"*: Evans, "Larry."

197 *"books that had missed"*: Ibid.

198 *"He argued that pornography"*: Ibid.

198 *"Max was a great companion"*: This and subsequent quotes from Mike Evans, "Larry."

199 *"I did . . . a lunch-counter"*: Literary Life, 121.

199 *"Henry sober"*: Books, 77.

199 *"I love you"*: Larry McMurtry, letter to Grace David, undated [1967], Special Collections, University of Houston Library.

200 *"I do love the Bookman"*: McMurtry to Grace David, August 31, 1967.

200 *"Dorman wandered over"*: Books, 81.

200 *"[W]e simply could not sell"*: Ibid., 82.

200 *"I'm quite sure"*: McMurtry to Grace David, undated [1967].

201 *"private; not so good"*: McMurtry to Grace David, undated [1967].

201 *"Larry is a writer"*: John Spong, Jeff Wilson, and Bill Wittliff, *A Book on the Making of Lonesome Dove* (Austin: University of Texas Press, 2012), 31.

201 *"I still have doubts"*: Gregory Curtis, "Forgery Texas Style," *Texas Monthly*, March 1989.

202 *"He lit a candle"*: Ibid.

202 *"survived Henry"*: Books, 83.

202 *"and he almost succeeded"*: James Bryan, Antiquarian Booksellers' Association interview with Larry McMurtry, Tucson, January 2014.

202 *"You know, I think all of you"*: Curtis, "Forgery Texas Style."

203 *"[It] could be argued"*: Patrick Lundberg, "Lysergic Pranksters in Texas," lysergia_2.tripod .com/MerryPranksters/IamaMerryPranksters.htm.

203 *Susan Walker*: Susan Walker in conversation with the author, December 5, 2014.

204 *"[They] were still beautiful"*: "On the Road," *The New York Review of Books*, December 5, 2002.

204 *"kind of spooky"*: Lundberg, "Lysergic Pranksters in Texas."

204 *"a weighty piece"*: This and other quotes from McMurtry concerning the Pranksters' visit to Houston are from "On the Road."

204 *"Jane said"*: "On the Road."

205 *"[T]he farm was loaded"*: Ken Kesey, *Demon Box* (New York: Viking, 1986), 38.

205 *"She's secreting"*: Kesey, *Demon Box*. In his pieces on the farm in *Demon Box*, Kesey—Prankster-style—refers to Faye as Betsy.

205 *"What can we do?"*: This and subsequent quotes are from Kesey, *Demon Box*, 47.

205 *"what in Prankster mythos"*: "On the Road."

206 *"Ken, through a combination"*: Ibid.

206 *"People aren't reading novels"*: Dianne Donovan, "Author Ken Kesey at Home on Farm

with 'Demon Box,'" *Los Angeles Times,* September 24, 1986, latimes.com/archives/la -xpm-1986–09–24-vw-8922-story.html.

206 *"This section":* Oppenheimer to McMurtry, January 10, 1968.

206 *"[W]hat most bothers me":* Oppenheimer to McMurtry, February 12, 1968.

207 *"[T]he editor's remark":* This and subsequent quotes concerning the essay manuscript, McMurtry to Oppenheimer, undated, 1968.

208 *"because it was my way":* Skip Hollandsworth, "The Talented Mr. Wittliff," *Texas Monthly,* February 2001, https://www.texasmonthly.com/articles/the-talented-mr-wittliff/.

208 *"toilet-hugging drunk":* Ibid.

208 *"set [him] on fire":* Ibid.

209 *"Starting the Encino Press":* Stayton Bonner, "The Serendipity Wrangler: Bill Wittliff and the Southwestern Writers Collection," *The Texas Observer,* April 18, 2008, https://www .texasobserver.org/2743-the-serendipity-wrangler-bill-wittliff-and-the-southwestern -writers-collection/.

209 *"peach farmer":* Joe Holley in conversation with the author, May 10, 2021.

209 *"By my father's grave": In a Narrow Grave: Essays on Texas,* epigraph page.

209 "In a Narrow Grave *had all these": A Book on the Making of* Lonesome Dove, 40.

210 *"irritated; fine, dry":* Oppenheimer to McMurtry, February 12, 1968.

210 *"inhibited reflection": In a Narrow Grave: Essays on Texas,* 52.

210 *"Midland":* Ibid., 121–122.

210 *"The Texas writer":* Ibid., xvi.

210 *"In Austin":* Ibid., 51.

210 *"essay is not a form":* Tom Pilkington, "The Dirt Farmer and the Cowboy: Notes on Two Texas Essayists," in ed. Clay Reynolds, *Taking Stock: A Larry McMurtry Casebook* (Dallas: Southern Methodist University Press, 1989), 93.

211 *"He seems very sure":* Ibid., 95.

211 *"Here is an honorable":* Dave Hickey, "McMurtry's Elegant Essays," in *Taking Stock: A Larry McMurtry Casebook,* 101.

211 *"the best-designed book": Literary Life,* 75.

211 *"skycrapers":* This and all subsequent details concerning the first edition of *In a Narrow Grave* are from Scott Brown, "In a Narrow Grave by Larry McMurtry—First Edition Identification," Downtown Brown Books, https://www.downtownbrown.com/pages /dispatches/6/in-a-narrow-grave-by-larry-mcmurtry-first.

CHAPTER 13

213 *"I could have fallen":* Babette Fraser Hale in conversation with the author, June 16, 2021.

213 *"looking very, very bored":* Larry McMurtry, *Hollywood* (New York: Simon & Schuster, 2010), 11.

213 *"[M]y imagination": Film Flam: Essays on Hollywood* (New York: Simon & Schuster, 1987), 17.

213 *"[I]t is a charming thing to watch":* Ibid., 17–18.

214 *"swamp chases":* Ibid., 18.

214 *"Wild Choke Cherry Place":* See Moises Gonzales, "The Genizaro Land Grant Settlements of New Mexico," *Journal of the Southwest* 56, no. 4 (Winter 2014), 588–92.

215 *"The canon":* This and all other quotes in this chapter from Babette Fraser are from the Babette Fraser Hale conversation.

216 *"he had a telephone":* Curtis conversation.

216 *"Larry's tinge"*: Mike Evans, "Larry," an unpublished memoir sent to the author, September 27, 2021.

217 *In fact, Marcia's youth:* Details from Marcia Carter's letters are from the Nell Goodrich DeGolyer Papers, 1896–1978, DeGolyer Library, Southern Methodist University.

218 *"go to Hell"*: Gordon Chaplin, "The Mouthpiece That Roared," *Washington Post Magazine*, June 22, 1980, https://www.washingtonpost.com/archives/lifestyle/magazine/1980 /06/22/the-mouthpiece-that-roared/508b4c1d-0767–4f54–9795–913f64397c88/.

218 *"Guns were an enormous part"*: Ibid.

218 *"We were always fantasizing"*: Ibid.

218 *"There seemed to be"*: Ibid.

219 *"Hit the floor!"*: Ann Waldron, *Hodding Carter: The Reconstruction of a Racist* (Chapel Hill, NC: Algonquin Books, 1993), 298.

220 *"[My dad and I] didn't have"*: Craig Clifford and Craig Hillis, editors, *Pickers and Poets: The Ruthlessly Poetic Singer-Songwriters of Texas* (College Station, Texas: Texas A&M University Press, 2016), 197.

221 *One day a driller:* Carl J. Schiro, Letter to the Editor, *Houston Chronicle*, April 4, 2021, https://houstonchronicle.com/opinion/letters/article/Opinion-A-true-story-about-Larry -McMurtry-16071053.php.

221 *"the spring of 1968"*: Evans, "Larry."

222 *"part of [his] life"*: Michael Korda, *Another Life: A Memoir of Other People* (New York: Random House, 2000), 285.

222 *"an Olympic-level kvetch"*: Ibid.

222 *"Shy, retiring"*: Ibid., 286.

222 *"East Coast reviewers"*: Ibid., 287. All subsequent quotes from *Another Life,* unless otherwise noted, 286–89.

222 *"publishers, by and large"*: Michael Korda, *Making the List: A Cultural History of the American Bestseller, 1900–1999* (New York: Barnes and Noble Books, 2001), 122.

222 *"and surrounded himself"*: Ibid., 123.

223 *"endlessly retyped"*: Korda, *Another Life,* 77.

223 *"adapt to any social habitat"*: *Literary Life,* 46.

224 *"the woman with whom I found"*: Larry McMurtry, *Moving On* (New York: Simon & Schuster, 1970), dedication page.

225 *"I have had a hard day"*: McMurtry to Dorothea Oppenheimer, December 28, 1967.

225 *"[N]ever, never write letters"*: Dorothea Oppenheimer to McMurtry, January 10, 1968.

225 *"was worrisome"*: Evans, "Larry."

225 *"a princely gift"*: Ibid.

225 *"I was beginning to feel"*: James Bryan, Antiquarian Booksellers' Association interview with Larry McMurtry, Tucson, January 2014.

225 *"That Michael Korda"*: Dorothea Oppenheimer to McMurtry, March 5, 1969.

226 *"The savage lusts"*: Larry McMurtry, *The Last Picture Show* (New York: Dell, 1971), cover.

226 *"third party"*: Dorothea Oppenheimer to McMurtry, June 26, 1969.

226 *"sold THE LAST PICTURE SHOW"*: Dorothea Oppenheimer to McMurtry, August 29, 1969.

226 *"It all sounds rather fuzzy"*: Dorothea Oppenheimer to McMurtry, October 20, 1969.

226 *"a lucky chance"*: Evans, "Larry."

227 *they wouldn't turn to sand:* Dorys C. Grover, "Roar of the Crowd: July 2021," *Texas Monthly,* July 2021, https://www.texasmonthly.com/the-stand-up-desk/roar-of-the-crowd -july-2021/.

227 *"Try not to get hurt":* See Sean Woods, "Larry McMurtry on the Old West and Modern Texas," *Men's Journal,* April 24, 2014, https://www.mensjournal.com/travel/larry-mcmurtry-on-the-old-west-and-modern-texas-20140424/.

227 *"Are you ok?":* Dorothea Oppenheimer to McMurtry, August 29, 1969.

228 *"I think you are living dangerously":* Dorothea Oppenheimer to McMurtry, December 9, 1971.

228 *"Be careful":* Dorothea Oppenheimer to McMurtry, July 17, 1969.

CHAPTER 14

231 *"[Larry] hated Washington":* David Streitfeld, "The Yellowed Prose of Texas," *Washington Post,* April 6, 1999, https://www.washingtonpost.com/archive/lifestyle/1999/04/06/the-yellowed-prose-of-texas/98598edd-b6a6-4c85-9a3e-fc72a836a5e7/.

231 *"I felt gloomy": Walter Benjamin at the Dairy Queen,* 71.

231 *The entire hamlet of Waterford:* For a history of Waterford and Loudoun County, see Robert A. Pollard, ed., "The History of the Loudoun County Courthouse and Its Role in the Path to Freedom, Justice, and Racial Equality in Loudoun County," Report of the Loudoun County Heritage Commission, March 1, 2019.

232 *"[b]eing around Waterford":* Steve Houk, "Music Notes: Things He's Come to Know," *Washington Life Magazine,* April 20, 2015, https://washingtonlife.com/2015/04/20/music-notes-things-hes-come-to-know.

232 *"In Richmond":* Mike Evans, "Larry," an unpublished memoir sent to the author, September 27, 2021.

232 *"I would take him camping":* Ibid.

232 *"I wanted to be Johnny Cash":* Lauren Daley, "James McMurtry talks redneck relatives, cruise ships, and a 'hell of a learning curve,'" *South Coast Today,* February 14, 2019, https://southcoasttoday.com/entertainmentlife/20190214/james-mcmurtry-talks-redneck-relatives-cruise-ships-and-hell-of-learning-curve.

233 *"It was his escape":* Richard Harrington, "The Roots of McMurtry," *Washington Post,* August 27, 1989, https://www.washingtonpost.com/archive/lifestyle/style/1989/08/27/the-roots-of-mcmurtry/bab69078-65ac-4955-a6a1-7295a24e0a8f/.

233 *"I was often":* Jo McMurtry letter.

233 *"[H]e explained to the judge":* Evans, "Larry."

235 *"power doyenne":* Staff, "Polly Kraft, 89, Artist and Doyenne," *East Hampton Star,* January 12, 2017, https://www.easthamptonstar.com/archive/polly-kraft-89-artist-and-doyenne.

235 *"way of communicating":* Michele Jacobson, "Polly Kraft," Citizens of Georgetown Interview, May 5, 2015, https://cagtown.org/2010/05/05/polly-kraft/.

235 *"the bright path":* James Barron, "Evangeline Bruce, 77, Hostess Known for Washington Soirees," *New York Times,* December 14, 1995, https://www.nytimes.com/1995/12/14/us/evangeline-bruce-77-hostess-known-for-washington-soirees.html.

235 *just as likely to do the Frug:* John Meroney and Patricia Beauchamp, "The Last of the Southern Girls," *Garden & Gun,* April/May 2021, https://gardenandgun.com/feature/the-last-of-the-southern-girls/.

235 *"The French would say":* Barron, "Evangeline Bruce."

235 *"The higher a monkey climbs":* Meroney and Beauchamp, "The Last of the Southern Girls."

235 *"the sheer, ice-covered face":* Larry McMurtry, *Cadillac Jack* (New York: Simon & Schuster, 1982), 40.

235 *"It was as if":* Ibid., 39.

236   *"age and beauty"*: Ibid., 194.

236   *"I immediately lose"*: Literary Life, 112.

236   *"fuck[ing] down"*: Cadillac Jack, 66.

236   *"Good God"*: Walter Benjamin at the Dairy Queen, 150.

237   *"I doubt"*: In a Narrow Grave: Essays on Texas, 137.

237   *"sound . . . like a bestseller"*: Michael Korda, Another Life: A Memoir of Other People (New York: Random House, 2000), 290.

238   *"Moving On was not the Great American Novel"*: Literary Life, 77.

238   *"Is Patsy Carpenter"*: John Leonard, "Moving On," New York Times, June 10, 1970, https://www.nytimes.com/books/97/12/07/home/mcmurtry-moving.html.

238   *"at the beginning of the evening"*: Moving On: A Novel (New York: Simon & Schuster, 1970), 11.

238   *"that old crazy Asian war"*: Ibid., 411.

238   *"a strong sense of being involved"*: Ibid., 525.

239   *"a cleanness and clarity"*: Ibid., 710.

240   *"foggy, mushy"*: Ibid.

240   *"She skipped from book to book"*: Ibid., 559.

240   *"two women in the same skin"*: Ibid., 556.

240   *"It was the question; she [can't] understand; hard to handle"*: Ibid., 343.

240   *"kissing had got lost"*: Ibid., 228.

241   *"that was Marcia Carter"*: Babette Fraser Hale in conversation with the author, June 16, 2021.

241   *"I saw Hud"*: Moving On, 223.

241   *"parents [she] knew slightly"*: Ibid., 789.

242   *"obese catastrophe"*: L. J. Davis, "Moving On," Book World, June 21, 1970, 6.

242   *"constructed like tumbleweed"*: Martha Duffy, "Moving On," Time, April 1972, 64.

242   *"Hemingway had decided"*: Elroy Bode, "Moving On . . . And On . . . And On," in ed. Clay Reynolds, Taking Stock: A Larry McMurtry Casebook (Dallas: Southern Methodist University Press, 1989), 228.

242   *"All about Sex"*: Reed Whitmore, "Texas Sex," New Republic 166, no. 14 (April 1972), 28–29.

242   *"about five coon-ass miles"*: cited in Kerry Ahearn, "More D'Urban: The Texas Novels of Larry McMurtry," in Taking Stock: A Larry McMurtry Casebook, 226.

242   *"quite simply ugly"*: Steven Barthelme, "McMurtry's Moving On," Texas Observer, January 8, 1971, 13.

242   *"I am indifferent to structure"*: Larry McMurtry, "Answer from McMurtry," Texas Observer, February 26, 1971, 22.

243   *"I frankly miss"*: Bode, "Moving On . . . And On . . . And On," 231.

243   *"There is the high-toned [diction]"*: Ahearn, "More D'Urban," 215–16.

243   *"penchant for repetition"*: Ibid., 221.

243   *"[At] least twenty times"*: Ibid., 220.

243   *"country traditions"*: McMurtry cited in Ahearn, "More D'Urban," 206.

243   *"exploit a given region"*: Ahearn, "More D'Urban," 206.

243   *"[E]ven though"*: Don Graham cited in Mark Busby, Larry McMurtry and the West: An Ambivalent Relationship (Denton, TX: University of North Texas Press, 1995), 125.

244   *"good ear"*: Leonard, "Moving On."

244   *"I'm not interested"*: Charles D. Peavy, Larry McMurtry (Boston: Twayne Publishers, 1977), 78.

244 *"I [still] had a good deal"*: Literary Life, 77.

244 *"simple novel"*: All My Friends Are Going to Be Strangers, 135.

244 *"I can't go on"*: Samuel Beckett, *The Unnamable*, ed. Paul Auster (New York: Grove Centenary Edition, 2006), 407.

245 *"I had ceased to like"*: Literary Life, 83.

245 *"[Writers] ought to be imprisoned"*: All My Friends Are Going to Be Strangers, 11.

245 *"All I had"*: Ibid., 275.

245 *"Being a writer"*: Si Dunn, "Ex-Native Son McMurtry," *Texas Observer*, January 16, 1976, 13.

246 *"It is true"*: Peavy, *Larry McMurtry*, 43.

246 *"It seems to me"*: McMurtry cited in Alan F. Crooks, "Larry McMurtry—A Writer in Transition: An Essay-Review," in *Taking Stock: A Larry McMurtry Casebook*, 235.

246 *"Texas was there"*: All My Friends Are Going to Be Strangers, 176.

247 *"Odysseus' visit"*: Ibid., 174.

247 *"falls somewhere"*: Louise L. Serpa, *Rodeo: No Guts, No Glory* (New York: Aperture, 1994), notes by McMurtry, 82.

247 *"clean cut"*: All My Friends Are Going to Be Strangers, 36.

247 *"My fate seemed to be"*: Ibid., 253.

247 *"Emma and I couldn't talk"*: Ibid., 238.

247 *"Why does everyone want sex, anyway?"*: Ibid., 138.

247 *"Despite all the good times"*: Ibid., 157.

248 *"[T]he flowing of rivers"*: Ibid., 278.

248 *"I had never felt"*: Ibid., 284.

248 *"the door to the ordinary places"*: Ibid., 281.

248 *"I [couldn't] see the great scenes"*: Ibid., 285.

248 *"It is a desperate"*: Jim Harrison, "All My Friends Are Going to Be Strangers," *New York Times*, March 19, 1972, https://www.nytimes.com/books/97/12/07/home/mcmurtry-friends.html.

249 *"McMurtry is coming to terms"*: Barbara A. Bannon, *Publishers Weekly*, February 1, 1972, 91.

249 *"a campus full"*: Literary Life, 87.

249 *"I [took] my money"*: Ibid., 89.

249 *"invitation from the great world"*: This and subsequent Stegner quotes are from Wallace Stegner, "Born a Square: The Westerner's Dilemma," *The Atlantic* 213, January 1964, 47–49.

250 *"fits Stegner's definition"*: Barbara Granzow, "The Western Writer: A Study of Larry McMurtry's All My Friends Are Going to Be Strangers," in *Taking Stock: A Larry McMurtry Casebook*, 242.

250 *"You can't take care of yourself"*: All My Friends Are Going to Be Strangers, 67.

CHAPTER 15

251 *"relationship people have; [She] bought"*: Books, 169–70.

251 *"museum-worthy"*: Sara Ossana, "On Collecting," *New England Home*, October 15, 2013, https://nehomemag.com/sara-ossana-on-collecting/.

251 *"willy-nilly"*: Books, 169.

251 *"an accumulator"*: Ossana, "On Collecting."

251 *"raffish splash of color"*: The phrase is David Montgomery's, from "D.C. Flea Market May Leap to Suburbs," *Washington Post*, September 1, 2000, https://www.washingtonpost.com/archive/local/2000/09/01/dc-flea-market-may-leap-to-suburbs/4d7d1959–04e2–4fad-a163–04d0496cdecc/.

252 *"hideous": Books,* 170.

252 *"[I] can get":* Ibid., 171.

252 *"craving for books; to come into New York":* James Bryan, Antiquarian Booksellers' Association interview with Larry McMurtry, Tucson, January 2014.

252 *"explosive; I believe":* Larry McMurtry, "Lost Booksellers of New York," *New York Times,* May 10, 2014, https://www.nytimes.com/2014/05/011/opinion/sunday/lost-booksellers -of-new-york,html.

252 *"She knew a rich girl":* James Bryan, Antiquarian Booksellers' Association interview with Larry McMurtry, Tucson, January 2014.

252 *"we would have to spend the night":* This and all subsequent quotes from Calvin Trillin are from "Scouting Sleepers," *The New Yorker,* June 14, 1976, 87–91.

253 *DC's great rare-book shop:* For a detailed history of W. H. Lowdermilk & Company, see Ames W. Williams, "The W. H. Lowdermilk Company," *Records of the Columbia Historical Society* (Washington, DC) 51 (1984): 158–65.

254 *"I think we quarreled":* McMurtry to Dorothea Oppenheimer, March 22, 1970.

254 *"I am sorry":* Ibid.

255 *"If you write me a letter":* Dorothea Oppenheimer to McMurtry, May 15, 1971.

255 *"[Y]our appearance":* Dorothea Oppenheimer to McMurtry, December 30, 1971.

255 *"We did it":* Robert G. Kaiser, Lee Lescaze, et al., "Ex-Rep. Lowenstein Fatally Shot by Gunman in N.Y. Law Office," *Washington Post,* March 15, 1980, https://www .washingtonpost.com/archive/politics/1980/03/15/ex-rep-lowenstein-fatally-shot-by -gunman-in-ny-law-office/a71c0d1f-ad7e-444c-9457–23feea55d71a/.

255 *"he was incredible":* John Curtis in conversation with the author, June 8, 2021.

256 *"I started fantasizing":* Rachel Abramowitz, "She's Done Everything (Except Direct)," *Premiere,* November 1993, https://www.maryellenmark.com/text/magazines/premiere/919V -000–004.html. For further background on Platt and Bogdanovich, I have drawn upon Peter Biskind's account in *Easy Riders, Raging Bulls: How the Sex-Drugs-and-Rock-'N'-Roll Generation Saved Hollywood* (New York: Simon & Schuster, 1998).

257 *"Holden Caulfield":* Abramowitz, "She's Done Everything (Except Direct)."

257 *"I watched Hawks":* Biskind, *Easy Riders, Raging Bulls,* 114.

257 *"[film] industry started dying":* John Simon cited in Joan Didion, "In Hollywood," in *The White Album* (London: Weidenfeld & Nicolson, 1979), 156.

258 *"changed everything":* This and all subsequent quotes from Jon Lewis unpaginated rough draft excerpts of *Road Trip to Nowhere: Hollywood Encounters the Counterculture* (Los Angeles: University of California Press, 2022), supplied to the author courtesy of Jon Lewis.

258 *"[in the] summer and fall":* Didion, "In Hollywood," 159.

259 *"it was a dirty movie":* Karina Longworth, "*Last Picture Show* Love Triangle" episode of "Polly Platt: The Invisible Woman," *You Must Remember This* podcast, youmustrememberthispodcast.com/episodes/2020/6/1/last-picture-show-love-triangle-polly-platt-the -invisible-woman-part-3.

259 *"I went from getting the laundry":* Biskind, *Easy Riders, Raging Bulls,* 115.

259 *"Polly was a very strong driving force":* Ibid., 116.

259 *"He's the locomotive":* Ibid.

259 *"If you really want to be":* Ibid., 115.

260 *"If I was in charge; You know, Howard; I think that was the day":* Ibid., 116.

260 *"Polly could be":* Ibid., 114.

260 *"She had funny little spit curls":* Ibid., 121.

260　*"get some nudity"*: Longworth, *"Last Picture Show* Love Triangle" episode.

260　*"I did not find"*: Ibid.

261　*"Everything that's in the book"*: Biskind, *Easy Riders, Raging Bulls,* 120–21.

261　*"pretty married"*: Hollywood, 38.

261　*"[I]t did nothing"*: Film Flam, 33.

261　*"Peter and Polly"*: Ibid.

261　*"It was immediately clear"*: Ibid., 33–34.

261　*Platt remembered him*: Longworth, *"Last Picture Show* Love Triangle" episode.

261　*"despite [his] efforts"*: Film Flam, 39.

261　*"I had wasted"*: Ibid., 41.

262　*"we had . . . normal script conference[s]"*: Hollywood, 29.

262　*"Old Choice and Rare Books"*: "Complete liquidation of the entire inventory of W. H. Lowdermilk & Co., Washington D. C.'s most famous bookstore," notice, Library of Congress, http://www.loc.gov./resource/rbpe.20808600.

262　*"the task of disposing"*: This and subsequent quotes concerning the Lowdermilk auction, *Books,* 99–100.

262　*"Where you wanna go?"*: Don Graham, "Picture Perfect," *Texas Monthly,* February 1999, https://www.texasmonthly.com/arts-entertainment/picture-perfect-2/.

263　*"emptiness"*: Hollywood, 30.

263　*"I was asleep"*: Graham, "Picture Perfect."

263　*"extension of [his] imagination"*: Film Flam, 19–20.

263　*"[W]e went into the McMurtry house"*: Ibid.

264　*"becom[ing] one of his favorites"*: Hollywood, 31.

264　*"working in a city"*: Film Flam, 47.

264　*"exactly the kind of novel"*: Ibid., 35.

265　*"scanty clothing"*: Graham, "Picture Perfect."

265　*"Nah, Pete"*: This and subsequent Johnson quotes are from Chris Nashawaty, "'The Last Picture Show': An Oral History," *Entertainment Weekly,* April 17, 2017.

265　*"If you ask"*: Graham, "Picture Perfect."

265　*"[Cloris and I]"*: Nashawaty, "'The Last Picture Show': An Oral History."

265　*"[Archer City]"*: Graham, "Picture Perfect."

266　*"kind of offhand"*: Ibid.

266　*"I didn't think I was like Jacy"*: Nashawaty, "'The Last Picture Show': An Oral History."

266　*"Most of our people"*: Steven V. Roberts, "Hollywood Sets Up Shop in Small Town on Texas Plain," *New York Times,* December 14, 1970, https://www.nytimes.com/1970/12/14/archives/hollywood-sets-up-shop-in-small-town-on-texas-plain-villagers-and-.html.

266　*"[This is] a savage"*: Ibid.

266　*"I don't know"*: George Hickenlooper, *Picture This: The Times of Peter Bogdanovich in Archer City, Texas* (Nelson Entertainment, 1989), dailymotion.com/video/xqdjx9.

266　*"I, for one, feel"*: Grover Lewis, "Splendor in the Short Grass: The Making of *The Last Picture Show,*" in ed. Jan Reid and W. K. Stratton, *Splendor in the Short Grass: The Grover Lewis Reader* (Austin: University of Texas Press, 205), 30.

267　*"I do not endorse"*: Ibid.

267　*"I could kill you"*: Hickenlooper, *Picture This.*

267　*"There ain't nothing else to do"*: Roberts, "Hollywood Sets Up Shop in Small Town on Texas Plain."

267　*"There's flat nothing to do"*: Lewis: "Splendor in the Short Grass," 20.

267 *The paper reported:* Roberts, "Hollywood Sets Up Shop in Small Town on Texas Plain."

267 *"When we were . . . shooting":* Graham, "Picture Perfect."

267 *"an actor's script":* Nashawaty, "'The Last Picture Show': An Oral History."

268 *"You might have a gas station":* Abramowitz, "She's Done Everything (Except Direct)."

268 *"She was Mom":* "The Last Picture Show 40th Anniversary Panel," youtube.com/watch?v
=EApoBmLc8uo.

268 *"Oh, fantastic, great":* Lewis, "Splendor in the Short Grass," 17.

268 *"amazingly tough":* Abramowitz, "She's Done Everything (Except Direct)."

268 *"[c]ast and crew conspire":* Cybill Shepherd, *Cybill Disobedience* (New York: HarperCollins, 2000), 85.

268 *"dated":* Nashawaty, "'The Last Picture Show': An Oral History."

268 *"[W]e all wanted to see her":* Graham, "Picture Perfect."

268 *"We were in Olney":* Ibid.

269 *"Cybill shot the shit":* Nashawaty, "'The Last Picture Show': An Oral History."

269 *"I felt ugly":* Longworth, *"Last Picture Show* Love Triangle" episode.

269 *"I just pretended":* Graham, "Picture Perfect."

269 *"Polly later told me":* Longworth, *"Last Picture Show* Love Triangle" episode.

270 *"Later in the day":* Hollywood, 39.

270 *"neatly tended tract":* Lewis, "Splendor in the Short Grass," 35.

270 *"It's Boot Hill, son":* Ibid.

270 *"I think Larry and Marcia":* Conversation with John Curtis.

271 *"I called it Booked Up":* Ibid.

271 *"[He] came from Australia":* Staff, *Washington Life* magazine, December 8, 2012, 51.

271 *"[O]pened a little bookshop":* McMurtry to Grace David, April 6, 1971.

272 *"She got elephantiasis":* James Bryan, Antiquarian Booksellers' Association interview with Larry McMurtry, Tucson, January 2014.

272 *"upper-class ladies":* Books, 118.

CHAPTER 16

273 *"Please don't call them used":* Wendi Kaufman, "Turn Up the Volumes," *Washington Post,* March 9, 2001, https://www.washingtonpost.com/archive/lifestyle/2001/03/09/turn-up
-the-volumes/a5937d39-a3fd-4027-abcf-9d1567e44923/.

273 *"Oh, there goes Yolanda":* Tom Shales, "Last Picture Show Author Still Longs for Peanut Patties," *Philadelphia Inquirer,* January 2, 1972.

273 *"like a tennis pro":* Ibid.

273 *"but I had written a lot":* Larry McMurtry, "The Author Who Sold Books," *Washingtonian,* August 1, 2008, https://www.washingtonian.com/2008/08/01/the-author-who
-sold-books/.

273 *"burned out":* Books, 149.

273 *"Scouts are the seed carriers":* Ibid., 110.

274 *"[T]he atmosphere in Booked Up":* Alan Bisbort, "Notes from the Secondhand Store," Literary Kicks, September 9, 2010, https://litkicks.com/NotesFromSecondhand/.

274 *"on penalty of death":* Shales, "Last Picture Show Author Still Longs for Peanut Patties."

274 *"nosebleed":* Tom Zito, "Larry McMurtry: The Last Bookseller (1936–2021)," *Alta,* March 31, 2021, https://www.altaonline.com/books/a35982235/larry-mcmurtry-bookedup
-appreciation-tom-zito/.

275 *"[T]he heaviest lifters":* Bisbort, "Notes from the Secondhand Store."

275 *"only one real book"*: "The Author Who Sold Books."

275 *"bought an excellent library"*: Ibid.

275 *"something of a social terror"*: *Books*, 131.

275 *"[We] didn't actually enter"*: Ibid.

276 *"Joanna wanted to buy a BMW"*: Ibid., 132.

276 *"I went and discovered"*: Larry McMurtry, "Splendors and Miseries of Being an Author/ Bookseller," https://www.abaa.org/member-articles/splendors-and-miseries-of-being-an -author-bookseller.

276 *"I had an expensive education"*: Skip Hollandsworth, "McMurtry Interview Compilation," provided to the author courtesy of Skip Hollandsworth.

276 *"street-level bookselling"*: Hollandsworth, "McMurtry Interview Compilation," 137.

277 *"We don't have it"*: Shales, "Last Picture Show Author Still Longs for Peanut Patties."

277 *"Better luck"*: Chris Nashawaty, "'The Last Picture Show': An Oral History," *Entertainment Weekly*, April 17, 2017.

277 *"not merely the best"*: See American Film Institute, "AFI Catalog of Feature Films: The First 100 Years, 1893–1993," https://www.catalog.afi.com/Catalog/moviedetails/54257.

277 *"nothing short"*: Ibid.

277 *"Bogdanovich is so plain"*: Pauline Kael, "*The Last Picture Show*," *The New Yorker*, October 9, 1971, https://scrapsfromtheloft.com/movies/last-picture-show-kael/.

277 *"written the best regional dialogue"*: *The Last Picture Show* 40th Anniversary Panel.

278 *"McMurdee"*: "*The French Connection* Wins Adapted Screenplay, 1972 Oscars," youtube .com/watch?v=Uad8qcBIRS4.

278 *"sat in his tux"*: *Hollywood*, 41.

278 *"Mr. Peter Bogdanovich['s] . . . lovely wife"*: "1971 (44th) Academy Award, Actor in a Supporting Role," Academy Awards Acceptance Speech Database, https://aaspeechesdb .org/link/044–21.

278 *"more than ever"*: *Film Flam*, 174.

278 *"[doesn't] help"*: *The Last Picture Show*, 265.

279 *"drive 'em on to Missouri"*: See Robert F. Wilson Jr., "Which Is the Real 'Last Picture Show'?," *Literature/Film Quarterly* 1, no. 2 (Spring 1973), 167–68.

279 *"Peter . . . coming to the material"*: *Film Flam*, 174.

279 *"[T]he film is extraordinary"*: Ibid.

279 *"[Ruth] finds the fact that she can feel"*: Ibid., 176–77.

279 *"rainy night"*: Rachel Abramowitz, "She's Done Everything (Except Direct)," *Premiere*, November 1993, https://www.maryellenmark.com/text/magazines/premiere/919V-000– 004.html.

280 *"I was soon deluged"*: *Hollywood*, 42.

280 *"In three months my fame"*: "The Author Who Sold Books."

280 *"All our famous friends"*: Karina Longworth, "Orson Welles, What's Up, Doc?, Paper Moon: Episode Four, Polly Platt: The Invisible Woman," *You Must Remember This* podcast.

280 *"Big Tony"*: Abramowitz, "She's Done Everything (Except Direct)."

281 *"I loved being with Larry"*: Longworth, "Episode Four, Polly Platt: The Invisible Woman."

281 *"The most poetic day"*: Ibid.

281 *"I was in love with Polly"*: Ibid.

282 *"a bruised optimist"*: Larry McMurtry, "Preface, *Cadillac Jack* (New York: Simon & Schuster, 1985), iii.

282 *"Billy Lee"*: Larry L. King, "Leavin' McMurtry," *Texas Monthly*, March 1974, https:// texasmonthly.com/arts-entertainment/leavin-mcmurtry/.

282   *"[T]he game [was] back on"*: Joan Didion, "In Hollywood," in *The White Album* (London: Weidenfeld & Nicolson, 1979), 158–59.

282   *"Is that Vietnam?"*: King, "Leavin' McMurtry."

282   *"So who's gonna know?"*: Ibid.

283   *"You know what your book's about?"*: Ibid.

283   *"appeared to be about two years older"*: Ibid.

283   *"It's not so bad; Lumet apparently"*: Ibid.

283   *"He was butted in the head"*: Bill Brammer, "Briar Patch," *Texas Monthly*, February 1973, https://www.texasmonthly.com/articles/briar-patch-11.

284   *"The night before the trip"*: Paradise, 22.

285   *"The next day the two of them"*: Ibid., 23.

285   *"and he had this beautiful young woman"*: Conversation with Joe Holley.

285   *"country; sentimental"*: These and other quotes from the Southwest Texas State University lecture, Larry McMurtry Speaking and Q & A at Texas State, 1974.

286   *"When arthritis and fatigue"*: Larry McMurtry, "Death of the Cowboy," *The New York Review of Books*, November 4, 1999, https://nybooks.com/articles/1999/11/04/death-of -the-cowboy/.

287   *"creeping socialism"*: Ibid.

287   *"separated from ours"*: Ibid.

287   *"On the last day"*: Ibid.

287   *"four or five conversations"*: Paradise, 40.

288   *"Suddenly, while waiting for a light"*: Ibid.

288   *"had never said a word"*: Ibid., 39.

288   *"took up with an elderly fellow"*: Ibid., 41.

CHAPTER 17

289   *"much pampered"*: Literary Life, 80.

289   *"had a rather different keyboard"*: Ibid.

290   *"Stop telling people"*: Cybill Shepherd, *Cybill Disobedience* (New York: HarperCollins, 2000), 139.

290   *"the silence of a woman"*: Ibid., 122.

291   *"You have brought joy and fragrance"*: Ibid., 186.

291   *"[He] sat with me in the lobby"*: Ibid., 185.

291   *"Ever since [I'd] known Peter"*: Literary Life, 93.

292   *"I will never forget the incongruity"*: John Spong, *A Book on the Making of* Lonesome Dove (Austin: University of Texas Press, 2012), 35.

292   *"serve as a kind of homage"*: Literary Life, 93.

292   *"I said it needed to be a trek"*: This and other quotes from Bogdanovich are from Spong, *A Book on the Making of* Lonesome Dove, 35–37.

292   *"The draft was welcomed"*: Ibid., 37.

293   *"You live in Europe?"*: See Bruce LaBruce, "Bruce LaBruce's Academy of the Under- rated: *Daisy Miller*," *Talk House*, https://www.talkhouse.com/bruce-labruces-academy -underrated-daisy-miller/.

293   *"[One day] my dad said"*: Geoffrey Himes, "James McMurtry: Landscape Artist," *Ameri- can Songwriter*, 2014, https://americansongwriter.com/james-mcmurtry/2/.

293   *"She did as she pleased"*: LaBruce, "Bruce LaBruce's Academy of the Underrated: *Daisy Miller*."

293   *"Peter was fundamental"*: Rachel Abramowitz, "She's Done Everything (Except Direct)."

294   *"[Larry] knew me"*: Karina Longworth, "Terms of Endearment: Polly Platt: The Invisible Woman, Episode Seven," *You Must Remember This* podcast.

294   *"What I was told"*: Ibid.

294   *"I wouldn't say"*: Rachel Abramowitz, "She's Done Everything (Except Direct)."

294   *"mulish, resigned silence"*: Larry McMurtry, "Unfinished Women," *Texas Monthly*, May 1977, https://www.texasmonthly.com/being-texan/unfinished-womenature/.

294   *"think I became a novelist"*: Ibid.

294   *"domestic victims"*: Ibid.

295   *"making no difficulties"*: Hollywood, 45.

295   *"Husband management"*: Larry McMurtry, "A Life for the Star," *The New York Review of Books*, April 26, 2012, https:www.nybooks.com/articles/2012/04/26/life-star.

295   *"The success of a marriage"*: Larry McMurtry, *Terms of Endearment* (New York: Simon & Schuster, 1975), 11.

295   *"Disgrace abounds"*: Ibid., 77.

295   *"had learned something about heat"*: Ibid., 70.

296   *"women in hats; stark"*: Ibid., 79, 81.

296   *"Suddenly, to Aurora's terror"*: Ibid., 22.

296   *"It is tempting"*: Ernestine P. Sewell, "The Houston Trilogy," in ed. Clay Reynolds, *Taking Stock: A Larry McMurtry Casebook* (Dallas: Southern Methodist University Press, 1989), 202.

297   *"women are at their best"*: Larry McMurtry, "Preface," *Terms of Endearment* (New York: Simon & Schuster, 1989), 7.

297   *"[T]he ending"*: Robert Towers, "An Oddly Misshapen Novel by a Highly Accomplished Novelist," *New York Times Book Review*, October 19, 1975, 4.

297   *"I consider it a process"*: Patrick Bennett, "Larry McMurtry: Thalia, Houston, and Hollywood," *Talking with Texas Writers: Twelve Interviews* (College Station, TX: Texas A&M University Press, 1980), 23.

297   *"One of the prime abilities"*: Ibid., 30–31.

297   *"Narrative is not"*: Film Flam, 175.

298   *"Tommy, be sweet"*: This and subsequent quotes from *Terms of Endearment, Terms of Endearment* (1975), 405–6.

298   *"inch backwards"*: Larry McMurtry Speaking and Q & A at Texas State, 1974.

299   *"[His] own long descent"*: "Death of the Cowboy."

299   *"cool distaste"*: "Preface," *Terms of Endearment*, 7.

CHAPTER 18

300   *"literary gloom"*: Literary Life, 84.

300   *"The Trash Trilogy"*: Mark Busby, *Larry McMurtry and the West: An Ambivalent Relationship* (Denton, TX: University of North Texas Press, 1995), 151.

300   *"glitzy but uncentered"*: Ibid., 152.

301   *"From the first it was apparent"*: This and all other quotes concerning the state dinner at the White House, are from Larry McMurtry, "A Night at the White House," unpublished rough draft, Susan Sontag Archives, Library Special Collections, Charles E. Young Research Library, UCLA.

302   *"One diplomatic couple"*: Sondra Gotlieb, "Joseph Alsop: One More Icon of the Bygone Beltway," *National Post*, February 4, 2013, https://nationalpost.com/life/joseph-alsop-one-more-icon-of-the-bygone-beltway.

302   *"part Maimonides"*: Sam Tanenhaus, "Wayward Intellectual Finds God," *New York Times*

Magazine, January 24, 1999, https://www.nytimes.com/1999/01/24/magazine/wayward
-intellectual-finds-god.html.

302 *"a fixture"*: Ibid.

302 *"dining regularly"*: Mike Evans, "Larry," an unpublished memoir sent to the author, September 27, 2021.

302 *"Clayton was also a musician"*: Ibid.

303 *"I saw Sam"*: Larry McMurtry, blurb for *Who the Hell Are We Fighting?: The Story of Sam Adams and the Vietnamese Intelligence Wars* by C. Michael Hiam, amazon.com/who-the
-hell-are-we-fighting-intelligence/dp/1586421042.

303 *"parochialism"*: John Spong, *A Book on the Making of* Lonesome Dove (Austin: University of Texas Press, 2012), 40.

303 *"Larry was respected"*: Ibid.

303 *"It was a little demoralizing"*: Tanenhaus, "Wayward Intellectual Finds God."

303 *"The novels got darker"*: Evans, "Larry."

304 *"mental and emotive"*: Larry McMurtry cited in Brooks Landon, "Larry McMurtry," in ed. Clay Reynolds, *Taking Stock: A Larry McMurtry Casebook* (Dallas: Southern Methodist University Press, 1989), 270.

304 *"determined to hang in there"*: "Preface" to *Cadillac Jack,* unpaginated.

304 *"[It] is ruinable"*: *Somebody's Darling,* 123.

304 *"the little roads"*: McMurtry cited in Landon, "Larry McMurtry," 273.

304 *"There's no getting away"*: *Somebody's Darling,* 160.

304 *"Texas is the ultimate"*: Ibid., 312–13.

305 *"about the horrors"*: Michael Granberry, "Texas Literary Giant Larry McMurtry Dies at 84," *Dallas Morning News,* March 26, 2021, https://www.dallasnews.com/2021/03/26
/texas-literary-giant-larry-mcmurtry-dies-at-84/.

305 *"[his speech] caused"*: Ibid.

305 *"what if we get McMurtry"*: Conversation with Joe Holley.

305 *"he went back and machine-gunned"*: A Book on the Making of Lonesome Dove, 42.

305 *"Texas has produced no major writers"*: Larry McMurtry, "Ever a Bridegroom: Reflections on the Failure of Texas Literature," *Texas Observer,* October 23, 1981, reprinted in *Range Wars: Heated Debates, Sober Reflections, and Other Assessments of Texas Writing,* ed. Craig Clifford and Tom Pilkington (Dallas: Southern Methodist University Press, 1989), 15.

305 *"high gift"*: Ibid., 39

305 *"high-risk modernist"*: Ibid., 25.

305 *"For some years now"*: James Lee Ward, "Arbiters of Texas Literary Taste," in *Range Wars,* 131–33.

305 *"Larry McMurtry implied Texas"*: Donald Barthelme, "Terms of Estrangement," in *Taking Stock: A Larry McMurtry Casebook,* 104–5.

306 *"I picked it up"*: A Book on the Making of Lonesome Dove, 42.

306 *"some twelve hundred pages"*: Larry McMurtry, "Preface" to *The Desert Rose,* viii.

306 *"I have always been attracted"*: Ibid., x.

307 *"brain-sphinctering"*: D. Keith Mano, "The Desert Rose," *National Review* 25, November 1983, 1405–96.

307 *"graced [his] life"*: Larry McMurtry, "Preface" to *The Desert Rose,* xi.

307 *"As a young writer"*: Clay Reynolds, "Come Home Larry, All Is Forgiven: A Native Son's Search for Identity," in *Taking Stock: A Larry McMurtry Casebook,* 287–88.

307 *"Where's Peter?"*: Rachel Abramowitz, "She's Done Everything (Except Direct)," *Premiere,*

November 1993, https://www.maryellenmark.com/text/magazines/premiere/919V-000–004.html.

307 *"Peter had always justified"*: Ibid.

308 *when Aurora slaps her daughter*: Karina Longworth, "Terms of Endearment: Polly Platt: The Invisible Woman, Episode Seven," *You Must Remember This* podcast.

308 *"genius"*: Abramowitz, "She's Done Everything (Except Direct)."

308 *"trying to seduce"*: Longworth, "Polly Platt: The Invisible Woman, Episode Seven."

308 *"You're killing me; He fought"*: Abramowitz, "She's Done Everything (Except Direct)."

309 *"wearing all my leftover"*: "Terms of Endearment," Santa Barbara International Film Festival notes, March 31–April 10, 2021, https://sbiff.org/terms-of-endearment/.

309 *"I know my marks"*: Ibid.

309 *"Polly was brilliant"*: Longworth, "Polly Platt: The Invisible Woman, Episode Seven."

309 *"A wonderful mix"*: Leonard Maltin, *2013 Movie Guide* (New York: Penguin Books, 2012), 1386.

309 *"an enormous contribution"*: James L. Brooks, Academy Awards acceptance speech, April 9, 1984, youtube.com/watch?v=6ErU36x31EQ.

310 *"other colors seem omitted"*: Larry McMurtry, unpublished, undated notes, Special Collections, University of Houston Library.

310 *"We met [once] in Washington"*: *Film Flam*, 220–21.

310 *"She was rummaging"*: Larry McMurtry, "Diane Keaton on Photography," *The New York Review of Books*, November 8, 2007, https://www.nybooks.com/articles/2007/11/08/diane-keaton-on-photography/.

310 *"If I could I'd wander"*: *Film Flam*, 213.

311 *"I was a farmer"*: Ibid., 217.

311 *"But like all true clowns"*: "Diane Keaton on Photography."

311 *"bulimia"*: Corrina Honan, "Bulimia, Woody and me: Diane Keaton reveals the eating disorder that blighted her affair with Woody Allen—and how doomed flings left her loveless and alone," *Daily Mail*, November 16, 2011, https://www.dailymail.co.uk/tvshowbiz/article-2061520/Diane-Keatons-Woody-Allen-affair-blighted-bulimia-Doomed-flings-left-loveless.html.

311 *"My own suspicion"*: Larry McMurtry, rough draft, undated, profile of Diane Keaton, Special Collections, University of Houston Library.

311 *"[T]hose who can read"*: Ibid.

311 *"all over the West"*: Ibid.

312 *"having decided"*: McMurtry to Grace David, May 23, 1982.

312 *"dumped"*: McMurtry to Grace David, September 5, 1982.

312 *"and also, unfortunately"*: Larry McMurtry, "The Author Who Sold Books," *Washingtonian*, August 1, 2008, https://www.washingtonian.com/2008/08/01/the-author-who-sold-books/.

312 *"I will be moving the contents"*: McMurtry to Grace David, May 23, 1982.

312 *"Writing lots of screenplays"*: McMurtry to Grace David, August 1, 1983.

312 *"an elaborate notation"*: *Film Flam*, 55.

313 *"not much more exciting"*: Ibid., 27.

313 *"not so much a hotel"*: Ibid., 59.

313 *"Mercedeses"*: Ibid., 60.

313 *"I must say I still like it"*: McMurtry to Grace David, August 1, 1983.

313 *"You never know where I'll be"*: Ibid.

314 *"I have been poorly"*: McMurtry to Grace David, January 24, 1985.

314 *"My doctors say"*: Ibid.

CHAPTER 19

317 *"I sing"*: Larry McMurtry, *Lonesome Dove* (New York: Simon & Schuster, 1985), 466.

317 *"On May 7, 1987"*: See "Dorothea Oppenheimer," *New York Times*, May 12, 1987, https://www.nytimes.com/1987/05/12/obituaries/dorothea-oppenheimer.html.

317 *"She remained"*: Hollywood, 78.

317 *"[She] had quality"*: Larry McMurtry, "Swifty Lazar: Evolved Heart, Evolved Style," *Los Angeles Times*, January 7, 1994, https://www.latimes.com/la-bk-larry-mcmurtry -1994–01–07-story.html.

317 *"Ideally"*: Oppenheimer to McMurtry, December 30, 1971.

317 *"She just didn't get Hollywood"*: Hollywood, 78.

318 *"who could step off an airplane"*: "Swifty Lazar."

318 *"Everybody who matters"*: Michael Korda, "The King of the Deal," *The New Yorker*, March 21, 1993, https://www.newyorker.com/magazine/1993/03/29/the-king-of-the-deal.

318 *"tastes and attitudes"*: "Swifty Lazar."

318 *"people who were perfectly willing"*: Korda, "The King of the Deal."

319 *"understood instinctively"*: This and subsequent quotes concerning Korda and Lazar are from Korda, "The King of the Deal."

320 *"He changed the rules"*: Korda, "The King of the Deal."

320 *"To build a writer's career"*: Michael Shnayerson and Annette Tapert, "'Swifty' Lazar's Legacy," *Vanity Fair*, April 21, 1994, https://www.vanityfair.com/news/1994/04/michael -shnayerson-199404.

320 *"Not for him"*: "Swifty Lazar."

320 *"McMurtry the attention and reviews"*: Michael Korda, *Another Life: A Memoir of Other People* (New York: Random House, 1999), 291.

321 *"[T]he vice presidency"*: Patrick Cox, "Not Worth a Bucket of Warm Spit," *History News Network*, https://www.historynewsnetwork.org/article/53402.

321 *"Welcome; Catfish"*: Literary Life, 101–2.

321 *"Coca-Cola girl made the apologies"*: Korda, "The King of the Deal."

321 *"as a relatively informal"*: Ibid.

322 *"I only invite friends"*: Irving Lazar, *Swifty: My Life and Good Times* (New York: Simon & Schuster, 1995), 11.

322 *"far too modest"*: This and subsequent quotes from Lazar concerning McMurtry are from from *Swifty: My Life and Good Times*, 225–26.

323 *"What do you have kicking around?"*: John Spong, *A Book on the Making of* Lonesome Dove (Austin: University of Texas Press, 2012), 63.

323 *"He said, $50,000"*: Ibid.

323 *"I don't know how to tell you this"*: Michael Hoinski, "*Lonesome Dove* Reunion Proves That the Three-Decade-Old Mini-Series Is Timeless," *Texas Monthly*, April 5, 2016, https:// www.texasmonthly.com/the-daily-post/lonesome-dove-reunion-proves-three-decade-old -mini-series-timeless/.

323 *"You know what?"*: Spong, *A Book on the Making of* Lonesome Dove, 63.

324 *"I never had any totally conscious plan"*: Skip Hollandsworth, "The Talented Mr. Wittliff," *Texas Monthly*, February 2001, https://www.texasmonthly.com/articles/the-talented-mr -wittliff/.

324 *"basically variations"*: Ibid.

324 *"There were so many reasons"*: Spong, *A Book on the Making of* Lonesome Dove, 63.

324 *"Can't we get them"*: Ibid.

324 *"Bill, listen to this"*: Ibid., 65.

325 *"letting go"*: Hoinski, *"Lonesome Dove* Reunion."

325 *"It would be nice to say"*: Hollywood, 81.

325 *"It all comes"*: Spong, *A Book on the Making of* Lonesome Dove, 43.

325 *"Gus is about affection"*: Ibid.

326 *"carefree banter"*: Don Graham, *"Lonesome Dove*: Butch and Sundance Go on a Cattle-drive," in ed. Clay Reynolds, *Taking Stock: A Larry McMurtry Casebook* (Dallas: Southern Methodist University Press, 1989), 315.

326 *"[B]efore we left"*: Ibid.

326 *"There was no timber"*: Ibid.

326 *"[T]he cowboys gathered"*: J. Evetts Haley, *Charles Goodnight: Cowman & Plainsman* (Norman: University of Oklahoma Press, 1949), 184.

326 *"Before [Call] reached Kansas"*: Lonesome Dove, 832.

327 *"served with me four years"*: Spong, *A Book on the Making of* Lonesome Dove, 46.

327 *"I did copy"*: Ibid., 47.

327 *"All along that trail"*: Haley, *Charles Goodnight,* 186.

328 *"I don't think these myths"*: Mark Busby, *Larry McMurtry and the West: An Ambivalent Relationship* (Denton, TX: University of North Texas Press, 1995), 183.

328 *"the battle"*: Lonesome Dove, 326.

328 *"If a thousand Comanches"*: Ibid.

328 *"I doubt there was"*: Ibid.

328 *"His own facts"*: In a Narrow Grave: Essays on Texas, 62–63.

329 *"the pleasure"*: Lonesome Dove, 356.

329 *"our emotional experience"*: In a Narrow Grave: Essays on Texas, 54.

329 *"I'm sorry you and Gus"*: Lonesome Dove, 831.

330 *"Titles are really important"*: "Larry McMurtry, Author of *Lonesome Dove,*" youtube.com /watch?v=14FinPjgd10.

330 *"really the Lonesome Dove"*: Ibid.

331 *"Captain. They say"*: Lonesome Dove, 838.

331 *"My life has been"*: Jeff Salamon, "A Tale of Two Endings," *Texas Monthly,* July 2010, https://www.texasmonthly.com/articles/a-tale-of-two-endings/.

331 *"The dern people"*: Lonesome Dove, 319.

331 *"poke"*: Ibid., 174.

332 *"How can it be"*: D. L. Birchfield, *"Lonesome Dove*: The Bluing of a Texas-American Myth," *Studies in American Indian Literatures* 7, series 2 (Summer 1995), 45–64.

332 *"we should be talking about these books"*: Joelle Fraser, "An Interview with Sherman Alexie," *The Iowa Review* 30, no. 3 (Winter 2000–2001), 60.

332 *"book [was] permeated"*: Spong, *A Book on the Making of* Lonesome Dove, 47.

333 *"supposed to de-mythologize"*: Ibid.

333 *"If Larry McMurtry's vision"*: Birchfield, *"Lonesome Dove*: The Bluing of a Texas-American Myth."

334 *"It really felt at times"*: Spong, *A Book on the Making of* Lonesome Dove, 133.

334 *"was gone in five hours"*: Ibid.

334 *"the lead steer"*: Ibid., 109.

334 *"[It's] as epic"*: Hoinski, *"Lonesome Dove* Reunion."

335 *"a rangy, hollow-cheeked cowman"*: Stephen Harrigan, "The Making of *Lonesome Dove*," *Texas Monthly*, June 1988, https://www.texasmonthly.com/articles/the-making-of -lonesome-dove/.

335 *"Larry McMurtry wasn't keen"*: Spong, *A Book on the Making of* Lonesome Dove, 71.

335 *"proves what television can achieve"*: Ibid., 146.

335 *"the most vividly rendered"*: Ibid.

335 *"a culmination"*: *Taking Stock: A Larry McMurtry Casebook*, 333.

335 *"The reviewers were beginning to feel"*: Spong, *A Book on the Making of* Lonesome Dove, 50.

335 *"I have a view"*: Ibid., 153.

336 *"I thought I had written"*: Peter Simek, "Trek the 'Lonesome Dove' Trail Across Texas," *Texas Heritage for Living*, November 20, 2020, https://texasheritageforliving.com/texas -travel/lonesome-dove-trail/.

336 *"not a despicable"*: Spong, *A Book on the Making of* Lonesome Dove, 153.

CHAPTER 20

337 *"The huge popularity"*: Hollywood, 114.

337 *"The mother was indignant"*: Ibid.

337 *"Is something the matter?"*: Ibid., 115–16.

337 *"He told me"*: Conversation with Michael Wallis.

338 *"a powerful, gripping"*: Thomas Doherty, "The Murder of Mary Phagan," *Cineaste* 36, no. 3 (Summer 2011), https://www.cineaste.com/summer-2011/from-the-archives-the-murder -of-mary-phagan.

338 *"Marcia was, in a small way"*: Books, 187.

338 *"filled the car"*: Ibid.

339 *"People do not always recognize"*: Thomas Curwen, "Larry McMurtry, Author of 'Lonesome Dove' and 'The Last Picture Show,' Dies," *Los Angeles Times*, March 26, 2021, https://latimes.com/obituaries/story/2021–03–26/larry-mcmurtry-author-of-lonesome -dove-and-the-last-picture-show-dies-at-84.

339 *"He operates on a different plane"*: Skip Hollandsworth, "The Minor Regional Novelist," *Texas Monthly*, July 2016, https://www.texasmonthly.com/arts-entertainment/larry -mcmurtry-minor-regional-novelist/.

339 *"I'd never known a man"*: Jan Reid, "Return of the Native Son," *Texas Monthly*, February 1993, https://texasmonthly.com/arts-entertainment/profile-return-of-the-native -son/.

339 *"At long last"*: Maureen Orth, "Remembering Larry McMurtry and His Friendships with Fascinating Women," *Vanity Fair*, March 26, 2021, https://www.vanityfair.com/style /2021/03/remembering-larry-mcmurtry.

339 *"a man who completely knows my heart"*: Maureen Orth, "Larry McMurtry—A Woman's Best Friend," https://maureenorth.com/1984/03/larry-mcmurtry-a-womans-best -friend.

339 *"loved, respected, and appreciated"*: Orth, "Remembering Larry McMurtry."

339 *"Through the years"*: Ibid.

340 *"normal; shoulder I cried on"*: Ibid.

340 *"I always wondered"*: Orth, "A Woman's Best Friend."

340 *"did not have very much"*: Orth, Ibid.

340 *"freest relationships"*: Ibid.

340 *"there has been a sexual aura"*: Ibid.

341   *"I can confide"*: Cybill Shepherd interview with Skip Hollandsworth, undated and unpublished [2016], courtesy of Skip Hollandsworth.

341   *"recklessness"*: Cybill Shepherd, *Cybill Disobedience* (New York: HarperCollins, 2000),
116.

341   *"is one of my treasures"*: Hollandsworth, Cybill Shepherd interview.

341   *"I've realized"*: John Beifuss, "Cybill Disobedience: Cybill Shepherd Returns to Her
Memphis Hometown," *Memphis Commercial Appeal,* March 16, 2018, https://
commercialappeal.com/story/entertainment/movies/2018/03/16/cybill-shepherd
-memphis-rose-screening-orpheum/426283002/.

341   *Once, in the fall of 1989:* This and all other details and quotes concerning Diane Keaton
are from Larry McMurtry, "Diane Keaton on Photography," *The New York Review of
Books,* November 8, 2007, https://www.nybooks.com/articles/2007/11/08/diane-keaton
-on-photography/.

343   *"[N]ot only did I not see"*: *Some Can Whistle,* 39.

343   *"If I'm a connoisseur"*: Ibid., 28.

343   *"would present his American Express card"*: Reid, "Return of the Native Son."

344   *"immunity from the common ills"*: *Some Can Whistle,* 44.

344   *Muhammad Ali; Zeppo Marx: Hollywood,* 53.

344   *"I can't be taking too many more"*: McMurtry to Max Crawford, October 21, 1990.

344   *"I'm trying to decide"*: McMurtry to Grace David, August 6, 1986.

345   *"Baptists don't always win"*: This and other quotes and details regarding Archer City,
unless otherwise noted, are from William K. Stevens, "New Life After 'The Last Picture
Show,'" *New York Times Magazine,* April 4, 1982, 43.

346   *"I learned early"*: Ray Isle, "Three Days in McMurtryville," *Stanford Magazine,* Novem-
ber/December 1999, https://stanfordmag.org/contents/three-days-in-mcmurtryville.

347   *"kindest, most generous"*: This and all other Judy McLemore quotes are from "Legendary
native son Larry McMurtry dies at 84," *Archer County News,* March 31, 2021, https:
//www.archercountynews.com/news/legendary-son-larry-mcmurtry-dies-84.

347   *"couple of local depressives"*: McMurtry to Max Crawford, October 21, 1990.

347   *"The mentality of the city"*: Julia Robb, "The Last Picture Show, for Real," *The Texas
Observer,* April 6, 2007, https://www.texasobserver.org/2471-the-last-picture-show-for
-real/.

348   *"I'm a polarizing figure"*: Ibid.

348   *"The love of my life"*: McMurtry to Grace David, August 15, 1986.

348   *"He was really cool"*: This and other Matt McLemore quotes, Matt McLemore in conversation with the author, July 2, 2021.

348   *"I like it fine"*: McMurtry to Grace David, August 15, 1986.

349   *"I'm an urban person"*: Evan Smith, "Larry McMurtry," *Texas Monthly,* September 2004,
https://www.texasmonthly.com/arts-entertainment/larry-mcmurtry/.

349   *Valley Fever:* Julie Cart, "Rapidly Growing Phoenix Finds Dust Unsettling," *Los Angeles
Times,* September 7, 1999, A1.

349   *"Everybody who lives here"*: Ibid., A24.

350   *"particularly pleasant"*: Smith, "Larry McMurtry."

350   *"involved with"*: McMurtry to Grace David, July 19, 1987.

350   *"I'm very much a creature"*: Smith, "Larry McMurtry."

350   *"We worked with the students"*: Leslie Silko, letter to the author, April 29, 2022.

350   *"the year of the supernova"*: Mary Ellen Snodgrass, *Leslie Marmon Silko: A Literary Companion* (Jefferson, NC: McFarland & Company, 2011), 8.

351 *"there were no beloved grandparents"*: Ibid., 11.

351 *"Indian Manifesto; US history"*: Josh Garrett-Davis, "Leslie Marmon Silko's *The Turquoise Ledge*," *Iowa Review*, September 6, 2011, https://iowareview.org/blog/leslie-marmon -silko's-turquoise-ledge.

351 *"ris[ing] near to greatness"*: Larry McMurtry, Introduction to *Ceremony* by Leslie Marmon Silko (New York: Penguin Books, 2006), xxi.

351 *"a long swim"*: Ibid.

351 *"criss-crossed with bird and animal tracks"*: Snodgrass, *Leslie Marmon Silko*, 19.

352 *"If gravity is distributed"*: Garrett-Davis, "Leslie Marmon Silko's *The Turquoise Ledge*."

352 *"Queen of Country Swing; See Sue"*: "Honkytonk Sue #1," *underground comix collection*, https://comixjoint.com/honkeytonksue1.html.

352 *city of murals:* See Tom Miller, "The Bold Murals of Tucson's Streets," *New York Times*, March 4, 1990, https://www.nytimes.com/1990/03/04/travel/the-bold-murals-of-tucson -s-streets.html.

353 *"I was having trouble"*: This and subsequent Silko quotes, Ellen L. Arnold, "Read a conversation with Silko from *Conversations with Leslie Marmon Silko*," Literary Birthdays Blog, https://litbirthdays.wordpress.com/2010/05/02/literary-birthdays-week-of -may-2–8/.

353 *"I had just finished"*: Casey Combs, "An Unlikely Team Produces 'Pretty Boy Floyd,'" *Los Angeles Times*, December 11, 1994, https://www.latimes.com/archives/la-xpm -1994–12–11-mm-7709-story.html.

353 *"Meanwhile"*: Ibid.

354 *"He would see me in Tucson"*: Bruce Newman, "Smile When You Say That, Partner," *Los Angeles Times*, October 30, 1994, https://www.latimes.com/archives/la-xpm-1994–10–30 -ca-56528-story.html.

354 *"Larry is a very private person"*: Ibid.

354 *"Things evolved"*: Ibid.

354 *"When I first met Larry"*: Michael Hoinski, "'Lonesome Dove' Legend Larry McMurtry on Fiction, Money, Womanizing, and Old Age," *Grantland*, May 22, 2014, https:// grantland.com/hollywood-prospectus/larry-mcmurtry-lonesome-dove-new-book -interview/.

354 *"I've been feeling not knowing you"*: McMurtry to Susan Sontag, December 9, 1988.

354 *"standing at the intersection"*: "About Us," PEN America, https://www.pen.org/about-us/.

354 *"I thought it was of some interest"*: McMurtry to Susan Sontag, December 9, 1988.

355 *"You certainly raised"*: McMurtry to Susan Sontag, June 10, 1988.

355 *"writing prose"*: "James McMurtry Biography," https://musicianguide.com/biographies /1608000705/James-McMurtry.html.

355 *"an old gal fiddler"*: Mary Andrews, "James McMurtry Remains the Harbinger of American Truth (Interview)," *Glide Magazine*, July 11, 2019, https://glidemagazine.com /228503/james-mcmurtry-remains-the-harbinger-of-american-truth-interview/.

355 *"I looked at the bullet holes"*: Graham Reid, "James McMurtry Interviewed (1990): In from the Wasteland," *Elsewhere*, September 6, 2010, https://www.elsewhere.co.nz /absoluteelsewhere/3493/james-mcmurtry-interviewed-1990-in-from-the-wasteland/.

356 *"Oh God"*: Richard Harrington, "The Roots of McMurtry," *Washington Post*, August 27, 1989, https://www.washingtonpost.com/archive/lifestyle/style/1989/08/27/the-roots-of -mcmurtry/bab69078–65ac-4955-a6a1–7295a24e0a8f/.

356 *"Larry, have your son call me"*: This and subsequent quotes, conversation between Mellencamp and James McMurtry.

356 *"[L]andscape . . . frames":* "James McMurtry Biography."

356 *"His songs [are] brown":* Ibid.

356 *"James's best songs":* J. Freedom du Lac, "His Songs? Bleak. His Future? Bright," *Washington Post,* June 1, 2008, https://www.conqueroo.com/jamesmcmurtrynewsclips.html.

356 *"it's harder":* Harrington, "The Roots of McMurtry."

357 *"a mini-novel":* Ibid.

357 *"We may have gotten":* Mario Tarradell, "James McMurtry Takes on Politics on Latest Album," *Dallas Morning News,* n.d., 2008.

357 *"[M]ore people":* du Lac, "His Songs? Bleak. His Future? Bright."

357 *"Why doesn't James like me?":* Ibid.

357 *"I used to think I was an artist":* Matt Fink, "James McMurtry and the Heartless Bastards Live in Aught-Three (Compadre)," *Paste Magazine,* June 1, 2004, https://www.pastemagazine.com/music/james-mcmurtry/james-mcmurtry-the-heartless-bastards/.

357 *"I tend to look at the dark cloud":* du Lac, "His Songs? Bleak. His Future? Bright."

357 *"theme is that tragedy":* McMurtry to Grace David, June 23, 1992.

CHAPTER 21

358 *"[T]he storyteller":* Walter Benjamin cited in *Walter Benjamin at the Dairy Queen,* 17.

358 *"The birthplace of the novel":* Ibid., 34.

359 *"The first [American] cowboys":* *Walter Benjamin at the Dairy Queen,* 64.

359 *"[m]y question":* Ibid., 25.

359 *"I wanted to know":* Ibid., 31.

359 *"Death is the sanctity; [S]o it certainly seemed":* Walter Benjamin cited in *Walter Benjamin at the Dairy Queen,* 37–38.

360 *"nothing around here to eat":* Ceil Cleveland, *Whatever Happened to Jacy Farrow?* (Denton, TX: University of North Texas Press, 1997), 153.

361 *"the Beginnings of Superstardom":* Larry McMurtry, *The Colonel and Little Missie,* title page.

361 *"west edge of town":* Larry McMurtry, *Texasville* (New York: Pocket Books, 1987), 25.

361 *"wicked":* McMurtry to Grace David, August 6, 1986.

361 *"He spent hours":* *Texasville,* 23.

363 *"hoping to meet":* Ibid., 163.

363 *"pedophilic community":* Ibid., 396.

363 *"'Texasville' often reads":* Louise Erdrich, "Why Is That Man Tired?," in ed. Clay Reynolds, *Taking Stock: A Larry McMurtry Casebook* (Dallas: Southern Methodist University Press, 1989), 338.

363 *"The entertainments":* Simon Raven and Martin Shuttleworth, "Graham Greene, The Art of Fiction, No. 3," *The Paris Review,* issue 3 (Autumn 1953), https://theparisreview.org/interviews/5180/the-art-of-fiction-no-3-graham-greene.

364 *"[I]n the main":* *Literary Life,* 103–104.

364 *"Time will sort us out":* Ibid., 104.

364 *"NOT TOO BAD":* Laura Furman, "Vanities: Lone Star Lit," *Vanity Fair,* July 1986, https://archive.vanityfair.com/article/1986/lone-star-lit.

364 *"What always impressed me":* Ibid.

365 *"It was one of the most deflating speeches":* Ibid.

365 *"I might as well have been living":* *Literary Life,* 113.

366 *"crowds of famous writers":* Ibid., 125–26.

366 *"labyrinth of projects":* Ibid., 129.

366 *"fern-bar writers"*: From a conversation with Donald Barthelme in 1989, I know the men discussed this topic; the wording here comes from Donald Barthelme, "Terms of Estrangement," in *Taking Stock: A Larry McMurtry Casebook,* 105.

366 *"You can kill this program"*: Abigail Santamaria, "Madelaine L'Engle's Private Correspondence with Ahmad Rahman," *Vanity Fair,* January 29, 2021, https://www.vanityfair.com /style/2021/01/madelaine-lengles-private-correspondence-with-ahmad-rahman.

367 *"The possibility of giving offense"*: This and further quotes from McMurtry's talk on censorship are from "Censorship and the Individual Talent," draft copy, Susan Sontag Papers.

367 *"brattish"*: McMurtry to Susan Sontag, October 30, 1990.

368 *"The Congress report"*: Larry McMurtry, "President's Report from the 55th International PEN Congress, Madeira, May 6–13, 1990," draft copy, Susan Sontag Papers.

368 *"PEN flops around"*: McMurtry to Susan Sontag, September 15, 1990.

368 *"[S]eeing what they have to deal with"*: McMurtry to Susan Sontag, October 30, 1990.

368 *"the West Texas Gogol"*: Inscription from McMurtry to Susan Sontag in a copy of *Some Can Whistle,* 1989, Susan Sontag Papers.

368 *"fearful of all forms"*: McMurtry to Susan Sontag, August 3, 1989.

368 *"my mother went"*: McMurtry to Susan Sontag, August 18, 1989.

368 *"would have dropped dead"*: McMurtry to Susan Sontag, August 20, 1989.

369 At one point, he estimated her papers: McMurtry to Susan Sontag, June 29, 1989.

369 *"you [could] stay"*: McMurtry to Susan Sontag, December 9, 1988.

369 *"the greatest living morbity collector"*: McMurtry to Susan Sontag, January 9, 1989.

370 *"Oh, wow!"*: *Literary Life,* 142.

370 *"I miss you very much"*: McMurtry to Susan Sontag, October 30, 1990.

370 *"Don't ever do that again"*: *Literary Life,* 144.

370 *"decimated"*: Benjamin Moser, *Sontag: Her Life and Work* (New York: Ecco, 2019), 591.

370 *"As a novelist"*: McMurtry to Susan Sontag, December 9, 1988.

370 *"I'm proceeding"*: McMurtry to Susan Sontag, January 16, 1990.

371 *"I'm smoking on"*: McMurtry to Susan Sontag, February 8, 1990.

371 *"I live mostly"*: McMurtry to Susan Sontag, October 8, 1990.

371 *"subvert the Western myth"*: *Walter Benjamin at the Dairy Queen,* 55.

372 *"debating with himself"*: Inscription from McMurtry to Susan Sontag in *Some Can Whistle.*

372 *"I was a loner"*: *Some Can Whistle,* 49.

372 *"brainy, sexual whistle"*: Ibid., 348.

372 *Mark Twain's polemic"*: See Mark Twain, "Fenimore Cooper's Literary Offenses," 1895, https://pbs.org/kenburns/mark-twain/fenimore.

372 *"[T]here's a really good movie"*: McMurtry to Susan Sontag, October 8, 1990.

373 *"I must say"*: Ibid.

373 *"When Larry said he was writing a sequel"*: George Hickenlooper, *Picture This: The Times of Peter Bogdanovich in Archer City, Texas* (Nelson Entertainment, 1989), dailymotion .com/video/xqdjx9.

373 *"a lot different this time"*: Nina J. Easton, "The Next Picture Show: Peter Bogdanovich and the cast of his 1971 classic reunite for a sequel's sake," *Los Angeles Times,* October 15, 1989, https://www.latimes.com/archives/la-xpm-1989–10–15-ca -476-story.html.

373 *"[T]here was no attention"*: Philip Wuntch, "'Texasville' Rekindled Tumult," *South Florida Sun-Sentinel,* September 29, 1990, https://www.sun-sentinel.com/news/fl-xpm -1990–09–29-9002160952-story.html.

373   *"confronting everything"*: Ibid.

373   *"[A]ll of a sudden"*: Andrew Yule, *Picture Shows: The Life and Films of Peter Bogdanovich* (New York: Limelight Editions, 1992), 235.

373   *"[I]t's rare in one's career"*: Easton, "The Next Picture Show."

374   *"some tension"*: Wuntch, "'Texasville' Rekindled Tumult."

374   *"On the day hundreds of people"*: Robert Medley, "Town Real to Reel Archer City Says Cheese to Film Sequel," *The Oklahoman,* September 11, 1989, https://www.oklahoman .com/story/news/1989/09/11/town-real-to-reel-archer-city-says-cheese-to-film-sequel /62601844007/.

374   *"I don't give a shit"*: Hickenlooper, *Picture This.*

375   *"What are you doing here?"*: Yule, *Picture Shows,* 237.

375   *"As we talked"*: This and subsequent quotes from Ceil Cleveland, *Whatever Happened to Jacy Farrow?* (Denton, TX: University of North Texas Press, 1997), 312–13.

CHAPTER 22

376   *"getting too delicate"*: McMurtry to Susan Sontag, November 21, 1990.

376   *"He's like a tiny holy man"*: McMurtry to Grace David, November 11, 1990.

376   *"the Baptists . . . will all get killed"*: McMurtry to Max Crawford, December 12, 1997.

377   *"and this Holstein"*: Bruce Newman, "Smile When You Say That, Partner," *Los Angeles Times,* October 30, 1994, https://www.latimes.com/archives/la-xpm-1994–10–30-ca -56528-story.html.

377   *"I was coughing"*: *Walter Benjamin at the Dairy Queen,* 141.

377   *"I had forgotten"*: Ibid.

377   *"didn't think I looked too good"*: Newman, "Smile When You Say That, Partner."

377   *"but I was in a room"*: Ibid.

378   *"She had . . . merely lived"*: Larry McMurtry, *The Evening Star* (New York: Pocket Books, 1992), 539.

378   *"an author's boredom"*: Thomas R. Edwards, "The Evening Star," *The New York Review of Books,* August 13, 1992, 54.

378   *"the Other Place"*: *The Evening Star,* 605.

379   *"a spiritual realm"*: Roger Walton Jones, *Larry McMurtry and the Victorian Novel* (College Station, TX: Texas A&M University Press, 1994), 69.

379   *"an indecisive sound"*: *The Evening Star,* 605.

379   *"the music had taken him"*: Ibid., 612–13.

379   *Dwight Harkin*: See "Pioneers of Heart Surgery," *Nova,* April 7, 1997, https://pbs.org /wgbh/nova/articles/pioneers-heart-surgery.

379   *"if the definition of a heart attack"*: McMurtry to Susan Sontag, November 26, 1991.

379   *"If I can't be an overworking overachiever"*: Ibid.

380   *"physical recovery"*: Larry McMurtry, "By Pass Surgery: A Patient's View," unpublished draft, Larry McMurtry and Diana Ossana Papers, 1890–2011, Woodson Research Center, Fondren Library, Rice University, 1.

380   *"healed and fine"*: McMurtry to Grace David, January 15, 1992.

380   *"the most minor soreness"*: McMurtry to Susan Sontag, December 22, 1991.

380   *"awful feeling of menace"*: Leslie Silko, excerpt from "The Border Patrol State," *Tucson Weekly,* September 26, 1996, https://www.tucsonweekly.com/tw/09–26–96/cover .htm.

380   *"We're kind of like Sancho and the Don"*: Josh Olson and Joe Dante, "Oscar Winning

Co-Writer of 'Brokeback Mountain' Diana Ossana," *The Movies That Made Me* podcast, Season 3, Episode 35, https://www.trailersfromhell.com/podcast/diana-ossana.

380 *"to resume"*: "By Pass Surgery: A Patient's View," 1.

380 *"I felt that I had become an outline"*: Ibid., 2.

381 *"I felt as if I were holding up the ceiling"*: Ibid., 3.

381 *"[A]ccording to current medical knowledge"*: Pim van Lommel, *Consciousness Beyond Life: The Science of the Near-Death Experience* (New York: HarperOne, 2010), vii.

381 *"I have felt largely posthumous"*: "By Pass Surgery: A Patient's View," 3–4.

382 *"I [grew up] observing people"*: Randy Haberkamp, "Discussion with Diana Ossana at the Samuel Goldwyn Theater," August 4, 2008, https://www.findingbrokeback.com /Interviews/Ossana/Ossana1.html.

382 *"My first real experience with film"*: Olson and Dante, "Oscar Winning Co-Writer of 'Brokeback Mountain' Diana Ossana."

382 *"He [went] to Vietnam"*: Ibid.

383 *"had come to Tucson"*: This and subsequent quotes concerning Joe Bonanno are from Olson and Dante, "Oscar Winning Co-Writer of 'Brokeback Mountain' Diana Ossana."

384 *"I [had] ceased to be able to be alone"*: "By Pass Surgery: A Patient's View," 3.

384 *"It just so happened"*: Casey Combs, "An Unlikely Team Produces 'Pretty Boy Floyd,'" *Los Angeles Times*, December 11, 1994, https://www.latimes.com/archives/la-xpm -1994–12–11-mm-7709-story.html.

384 *"He was falling apart"*: Mark Horowitz, "Larry McMurtry's Dream Job," *New York Times*, December 7, 1997, https://archive.nytimes.com/www.nytimes.com/books/97/12/07 /home/article2.html?_r=2.

384 *"because he seemed to be comfortable"*: Combs, "An Unlikely Team Produces 'Pretty Boy Floyd.'"

384 *"heaviness behind my eyes"*: "By Pass Surgery: A Patient's View," 8.

384 *"but it came rapidly"*: *Walter Benjamin at the Dairy Queen*, 145.

384 *"I was in the rhythm"*: Horowitz, "Larry McMurtry's Dream Job."

385 *"As I was doing it"*: Anne Thompson, "How Larry McMurtry's 'Brokeback Mountain' Writing Partner Diana Ossana Saved Him from Despair," IndieWire, March 27, 2021, https://www.indiewire.com/2021/03/larry-mcmurtry-diana-ossana-brokeback-mountain -oscar-1234626324/.

385 *"He would have to live"*: Horowitz, "Larry McMurtry's Dream Job."

385 *"For about ten minutes"*: Ibid.

385 *"Mama"*: Ibid.

CHAPTER 23

386 *"batting them away"*: Anne Thompson, "How Larry McMurtry's 'Brokeback Mountain' Writing Partner Diana Ossana Saved Him from Despair," IndieWire, March 27, 2021, https://www.indiewire.com/2021/03/larry-mcmurtry-diana-ossana-brokeback-mountain -oscar-1234626324/.

386 *"It was like his essence"*: Michael Hoinski, "'Lonesome Dove' Legend Larry McMurtry on Fiction, Money, Womanizing, and Old Age," *Grantland*, May 22, 2014, https:// grantland.com/hollywood-prospectus/larry-mcmurtry-lonesome-dove-new-book -interview/.

386 *"fascinated with the difference:"* Thompson, "How Larry McMurtry's 'Brokeback Mountain' Writing Partner Diana Ossana Saved Him from Despair."

386   *"I wanted to get Larry back"*: Mark Horowitz, "Larry McMurtry's Dream Job," *New York Times,* December 7, 1997, https://archive.nytimes.com/www.nytimes.com/books/97/12 /07/home/article2.html?_r=2.

386   *"I can't make this character sympathetic"*: Bruce Newman, "Smile When You Say That, Partner," *Los Angeles Times,* October 30, 1994, https://www.latimes.com/archives/la-xpm -1994–10–30-ca-56528-story.html.

386   *"I was getting sort of desperate"*: Ibid.

386   *"I could see something sparkling"*: Thompson, "How Larry McMurtry's 'Brokeback Mountain' Writing Partner Diana Ossana Saved Him from Despair."

387   *"first-stage-of-the-rocket"*: Newman, "Smile When You Say That, Partner."

387   *"his juices going"*: Ibid.

387   *"a database with opinions"*: Skip Hollandsworth interview with Larry McMurtry and Diana Ossana, Arts & Letters Live, May 17, 2014, youtube.com/watch?v=rsa1yEvE3Cg.

387   *"we still had a certain amount"*: Newman, "Smile When You Say That, Partner."

387   *"I was very worried about our styles"*: Casey Combs, "An Unlikely Team Produces 'Pretty Boy Floyd,'" *Los Angeles Times,* December 11, 1994, https://www.latimes.com/archives/la -xpm-1994–12–11-mm-7709-story.html.

387   *"I realized"*: Ibid.

387   *"I was excited"*: Newman, "Smile When You Say That, Partner."

388   *"Larry and Diana's novel"*: Conversation with Michael Wallis.

388   *"rather inert quality"*: Newman, "Smile When You Say That, Partner."

388   *"What is a guy like Larry McMurtry"*: Sidney Zion, "A Legend in J. Edgar Hoover's Time," *New York Times,* October 16, 1994, https://www.nytimes.com/books/99/01/10/specials /mcmurtry-floyd.html.

388   *"slow, leisurely"*: Joyce Maynard, "The Eve of Destruction," *Los Angeles Times,* January 19, 1997, https://www.latimes.com/archives/la-xpm-1997–01–19-bk-19963-story.html.

388   *"Mr. McMurtry and Ms. Ossana"*: Scott Martelle, "Zeke and Ned," *New York Times,* January 19, 1997, https://www.nytimes.com/books/07/01/19/bib/970119.rv124037.html.

389   *"[I]f you try to do something different"*: Newman, "Smile When You Say That, Partner."

389   *"I didn't want to deal with Hollywood"*: Combs, "An Unlikely Team Produces 'Pretty Boy Floyd.'"

389   *"riding on Larry's coattails"*: Newman, "Smile When You Say That, Partner."

389   *"the icon"*: Combs, "An Unlikely Team Produces 'Pretty Boy Floyd.'"

389   *"Everybody at [Simon & Schuster]"*: Newman, "Smile When You Say That, Partner."

389   *Yoko Ono:* Ibid.

389   *"It was so odd to me"*: Ibid.

389   *"companion"*: Ibid.

389   *"There's bound to be speculation"*: Ibid.

389   *"Well, I love Larry"*: Michael Hoinski, "'Lonesome Dove' Legend Larry McMurtry on Fiction, Money, Womanizing, and Old Age," *Grantland,* May 22, 2014, https:// grantland.com/hollywood-prospectus/larry-mcmurtry-lonesome-dove-new-book -interview/.

389   *"She's a force of nature"*: Beverly Lowry email to the author, June 8, 2021.

389   *"Everyone was suspicious"*: Skip Hollandsworth interview with Susan Freudenheim, undated, unpublished, courtesy of Skip Hollandsworth.

389   *"I don't know"*: Thompson, "How Larry McMurtry's 'Brokeback Mountain' Writing Partner Diana Ossana Saved Him from Despair."

389   *"Call it an* amitié amoureuse*"*: Newman, "Smile When You Say That, Partner."

390 "Father Freakin' Knows Best?": Ibid.

390 *"I think they [saw] it"*: Ibid.

390 *"One thing"*: Ibid.

390 *"I'm very annoyed"*: Ibid.

390 *"I want to give good seats"*: Michael Shnayerson and Annette Tapert, "'Swifty' Lazar's Legacy," *Vanity Fair,* April 21, 1994, https://www.vanityfair.com/news/1994/04/michael-shnayerson-199404.

390 *"world-class haircut"*: Larry McMurtry, "Swifty Lazar: Evolved Heart, Evolved Style," *Los Angeles Times,* January 7, 1994, https://www.latimes.com/la-bk-larry-mcmurtry-1994–01–07-story.html.

391 *"geriatric table"*: Larry McMurtry, "A Life for the Star," *The New York Review of Books,* April 26, 2012, https:www.nybooks.com/articles/2012/04/26/life-star.

391 *"perhaps to say hello"*: Ibid.

391 *"sort of the end"*: Hollywood, 88.

391 *"such happy news"*: Ibid., 83.

392 *"he rose out of sedation"*: "Swifty Lazar: Evolved Heart, Evolved Style."

392 *"There are already new areas"*: John Brodie, "WMA Inks McMurtry and Ossana," *Variety,* March 28, 1994, https://variety.com/1994/biz/news/wma-inks-mcmurtry-and-ossana-119717/.

392 *"was willing to entertain bids"*: Sarah Lyall, "McMurtry Keeps Publisher after Seeking Other Offers," *Deseret News,* February 5, 1994, https://www.deseret.com/1994/2/5/19090309/mcmurtry-keeps-publisher-after-seeking-other-offers.

392 *"Wylie's inquiries"*: Ibid.

393 *"I worry about where the next million dollars"*: Hoinski, "'Lonesome Dove' Legend Larry McMurtry on Fiction, Money, Womanizing, and Old Age."

393 *"name had little pull"*: Hollywood, 91.

393 *"the executives at the various studios"*: Ibid., 90–91.

393 *"I really wanted to be [Aurora]"*: Karina Longworth, "Polly Platt: The Invisible Woman: Episode Ten: How Did It End?," *You Must Remember This* podcast.

393 *"Terms of Endearment every year"*: Joe Leydon, "On Its Own Terms," *Los Angeles Times,* April 7, 1996, https://www.latimes.com/archives/la-xpm-1996–04–07-ca-55802-story.html.

393 *"He did not trust me"*: Longworth, "Polly Platt: The Invisible Woman: Episode Ten."

394 *"I'm coming for you"*: Ibid.

394 *"a tragedy"*: Ibid.

394 *"haunting tale"*: Ibid.

394 *"On the weekends"*: Ibid.

394 *"She lost her agency"*: Ibid.

394 *"If you could bring back to life"*: Noah Charney, "Larry McMurtry: How I Write," *The Daily Beast,* July 11, 2017, https://www.thedailybeast.com/larry-mcmurtry-how-i-write.

395 *"new areas of . . . business"*: Brodie, "WMA Inks McMurtry and Ossana."

395 *"The advantage we had"*: Hollywood, 93.

395 *"meander"*: John J. O'Connor, "A 'Lonesome Dove' Sequel by McMurtry Himself," *New York Times,* November 10, 1995, https://www.nytimes.com/1995/11/10/arts/tv-weekend-a-lonesome-dove-sequel-by-mcmurtry-himself.html.

395 *"I think the members of Congress"*: Allen R. Myerson, "Following Capt. McMurtry, Take by Take," *New York Times,* May 12, 1996, https://www.nytimes.com/1996/05/12/arts/television-following-capt-mcmurtry-take-by-take-html.

395   *"We've had to do it"*: Ibid.

396   *"He gets away with things"*: Ibid.

396   *"Apparently you can slice and dice"*: Tom Shales, "Tome on the Range," *Washington Post*, May 12, 1996, https://www.washingtonpost.com/archive/lifestyle/style/1996/05/12 /tome-on-the-range/5f551d15–9f8a-43e2–65a1–039e76ee6a95/.

396   *"I did it"*: This and subsequent dialogue is from Myerson, "Following Capt. McMurtry, Take by Take."

396   *"overalls and blond bangs"*: Ibid.

396   *"The kids were up"*: Ibid.

396   *"You can't let anything slip by"*: Ibid.

396   *"tedious"*: Brian Lowry, "Comanche Moon," *Variety*, January 10, 2008, https://www .variety.com/2008/scene/markets-festivals/comanche-moon-1200553680.

399   *"Whipped they might be"*: *Lonesome Dove*, 27.

399   *"huge Indian"*: Ibid., 33.

399   *"at how thin and poor"*: Ibid., 505.

400   *"atheisticall"*: Mary Rowlandson cited in Alexander Lalrinzama, "Critiquing the Representation of Native Americans in Selected Narratives of Louis L'Amour and Larry McMurtry," Department of English, Mizoram University, April 2009, 68–69.

400   *"[T]he Westerner"*: Edward Said cited in Lalrinzama, "Critiquing the Representation of Native Americans," 66.

401   *"You don't always get better"*: Kathryn Jones, "I've Written Enough Fiction," *Texas Monthly*, December 1997, https://www.texasmonthly.com/articles/ive-written-enough-fiction/.

402   *"McMurtry sounds a little like"*: Horowitz, "Larry McMurtry's Dream Job."

402   *"It's wonderful"*: Jones, "I've Written Enough Fiction."

402   *"not-quite-relationships"*: Mary Kaye Schilling, "How Larry McMurtry Went from Cowhand to Top Novelist," *Entertainment Weekly*, November 23, 2003, https://www.ew.com /articles/2003/11/23/how-larry-mcmurtry-went-from-cowhand-to-top-novelist/.

402   *"[H]e would be frantic"*: Newman, "Smile When You Say That, Partner."

402   *"renovating the cowboy"*: Mervyn Rothstein, "A Texan Who Likes to Deflate the Legends of the Golden West," *New York Times*, November 1, 1988, https://www.nytimes.com /1988/11/01/books/a-texan-who-likes-to-deflate-the-legends-of-the-golden-west.html.

403   *"Archerites"*: McMurtry to Max Crawford, December 3, 1995.

403   *"the eyes of assassins"*: Ray Isle in conversation with the author, June 1, 2021.

403   *"I'd go running"*: Conversation with Mike Evans.

404   *Booked Up's offerings*: See David Streitfeld, "Lonesome Trove," *Washington Post*, February 22, 1998, https://www.washingtonpost.com/archive/lifestyle/travel/1998/02/22 /lonesome-trove/8c9cea6f-0855–4f7e-99d2–27c1f671e8cf/. See also Ray Isle, "Three Days in McMurtryville," *Stanford Magazine*, November/December 1999, https:// stanfordmag.org/contents/three-days-in-mcmurtryville.

404   *"Dear sir"*: Isle, "Three Days in McMurtryville."

404   *"In your heart; A woman's love"*: Thomas Swick, "Book Rancher McMurtry Rides Herd Over Words," *Chicago Tribune*, May 23, 2001, https://www.chicagotribune.com/sns -archercity-texas-story.html.

404   *"Say you were looking for minor writers"*: Isle, "Three Days in McMurtryville."

404   *"He's pretty calm now"*: Jones, "I've Written Enough Fiction."

404   *"I spent a lot of time in New York"*: Horowitz, "Larry McMurtry's Dream Job."

405   *"evil woman"*: Isle, "Three Days in McMurtryville."

405   *"I'll make you something smaller"*: Isle, "Three Days in McMurtryville."

405 *"as indifferent"*: Jones, "I've Written Enough Fiction."

405 *"The old folks don't read"*: Ian Buruma, "Driving Texas: A European Take," *Travel and Leisure,* April 1, 2009, https://www.travelandleisure.com/trip-idea/driving-texas-a-european-take.

405 *She and Ceil:* See Jean Simmons, "Texas Town Takes a Page from Literary Legend," *Orlando Sentinel,* February 28, 1999, https://www.orlandosentinel.com/news/os-xpm -1999–02–28–9902240509-story.html.

405 *"We only have enough business"*: Streitfeld, "Lonesome Trove."

406 *Susan Sontag: Walter Benjamin at the Dairy Queen,* 77.

CHAPTER 24

407 *"low, almost vegetable form"*: Paradise, 75.

410 *"Hi Mom, I'm back"*: Ibid., 159.

410 *"I hope my left eye"*: Michael Hoinski, "'Lonesome Dove' Legend Larry McMurtry on Fiction, Money, Womanizing, and Old Age," *Grantland,* May 22, 2014, https://grantland .com/hollywood-prospectus/larry-mcmurtry-lonesome-dove-new-book-interview/.

411 *"Tired of fiction"*: McMurtry to Max Crawford, October 17, 1997.

411 *"I've written enough fiction"*: Kathryn Jones, "I've Written Enough Fiction," *Texas Monthly,* December 1997, https://www.texasmonthly.com/articles/ive-written-enough-fiction/.

411 *"[Larry's] views"*: Sara Ossana in an email to the author, October 5, 2021.

411 *"pleasures"*: Verlyn Klinkenborg, "Once More, with Harmony," *New York Times,* May 21, 1995, https://www.nytimes.com/books/99/01/10/specials/mcmurtry-late.html.

411 *"You're cutting all ties"*: Larry McMurtry, *Duane's Depressed* (New York: Simon & Schuster, 1999), 281.

411 *"Mr. McMurtry's career"*: Klinkenborg, "Once More, with Harmony."

412 *"One of the things I've always found compelling"*: David Ulin, "'The Late Child' by Larry McMurtry," *Los Angeles Times,* November 14, 2008, https://www.latimes.com/la-bk-larry -mcmurtry-1995–06–04-story.html.

413 *"So those two stories are ended"*: Duane's Depressed, 430.

413 *"to say something simplistic"*: Ibid., 133.

414 *"Thunder had rumbled"*: Ibid., 384.

414 *"As he watched the river"*: Ibid., 278–79.

414 *"[McMurtry] proves again"*: Robert Houston, "Happy Trails," *New York Times,* February 21, 1999, https://www.nytimes.com/books/99/02/21/reviews/990221.21houst.html.

415 *"full auto"*: This and all other quotes regarding the Branch Davidian standoff Larry McMurtry, "No More Cane on the Brazos: The Destruction of the Branch Davidians," rough draft, 1993, Larry McMurtry and Diana Ossana Papers, 1890–2011, Woodson Research Center, Rice University.

417 *"awesome"*: Larry McMurtry, "On the Road," *The New York Review of Books,* December 5, 2002, https://www.nybooks.com/articles/2002/12/05/on-the-road/.

417 *She addressed lawsuits:* See Lance Kramer and Aaron Mesh, "Sometimes a Great Lawsuit," *Willamette Week,* August 26, 2008, https://www.week/com/portland/article-9448 -sometimes-a-great-lawsuit.html.

418 *"finally detonated"*: "On the Road."

CHAPTER 25

419 *"launched her ascent"*: Literary Life, 145.

419 *"Hope these photographs"*: McMurtry to Susan Sontag, August 3, 1989.

419 *"After all"*: Larry McMurtry, "The Trouble with Arizona," *The New York Review of Books,* June 24, 2010, https://nybooks.com/article/2010/06/24/the-trouble-with-arizona.

420 *"a really ugly city"*: Phil Villarreal, "He's Smart & Lucky," *Tucson,* April 10, 2008, https://tucson.com/entertainment/hes-smart-lucky/article_7188f460–8f9c-5718–87b8 -e80803eb4d3.html.

421 *"The claim is"*: James Atlas, "McMurtry Country," *Architectural Digest,* September 30, 2000, https://www.architecturaldigest.com/story/mcmurtry-article-102000.

421 *"Sunset is the magic time"*: Ibid.

421 *"There is something hallucinatory"*: Ibid.

421 *"What I have in Archer City"*: Ibid.

422 *"I went out there"*: Villarreal, "He's Smart & Lucky."

422 *"There's a story"*: Randy Haberkamp, "Discussion with Diana Ossana at the Samuel Gold-wyn Theater, Part 1," August 4, 2008, https://www.findingbrokeback.com/Interviews /Ossana/Ossana1.html.

422 *"I have insomnia"*: Ibid.

422 *"If I recall"*: Ibid.

422 *"I was very anxious"*: Ibid.

423 *"I asked Larry"*: Ibid.

423 *"We admired your story"*: Ibid.

423 *"I had noticed an older ranch hand"*: Annie Proulx, "Getting Movied," in *Brokeback Mountain: Story to Screenplay*, Annie Proulx, Larry McMurtry, and Diana Ossana (New York: Scribner, 2005), 129–30.

424 *"I was an aging female writer"*: Ibid., 133.

424 *"long bones; enrich"*: Amy Dawes, "Larry McMurtry and Diana Ossana," *Variety,* December 18, 2005, https://variety.com/2005/film/awards/larry-mcmurtry-and-diana-ossana -1117934900/.

424 *"story that had been sitting there"*: Larry McMurtry, "Adapting Brokeback Mountain," in *Brokeback Mountain: Story to Screenplay,* 140.

424 *"strong, long American tradition"*: Ibid.

424 *"[T]he Code of the West"*: In a Narrow Grave: Essays on Texas, 61.

425 *"All you two done"*: Lonesome Dove, 831.

425 *"evident on the front page"*: McMurtry cited in David Lamble, "Brokeback's Back Story," *Bay Area Reporter*, February 28, 2006, https://www.ebar.com/arts_&_culture/books /223900.

425 *"inward"*: Ibid.

425 *"felt like someone was pulling"*: Annie Proulx, "Brokeback Mountain," in *Brokeback Mountain: Story to Screenplay*, 9.

425 *"ENNIS rides"*: Larry McMurtry and Diana Ossana in *Brokeback Mountain: Story to Screenplay,* 20.

425 *"highway crew"*: Annie Proulx in *Brokeback Mountain: Story to Screenplay,* 9.

425 *In the screenplay, roads*: For an extended discussion of *Brokeback Mountain*'s cinematic imagery, see Rodney Stenning Edgecombe, "The Formal Design of 'Brokeback Mountain,'" *Film Criticism* 31, no. 3 (Spring 2007), 2–14.

425 *"accumulation of very small details"*: Annie Proulx, "Getting Movied," 138.

425 *"I pretty much gave up"*: Ibid., 135.

426 *"the biggest obstacle"*: Haberkamp, "Discussion with Diana Ossana."

426 *"I read fifteen pages"*: Johnni Macke, "Stars Who Turned Down Roles in 'Brokeback Mountain': Josh Hartnett, Leonardo DiCaprio, Mark Wahlberg, More," *Us,* December 13, 2021, https://www.usmagazine.com/entertainment/pictures/celebrities-who-turned -down-brokeback-mountain-roles/mark-wahlberg-13/.

426   *"sent it to four or five different directors"*: Haberkamp, "Discussion with Diana Ossana."

426   *"Diana, don't worry"*: Ibid.

426   *"You really ought to look"*: Ibid.

426   *"I don't want to watch anymore; That young man's"*: Ibid.

426   *"wasn't macho enough"*: Macke, "Stars Who Turned Down Roles in 'Brokeback Mountain.'"

426   *"It's the most beautiful script"*: Ibid.

427   *I shared my trailer"*: Haberkamp, "Discussion with Diana Ossana."

427   *"[T]hey found Matthew's body"*: Diana Ossana, "Climbing Brokeback Mountain," in *Brokeback Mountain: Story to Screenplay,* 146.

427   *"Whenever I would feel"*: Ibid., 149–50.

427   *"Hasn't anyone told him"*: Patrick Goldstein, "Grumpy Charm Shines Through," *Los Angeles Times,* December 13, 2005, https://www.latimes.com/archives/la-xpm-2005-dec-13-et-goldstein13-story.html.

427   *"Larry is such an odd fellow"*: Randy Haberkamp, "Discussion with Diana Ossana at the Samuel Goldwyn Theater, Part 2," August 4, 2008, http://www.findingbrokeback.com/Interviews/Ossana/Ossana2.html.

428   *"I was not at all prepared"*: Ossana, "Climbing Brokeback Mountain," 150.

428   *"Moving"*: Dawes, "Larry McMurtry and Diana Ossana."

428   *McMurtry and Ossana were feted:* See *Backstage* staff, "Nominees Reflect on Their 'Great News,'" *Backstage,* December 13, 2005, https://www.backstage.com/magazine/article/nominees-reflect-great-news-27154/.

428   *"Marriage in this state"*: Texas Proposition 2, passed November 8, 2005, https://en.wikipedia.org/wiki/2005_Texas_Proposition_2.

428   *"If there is some other state"*: Daniel Kusner, "CAN'T QUIT—EVER: McMurtry promises that 'Brokeback' will stem trend of Texas homophobia," https://www.danielkusner.com/blog/mcmurtry-promises-that-brokeback-will-save-texas.

428   *"If the governor wants to say"*: Ibid.

429   *"You know about that McMurtry?"*: Paul Knight, "Broken Brotherhood," *Center and Main,* October 15, 2013, https://centerandmain.org.

429   *"while strangers prodded"*: This and all other quotes regarding the Hollywood awards season, unless otherwise noted, from Larry McMurtry and Diana Ossana, "Mixed Pickles in Hollywood," *The New York Review of Books,* March 1, 2011, https://nybooks.com/articles/2011/03/01/mixed-pickles-in-hollywood.

430   *Annie Proulx noticed a purple tinge:* Annie Proulx, "Blood on the Red Carpet," *The Guardian,* March 11, 2006, https://www.theguardian.com/books/2006/mar/11/awardsandprizes.oscars2006.

431   *"If you are looking for smart judging"*: Ibid.

431   *"The duty of art"*: Diana Ossana Academy Awards acceptance speech, 78th Academy Awards, March 5, 2006, youtube.com/watch?v=0-W1RmiyN5M.

432   *"smarts, guts, drive"*: Larry McMurtry Academy Awards acceptance speech, March 5, 2006, youtube.com/watch?v=0-W1RmiyN5M.

CHAPTER 26

433   *"There's something about him"*: Patrick Goldstein, "Grumpy Charm Shines Through," *Los Angeles Times,* December 13, 2005, https://www.latimes.com/archives/la-xpm-2005-dec-13-et-goldstein13-story.html.

433   *Diana and Sara left:* McMurtry relates part of this incident in *Hollywood,* 145–46.

433   *"French woman in Tucson":* Literary Life, 9.

434   *He remembered he had been driving:* For a description of this incident from James McMurtry's point of view, see jamesmcmurtry.com/blog-archive.html.

436   *"I'm funnier the grouchier I get":* Phil Villarreal, "McMurtry, Ossana Have Special Bond," *Tucson,* February 14, 2010, https://tucson.com/entertainment/books-and-literature /mcmurtry-ossana-have-special-bond/article_920be603–0c2a-50a1–899e-c4560fcabf6c .html.

436   *"wide red tie":* Patt Morrison, "From Lonesome Dove to Lonesome Book Lover," *Huffington Post,* May 1, 2008, https://www.huffpost.com/entry/from lonesome-dove-to-lon_b_99622.

436   *McMurtry said that, in 1963:* Ibid.

436   *"Even thinking about them":* Ibid.

436   *"I fear for libraries":* Los Angeles Public Library, "An Afternoon with Larry McMurtry," hosted by William Deverell, May 1, 2008, lapl.org/books-emedia/podcasts/aloud /afternoon-library-mcmurtry.

437   *"can't bring us love":* Morrison, "From Lonesome Dove to Lonesome Book Lover."

437   *"The great majority":* "An Afternoon with Larry McMurtry."

437   *"However, there is a point":* Ibid.

437   *"Curtis was a big, big reader":* Ibid.

437   *"I don't think":* Morrison, "From Lonesome Dove to Lonesome Book Lover."

437   *"tsunami of technology":* David D. Medina, "Lonesome Larry McMurtry Ponders the Fate of Books," *Literal,* issue 17 (2008), https://literalmagazine.com/lonesome-larry -mcmurtry-ponders-the-fate-of-books/.

437   *"internalized some of the store's":* Jeff Tietz, "A Bookish Paradise," *Texas Co-op Power,* August 2009, https://texascooppower.com/a-bookish-paradise/.

437   *"She'd hung a guide":* Ibid.

438   *"Having hog problems?":* Ibid.

438   *"teenage bands":* Morrison, "From Lonesome Dove to Lonesome Book Lover."

438   *"people come from":* Tietz, "A Bookish Paradise."

438   *"I did everything I could do":* Julia Robb, "The Last Picture Show, for Real," *The Texas Observer,* April 6, 2007, https://www.texasobserver.org/2471-the-last-picture-show-for -real/.

439   *"He's what's keeping the town alive":* City Confidential, "Archer City Under Suspicion," narrated by Paul Winfield, dailymotion.com/video/xZrmfi.2.

439   *"He's been a bear":* Villarreal, "McMurtry, Ossana Have Special Bond."

439   *"house of many creatures":* Ibid.

439   *"restless, roving intellect":* Skip Hollandsworth, "The Minor Regional Novelist," *Texas Monthly,* July 2016, https://www.texasmonthly.com/arts-entertainment/larry-mcmurtry -minor-regional-novelist/.

440   *"when my whole family was here":* Ibid.

440   *"The older the violin":* Ibid.

440   *"become the party of stale air":* This and other quotes regarding Rick Perry are from Larry McMurtry, "The Rick Perry Hustle," *The New York Review of Books,* October 1, 2011, https://www.nybooks.com/online/2011/10/01/larry-mcmurtry-rick-perry-hustle/.

440   *"More people died":* Larry McMurtry, "American Tragedy," *The New York Review of Books,* January 11, 2011, https://www.nybooks.com/online/2011/01/11/american -tragedy/.

441 *"created a centralized multilevel political system"*: Cited in Larry McMurtry, "The Conquering Indians," *The New York Review of Books,* May 29, 2008, https://nybooks.com/articles/2008/05/29/the-conquering-indians/.

441 *"How can the Comanche empire"*: Ibid.

442 *"If we were to conceive"*: Patricia Limerick, "The Midnight Rodeo: Larry McMurtry, Me, and Our Abject Failure to Feud," Center of the American West, University of Colorado Boulder, March 2021, https://www.centerwest.org/archives/25197.

442 *"[W]e were regarded with astonishment"*: "The Conquering Indians."

443 *Rudolph Muus:* See Larry McMurtry, "The West Without Chili," *The New York Review of Books,* October 22, 1998, https://www.nybooks.com/articles/1998/10/22/the-west-without-chili/.

443 *"the battery of Venus"*: Cited in Don Graham, "Not Moving On," *Texas Monthly,* May 2003, https://www.texasmonthly.com/articles/not-moving-on/.

443 *"the Berrybender version"*: Verlyn Klinkenborg, "Plunging In," *New York Times,* December 7, 2003, https://www.nytimes.com/2003/12/07/books/plunging-in.html.

444 *"boredom is the essence"*: Don Graham, "Father Knows West," *Texas Monthly,* December 2011, https://www.texasmonthly.com/articles/father-knows-west/.

444 *"unedited"*: Chelsea Cain, "Cowboys Are My Weakness," *New York Times,* June 18, 2006, https://www.nytimes.com/2006/06/18/books/review/18cain.html.

444 *"Mr. McMurtry . . . hasn't made it easy"*: Dwight Garner, "Bookish Cowboy Heads Off to the Corral," *New York Times,* December 11, 2009, https://www.nytimes.com/2009/12/11/books/11book.html.

444 *"She had been a caregiver too long"*: Larry McMurtry, *Loop Group* (New York: Simon & Schuster, 2004), 47.

444 *"the book's primary classification"*: Liesl Schillinger, "'Loop Group': 60-Plus Sunset Strip," *New York Times,* January 2, 2005, https://www.nytimes.com/2005/01/02/books/review/loop-group-60-plus-sunset-strip.html.

445 *"The Chick Lit genre"*: Janet Maslin, "Older, but Keeping Up With the Bridget Joneses," *New York Times,* December 14, 2004, https://www.nytimes.com/2004/12/14/books/older-but-keeping-up-with-the-bridget-joneses.html.

445 *"He's too good"*: Norman Mailer cited in Hollandsworth, "Minor Regional Novelist."

445 *"Every great writer has his failures"*: Benjamin Moser, "A Prophet at the Barbecue: Larry McMurtry, 1936–2021," *The Nation,* May 17/24, 2021, https://www.thenation.com/article/culture/larry-mcmurtry-texas-bookstore/.

CHAPTER 27

446 *"It got romantic quickly"*: Skip Hollandsworth, undated, unpublished interview with Larrry McMurtry, Diana Ossana, Faye Kesey (2016), courtesy Skip Hollandsworth.

446 *"sound[ed] like an old married couple"*: Sara L. Spurgeon, "Talking with Larry McMurtry," *Southwestern American Literature* 40, no. 1 (Fall 2014), htps://go.gale.com/ps/i.do?id=GALE%7CA405925312&sid=googleScholar&v=2.1&it=r&linkaccess=abs&issn=00491675&p=AONE&sw=w&userGroupName=Oregon_oweb.

446 *"Faye didn't like to be on the phone"*: This and subsequent quotes regarding the McMurtry-Kesey marriage, unless otherwise noted, are from Hollandsworth unpublished interview.

447 *"very sweet"*: Jeff Baker, "Ken Kesey's Widow Married Larry McMurtry in Texas," *The Oregonian,* May 9, 2011, https://www.oregonlive.com/books/2011/05/ken_keseys_widow_married_larry_mcmurtry.

447 *"I promise I'll always be interesting"*: Skip Hollandsworth, "The Minor Regional Novelist," *Texas Monthly,* July 2016, https://www.texasmonthly.com/arts-entertainment/larry -mcmurtry-minor-regional-novelist/.

447 *"was the person who knew Faye"*: Conversation with Laurence McGilvery.

448 *"Larry was kind of a prick"*: Benjamin Moser, "A Prophet at the Barbecue: Larry Mc-Murtry, 1936–2021," *The Nation,* May 17/24, 2021, https://www.thenation.com/article /culture/larry-mcmurtry-texas-bookstore/.

448 *"good relationship"*: Hollandsworth unpublished interview.

449 *"Book prices dropped"*: McGilvery conversation.

449 *"Miraculous birth!"*: Paul Knight, "A Literary Hero, Keeping the Last Bookshop Alive," *New York Times,* August 19, 2012, https://www.nytimes.com/2012/08/19/larry -mcmurtry-keeping-his-last-hometown-bookshop-alive.html.

449 *"I . . . need a sabbatical"*: Richard Mize, "Author McMurtry Has Novel Approach to Hometown Realty," *The Daily Oklahoman,* August 20, 2005, https://www.oklahoman .com/article/2908262/author-mcmurtry-has-novel-approach-to-hometown-realty.

449 *"It's nice to be missed"*: Ibid.

449 *"The economic crisis"*: Ibid.

450 *"I don't know if [my problem]"*: Michael Lindenberger, "The Great Book Sale of Texas: Larry McMurtry Gives Up His Collection," *Time,* August 15, 2012, https://nation .time.com/2012/08/15/the-great-book-sale-of-texas-larry-mcmurtry-gives-up-his -collection/.

450 *"it's [getting] toward"*: Ibid.

450 *"a potential liability"*: Ibid.

450 *"cracker-jack team"*: Larry McMurtry, "The Last Book Sale," *The New York Review of Books,* August 17, 2012, https://www.nybooks.com/online/2012/08/17/larry-mcmurtry -last-book-sale/.

450 *"It's bittersweet"*: Knight, "A Literary Hero, Keeping the Last Bookshop Alive."

450 *"In a summer"*: "The Last Book Sale."

451 *"an atmosphere of coolness"*: Kurt Zimmerman, "Thinning the Herd: Larry McMurtry Cuts 300,000 Books Loose in a Two Day Auction," *American Book Collecting,* August 20, 2012, https://www.bookcollectinghistory.com/2012/08/thinning-herd-larry-mcmurtry -cuts.html.

451 *"I'm a fiction writer"*: Geoffrey Himes, "The Curmudgeon: James McMurtry and the Family Business," *Paste,* August 18, 2021, https://www.pastemagazine.com/music/james -mcmurtry/james-mcmurtry-the-horses-and-the-hounds-feature-i/.

452 *"We had a good time together"*: Mike Evans, "Larry," an unpublished memoir sent to the author, September 27, 2021.

452 *"approach of mixing"*: Michael Agresta, "The Last Book Sale: An Era Ends for an Author, a Town, and a Culture," *The Atlantic,* August 22, 2012, https://www.theatlantic.com /entertainment/archive/2012/08/the-last-book-sale-an-era-ends-for-an-author-a-town -and-a-culture/261426/.

452 *"free same-day bike delivery"*: Ibid.

452 *"self-made wildcatter"*: Lindenberger, "The Great Book Sale of Texas."

452 *"tattooed furniture"*: Judy Wiley, "Writer Larry McMurtry auctions most of 450,000 book collection," *Reuters,* August 11, 2012, https://www.reuters.com/entertainment-us-usa -book-auction-idCABRE87A0B220120811.

452 *"great in mind"*: Oklahoma Hall of Fame, Gaylord-Pickens Museum, https://www .oklahomahof.com/member-archives/johnson-roy-1953.

452 *"jaded virility"*: Stephen J. Gertz, "The Celebrated Stable of Clandestine Erotica Writers Part I: The Man, His Plan," *Fine Books,* May 2009, https://finebooksmagazine.com/blog /celebrated-stable-clandestine-erotica-writers-part-i-man-his-plan.

452 *"could only erect"*: "Erotic Typescripts [circa 1940]," Between the Covers Rare Books Inc., https://www.betweenthecovers.com/pages/books/381515/82-erotic-typescripts.

453 *"what in my high school days"*: Books, 174.

453 *"not-particularly-comfortable hotel"*: Books, 176.

453 *"Power to the young dealers!"*: Agresta, "The Last Book Sale."

454 *"He could have made a lot more money"*: Ibid.

454 *He had once asked her:* Cheryl Beesinger email to the author, July 10, 2012.

454 *"There isn't the next generation"*: Agresta, "The Last Book Sale."

454 *"You can't spend a lifetime"*: Lindenberger, "The Great Book Sale of Texas."

454 *"The oil business is gone"*: Knight, "A Literary Hero, Keeping the Last Bookshop Alive."

454 *"The proceedings had the aspect"*: Agresta, "The Last Book Sale."

455 *"[It] took a lot of strength"*: James Bryan, Antiquarian Booksellers' Association interview with Larry McMurtry, Tucson, January 2014.

455 *"tired"*: Los Angeles Public Library, "An Afternoon with Larry McMurtry."

455 *"We had a lot of good porcelain books"*: Antiquarian Booksellers' Association of America interview with McMurtry.

455 *"hugely influential"*: TW Editors, "True Westerner of 2013," *True West,* January 2013, https://www.truewestmagazine.com/article/true-westerner-of-2013/.

455 *"Larry McMurtry bugs the hell"*: Bob Boze Bell, quoted in "True Westerner of 2013."

456 *"He wasn't doing too well"*: Conversation with Michael Wallis.

456 *"low key"*: Larry McMurtry and Diana Ossana, "True Westerners," *Flash and Filagree,* March 14, 2013, https://flashandfil-igree.com/2013/03/14/true-westerners/.

456 *"He was very self-effacing"*: Conversation with Michael Wallis.

456 *"deepened the nation's understanding"*: Cited in Maggie Galehouse, "Larry McMurtry to Receive National Humanities Medal," *Houston Chronicle,* September 3, 2015, https: //www.houstonchronicle.com/entertainment/books/article/Larry-McMurtry-to-receive -National-Humanities-6484194.php.

456 *"I always do pretty good"*: This and subsequent Obama quotes are from Office of the Press Secretary, The White House, "Remarks by the President at the National Medals of the Arts and Humanities Awards Ceremony," September 10, 2015, https://obamawhitehouse .archives.gov/the-press-office/2015/09/11/remarks-president-national-medal-arts-and -humanities-awards-ceremony.

457 *"an aide called"*: Michael Lindenberger, "Novels, Larry McMurtry Told Me Nine Years Ago, Are a Younger Writer's Game. He Was Done," *Houston Chronicle,* March 26, 2021, https://www.houstonchronicle.com/opinion/outlook/article/Lindenberger-Novels-Larry -McMurtry-told-me-nine-16056850.php.

457 *"excited about us coming out here"*: Michael Lindenberger, "President Obama Honors Larry McMurtry in Elegant White House Ceremony," *Dallas Morning News,* September 10, 2015, https://www.dallasnews.com/news/politics/2015/09/10/president-obama -honors-larry-mcmurtry-in-elegant-white-house-ceremony/.

CHAPTER 28

459 *"When I lay abed"*: Roads, 20.

459 *"Never eat at a place called Mom's"*: Nelson Algren cited in *Roads,* 26.

459 *"a skim-milk light"*: Roads, 28.

459   *"The killings"*: Ibid., 39.

460   *generations of . . . farmers"*: Ibid., 37.

460   *"was an awful tragidy"*: *In a Narrow Grave: Essays on Texas,* 152.

460   *"What does PhD stand for?"*: Ibid., 151.

461   *"forgiving form"*: Allen Barra, "A Dynamic Duo: McMurtry, Ossana," *Tampa Bay Times,* January 18, 2008, https://www.tampabay.com/archive/2008/01/11/a-dynamic-duo -mcmurtry-ossana/.

461   *"If I could not write another word"*: Evan Smith, "Larry McMurtry," *Texas Monthly,* September 2004, https://www.texasmonthly.com/arts-entertainment/larry-mcmurtry/.

461   *"Larry is like an old cowboy"*: Skip Hollandsworth, "The Minor Regional Novelist," *Texas Monthly,* July 2016, https://www.texasmonthly.com/arts-entertainment/larry-mcmurtry -minor-regional-novelist/.

461   *"I might* have one more novel": Hollandsworth, "The Minor Regional Novelist."

461   *"Larry McMurtry closed the book"*: John Leland, "Duane's Depraved," *New York Times,* March 18, 2007, https://www.nytimes.com/2007/03/18/book/review/Leland.t.html.

461   *"marathon [sex] session"*: Ibid.

462   *"growing lonelier and older"*: Larry McMurtry, *When the Light Goes* (New York: Simon & Schuster, 2007), 41.

462   *"Duane Moore quietly keeled over"*: Larry McMurtry, *Rhino Ranch* (Waterville, ME: Wheeler Publishing, 2009), 458.

462   *"An old Mississippi mule trader"*: Tim Gautreaux, "A Review of Larry McMurtry's 'Rhino Ranch,'" *Washington Post,* August 15, 2009, https://www.washingtonpost.com/wp-dyn /content/article/2009/08/14/AR2009081403109.html.

462   *"woman-superior"*: *When the Light Goes,* 88.

462   *"I'm about at the end"*: Marjorie Kehe, "No More Novels for Larry McMurtry?," *The Christian Science Monitor,* August 3, 2009, https://www.csmonitor.com/Books/chapter -and-verse/2009/0803/no-more-novels-for-larry-mcmurtry.

462   *"Oh, I don't know"*: Michael Granberry, "Larry McMurtry Shirks Retirement for New Book," *Houston Chronicle,* June 3, 2014, https://www.houstonchronicle.com/entertainment /books/article/Larry-McMurtry-shirks-retirement-for-new-book-5525479.php.

463   *"They seemed to be having trouble"*: Michael Hoinski, "'Lonesome Dove' Legend Larry McMurtry on Fiction, Money, Womanizing, and Old Age," *Grantland,* May 22, 2014, https://grantland.com/hollywood-prospectus/larry-mcmurtry-lonesome-dove-new-book -interview/.

463   *"I'd always been a midlist writer"*: Ray Isle, "Three Days in McMurtryville," *Stanford Magazine,* November/December 1999, https://stanfordmag.org/contents/three-days-in -mcmurtryville.

463   *"Larry is like Charles Dickens"*: Hoinski, "'Lonesome Dove' Legend Larry McMurtry on Fiction, Money, Womanizing, and Old Age."

463   *"a ballad in prose"*: Larry McMurtry, *The Last Kind Words Saloon* (New York: Liveright, 2014), author's note, unpaginated.

463   *"nearly in Kansas"*: Ibid., 13.

463   *"about all the female I can handle"*: Ibid., 6.

464   *"It's as if Vladimir and Estragon"*: Joyce Carol Oates, "The Real West, at Last," *The New York Review of Books,* June 5, 2014, https://www.nybooks.com/articles/2014/06/05/larry -mcmurtry-real-west-at-last/.

464   *"damn waste of time"*: *The Last Kind Words Saloon,* 192.

464   *"You fool"*: Ibid., 193.

464 *"So much for legend"*: Oates, "The Real West, at Last."

464 *" [t]orturing whites"*: *The Last Kind Words Saloon,* 24.

464 *"lived in a dilapidated"*: Ibid., 197.

464 *"There was nothing to be had"*: Ibid., 197–98.

464 *"radically-distilled"*: Oates, "The Real West, at Last."

465 *"Things yet to come"*: Donald Barthelme, *The King* (New York: Harper & Row, 1990), 102.

465 *"I want this book"*: Hoinski, "'Lonesome Dove' Legend Larry McMurtry on Fiction, Money, Womanizing, and Old Age."

465 *"my partner [Diana]"*: This and all other quotes from the Dallas Museum of Art event, Skip Hollandsworth, "Arts & Letters Live," May 17, 2014.

466 *"We speak of great world writers"*: This and all other quotes from the Miami Book Fair International event, Robert Weil, are from "Miami Book Fair International Interview with Larry McMurtry and Diana Ossana," March 11, 2015, youtube.com/watch?v =bfMdwEjptv8.

466 *"Old age comes on apace"*: Hollandsworth, "The Minor Regional Novelist."

466 *"The depression that had always stalked him"*: Mike Evans, "Larry," an unpublished memoir sent to the author, September 27, 2021.

467 *electroconvulsive therapy*: For an overview of electroconvulsive therapy, see R. Douglas Fields, "Beyond the *Cuckoo's Nest*: The Quest for Why Shock Therapy Can Work," *Scientific American,* November 17, 2017, https://www.scientificamerican.com/article/beyond -the-cuckoos-nest-the-quest-for-why-shock-therapy-can-work/.

467 *"For some time"*: Evans, "Larry."

467 *"What's happening to me"*: Sara L. Spurgeon, "Talking with Larry McMurtry," *Southwestern American Literature* 40, no. 1 (Fall 2014).

468 *"There's nobody to talk to"*: Ibid.

468 *"made a cautious approach"*: Larry McMurtry Facebook page, facebook.com /larrymcmurtrywriterbookseller.

468 *"I am in no way a spiritual person"*: This and all other last interview quotes with Benito Vila are from "Looking West with Larry McMurtry," June 8, 2021, *Please Kill Me,* https: //pleasekillme.com/larry-mcmurtry/.

469 *"There is a fair amount"*: Charles Ealy, "Assessing the State of Texas Letters," *Austin Statesman,* December 11, 2018, https://www.statesman.com/story/news/2013/10/26/assessing -state-texas-letters/6713647007/.

469 *"the twentieth century's most frightening image"*: Ibid.

469 *"the military-industrial complex"*: Ibid.

470 *"headspace of women"*: Eric Kohn, "Jane Campion Is Not Alone: Women Are Reinventing the Western, One Movie at a Time," *IndieWire,* September 7, 2021, https://www.indiewire .com/2021/09/jane-campion-women-directors-reinventing-western-1234662548/.

470 *"focus on strong women"*: Diana Finlay Hendricks, "Larry McMurtry: An Accidental Feminist?," https://www.dianahendricks.com/larry-mcmurtry-an-accidental-feminist.html.

470 *"There is a kind of writing"*: Madeleine Watts, "Larry McMurtry Couldn't Write Women," April 13, 2021, https://madeleinewatts.substack.com/p/larry-mcmurtry-couldn't-write -women.

471 *"We're talking about"*: Thomas Curwen, "Larry McMurtry, Author of 'Lonesome Dove' and 'The Last Picture Show,' Dies," *Los Angeles Times,* March 26, 2021, https://latimes .com/obituaries/story/2021–03–26/larry-mcmurtry-author-of-lonesome-dove-and-the -last-picture-show-dies-at-84.

471 *"He cast a big shadow"*: Ibid.

471   *"masterpieces":* Benjamin Moser, "A Prophet at the Barbecue: Larry McMurtry, 1936–
      2021," *The Nation,* May 17/24, 2021, https://www.thenation.com/article/culture/larry
      -mcmurtry-texas-bookstore/.

471   *"Larry took us":* Jane Summer, "Not Finished Yet: Larry McMurtry Talks About His New
      Novel," Skip Hollandsworth notes, courtesy Skip Hollandsworth.

471   *"WHEREAS":* "Bill Text: TXSR305/2021–2022/87th Legislature/Enrolled Texas Senate
      Resolution 305," *LegiScan,* https://legiscan.com/TX/text/SR305/id/2383605.

471   *"I* am *a minor regional novelist":* James Bryan, Antiquarian Booksellers' Association inter-
      view with Larry McMurtry, Tucson, January 2014.

472   *"There'll be some kind of biography":* Spurgeon, "Talking with Larry McMurtry."

472   *"What I have hoped to be":* Literary Life, 174.

472   *"Larry didn't go to the big cattle drive":* Leslie Silko, letter to the author, April 29, 2022.

472   *"He was my friend":* Diana Ossana in an email to the author, September 27, 2021.

472   *"I keep walking":* Hollandsworth, "The Minor Regional Novelist."

473   *"I'm not going to write about women":* Ken Whyte, "Making Larry McMurtry Woozy,"
      April 2, 2021, https://shush.substack.com/p/making-larry-mcmurtry-woozy.

473   *"a very polite":* "Legendary Native Son Larry McMurtry Dies at 84," *Archer County News.*

473   *"The rules of happiness": Some Can Whistle,* 341.

INDEX